Sociological Reality: A Brief Introduction

BETTY YORBURG

City College and the Graduate Center
City University of New York

DPG

The Dushkin Publishing Group, Inc.
Sluice Dock, Guilford, Connecticut 06437

Printed in the United States of America

Library of Congress Catalog Card Number 94-060669

International Standard Book Number (ISBN) 1-56134-313-7

First Printing

10 9 8 7 6 5 4 3 2 1

This book is printed
on recycled paper

Credits & Acknowledgments
Cover: Will Barnet, *Family and Pink Table,* 1948. © 1994 Will Barnet/VAGA, New
York. Cover design by Harry Rinehart.

Credits & Acknowledgments are continued on page lxxxiii, which constitutes an
extension of the copyright page.

Sociological Reality: A Brief Introduction

Betty Yorburg is Professor of Sociology at the City College of New York and is on the faculty at the Graduate Center of the City University of New York. She is the author of a number of books and papers in the areas of political sociology, the family, and women. She is currently at work on a large-scale interview research project on aging. Her professional memberships include the American Sociological Association, Sociologists for Women in Society, The National Council on Family Relations, and the Society for the Study of Social Problems. Professor Yorburg has a special interest in students who have interrupted their education; she has been in charge of the Sociology Department Evening Session at the City College of New York since 1970. Over the years, she has advised and encouraged students from a wide variety of social backgrounds, ranging in age from 18 to almost 70. She enjoys teaching introductory sociology and has been teaching the course for more than two decades.

Preface

The need for sociological information about public issues and private concerns is greater now than ever. We live in a time when crisis is commonplace, old solutions are increasingly questioned, and informed decision making by citizens and governments is imperative. The discipline of sociology has much to offer to those who would listen. Here, I will attempt to show how this discipline expands understanding and promotes thought about the various social realities humans have lived in since the beginning of history.

Students in introductory sociology courses complain that the texts are too expensive, the language too technical, and the content not relevant enough to the realities of their daily lives. Professionals in the field too often are bound up in controversies about the field that stem from differences in political and economic values rather than observed fact. They disagree about the meaning of basic concepts, interpretations of facts and generalizations, and the implications of sociological knowledge for public policy and the good life.

The general public tends to view sociologists (when they do not confuse us with social workers or socialists) as academics who do elaborate studies of the obvious, or who attempt to peg, classify, and quantify that which is not classifiable or quantifiable—the uniqueness of each individual human being. These objections and judgments can be answered and corrected. This is what I hope to do here.

What is still needed is a description of the field of sociology that makes sense to professionals, students, and general readers; that attempts to integrate rather than reinforce competing points of view; and that demonstrates the value of the discipline of sociology to people who want a better understanding of themselves and their social situations.

Sociological knowledge about self, community, and society is crucial in societies where alternatives and choices exist. If we could not change our individual and collective destinies, we would not need this knowledge. As long as we can, however, it becomes as essential to know our society as it is to know ourselves.

What follows is a description of the human experience in major areas of life as societies, cultures, and human relationships have become increasingly complex, a process we call sociocultural evolution. Societies are classified as hunting and gathering, horticultural, agricultural, industrial, and postindustrial, according to their level of cultural complexity, technological development, and scientific knowledge about the world. Using this basic classification, I describe and explain changing human relationships in major spheres of social life—economic, political, familial, educational, and religious—with particular emphasis on roles, values, power, and conflict.

The social location of people and societies in time and in physical and cultural space will be the focus and the organizing principle for describing the various social realities that have marked human history. The concept of role will be the connecting link between culture and subculture and the typical ways of thinking, feeling, and behaving of people located in various societies, or segments of a society, at various times and in various places.

Economic changes that occur as cultures, science, and technology become more complex will be given great weight in explaining certain historical and current changes in all areas of life. Values are also given great weight, particularly as these hasten or slow the process of cultural change. Power and conflict will be related to changing resources, particularly economic resources. The spread of urban values in human relationships—individualism, achievement, egalitarianism, and rationalism—will be traced to the rise in opportunities and in resources of various kinds, especially education as societies become more complex.

The focus on sociocultural evolution as a basic explanatory perspective provides a logical framework for tying together the major concepts and subfields of sociology. I start with basic information about the field of sociology, its theories, methods, and concepts. This is followed by a historical description of major types of human societies and major social trends. I then proceed to a discussion and explanation of more specific changes in important areas of life—at home, at work, at school, and in religion—as societies and cultures become more complex.

Most of the traditional topics found in introductory sociology texts are discussed, but they are integrated within the sociocultural evolution framework. Students do not have to ask, "Why does the topic of social change come at the end of the book and not at the beginning?" Social change and social stability, the two ultimate concerns of sociology, are discussed throughout the book. Two prominent perspectives in contemporary sociology with different emphases, structural-functionalism and conflict theory, are reconciled where possible.

The text is organized into 13 chapters, with a prologue and an epilogue. Tables are included to summarize complicated ideas or complex information at a glance. Some of these tables represent a synthesis of a great number of studies on particular topics. They could be helpful in other, more specialized courses in sociology, such as courses on minorities, deviance, social stratification, or family relationships.

At the end of each chapter is a built-in study guide. This consists of a set of review objectives; a summary of major topics covered; a glossary with concise definitions of new concepts; a practice test on the chapter, including true/false, multiple-choice, and matching questions; a comprehensive selection of review questions; and a section called "Applying Sociology" in which students are asked to apply newly introduced sociological concepts and generalizations to their own lives. At this point, what has been learned and what needs further review should be clear to the student.

I have attempted to use straightforward, clear, and informal language throughout the text. Even the most complicated ideas can be meaningful and intriguing when presented with clarity and enthusiasm. An introductory text, particularly in sociology, can be both scholarly and useful. It can communicate new ideas as well as basic knowledge. And, in sociology, it can promote informed, critical thought about self, society, and the world. It can give students the means to think sociologically on their own.

This book is a result of the years I have spent thinking, learning, and changing my ideas about sociology—its meaning, direction, goals, and purposes. It parallels my own personal search for answers to the riddles of time and of history. Over the centuries, a model of the universe based on faith and philosophy has been supplanted, increasingly, by one based on science—a crucial addition for those who search for valid and reliable information about historical and contemporary changes in human social realities.

We know more about the world now than we have ever known. We have a greater possibility of changing this world, rationally, than we have ever had—if only we would.

ACKNOWLEDGMENTS

The American Sociological Association now lists 34 separate membership sections. This reflects the enormous increase in the number of specialties within the field of sociology over the years. Keeping up with the developments in the various specialties becomes extremely difficult. I am grateful to colleagues at the various branches of the City University of New York who talked to me about the latest trends in their special areas and gave me names of good, recent references to check out. Among these colleagues, I particularly want to mention Ibtihaj Arafat in the area of demography, Gerald Handel in family and childhood socialization, Catherine Silver in aging, Charles Winick in criminology and drug abuse, and Julia Wrigley in education. Dana Fenton was extraordinarily helpful with the chapter on the sociology of religion.

John A. Rome of Information Conveyance, Inc., and Stephen D. Rappaport, a telecommunications consultant, provided me with invaluable information about the latest trends in the uses of electronic technology in the workplace.

The suggestions of reviewers, including Donald Bylsma of Washtenaw Community College, Manuel Gil of Delgado Community College, and James T. Mathieu of Loyola Marymount University in Los Angeles, were very helpful in the almost endless process of adding, deleting, and polishing my manuscript.

In particular, I would like to thank Kurt Finsterbusch of the University of Maryland and Martha L. Schwayder of Metropolitan State College of Denver for their thoughtful, detailed comments.

The high morale and the support of the staff at The Dushkin Publishing Group were unique in my long and varied experience with publishers. I am especially grateful for the conscientious and encouraging memos I received from Irv Rockwood, publisher at Brown & Benchmark, who knows the field and cares about authors and their concerns. The copyediting of Josh Safran and Catherine Leonard was extraordinarily meticulous. Their queries about content, on practically every page of the manuscript, helped me clarify a number of points that needed reformulating or expansion. They were also gracious enough to leave my writing style largely intact. Acquisitions Editor Michael Alread was especially helpful in providing ideas for the built-in study guide and Focus on Social Issues boxes that appear in the text.

Betty Yorburg

Brief Table of Contents

Topic Guide

Contents

2 Models and Methods 30

3 The Language of Sociology: Social Stability 72

PART II   *Human Societies: Major Social Trends* **143**

 Human Societies 144

PART III   *Major Institutions* **285**

 9 Families 286

12 Education 393

13 Religion 429

Sociological Reality: A Brief Introduction

Prologue

Reality is out there for anyone to experience and interpret. Our view of reality, however, can be clear or hazy, accurate or distorted, rigid or constantly shifting, frightening or benign. Religion, philosophy, the sciences, and common sense have provided models or perspectives for viewing reality. Each has its advantages; each, its limitations.

Religion can transcend reality and rely on faith in interpreting the human experience. Philosophy is bound by reality, but like religion it can include values in its ordering of reality; it can go beyond what *is* to what *ought* to be. Science, at least in its immediate concerns, is limited to what is. Common sense also focuses on reality, but as reality becomes increasingly complex and complicated in advanced industrialized societies, common sense becomes inadequate and inaccurate as a means for understanding what is actually going on. Common sense also becomes increasingly ineffective in coping with the more numerous challenges and demands of adaptation and survival.

Ultimately, all sciences, natural or social, have implications for understanding and changing social reality. Science in general and sociology in particular are judged by the standard of "rationalism"—the ability to provide logically more effective and efficient means for accomplishing goals—whatever these goals are and however they may change.

The Need for Sociology

Sociologists become indispensable in modern times because governments become increasingly responsive to the needs and desires of their people. They must know what these needs and desires are. Also, citizens in modern societies must be literate and skillful to function in these societies, for educated people have a lower tolerance for greed, corruption, and deception. They are less susceptible to propaganda, and they get the facts sooner or later, despite the confusing complexity of many issues in advanced industrial societies.

Governments must also have valid information about their societies if they are to plan for the future—the near as well as the distant future—in rapidly changing societies. An attitude of live and let live does not work well when people start out very unequally and are increasingly unlikely to accept this inequality, and when the possibility of world destruction is very real. Governments must plan or else collapse in chaos.

Governments in highly industrialized societies must plan not only because their citizens are well educated and knowledgeable, but also because the unanticipated results of technological change may kill us all if we do not plan. Uncontrolled pollution could eliminate both governments and citizens.

Citizens also need the knowledge and understanding that sociology can provide so that they can better understand the choices and alternatives available to them. A knowledge of sociology can enable us to understand better how our individual destiny is affected by historical trends and contemporary economic and political circumstances that are not beyond our control.

Purpose and Plan

My goal here is to portray, as clearly as possible, my own understanding of sociology. I will describe sociology as a discipline and as an approach to explaining social stability and social change. Ultimately, human social life will be viewed in terms of the fulfillment of human needs and the curbing of human destructiveness.

At a more concrete level, I will try to convey a sociological perspective on people and their typical relationships, in major areas of life, in various parts of the world, during major eras of human history. I will focus on the typical struggles, accomplishments, gratifications, and frustrations that humans have experienced since the genus *Homo* first appeared on earth about 4 million years ago.

The Discipline of Sociology

We will begin with a definition of the field of sociology—its focus, history, uses, and limitations. When and why did sociology arise as a field of study? Who are some of the pioneers in the field—the people who pointed to the questions about human social life that needed answering and provided some initial guidelines, right or wrong, about how these questions could be answered? To some extent, every field of knowledge, every occupation, and all groups share a certain perspective on the world. What is the sociological perspective, and how does this perspective differ from that of the other social sciences?

Theories, Methods, and Language

What are the major theories, methods, and basic concepts that sociologists have used to observe and to explain the facts of social order and social change in human societies? What theories do we use to explain why we have stability and not chaos in our daily social lives? Under what circumstances do we have chaos and not stability? How do the various theories in sociology differ with respect to their focus or emphasis on roles, values, power, and conflict?

Every scientific field has its own technical language that makes the communication of information more efficient, particularly for other scientists in the field. What is the language of sociology—the basic vocabulary that sociologists use to focus our observations and to communicate what we see?

Major Types of Societies

Given the sociological view of reality, I will then describe the major kinds of societies—hunting and gathering, horticultural and herding, agricultural, industrial, and postindustrial—that have existed since the first appearance of the human animal on earth. We will see how inventions, discoveries, and the borrowing of knowledge, customs, techniques, tools, and weapons from other societies have changed human reality and the human experience over the ages.

Major Social Trends

More specifically, we will focus on basic social trends as societies have become more complex. Among these trends, for example, are the shift from rural to urban life and the tremendous increases in population size and mobility, in economic resources, in nonconforming behavior of all kinds, and in minority group/dominant group conflict in human societies.

Major Institutions

We will see how roles, values, power, and conflicts have changed in major areas of life—within institutions such as the family, economy, government, education, and religion—as resources and opportunities have increased in modern societies. What needs do these various institutions satisfy, ideally and actually, in human societies?

The Family

The family is a social group found in all human societies, regardless of how it has varied in form and functions historically. What is a family? Why is the family universal? What are the biological foundations of family life? How and why has family life typically changed as societies have developed technologically and as scientific knowledge has accumulated? More specifically, how have developments in scientific knowledge, technology, and economics affected family structure, power, gender roles, premarital sexual behavior, marital choice, parent-child relationships, and divorce rates? What are some of the most significant recent changes in family life in the United States, and why are these changes occurring? Why, for example, are nontraditional families—single-parent families, marriages without children, and unmarried, living-together couples, with or without children—becoming more prevalent? What is the probable future of the family in the United States, and elsewhere?

The Economy

The way goods and services are produced and distributed in a society is the economic system of that society. Changes in the possession of economic resources by individuals, groups, societies or segments of societies, as societies become more complex, are a major factor in explaining the changes that have occurred in human relationships in all areas of life, historically. How have developments in science and technology affected not only the amount but also, more important, the distribution of economic resources (who gets what and how much) in major kinds of societies? Why does inequality persist in human societies? How are economic resources distributed and redistributed in the United States today? How does this compare with other contemporary societies? How do the various social classes in the United States today differ in values, beliefs, and behavior? How do work, leisure, longevity, and psychological well-being vary according to social class location? How does this differ in other contemporary societies?

Power and Politics

Individuals, groups, and governments that have the ability to carry out their will, especially against resistance, have power. All human relationships involve the exercise of power by one member over another at certain times and in certain situations. Political power refers to the power of rulers and leaders of societies, states, and social movements over citizens and followers. Politics is the struggle for political power. How have the bases, justifications, and distribution of political power varied as societies have become more complex? What is the difference between power, authority, and influence? How have social movements of various kinds affected the distribution of power and resources in human societies? Under what circumstances do revolutions arise and what makes for the success or failure of revolutions? What is the relationship between wealth, power, and influence in the United States today? How does this compare with other contemporary societies?

Education

In all societies, newborn members must be deliberately trained so that they can function adequately as adults—as citizens, workers, family members, and so on. Education is a special aspect of a more general process known as "socialization" by which the culture is transmitted and people learn how to function in the societies in which they live and in the groups to which they belong.

Throughout the centuries and across the continents, education, in the long view, has become more formal and specialized in terms of what is taught and who does the teaching. In the simplest societies, no one reads or writes. In agricultural societies, only a small number of very privileged citizens are literate—priests, scribes, and some, but not all, kings, queens, and other aristocrats. In industrialized societies, all citizens are required by law to be educated. In modern societies, who is educated, how, to what extent, and for what purpose are matters of concern. How and why has education changed in these respects as societies have become more complex? What are the major issues and problems of education in the United States today? Are ability and drive or class, gender, and ethnic origin more important in determining adult occupational achievement and rewards? How does this compare with other contemporary societies? In the United States, what are some recent trends in education that are likely to continue—in testing, tracking, preschool, and adult education? How can these trends be explained?

Religion

Religion, like other major areas of life, also becomes increasingly separate, formal, and specialized in structure and function as societies become more complex. Religious values have been important in affecting the rate of technological development in human societies. At the same time, religious beliefs and practices have been strongly affected by developments in science, changes in the distribution of power, resources, and opportunities, and the spread of urban values in modern societies. What is religion, and why is religion found in all human societies? How have religious beliefs and practices varied in major kinds of societies? What functions does religion serve for individuals, groups, and societies? What functions does religion have for maintaining social order and promoting social change? What is the relationship between religious beliefs and social class, historically, and in the United States today?

Why are religious beliefs and confidence in organized religion stronger in the United States than in other contemporary industrialized societies? Will religion survive, grow stronger, change in direction, or disappear as science and technology continue to encroach on the realm of the unknown, uncertain, and uncontrollable?

Sociology and Prediction

The natural sciences cannot predict the timing of major scientific discoveries, such as the development of substitutes for natural fuels or the cure (or cures) for cancer. Natural scientists can predict more specific and less complicated occurrences, however, especially in laboratory settings. Outside the laboratory, they can predict an eclipse and are getting better at predicting snowstorms and even earthquakes.

In the social sciences, the problem of prediction is far more complicated. Many more factors have to be considered, including human motivation and the uniqueness of each human being. At best, social scientists can point to general trends and to the likelihood that these trends will continue—if only because we know of no reason why they should *not* continue.

The Epilogue summarizes some of the major insights that sociology has contributed to the understanding of the human experience at different times, on different continents, and in different societies. Sociology illuminates the effects of sociocultural evolution and economic change on roles, values, power, and conflict in groups and in societies.

The social worlds of modern women and men continuously expand and become more complicated. For total societies, and for all humankind, the possibility of world destruction now exists. But for most individuals in industrialized societies, the possibilities for choice, intellectual and psychological growth, and life itself are greater now than ever, despite this threat.

Many questions have been posed in this short preview of what is to come. Why do sociologists focus on these questions—and how do we answer them?

B. Y.

PART I

Sociology:
Definition, Theories, Methods, Language

An introduction to a new field of knowledge should provide a solid base for understanding the field and its contributions to scientific knowledge. The definition of sociology given in chapter 1 emphasizes what is unique about the sociological focus on human social life. The history of the field is described in terms of the ideas of classical thinkers that are still relevant today. The discussion of the relationship of the other social sciences to sociology focuses especially on overlapping trends in the various fields. The description of sociology as an occupation emphasizes the usefulness of a sociological background in a large variety of job settings. Chapter 2 discusses the major theoretical perspectives in sociology, focusing on the different weight researchers using them give to various explanatory factors. Research methods are explored with an emphasis on the advantages and limitations of each method and the special difficulties in doing research on humans. Chapter 3 outlines the basic concepts in sociology that refer to conditions that promote social stability in human societies and predictability in human relationships. In chapter 4, the discussion is centered on sociological concepts that are most helpful in explaining major changes in human societies and relationships, historically and in various parts of the world today.

1

What Is Sociology?

What is sociology? Definitions vary. Some definitions are too vague or too broad to be useful or meaningful—defining sociology as the "science of society" without clarifying what these terms mean, for example. The following definition describes what is unique about sociology, both as a field of study and as a way of looking at the world:

> **Sociology** is the scientific study of the typical ways of thinking, feeling, and behaving of people who are similarly located in time and in physical and cultural space.

The term "scientific" means that sociologists in their research must abide by the standards of validity (truthfulness and accuracy) and reliability (other people studying the same reality and using the same methods obtain the same results). All scientists must conform to these standards.

The word "typical" in our definition means that a particular custom, belief, or behavior is true of a majority of people in a society, or part of a society (a class, an ethnic population, males or females, children or adults). It may apply to 90 percent of the people, but even if it applies to only 51 percent, it is still true of a majority of the people being studied.

Location in time refers to those who live or have lived during a certain historical period. Historical eras leave their special mark on people because cultures are time-bound, and historical events do not repeat themselves in exactly the same way and in exactly the same detail.

Location in time also includes age and generation. Especially in constantly changing industrial societies, the experiences of individuals in different generations vary, sometimes enormously. The memories, experiences, and outlooks of people in the United States who entered the labor market during the Depression, after World War II, or after the end of the cold war, for example, differ in very important ways (Elder, 1974; Esterlin, 1987; Schuman and Scott, 1989; Schuman and Reiger, 1992).

The Depression generation has vivid lifelong memories of severe economic deprivation experienced in childhood. The baby boom generation, born after World War II and now middle-aged, has unforgettable memories of Vietnam and the civil rights, student, and women's movements. The generation coming of age in the 1990s does not yet have comparable memories. But its members have experienced great economic uncertainty, grave environmental threats, and explosions of racial violence such as the 1992 riots in Los Angeles. These experiences, and the reasons for them, will leave their special mark on this particular generation.

Location in physical space refers to geography—to urban or rural residence or to residence in Asia, Africa, or Latin America, for example. It also refers to location in a particular community, neighborhood, organization, or household. Cultures and subcultures are attached to geographic locations. They continue to affect typical beliefs and behavior. This is true despite increased change, ambiguities, and contradictions in the traditions we inherit.

Social location, generally, affects what we think and do, how we feel, what we value, and how others value us. Locating factors determine our social worlds. The adjective "sociological" usually refers to social location. When newspaper reporters point to sociological causes of delinquency, for example, they are usually referring to the effects of particular locating factors, such as neighborhoods, youth gangs, or poverty, on the behavior of adolescents.

Sociologists try to understand how and why women's self-images, behavior, and views of the world have differed, typically, in nineteenth-century African tribal societies, among the Chinese aristocracy before the first Chinese revolution in 1911, or among African American single mothers in New York City in the 1990s, for example. We study and try to explain why divorce rates, childrearing practices, gender roles, and sexual behavior have varied from one generation to another in the United States. What has changed? What is the same? Why, or why not?

Sociologists are also interested in what is not typical. We study nonconforming or "deviant" behavior not only because this behavior is socially located, but also because what is nontypical may become typical, after a while. We do not focus on unusual behavior, ideas, or emotions simply because we are intrigued by the strange or the bizarre. The study of non-

Note: Definitions for **boldface** terms may be found in the study guide at the end of each chapter and in the glossary.

conforming behavior can help sociologists better understand what makes for conformity and social stability and what makes for new ideas, new behavior, and social change in human societies.

Sociological information is essential in modern societies for many reasons. One important function of our research is to debunk widely held stereotypes and myths (false beliefs) about other people and about what is actually going on in a society. What "everyone knows" is often wrong. Getting the facts is essential, not only for public policy decisions, but for private decision making as well.

WHAT "EVERYONE KNOWS"

It is commonly believed—"everyone knows"—that the United States is the land of opportunity. Sociologists know that class origin, family, ethnic origin, and community background are most important in the academic and occupational achievements of most children (Hauser and Sewell, 1986; Corcoran et al., 1990; Mayer, 1991). The late-nineteenth-century novelist Horatio Alger was the champion salesman of the "American Dream," the belief that success is possible for everyone and that those who fail simply do not try hard enough. If we look closely at Alger's novels, however, we see that his rags-to-riches heroes, Ragged Dick and Tattered Tom, make it by luck and pluck (marrying the boss's daughter after saving her from certain death, for instance) and not simply by hard work, dedication, and determination. Even in popular folktales, opportunity in the United States is hedged by luck.

"Everyone knows" that poverty breeds crime. Sociologists know that the rich commit crimes that are less publicized but more costly to taxpayers and consumers. Nonviolent upper- and middle-class crimes—investment fraud, embezzling, bribery, corruption, pollution, and the sale of unsafe products—are less obvious. And they are far less severely punished, because their perpetrators come from higher-income groups and are treated with greater leniency because of their higher prestige (Pizzo and Muolo, 1993; Day, 1993). The savings and loan scandal in the late 1980s added $13 billion a year in interest to the national debt. Four years after the scandal become public, two-thirds of the charges had been dropped and only 5 percent of the fines imposed had been collected (Day, 1993).

"Everyone knows" that family life in the United States is deteriorating. Sociologists know that over three-quarters of those who divorce eventually remarry, half within the 3 years after their divorce becomes final (Martin and Bumpass, 1989). On repeated surveys, two-thirds of those who are married (and have stayed married) report themselves to be very happy or very satisfied with their marriages (Glenn, 1990). Ninety percent of families in the United States live near at least one other set of relatives. Most older parents (about 70 percent) see at least one of their adult children once a week, and usually more often. And help between the generations—baby-sitting in emergencies, loans, and gifts—is widespread, especially from older parents to their adult children (Goetting, 1990; Hoyert, 1991; Eggebeen, 1992). In times of crisis or disaster, most people still turn to their families first. On surveys, a majority of married people with children list family rather than friends as the source of their closest relationships outside of their immediate households. This is especially true among lower-income groups and among more recent immigrants to the United States. The family is changing. But it will not disappear and, in important respects such as communication, companionship, and friendship, it is stronger than ever (Kain, 1990; Skolnick, 1991; Coontz, 1992; Yorburg, 1993).

"Everyone knows" that unmarried career women are lonely. Sociologists know that career women who have never married are usually not lonely. They are very active with family and friends, as well as at work. Married career women who enjoy their work and do not find it excessively demanding have higher self-esteem and are physically and mentally healthier than full-time homemakers (Spitze, 1988). Married women who are at home full time but would prefer being out working are the women most likely to report being depressed (Ulrich, 1988). The higher self-esteem of successful career women stems from doing relatively well-paying work. In a business civilization, level of self-esteem tends to coincide with level of income (Kohn et al., 1990).

"Everyone knows" that the children of working mothers are more likely to be disturbed, delinquent, or deficient in some way. Sociologists and psychologists know, however, after many careful studies of the effects of maternal employment on children, that there is no hard evidence that this is true (Jay Belsky, 1990; Greenstein, 1993). Children reared in day care centers tend to be more outgoing, and they are usually somewhat slower in developing language skills (they have less exclusive, one-to-one teaching and contact with adults). But they catch up. Warmth, acceptance, encouragement, and emotional support by caregivers, whoever they are, are the most important factors associated with psychological security in children (Ainsworth and Bowlby, 1991). And a little bit of love goes a long way, particularly when this love is consistent and relatively unambivalent. Furthermore, the mother's emotional availability is not guaranteed by her full-time presence at home (Lerner, 1993).

"Everyone knows" that in the United States we worship the almighty dollar. Sociologists know that the occupations in this country that are consistently rated as having the highest prestige, according to repeated National Opinion Research Center surveys going back to the 1940s, are those involving responsibility for the public welfare. Physicians, college professors, and scientists rank higher than bankers.

And, finally, "everyone knows" that ignorance is bliss—that intellectuals are more nervous, high strung, and sensitive. But sociologists know that more highly educated people have higher self-esteem and better physical and mental health, live longer, and are more likely to report themselves as very happy (Kohn et al., 1990; Williams, 1992). We also know that it is not education alone that affects the general level of health and mood, but the better income associated with higher levels of education. Money does not buy health and happiness—but it helps.

In complex, constantly changing societies, sociologists go out and do the legwork for the powerful, the curious, the thoughtful, and the needy. Speculation, myth, ideology, and intuition are poor substitutes for knowledge if human destinies are to be changed rationally.

TECHNICAL LANGUAGE IN SOCIOLOGY

All scientific fields have their own specialized, technical vocabulary. This vocabulary helps colleagues in a particular field to communicate with each other more efficiently. In sociology, abstract technical terms—bureaucracy, class, status, and role, for example—can summarize dozens of ideas in one word or phrase. To the sociologist, the concept of **bureaucracy** means an administrative staff, the coordination of large-scale activities, large numbers of people, the flow of authority from the top down, written rules and regulations, hiring on the basis of skills and qualifications (such as degrees and licenses), paperwork, daily routine, predictability, impersonality, orderly promotion through the ranks, accountability, and so on.

One of the problems that sociologists encounter is that many sociological concepts are also used by the general public. Sociologists refine these concepts so that they can perceive, observe, and explain social reality more clearly and sensitively. But because sociologists use a common language and often study familiar experiences and behavior, laypersons are more likely to argue with the facts sociologists uncover than with natural scientists' observations and conclusions.

When biologists describe the workings of a human cell, they do not get arguments, except from other biologists. When sociologists describe the workings of a human society, however, we are likely to get an argument, particularly if the facts we find suggest a need for policies that some people oppose. Amateur biologists are rare; amateur sociologists are everywhere.

Sociologists use technical language when they write for each other. Sociologists write simply, by contrast, when their work is directed toward political leaders, the helping professions, people in business, and ordinary citizens. Many sociologists are particularly concerned with human needs and how these needs are or are not being met in a society; they must be understood if their work is to be useful.

THE DEVELOPMENT OF SOCIOLOGY

Sociology and the other social sciences arose, in part, as a consequence of destroyed political systems (such as feudalism) and the fallout of new economic systems, especially unregulated capitalism. By the nineteenth century, industrialization had increased opportunities for the small but growing middle classes in Europe. But it had not alleviated the suffering of the majority—serfs, slaves, workers, and women—who were becoming increasingly aware of their deprivations and increasingly unwilling to accept them. Revolts, reform and revolutionary movements, and violent crime were multiplying, and family breakdown, prostitution, and destitution were becoming pervasive.

Most of the pioneers in sociology were deeply concerned by the widespread human suffering they observed. They hoped to relieve such suffering by providing scientifically verified information that could be used as a basis for rational and effective government policy.

Sociology in Europe: The Pioneers

The idea that societies and humans can be studied scientifically goes back to at least the seventeenth century. Social philosophers of that time argued for the accumulation of knowledge based on observation, experimentation, and reason rather than on intuition, divine revelation, tradition, or guesswork. It took more than 200 years, however, before these ideas were actually applied to the study of human social life using valid and reliable scientific methods.

In the history of modern science, objects furthest removed from human beings (the planets and the stars) were the first to be withdrawn from the realm of the sacred and the forever mysterious. The social sciences were the last to achieve the status of distinct sciences, as human beings and their social worlds came to be viewed as legitimate objects of study and rational change.

Auguste Comte (1798–1857)   The French philosopher Auguste Comte, who gave sociology its name in the 1830s, is usually credited with founding the discipline. He would have preferred to call the new field "social physics," but that name had already been taken by the founders of the field now known as statistics. Comte (1915 [1830–1842]) argued that the research methods of physics should be applied to a science of society, an approach he called **positivism**. For Comte, only those aspects of social reality that could be measured and observed directly by the senses were facts. Comte believed in the possibility of formulating laws of social life based on observed fact that would be the equivalent of the laws of physics.

Comte maintained that all societies, ideas, and beliefs about the world go through three inevitable, step-by-step, evolutionary stages: (1) the theological stage, in which explanations are supernatural; (2) the metaphysical stage, in which explanations are not supernatural, but are based on tradition, intuition, or theories that are unsupported by scientific evidence; and (3) the positive stage, in which explanations are based on observed facts and on logical reasoning from these facts. He also distinguished between two basic aspects of the study of human societies—"social statics," concerned with social stability and social order, and "social dynamics," concerned with social change.

For Comte, "progress" toward the "perfect" society would be inevitable, given the determined and deliberate efforts of a "priesthood of positivism," political leaders trained in sociology and scientific methods. Power would be turned over to these leaders voluntarily, because the need to use their knowledge in solving social problems would be recognized and accepted.

Like many other social thinkers of the nineteenth and early twentieth centuries, Comte was an optimist. But he lived in an era when humans were not threatened by the destruction of the world they had made. Comte was also premature (if not deluded) in his beliefs about the potential power of social scientists. But Comte's focus on social order and social change, his emphasis on the scientific method (although very narrowly defined), and his belief in the potential usefulness of sociological research for designing and evaluating social programs are still relevant.

Karl Marx (1818–1883)   Karl Marx was another important nineteenth-century thinker who contributed some lasting insights to the understanding of human history, though his ideas were inaccurate in important respects. In his writings, Marx focused on social location, especially class, and the effects of class membership on the typical attitudes, values, and beliefs of people in a society. Marx claimed that "man's ideas, views, and conceptions, in one word, man's consciousness, changes with every change in the conditions of his material existence, in his social relations, and in his social life" (Marx and Engels, 1955 [1848], pp. 30–31). For Marx, **economic class**–rank in society based on possession of economic resources–determined consciousness (see chapter 2, p. 34).

Marx viewed changes in technology and in work relationships from a historical and evolutionary perspective. Labor evolved from slavery, to serfdom, to wage labor, and, finally, under socialism, to labor in publicly owned factories and farms. Marx gave greater weight than Comte to **class conflict**, the struggle in industrial society over economic resources between the owners of productive property (the bourgeoisie) and the workers (the proletariat), and to revolution as a source of social change. He did not believe that those in control would ever voluntarily give up their power to a priesthood of positivism, or to anyone else for that matter. Only by violent revolution would the ruling class be overthrown. And only then would the working class be able to rid society of "the accumulated rubbish of the past and become capable of reconstructing society" (Marx, 1964 [1844], p. 70).

Like Comte, Marx had great respect for science; in fact, he called his system "scientific socialism." He believed that the natural and social sciences would someday be unified into a single science.

For Marx and his followers, the perfect socialist society would be one in which economic classes would disappear. People would be given economic rewards according to their needs and not on the basis of their ownership or nonownership of productive property (land or factories). Opportunity would be equal for all, and, therefore, all people would work according to their abilities. The state as an instrument of political control would "wither away." This function of the state would disappear, because the conflicts that result from the struggle over economic resources would vanish forever from human societies.

Marx's emphasis on class conflict and social change, on class as a determinant of attitudes, values, and beliefs, and on the importance of economic factors in human relationships provides insights of enormous importance in understanding social life. In contemporary sociology, the conflict theorists, discussed in the next chapter, give the greatest weight to economic factors in their explanations of the world around us.

Herbert Spencer (1820–1903)   Herbert Spencer applied Charles Darwin's principle of biological evolution to social change in human societies and to historical changes in human ways of doing things. He believed that societies and their ways of life (their beliefs, morals, and customs) also followed an evolutionary pattern—a step-by-step, one-way, inevitable pattern of change—from the less adaptive to the more adaptive. Spencer's perspective was labeled **social Darwinism** specifically because of his use of Darwinian concepts of a struggle for existence and natural selection in his analysis of human societies. But Spencer added the notion of "survival of the fittest" to Darwin's ideas. He did this to explain and justify the privileges and power of the societies and people who were dominant at the time he wrote.

According to Spencer, the British, males, and the upper classes were superior morally and intellectually because they were genetically superior. They were the biological victors in the struggle for survival, and they had rightly inherited the earth (the nineteenth-century earth, that is).

Spencer, like Comte, believed in the inevitability of progress. But he did not believe that governments should help the less privileged and less fortunate—the poor, unemployed, uneducated, disabled, or diseased. He believed that economic reforms would interfere with the weeding out of biologically inferior people by the process of natural selection. This would preserve the unfit and weaken the "great white race."

A look at the table of contents of Spencer's *Principles of Sociology* (1898) indicates that the broad topics he discussed—the family, politics, religion, and the economy—are still major areas of study in sociology. Spencer suggested that sociologists should discover the relationships between these major areas of life—the relationship between government and religion in regulating social life and maintaining social order (Comte's social statics), for example. He was also interested in studying social change in these basic areas of life throughout human history. Here, he advocated what is now called the "comparative historical method," in which sociologists compare "societies of different kinds and societies in different stages" to understand the principles of social change. The main divisions of sociological research that were suggested by Comte—social statics and social dynamics—appear in Spencer's work as well.

The comparative historical method is still important in sociological research. If used properly—that is, without omitting certain societies and selecting only those that support our theories—the comparison of different societies at the same or at different times is like an experiment. We look for effects when certain conditions (particular climates, customs, or values, for example) in the societies we are comparing are present or absent. But we cannot add or subtract these conditions deliberately as we do in a laboratory experiment. That is why this technique of research is called a **natural experiment**.

Spencer's social Darwinism as a way of explaining and justifying human inequality is still popular, despite the absence of evidence to support it. Spencer's evolutionary perspective is useful, however, when it is not taken to imply a necessary or inevitable, one-way, step-by-step change in any particular society. And we cannot assume the biological superiority of any nation or any large category of people in relation to the pace and direction of social change. Stripped of these presuppositions, the evolutionary perspective, now called sociocultural evolution, is a valuable way to understand social change in human societies. Sociocultural evolution refers to the historical trend in human societies toward more complex social relationships and cultures. This trend occurs as scientific knowledge accumulates and as tools, weapons, techniques, and sources of energy become more efficient and effective. Sociocultural evolution is an increasingly important perspective in interpreting human history (Lenski, 1966; Yorburg, 1973, 1974, 1983; Parsons, 1977; Lenski, 1988; Lenski, Lenski, and Nolan, 1991).

Émile Durkheim (1858–1917)   Another French pioneer sociologist, Émile Durkheim, who became the first professor of sociology in France, also viewed social change from an evolutionary perspective. Durkheim was primarily interested in social order and in the question of why social life is stable and predictable. He attributed the stability of human societies to the norms or rules of behavior, thought, and feeling that individuals learn in their groups and communities. He called these norms, including customs, morals, and traditions, **social facts**. According to Durkheim, social facts exist outside individuals as collective conceptions of right or wrong exist outside individuals as collective conceptions of right or wrong that guide and control people. They are a part of what we now call "culture."

Durkheim was aware that norms vary according to social location. Each social fact is related to "a particular social milieu, to a definite type of society" (Durkheim, 1938 [1895], p. 3). The norms or rules that guide human feelings, attitudes, and behavior are not "suspended in a void" and can only be described and understood in relation to various locating factors, such as class, ethnicity, gender, age, and so on. Durkheim observed that when group ties are strong, the controlling effects of social facts are strong, and, conversely, when group ties are weak, social control is weak, a condition he called **anomie** (literally, normlessness), an absence of norms or rules to guide behavior.

Like Comte, Durkheim was passionately devoted to developing a science of society. Like Spencer, he advocated the use of the comparative historical method:

> One cannot explain a social fact of any complexity except by following its complete development through all social species. Comparative sociology is not a particular branch of sociology; it is sociology itself. (1938 [1895], p. 139)

Durkheim applied this method in his study of religion (1947 [1912]), in which he collected and analyzed large quantities of anthropological and historical information on religious beliefs and practices in various societies.

But Durkheim is best known, at least in the United States, for his application of statistical methods to support his theories about group ties and the controlling effects of norms as these vary among people in different social locations. He illustrated his theory of the "sociological causes" of suicide by collecting and analyzing suicide statistics from various European countries over a period of years (Durkheim, 1951 [1897]).

Durkheim found, as he expected, that people who have weaker group ties—men, single people, and Protestants—have higher suicide rates than women, married people, and Catholics, who generally have stronger group ties. He called suicide attributable to this factor **egoistic suicide**.

Durkheim also found that suicide rates vary among different societies and within the same society at different times. Within a society, he found that rates increase (1) during times and situations of rapid social change; (2) when the rules governing behavior are vague, contradictory, or confusing; and (3) when the usual expectations in human relationships do not apply, such as during natural disasters. This is the social condition that Durkheim identified as anomie. The increased suicide rates that occur under these circumstances—particularly during periods of economic crisis, political upheavals, after a defeat in war—he called **anomic suicide**.

Not only can group ties be too weak to constrain people from destroying themselves, but they also can be so strong that individuals place the mikaze pilots who flew suicide missions placed more importance on the value of patriotism than on self-preservation. This type of suicide Durkheim called **altruistic suicide**. Durkheim believed that altruistic suicide was more characteristic of agricultural societies, where group commitment tends to be stronger, than of competitive, individualistic urban industrial societies. The urbanized and industrialized Japan of the 1940s represents a partial exception to Durkheim's theory.

Durkheim's analysis of suicide rates is sociological rather than psychological. The reason why any *particular* individual chooses to commit altruistic suicide can be explained psychologically. The greater or lesser "suicidal tendency" of large numbers of people by virtue of their location in a particular society, however, is a sociological phenomenon.

Durkheim's work has had tremendous influence on contemporary sociology. His focus on social facts, particularly moral values, as a basis for the social stability of societies is a major point of emphasis among contemporary structural-functional theorists, whose work is described in the next chapter.

Max Weber (1864–1920)   By the end of the nineteenth century, a disenchantment with Comte's positivism and with the supposed necessity of rigidly applying the methods of the natural sciences to the study of humans and of their ways of life had begun to set in. Although humans are motivated creatures, the meaning of their behavior cannot be measured directly by quantitative methods. The senses cannot directly observe what motivates people. We cannot see, hear, touch, smell, or taste a motive. We can ask people why they think or behave as they do, but they may not know why. Or they may be unwilling to tell us, even if they do know. One of the first to address this basic problem in social scientific research was Max Weber.

Weber defined sociology as "a science which attempts the interpretive understanding of social action in order thereby to arrive at a causal explanation of its course and effect" (1947 [1925], p. 88). Weber advocated what we now call identification and empathy on the part of social scientists to achieve *Verstehen* (the German term for understanding or insight) to determine the "intents and purposes" of behavior. We must identify with the people we study—imagine ourselves in their place—and empathize with them—feel what they are feeling and think what they are thinking. Weber believed that it was possible for social scientists to be objective and scientific, despite the complexity of their data and the necessity to use the **Verstehen** method to obtain information indirectly (1949 [1903–1917]).

Weber also believed that the information gathered by social scientists can and must be **value free**—unbiased and undistorted by the observer's own judgments about what is good or bad, desirable or undesirable, valuable or valueless. He recognized that values determine what a researcher decides to study, what knowledge is sought at a particular time in a society, and how knowledge is used. But facts are facts, and they should be reported objectively. Few social scientists would disagree with this idea.

But Weber also called for the pursuit of scientific knowledge regardless of the consequences. He argued that ends cannot be determined by science. Ends are given; science can only provide rational means for accomplishing these ends (1946 [1919], pp. 129–156). With the advent of nuclear warfare and the possibility of world destruction, scientists are increasingly concerned about the consequences of their research, in terms of both the means they supply and the ends for which these means are used. The quest for scientific knowledge is often undermined by public morality. In studying highly charged topics such as changes in sexual behavior, for example, research scientists tend to avoid any sort of confrontation with policy makers, which has made it easier for these policy makers "to use research evidence any way they [have] wished—including ignoring it, misinterpreting it, or *banning* it" (Reiss, 1993, p. 9).

Weber classified types of motivated action as emotional, traditional, rationally oriented toward an end, or rationally derived from values. He provided precise definitions of many terms, such as "power," "authority," "nation," "state," "bureaucracy," and "charisma," that are still useful to sociologists today. He used the comparative historical method to trace the evolutionary development of rational social action in Western economic life, religion, music, art, government and other large-scale organizations, and bureaucracies. He defined **rational social action** as a means-end orientation in which the means chosen are calculated logically and are the most effective available for achieving desired ends. He related the greater efficiency and effectiveness of social action in modern societies to developments in scientific knowledge and technology.

Weber believed that Marx's analysis of class and economic life was oversimplified. In the case of class, Weber described two other ways, aside from income and property, in which individuals are ranked as superior or inferior to each other—on the basis of power and according to differences in prestige, or "social honor." He pointed out that power and prestige hierarchies do not necessarily coincide with rankings on the basis of economic resources or class. It is possible to rank high on power and wealth, but low on prestige, as an unpopular military dictatorship would, for example.

Weber also felt that Marx's analysis of the separation of workers from the ownership of their tools when they went to work in factories was just a special case of a broader trend in industrial societies. This trend has been toward increasing bureaucratization in all spheres of life outside of family groups. Not only factory workers, but soldiers, scientists, and civil servants in modern societies are also separated from the ownership of their tools or equipment. Weber felt that socialism, by turning over the means of production to governments, would simply enhance the trend toward bureaucracy in modern societies. And Weber hated the impersonality, routine, and regimentation of bureaucratic organizations (Marianne Weber, 1975 [1926]).

Focus on Social Issues

A PIONEER WOMAN SOCIOLOGIST

[Women now make up a large part of the sociology profession and occupy many national leadership positions in the field. Before the women's movement of the 1960s and 1970s, however, women sociologists frequently encountered discrimination, sometimes from men unwilling to acknowledge that women could do serious sociological work. In the following passage, Matilda White Riley, who would later be elected president of the American Sociological Association, describes what it was like to enter the field in the 1930s and 1940s.]

Coming from the 1911 birth cohort, . . . sex discrimination was taken for granted; to advance, an enterprising woman had to find her own way around the obstacles. When a publisher refused to put my name on a book (on gliding and soaring!) that I had written during a college vacation "because no one will read a book written by a girl," I changed my name from Matilda to Mat, and the book sold quite well. When I sought a job to help support us during my husband's graduate studies, the professor who wanted to appoint me for the only available teaching assistantship was turned down by his dean because "as a woman she will not continue a career." Thereupon, through a stroke of good fortune, my summer vacation experiences in market research and my knowledge of foreign languages qualified me for the first research assistantship in the newly formed Harvard Department of Sociology.

–Matilda White Riley, ed., *Sociological Lives*, 1988, Newbury Park, CA: Sage Publications

What Do You Think?

1. How and why have the relative positions, prestige, and power of women and men changed, especially in the past 25 years in the United States?
2. How do you feel about the changes that have taken place?
3. Answer the preceding question again after completing this course and compare this answer with your earlier response.

Many of the ideas of Durkheim, Marx, and Weber are still useful. Weber's *Verstehen* technique, for example, is used by sociologists who observe relationships in groups. We study people intensely—observing not only what they say and do, but their gestures, facial expressions, and other nonverbal cues as well—to determine the real meaning of what is going on in a family, a gang, an office, school, or neighborhood. This kind of work, an example of *qualitative* research, is important in contemporary sociology, as are *quantitative* measures of what we can directly see or hear. Both types of knowledge are necessary if sociologists are to learn as much as they can about people and the social worlds in which they live and have lived.

14

The European pioneers gave sociology its name, its focus and perspective, some of its basic language, and a start with its quantitative and qualitative methods of scientific research. Each pioneer had his own special interests that were related to his own social location. Comte was responding to the ultimate failure of the first modern political revolution in France with a concern for social reconstruction. Marx, outcast and impoverished, focused on economics and exploitation. Spencer, an upper-class Englishman, was concerned with justifying the privileges of his gender, class, and country. Durkheim, son of a rabbi, studied religion, solidarity, and social control. And Weber, citizen of highly bureaucratic Germany, was preoccupied with bureaucracy and rationalism. Together, their insights have provided a solid foundation for other sociologists to build on.

Sociology in the United States

The first sociologists in the United States were the academic counterparts of the muckrakers of the turn of the century and the investigative reporters of today. They were perhaps more restrained and less sensationalist, but strongly oriented toward reform and the relief of human suffering. Many of the early members of the American Sociological Society were ministers or sons of ministers.

In addition to the problems of rapid urbanization and industrialization that plagued Europe, the United States experienced the problems caused by widespread racial, religious, and ethnic prejudice and discrimination. To the shock and confusion that arose from rural-urban migration within the same society were added the more profound upheavals experienced by over 35 million immigrants from very different societies. For many, the streets of New York and San Francisco, the major ports of arrival, were not paved with gold as anticipated, nor was America the melting pot they had envisioned.

After World War II, the emphasis in American sociology shifted increasingly toward positivism and the development of more refined quantitative, or statistical, methods. Earlier research had focused primarily on social problems, using qualitative methods or unsophisticated statistics. The new trend was promoted by (1) the explosion of advanced technology and scientific knowledge in the United States, (2) economic affluence and the decline in economic suffering after World War II, and (3) a strong desire to increase the reliability of sociological knowledge. Today, in a time of rising expectations, growing economic frustration, and increasing political and environmental threat and terror, all perspectives and research techniques, qualitative as well as quantitative, are needed. There is too much to know and too much to be done for sociologists to limit themselves methodologically.

Since the early days of sociology in Europe and the United States, sociologists have collected more and more accurate information to test theories about social stability and social change. We know much more about power and conflict, about values and roles, and about the effects of social

TABLE 1.1

Membership Sections, American Sociological Association

Undergraduate Education	Sociology of Aging
Methodology	Sociology of Mental Health
Medical Sociology	Collective Behavior/Social Movements
Crime, Law, and Deviance	Racial and Ethnic Minorities
Sociology of Education	Comparative Historical Sociology
Family	Political Sociology
Organizations and Occupations	Asia/Asian American
Theory	Sociology of Emotions
Sex and Gender	Sociology of Culture
Community and Urban Sociology	Science, Knowledge, and Technology
Social Psychology	Microcomputing
Peace and War	Latino/a Sociology
Environment and Technology	Alcohol and Drugs
Marxist Sociology	Sociology of Children
Sociological Practice	Sociology of Law
Sociology of Population	Rational Choice
Political Economy and the World System	Sociology of Religion

Source: American Sociological Association, 1994.

location on human thought, emotion, behavior, and destiny. With technological advances, more efficient and precise ways of collecting and processing data have been developed, using video cameras, tape recorders, and computers, for example.

The amount of knowledge in the field of sociology has increased to such an extent that there are now 34 membership sections listed by the American Sociological Association (see Table 1.1). These sections represent specialized areas or subfields within the discipline. As knowledge continues to accumulate, new specialties are created and new sections are added to the list.

Sociology as a scientific discipline has had its greatest flowering in the United States. Most of the vast amount of research described in succeeding chapters was conducted by sociologists in the United States. We will become familiar with their contributions throughout the text. Sociology is a discipline that does not flourish in repressive or totalitarian societies. In these societies, leaders usually define social reality by government edict and prescribe the truth about their citizens' needs in a way that best serves the leaders' interests.

SOCIOLOGY AND THE SOCIAL SCIENCES

Sociologists were the first to synthesize or combine the facts provided by other social scientists to present a more complete picture of human social life. We combine these facts and we generalize. We look for general patterns and major trends in human history. Historians, for example, will study a particular dictatorship in great and careful detail, whether it be German, Latin American, Italian, or Spanish. Sociologists more often use this information to look for what is common to all dictatorships. Under what conditions do dictatorships usually arise? What do all or most dictators, and all or most societies they rule, have in common? To answer these questions, we need accurate information not only from history, but also from anthropology, psychology, political science, and economics.

Initially, social scientists jealously carved out their domains more or less neatly. In recent years, however, these often-arbitrary boundaries have become increasingly blurred. More social scientists are now exchanging concepts, information, and perspectives in their research. In the most complex societies, interdependence increases tremendously as people become increasingly specialized in their activities, training, and knowledge. No one person can become equally expert in all fields. Knowledge accumulates too quickly, and it becomes impossible to keep up with it all. Researchers need the input of other specialists for a more complete understanding of what they are studying.

Anthropology, History, and Sociology

The work of anthropologists and historians is especially helpful to sociologists who do cross-cultural or cross-national research, comparing different societies at the same or at different times. Such comparative research has become increasingly popular in our global era. An example is studies focused on the question of whether certain personality traits, such as passivity among females or aggression among males, are primarily biologically or culturally determined. Sociologists have used anthropological studies of societies in which females are not passive and males are not aggressive to conclude that these and other male and female personality traits are highly variable. They vary depending on the society, the culture, and changing political and economic conditions (Yorburg, 1974; Epstein, 1988; Blumberg, 1991). This means that culture, learning, and social circumstances can, and do, override genetic hormonal, chromosomal, and anatomical differences that exist between the sexes.

Another example of the value of comparative, historical research is in addressing the question, Do men have a stronger genetic sex drive than women? The answer is that it doesn't matter, really, whether they do or they do not. The important point is that in societies where the culture does not *define* men as having a stronger sex drive, their sexual behavior is no different, typically, from that of women. In these societies, women are as likely to pursue sexual partners and enjoy sexual activity as men (Mead, 1935; 1949).

Psychology and Sociology

Psychologists study motivation, perception, thinking, learning, personality development, and abnormal behavior. Sociologists are also interested in these topics, but we ask, "How does social location–gender, class, or historical era, for example–affect these characteristics of human beings?" Do women in the United States today have higher rates of depression than men? (They do.) Do the rich have lower reported rates of mental illness than the poor? (They do.) Was mental illness more prevalent in industrializing societies than it is today? (Apparently, but we don't know for certain.)

Psychologists have long been interested in what makes for high levels of achievement motivation in children. What kind of parent-child relationship produces "A" students, children who have a strong drive to succeed in competition with others? The answer is a relationship in which mothers set very high standards and use powerful rewards and punishments to encourage successful competition. Fathers in such families, if they are present, are supportive, but not dominant or authoritarian (McClelland, 1961). Parents of high-achieving children do not dominate, overprotect, or overindulge their children because this discourages the independence, self-discipline, and resourcefulness necessary to be successful in any field (Kohn, 1969).

Sociologists have also been interested in this question. But we investigate how and why these kinds of parent-child relationships are more or less frequent in various classes, racial/ethnic populations, societies, and centuries. Sociologists emphasize and give more weight to social location in explaining typical differences in personality development and behavior. We are more interested in *rates* of crime, mental illness, achievement motivation, or suicide in various societies or among various categories of people in a society than in the *individual* reasons for these events (see Figure 1.1).

It is essential to understand the basic difference between the sociological view and the psychological view of human behavior and experience, because this understanding has crucial implications for social policy. Ultimately, it is individuals who act. And they act, ultimately, for psychological reasons, of course. But social location *channels* individual behavior. It provides means, mechanisms, and opportunities for this behavior. It reinforces or extinguishes constructive or destructive behavior.

To put all the blame on parental neglect, abuse, or rejection for human failure and violence diverts attention from the political and economic conditions that promote family stress. Any other approach that reduces behavior and achievement to psychological factors alone has the same effect. Psychological explanations have been especially popular in the United States, where individualism is a strong value. Psychology, after all, focuses on the individual. But we must also understand how the social climate–the culture, the economy, and government policy (or lack of policy)–encourages or discourages love or hate and good or evil in everyday life.

FIGURE 1.1

Sociology and the Social Sciences

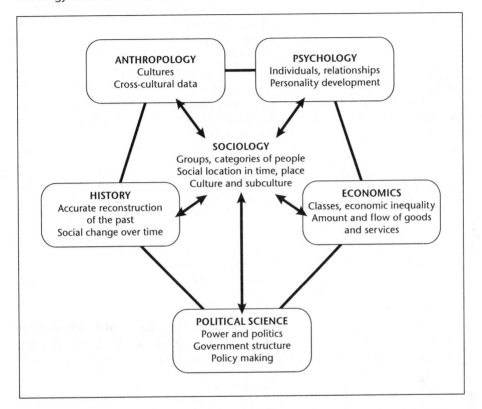

This figure shows the key concepts and areas of focus of sociologists and other social scientists, and the kinds of data that they collect and exchange in doing scientific research. Sociologists, for example, often use data collected by anthropologists in doing cross-cultural research. Psychologists increasingly include the effects of social location, a major concept and focus of sociologists, in their studies of personality development. Economists and political scientists now routinely use survey research methods developed by sociologists.

SOCIOLOGY AS AN OCCUPATION

Most sociologists with Ph.D. degrees teach and do research. According to the latest figures collected by the American Sociological Association, about 78 percent of its members work in colleges and universities, and 22 percent work outside of academia (American Sociological Association, 1993). Actually, many more sociologists with B.A. degrees, who are not usually members of the association, work in a large variety of occupations (see Table 1.2).

(Continued on page 21)

TABLE 1.2

Job Titles of Sociology Degree Recipients, B.A. Level

Research
Social research assistant
Survey research technician
Data analyst
Market researcher
Interviewer
Statistician
Public survey worker
Census research assistant
Demographer assistant
Criminology assistant
Consumer researcher

Education
Teacher
Student personnel worker
Affirmative action assistant
Admissions counselor
Alumni relations worker
College placement worker
Extension service specialist
Public health educator

Community and Social Services
Fund-raising assistant/director
Child care worker
Caseworker/aide
Environmental organizer
Community organizer
Youth outreach worker
Family planning worker
Substance abuse counselor
Occupational/career counselor
Hospital administrator
Medical records worker
Community aid workers
Homeless/housing worker
Case manager
Child development technician
Recreation worker
Public assistance worker
Resident planning aide
Group home worker
Rehabilitation program worker
Public health supervisor
Rural health supervisor
Housing coordinator

Justice System
Corrections officer
Corrections staffer
Criminal investigator
Juvenile court worker
Parole officer
Police officer
Police department staffer
Special agent
Correctional counselor
State trooper
Rehabilitation counselor

Business and Industry
Sales representative
Sales manager
Advertising staffer
Consumer relations worker
Market analyst
Real estate agent
Issues manager
Public relations staffer
Training assistant
Insurance agent
Production manager
Labor relations staffer
Administrative assistant
Planning assistant
Quality control manager
Merchandiser/purchaser
Computer analyst
Data entry manager
Publishing staffer
Banker
Human resources manager

Government
Employee specialist
Foreign service officer
Human rights officer
International worker
Personnel coordinator
Program supervisor
Special agent
Urban planner
Information officer
Legislative aide
Peace Corps volunteer
Affirmative action worker

Source: American Sociological Association. Based on reports from placement offices and sociology departments of three major universities.

And the number of sociologists employed in business, industry, and government has been increasing for decades, as **applied sociology**—the use of sociological research to achieve immediate, practical goals—becomes more recognized. In applied settings, employers define the goals they want to achieve. And sociologists advise on the best means for accomplishing these goals, given our present state of knowledge.

Sociologists in Business, Industry, and Government

In business and industry, the goals are to increase productivity and profit and produce goods that will sell well. In these settings, sociologists advise on public relations and employee relations, especially on techniques for improving employee morale. Here, sociologists have been in the forefront in programs to increase worker participation in executive decision making. Sociologists were among the first to design and evaluate experimental programs such as the 4-day workweek, work sharing, and profit-sharing plans. Sociologists in business and industry also do **market research**. They survey the tastes and desires of the buying public and test reactions to new products or product changes that are in the planning stage.

In government, sociologists collect statistical information about the population and its needs in agencies such as the Bureau of the Census. They also do **evaluation research**, follow-up studies that measure the long-term effectiveness of various social programs such as job training, Head Start, and welfare. Sociologists have also been active on the community level, especially in self-help programs that attempt to mobilize local talent to cope with local problems, mainly in inner-city ghettos.

Sociology and the Helping Professions

Sociologists also work with members of the helping professions: social workers, medical students, doctors, and lawyers. They evaluate new social service programs. And they provide information about ethnic and class subcultures. This improves communication and increases understanding between professionals and their clients or patients. It was sociologists who first pointed out that conventional insight psychotherapy (helping patients become more aware of their defenses and motives) does not work well with poorly educated mental patients. Direct advice and medication are usually more effective, given the values, educational level, and previous life experiences of these patients.

Courses in undergraduate sociology are valuable for students anticipating any profession that involves working with people and their environments, such as architecture and engineering. High schools are increasingly offering sociology as a separate course, or as a unit in social studies programs. Many civil service positions, when they are available, have been filled by young men and women with undergraduate degrees in sociology. And the spread of various action programs—consumer and urban advocacy groups, fair employment practices commissions, and human relations programs—has provided additional employment for sociologists in applied fields.

The increasing role of sociologists in complex societies goes hand in hand with rising expectations and the increased awareness of individual and group interests that more educated citizens have. The work of sociologists and social scientists, generally, is essential to political democracy, regardless of whether the economic system is capitalist, socialist, or something in between. Sociological knowledge is vital in all countries where citizens have the right to make their needs known and to have their wishes respected.

A knowledge of sociology can also be quite helpful in our own individual lives. It can be reassuring to know, for example, that what seems to be a personal problem is really a widespread social problem. It helps to know that we are not alone. We are less likely to blame ourselves (or others who are not really responsible) for our problems. We can also act more effectively in coping with our environment if we understand what is actually going on in our society. And we can avoid costly mistakes if we understand better the probable long-term consequences of making certain choices rather than others, whether in political, economic, family, or educational areas of life.

Study Guide

REVIEW OBJECTIVES

After studying this chapter, you should be able to:

1. Define sociology clearly.
2. Explain how sociological knowledge often dispels false commonsense beliefs.
3. Discuss why sociologists sometimes use technical terms.
4. Identify the basic ideas of the pioneer sociologists in Europe.
5. Describe the special concerns and interests of sociologists in the United States.
6. Explain how sociology differs from the other social sciences.
7. Describe the kind of work sociologists do.
8. Discuss the usefulness of sociology to governments and citizens.

SUMMARY

1. Sociologists study the typical thoughts, emotions, and behavior of people who live and have lived in different social worlds. These worlds are located in time (the past or the present), in physical space (continents, countries, regions, communities, neighborhoods, buildings, groups), and in social or cultural space (classes, ethnic groups, genders, generations, religions, nationalities).

2. Sociologists also study the atypical: nonconforming or deviant behavior, ideas, and feelings. These, too, are socially located. The study of what is atypical helps us understand better why societies remain stable and why they change.

3. Sociological research as a means for collecting factual information about human societies becomes essential in complex, rapidly changing societies. Common sense is a poor guide to what actually goes on in such a society.

4. Sociologists, like other scientists, use technical language to guide and sensitize their observations of social reality and to communicate information more efficiently. We define familiar words used in the popular language more precisely, however, to increase awareness and understanding of what we study.

5. Sociology arose in Europe in the nineteenth century in response to the problems created by industrialization and urbanization. The European pioneers were concerned with human suffering and social reform. They provided a definition of the field, an outline of major areas for research, some basic concepts that are still used, and a discussion and application of qualitative

and quantitative methods, which continue to be significant in sociological research.

6. The first American sociologists were also motivated primarily by a concern for human suffering. In addition to the problems created by industrialization and urbanization, sociologists in the United States were, and still are, concerned with the consequences of massive immigration to the United States. This immigration peaked in the early twentieth century and increased again, dramatically, in the 1980s.

7. Sociology in the United States has also been characterized by a strong emphasis on quantitative methods. Sociologists have been in the forefront in the development of highly sophisticated statistical methods and in the use of advanced technology in the collection and processing of data.

8. Sociologists have long used the data collected by the other social sciences to provide a more complete understanding of human social life. Many social scientists are now borrowing concepts, methods, and information from each other.

9. Most sociologists with Ph.D. degrees teach and do research at colleges and universities. In recent years, however, the usefulness of sociologists as researchers and consultants in government, business and industry, and professional service settings has been increasingly recognized.

10. Sociological knowledge helps citizens in political democracies become more aware that what seem to be purely personal problems are often also social problems that require political as well as personal solutions.

GLOSSARY

Altruistic suicide Suicide that is motivated by a very strong commitment to a group and its goals.

Anomic suicide Suicide that stems from rapid social change and the breakdown of the norms that previously controlled people.

Anomie A social condition in which norms are weak or absent and do not control people.

Applied sociology The use of sociological research and knowledge to achieve practical goals.

Bureaucracy A complex administrative organization that coordinates the activities of large numbers of people in carrying out large-scale tasks.

Class conflict The struggle over economic resources by members of different economic classes.

Economic class Rank in society determined by possession of economic resources (property and income); large category of people sharing the same rank.

Egoistic suicide Suicide that stems from a lack of strong group ties.

Evaluation research Follow-up studies that measure the effectiveness of social programs.

Market research Surveys of the buying habits of the public and tests of consumer reaction to proposed new products or changes in products.

Natural experiments The comparison of societies with different social conditions to determine the effects of the presence or absence of these conditions on whatever it is we are investigating. This is also called the comparative historical method, or, more simply, cross-cultural research.

Positivism The application of the methods of the natural sciences to the study of societies and social relationships.

Rational social action A choice of means that are logically the most efficient and effective for achieving desired ends.

Social Darwinism The application of Darwin's theory of biological evolution to explain inequality between different societies and among various categories of people in the same society.

Social facts Rules that exist outside of individuals and have a controlling force over them. They define right and wrong behavior, thought, and emotion within groups, communities, and societies.

Social location Location within a particular society or major category of people in a society at a particular time.

Sociology The study of the typical ways of thinking, feeling, and behaving of people who are similarly located in time and in physical and cultural space.

Value free The principle that research techniques, observations, and conclusions must not be distorted by the investigator's values.

***Verstehen* method** A qualitative method of sociological research involving identification and empathy with subjects.

PRACTICE TESTS

Answers to practice tests may be found on page xliii at the end of the text.

True ▪ False Test

___ 1. Sociologists usually are not concerned with nontypical or deviant behaviors.

___ 2. Sociological research strongly supports the argument that maternal employment is bad for children.

___ 3. Sociologists have found that the majority of married people are happy/satisfied in their marriages.

___ 4. Sociologists try to avoid the use of such common terms as "bureaucracy," "role," and "status," believing that such terms are of little scientific value.

___ 5. Durkheim coined the name "sociology."

___ 6. Marx believed that the ruling class could be overthrown only by revolution.

___ 7. Spencer advocated the use of the comparative historical method.

___ 8. Durkheim's concept of sociology was diametrically opposed to that of Spencer.

___ 9. The work of the early pioneers of sociology is now considered to have only very limited applications to the science.

___ 10. Other disciplines besides sociology, such as psychology, are of value in the study of the family.

Multiple-Choice Test

___ 1. Of the following choices, an example of the sociological concept of a location in time is:
   a. survival of the fittest.
   b. a rural town threatened by pollution.
   c. sexual attitudes during the Victorian era.
   d. changes in India's caste system.

___ 2. In the sociological sense, holding a job as an adult is a behavior that could be termed:
   a. typical.
   b. social location.
   c. luck and pluck.
   d. positivism.

___ 3. Age and generation are both aspects of the sociological concept or perspective known as location in:
   a. physical space.
   b. myth.
   c. class.
   d. time.

__ 4. The philosophical and scholarly foundations of sociology were laid in:
   a. Europe.
   b. the United States.
   c. ancient China.
   d. the Islamic Middle East.

__ 5. The founder of sociology is usually identified as:
   a. Weber.
   b. Spencer.
   c. Engels.
   d. Comte.

__ 6. The early contributor to sociology whose ideas are most closely associated with theories related to class membership is:
   a. Marx.
   b. Darwin.
   c. Durkheim.
   d. Comte.

__ 7. Social Darwinism:
   a. was the precursor of scientific socialism.
   b. led to Comte's positivist approach.
   c. is not supported by extensive scientific evidence.
   d. rejects the inevitability of progress.

__ 8. Sociological research that compares and contrasts information about different societies is called:
   a. evolutionary.
   b. cross-cultural.
   c. anthropological.
   d. generalized.

__ 9. Most sociologists with Ph.D. degrees work in:
   a. government.
   b. colleges and universities.
   c. market research.
   d. nonprofit community outreach programs.

__ 10. It is incorrect to believe that sociology:
   a. is applicable to many government and business decisions.
   b. has no value to an individual seeking to solve a personal problem.
   c. is a social science.
   d. has increased in importance during the twentieth century.

Matching Test

Match each concept with its definition, illustration, or explication below.

1.

___ (1) Location in physical space
___ (2) Location in time
___ (3) Typical
___ (4) Sociological
___ (5) Myths

a. Occurs among a majority
b. Refers to social location factors
c. Geography
d. False beliefs about a society
e. Historical period

2.

___ (1) Embezzlement
___ (2) Good pay
___ (3) "Everyone knows"
___ (4) Speculation
___ (5) Sociological knowledge

a. Commonly believed
b. Not necessarily true
c. Based on fact
d. Heightens self-esteem
e. Middle- and upper-class crime

3.

___ (1) Social physics
___ (2) Bureaucracy
___ (3) Social statics
___ (4) Social dynamics
___ (5) Metaphysical stage

a. Top-down authority
b. Unsupported by scientific evidence
c. Order, stability
d. Statistics
e. Concerned with change

4.

___ (1) Weber
___ (2) Comte
___ (3) Spencer
___ (4) Durkheim
___ (5) Marx

a. Positivism
b. Scientific socialism
c. Anomie
d. Evolutionary perspective
e. *Verstehen* technique

5.

___ (1) Was optimistic about the power of social scientists
___ (2) Believed in social "survival of the fittest"
___ (3) Emphasized economic factors in human relationships
___ (4) Termed norms of behavior "social facts"
___ (5) Advocated value-free social science

a. Spencer
b. Durkheim
c. Comte
d. Weber
e. Marx

REVIEW QUESTIONS

1. What is sociology? Why is it a science?
2. What are some of the basic ideas of Auguste Comte, Karl Marx, Herbert Spencer, Émile Durkheim, and Max Weber that are still useful today?
3. What have been the major contributions of sociologists in the United States to the development of the field?
4. How do sociologists use information from history and anthropology to answer sociological questions?
5. How does sociology differ from psychology? Give examples of research questions and conclusions that illustrate this difference.
6. How is sociological knowledge useful in business, industry, government, and in the helping professions?
7. How can sociological knowledge be helpful to individuals, especially in democratic industrial societies?

APPLYING SOCIOLOGY

1. Discuss how a sociologist might investigate the truth or falsity of certain commonsense beliefs that are contradictory, such as these:
   a. Absence makes the heart grow fonder.
      Out of sight, out of mind.
   b. Opposites attract.
      Birds of a feather flock together.
2. Can you think of possible situations in which sociologists would refuse to investigate the most effective means for accomplishing certain goals—in government and industry, for example—that they do not approve of?
3. How might a researcher in each of the different social sciences view the following social conditions, institutions, or movements in the United States differently?
   a. poverty
   b. race relations
   c. the educational system
   d. the civil rights movement
   e. the women's movement
4. How might a sociologist be useful as a consultant in carrying out the following goals?
   a. improving morale in the army or in industry
   b. lowering rates of crime and delinquency, mental illness, alcoholism, and drug addiction
   c. diminishing conflict between ethnic groups
   d. lowering unemployment rates
   e. improving the effectiveness of public education
   f. improving relationships between professionals and their clients

5. How could a knowledge of sociology help us better understand an individual with the following personal problems? (First locate the person socially, and proceed from there.)
   a. poor ability to read or write
   b. inability to get a job
   c. alcoholism
   d. lack of ambition or drive
   e. a divorce in the family
   f. a nervous breakdown
   g. suicidal impulses
   h. loneliness
6. Locate yourself socially and think of possible sociological explanations for some of your problems.

   Toward the end of the semester, answer these questions again. A comparison of your answers then and now will be an indication of the extent to which you have learned to think sociologically.

2

Models and Methods

Researchers use **theories** to explain why or how things happen. Theories tell us what it's all about, why we suffer or despair, why we love or hate, why we succeed or fail. Theories answer questions. Some historical questions have been the source of much controversy in sociology. Why did the West industrialize sooner than the East? Why has economic inequality been more extreme in agricultural societies than in industrial societies? Why has there never been a society ruled by women as a class? Researchers with different theoretical perspectives have given different answers to these questions. We will return to these questions later in the chapter.

Theories point to relationships between **variables**. Variables are characteristics that differ in degree or type. They can be observed either directly or indirectly. An attitude cannot be observed directly; an opinion, which is a verbal expression of an attitude, can be observed directly. It can be heard or read. Some of the more important variables used by sociologists interested in answering historical questions have been differences in human biology, climate and geography, sociocultural evolution, economic resources, and cultural values.

For contemporary problems, researchers usually look at variables such as changing economic and political conditions and values. They also study the effects of locating factors such as gender, social class, racial/ethnic origin, or age and generation to explain differences in human experiences, prospects, and outcomes. It is important to emphasize at the outset, however, that when social scientists study human beings and their changing realities, we look to many causes. Causation in the social sciences is enormously complicated. Almost nothing can be explained as the result of a single variable. Usually we focus on how various factors interrelate to produce a particular result.

Researchers will give different explanations for some of the major problems of our time—high crime rates, poverty, unemployment, inequalities in educational achievement, and high divorce rates—depending on the variables they select and the relative weight they give to these variables. In explaining high adolescent pregnancy rates in inner-city areas of the United States, for example, are personality, personal values, family structure (single- or two-parent), racial/ethnic subcultural values, or poverty the most important factors? If all these variables are important, how much weight do we give to each? How do they interrelate? Does premarital childbearing result in poverty, or does poverty result in premarital pregnancies? Or are both true and, if so, to what extent and for whom?

According to one national study of over 13,000 households, poverty is the most important variable in explaining differences between minority and nonminority rates of premarital pregnancy (Wu and Martinson, 1993). Other factors, such as family instability (divorce or separation) and psychological factors, are more important among higher-income groups. Most teenage mothers, however, regardless of social class, experience long-term disadvantages in education and occupational achievement (Hoffman, Foster, and Furstenberg, 1993) (see Figure 2.1).

Theories differ in the *weight*, or emphasis, they place on particular variables. Since causation is difficult to prove in the social sciences, we do not have a single theoretical perspective that is used by most, or all, sociologists at the present time. Different theories are not necessarily contradictory, however. Often, researchers ask different questions and seek to explain different facts. Sociologists may focus primarily on social stability or on social change. They may focus on whole societies, particular aspects of a society (the government or the economy, for example) or on large

FIGURE 2.1

Risk Factors Associated with Early Adolescent Sexual Activity

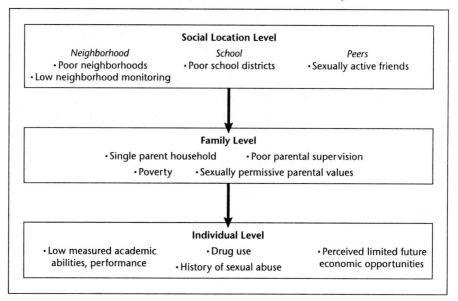

Source: Adapted from Stephen A. Small and Tom Luster, "Adolescent Sexual Activity: An Ecological, Risk-Factor Approach," *Journal of Marriage and the Family* 56 (1994), pp. 181–192. Used by permission.

Conditions and patterns at several different social levels are associated with sexual activity at an early age.

categories of people within a society (races or classes, for example). Or they may focus on day-to-day relationships (interaction) in small or large groups, from families to corporations.

THEORIES AND MODELS

A **model** is a perspective that orients us to reality. It consists of a set of interrelated concepts that sensitize us to certain aspects of reality. Models determine what we look for and, to some extent, what we see. They focus our attention on specific variables such as climate, sociocultural evolution, social location, economics, values, genes, or personality that may explain what we observe. **Concepts** are abstract terms or phrases that classify or characterize various aspects of realty. The concepts in a model, such as "class struggle" in the Marxian model or "defenses" in the psychoanalytic model, encourage researchers to look for these things in their observations and explanations. Current models and theories cannot answer all questions of human existence. But they steadily improve as accurate scientific information about people, places, things, and events continues to accumulate.

Theoretical models can be religious, emphasizing supernatural causation, divine dispensation, or God's will, for example. They can be scientific, focusing on observable, verifiable evidence. They can be philosophical or based on common sense. Or they may have a combination of these characteristics. All widely used scientific perspectives approach the truth; none exhausts it. Scientific models and theories, however, generally have an edge with respect to predicting events and behavior.

The term "class" is a basic concept in the Marxian theoretical model. Other related concepts, each of which has come into popular use as well as having a more precise meaning within the Marxian model, include "exploitation," "alienation," "class consciousness," and "class struggle." Though it is now declining in influence, this model provided meaning and answers to basic questions of human existence for millions of people in the past. Religious, philosophical, and psychological models have functioned in a similar way for those who use them.

To a much greater extent than in the natural sciences, sociological models and concepts, especially those that are tied to social location, change. Concepts such as "counterculture," "hippies," "yuppies," and "generation gap" are examples. This reflects rapidly changing social realities in modern societies. What may have been true for one generation is not necessarily true for the next, or even for the same generation as it gets older. Most hippies of the 1960s counterculture generation, who distanced themselves from their "uptight" parents, are now respectably employed in conventional occupations. Things change for generations as well as for individuals.

Materialistic yuppies (young urban professionals) of the 1980s are now more likely to persuade themselves that less is more. Many are shifting to simple pleasures like family, fidelity, and frugality and to spiritual values. M.B.A. enrollments are down and applications to medical school are increasing (Altman, 1993).

Job security and financial security have become major factors in occupational choices as a result of more than 20 years of recurring recessions in the United States, a national debt that quadrupled in the 1980s, and widespread layoffs and plant closings in the 1990s. This partly accounts for the resurgent interest in medicine; teaching and nursing have also become more popular choices recently. Business careers, involving greater risk taking and uncertainty about the future, are no longer as fashionable as they were in more affluent times.

As for the generation gap—disagreements about values between parents and their children—we now know that generations in specific families are more likely to agree than disagree about basic values in the long run. This is especially true of close-knit, nonimmigrant, middle-class families (Rossi and Rossi, 1990). Adolescents, seeking psychological independence from parents, may dress, speak, and behave sexually in ways that offend their parents. But they tend to return to the values of their parents eventually, especially after they have children of their own.

Many sociological concepts have become part of the popular vocabulary in watered-down versions. Terms such as "charisma," "conspicuous consumption," "counterculture," "power structure," and "lifestyle" were originally used in very specific ways by sociologists. These terms are now in wide use in the United States. But they have lost much of their precisely defined original meaning.

The term "charisma," for example, was originally a biblical term referring to the gift of grace. It was used by Max Weber to refer to the extraordinary or even magical qualities that are attributed to certain political or religious leaders. These leaders arise, outside of mainstream religion or government, in times of crisis. The enormous persuasiveness of charismatic leaders is based on the magical faith that followers have in their ability to restore or cure the ills of the soul or the society in crisis. Jesus, Joan of Arc, Mao Zedong, and Malcolm X were all charismatic leaders. As the concept is now used in the popular media and by the general public in the United States, however, charisma refers to "presence" or "sex appeal" and, as such, it is now the name of a perfume.

Some concepts in theoretical models are more difficult to support by facts than others. The concept of economic class in the Marxian model refers to something that can be measured. It is determined by the amount of income or wealth individuals or families have and the productive resources they own or control. In contrast, when placing people in the class structure, sociologists usually measure income and property, educational level, and occupational prestige. These factors, along with ancestry (family and racial/ethnic origin) and gender, determine overall prestige (respect, acceptance, and esteem) in a society. They are the basis of what we will call **social class** or overall **social status**, a rank that is much more difficult to measure than economic class. There are no rigid boundaries between social classes in industrial societies.

Concepts such as **class consciousness**—awareness or lack of awareness of how one's economic needs are being served in a society—are also more difficult to measure. They refer to subjective, internal states—to beliefs, knowledge, class identifications, and feelings of identity. These things are more complicated to observe, measure, and explain.

Before turning to the specific theoretical models that have been most popular in the field of sociology, it would be helpful to discuss some of the basic variables that have most often been used by social scientists to explain changing human realities.

MAJOR VARIABLES IN THE SOCIAL SCIENCES

In the history of social scientific theory, many different variables—human biology, climate and geography, scientific knowledge, technology, economics, power, values, and psychology—have been given primary weight in explaining the course of human history. Actually, all these factors (and more) must be accounted for in an adequate model of human history and human prospects. The problem, again, is to explain—if we can—how these factors all interrelate and how much weight to give to each.

Human Biology

Human biology underlies all other factors; it explains certain universal social forms that have been found in all societies. Among these are the family, marriage, the incest taboo, and male dominance. The biological reasons for the existence of these universals are (1) the far greater dependency of the human infant at birth compared to other animals, (2) the continuous sex drive of the human female, and (3) the greater average size and strength of the human male.

Human beings have the most complex nervous systems and physiology of any animal species. They live longer than most other animals. They are born more completely helpless and dependent, and they take much longer to reach adulthood. Most animals reach maturity in a few weeks or months. Nonhuman primates, such as chimpanzees, take from 10 to 12 years to become physically and sexually mature. Humans take anywhere from 14 to 20 years before growth ends and full biological maturity is reached.

Humans require more intense and prolonged care and are far more dependent on learning than any other animal. Possessing a more highly developed cortex (the center of memory and learning), however, humans have a unique capacity to use **language**. Other animals generally communicate by signs or signals (gestures)—hostile or friendly—that represent immediate motives and feelings. Humans operate at a more sophisticated level. Language is made up of arbitrary written or oral symbols whose meaning is agreed upon by two or more people (see chapter 3, pp. 79–80). These symbols represent more abstract and not necessarily immediate conditions, motives, or feelings. Humans can refer to the future or the past when they communicate. They can warn, predict, remind, encourage, and teach by talking, not doing, thereby eliminating the necessity for much trial-and-error behavior by the human young. The necessity to learn language and the dependence on language in coping with potential threats in the environment increases the dependence of human infants—and the survival and adaptability of humans of all ages.

These differences underlie the fact that all human societies have a recognizable family unit, no matter how this unit has varied in form and function. Humans cannot depend on hereditary instincts or hormones to provide the intense and lengthy care that their young require to achieve physical, emotional, and intellectual maturity. The universality of the family as a social form stems from the necessities of human biology. Nonfamily units have, in some circumstances, provided physical and intellectual care for the human young more effectively than the family. But in no society has the satisfaction of the basic emotional needs of a majority of its members been left to nonfamily groups.

Another biological characteristic of humans that has important consequences for human social life is the continuous sex drive of the human female. The female does not have to be in heat before mating can take place. Humans have no mating season—at least not one determined by biology.

This means that sexual jealousies and conflicts are always a possibility in human societies. Uncontrolled sexual behavior could undermine the prolonged and stable care that infants and children need. The **incest taboo** prohibits sexual relationships between close relatives in the immediate family, although it can and has been extended arbitrarily to include various other relatives. And, of course, it has often been broken (deMause, 1991). When it is effective, however, this taboo prevents sexual rivalry between mother and daughter or father and son, a rivalry that could break up families and be destructive to the very dependent human young.

Marriage is another means for controlling sexual competition in human societies. It is a socially controlled, sexual relationship that is more or less exclusive and more or less permanent, depending on the society. Adultery, divorce, or separation are as universal as marriage. But to the extent that they work, the controls surrounding marriage do limit sexual relationships and potential sexual conflicts in human societies. The incest taboo and marriage are human inventions that help control and set limits to human sexual behavior. Both are **cultural universals** that are found in every known society and culture.

One final biological characteristic of humans (and most other animals) is the greater average size and muscular strength of the human male as compared to the human female. Males, generally, have had more power than females in human societies. The ultimate source of power is physical force. When all else fails, males can get what they want, even against resistance, by using their generally superior strength. For this reason, even though we have had women queens, prime ministers, and presidents, no known society has been ruled by women only.

As societies develop technologically, however, and as machines replace muscle power, the greater average size and strength of males becomes increasingly irrelevant to differences in the power and prestige of the sexes. Anyone can push a button, dial a service, pull a trigger, or fly a plane. Historically, however, male dominance has been grounded in biology, at least as far as greater size and strength reinforce the ability to win in situations of conflict.

Sociobiology is the current model in which biology is given the greatest weight in explaining complex human personality tendencies such as aggression, selfishness, tribalism, and male dominance hierarchies. Sociobiologists believe these personality dispositions became genetically established and inherited by selection in the evolutionary process because they were more adaptive in the struggle for food, shelter, and living space and generally, for survival (Wilson, 1975).

Most sociologists (and anthropologists) have questioned the evidence presented by sociobiologists, especially as this model has been used by some researchers to explain (and justify) differences in the power and privileges of large categories of people such as men and women (Goldberg, 1993). These researchers assume the existence of universal biologically based traits, such as passivity in women, to explain such things as why women, as a class, have never ruled human societies (Goldberg, 1993). Researchers who use this model believe that certain personality traits are a part of "human nature" and are fixed and unchanging because they are based on biology.

Most sociologists, however, are likely to argue that human nature is quite flexible. If personality traits such as selfishness or aggression were biological and universal, they would be widespread in all societies—but they are not. To a large extent, the concept of human nature tends to mean that which is defined as human nature in a particular culture and society at a particular time. In the nineteenth century, in Europe and the United States, newborn infants were defined as born evil and in need of "taming"—in other words, beating (deMause, 1974). In the twentieth century, infants tend to be viewed as blank tablets—aside from individual differences in intelligence and temperament—on which family, experts, friends, and models in the media write their messages. And parental discipline, therefore, is kinder, or at least gentler: "time-out" replaces the slap or the strap in disciplining young children, at least in the middle social classes.

Inherited genetic differences among humans are certainly important for individuals. Individual differences in **temperament**, for example—in emotional intensity, energy level, and frustration tolerance—are observable at birth. For the newborn infant, these differences seem to override the effects of prenatal care of the mother and other environmental differences that might affect temperamental characteristics of infants at birth (Buss, 1994).

Certain assumptions in the sociobiology model, especially about inborn selfishness and tribalism, have important implications for social policy and the future of the human animal. These assumptions are inherently pessimistic: that war between societies is inevitable because of our aggressive genes, for example. In the public policy arena, if selfishness and destructiveness are innate and inflexible human traits, we cannot expect citizens to sacrifice their own self-interests for others who are less fortunate. And the future prospects of humans and other inhabitants of the earth, in an era of global threat to our natural environment, are very dim indeed. Those sociobiologists known as evolutionary biologists tend to believe that "[p]eople are programmed by their genetic heritage to be so selfish that a sense of global responsibility will come too late" (E. O. Wilson, 1993, p. 26).

Climate and Geography

Climate and geography are also important factors that affect social stability and social change in human societies. Countries with a tropical climate or a year-round growing season have been slower to industrialize than those with a temperate climate. Tropical countries have felt less pressure to shift their energies and talents to the invention of more efficient techniques for increasing their material resources. Food is usually plentiful in all seasons. In temperate climates, sections of a country located in the colder climates of the north have usually industrialized faster than southern areas—in the United States, Italy, and the United Kingdom, for example.

The geographic location of a given society has also been a basic factor in determining its history (Lenski, 1988). The societies that have been most isolated geographically (those in forests, deserts, and arctic areas) have been least likely to experience the effects of **cultural diffusion**. This process involves the spread of scientific knowledge, customs, tools, weapons, and skills from one society to another. It is isolated societies that have been most likely to survive into the present as hunting and gathering or herding societies.

Geography affects the amount of contact with other societies through trade, migration, and war. This contact, in turn, affects the rate of sociocultural evolution in a society. The pace of sociocultural evolution speeds up when societies borrow more efficient techniques, tools, and weapons from other societies. This also happens when new technologies are imposed on conquered societies by victorious, more technologically advanced societies. Isolated societies are safe from conquest, but they are less exposed to the fruits of the inventions and discoveries of other societies. Ancient empire builders, such as the Romans, taught their conquered populations the techniques of road building and irrigation, even as they exploited these populations. Other colonizers exported their knowledge of agriculture, mining, and manufacturing to conquered territories, as well as their customs, values, and morals.

Science, Technology, and Economics

Developments in scientific information and technology reinforce each other. Science provides the discoveries that improve technological efficiency, and technology provides the tools that increase the accuracy of scientific investigations, tools such as microscopes, tape recorders, and computers. The germ theory of disease, a scientific model in which certain diseases are explained by the presence of specific bacteria in the body, was not possible until the invention of the microscope allowed scientists to see bacteria.

The efficiency of tools and weapons in a society directly affects the economy of that society. It determines the amount, kind, and distribution of economic goods and services available to its members. The discovery of plant cultivation and the invention of the tools used in planting—first the digging stick, then the hoe, then the plow, and then, finally, the tractor—increased food supplies in human societies enormously over time. Land became the basic economic resource. Later, with increased trade and the invention of machines, money and other forms of capital became the basic source of wealth.

Weapons especially affect the distribution of economic resources in a society. Everywhere and at all times, when there has been an economic surplus (more food and other products for consumption than needed) in a human society or societies, weapons have been used in conflicts over who gets what and how much. And the spoils of victory (food and other material goods) have often, although not always, gone to those who have better weapons.

Initially, societies become more stationary and permanent as they accumulate more economic resources, especially food. They have (1) larger populations, (2) more specialized occupations, (3) more trade and commerce, (4) greater economic inequality, (5) more competition and conflict between groups and between societies, and (6) more complex and elaborate political, educational, and religious institutions. Some trends—the rate of population increase and the exclusive concentration of wealth in upper-class families, for example—diminish somewhat as societies become highly industrialized (Lenski, 1966; 1988). In these societies, values change in favor of smaller families and the middle classes increase in size.

Whatever the direction of change, however, all areas of life are profoundly affected by inventions, discoveries, the growth and diffusion of scientific knowledge, more efficient and effective tools, weapons, and skills, and the economic changes that result. This is the essence of sociocultural evolution.

Values

The term **values** refers to beliefs about what is good, right, desirable, or important. Values determine an individual's and a society's goals, choices, and priorities. The cultural values of a particular society are important in explaining its history. Values speed up or delay sociocultural evolution. They affect the distribution of economic resources in a society. Societies that value internal economic reforms do not usually value diversionary external wars. Some sociologists have given primary weight to values in interpreting social change. Others view sociocultural evolution and economics as more basic factors.

In trying to explain why capitalism arose first in the West, for example, Weber gave great weight to the values of the Protestant religion. Protestant doctrine emphasized individual, materialistic success rather than other-worldly spiritual goals. Spiritual values were central to the Catholic religion and the religions of the East (Weber, 1958 [1904]). Karl Marx (1906 [1867]), on the other hand, gave less weight to values and more to changes in technology and the changing economic relationships between the classes that result from technological development. This is a very complicated issue in sociology; it has been the source of argument and controversy among social scientists to this day.

At present, the weight of the evidence indicates that developments in science, technology, and economics are more important factors in explaining social change. Values certainly affect the speed and direction of change in a society. But values do not exist in a vacuum. They themselves change, usually in response to widespread changes in the scientific, technological, and economic spheres in a society. An example will make this clearer. Because of declining real purchasing power (corrected for inflation) in the United States over the past two decades, it now takes two paychecks to support most families comfortably, or even adequately. Husbands, especially those in the middle social classes, are now more likely to approve of their wives' employment than to feel threatened by it as they were in the 1950s and 1960s (Perry-Jenkins and Crouter, 1990; Wilkie, 1993).

In chapter 4, we shall see why certain values such as individualism, egalitarianism, rationalism, and achievement become more widespread as societies industrialize. The spread of these values in modern times is directly related to the spread of mass education and the increase in choices and alternatives that developments in scientific knowledge, technology, and economics make possible.

Psychological Factors

The psychological motivation of individuals or groups has sometimes been given the greatest weight in explaining human history, especially by psychologists and historians. An example of this is the "great man" (or woman) theory of history. Here, it is argued that the major events that have changed the face of the earth and the fate of its inhabitants have been caused by certain individuals (and their supporters) who happen to come along at a particular time in history. The assumption is that these events would not have occurred were it not for the unique psychological characteristics of certain leaders. (The leaders are "great" in the sense of their historical impact, whether or not it is positive.) In other words, without Lenin, the Russian Revolution would not have occurred and without Hitler, there would have been no World War II.

Most social scientists at present would give greater weight to political and economic conditions than to the psychological characteristics of particular political leaders in explaining events such as wars and revolutions. They would argue that wars and revolutions may have been precipitated at certain times by particular leaders and their followers. But underlying economic and political conditions are the predisposing and basic reasons for these events.

Some social scientists (usually psychologists, not surprisingly) give psychological factors the greatest weight in explaining historical changes in human social life. They explain sociocultural evolution, for example, as a result of typical childrearing practices in societies that promote achievement motivation (a strong drive to succeed in competitive situations) in children (McClelland, 1961, 1975).

Human history, according to this model, is determined by the relationships between parents and children, and these have varied in different societies at different times. As typical parent/child relationships have changed, individuals' needs for achievement, power, or love have changed as well. Individual motivation, either of leaders or citizens, is given the greatest weight in this model of social stability and social change.

The problem with the psychological model when applied to entire societies is that it cannot explain widespread historical changes in childrearing practices and in values and motivation. Techniques of childrearing, like values, do not exist in a vacuum.

According to the evidence currently available, parents, in their childrearing values and methods, respond to changing economic and political conditions. Parents try to bring up children who will function adequately in the circumstances under which they will live. If they expect their children to have economic and educational opportunities, parents encourage achievement, self-reliance, and individualism. If not, parents emphasize conformity, obedience, and fatalism (Kohn, 1959, 1969; McLoyd, 1990; Jay Belsky, 1990; Kohn et al., 1990). In the United States, with its open frontier, rapid rate of industrialization, and the belief in the American dream, childrearing practices have emphasized competitive success, individualism, and self-reliance to a greater extent than practices in older, more traditional societies in Europe and Asia.

MAJOR THEORETICAL MODELS: MACROLEVEL

The theoretical models that have been most important in sociology are the sociocultural evolution model, the conflict model (including feminist models), the structural-functional model, and the interactionist model or role theory model. These models differ in the weight they give to various factors, especially developments in scientific knowledge and technology, values, and power and economics, in explaining social change (see Table 2.1 on p. 42).

Models also differ in their focus on time and space. Some are primarily historical and evolutionary in focus, emphasizing change through time. Some concentrate on stability in societies at a certain point in time, usually the present. The focus of various models also differs in the extent that they apply to the *macrolevel*—to entire societies, cultures, and subcultures, and

TABLE 2.1

Sociological Models and Concepts

Variables in Social Scientific Models

Biology, climate and geography, science and technology, economics, values, psychological factors

Major Models in Sociology

The Sociocultural Evolution Model

Basic Concepts: evolution, science, technology, economics, complexity, efficiency, invention, discovery, cultural diffusion, cultural lag, social stability, social change

Greatest Weight: developments in science, technology, economics

Structural-Functionalism

Basic Concepts: group or societal needs, structure, functions, values, consensus, social stability

Greatest Weight: structure, values, social stability

The Conflict Model

Basic Concepts: human needs, economic resources, power, conflict, social change

Greatest Weight: economic resources, power, social change

The Interactionist Model

Basic Concepts: status, role, cultural and subcultural role prescriptions, role perceptions, role performance, socialization

Greatest Weight: role perceptions and performance (the ideal vs. the real)

---

the norms, values, ways of organizing power, and conflicts of large categories of people. The role theory or interactionist model takes primarily a *microlevel* (small-scale, as in microscopic) approach, focusing on actual, ongoing interaction in the day-to-day relationships of human beings in groups.

When those who use the interactionist model turn away from actual group interaction and back toward role prescriptions in the cultures and subcultures of these groups (the ideal role of mother or father, for example, as defined in various social locations), they shift to a macrolevel perspective. The role theory model provides a framework for understanding social life in small, bounded social universes—in family, work, religious, political, educational, and recreational groups.

Sociocultural Evolution

Like the social Darwinists, those who use a sociocultural evolution perspective focus primarily on evolutionary change through time and on entire societies, a macrolevel approach. Unlike social Darwinism, however, the evolutionary principle is not applied to values, morality, and such elusive qualities of life as human happiness. And there is no assumption that the rate of sociocultural evolution in particular societies is related to the genetic, intellectual, or moral superiority or inferiority of citizens in these societies. Marx (Marx and Engels, 1848) was one of the first to employ a model of sociocultural evolution. In this century, anthropologist V. Gordon Childe (1951, 1964) and sociologists William F. Ogburn (1922), Talcott Parsons (1977), and Gerhard Lenski (Lenski, 1966; Lenski, Lenski, and Nolan, 1991) are among those who have used this model to increase our understanding of human history.

The **sociocultural evolution model** views developments in scientific knowledge and technology as both *cumulative* and increasingly *adaptive*, facilitating greater efficiency and effectiveness in accomplishing material goals—whatever these might be. This scientific and technological trend and related economic changes are given the greatest weight in explaining the human experience, historically and at the present. At the worldwide level, technology is seen as evolving in a one-way direction, from the simple to the complex, and from the less efficient to the more efficient.

Researchers who use the sociocultural evolution model see the accumulation of accurate and valid information about the world and its inhabitants as a process that occurs at varying rates. Such knowledge grows much more rapidly in modern times, however; scientists estimate that the amount of accurate scientific information available now doubles every 10 to 15 years (E. O. Wilson, 1993).

The development of technology and the accumulation of knowledge occurs despite reversals in its progress, at times, in particular societies. Such reversals of progress have usually resulted when families guarding a secret knowledge of a certain technique died out. Reversals have also occurred when nations with less complex and less efficient technology have conquered and destroyed the citizens of more technologically advanced societies. The victors have buried the knowledge and skills along with the bodies of their enemies. The defeat of Rome that ushered in the technologically impoverished Dark Ages is an example.

Some of the basic concepts in the sociocultural evolution model are technology, evolution, efficiency, discovery, invention, complexity, cultural diffusion, and cultural lag. **Technology** refers to tools and weapons and the skills necessary to operate these objects. **Evolution**, in this model, involves step-by-step improvements over time in the efficiency of tools, from digging sticks to computers; weapons, from spears to atomic bombs; and information storage, from hieroglyphics carved in stone to electronic libraries. **Efficiency** means increasing effectiveness in achieving goals (better performance and greater productivity) in shorter periods of time using higher levels of skills.

A **discovery** is accidental and unplanned; an **invention** is deliberate and intentional. **Complexity** refers to the process in which inventions and discoveries build on each other and tools and weapons become more differentiated, containing more working parts and performing more diverse functions. The steam engine is more complex than the water mill. The adding machine adds and subtracts; the calculator adds, subtracts, multiplies, and divides.

A parallel to the increased differentiation in technology in human societies is the increased specialization of work activities in the economic sphere. The jack-of-all-trades disappears in highly industrialized societies. There is too much to know; no single individual can know it all.

Human relationships also become more segmented and differentiated as societies become more complex. People have more titles (positions and statuses), perform more roles, and experience more conflict in the roles they perform. The time and energy we have is limited. But demands and obligations tend to become more pressing, contradictory, and unclear as societies become more complex and change more rapidly.

We have already discussed cultural diffusion. **Cultural lag** is a concept coined by sociologist William F. Ogburn (1922). In his analysis of social change, Ogburn pointed out that the material culture (applied science and technology) tends to change faster than the nonmaterial culture (values, attitudes, and beliefs) in human societies. In currently industrializing societies, in Asia and Africa, for example, the diffusion of both medicines (especially antibiotics) and advanced medical technology from industrialized societies is keeping more people alive longer. It is no longer necessary to have large numbers of children, since fewer children (in nonfamine areas) will die before reaching adulthood. In addition, children are not an economic resource in urban industrial societies. They do not increase family wealth by working in the fields; they are a luxury, expensive to raise and to educate. Moreover, standards of health, cleanliness, and functioning are higher and more difficult for parents to achieve in bringing up children. In urban industrial societies, according to surveys, large families are usually not happy families.

And yet, having large numbers of children continues to be valued by many families in industrializing societies, despite sometimes harsh government efforts to control population growth. For more than 20 years, the government of China has imposed a legal limit of one child per family. Severe punishments (fines and loss of jobs or government-owned apartments) have been imposed for disobedience. In 1993, the birth rate in China finally dropped to below replacement level (Haub, 1993). But government officials remain cautious about predicting the future population of the world's largest society. Traditional values change slowly, more slowly than science, technology, and economics.

The sociocultural evolution model is basic for explaining much that has happened in human history. It is historical and contemporary, global

THE LATENT FUNCTIONS OF POPULATION CONTROL IN CHINA

China's strict law limiting married couples to one child, imposed in the late 1970s to control population growth, has led to a number of unintended and unanticipated consequences. Since male children are greatly preferred in China, there are about 118 male newborns for every 100 female newborns (Shenon, 1994). The normal worldwide sex ratio for newborns is 105 males for every 100 females.

The very latest technology, ultrasound imaging, is used to check the sex of fetuses. Readily available abortions enable many couples to abort a female fetus and keep trying until they have the male child they desire. This had led to a huge surplus of males in China, many of whom will never be able to find a wife to marry.

At the same time, the relative scarcity of women has increased their prestige and value in a society that is converting to a market economy of supply and demand, in marital partners as well as in material goods and services. Women are new exercising higher standards in their marital choices and fewer older, highly educated women are remaining unmarried. Government leaders are now concerned about other unanticipated consequences of population control policies—an increase in prostitution and male suicide, for example (Shenon, 1994).

What Do You Think?

1. How did traditional values affect the consequences of family planning policies in China?
2. For whom and under what circumstances might family planning policies be dysfunctional in other industrializing societies?
3. Can you think of recent examples of latent functions of government policies in the United States?

and national, and macrolevel-focused but with strong links to the microlevel through its focus on the culturally defined roles people learn and perform. It applies to all aspects of the human experience, at all times, across all continents. Two other important models in sociology, structural-functionalism and the conflict model, have been used to focus more specifically on particular aspects of human reality—mainly social stability in the case of structural-functionalism, and mainly social change in the case of the conflict model, though neither model excludes other aspects.

The Structural-Functional Model

Those who use the **structural-functional model**, usually called "functionalists," tend to give more weight to values than to developments in science, technology, and economics in explaining human social life. Functionalists emphasize **consensus**–the sharing of common values and interests in a society–rather than conflict. They view consensus as the most important factor in maintaining social stability. They tend to place more emphasis on the rule of law and are less likely to focus on the role of power and political repression in preserving social stability in human societies.

The concept of **structure** in this model refers to the various parts of a whole (a cell, a group, or a society, for example) that are related to each other in regular and recurring ways. The structure of a family consists of several people, related by blood, marriage, adoption, or mutual definition, who react with one other on a regular, fairly predictable basis. Marriage, divorce, separation, childbirth, and death change the structure of the family by either adding or removing individual members from the group.

The concept of **function** is used in this model to explain the existence of particular conditions in a society or group–economic inequality, for example–in terms of the role the conditions play in maintaining the stability ("equilibrium") of the society or group (Merton, 1968). Not all social conditions, however, have positive effects for a group or society. **Dysfunctions** are the negative consequences that some social conditions have for group or societal survival (Merton, 1968). The high birth rate in industrializing countries is dysfunctional for these countries. Resources must be diverted toward feeding rapidly increasing populations and away from building up the industrialized economy that most of these societies want. Wars may be functional for maintaining societies, but they are not functional for family groups whose members are killed in combat or on the streets.

Functionalists also distinguish between latent and manifest functions (Merton, 1968). **Manifest functions** are those "intended and recognized" by a group or society; **latent functions** are neither intended nor obvious. The manifest function of legally requiring students to remain in school until age 16 in the United States is to ensure that young people will have the necessary skills to function adequately in a technologically advanced society. The latent function of this policy is to keep young, untrained people off the streets and out of unemployment offices, at least until they are older.

One of the manifest functions of the women's movement was to increase economic equality for women. This happened mainly for highly educated, young, nonminority women, however (Fuchs, 1988). An unintended latent consequence has been the rise in births to never-married professional and managerial women between 18 to 44 over the past 10 years (from 3.1 percent to 8.3 percent of all births) (Bachu, 1993; National Center for Health Statistics, 1993). Middle-class women are now more likely to be economically independent and go it alone in all industrialized societies with the exception of Japan.

Functionalists have argued that social inequality, from the point of view of the society, is functional for the maintenance of the society. Social inequality motivates people to perform more difficult tasks that require the greatest amount of training or talent. If doctors, for example, had the same income and prestige as factory workers, few people would be motivated to go through the stressful and strenuous training that it takes to become a doctor. And societies might suffer a shortage of doctors.

Functionalists view *extreme* inequality as dysfunctional, however. At the societal level, it threatens social stability and democracy, and it is economically inefficient and irrational. Extreme economic inequality destroys people, wastes human resources, and promotes conflict, envy, hatred, and hostility between societies and within societies. Many of the wealthiest members of human societies inherit their wealth. Their economic resources do not stem from unique or scarce talent or from long years of difficult and stressful effort. Their rewards are a chance circumstance of the lottery of birth. Schoolteachers in some parts of the United States earn $250 a week in decaying school systems with increasingly crowded classrooms and declining reading scores. Do schoolteachers contribute less to the maintenance of society than do television, rock, baseball, and movie stars? Is learning less functional for survival than being entertained? Economic rewards depend on societal values as well as other factors. And values can be dysfunctional for societies.

Functionalists focus primarily on social stability, but they do not ignore social change (Moore, 1960; Parsons, 1977). They cannot, in modern times. Similarities in interests and values do bind groups and societies to each other. But in highly mobile, complex societies, diversity flourishes. In societies that are ethnically, religiously, economically, and culturally diverse, differences in values and interests multiply. Differences in needs, desires, tastes, and preferences become widespread in education, politics, work, leisure, and family life. More recently, functionalists have increased their efforts to understand how values and social conditions interact in affecting the fate of societies, groups, and individuals. Values usually do change more slowly than science, technology, and economics. But we should also recognize that the values underlying the socialist revolutions in countries such as China and the Soviet Union resulted in profound scientific, technological, and economic changes in these countries.

The Conflict Model

Those who use the **conflict model** focus primarily on conflict over economic resources and on power as something that is based on the possession of resources of various kinds. A situation of **conflict** exists when there are opposing or contradictory impulses, feelings, needs, or wants within an individual or between people, groups, or societies. **Power** is the ability to get what you want "despite resistance" (Weber, 1947 [1925], p. 152). **Resources** are characteristics or possessions that are valued in a society because they reduce stress, promote survival, or gratify needs and desires. Resources are viewed both as a source of power and a means for obtaining and maintaining power at the level of the individual, group, or society.

For individuals in groups (in families, for example), personal resources such as intelligence, education, drive, physical strength, psychological strength (self-esteem and confidence), health, wealth, and income determine power (Kemper and Collins, 1990). At the societal level, scientific know-how, technological efficiency (particularly in weapons), and economic resources (natural resources and gross national product, for example) are seen as sources of power.

The conflict model applies at the macrolevel to conflicts between societies and between various categories of people—rich and poor, male and female, young and old—within societies. It also applies to microlevel relationships—to face-to-face conflicts in families, for example. Research studies on power and violence in families have multiplied in recent years (Straus and Gelles, 1990). This increase parallels the rise in the resources and prestige of women since the 1960s, as the women's movement has continued and more married women have begun to work outside the home and earn independent income. At the same time, researchers have found that, from a macrolevel perspective, the social class location of families is a major factor affecting family satisfactions, stresses, and conflicts (Chilman, 1991; Yorburg, 1993).

The most famous conflict theorists have been Karl Marx and his followers. Marx, as we saw in chapter 1, related the basic conflicts, distribution of power, and direction of social change in human societies to the way in which goods and services are produced and distributed in these societies. According to his model, conflicts between societies, classes, and men and women reflect the differences in the ownership of productive property (first land, then machines, and then, finally, liquid capital). Social location, especially in the class system, determines what Marx called the "relations of production." Differences in economic interests are viewed as responsible for wars, riots, revolutions, and other social movements. Social change is a result, ultimately, of technological development that affects the kind and amount of economic resources available in a society. More immediately, social change occurs because of conflicts between classes or interest groups over economic resources.

Among the more prominent sociologists who have used the conflict model in the past are Georg Simmel (1955 [1908]); Louis Coser (1956); Ralf Dahrendorf (1959); and C. Wright Mills (1959). Sociologists who use the conflict model focus not only on economic conflicts but also on conflicts that have no clear economic basis, conflicts over *values, ethics,* and *behavior.* Current controversies in the United States over sex education and sexual behavior, tolerance of gay men and lesbians, abortion rights, and gun control, for example, cannot be explained primarily by differences in economic resources of competing social classes or interest groups. Other conflicts—

between residents of inner cities and suburbs, among North, South, and West (on energy tax programs, for example), and among racial/ethnic populations and social classes (on taxes and government spending programs, for example)—have a clearer economic basis.

The three theoretical models discussed so far are most useful for explaining stability and change in whole societies or parts of societies, analysis on the macrolevel. They help us understand why some societies have gone in certain economic, political, and cultural directions and why other societies have had very different histories.

MAJOR THEORETICAL MODELS: MICROLEVEL

We also need a model that links the individual in the group to the larger society and the culture. The interactionist or role theory model provides this link.

The Interactionist Model

Role theorists focus on interaction—on actual, ongoing, face-to-face relationships in groups. They observe these groups directly. They may do this as *participants* in the group—as members of a gang or club, as workers in a factory or office, or as residents of a community or homeless shelter, for example. Or they may do this as *detached observers,* hired to improve the morale and functioning of a group (in businesses or in family therapy, for instance).

Observers look at the roles people play. **Roles** are attached to statuses. They are the typical scripts people follow as occupants of a particular status. A **status** is a widely recognized position in a group or in a society—mother, teacher, working class, poor. We occupy a status; we play a role. Role conceptions tend to be typical and recurrent in particular social locations, specific societies, communities, groups, and historical periods. These conceptions provide guidelines for thinking and feeling, as well as behaving. They define the rights and obligations of people in various statuses.

Roles are learned through a process sociologists call **socialization**. We look at how socialization occurs in great detail in chapter 3 because socialization is the essence of stability and predictability in human relationships and societies.

Where there is no conflict or disagreement about rights and obligations, roles involve mutual expectations. Because we know what to expect, we can usually predict who will do what in a group—who will make the beds, cook, do laundry, or mow the lawn and wash the car at home; who will make the coffee, do the clerical tasks, or make the decisions at work.

Routine and ritual are the end products of successful role learning (Goffman, 1967).

Sociologists who use the **interactionist model** focus on the learning and performing of roles. They make their unique contributions to understanding group relationships when they focus on the role perceptions of the people who are interacting—on what Max Weber called the motives or the meaning of social action. They also focus on the messages—intentional and obvious, but sometimes unintentional and not so obvious—that people convey in their relationships. The desire for power, for example, is a subtle motive that may not be obvious or appropriate in a specific relationship between friends or between romantic or marital partners. People who successfully manipulate others are powerful, but they get what they want by playing on guilt or gratitude rather than directly asking or arguing for what they want.

When role theorists focus on typical role prescriptions in the culture, rather than on actual role playing in groups, they do macrolevel analysis (Yorburg, 1974; Stryker, 1980; 1987). Here, they may be more interested in explaining why cultural role prescriptions change. They analyze the economic and political conditions that have led to these changes, historically or currently. They focus, usually, on developments in scientific information, technology, and economics, or on changing values to explain changing roles.

Symbolic Interaction   Some role theorists believe that there are few widely accepted, culturally prescribed roles attached to specific statuses in constantly changing, multicultural modern societies (Blumer, 1969). These theorists focus primarily on the unique versions of roles—on the conflicts, negotiations, compromises, and agreements—that are worked out by individuals interacting in groups (Handel, 1985, 1994). This working out of roles is done by means of communication, using symbols such as language, or through nonverbal cues (a tone of voice, a smile, a frown) and gestures. Hence the name **symbolic interaction**.

Speaking so softly that one cannot be heard, or leaving out an essential piece of information in explaining something, may reinforce dominant-subordinate roles in a relationship, for example, by making the listener feel deaf or stupid (Tannen, 1990; Ng and Bradac, 1993). This kind of role playing falls between the cracks of cultural role prescriptions; it depends more on personality. In families, the role of scapegoat, black sheep, substitute parent, mediator, rescuer, or clown is not prescribed by cultures (Yorburg, 1993). Cultural role definitions are modified in important ways in particular groups. They are mediated by personality differences among the people who are interacting. Symbolic interactionists look beyond the surface to get at the real (and not obvious) meanings that people give to roles they are playing. For example, the volunteer work that some upper-class women do has the same meaning for them as demanding careers have for women in top business or professional jobs (Daniels, 1988). Successful volunteer work raises self-esteem and involves the same ambition, competitiveness, hard work, and confidence as success in business or the professions. It is a major source of prestige for women in this social class who are not employed.

Ethnomethodology　Symbolic interactionists look at how culturally defined roles are changed and new roles created in specific groups. In contrast, other role theorists known as ethnomethodologists are more interested in illuminating conformity to cultural role prescriptions. They study rules that are so taken for granted that individuals are not even aware of them.

Ethnomethodology refers to the techniques or methods used by various people to relate to others in their everyday lives. As a way of understanding sociological reality, it draws from Weber's emphasis on *Verstehen* and Émile Durkheim's focus on social facts. As a theoretical perspective, it is becoming more influential in other "human sciences," especially psychology, cultural anthropology, and linguistics (Button, 1991; Watson and Seiler, 1992; Hilbert, 1992). Sociologist Harold Garfinkel (1967) gave the perspective its name and designed some of the pioneering studies using this approach.

Garfinkel and his students conducted a number of experiments or "demonstrations" in which they deliberately violated cultural rules and role definitions. They "start with familiar scenes and ask what can be done to make trouble" (Garfinkel, 1967, pp. 37–38). In one experiment, students were instructed to draw closer and closer to someone they were talking to, without letting the person know about the experiment. At the point where noses were practically touching, the "victims" reacted with extreme irritation, anger, embarrassment, or anxiety.

In another experiment conducted by ethnomethodologists, students were instructed to go home and, for 15 minutes to 1 hour, to assume the status and play the role of a boarder rather than a son or daughter in relating to their families. They were instructed to address their parents as Mr. and Mrs., to speak only when spoken to, to ask permission to go to the refrigerator, to be polite and impersonal. Families reacted with shock, bewilderment, anxiety, embarrassment, or anger. They accused the students of being mean, crazy, selfish, or nasty. Anyone who attempts similar experiments will quickly realize how important cultural role definitions are in guiding behavior and defining expectations in typical social situations, however much traditional roles have changed and are changing.

The Dramaturgical Approach　Another role theorist, Erving Goffman (1922–1982) also focused on the subtle, unspoken rules that bind us in social relationships, but especially on the little niceties people engage in to create a good impression, a process he called impression management (1959). Goffman described the scenery and the props (clothing, furniture, language, and gestures) that people use to confirm their ideal selves or desired statuses. He distinguished between "front-stage" behavior and "back-stage" behavior—where, in private, the real self emerges. He also focused on public and private selves and the loss of the private self among those who are subject to total control by authorities in mental hospitals and other institutions (1961). Privacy is a value that initially became widespread in industrial societies as the middle classes increased in size. They increasingly needed privacy to hide nonconforming behavior, which more living space allowed them to do, at a time when public conformity was far more important than it is today. In an era of constant change and instant, worldwide electronic communication and invasion, private and public spheres tend to merge, however. The realm of the sacrosanct declines, and "telling it like it is" becomes the norm. Pretense and playacting diminish, but they do not disappear. There is still work for Goffman's followers to do. For Goffman (1967), all the world is not a stage, but it is *like* a stage, on which people act out the ritualized little dramas of daily life. Hence, his perspective is called **dramaturgical**, after the art or technique of composing dramas. The sociologist, in this approach, unmasks the pretenders and exposes the pretenses to arrive at the hidden or real meanings, purposes, and intentions of actors in groups.

This completes our introduction to theoretical models in sociology, historical and ahistorical, macrolevel and microlevel, with major emphasis on one or another factor in explaining how social location defines, and has defined, human reality. We will come back to these models throughout the book, as we review current sociological research on various topics. We turn now to the methods sociologists use in collecting information about people and their environments.

SOCIOLOGICAL RESEARCH

In complex industrial societies, where more alternatives are available and more decisions are necessary, accurate information about the population and changing political and economic conditions is essential for prediction and planning. Planning is based on predictions about many factors, such as the economy, immigration, and rates of birth, death, marriage, and divorce. Neither governments nor individuals can plan for the future unless they know what is actually going on in their society.

Sociologists are bound by **facts**, information that is both *valid* and *reliable,* when they do research. A scale that weighs 2 pounds light will give us the same result every time we weigh ourselves. The scale is reliable. But the results are not valid, that is, true or accurate. Results on IQ tests tend to be reliable and verifiable, regardless of who does the testing. Individuals usually score within a 5-point range on repeated testing in large groups by anonymous administrators. But do these tests measure inherited

Instructor's Resource Guide and Test Bank Sampler

Sociological Reality: A Brief Introduction

by Betty Yorburg

City College and the Graduate Center, City University of New York

Suggested Student Price of Text: $17.95

This booklet contains chapter 9 of the Instructor's Resource Guide and Test Bank to accompany *Sociological Reality: A Brief Introduction.*

It includes:

- A chapter outline
- Review objectives for the chapter
- A list of glossary terms
- An overview/discussion of the chapter
- A test bank of 80 multiple-choice, true/false, short-answer, and essay questions on the chapter

The complete test bank of over 1,000 questions is also available in computerized format via TestPak 3.0.

For additional information or materials, please contact your local Brown & Benchmark Sales Representative or call Educational Resources at 800-338-5371.

The Dushkin Publishing Group/Brown & Benchmark Publishers
Sluice Dock, Guilford, Connecticut 06437

Chapter 9

Families

Outline

Review Objectives

After studying this chapter, students should be able to:

1. Give some reasons why family groups are universal.

2. Describe how and why family functions and forms, pre-marital sexual behavior, marital choice, and husband-wife and parent-child relationships have changed during the course of sociocultural evolution.

3. Define the characteristics of heterosexual and same-sex living-together relationships and single-parent families as alternative family forms.

4. Describe demographic patterns in living-together relationships with respect to geographic location; duration; class, ethnic, and gender differences; and divorce rates for those who marry.

5. List possible reasons for the the recent, slight decline in divorce rates in the United States, and the decades-long increase that preceded this decline.

6. Assess the probable future of families worldwide, especially with respect to marital and parental roles, power, and role conflict.

Glossary

Authoritarian childrearing (parenting): An adult-centered parenting style characterized by strict obedience to nonnegotiable rules that are not explained or justified. This parenting style is typical in agricultural societies and among more traditional segments of industrial societies. **302**

Authoritative childrearing (parenting): A parenting style characterized by consistent, strict but democratic discipline, warmth, and affection that is typical in the middle social classes in industrial societies. Also called **democratic childrearing. 304**

Cohabitation: Unmarried, living-together sexual relationships. **305**

Double standard: The social norm that allows sexual freedom to men but not to women. **295**

Extended family: Two or more nuclear families or parts of nuclear families that live in daily contact and are economically and psychologically interdependent. **289**

Matriarchy: Rule or dominance by females in a society or family. **300**

Matrilineal societies: Societies in which the female line is most important in descent and inheritance of property. **312**

Monogamy: Marriage limiting partners to one husband and one wife. **292**

Nuclear family: Parents and their children; the immediate family. **289**

Parenting styles: Parent-child relationships that vary with respect to expression of emotion, discipline, flexibility of rules, and emphasis on obedience versus self-reliance. These vary, typically, in different types of societies and in different social classes in the United States today. **302**

Patriarchy: Complete and absolute power of males in societies and families. **300**

Patrilineal societies: Societies in which the male line is most significant in descent and inheritance of property. **311**

Permissive childrearing: A child-centered parenting style characterized by very flexible rules. **303**

Polyandry: Marriages involving one wife with several husbands. **292**

Polygamy: Marriages involving one husband or wife with more than one spouse. **291**

Polygyny: Marriages involving one husband with several wives. **291**

Sexual revolution: A time of rapid change in sexual values, attitudes, and behavior that occurred in the middle social classes in the United States and Europe before, during, and after World War I. **293**

Chapter Overview

Despite the increasing social and economic stresses on families and the proliferation of alternative family forms over the past few decades, sociologists can agree that families will survive into the discernible future. However one defines the family, there appears to be a basic, perhaps inborn, human need for emotional connection with the family and for the emotional support it provides. It is important for students to gain an understanding of individuals' need to belong to a reliable, stable social unit. Ask students to consider the emotional meanings of family as well as its practical functions.

In industrialized and postindustrial societies, the notion of what constitutes a family is clearly less restrictive than agricultural and horticultural societies. Yet—a point that is implicit throughout the chapter—in every type of society there is variance in individuals' experience of what family means. Even in the most traditional of societies, nonconformity of family form has existed. And even in the most nonconformist of subcultures, norms and ideals exist regarding the meaning and form of family. (These principles, students may observe, also apply to other major social institutions, economic, political, educational, and religious.)

One approach to putting the chapter into context for students is to ask them to describe their personal experiences and perceptions of family. Chances are that the class as a whole will evidence classification into a wide range of family forms, from extended family to isolated nuclear family to alternative family. Ask students whether or not their impressions of their own or others' families bear out the theories and statistics presented in the chapter. For example, do students' experiences and observations support statistics that indicate that couples with severe economic pressures in more complex societies are more likely to divorce than wealthy couples? That families headed by single women are more likely than two-parent families to be poor? That cohabitation is more closely correlated with divorce than noncohabitation?

A major theme in the chapter is the resemblance between the family forms and interactions in the most simple and the most complex societies in human history. That is, family forms and interactions in hunting and gathering societies and postindustrial societies bear astonishing similarities to each other. As students will note, the text describes substantial differences between life and relationships in the two societies, but at the same time there exist clear parallels in family form and function (see Table 9.3 on text page 305). Ask students to delineate these parallels. The most obvious are in communication, parent-child relationships, husband-wife relationships, marital choice, premarital sexual activity, and family structures. How do they explain these parallels?

In a related vein, students might be asked to consider the family from different theoretical perspectives used in sociology. How do the students think the persistence of family would be explained by conflict theorists? By functionalists? By sociocultural evolution theorists? In the chapter, the forms and functions of families in different types of societies are described in some detail; how would different theorists explain the evolution and future of family? How do students think these theorists would explain divorce? Remarriage? Single parenthood?

Finally, ask students to identify what social, technological, and economic trends are likely to influence the functions of family and the roles of specific family members in the future. How do they define their ideal for their own families in coming decades, and how can they help to bring their ideal about?

Multiple-Choice

1. Which of the following is *not* among the reasons for the decline in some traditional family ideals and expectations?
   a. scientific changes
   *b. fundamental defects in family groups

   c. technological changes
   d. economic shifts
Text pg: 287   Type: A   Diff: M   Obj: 1

2. The family:
   a. has already vanished.
   b. is on its way to extinction.
   c. is a perfect social unit.
 *d. cannot be replaced in society.
Text pg: 287   Type: A   Diff: M   Obj: 1

3. People are a family:
   a. only if they have blood ties.
   b. only if they have marital ties.
   c. if they help each other.
 *d. if they so define themselves.
Text pg: 287   Type: F   Diff: M   Obj: 1

4. The basis of family relationships is:
   a. the blood tie.
   b. economic responsibility.
 *c. emotions.
   d. religious obligation.
Text pg: 287   Type: F   Diff: M   Obj: 1

5. Unmarried parents with children now outnumber married parents with children in:
   a. the United States.
   b. France.
 *c. Sweden.
   d. China.
Text pg: 288   Type: F   Diff: M   Obj: 1

6. Family relationships:
 *a. follow similar patterns in hunting and gathering societies and postindustrial societies.
   b. not only show differences in culture and conditions but also vary widely from the least complex societies to the most complex ones.
   c. bear absolutely no resemblance from one type of society to another.
   d. cannot truly be said to exist in the more complex types of societies.
Text pg: 288   Type: F   Diff: M   Obj: 2

7. Families in most complex societies differ most significantly from families in the simplest societies in their:
   a. size.
 *b. function.
   c. amount of contact.
   d. form.
Text pg: 289   Type: F   Diff: M   Obj: 2

8. The most common family form in both postindustrial and hunting and gathering societies is:
   a. the single mother with children.
   b. the extended family.
 *c. the nuclear family.

   d. the single person with no children, with the extended family living elsewhere.
Text pg: 289   Type: F   Diff: E   Obj: 2

9. Which of the following is most likely *not* part of an extended family?
   a. John is a single father whose parents, who live down the block, and cousin, who lives a few miles away, help with child care on a daily basis.
   b. Sandra and Tomás have no children but spend a lot of time with their three nieces and nephews.
 *c. David and Leslie, who live in Los Angeles, have literally dozens of cousins, aunts, and uncles back east but rarely see or talk to them.
   d. Dina, a single woman who lives alone, travels a lot for her job but tries to attend as many family gatherings as possible.
Text pg: 289   Type: A   Diff: H   Obj: 2

10. Factors that break up extended families in industrial and postindustrial societies include all of the following *except:*
   a. conflict between generations.
 *b. poverty, which makes it too difficult to support large extended families.
   c. moving away from the family to take a new job.
   d. social mobility.
Text pg: 289-290   Type: F   Diff: H   Obj: 2

11. The isolated nuclear family is most common among which of the following social classes?
   a. the poor
   b. the middle class
 *c. the upper middle class and new upper class
   d. the "old money" class
Text pg: 290   Type: F   Diff: M   Obj: 2

12. A close extended family network is most prevalent among which of the following social classes?
 *a. the poor
   b. the middle class
   c. the upper middle class and new upper class
   d. the "Old money" class
Text pg: 290   Type: F   Diff: M   Obj: 2

13. Semi-nuclear families:
   a. receive emotional, but not financial, help from relatives.
   b. never approach relatives for loans.
   c. keep their private lives private from relatives who do not live with them.
 *d. get financial help from relatives only in emergencies.
Text pg: 291   Type: F   Diff: M   Obj: 2

14. Which family form is most common among middle-income groups in industrial societies?
   a. isolated nuclear
 *b. semi-nuclear
   c. semi-extended

d. truly extended
Text pg: 291   Type: F   Diff: M   Obj: 2

15. Polyandry:
  *a. is rare.
  b. no longer exists.
  c. is most common in agricultural societies.
  d. occurs only in the wealthiest families in a given society.
Text pg: 291-292   Type: F   Diff: H   Obj: 2

16. Throughout history, the majority of families have practiced:
  a. polygamy.
  b. polygyny.
  c. polyandry.
  *d. monogamy.
Text pg: 291-292   Type: F   Diff: M   Obj: 2

17. The family form in which one man is married to one woman is called:
  a. polygamy.
  b. polygyny.
  c. polyandry.
  *d. monogamy.
Text pg: 291-292   Type: F   Diff: E   Obj: 2

18. In agricultural societies, the cultural ideal is:
  *a. the extended family.
  b. the isolated nuclear family.
  c. celibacy.
  d. polyandry.
Text pg: 292   Type: F   Diff: M   Obj: 2

19. In hunting and gathering societies:
  a. the mating activities of children are crucial to the economic future of the family line.
  *b. premarital pregnancy is rare for biological reasons.
  c. puberty occurs at an earlier age than in more complex societies.
  d. there are profound socioeconomic class differentials.
Text pg: 292-293   Type: F   Diff: M   Obj: 2

20. In the United States, the sexual revolution started around:
  *a. World War I.
  b. the Depression.
  c. World War II.
  d. the 1960s.
Text pg: 293   Type: F   Diff: M   Obj: 2

21. Sexual activity during the 1960s differed from earlier decades primarily in:
  a. crossing racial and class lines.
  b. private morality.
  *c. public morality.
  d. the range of sexual activities pursued.
Text pg: 293   Type: A   Diff: M   Obj: 2

22. What sociologist Andrew Greeley termed the "fidelity epidemic" is most likely the result of:
  a. changes in the double standard.
  b. people's diminishing interest in sex.
  c. improved birth control techniques.
  *d. fear of AIDS.
Text pg: 295   Type: A   Diff: E   Obj: 2

23. In the United States, people who are virgins at marriage are usually:
  *a. deeply religious.
  b. afraid of the opposite sex.
  c. undersexed.
  d. afraid of sex.
Text pg: 295   Type: A   Diff: M   Obj: 2

24. The patterns of sexual behavior of the young common in horticultural societies are most closely mirrored by those patterns in:
  *a. herding societies.
  b. agricultural societies.
  c. industrializing societies.
  d. postindustrial societies.
Text pg: 295   Type: F   Diff: M   Obj: 2

25. An individual's choice of marital partners is freest in:
  a. agricultural societies.
  b. industrializing societies.
  c. patriarchal societies.
  *d. both the simplest and the most complex societies.
Text pg: 296   Type: F   Diff: M   Obj: 2

26. In which of the following types of societies is arranged marriage most common?
  a. hunting and gathering societies
  b. industrializing societies
  *c. agricultural societies
  d. postindustrial societies
Text pg: 297   Type: F   Diff: E   Obj: 2

27. Which of the following factors has probably had the most important impact on decisions of who marries whom, why, and when?
  a. lengthening life expectancy rates
  b. the growth of the service economy
  *c. women's changing economic roles
  d. changes in school dropout rates
Text pg: 297   Type: A   Diff: M   Obj: 2

28. Marriage between partners of equal status in age, education, and potential or actual earnings is most likely in which of the following societies?
  a. agricultural societies
  b. industrializing societies
  c. industrialized societies
  *d. postindustrial societies
Text pg: 297   Type: A   Diff: M   Obj: 2

29. Husband-wife relationships are most likely to be egalitarian in:
    *a. the simplest and the most complex societies.
    b. agricultural societies.
    c. horticultural societies.
    d. industrializing societies.
    Text pg: 299   Type: A   Diff: M   Obj: 2

30. Rule by men as a class is termed:
    a. polygamy.
    *b. patriarchy.
    c. matriarchy.
    d. monogamy.
    Text pg: 300   Type: F   Diff: E   Obj: 2

31. In the United States today, most married women feel that the most important aspect of marriage is:
    *a. companionship.
    b. economic support.
    c. social mobility.
    d. the opportunity to have children.
    Text pg: 301   Type: A   Diff: M   Obj: 2

32. Psychologist Diana Baumrind's classification of parenting styles uses all of the following measures *except:*
    a. expression of emotion.
    *b. quality of care, material support, and protection.
    c. type of rules.
    d. style of discipline.
    Text pg: 301-302   Type: F   Diff: H   Obj: 2

33. Which of the following cases is an example of an authoritarian parenting style?
    a. Josephine and Leroy are very warm and loving toward their children and expect the children to perform certain household tasks on a daily basis.
    b. Jason and Andrew believe in following rules of democratic childrearing in how they treat their adoptive daughter.
    c. Sally and Manuel avoid punishing their son's bad behaviors and instead reward his good behaviors.
    *d. Vernon and Lillian believe that being firm and distant toward their children will help them to become strong, contributing members of society as adults.
    Text pg: 302-304   Type: A   Diff: H   Obj: 2

34. Psychologically correct parenting is most likely to occur in:
    a. herding societies.
    b. industrializing African societies.
    *c. postindustrial societies.
    d. technologically simple societies.
    Text pg: 303   Type: A   Diff: M   Obj: 2

35. Family life in hunting and gathering societies is probably most similar (though still very different) to family life in:
    *a. postindustrial societies.
    b. agricultural societies.
    c. horticultural societies.

    d. authoritarian societies.
    Text pg: 288   Type: A   Diff: M   Obj: 2

36. Living together in a sexual relationship is often termed:
    a. bigamy.
    *b. cohabitation.
    c. open marriage.
    d. illegitimacy.
    Text pg: 306   Type: F   Diff: E   Obj: 3

37. Living-together relationships:
    a. occur almost exclusively in industrializing societies.
    b. are uncommon among middle and upper classes in any society.
    c. are usually of longer duration than marriages in postindustrial societies.
    *d. are a global trend among postindustrial societies.
    Text pg: 306-307 Type: A   Diff: M   Obj: 3

38. In the United States today, which of the following groups is most likely to enter a living-together relationship?
    a. people with at least some college education
    *b. African Americans
    c. college-educated women
    d. upper-middle-class people
    Text pg: 307   Type: F   Diff: M   Obj: 4

39. Which of the following groups would you expect to be the one most likely to be living in poverty?
    a. same-sex living-together couples
    b. married couples
    c. heterosexual living-together couples
    *d. single-parent households headed by women
    Text pg: 310-311 Type: A   Diff: E   Obj: 4

40. The effects of single parenting on children are largely dependent on:
    *a. social location.
    b. race.
    c. a child's gender.
    d. geographical location.
    Text pg: 310   Type: F   Diff: H   Obj: 4

41. Research studies since the 1970s on the effects of single parenting on children have focused on:
    a. the economic and social stigma of illegitimacy.
    b. psychological effects.
    *c. the effects of poverty.
    d. health effects.
    Text pg: 310   Type: F   Diff: M   Obj: 4

42. In which of the following sentences is the woman described most likely, from a sociological perspective, to get divorced?
    *a. Janine has a secure, well-paying job as an accountant and a broad middle-class social base in her community.
    b. Nancy is a traditional wife and mother who depends entirely on her husband's upper-level income.

c. Nadia and her husband both have low but rising wages in their jobs in the service sector.

d. Anna and her fiancé both live with their families and are planning to marry next year, after they both graduate from college.

Text pg: 312-313   Type: A   Diff: H   Obj: 5

43. In the United States, the divorce rate began to level off in:

*a. 1977.

b. 1982.

c. 1989.

d. 1993.

Text pg: 313   Type: F   Diff: M   Obj: 5

44. In the United States, the group with the highest separation and divorce rates is:

*a. the poor.

b. the middle class.

c. the wealthy.

d. middle-class Latinos.

Text pg: 313   Type: F   Diff: M   Obj: 5

45. In 1990, the largest percentage of household types consisted of:

a. single-parent households.

b. single-person households.

*c. married couples without children.

d. married couples with children.

Text pg: 315   Type: F   Diff: H   Obj: 5

46. Among stepfamilies:

a. conflicts are rare.

*b. certain typical problems exist that are infrequently found in other families.

c. in-law problems are uncommon.

d. children are usually happy to see their parents remarry.

Text pg: 316   Type: A   Diff: M   Obj: 5

47. Role conflicts occur in stepfamilies when:

a. economic problems no longer distract family members from relationship problems.

b. cultural guidelines show family members how to feel and behave.

c. the children and stepparents know each other well.

*d. the new family members do not know what is expected of them.

Text pg: 316   Type: A   Diff: M   Obj: 5

48. Conflicts in remarriages often center on all of the following factors *except:*

*a. clear cultural guidelines on how to behave and feel.

b. finances.

c. discipline of children.

d. marital versus parental obligations.

Text pg: 316   Type: F   Diff: M   Obj: 5

49. The primary caregiver to older adults is:

a. a married son.

*b. a daughter.

c. an unmarried son.

d. a neighbor or friend.

Text pg: 317   Type: F   Diff: M   Obj: 6

50. Which of the following is likely to be a trend that will continue in the United States?

a. Role conflict among family members will diminish.

b. Single-parent households will decrease in number.

c. Premarital sex will no longer be as accepted by society.

*d. There will be more emphasis on egalitarianism between husband and wife.

Text pg: 317-318   Type: A   Diff: H   Obj: 6

True/False

51. Family relationships are of relatively little importance in postindustrial societies.   F

Text pg: 287   Type: A   Diff: E   Obj: 1

52. As societies become increasingly complex, families lose their monopoly over providing for their members' needs.   T

Text pg: 289   Type: F   Diff: M   Obj: 2

53. In hunting and gathering societies, the major family form is the large, extended family.   F

Text pg: 289   Type: F   Diff: M   Obj: 2

54. Extended families rarely own economic resources in common in industrial societies.   F

Text pg: 290   Type: F   Diff: M   Obj: 2

55. Extended families were the norm as well as the ideal in agricultural societies.   F

Text pg: 292   Type: F   Diff: H   Obj: 2

56. AIDS has had a significant impact on many people's sexual behavior.   T

Text pg: 294   Type: F   Diff: E   Obj: 2

57. The so-called double standard is the universal norm in every society, from the most simple to the most complex.   F

Text pg: 295   Type: F   Diff: H   Obj: 2

58. Women and men have, in most societies, had different priorities in their search for a marital partner.   T

Text pg: 297   Type: F   Diff: M   Obj: 2

59. The current formula for bringing up children in middle-class households in industrial societies is "strictness with affection."   T

Text pg: 304   Type: F   Diff: E   Obj: 2

60. Cohabitation has decreased sharply in the United States over the past 5 years.   F

Text pg: 307   Type: F   Diff: M   Obj: 4

61. Divorce rates for people who lived together before marrying are much lower than for those who did not.
F
Text pg: 308   Type: F   Diff: M   Obj: 4

62. Same-sex couples have the same legal disadvantages as heterosexual living-together couples.   T
Text pg: 308   Type: F   Diff: M   Obj: 4

63. Studies indicate that children of single parents are more likely than children raised in two-parent households to have long-term economic and psychological disadvantages.   T
Text pg: 310-311   Type: F   Diff: M   Obj: 4

64. In the United States, approximately 50 percent of first *and* second marriages end in divorce.   F
Text pg: 313-315   Type: F   Diff: M   Obj: 5

65. In postindustrial societies, occupations are so specialized that the functions of family have been rendered obsolete.   F
Text pg: 317   Type: A   Diff: H   Obj: 6

Short Answer

66. Why has the family been the only major institution that has not been transformed by complex societies into a bureaucratic organization?
The family is based on emotional ties; the stability, security, and depth of emotional support that ideally exist in family groups are impossible in bureaucratically organized large groups.
Text pg: 287-288   Type: A   Diff: M   Obj: 1

67. Why in simpler societies do extended families, while representing the ideal, often not exist?
Low life expectancy; frequently, three generations do not survive to share the same household or live close to one another.
Text pg: 292   Type: F   Diff: M   Obj: 2

68. Which population groups have been most directly affected by the so-called sexual revolution in the United States and Europe?
Mainly the middle class; mainly women.
Text pg: 296   Type: A   Diff: M   Obj: 2

69. In which societies do women have the most control over economic resources? How does this affect marital relationships?
In the most simple and the most complex societies; their control of economic resources is one of several factors that have an impact on the relationship's egalitarianism and the couple's commitment.
Text pg: 299   Type: A   Diff: M   Obj: 2

70. Summarize the main characteristics of authoritarian parenting.
An insistence on children's strict obedience to rules and respect of parents; emotional distance; little expression of affection; the use of punishment as a way of control.
Text pg: 302   Type: F   Diff: M   Obj: 2

71. Which factors explain the spread of living-together relationships to the middle class?
Factors include more liberal sexual attitudes, better contraception, extended adolescence, delays in marriage age due to job market, a high divorce rate, and higher expectations of marriage.
Text pg: 307   Type: A   Diff: M   Obj: 3

72. What is unique about the single-parent households headed by women in industrial and postindustrial societies?
In no known nonliterate or agricultural societies were mothers the exclusive caretakers of young children as they are in these households.
Text pg: 309   Type: A   Diff: H   Obj: 4

73. Briefly describe what studies have shown to be the likely effects on children of single parenting.
The effects are more often negative than positive: children are likely to have more economic and psychological disadvantages, to achieve lower levels of education, to commit crimes, and to engage in substance abuse.
Text pg: 310-311   Type: F   Diff: H   Obj: 4

74. How is the high divorce rate in the United States often explained?
It is attributed to the high and unrealistic expectations placed on marriage in the United States as compared to other societies.
Text pg: 312   Type: F   Diff: M   Obj: 5

75. How can ex–marital partners and in-laws cause conflicts in a stepfamily?
They may have influence stemming from ongoing contact with children and grandchildren, and there may be financial conflicts, both of which may cause problems involving boundaries, privacy, and independence.
Text pg: 316   Type: F   Diff: M   Obj: 5

Essay

76. What is a family?
It is a relatively enduring group based on marriage, birth, adoption, or mutual definition; involves feeling of belonging and identity; not always sanctioned by law or religion.
Text pg: 288   Type: F   Diff: M   Obj: 1

77. In which types of societies is premarital sexual behavior less closely controlled? Why?
Premarital sexual behavior is less closely controlled in the most simple and the most complex societies, because the family's future is not so heavily dependent

on a child's marital choice in these societies as it is in,
for example, agricultural or horticultural societies.
Text pg: 292-293   Type: A   Diff: M   Obj: 2

78. Describe husband-wife relationships, specifically the
distribution of power and responsibility, in various sorts
of societies.
These relationships are most equal in the simplest and
the most complex societies. Other factors heavily influ-
ence power in the marital relationship, such as personal
qualities and degree of commitment. Women are more
likely to be caregivers for both their children and those
in their parents' generation, though caregiving work
is shared more in the simplest and the most complex
societies. Male dominance is most extreme in herding
and agricultural societies.
Text pg: 299-301   Type: A   Diff: H   Obj: 2

79. Choose one type of society and characterize family
life—for example, forms, functions, and relationships—
in that society.
Examples will vary but should identify the society
chosen and summarize such characteristics as gender
roles, marital choice, family structures and forms, and
husband-wife and parent-child relationships.
Text pg: 305   Type: A   Diff: M   Obj: 2

80. In what way might remarriage rates in modern societies
be indicative of the future of the family?
Remarriage now more frequently follows divorce than
the death of a spouse; perhaps people's desire to remarry
mirrors the universal human need people have to be
emotionally connected, to belong to a reliable and
enduring social unit; the future of the family, despite
strains, seems secure.
Text pg: 314-318   Type: A   Diff: H   Obj: 5.6

Sociological Reality: A Brief Introduction by Betty Yorburg was written to provide a brief, inexpensive, straightforward description of the field of sociology that makes sense to students, professionals, and general readers; that integrates rather than reinforces competing points of view; and that demonstrates the value of the discipline of sociology to people who want a better understanding of themselves and their social situations.

Key Features:
- 460 pages, 7 ⅜" x 9 ¼", paperbound
- 13 chapters
- Built-in study guide with practice tests and glossary at the end of each chapter
- "Applying Sociology" sections where students assess the meaning of new sociological concepts for their lives
- "Focus on Social Issues" boxes followed by "What Do You Think?" questions that provoke critical thinking about current sociological topics
- Sociocultural evolution model that integrates the traditional perspectives of sociology on social order and social change
- Cross-cultural, cross-national, global view of changing human realities, both historically and today
- Focus on concept of social location in time and in physical space, with emphasis on major historical trends in power, conflict, values, and roles
- Almost 1,000 references from a vast array of sources, with emphasis on the very latest developments in the discipline
- Suggested student price: $17.95

Betty Yorburg is a Professor of Sociology at the City College of New York and is on the faculty at the Graduate Center of the City University of New York.

intelligence? Or, do they reflect social inequality and success or failure in middle-class educational systems? The controversy continues. The fact is, however, that the average IQ scores of immigrants in various countries around the world (Israel, Germany, and the United States, for example), where immigrants and their descendants have been tested, improves in successive generations, after the time of initial immigration. This would not happen if IQ tests measured actual genetic differences in the average intelligence of immigrant groups.

In doing research, sociologists generalize; they do not stereotype. A **generalization** is a conclusion based on research and observed facts. A **stereotype** is a belief about a category of people (such as men, women, immigrants, or minorities) that is not based on research and is applied indiscriminately to all people in the category. Stereotypes are not facts.

In sociological research, what people *do* and *say* are facts, even if what they say is defensive or untrue. We do not have the poetic license that novelists have. We may need the sensitivity of a good novelist, however, to understand what people are really thinking or feeling. Describing sociological reality often requires the skills of a good detective in searching out the evidence that confirms or denies what we see and hear. And facts do not speak for themselves. We must explain the facts we find. We do this using particular theoretical perspectives. But first, we must collect our facts. Like other scientists, sociologists use the **scientific method** to collect verifiable information about physical and social reality. The information that sociologists collect is often summarized in the form of tables or graphs (see "How to Read a Table" and "How to Read a Graph" on pp. 54 and 58).

STEPS IN THE SCIENTIFIC METHOD

The scientific method consists of a series of steps that researchers typically go through in acquiring accurate, verifiable knowledge. We use the same steps in writing scientific papers, incidentally, but research for papers is usually done in the library and not in the laboratory or out in the field.

Selecting a Problem

The problems that researchers choose and their interpretations of results are affected by historical period, place, and the social location (especially class, gender, age and generation, and ethnic origin) of the researcher. In sociology, the study of the effects of social location on the kind of knowledge sought and the conclusions reached is known as the **sociology of knowledge** (Mannheim, 1952 [1928]). The work of specialists in the soci-

(Continued on page 55)

HOW TO READ A TABLE

Tables are designed to summarize data at a glance. They reveal amounts, types, or trends (degree of change) in data. To interpret the table reprinted below, certain steps should be followed:

1. *Determine the Source of the Data* The source (U.S. Bureau of the Census or a private interest group, for example) may provide some indication of the possible validity and reliability of the data. Also check the methods used in the study for an indication of validity. The published source usually describes both.

2. *Read the Title* The title indicates what information is contained in the table. In Table 2.2, information is presented about current birth rates and projected total fertility rates of women in major racial/ethnic groups in the United States. The total fertility rate is the total number of births that 1,000 women in a particular age category will have during their lifetime. The projections in this table do not include immigration.

3. *Read the Headings* Horizontal columns in the table indicate the major ethnic groups in the United States. Vertical headings indicate total fertility rates for all women and the birth rates for different age categories of women.

4. *Study and Compare the Figures* The table indicates that American Indians, Eskimos, and Aleuts have the highest birth rates, followed by Hispanics, blacks, Asian and Pacific Islanders, and whites, in descending order. It also indicates that minorities have higher birth rates at younger ages, compared to whites. This is particularly true of blacks, who have the highest birth rates in the teenage categories. A total fertility rate of 2,110 is required for a particular racial/ethnic category to maintain its numbers in the population. The rate for whites is below replacement level; it is above replacement level for all racial/ethnic minorities.

5. *Draw Conclusions* If current trends continue, the proportion of the population that is of minority racial/ethnic origin will increase significantly, relative to whites, by the year 2010, without taking immigration into account.

TABLE 2.2

Projected U.S. Fertility Rates, by Race and Age Group: 1992 and 2010

Age Group	All Races[1] 1992	All Races[1] 2010	White 1992	White 2010	Black 1992	Black 2010	Asian and Pacific Islanders 1992	Asian and Pacific Islanders 2010	American Indian, Eskimo, Aleut 1992	American Indian, Eskimo, Aleut 2010	Hispanic[2] 1992	Hispanic[2] 2010
Total fertility rate	2,054	2,092	1,953	1,981	2,468	2,459	2,335	2,271	2,874	2,855	2,655	2,588
Birth rates:												
10 to 14 years old	1.4	1.5	0.6	0.7	5.3	5.2	0.6	0.6	1.9	1.9	2.3	2.2
15 to 19 years old	57.3	58.7	46.7	48.5	113.7	112.7	28.3	27.2	105.9	105.5	86.3	84.1
20 to 24 years old	118.0	120.0	109.8	112.1	161.6	160.8	95.8	93.1	210.5	209.0	163.2	159.1
25 to 29 years old	120.0	121.0	119.8	120.0	113.8	113.6	152.2	149.1	142.1	141.1	139.1	135.6
30 to 34 years old	79.2	80.5	79.7	79.9	66.6	66.6	123.8	120.7	76.2	75.8	88.6	86.4
35 to 39 years old	29.6	31.0	29.1	29.9	27.2	27.3	53.6	52.2	31.2	31.1	41.3	40.2
40 to 44 years old	4.9	5.4	4.7	5.0	5.2	5.3	11.3	11.0	6.7	6.8	9.7	9.5
45 to 49 years old	0.2	0.3	0.2	0.2	0.3	0.3	1.3	1.2	0.4	0.4	0.6	0.6

[1] Includes other races not shown separately.　　[2] Persons of Hispanic origin may be of any race.

Source: U.S. Bureau of the Census, *Current Population Reports*, series P25-1092; and unpublished data.

ology of knowledge helps us become aware of why we choose the problems we choose and how our values might influence the facts we collect and distort the conclusions we reach.

The interests, values, and skills of researchers and the needs of governments and citizens determine the problems that are selected for study at any particular time. In the 1930s, for example, it was important to keep married women out of the labor force because of the unemployment among men caused by the Depression. Social scientists produced dozens of studies pointing to the ill effects on children of "maternal deprivation." Studies of maternal deprivation peaked again in the 1950s (Bowlby, 1953), a time of return to tradition after the upheavals experienced by families during World War II. Rosie the Riveter returned home from the defense plants, and four children, a station wagon, and a house in the suburbs became the middle-class ideal in the United States (Halberstam, 1993).

The implication of these studies was that the absence of the employed mother from the home had very damaging emotional effects on children. Researchers studied cases of severe maternal deprivation, focusing on hospitalized or orphaned children who were completely separated from their mothers, permanently or for long periods of time. They then drew general conclusions from the severe depression they observed about the effects on children of separation from their mothers.

The separation that the child of a working mother experiences is hardly comparable to the experiences of orphaned or long-term hospitalized children. These studies have, however, had important consequences. Mothers (and sometimes fathers) now routinely stay with their children when they are hospitalized. Since the 1970s, as more mothers have joined the paid work force, fathers have been participating more in child care. Paternal deprivation has became a focus of research (and controversy) in the United States. By 1993, the "guilt, joy, fear, and fun" of the changing role of fathers was the cover story of an issue of *Time* magazine (Gibbs, 1993a). And child care guides for fathers (*How to Father, Fathers Almanac, Father Power*) are now a prime growth market in bookstores.

Reviewing the Literature

After selecting a problem to study, most investigators do what is called a "review of the literature." They look up previously published research that has been done on the topic. They do this to see what is known about the problem and how they can add to this knowledge. They also get ideas about how to design their own research and how to avoid errors made by previous investigators.

Formulating a Hypothesis

A research problem is usually expressed in the form of a **hypothesis**, a statement of an anticipated relationship between two or more variables. The variables may be income and power in families, social class location and divorce rate, educational level and degree of prejudice, or occupational prestige and retirement rates, for example. **Independent variables** are conditions or factors that result in certain consequences. The consequences are called **dependent variables**. Hypotheses usually reflect a theoretical point of view: researchers believe there *is* a relationship between the variables they select to study. The basic hypothesis in this book is that inventions and discoveries are the major historical factors (independent variables) explaining changes in economics, values, roles, and power in human societies (dependent variables).

Designing the Research Project and Collecting the Data

Depending on what they want to study, researchers decide how they can best obtain their facts, using methods that ensure the greatest accuracy and precision possible (Marsden, 1992). Technological advances such as tape recorders, videotapes, and computers have improved observation and data collecting enormously in recent years. Human errors of perception, memory, or judgment are much reduced. Also, computers do not suffer from fatigue, emotions, prejudices, or other possible sources of bias.

Survey research is the most common method used by sociologists. This is because we usually study whole societies or large categories of people in a society. In studying small groups or small numbers of people, we are more likely to do case studies or experiments. Sociological experiments are usually carried out as *field experiments* in natural settings, in schools or communities, however, and not in laboratories. Finally, we may do secondary research, analyzing information collected by others, usually for other purposes. Each method has advantages; each has limitations (Marsden, 1992) (see Table 2.3).

Survey Research   If we decide to do **survey research**, we mail questionnaires, phone large numbers of people, or do personal, face-to-face interviews in the community. On national surveys, we question a **sample** of the total population (usually about 500 to 1,500 people) who reflect the attitudes, behavior, and feelings of the wider population as accurately as possible. A representative national sample accurately reflects the actual composition of the total population. Respondents are chosen on a regular or random basis.

The personal interview is used when mailed questionnaires are not feasible, when more detailed, deeper information is necessary, or when

TABLE 2.3

Research Methods in Sociology

Surveys	Experiments

Surveys

Advantages:
1. Large amounts of information can be gathered quickly and easily.
2. Essential for documenting national and regional trends and the needs of various categories of the population, government planning, evaluating social programs.

Limitation:
Respondents may lie (giving more socially acceptable responses), refuse to answer, respond defensively, misunderstand the questions.

Case Studies

Advantages:
1. Can penetrate defenses, reveal deeper motives, feelings.
2. Can yield unexpected, new, and valuable insights that can then be tested out on larger populations.

Limitations:
1. Greater danger of emotional involvement of researcher, less objectivity in observations, interpretations, reporting results.
2. Results may not be representative of other examples of the single case that is intensively studied (other suburbs, schools, hospitals, and so on).

Experiments

Advantage:
Can determine the relative importance of different variables.

Limitations:
1. Difficulty recreating very complex social realities, selecting most important variables to observe, measure.
2. Subjects may change their behavior when they know they are being observed.

Secondary Analysis

Advantage:
Expands the analysis of available research data.

Limitation:
Incomplete records, inaccuracies, omissions.

people might not understand the questions or might not return the questionnaires. Mailed questionnaires save time and are cheaper, but there is often a built-in bias in questionnaire returns. This occurs because people at the extremes of opinion or concern about a particular problem or issue are more likely to return questionnaires. Our results may not be representative of the total population.

The use of telephone interviews has increased tremendously in recent years. Telephone interviews save time and money. There is no problem about being admitted into the home, and callbacks are easy if respondents are not at home. Comparisons of results from telephone interview and face-

(Continued on page 59)

HOW TO READ A GRAPH

A graph is a pictorial outline of a set of facts or data. Quantitative data are depicted along two axes: a horizontal one, called the "*x*" axis, and a vertical one, called a "*y*" axis. Headings along the left side and across the bottom indicate the amount or value of what is being measured. This value or amount goes up as you go up the "*y*" axis and to the right on the "*x*" axis.

Figure 2.2 indicates that the median age at first marriage in the United States was lowest for men and for women in 1955, a time of economic affluence. In part, the age at first marriage tends to reflect economic conditions. The decline in age at first marriage began after the beginning of World War II, when many hasty marriages were contracted by very young adults who were soon to be separated by the exigencies of war. Servicemen had guaranteed income from the military, and many women went out to work during a period of labor shortages, especially in defense industries. The upward trend, after the 1960s, in part re-flects recurring recessions in the United States since the 1970s. Higher rates of un-employment and poverty are associated with delays in marriage.

The upward trend in the median age at first marriage also reflects, in part, the ad-vent of the women's movement and the increase in the divorce rate. Women, espe-cially in the middle social classes, are now more likely to complete their own training rather than drop out to support husbands who are in training for professional and managerial positions. Poor and working-class men and women, especially those who are unemployed or underemployed, are delay-ing marriage and are most likely to live to-gether rather than marry. Figure 2.2 also reveals a closing of the age gap between men and women in age at first marriage between 1920 and 1992, from approxi-mately 4 years to 2 years. In first mar-riages, partners are now more likely to be status equals.

FIGURE 2.2

Trends in the Median Age at First Marriage in the United States

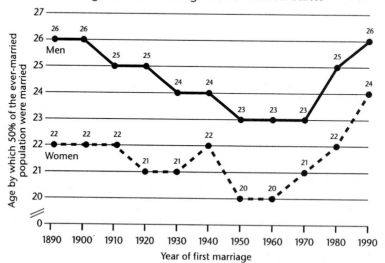

Note: Ages are rounded off to the nearest years.

Sources: Alan Guttmacher Institute, *Sex and America's Teenagers*, 1994, p. 24; U.S. Bureau of the Census, "Marital Status and Living Arrangements, 1990," *Current Population Reports*, Series P-20, No. 450, 1991, Table A, p. 1.

to-face interview studies indicate that results are similar. In fact, respondents may be more honest and less likely to give defensive, socially acceptable replies when the interviewer is an anonymous voice on the telephone.

The problem with this technique, however, is that it cannot reach people with unlisted numbers and those on the fringes of society who do not have telephones, especially poor, homeless, or transient people and illegal immigrants. Also, people are increasingly refusing to participate in telephone surveys because they feel pressured by lack of time or bombarded by too many telephone sales pitches for products or services.

Case Studies If we want to study small numbers of people in their natural settings, we use the **case study** method. Within a larger category of social groups or situations, we do intensive, in-depth observation of a single example—one particular street corner gang, mental hospital ward, old-age home, assembly line, suburban community, commune, religious group, or political club. We either interview the people being studied very intensively, or we become a member of the group, using **participant observation**.

The case study method is time consuming and demanding. The possibility of becoming emotionally involved is much greater than in survey research. Detached and objective observation may become difficult, perhaps impossible. Moreover, since only one example of a social situation or group is being studied, our results may not be typical or representative of other, similar groups or situations in a society. The old saying "If you've seen one, you've seen them all" is a stereotype.

The case study technique has one great advantage, however. With this method, we can penetrate defenses and obtain a deeper and more complete understanding of our respondents' perceptions of the world. It is Weber's *Verstehen* method in action. If people talk long enough, they are more likely to reveal their true feelings and motives, especially those they are less aware of or less willing to admit. The valuable and sometimes unexpected insights yielded by case study research can also be formulated into new hypotheses. Questionnaires can then be mailed out nationally to determine just how typical or atypical the particular group or situation is in the wider society.

Experiments Laboratory experiments are not common in sociology because of the difficulty of duplicating very complex social realities. We are more likely to do field experiments, conducted out in the community. In all experiments, we observe a group of people under rigidly controlled conditions. We may vary one factor (the independent variable), holding all others constant, and compare the **experimental group** that experiences a change with another group, the **control group**, that does not experience this change. We match the experimental and control groups as closely as possible, in terms of locating variables such as social class, ethnic origin, age, and neighborhood. The experimental group experiences a change: enrollment in a Head Start program, psychological counseling, job training, busing, or a move into integrated housing, for example. The control group experiences no change. We then compare the two groups at a later point in time to try to determine the effects of the change on the experimental group. Field experiments are a major way to evaluate the short- and long-term consequences of specific social programs (Zigler and Styfco, 1993). Evaluation studies conducted by sociologists determine whether programs work, or how they work best. In recent years, field experiments have received increasing recognition by the federal government. They provide necessary evidence for more rational government planning and public policy. Differences in political values and economic interests, however, continue to determine how (or whether) information collected by this method is used.

Secondary Research   Sometimes the question we are interested in can best be answered by collecting and analyzing information already available. We use published or unpublished information, such as statistics issued by government agencies or businesses, letters, diaries, newspapers and magazines, historical records, or studies done by other sociologists and social scientists. The major advantage of this method is that we can test out our hypotheses over a wider period of time and on many different cultures and societies. Historical records may be incomplete or inaccurate, however, and important questions may not have been asked in the original studies, especially if the researchers were interested in answers to different questions. An example of this kind of research is a study done by sociologist Claude Fischer (1991). Fischer was interested in the relationship between gender (the independent variable) and telephone use (the dependent variable) during the 50 years before World War II. Phones were expensive and not in common use among the poor and working classes at that time. Fischer reviewed research indicating that women are more sociable, generally, than men, and are usually more responsible than men for maintaining extended family, friendship, and community ties outside of the household. He also knew that middle-class women before World War II were unlikely to be out in the paid workforce, were more isolated, and probably more in need of social contact than employed women.

His hypothesis was that middle-class households containing women (mothers and daughters) would be more likely to have phones and that these phones would be used more frequently than in households containing fathers or sons only. His hypothesis was confirmed. To collect his evidence, Fischer used studies of phone use conducted by AT&T, advertisements (which were mainly directed toward women), U.S. Census Bureau data from 1900 to 1910 on phone use and household composition, a U.S. Bureau of Labor Statistics study of the spending patterns of 12,000 families in 1918 and 1919, and various surveys of women in rural and urban households from the turn of the century to World War II.

FIGURE 2.3

Steps in the Scientific Method

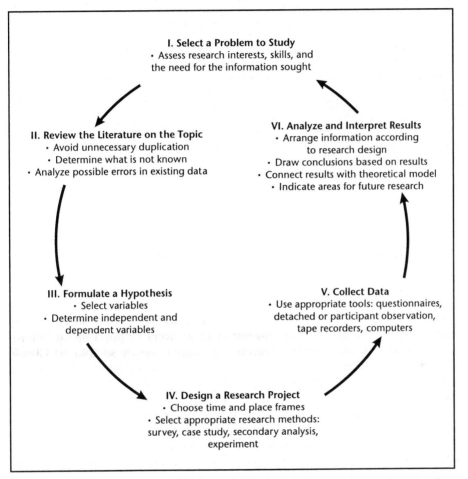

The six steps in the scientific method may be understood as forming a circle, because one of the objectives of the last step, analyzing and interpreting results, is to indicate areas for future research.

Analyzing and Interpreting Results

At this stage, we examine our results and draw a conclusion. Here, the most important consideration is that we do not distort our findings and draw conclusions that are not supported by our study. If our hypothesis is not confirmed, we say so, and try to explain why. If it is confirmed, we usually spell out the broader implications of our study (for public policy, for example), or we indicate additional research that is needed on the topic.

TABLE 2.4

Special Problems in Sociological Research

Problems in Explanation	Problems with Human Subjects
• Problem of selecting the most important variables • Problem of giving appropriate weight to different variables • Problem of constantly changing variables: changes in political and economic conditions, science and technology, values, demographics, environment	• Problems of prediction: individual variability, uniqueness • Ethical problems: Obtaining informed consent; avoiding dishonesty, harm, coercion, unnecessary invasion of privacy, discrimination • Problems of bias: possible distorting effects of the researcher's social location, values, expectations on observations, interpretations, and conclusions

SPECIAL PROBLEMS IN DOING SOCIAL SCIENCE RESEARCH

In doing research, social scientists encounter special difficulties. To begin with, we need to obtain the consent and cooperation of the people we want to study. Natural scientists do not have to worry about the willingness to be studied of mice, molecules, masses, or machines, although monkeys may pose a problem. The closer one gets to studying human beings, the greater is the problem of obtaining consent. Social scientists must also abide by certain ethics in conducting research. They must not deceive, harm, coerce, or discriminate against their research subjects. Judgments about ethics must be clear.

Another difficulty in doing social science research is that facts in the social sciences are very complex. It is almost impossible to duplicate social situations in all their infinite variety in the laboratory, and people change their behavior when they know they are being observed. The number of variables is greater than in the natural sciences. We must select the most important variables and give each the proper amount of weight, relatively. How can we be sure we have done this? Also, our facts are constantly changing.

Explanations in the natural sciences are more stable and more concrete. The causes of cancer will eventually be understood and brought under control; the problem of understanding and controlling crime may never be resolved for all time. The very definitions of crime keep changing. Economic, political, and material conditions keep changing. Values, beliefs, and opinions keep changing. Our work is quickly outdated and is never done. Outdated sociology, however, is good history.

Study Guide

REVIEW OBJECTIVES

After studying this chapter, you should be able to:

1. Describe what theoretical models are.
2. Identify some basic factors that have been used to explain social stability and social change in human societies.
3. Explain how major macrolevel and microlevel theoretical models differ in focus and emphasis (explanatory variables).
4. Identify the steps in the scientific method.
5. Describe the basic research methods that sociologists use.
6. Discuss special problems in doing social scientific research.

SUMMARY

1. It is important to be aware of the particular theoretical model being used in a research study. With such knowledge, we are better able to judge the validity of the explanations of research results. We are more alert to the investigators' assumptions and the possible omission of variables from their studies; causes not mentioned may be more important than the ones the investigators have emphasized.

2. Models are made up of related concepts that sensitize people to particular aspects of reality. Models differ in focus; they may be macrolevel or microlevel, and historical or ahistorical. Theories derived from models differ in the emphasis or weight they give to different possible factors that affect social conditions, factors such as crime, poverty, unemployment, and discrimination.

3. In the social sciences, macrolevel theoretical models have variously given the greatest weight to biology, climate and geography, science, technology, economics, values, or psychology in explaining the facts of human

social life. All these variables, and more, are necessary for an adequate understanding of the past and present. And they are all necessary for predicting the probable future of human societies.

4. Social Darwinists have a macrolevel and historical focus. They give the greatest weight to biology in explaining human history and human behavior. The sociocultural evolution model also has a macrolevel, historical focus, but researchers give the greatest weight to developments in science, technology, and economics in explaining social change. Functionalists can have a macrolevel or microlevel focus. Their perspective is usually ahistorical. They give the greatest weight to values in explaining the facts of social life—particularly social stability. Conflict theory also applies to the macrolevel or microlevel. It is historical as well as contemporary, because its primary focus is on social change. In their explanations, conflict theorists give the greatest weight to economic resources and how

these are distributed and used in groups or societies.

5. Interactionists or role theorists focus on the macrolevel when they are analyzing cultural and subcultural role definitions. They focus on the microlevel when they describe role learning and role performing in groups or in typical social situations. In explaining changing role definitions, they use one of several models currently in use in sociology.

6. Symbolic interaction, ethnomethodology, and the dramaturgical perspective are three influential interactionist models in contemporary sociology. Symbolic interactionists emphasize the real meanings and messages that people convey in their social relationships. They also focus on how old roles are changed and new roles are created. Ethnomethodologists explore the taken-for-granted world around us. They expose the petty conformities of everyday life that we are largely unaware of. In the dramaturgical approach, the focus is primarily on the fictions people maintain to present a favorable or acceptable impression of themselves to others.

7. Scientific researchers gather facts, which consist of accurate information, based on observation, that can be verified by others. Such verification is not always easy. Unlike stereotypes, social scientific generalizations are based on facts.

8. Most scientists use the same series of steps in studying a problem. First, they select a problem to study. In so doing, sociologists are influenced by the changing needs of society, but also by their own values, interests, and needs. They should be aware of these possible sources of bias so that they are less likely to influence the results they obtain and the conclusions they reach.

9. The next step is to review related research on the topic. Researchers do this to learn what is known, so that they do not duplicate knowledge unnecessarily. They

also get ideas about what methods to use. And they may learn how to avoid errors made in previous studies.

10. Researchers next formulate a hypothesis about the relationship between the variables—class and childrearing techniques, generation and economic opportunities, or religion and values, for example—that they are studying. Hypotheses usually reflect a certain theoretical point of view. Researchers choose particular variables to study or measure because they believe these are the factors that will explain the results they obtain. Their theoretical point of view also tells them how and why variables are related and how much weight to give different variables, such as economics and values, in explaining rates of sociocultural evolution in specific societies.

11. They then choose the one or more research methods that will best serve their needs: survey research, the case study, experiments, or library research, most frequently. Each method has both advantages and limitations.

12. When they have completed the collection and processing of their data, they are at the final stage of the scientific method: the analysis and interpretation of results. They state their conclusions. Here, they must not make claims that are not supported by the data. If their hypothesis was mistaken, they admit it. If the knowledge they have gathered has implications for further research, or for explaining and predicting future trends in human behavior or needs, they point these out.

13. Doing social scientific research involves certain unique difficulties. Our data are very complex, constantly changing, and frequently not directly observable. In addition, we must have the informed consent of the people we study, and we must not deceive, harm, coerce, or discriminate against them.

GLOSSARY

Case study Intensive observation of a single example, or small sample, of a much larger category of social groups or situations.

Class consciousness Awareness of how the economic interests of one's class are being served, or not being served, in a society.

Complexity In the sociocultural evolution model, a trend toward increasing differentiation of parts and functions in the material and nonmaterial cultures of human societies.

Concepts Abstract terms or phrases that classify or characterize various aspects of reality.

Conflict A situation of opposing or contradictory needs, impulses, feelings, or desires within an individual or between people, groups, or societies.

Conflict model A theoretical model in which economics and conflict are given the greatest weight as explanatory factors.

Consensus The sharing of common values and interests in a society.

Control group A group, as similar to an experimental group as possible, that does not experience a change.

Cultural diffusion The spread of knowledge, values, skills, and material products from one society to another.

Cultural lag The tendency for the material culture (applied science and technology) to change faster than the nonmaterial culture (values, attitudes, and beliefs).

Cultural universals Ways of life found in every known society.

Dependent variable A condition that is the consequence of another factor or condition.

Discovery A sudden awareness of something in the environment that already exists.

Dramaturgical model A focus on the fictions that people create to be accepted or maintain a favorable impression.

Dysfunctions The negative consequences of a condition or an action for the maintenance of a group or society.

Efficiency In technological evolution, increasing effectiveness in achieving goals in shorter periods of time using higher levels of skills.

Ethnomethodology The study of the taken-for-granted techniques used within various groups in coping with typical, everyday life situations.

Evolution In the technological sphere, step-by-step improvements in efficiency, effectiveness, and complexity.

Experimental group A group that experiences a change under controlled conditions.

Facts Information, data, and evidence, based on observation, that can be checked or verified by others.

Function The positive consequences a condition or an action has for maintaining a group or society.

Generalization A statement about people, places, things, or events based on research evidence.

Hypothesis A statement of an expected relationship between two or more variables or conditions.

Incest taboo Prohibition on sexual relationships between close relatives in the immediate family.

Independent variable A factor or condition that results in another condition.

Interactionist model A focus on the learning and performing of roles within groups.

Invention The deliberate creation of something new from existing elements in the culture.

Language System of arbitrary written or oral symbols whose meaning is agreed upon by two or more people.

Latent functions The consequences of a condition or action that are not intended or obvious.

Manifest functions The consequences of a condition or an action that are intended and recognized.

Marriage A socially sanctioned sexual relationship requiring some degree of permanence and faithfulness.

Model A perspective or orientation toward reality made up of interrelated concepts.

Participant observation A research technique in which investigators assume a status and play a role in the group they are studying.

Power The ability to get what you want despite resistance.

Resources Characteristics or possessions valued in a society because they promote survival, reduce stress, or gratify needs and desires.

Roles Scripts people follow as occupants of a particular status.

Sample In survey research, a smaller number of people chosen to represent a larger population.

Scientific method A series of steps that researchers follow in accumulating accurate and verifiable knowledge.

Social class A large category of people who share a similar rank in a prestige hierarchy. Rank is based on property and income, education, occupation, ancestry, and gender. Also known as **social status**.

Socialization The process by which individuals learn to function in their groups and societies.

Sociobiology A model in which complex personality dispositions such as aggression, selfishness, tribalism, and male dominance are believed to be genetically determined.

Sociocultural evolution model A theoretical model in which developments in science, technology, and economics are given the greatest weight as explanatory variables.

Sociology of knowledge The investigation of how location in time and social space affects the knowledge that is sought and the interpretation of this knowledge.

Status A widely recognized position in a group or society.

Stereotype An exaggerated or untrue belief that is applied to an entire category of people.

Structural-functional model A theoretical model in which social structure, values, and the tendency toward social stability are given the greatest weight as explanatory factors.

Structure Parts of a bounded whole (a cell, a group, or a society) that are related in a recurring, interdependent way.

Survey research The study of large numbers of people, using personal interviews or mailed questionnaires.

Symbolic interaction model A focus on perceptions and performance of roles as these are based on the use of mutually understood symbols, especially language, gestures, and cues (body language).

Technology Tools, weapons, and the skills necessary to operate these objects.

Temperament Levels of emotional intensity, energy, and activity within individuals that are biologically grounded.

Theories Statements of the relationship between variables that explain why certain conditions exist or how they came about.

Values Beliefs about what is good, right, desirable, or important.

Variables Characteristics that vary in degree or type.

PRACTICE TESTS

True ▪ False Test

___ 1. Almost every sociological phenomenon or problem can be explained to exist as the result of a single variable.

___ 2. "Concepts" is a more contemporary term for "theory" or "hypothesis."

___ 3. Social class and social status are still considered important sociological concepts.

___ 4. All human societies have a recognizable family unit.

___ 5. Male dominance in human society has not been found to have a basis in biology.

___ 6. Climate and geography are important variables affecting human societies.

___ 7. Marx was one of the first theorists to use a model of sociocultural evolution.

___ 8. Macrolevel studies are too generalized to be of much value to sociologists.

___ 9. Generalizations are beliefs about categories of people that are not based on research and are applied indiscriminately to all people in a category.

___ 10. Sociologists are under no special obligation to obtain the consent of the people whom they wish to study.

Multiple-Choice Test

___ 1. Of the following choices, the statement that could most accurately be called a "theory," as defined in the chapter, is:
   a. Christopher Columbus was seeking a new route to India when he first sailed to the Americas.
   b. Poor people tend to seek out care from physicians less frequently than do wealthier people.
   c. The incest taboo exists in virtually all human societies.
   d. Sociocultural evolution is a result of typical childrearing practices in societies that promote achievement motivation.

___ 2. All of the following can be considered types of variables in sociological research *except:*
   a. socioeconomic class.
   b. education level.
   c. family structure.
   d. luck.

___ 3. Of the following, the selection that is not a basic concept in the Marxian theoretical model is:
   a. counterculture.

    b. exploitation.

    c. class struggle.

    d. alienation.

__ 4. Of the following variables, the most important is:

    a. human biology.

    b. economics.

    c. family.

    d. the incest taboo.

__ 5. Historically, which of the following countries would you say has been least affected by cultural diffusion?

    a. France

    b. Iceland

    c. England

    d. India

__ 6. Sociocultural evolutionists are likely to believe that a people's economic and political problems can be solved by:

    a. advances in science and technology.

    b. religious faith.

    c. social role change.

    d. changes in societal values.

__ 7. Discoveries may be said to be similar to latent functions in that both are:

    a. obvious to the unbiased observer.

    b. unintended rather than deliberate.

    c. simple.

    d. of more importance in the twentieth century than they were in earlier centuries.

__ 8. The first step in the sociological scientific method is to:

    a. formulate a hypothesis.

    b. design the research project and collect the data.

    c. select a problem.

    d. review the literature.

__ 9. The most common research method used by sociologists is conducting:

    a. surveys.

    b. experiments.

    c. secondary analysis.

    d. case studies.

__ 10. The group that does not experience change in a sociological research experiment is termed the:

    a. secondary group.

b. control group.
c. participant observer.
d. case student.

Matching Test

Match each concept with its definition, illustration, or explication below.

1.
__ (1) Attitudes
__ (2) Theories
__ (3) Class
__ (4) Variables
__ (5) Models

a. Attempt to explain
b. Can be observed directly or indirectly
c. A perspective that orients one to reality
d. Cannot be observed directly
e. Marxian concept

2.
__ (1) Ancestry
__ (2) Gender
__ (3) Economic class
__ (4) Materialism
__ (5) Social status

a. Family and racial/ethnic origin
b. Rank
c. Measurable concept
d. Male or female sex
e. Value ascribed to yuppies

3.
__ (1) Family unit
__ (2) Physical force and/or weaponry
__ (3) Temperament
__ (4) Values
__ (5) Great man theory

a. Facilitates dominance
b. Cultural universal
c. Psychological motivation
d. Individual characteristics
e. Beliefs

4.
__ (1) Focuses on developments in science and technology
__ (2) Uses a sociocultural evolution perspective
__ (3) Focuses on human needs, power
__ (4) Role perceptions and performance
__ (5) Values consensus and stability

a. Structural functionalism
b. Conflict model
c. Interactionist model
d. Sociocultural evolution model
e. Social Darwinism

5.
__ (1) Hypothesis
__ (2) Dependent variables
__ (3) Case study method
__ (4) Sample
__ (5) Research bias

a. The expression of a research problem
b. Can be insightful but subjective
c. Group reflects wider population
d. Distorting
e. Consequences

REVIEW QUESTIONS

1. What is the relationship among theories, models, and concepts in social scientific research?
2. How do variables such as biology, psychology, climate and geography, science, technology, economics, and values help explain social stability and social change in human history?
3. What are the basic concepts of the sociocultural evolution model, the structural-functional model, and the conflict model?
4. Which explanatory variables are most important in each of these models?
5. How do the major models at the microlevel—symbolic interactionism, ethnomethodology, and the dramaturgical approach—differ from one another?
6. What are sociological facts? Give examples of generalizations and stereotypes.
7. What are the steps in the scientific method and some possible problems in doing research at each stage?
8. What are the advantages and limitations of survey research, experiments, case studies, and secondary analysis?
9. Discuss some special problems that social scientists have in conducting their research.

APPLYING SOCIOLOGY

1. Using the concepts in parentheses to answer the questions, indicate how a functionalist and a conflict theorist would explain the following facts:
   a. the higher rates of poverty among African Americans (subcultural values, economic discrimination).
   b. high crime rates in the United States (anomie, economics).
   c. the increase in the social status of women since the 1960s (changing societal or family needs, economics).
   d. prostitution (functions in maintaining family groups, economics and exploitation).
2. What are some norms that you follow in major areas of life that are so automatic you are not usually aware of them (greeting behavior and gestures, particularly)?
3. Describe the differences in scenery and props (dress, language, equipment, and so on) among different statuses that you occupy. What techniques have you used to maintain or save face in embarrassing or threatening situations?

4. Analyze a situation you have experienced that is new or not clearly defined in your culture. To what extent did traditional norms apply? To what extent did new and different norms arise?
5. Design a field experiment involving two groups of mothers on welfare who have newborn infants. One group is coached in teaching their infants certain skills; the other group is not coached. Describe the stages of the scientific method you would go through in carrying out this research.
6. Design a survey research project to evaluate the effect of bilingual educational programs in inner-city public schools. What precautions would you take to see that a survey you might conduct would yield valid, reliable, and representative results?

3

The Language of Sociology:
Social Stability

To understand any science, we must first learn the basic language, or concepts, used by scientists in the field. Concepts are a scientific shorthand that enables researchers to communicate abstract ideas more quickly and easily. The concepts that sociologists use to classify or characterize people, places, things, or events differ in their degree of abstractness. The **family** is a concept that helps classify people into groups related by

72

birth, marriage, adoption, or mutual definition (as in unmarried-couple households or gay or lesbian domestic-partner households). Mutual definition means that members are tied by psychological bonds, in relationships not sanctioned by birth, law, or tradition. The concept of the family includes a great variety of groups, but it is not very abstract or difficult to define. The concept of social class, however, is relatively abstract and difficult to define, as we have seen. This is also true of the concept of society.

The term "society" sometimes means a group of people who share a common interest and meet more or less regularly to further this interest. Examples are the Society of American Magicians, the Society for the Prevention of Cruelty to Animals, various professional societies, and "high society." To sociologists, however, a **society** is any number of people who share a specific territory and a common identity, language, and culture. In addition, a society is politically independent, or its members—especially in modern times—believe it should be. Political autonomy distinguishes societies from communities, neighborhoods, or street gangs (Lenski, Lenski, and Nolan, 1991). As used here, the concept of society also applies to populations that once were politically independent and are seeking to reestablish their independence.

For now, we should also know the distinction between preindustrial and postindustrial societies. Historically, **preindustrial** (agricultural) societies were those in which a majority of workers extracted raw materials from land and sea—in farming, mining, and fishing. **Postindustrial** societies are those in which a majority of workers are in service occupations (Bell, 1973; Naisbitt and Aburdene, 1989). They do not provide basic resources or manufacture products; they sell their services as domestic workers, salespeople, teachers, case workers, administrators, computer programmers, and so on. At the higher levels, they mainly work with or provide information and use communication skills.

A society may or may not coincide with actual, legal political boundaries. Palestinian society at present is located primarily in a political vacuum between Jordanian and Israeli societies. Quebec is legally and politically a part of Canada. But those whose ancestors were originally French continue to speak French, maintain a separate identity, and periodically threaten to secede from Canada. The Czechs and the Slovaks have, in fact, separated and are now two politically independent societies, as are the societies that formerly made up the Union of Soviet Socialist Republics.

Concepts focus our observations. They determine what we look for and—to an extent—what we see. If we did not have the concept of the family, we would not be able to analyze what is unique or typical about human relationships in this particular type of group. We would not even perceive that there is this type of group that is different from all others in human societies. If we did not have the concept of social class, we would not be sensitive to what is probably the most important variable in explaining widespread similarities or differences in attitudes, values, and life experiences in complex societies. And if we did not have the concept of society, our observations about human populations would lack logical boundaries. We would be unable to classify these populations or compare them. And we would lose an important source for understanding our own society better.

Concepts such as culture, norms, institutions, and socialization, as well as others to be introduced in this chapter, are used to explain why societies are stable. We use these concepts to explain why social life is fairly predictable from day to day—barring natural (and unnatural) disasters. They help us understand why most people know pretty much what to do and what to expect in most typical situations, most of the time, in the groups and societies in which they live.

CULTURE

Émile Durkheim did not use the concept of culture, but he came close with his concept of "social facts" (Durkheim, 1938 [1895]). He defined social facts as collective (common and widespread) ideas about right and wrong that exist outside of individuals and have a controlling effect on their lives. Social facts—norms—are an important aspect of what we now call culture.

Norms

People learn certain rules about how they should or should not perceive the world, act, and relate to others. These rules, called **norms**, apply in familiar, recurring situations. Norms differ in the degree of importance attached to conformity and the severity of punishment for nonconformity.

These distinctions were made at the turn of the century by sociologist William Graham Sumner (1906). Sumner identified two types of norms, which he called folkways and mores. **Folkways** are the traditional customs and manners that are widespread in a society. Norms of speech, dress, greeting behavior, and table manners are examples of folkways. People do not usually have strong feelings of right and wrong about these particular customs. Nonconformity may bring ridicule, mild disapproval, or avoidance, but people do not define this behavior as destructive to self or society. **Mores** are norms that have a conception of "societal welfare" and more intense feelings of right and wrong attached to them. Nonconformity to mores is defined as immoral and brings more severe punishment, although not always by recognized authorities such as judges or police officers. The Ten Commandments are mores. Ostracism and expulsion from the group are examples of more severe punishment for nonconformity.

According to Sumner, the mores of a society "make anything right"—brother/sister marriages among the royalty of ancient Egypt, the blood revenge of family feuds and vendettas, the killing of surplus infants (usually females), the selling of children. In certain impoverished nonliterate societies, the mores defined the voluntary suicides of disabled old people as a "regretted necessity," but right, nevertheless (Keith, 1990). **Taboos**, on the other hand, are norms that define wrong behavior, ranging from mildly disapproved behavior such as eating with one's fingers to behavior such as cannibalism or incest that is strongly disapproved in almost all societies.

Laws are norms that are written out and enacted by specific groups (legislatures). They prescribe explicit punishments for behavior that is taboo. Laws are enforced by trained specialists: police, attorneys, judges, wardens, and parole officers. Laws become necessary, as Sumner pointed out, when societies become larger and more complex and the mores begin to lose their effectiveness in controlling human behavior.

In describing the norms of a society or group, sociologists often make a distinction between the *ideal* norms of a culture and the *real* norms by which people actually live. The latter may be more difficult to uncover. Ideal norms such as equality of opportunity, tolerance and sympathy toward all people regardless of ethnic origin or religion, or respect for the aged regardless of their economic circumstances may be given lip service in a society. Frequently, however, these ideal norms do not actually control the behavior of a majority of people in that society. It is important to make the distinction between the ideal and the real if we are to understand what is actually happening in a society, particularly one that is changing rapidly. Ideal norms have an aura of goodness and sanctity about them and nonconformity tends to be denied. Reality, however, consists of what people actually do, as well as what they say they do.

Anthropologists were the first to invent the social scientific concept of **culture**. Edward B. Tylor, a pioneer in the field of anthropology, defined culture as the "knowledge, beliefs, art, morals, law, custom, and any other capabilities and habits acquired by . . . a member of a society (1871, p. 1). Acquired means learned—not transmitted by heredity, not in the genes, not an aspect of "human nature." Culture is our "social heredity" (Linton, 1936, p. 69), in contrast to our biological heredity. This social heritage is acquired through a process called "socialization," another concept of social stability to be discussed shortly.

There are four important things to remember about culture (see Table 3.1). Culture is attached to a particular society. The ways of life in a culture are learned. They are shared by most people in a society. And aspects of culture are long lasting. The language, norms, values, beliefs, skills, and other parts of a culture are passed down from generation to generation in the society.

Culture affects humans from the moment of conception to the moment of death. It affects what pregnant women eat and drink, how much exercise they get, how much stress they experience, and how they view motherhood, childbirth, and childrearing. At the other end of the life cycle, culture

TABLE 3.1

Characteristics of Cultures

1. Cultures are attached to specific societies.	3. The culture is transmitted to a majority of people in a society.
2. The nonmaterial culture (language, norms, values, beliefs, knowledge, skills) is learned by individuals in a society through the process of socialization.	4. Aspects of culture are enduring; they are passed down from one generation to the next, although they may change greatly in the process.

affects how people react when they are dying and how they are responded to by those who care for them (Sudnow, 1967). These roles, too, are culturally defined and vary in different classes, racial/ethnic groups, societies, and time periods.

Cultural norms affect a majority of people in a society. Most people in the United States speak English, eat hamburgers and hot dogs, and value education, democracy, religion, and family life. And cultural patterns are enduring. A fad or a fashion, which is a learned behavior, may spread to most people in a society at a particular time. But it does not become part of the culture unless it is taught to succeeding generations.

Material Culture

Some anthropologists and sociologists also include arts and crafts, tools and weapons, and other things in their definition of culture (Kroeber and Kluckhohn, 1963). The things that are made or used in a society are called **artifacts,** and they are part of the *material* culture. Even here, however, the emphasis is on the knowledge, skills, values, and other ideas that go into producing and using artifacts—the ideas that are incorporated in these things and taught to succeeding generations so that the material culture survives.

A work of art is part of the material culture. But it is not only a concrete object. It represents certain technical skills, perceptions of the world, and economic and political conditions that are current in a society at a particular time in history. Fast-food drive-ins, for example, are a part of the material culture. They are material things—buildings, cooking and seating facilities—that require technical know-how to build and operate. But they also reflect currently changing cultural values and economic circumstances: most married women are now employed, almost half of the food dollar is spent on food prepared outside the home, and the automobile is the primary source of transportation for an increasingly suburbanized population.

Culture and Conformity

In rapidly changing, complex societies, cultural norms may be unclear or outmoded. In new situations, they may not exist. Nonconformity increases and may even be highly valued. There are vast gray areas where we must reinterpret the rules, make up our own rules, or decide whether or not the rules apply. In a nationwide Harris poll of American high school and junior high students in 1992, many students reported confusion about where to draw the line between flirting and harassment, advances and abuse, right and wrong in their relationships with the opposite sex (Henneberger, 1993). Those who reported less confusion, incidentally, attributed this to strong family ties or deep religious faith.

We should never underestimate the power of tradition in regulating behavior, however, especially at levels that are so automatic that we are not aware of being controlled, or even of being affected. An example is greeting behavior. Some people bow when they greet each other (in Japan), some people shake hands (men more often than women), and some people kiss (Italian Americans).

Most people in the United States are taught that they must say please or thank you when they ask for or are given something, and we are quite aware of these rules. But we are less aware of being taught the various proper distances to maintain between ourselves and strangers, family, friends, or lovers when we talk (Hall, 1959). We become aware of these silent norms, however, when we violate them, or when we are talking to someone from another culture with different rules. Latin Americans, for example, tend to stand closer in polite conversations. North Americans back away, or may misinterpret an attempt to engage in friendly conversation as a sexual advance. Affectionate touching, a norm in Latin America, may be perceived as sexual harassment in the United States.

Cultural rules define who can touch whom, how, and under what circumstances (Thayer, 1988). Northern European countries and the United States are "low touch" cultures. Mediterranean and Latin American cultures permit much higher rates of touching, even among strangers (Montagu, 1986). Psychologist Sidney Jourard observed the amount of touching in one hour between couples sitting in coffee shops in various parts of the world. Couples touched each other 180 times in one hour in San Juan, Puerto Rico; 110 times in Paris, France; twice in Gainesville, Florida; and not at all in London, England (cited in Thayer, 1988).

Culture and Instinct

Before the concept of culture was invented, social scientists believed human behavior to be caused by hereditary **instincts**, biological tendencies to react in certain specific ways. People who committed crimes or suicide were believed to have inherited criminal or suicidal instincts in the genes of their particular family lines.

The problem with the instinct theory of behavior is that, taken alone, it cannot explain changes in human behavior in individuals during their lifetime, or in the same society during different periods of time. If human behavior is determined primarily by fixed biological instincts, humans should behave in the same fixed, unchanging way throughout their lives. But they don't. If biology is the most important factor in determining human behavior, then changing political and economic conditions should have little or no effect on typical behavior in societies at different stages of sociocultural evolution. But they do have an effect. And certain instincts that were believed to be universal, such as the maternal instinct, should have been found in all societies. But they were not.

As scholars in the nineteenth century compiled longer and longer lists of instincts that supposedly determined all human behavior, anthropologists began to report on little-known societies where what was believed to be universal instinctive behavior did not occur. The maternal instinct, for example, was absent among the fiercely competitive Mundugumor tribe in New Guinea, where women dreaded pregnancy and nursed their children grudgingly and unlovingly (Mead, 1935). More recent research indicates that aggressive behavior is also not universal or fixed in human societies. Infanticide and child abuse, for example, were widespread in agricultural societies, but are less frequent (although more publicized) in the same societies as they become industrialized (deMause, 1991). Animal research indicates that even the supposedly instinctive behavior of lower animal forms also depends, to some extent, on learning. Monkeys and seagull chicks isolated from other animals at birth, for example, are unable to respond sexually when they reach adulthood and cannot reproduce (Harlow and Harlow, 1962; Hailman, 1969). The sexual drive is biological, but sexual behavior is learned.

We now recognize that human beings are born with certain biological reflexes and drives, such as hunger, thirst, and sex, but learning, socialization, and environment channel these in directions that are socially defined as acceptable or unacceptable in particular groups and societies. Hunger is a biological drive, but whereas people in China eat the heads of fish, people in the United States do not. Thirst is a biological drive, but the French prefer wine to water. Sex is a biological drive, but women in the Victorian era who greatly enjoyed sex were defined as abnormal. Currently, in the United States, women who do not enjoy sex are defined as "inhibited," or worse (Kaplan, 1979).

Culture and Language

The key to culture is language, a uniquely human attribute. It is largely through language that culture is transmitted. As noted in chapter 2, language is made up of arbitrary, agreed-upon **symbols** whose meanings are shared by two or more individuals. Symbols are concrete things that stand for more complex or abstract things. A flag, for example, is a symbol of a group or a society. In language, certain sounds or written words stand for other things. All animals respond to **signs**, symbols such as cues or gestures that refer mainly to present conditions. Smiles or frowns are signs. Chimpanzees can learn and respond to primitive sign language. But humans can, in addition, respond to oral or written symbols that refer to conditions or events that are not present. Humans can be warned in advance that fire burns. Much trial-and-error behavior in which people learn to adapt to their environment is avoided by humans because they can be reminded of past situations and can be told what to expect in future situations. Humans can be controlled by promises or threats of future rewards or punishments, or by reminders of past behavior that induce guilt, fear, or gratitude.

Culture is communicated to members of society by signs and symbols. The elements of the culture are symbolized in the form of ideas that people learn. Culture gives meaning to what people experience and strongly affects perception. Individuals entering a new, different society for the first time often experience **culture shock**. They become confused and anxious because they do not understand the new symbols and signs, the new norms, the new attitudes. The new language does not communicate; the people behave unpredictably (they laugh at things that are not funny; a nod means no rather than yes); traffic signs are unfamiliar or absent; the cooking is strange and perhaps inedible. The familiar ways of life dictated by the previous culture are gone, and the individual experiences a feeling of shock, bewilderment, and, often, loss (Sontag, 1993).

Most societies and groups are characterized by **ethnocentrism**, the tendency to view one's own group and culture as the center of the universe, not only different from but superior to all others (Sumner, 1906). Labels such as "savages," "pagans," and "infidels" reflect ethnocentric beliefs and attitudes. Extreme patriotism, or nationalism, is a form of ethnocentrism. It derives its strength from prejudice against outsiders (Pfaff, 1993). Ethnocentrism promotes loyalty, solidarity, and stability in groups by reinforcing the cultural norms of the group. But extreme ethnocentrism reinforces hatred and misunderstanding between groups. It is an attitude that discourages cultural change because it prevents the acceptance of other people's ways of life.

In the past, the "ugly Americans" were ethnocentric tourists or foreign service officers who ignored or ridiculed the cultural norms of the societies they were visiting and offended the local people (Lederer and Burdick, 1958). Now, professional foreign service officers (and, ideally, political appointees as well) are briefed about the customs and traditions of the society in which they will be stationed and are usually required to know the language.

Subculture and Counterculture

When anthropologists first conceived of the concept of culture, they based their observations on small, nonliterate (without a written language) hunting and gathering or tribal societies in which all members shared a common culture. Even in these societies, however, social location with respect to age and gender typically determined certain differences in how people related to one another. In larger, more complex societies there are different

80

ethnic groups, classes, religions, and regions, as well as different generations and the two genders. Large numbers of people learn certain different
ways of life as a result of their more specific social location in the wider
society. Cultures are attached to societies; subcultures are attached to more
limited social locations within the larger society.

Members of a **subculture** accept most of the basic cultural norms of
a society, but their customs differ in some ways. The prefix "sub," incidentally, does not mean lower, or inferior; it simply means different. Apple pie
is a cultural taste. Shoofly pie is subcultural (Pennsylvania Dutch). Should
the taste for shoofly pie spread to a majority of citizens in the United States,
shoofly pie would become a part of the culture. This has happened with
salsa, originally a Mexican American food. Salsa now outsells ketchup in
the United States. Country music is now urban and suburban music, as well.
Hot dogs, french fries, apple pie, and pizza were all originally subcultural
tastes.

Members of some subcultures can be recognized by distinctive language and dress. This is particularly true of age and ethnic subcultures.
Young adults in the United States rarely wear a grass skirt or a loincloth,
for example, but many young women wear cutoff blue jeans, miniskirts,
and bikinis. This dress is rare among women over 65, however. Most young
adults in the United States use certain slang words or phrases that are not
used by older people (and that bewilder immigrants and visitors who come
to the United States with a textbook knowledge of English).

Older people who work with the young, or who identify with the
young, will sometimes use their language. Language, gestures, makeup, and
dress are evidence of actual group membership. But they may also indicate
desired group membership by those who are not actually members of a
subculture.

People who share a similar subculture, especially age, class, and ethnic
subcultures, also very often share a common "territory"—ghettos, high
school and college campuses, communes, gay male or lesbian neighborhoods, singles' apartment complexes, or retirement communities, for example. One of the latest subcultures in the United States, incidentally, is based
on a computer-connected "virtual community." Here, the shared territory
is cyberspace. Community members are joined by computer networks and
the need for instant, non-face-to-face information. As in other subcultures,
members of the cyberspace subculture have a special language, shared interests and values, and a feeling of belonging together (Raymond, 1993).

In the United States, at the moment, the "melting pot" cultural ideal
(in which all ethnic groups are supposed to become homogenized according
to the standards of English immigrants) is competing with the ideal of **cultural pluralism**. This ideal prescribes the coexistence and mutual tolerance
of all ethnic groups and their ways of life. The real culture in the United
States is more accurately described by the more neutral, descriptive concept
of cultural diversity, however.

In the 1960s, some sociologists added the concept of **counterculture** (originally "contraculture") to their vocabulary (Yinger, 1960; 1977). Countercultures not only differ in certain respects from the dominant culture, but also reject some (or most) of the basic norms, values, and beliefs of the wider society. Most members of the youth movement of the 1960s rejected the norms of hard work and material success (the "uptight" ethic) and military preparedness (instead proclaiming "make love, not war"). The majority of the members of this counterculture shared a similar social location with respect to age and social class. Most were under 30 and middle- or upper-class in social origins. Current examples of counterculture groups in the United States are drug syndicates, Satanic cults, and white supremacists.

If they isolate themselves, counterculture groups may promote social stability by removing potential rebels from the wider society. But the norms of countercultures may spread to the wider society and hasten social change. The politically radical countercultures of the 1920s and 1930s in the United States contained certain ideas that were adopted, in watered-down versions, by New Deal Democrats in the 1930s (Yorburg, 1969). The less inhibited expression of feelings and beliefs ("telling it like it is") and the sexual liberalism of the youth counterculture of the 1960s have become part of the culture in the United States. Greater sexual freedom was also the result of advances in birth control technology (Yorburg, 1993).

Traditional Values

Norms are based on values, defined earlier as ideas people have about what is good, desirable, and important. Values, like norms, are an important part of a culture, but they are less likely than norms to vary in the subcultures of a society, and they change more slowly than norms, even in rapidly changing, complex societies.

Traditional values are those that have been part of a culture for many generations, such as authoritarianism or monogamy, for example. Insofar as these values are shared by large numbers of people in a society, they tend to promote social order and stability. If aggression and violence are valued in a society, however, as is happening increasingly in the United States today (Nisbett, 1993), values do not promote stability.

In contrast to traditional values, new values—those of successful social movements, for example—can lead to widespread changes in all spheres of life. The values of the Protestant Reformation of the sixteenth century, the various socialist revolutions of the early twentieth century, and the women's movements in the later part of the twentieth century transformed the lives of millions of people.

Values are used to judge reality. They justify choices. Goals are derived from values, as well as the means we use to achieve our goals. Those who value learning may work for Ph.D.'s and professorships; those who value independence and risk taking will start small businesses; those who value security will go into government employment; those who value athletics will channel their time and energy into sports activities. Other life choices rest on values. If duty is the uppermost value in an unhappy marriage, husband and wife will probably remain married, despite conflicts and differences. If personal well-being is a more important value, divorce is, at least, more likely.

If we want to know what the values of a society are, we conduct surveys, analyze census data, study entertainment preferences (especially movies, television programs, and popular music and magazines), or examine government policies. A government that capitulates to the threats of another government may do so because it values peace at any price. If it invests resources into industrial plants rather than consumer goods, it values industrialization. If it segregates and legally deprives its minority populations of economic, educational, and political opportunities, it values racism.

China did not value industrialization until the twentieth century, although many inventions—gunpowder and printing, for example—occurred in China first. Certain values in the traditional upper-class Mandarin subculture—the emphasis on learning and Confucian ethics—slowed the rate of sociocultural evolution in that country.

Traditional values, as pointed out earlier, promote solidarity within a society when they are generally accepted. But they may also create much personal distress when they conflict with changing social conditions, especially changing economic conditions. The traditional value of **familism** requires that the needs of the family come before those of any individual member of the family. Duty and obligation to the family are valued more than personal interests and goals. But modern economic conditions often require a tremendous investment of time and energy in careers, and more so in the United States than in Western European industrial societies (Schor, 1992; Reich, 1993). According to U.S. Labor Department surveys of multiple jobholders, three-job marriages, in which one partner holds two jobs and the other partner is also employed, are increasing rapidly in the United States (Uchitelle, 1994).

Women senior executives in the United States are more likely to be married and have children now than they were 10 years ago (Noble, 1993). "Having it all" (career *and* family) is the current cultural standard for educated, successful women. On recent surveys, however, women executives are much more likely to report feeling stressed and burned out than male executives. This is largely because they continue to have the major responsibility for childrearing and homemaking (Ferree, 1991; Lye and Biblarz, 1993; Presser, 1993). They get more help from husbands or partners than in the past, and men also report frequent work/family conflicts. The conflict between traditional family obligations and career responsibilities, however, continues to be stronger for women than men.

GROUPS AND SOCIAL RELATIONS

The term *group* at the microlevel is comparable to the concept of *society* at the macrolevel. Some sociologists, in fact, define sociology as the study of group interaction or group relationships. This definition is too narrow, since we also study cultures and subcultures, social stability and social change, and major institutions. But it is certainly an important focus in the field.

A **group** consists of two or more people who relate to each other on a regular basis. Members of a group define themselves as members and usually share common values and norms. They occupy established positions and play out recognized roles. They use rewards and punishments (sanctions) to promote conformity to group norms.

Audiences, crowds, and mobs are not groups. They come together for a while and then depart. They have little or no interest in one another. There is no conception of being members of an ongoing, cooperative enterprise dedicated to carrying out certain goals and fulfilling certain needs. Families, gangs, classmates, political clubs, religious congregations, boards of directors, unions, and Weight Watchers are groups. Groups teach, control, liberate, amuse, bore, support, and sometimes destroy their members. They are the setting for much that is human (and inhuman) in social life.

Groups differ in size, permanence, and purpose. But members of groups usually share a set of norms and values that define good and bad, right and wrong, and, often, true and false. Members have mutual expectations (and, more often in modern times, conflicts) about who should do what in the group (in families, for example). They use techniques ranging from love and affection to physical violence to persuade others to conform to their expectations.

Groups and Networks

Networks refer to the total number of direct and indirect contacts individuals have with other people. Networks are not necessarily groups, since we do not relate on a regular basis with all members of our network. But networks contain groups, and they provide access to other groups who may be helpful in fulfilling our needs and desires. Networks are particularly useful in the obtaining of jobs, especially at higher occupational levels. They are a major reason why some people attend professional meetings, join country clubs, or go to parties—to meet people who might be helpful in advancing a career.

The inheritance of jobs within family lines—**nepotism**—indicates the importance of networks in industrialized societies. Sons and daughters of Hollywood actors need talent to succeed in acting, but their parents' contacts give them a tremendous edge over equally talented, or even more talented, men and women who are outside the Hollywood inner circle.

Status and Role

Individuals in groups and in recurring social situations have widely recognized positions, such as student, teacher, customer, salesperson, prisoner, and warden. Each of these positions, as noted in chapter 2, is a status. Sociologists distinguish between **ascribed** and **achieved** statuses. An ascribed status, such as sex, ethnic origin, or age, is one we do not have control over and cannot change—at least not very easily. An achieved status is the result of effort and choice. In modern societies, achieved statuses include occupation, marriage, and parenthood.

This distinction can be very important. Minority status, for example, is usually based on birth. We do not choose our ancestors, our gender, or our year of birth. In the United States there are legal protections against discrimination on the basis of national origin, race, gender, or age. In the case of gay men and lesbians, some researchers have argued that a same-gender sexual orientation may be genetic and, therefore, an ascribed status (Bailey, 1991; Hamer et al., 1993). If this is true, and becomes accepted as true, being gay or lesbian would then be defined as a matter of birth, not choice. Gay men and lesbians could then claim the same legal protection against discrimination as women and racial/ethnic minorities. The genetic basis of homosexuality, however, is far from established at the present time (Hubbard and Wald, 1993).

The statuses of mother, foreman, president, or priest call forth images—however vague, changing, or contradictory—about how people who occupy these positions should conduct themselves. The scenarios we act out as occupants of a status are **roles**. As occupants of a particular status, we play a variety of roles (see Figure 3.1 on p. 86). In learning roles, we are taught the values, norms, and skills defined as appropriate to that status in our culture or subculture (see Table 3.2 on p. 88).

When we go into a store to make a purchase, why do we behave as we do and why do salespeople behave as they do? We follow the script; we play out the role. We behave predictably in this situation because we have learned the role that is attached to the status of customer or salesperson in our society or group. In industrialized societies, customer/salesperson relationships are usually polite and impersonal. The people involved know how to read, count, and write. The price of the merchandise is clearly marked. The salesperson writes up the sale and gives a receipt for the merchandise so that the purchase can be returned, if necessary, without squabbling. Most customers in industrialized societies look at the merchandise, make a selection, and pay the price that is marked. They pay cash for their purchases or charge them. They do not bargain or barter. They do

FIGURE 3.1

Status and Role

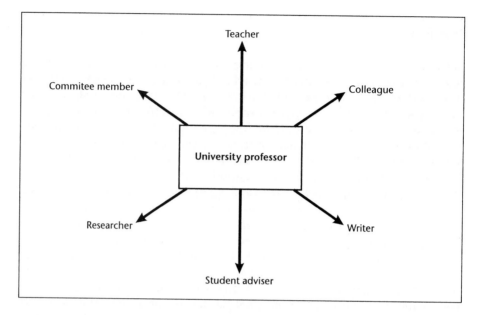

A status, such as university professor, carries with it a role with a number of responsibilities and privileges. In performing roles, we may relate to a variety of people who have similar or different statuses and roles.

not take the item and run. These are the norms of retail buying and selling in industrialized societies, with some differences in middle-class as compared with working-class stores or mom-and-pop stores in ethnic neighborhoods.

In the outdoor marketplaces of currently industrializing societies in Latin America or Africa, on the other hand, prices are not marked and bargaining over price is expected. The final price for the same item will vary depending on who is doing the bargaining. There are no charge accounts, no credit cards, and no refunds. Buying and selling are less impersonal and more sociable activities, involving gossip and friendship relationships.

Since no two people are identical psychologically, however, no two people will play out a role in exactly the same way. College students must abide by certain norms in their role as student. They enter the classroom. They take a seat. They sit quietly as the professor lectures. They take notes. They raise their hands if they want to speak. They use formal, polite language when they do speak. They do not swear; they rarely joke. By speech or written word, they must provide evidence of knowledge gained or work performed. The students' obligation is to do the required work. Their right is to receive a grade and course credit for this work.

Students play the role differently, however, depending on their personalities. They will attend class and speak up in class more or less often, work more or less hard, feel more or less confident or fearful. Personality is the basic source of individual differences in the playing out of a role. But college student role definitions also vary, typically, between small and large colleges, between public and private colleges, and between secular and religious colleges. They differ, typically, in Japan, England, and Germany, and in the twelfth, nineteenth, and twentieth centuries. In other words, they vary in different cultures, subcultures, and social locations.

It is also important to understand that culturally defined role expectations prescribe right and proper feelings and values as well as behavior (Hochschild, 1983). Professional licensing organizations define the role of doctors, lawyers, and other members of the helping professions. But they do not limit themselves to establishing standards, such as keeping up with the field, for members in good standing. Inherent in the concept of professional ethics is the idea that professionals should also have certain attitudes (helping and unselfish) and certain emotions (sympathetic, but detached and objective) in dealing with their clients. Ideally, at least, the helping professional should be service oriented rather than profit oriented. Those who grossly violate professional ethics, and are caught, are expelled from their professional organizations by disbarment or revocation of their licenses.

Our identities, self-conceptions, and personalities are, very largely, a result of the roles we play and have played. In large measure, we are what we do. Role definitions change and people change, but role conceptions, insofar as they are mutually shared in a group or society, promote stability. If we did not learn what to expect from others and they did not learn what to expect from us, at least within broad limits, then orderly, predictable social life would be impossible.

Social Status

From a macrolevel perspective, individuals have a status in the society as a whole as well as in various groups within it. This position is called a **social status**. It is a rank, from very high to very low, relative to other people in the society, with respect to prestige, or what Max Weber called "social honor." This is a global, cross-cultural way of defining social status that applies to all societies—past, present, and future. Even in the simplest societies, where there are usually no differences in *economic* resources, individuals are ranked in terms of relative prestige. In these societies, however, prestige is determined by *personal* resources such as bravery, strength, intelligence, and resourcefulness. In the most complex industrialized socie-

TABLE 3.2

Characteristics of Roles

---

1. Roles are attached to statuses and are defined by the culture (or the subculture).

2. Roles define the rights and obligations of individuals in widely recognized statuses.

3. Roles are performed in different ways by individuals because of differences in personality.

4. Roles define right and proper feelings and values as well as behavior.

5. Roles provide the link between the culture (or subculture) and the individual.

---

ties, social class (prestige ranking) is determined by a combination of achieved characteristics (wealth and income, education, and occupation) and ascribed characteristics (ancestry, ethnic origin, and gender).

Social Control and Sanctions

Why do we often play out the roles we have learned without conviction or commitment in modern times? We usually do what is expected of us because our groups and our society exert **social control**. This involves the use of **sanctions**, rewards or punishments that enforce conformity to group and societal role expectations and norms.

Positive sanctions are rewards such as affection, love, praise, friendship, promotions, salary increases, honorary degrees, and other privileges that are granted to those who conform. Negative sanctions are punishments such as disapproval, ridicule, scorn, withdrawal of love, expulsion from the group (through firing or dishonorable discharge, for example), imprisonment, torture, and death. A grade for a course can be a positive or negative sanction, depending on what the grade is.

When it is successful, social control ensures conformity, and conformity ensures stability. People who conform experience few surprises or disappointments in their relationships with each other. The boat does not rock—except, perhaps, when it is about to sink. Punishment fits the crime of nonconformity, at least to the extent that people believe very strongly in some norms and care much less about others (street crimes are punished more harshly than fraud). In modern societies, the term conformity is sometimes associated with negative images—images of restriction, repression, routine, and boredom. But without some degree of conformity, social life could not continue and societies could not exist.

Even in situations in which preexisting norms are inadequate—new, temporary situations created by unexpected disasters such as tidal waves, earthquakes, floods, blackouts, or invasions—people choose leaders, new roles are created, new norms are laid down to cope with the crisis, and life goes on. Without norms the cooperation necessary for human survival would be impossible. Chaos and catastrophe, unpredictability and uncertainty—always potentially possible in human social life—would be everywhere.

Institutions

The stable sets of related norms, values, roles, and procedures that are organized to satisfy basic human needs are called **institutions**. In the popular language, institutions refer to buildings that house large numbers of people, such as hospitals or prisons, and to important traditions, such as Thanksgiving family dinners and Fourth of July parades. Sociologists usually focus on five major institutional areas—the familial, economic, religious, educational, and political—that reflect universal human needs and the solutions to these needs that have been worked out by various peoples. Activities in these major areas of life are bound by a set of values and norms that are usually widely accepted in a society and strongly believed in, although they are constantly changing in industrial societies.

What are the human needs that major institutions are concerned with—again, ideally? Family groups control sexual rivalry and conflict, produce new members of the society, and provide for the physical, emotional, and intellectual needs of the biologically very dependent human young. The economy functions to produce and distribute goods (such as food, shelter, and clothing) and basic services necessary for survival. Education is concerned with the need to train members of a society to function adequately as adults. Religion provides meaning and purpose for believers and the motivation to continue functioning, despite injustice, tragedy, and adversity. Religion helps believers cope with the question "Why me?" when there is no rational answer. Governments are concerned with protection against violence and destruction (from within the society or from other societies) and with the distribution of rewards and privileges in the society.

In the United States, marriage, monogamy, fidelity, and legitimacy are values followed by most people in families. In economic life, widespread values are free enterprise, hard work, achievement, and material success. In educational life, high levels of academic achievement and equal access to educational opportunity are valued. In religious life, freedom of worship, church attendance, the giving of charity, and voluntary social service are valued. In political life, democracy (the will of the people) is a strongly felt value, as is the rule of law in dealing with crime. Frequently, these values and norms are reflected in the laws of agricultural and industrial societies

TABLE 3.3

Institutional Areas in the United States: Ideal Values

Institutional Area	Ideal Values
Family	Monogamy, marriage, fidelity, legitimacy
Economic Life	Free enterprise, hard work, achievement, material success
Education	High levels of academic achievement, equal access to educational opportunities
Religion	Freedom of worship, church attendance, the giving of charity, voluntary service to the community
Political Life	Democracy (the will of all of the people); equal justice under the law (due process)

because conformity is believed to be essential to survival, for the individual and for the society (see Table 3.3).

SOCIALIZATION

The process by which we learn to become functioning members of our groups and our society is termed **socialization**. With this concept we can explain how people become what we define as "human" or "inhuman." It explains how people in various social locations become typically aggressive or passive, selfish or altruistic, hopeful or fatalistic, and so on. Individual differences in heredity, temperament, intelligence, and unique life experiences diminish the steamroller effects of unbridled socialization. But people in similar social locations are generally more alike than they are unlike, at least in their interests and values.

The Socialization Process

How, then, do people become recognizably and predictably human in various social settings? Charles Horton Cooley (1864–1929) and George Herbert Mead (1863–1931) are generally regarded as pioneering contributors to a sociological understanding of the process of socialization.

Cooley (1964 [1902]) focused on the development of a self-image in humans. According to Cooley, our ideas of who we are and our judgments about ourselves (what we now call self-esteem) arise as a result of communication and "sympathy" with important figures in our environment. We enter into and "share the mind" of these figures, who evaluate us and transmit the culture or subculture—"the history, institutions, and tendencies"—of the society in which we live (p. 102).

The result is a sense of self, or a self-image, that is a mirror image of the judgments of people with whom we identify. Cooley called this self-image the **looking-glass self**. The self-concepts that people develop are important in understanding and predicting human behavior, because to some extent we tend to become what we and others think we can or will become. In sociology, this is known as a **self-fulfilling prophecy**; in psychology it is called the **pygmalion effect.**

In George Bernard Shaw's play *Pygmalion* (performed on Broadway as *My Fair Lady*), Eliza Doolittle is transformed from a cockney ragamuffin to a high-society aristocrat by the strong conviction of another person that this could be done. Eliza learns the superficial status symbols of membership in the new subculture: language and dress. She succeeds, despite tremendous disadvantages, because someone she trusts (and sometimes hates) believes she could do it.

The judgments and expectations of important figures (parents, teachers, or friends) can sometimes have very powerful effects on human destinies, regardless of objective social circumstances. These objective circumstances set the scene, but the reactions of important figures in our environment can reinforce or override them. Parents who strongly believe that their children will be very successful tend to have children who are successful, even when the odds are otherwise poor. And, of course, parents who expect that their children will fail tend to have children who fail, regardless of the children's actual opportunities and abilities. The power of positive (or negative) thinking, at the psychological level, is very real.

George Herbert Mead (1934) was familiar with Cooley's ideas and built on them by describing stages in the development of the self and distinguishing two major aspects of the self. He, too, emphasized the importance of communication in the process of socialization, first through nonverbal cues and gestures (smiles, frowns, holding, and touching) and then through the shared meanings of language, learned through social interaction with "significant others." These significant others are parents, or others who serve in parenting roles, in early childhood and teachers and friends later on.

Mead described the phenomenon that Cooley called sympathy as "taking the role of the other." In doing so, the child imagines the feelings and thoughts of others and internalizes these thoughts and feelings, gradually making them a part of his or her own personality. At first, children do this only with immediate figures in their environment—significant others. Children act out the process of taking the role of the other in their play, for example, by dressing up and imagining themselves as mothers and fathers and acting out the specific roles played by these significant others in their lives.

Later, children develop the capacity to form a generalized, more impersonal, and less specific conception of the roles people play. They learn not only the rules that they themselves must follow but also the roles of all people in their groups or communities. Mead called this the "generalized other." To use Mead's illustration, children learning to play baseball first learn the specific rules they must follow as a pitcher or batter. Later, they are able to keep in mind all the "rules of the game." They know the roles of all members of the team.

Mead further pointed out that human beings are never simply carbon copies of significant or generalized others. He divided the self into two parts—the "I" and the "me." The *me* is the conventional self, the part that has learned and conforms to the general rules of the game. The *I* is the unique individual in all of us. It is the part that is spontaneous and creative. We act within the demands and expectations of the role, but with the stamp of our unique personality and life experiences.

In modern language, the process of childhood socialization as analyzed by Cooley and Mead would be described as follows: children identify with and internalize the attitudes, norms, and values of models in their environment. **Identification** is the act of imagining oneself in the place of others. This is what Cooley called sympathy and what Mead called taking the role of the other. **Internalization** is the process whereby the attitudes, values, and norms of people with whom we identify become a part of our personality.

We now know that identification and internalization in childhood occur when caregivers are viewed as warm, supportive, and approving (Ainsworth and Bowlby, 1991). Throughout life, we identify with models who have resources—intellectual, emotional, physical, or economic—that we value or admire. We also know that if parents or other socializing agents are unreliable, unavailable, very critical, or rejecting, children will have low self-confidence and self-esteem. They are likely to have difficulty trusting and accepting others during childhood and adolescence and in adulthood as well (Shaver, Hazan, and Bradshaw, 1988; Feeney and Noller, 1990; Mayseless, 1991).

In cases of severe abuse, the child may obey when the parent is around to observe and punish, but will feel little or no guilt about disobeying when the parent is not present. People who are labeled "psychopaths" or "sociopaths"—who seem to have no conscience or sense of morality—have usually experienced severe abuse and rejection in their early childhood socialization experiences (McCord and Tremblay, 1992). They have not internalized strong feelings about right and wrong behavior. They are unable to feel sympathy or compassion for their victims. They are ruthless, expedient, and destructive. In short, they are failures of the socialization process.

Mead confined his discussion to socialization in groups to which individuals belong—family, school, play, and community groups. Cooley, however, also discussed the socializing influence of the mass media and pointed out that adults can identify with people about whom they read. (He wrote before the days of television.) This, according to Cooley, enables "like-minded people in religion, politics, art, or whatnot, to get together in spirit and encourage one another in their peculiarities" (Cooley, 1909, p. 92). Cooley's like-minded people are now called **reference groups** (Hyman and Singer, 1968). These are groups to which we may or may not belong; they serve as a standard of comparison in evaluating ourselves and our life circumstances.

Not all reference groups are like-minded people. Some reference groups are used only as a standard for comparison. Revolutionaries will view the power and privileges of the ruling groups in their society in this way. They do not identify with these groups or share their values and norms. Social climbers, on the other hand, do want to be like their wealthier, more prestigious, or more powerful reference groups. They imitate these people, sometimes with grotesque or tragic consequences (as in *The Great Gatsby*). In either of these examples, the reference group is not a membership group to which the revolutionary or the social climber actually belongs. Ambitious people on their way up are more likely to identify with or compare themselves with higher-status, nonmembership reference groups.

Relative Deprivation

A concept that is closely related is **relative deprivation**, the tendency to feel more or less deprived about our life circumstances, depending on whom we compare ourselves with—our reference groups. Students who receive a "C" in a course will feel less deprived if their reference groups are also "C" students. They will feel very deprived, however, if their reference groups are "A" students. The concepts of reference group and relative deprivation have tremendous significance for an understanding of the socialization process and why people feel and act as they do.

In a classic study, conducted during World War II, sociologists were asked to investigate the sources of high or low morale in the army. They found that draftees had high morale and learned the new role more easily when they identified with and took as their reference groups other soldiers in their units or the army hierarchy (Merton and Kitt, 1950). Those draftees who continued to identify with their friends back home (who were not drafted) experienced low morale, feelings of severe deprivation, and much greater difficulty learning the role attached to their new status.

This was a profound discovery. It helped answer two long-standing questions: First, why are people who start revolutions usually not the poorest or most deprived citizens in the society? Part of the answer is that people who have achieved some betterment in their life circumstances tend to identify with and compare themselves to reference groups who are even

FIGURE 3.2

Social Location and Socialization

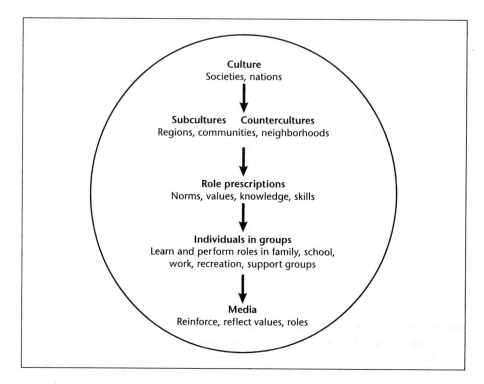

Role conceptions stem from a variety of sources.

better off. They will feel more deprived than those who are actually the most deprived members of a society.

Second, why do wealthier members of ethnic minorities tend to ghettoize themselves voluntarily in what have been called "gilded ghettos" when they could afford to live just about anywhere? The answer is that people feel more comfortable and relatively less deprived when they live in ethnic communities. They avoid contact with reference groups whose members do not experience the prejudice and discrimination they themselves experience.

Reference Group Choices

This still leaves open the question of why people choose the particular reference groups they choose. Why did some draftees during World War II identify with their fellow draftees in the army, and why did others identify with their friends back home? We need more research on these questions, but at least part of the explanation has to do with the preexisting values and personalities of the people who are undergoing an experience of socialization. Those who value conformity highly and are very sensitive to group sanctions are more likely to identify with their membership groups. Those who value success may identify with nonmembership groups if they do not consider themselves successful.

Another, and possibly more important, reason has to do with whether the individual's participation in a new group, such as the army, is voluntary. A volunteer into the army presumably believes in the goals of the army and will shift reference groups and conform; a draftee may not.

Redoing Socialization

This brings us to another concept that has become increasingly useful in recent years. The socialization experience is an ongoing one that takes place every time we enter, or anticipate entering, a new status, from infancy to old age. Sometimes, however, we enter a situation, voluntarily or not, in which an attempt is made to change our previous socialization experiences and wipe out certain of our ways of thinking and behaving. This is called **resocialization**. Brainwashing is an extreme example of resocialization.

Resocialization may take place in what is called a **total institution**, a place in which the individual is segregated from the rest of society and is under the total control of the new authorities. Prisons, mental hospitals, residential drug treatment centers, religious communes, and military organizations are total institutions. Encounter groups, Weight Watchers, and Alcoholics Anonymous also attempt to resocialize their members, but without removing them from their environments.

To be most effective, resocialization requires voluntary participation, complete removal of the individual from the previous environment and previous social contacts, a shift in identification to the new reference group, constant supervision, the application of very powerful group sanctions to enforce conformity to the new norms, and permanent reinforcement, or lifetime support (Yorburg, 1983) (see Table 3.4 on p. 96).

Prisons do not usually succeed in resocializing prisoners (about two-thirds return to prison), because participation is not voluntary. Prisoners are not removed from like-minded people. Fellow inmates who share similar values are the new reference group. Sanctions promote conformity to prison rules. Prisoners learn the role of prisoner; they do not learn the role of conforming member of the wider society. Prisons temporarily or permanently remove nonconformists from the wider society, but do not usually resocialize them.

TABLE 3.4

Conditions of Successful Resocialization

• Voluntary participation	• A shift to a new reference group
• Complete or partial removal from previous social contacts	• The use of powerful group sanctions to enforce conformity to the new norms
• Constant supervision (in total institutions) or regular meetings	• Permanent reinforcement (lifetime support)

A similar situation prevails in mental hospitals (Goffman, 1961). The invention, starting in the mid-1950s, of certain psychoactive drugs—tranquilizers, antidepressants, and antipsychotic medications—has underwritten the trend in industrial societies toward discharging mental patients who have not been judged criminally insane into the community. The underlying logic is that people are more likely to be able to resume the full rights and obligations of functioning members of society if these rights and obligations are not completely taken away from them.

Voluntary residential drug rehabilitation centers have had more success than prisons or mental hospitals in resocializing members. The most successful have fulfilled all the necessary preconditions for permanent change. In the early days, and before they came on hard times, the Synanon centers on the West Coast would only accept recruits who were very anxious to enter (Yablonsky, 1969). New arrivals were not permitted outside contacts—no letters, telephone calls, or visits from relatives or friends. Previous statuses were symbolically destroyed: members were given new birth dates on the day they entered Synanon. The new rules were explicit: no drugs, no fighting, hard work. "Squealing" was also a norm. Members were required to report others who were disobeying group rules. If they did not, they were punished more severely than the offenders—sometimes by expulsion from the center.

Educational seminars, held three times a week, were leaderless. The group listened, encouraged, or criticized. The sanctions were powerful—public shame and shaving the head for more serious offenses (going back on drugs), or demotion to cleaning toilets for less serious offenses (stealing or lying). Conformity was rewarded by promotion up the ranks to more pleasant and more prestigious work. Morale was very high at Synanon. Long-time members were ferocious in their loyalty to an organization that had probably saved their lives.

The pioneering success of this type of treatment center is currently mirrored by other groups that attempt to help members cope with problems of addiction to food, alcohol, or smoking. These groups work with people whose addictions are not so severe that they need to be isolated to be resocialized. But the principle is the same: the use of group sanctions and support by others who have the same problem. Withdrawal from the addictive substance is less painful because it is shared by others, members of the new reference group who are also feeling deprived.

Fellow sufferers can help members accomplish incredible transformations quickly and much more effectively than well-meaning friends, relatives, or therapists who do not have the problem themselves. But individuals who are so transformed usually need permanent reinforcement. They must continue to meet with ex-addicts, the new reference group, formally or informally, because the impulse to eat or drink excessively, or to smoke, rarely disappears entirely. Support groups and self-help groups have become common in industrial societies. They are becoming the functional equivalent of traditional support groups, such as family or friends.

Socialization and the Life Course

Socialization is a lifelong process. We all learn new roles as we enter new statuses. We all change over time as we pass through various phases of our lives, from infancy to childhood, adolescence, adulthood, middle age, and old age. Developmental psychologists focus on biologically grounded individual development over the life cycle, as this is affected by different types of relationships with significant people in the individual's environment.

Sociologists also focus on change over the life cycle, but we are more likely to focus on the effects of changing cultural, economic, and political conditions on the socialization experiences and other life experiences of specific generations. We use the concept *life course* to distinguish our approach from the more microlevel approach of psychologists to interpreting life cycle changes (Aldous, 1990; Elder, 1992).

We locate a particular generation of children, adolescents, or old people, for example, and try to understand how the experience of being in this stage of life is different because they were born, grew up, or grew old during a particular period in history. Because of major sociocultural changes during the twentieth century in the United States (and even more so in most other postindustrial societies), members of the current over-65 generation (excluding impoverished recent immigrants) are in much better material circumstances than people of that age were at the turn of the century. They will live longer, are in better health, are better educated, and are more secure economically through pensions and entitlement programs. They have also had different childhood socialization experiences as children, typically, than nineteenth-century older people did. They were less likely to experi-

FIGURE 3.3

Generations and Gender Equality

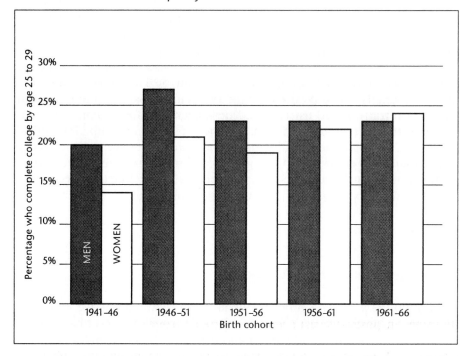

Sources: Campbell Gibson, "The Four Baby Booms," *American Demographics 15*(11) (November 1993), p. 40; based on data from U.S. Bureau of Labor Statistics, *Current Population Survey.* Reprinted by permission.

While before-age-30 college completion rates have varied in successive birth cohorts since 1941, the gap in rates between men and women has disappeared.

ence the trauma of the early death of parents or siblings and more likely to have had living grandparents around to relate to, for example.

Most of these positive changes should become even more widespread as the oldest members of the post–World War II "baby boom" generation (born between 1945 and 1964) turn 65, starting in 2010—barring unforeseen and large-scale environmental, military, or economic catastrophe. Baby boom couples, for example, delayed getting married, were economically more secure when they did marry, and had lower fertility rates than previous generations. Gender roles are more equal among baby boomers (see Figure 3.3). They are more likely to be living in two-earner households and will be more likely to be living in two-pension households in 2010 (Esterlin, Macdonald, and Macunovich, 1990). These trends can be expected to affect the life conditions, roles, and relationships of older people in future generations.

Stages in the Life Course

For years, psychologists have tried to pinpoint universal, unvarying, and inevitable *life stages* in individual life histories (Erikson, 1963; Vaillant, 1977; Levinson, 1978; Erikson, 1982). Each stage of the life cycle is supposed to be characterized by specific positive or negative psychological consequences for individuals. In middle age (around age 45), for example, it was found that men typically experience a **midlife crisis**, a period of increased anxiety and acting out—drinking, divorcing, and/or quitting jobs—because of disappointed expectations and a fear of aging.

The problem with these studies is that they did not take into account other locating factors such as age and generation, social class, and gender in interpreting their results, as sociologists would be more likely to do. The individuals studied were small numbers of upper-middle-class, very ambitious, nonminority males, born before or during the Depression, with very high expectations that were not fulfilled. Do most women, working-class individuals, or poor people, who have never had enormously high expectations, experience a midlife crisis when they take stock and perhaps find their marriages wanting or their careers at a standstill? Nationwide surveys do not support this conclusion (Tamir, 1989). People in their twenties, in fact, are more likely to experience economic and psychological crises. From a life course perspective, we can now draw several major conclusions about life stages in postindustrial societies (Yorburg, 1993):

A Greater Number of Stages   First, in postindustrial societies, there are more stages in the life cycle. Adolescence—a time of learning and experimenting in anticipation of more complex adult roles—was unknown in pre-industrial societies. Children went to work in fields or as apprentices in workshops at age 5 or sooner if they were able to (deMause, 1974). Another stage, youth, a postadolescent phase that occurs before the individual becomes fully adult and self-supporting, is also new, but it is mainly experienced by middle-class college students (Keniston, 1970). Middle age was unknown in preindustrial societies because people aged much more rapidly and did not typically live beyond age 50 (Crews, 1993). Finally, most human development researchers and gerontologists now divide old age (starting legally at age 65) into young-old and old-old, depending on ability to function and chronological age (Neugarten, 1974). The old-old are usually over 85, but disabled older people may reach this status much earlier.

The Blurring of Boundaries   The boundaries between stages also become blurred in postindustrial societies. More people are in mixed stages—working full time in an adult occupational role, but continuing to live at home, for example. Or they are in between stages, finished with their training but unable to find a job. More people are returning to school at older ages after having finished, or dropped out, earlier. More are starting second

TABLE 3.5

Characteristics of the Life Course in Postindustrial Societies

1. There are more life periods or stages (delays before occupying adult economic, marital, and parent statuses, especially in the middle class; greater longevity, young- and old-old stages).	3. Timing of change from one period to the next is more flexible (more skipping of stages, returning to earlier stages).
2. Boundaries between stages are blurred (more in-between, mixed stages, extension of stages).	4. Less conformity occurs on the basis of age (cultural age norms are less binding at any particular stage, especially among middle and upper social classes).

or even third careers—and not only because they have lost their jobs. Many young adults are returning home again, usually after a divorce or the loss of a job (Aquilino, 1990). When does middle age start and when does it end? In the middle classes, those who are in good health—neither senile nor physically disabled—continue to think of themselves, and refer to themselves, as middle aged into their 70s and even their 80s (Hunter and Sundel, 1989).

More Flexible Transitions   The timing of major status changes is much more variable now than it was 25 years ago (Neugarten and Neugarten, 1987). First marriages and remarriages are taking place anytime from ages 13 to 80 or older. Women are having their first child anytime from their teens up to their 40s (and, in a few cases, in their 50s). Men and women are becoming grandparents for the first time in their 30s and up into their 70s, or 80s. Conceptions of the "right time" to do anything are not as clear as they once were and more people are likely to be "off time" (Neugarten and Neugarten, 1987; Crews, 1993).

Less Binding Age Norms   Age norms ("act your age") are much more ambiguous and less binding than in the past. Cultural definitions of right and proper behavior at any particular age are more flexible and negotiable than in the past.

BUREAUCRACIES

Complex administrative organizations that direct the carrying out of large-scale activities by large numbers of people are called **bureaucracies** (Weber, 1947 [1925]). The first bureaucracies arose in agricultural societies, when it became necessary to oversee the activities of large numbers of slaves, laborers, soldiers, and tax collectors in building pyramids, roads, and walls and collecting taxes from far-off conquered societies. As sociocultural evolution results in more populous and complex societies, all major institutions except the family become bureaucratized.

Ideal Bureaucracies

The purest form of bureaucracy (in government and public service places such as schools and hospitals) has written rules and regulations that define qualifications for hiring (except at the very top), job activities (very specialized and standardized), salaries, job security (with career paths, seniority, tenure, and pensions), and lines of authority (from the top down) (Weber, 1947 [1925]). Top administrators in political bureaucracies are elected or are political appointees. They may change as governments change, but the bureaucracy carries on. Written (or electronic) records are kept of the structure of the organization (personnel, background checks) and all official activities (clients, services performed, meetings, discussions, and decisions). These records are placed in files (or on computers).

Ideally, bureaucracies are the most efficient way of getting things done because they are rational and impersonal. They are rational because "the exercise of control [is] on the basis of knowledge" (Weber, 1947 [1925], p. 337). This is assured because hiring is based on technical training and ability, as measured by exams and certified by diplomas. Also, emotions do not get in the way of efficient functioning because officials are bound by "duty without regard to personal considerations" and "impersonality . . . without hatred or passion, and hence without affection or enthusiasm" (p. 340).

Weber believed that the growth of bureaucracies in large, complex societies "levels" the power of the upper social classes because authority in bureaucracies is based on training and competence (merit) rather than wealth. He argued, therefore, that bureaucratic organization "everywhere inevitably foreshadows the development of mass democracy" (p. 340). Currently, the idea of authority on the basis of competence is contained in the concept of **meritocracy**. In meritocracies, power and authority are based on personal qualities such as drive, talent, training, and knowledge, rather than birth or wealth. In government, think tanks that produce knowledge and information become increasingly important in decision-making processes (Ricci, 1993), although political values often override reason.

The Ideal and the Real

Since Weber's time, and especially in recent years, an enormous amount of research has been done on the actual operations of bureaucracies (Kantor,

1977; Glassman, Swatos, and Rosen, 1987; Stinchcombe, 1990; Wilson, 1990; Romanelli, 1991). To begin with, no bureaucracy functions strictly according to the written rules and regulations and formal lines of authority. There is an informal or unofficial structure composed of cliques and networks. Subordinates may actually be in control, especially if the person in charge of a particular unit is incompetent, or less competent than someone who is on the way up. There are secrets, shortcuts, grapevines, and rumors in the actual operations of bureaucracies. Rules are broken or bent for powerful persons. These tendencies lead to the dysfunctions of bureaucracies (see Figure 3.4). Other common patterns that greatly diminish the rationalism and efficiency of bureaucratic operations are the following:

Irrational Growth   Organizations tend to grow to the point of inefficiency, and bloated staffs become entrenched. Also, the more time available, the more time it will take to do the same job. This is known as Parkinson's Law (Parkinson, 1957).

Compulsive Conformity   There is a tendency toward a narrow, rigid insistence on enforcing the rules in bureaucracies. Clients are frustrated and lower-level employees are unable or unwilling to deal with atypical cases that fall outside of official guidelines.

Protection of the Inept   The Peter Principle states that employees tend to be promoted beyond their level of greatest competence (Peter and Hull, 1969). Talent in working with people, for example, may not translate into talent in doing paperwork. Outstanding teachers who are promoted to administrative levels may make poor principals or deans.

Communication Difficulties   As organizations grow in size, forms, files, and facilities also expand, so do secrets, cover-ups, backups, and distorted messages. Communication between the ranks does not flow freely, usually, in authoritarian settings. Resolving conflicts between the ranks, which requires communication and compromise, may be difficult to accomplish.

POWER AND SOCIAL STABILITY

Several concepts are useful in explaining both social stability and social change. Among these is power, defined by Max Weber as the ability to carry out one's will despite resistance (see chapter 2, p. 47). Political leaders in a society may be able to maintain order because they are obeyed willingly. The leaders' right to carry out their will—to make decisions and see that these decisions are acted on—may simply be accepted by citizens, with little or no resistance. But leaders can also carry out their will by the use of force. This, too, will maintain social stability. Force will destroy dissent, at

FIGURE 3.4

Bureaucracy: The Ideal and the Real

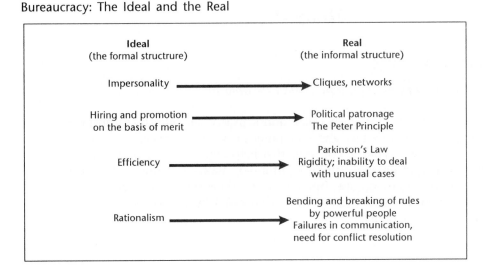

Actual bureaucracies characteristically diverge from the ideal model of bureaucracy; they possess an informal structure that parallels ideal bureaucracy's formal structure.

least temporarily. Military dictatorships will maintain order, unless or until they are overthrown.

Power can also bring about social change, however. The wealthiest nations in the world use military and economic sanctions such as trade embargoes, as well as assistance in the form of aid or loans, to impel change in countries throughout the world, from Russia and South Africa to Iraq, Haiti, and Cuba. In the next chapter, we will examine social movements and other forms of collective behavior, which provide another example of power being used to promote social change.

Study Guide

REVIEW OBJECTIVES

After studying this chapter, you should be able to:

1. Discuss how concepts help guide and sensitize sociologists to observe certain aspects of reality and communicate what they see.
2. Define basic sociological concepts that help explain social stability: culture, norms, traditional values, institutions, status and role, social control and sanctions, groups, bureaucracies, socialization, power.
3. Explain how each of these concepts specificially contributes to maintaining social stability.

SUMMARY

1. Concepts are essential in any science. They sensitize scientists to important aspects of reality and provide a technical language that makes for more efficient communication of information.

2. Certain concepts in sociology are essential in explaining the stability of human societies—why social life goes on from day to day and from generation to generation in fairly predictable ways. These concepts explain how people in particular social locations learn to perceive and react to reality in similar and predictable ways. They represent a tremendous advance in knowledge over earlier, more speculative attempts to explain human behavior only in terms of such concepts as heredity or instincts.

3. Cultures are attached to societies. With sociocultural evolution, the size of human populations increases greatly, as does immigration. Complex societies have subcultures and countercultures. Elements of culture are learned through the process of socialization. They are taught to a majority of citizens in a society. And they are transmitted from generation to generation. The things (artifacts) made and used in a society are part of the material culture.

4. Norms vary in the degree of importance attached to conformity and the severity of punishment for nonconformity. Values determine perception of reality and justify choices and goals. Cultural values in major institutional areas of life change more slowly than norms.

5. We are either born with the statuses we occupy or we achieve them. We occupy a status; we play the culturally defined role attached to this status. The effects of culture are much less pressing in modern times, but they persist in ways that are often quite subtle. Differences in personality strongly affect role playing, regardless of the strength of social control and sanctions in a group or society. Social location strongly affects socialization experiences.

6. With sociocultural evolution, all institutional spheres of life except the family become bureaucratized. Since Weber's analysis, researchers have focused primarily on the informal structure and the dysfunctions of bureaucracy.

GLOSSARY

Artifacts: Things that are made or used in a society.

Achieved status: A position in a group or society we attain because of choice or effort.

Ascribed status: A position in a group or society that is based on birth and cannot usually be changed.

Bureaucracies: Complex administrative organizations that coordinate the activities of large numbers of people in carrying out large-scale tasks.

Counterculture: A subculture containing norms and values that conflict with certain basic values of the dominant culture.

Cultural pluralism: A cultural ideal precribing coexistence and mutual tolerance of all ethnic groups in a society.

Culture: The total social heritage attached to a society that is learned, shared by most people, and transmitted from generation to generation.

Culture shock: The feeling of bewilderment experienced by people who enter a new and unfamiliar society or group with a different culture or subculture.

Ethnocentrism: The belief that our own groups and culture are the center of the universe and superior to all others.

Familism: The doctrine or custom that requires that the needs of the family come before those of any individual member of the family.

Family: A group related by blood descent, marriage, adoption, or mutual definition (such as unmarried-couple households with children).

Folkways: Norms such as customs and manners that are not crucial for group survival and are not enforced by severe sanctions.

Group: Two or more people involved in a recurring social relationship.

Identification: The act of imagining oneself in another person's place.

Instincts: Inborn biological tendencies to behave in certain very specific ways.

Institutions: Major areas of social life in which activities are directed toward the satisfaction of basic human needs.

Internalization: The process by which the norms, values, and beliefs of others become a part of our personality.

Laws: Norms that are written out and enacted by legislators in complex societies.

Looking-glass self: A self-image we develop that mirrors the judgments of those whom we relate to and who are important to us.

Meritocracy: A system of power and authority in a society organized on the basis of merit—training, talent, and drive.

Midlife crisis: A period of severe stress and acting out that is believed to occur in highly ambitious middle-aged men who fear aging or are dissatisfied with their lives.

Mores: Norms that have intense feelings of right and wrong attached to them.

Nepotism: The inheritance of jobs within family lines.

Networks: The total number of direct and indirect contacts we have with other people.

Norms: Rules we learn that guide thinking, feeling, and behaving in typical situations.

Postindustrial societies: Societies in which a majority of the labor force works in service occupations.

Preindustrial societies: Societies in which a majority of workers extract raw materials from land and sea by farming, fishing, and mining.

Pygmalion effect: Doing and becoming what other people expect you to do and become.

Reference groups: Groups that we identify with and compare ourselves with.

Relative deprivation: The idea that the subjective feeling of being deprived is relative and depends on whom we compare ourselves with.

Resocialization: The learning of a new role that requires the rejection of certain previous values, beliefs, and behaviors.

Roles: The scripts we play out as occupants of a particular status. Roles include beliefs about rights and obligations.

Sanctions: The rewards and punishments used by groups and individuals to enforce conformity to norms.

Self-fulfilling prophecies: Doing or becoming what others predict you will do or become, regardless of social circumstances.

Signs: Symbols such as cues or gestures that refer mainly to present conditions.

Social control: The use of sanctions (rewards and punishments) to enforce conformity to group and societal norms.

Social status: A ranked position in the total society.

Socialization: The process whereby we learn to become functioning members of our groups and our society.

Society: A number of people who occupy a specific territory, share a common culture and identity, and are, or would like to be, politically independent.

Subculture: Customs and traditions of particular segments of a society that differ in certain ways from those of the wider society.

Symbols: Concrete things that stand for more complex or abstract phenomena.

Taboos: Norms that define prohibited behavior.

Total institution: A place in which people are confined and are under total control of the authorities.

Traditional values: Values that have been part of a culture for many generations.

PRACTICE TESTS

True ▪ False Test

___ 1. In preindustrial societies, most people are service workers.

___ 2. Characteristics of postindustrial societies suggest that laws are not—or eventually will not be—necessary in those societies.

___ 3. Tradition is very powerful in societies like Japan, but it has lost all influence in less isolated industrialized countries like those of North America and Western Europe.

___ 4. Wearing a certain clothing style may be evidence of a person's desire to gain membership in a group.

___ 5. Not all values are necessarily good for a culture.

___ 6. One individual may have many roles and statuses.

___ 7. Social sanctions are always negative.

___ 8. Mead and Cooley would agree that communication is important in the socialization process.

___ 9. Socialization is a process that occurs primarily, if not exclusively, in childhood.

___ 10. Parkinson's Law states that employees tend to be promoted beyond their level of greatest competence.

Multiple-Choice Test

___ 1. Of the following, which is most likely to be the most controversial classification of family?
   a. groups related by birth
   b. groups related by mutual definition
   c. groups related by adoption
   d. groups related by marriage

___ 2. An example of a peculiarly American folkway is the foods and family celebrations associated with:
   a. Thanksgiving.
   b. New Year's Eve.
   c. Christmas.
   d. Yom Kippur.

___ 3. Biological tendencies to react in certain specific ways are termed:
   a. mores.
   b. cultural lag.
   c. folkways.
   d. instincts.

___ 4. Culture is transmitted among humans by:
   a. traditional values.
   b. cultural pluralism.
   c. language.
   d. biological heredity.

___ 5. A characteristic that could be classified as opposite to familism is:
   a. cultural pluralism.
   b. "having it all."
   c. traditional values.
   d. individualism.

___ 6. "Groups," as defined sociologically, differ in all of the following ways *except* in:
   a. norms and values.
   b. size.
   c. permanence.
   d. purpose.

___ 7. Cooley and Mead were two sociologists who contributed significantly to the understanding of:
   a. cultural diffusion.
   b. familism.
   c. socialization.
   d. midlife crisis.

__ 8. Sociologists believe that identification and internalization in childhood are most reliant on the quality or type of:
   a. educational facilities.
   b. caregiving.
   c. outlets for physical activities.
   d. arts and crafts play.

__ 9. What Cooley termed "like-minded people" are now known as:
   a. looking-glass selves.
   b. bureaucracies.
   c. artifacts.
   d. reference groups.

__ 10. A kidnap victim who is brainwashed into rejecting his or her group's values and norms in favor of the kidnappers' ways of thinking and behaving could be said to be:
   a. resocialized.
   b. countercultured.
   c. bureaucracized.
   d. culturally pluralized.

Matching Test

Match each concept with its definition, illustration, or explication below.

1.
__ (1) Meritocracy
__ (2) Bureaucracy
__ (3) Preindustrial
__ (4) Postindustrial
__ (5) Total institution

a. Place of confinement
b. Organized on basis of ability/drive
c. Complex administrative institution
d. Service-based
e. Agricultural

2.
__ (1) Émile Durkheim
__ (2) Charles Horton Cooley
__ (3) Max Weber
__ (4) George Herbert Mead
__ (5) William Graham Sumner

a. Self-image
b. Social facts
c. Folkways
d. Stages in development of the self
e. Analyzed bureaucracies

3.
__ (1) Laws
__ (2) Folkways
__ (3) Incest
__ (4) Culture
__ (5) Mores

a. Universal taboo
b. Traditional customs and manners
c. Intensely protected norms
d. Social heredity
e. Written norms

4.
__ (1) Reference groups
__ (2) Relative deprivation
__ (3) Identification
__ (4) Self-fulfilling prophecy
__ (5) Internalization

a. Depends on reference group
b. One may or may not belong
c. Psychology's pygmalion effect
d. Adopting others' attitudes, values, norms
e. Cooley's sympathy

5.
__ (1) Voluntary participation
__ (2) Disappointed expectations
__ (3) Blurring of life-cycle stages
__ (4) More flexibility
__ (5) An ideal bureaucracy

a. Midlife crisis
b. Age norms
c. Meritocracy
d. Postindustrial society
e. Successful resocialization

REVIEW QUESTIONS

1. What are the three distinguishing characteristics of societies? How do preindustrial societies differ from industrial societies?
2. What are the four important things to remember about culture? Give examples of material and nonmaterial culture.
3. How does culture promote social stability? Give examples.
4. What are the basic distinctions among culture, subculture, and counterculture? Give examples.
5. How and why do sociologists classify types of norms in human societies? Give examples of the various types of norms.
6. What are some important traditional values? Why do they change in industrial societies?
7. What are basic values in the five major institutional areas (family, economics, politics, religion, and education) in the United States today?
8. How does the concept of role link the culture with the individual?
9. What are the basic ideas of Cooley and Mead? How do their ideas relate to the concepts of reference group and relative deprivation?
10. What are the preconditions of successful resocialization?
11. How and why does the life course change in postindustrial societies?

APPLYING SOCIOLOGY

1. Describe some subcultural norms that you abide by—of social class, age, ethnic origin, or region—that differ in some way from those of the wider society. The easiest to identify are dress, language, food, drink, and recreational tastes.
2. Have you ever experienced culture shock? If so, describe the experience.

3. What are your major values in order of importance? Some major values are love, power, fame, material success, hard work, having fun, physical fitness, and popularity.

4. Answer the question "Who am I?" in terms of the various statuses that you occupy. To do this, locate yourself in groups in major institutional areas such as family, school, religion, economy, and government, and in friendship and recreational groups.

5. Describe an experience of socialization that you went through during a major change in status, such as a move to a new neighborhood, your first job, the shift from high school to college, the shift from single to married status, or to parenthood.

6. Have you ever gone through a resocialization experience? If so, describe this experience using sociological concepts such as reference group, sanctions, new norms, relative deprivation, and others, if applicable.

7. What are your reference groups? How and why have they changed during your lifetime?

4

The Language of Sociology:
Social Change

We will be spending less time on concepts of social change than we spent on concepts of social stability. This is because the fact that societies exist and continue to exist is far more mysterious than the fact that societies change, decline, develop, or disappear. We have fewer concepts to explain social change, but these concepts are no less important for understanding human societies than concepts of social stability. In modern times, in fact, they are even more important.

Social change refers to large-scale changes in culture and in the social location of human beings in a society. One person moving up from the middle class to the upper class is not social change. Also, little if anything changes if one ruling military group replaces another ruling military group of the same social class, as in a coup d'état. Social change does occur, however, if large numbers of middle- or working-class people become the new rulers, as in a successful **revolution**.

This applies also to changes in attitudes and behavior. One person experiencing a reduction in prejudice and behaving more kindly toward members of a particular out-group is personal or individual change. But large numbers of people becoming less ethnocentric and more tolerant is social change.

We have already defined conflict at the macrolevel, among groups and societies, and have begun to discuss role conflict of individuals in groups. In this chapter, we will explore in greater depth the ways in which each promotes social change, and we will introduce several new concepts of social change.

HUMAN RELATIONSHIPS AND CONFLICT

Human relationships are usually oriented toward obtaining rewards and resources—at some level, to some degree, and at some time—if this is at all possible. When individuals, groups, and societies relate to each other, they can **exchange** or trade resources and rewards—for example, economic support for sexual gratification and children, as in the traditional husband-wife relationship in preindustrial societies. Both parties get something from the exchange; they trade on the basis of different needs. At the societal level, industrialized nations trade medicine and economic aid for military bases, democracy, or human rights.

When resources are scarce, **cooperation** is a possibility. People work together in a common effort to obtain and share resources and rewards. Everyone gets something, and conflict is reduced. At the international level, cooperation is most evident in nonmilitary scientific research, such as the development of new drugs, for example.

At the group level, the cooperation of blacks and whites in integrated housing projects to form safety patrols and ground maintenance crews or to organize rent strikes reduces conflict and prejudice. The shared benefits of cooperation promote mutual tolerance and the breakdown of irrational barriers and hostility. Something similar occurs when people of very different social backgrounds cooperate to cope with a sudden crisis or disaster.

During the Mississippi River floods of 1993, farmers in one local community in Illinois were helped by convicted black and Latino drug dealers from Chicago, released from a nearby "boot camp" prison (Rimer, 1993). Each group expected the worst, but friendship, generosity, and good will prevailed. Despite all efforts, the levee broke and the town was flooded. The farmers had a meeting following the flood. "We had a choice between having college students or the boot campers come back and help us clean up. . . . Everyone wanted the boot campers" (Rimer, 1993, p. D23). The short-lived awareness of a common threat and the ultimate vulnerability of all mortals brings everyone together, at least for a while.

When rewards and resources are scarce or unequally distributed, individuals, groups, and societies can also engage in **competition**. Here, some win and some lose, but efforts are bound by explicit norms and rules. Rewards are not shared; losers get less or nothing, as in a zero sum game. Conflict and hostilities are aroused, but they are usually under control. Good losers follow rules; they shake hands, smile, and congratulate their opponents. They decide that everything happens for the best, that they didn't want what they lost, or that they will win next time.

People can also react in the battle for resources and rewards by engaging in open **social conflict**, ignoring rules and hurting or weakening their opponents in some way. The breaking of rules that occurs when groups and societies engage in open conflict most obviously promotes social change. The winners redefine old rules or make new ones. They redistribute resources and rewards. The losers accommodate or withdraw, and groups and societies change.

Around the world we are seeing conflict between rich and poor societies, racial/ethnic minorities and dominant groups, the classes, the religions, and the sexes. Such conflict is today a major source of social change.

Macrolevel Conflicts

Conflicts at the macrolevel—between groups and between societies—are as old as conflicts within groups (Ross, 1993). Conflict increases in destructiveness, proportionately, as sociocultural evolution provides more material resources (such as oil, gas, and food) and nonmaterial resources (such as power, prestige, and influence) to fight over and more effective means (better weapons) to fight with. Sociocultural evolution also increases the scale of conflict in and between societies. With technological advances in transportation and communication, conflicts become increasingly global. The cold war era of conflict between East and West seems benign compared to the current explosion of nationalistic ethnic hatreds, as well as the spread of nuclear capabilities in more developed industrializing societies such as Pakistan, Brazil, and North Korea.

The violent fringe of Islamic fundamentalism is strongest in currently industrializing societies with the severest economic problems. Economic conditions also underlie the surging nationalism and the scapegoating of weaker minorities in Eastern European and Asian societies, as these societies shift from planned socialist to competitive market economies. The wave of violence against Turkish immigrant "guest workers" in Germany, Pakistanis in Britain, and Algerians in France exemplifies rising nationalism in European industrial societies, which experienced their worst recession in decades in the early 1990s (Darnton, 1993).

Technological advances in communication bring dissidents from all over the world into contact with each other through moving pictures, sounds, and symbols. Identical electronic messages bombard households practically everywhere, in villages and metropolises, daily and relentlessly, recruiting new members for groups that want to speed up or prevent social change. Global telecommunication networks depict shots heard around the world almost at the moment they are fired. The student movement of the 1960s began with demonstrations at various college campuses in the United States. Within a few days after these events appeared on television, students all over the world were out demonstrating.

The rate of social change in societies also increases as strikes, wars, riots, revolts, revolutions, and counterrevolutions increase, particularly in societies that have very unequally distributed economic resources. More educated, better informed, and less isolated populations become more aware of their economic and political interests. Their reference groups expand, and they feel more deprived and frustrated, regardless of their objective economic circumstances.

On the other hand, as reference groups expand, the feelings of shared hardship can lead to an additional identity that overrides national borders. Currently, in a time of severe economic recession throughout Europe, well-educated Europeans in their twenties are more likely than previous generations to identify themselves as European, in addition to being French, German, English, and so on. "I probably feel more Spanish, but I like feeling European. . . . Europe means unity and strength." "We've been through so much together, that it's very unifying. I am British first, but I am also proud to be European" (Riding, 1993, p. A1).

According to the polls, three out of four Europeans between 15 and 24 support the idea of a European Economic Community with free trade and a single European currency (Riding, 1993). Their parents are less likely to feel this way. Unlike their parents, most of the younger generation have visited other European countries as exchange students or tourists. Many speak at least one language (usually English) other than their own. Their reference groups and identifications go beyond national borders.

Microlevel Conflicts

Microlevel conflicts within groups—between husband and wife, parent and child, employer and employee, teacher and student, priest and parishioner—also increase as sociocultural evolution provides more information, alternatives, and choices. Changes in the wider society are mirrored in the increased conflicts experienced by all individuals at the face-to-face, person-to-person level (Yorburg, 1993). This is the cauldron in which new values and norms are brewed, because old values and norms are inadequate to meet the demands of new political and economic conditions. Faced with this inadequacy, people become more willing to change their ways, which also serves as an important source of social change (Stacey, 1990).

Sociologists have studied exchange, cooperation, competition, and conflict as ways in which people fulfill needs and obtain resources and rewards, especially at the macrolevel. At the microlevel, we also study conflict as a subjective, internal feeling that is only indirectly related to economic or other resources, however. This type of conflict may be destructive, but it is destructive mainly to the self. Resources such as income and wealth or psychological strength help reduce this type of conflict, but the conflict does not arise from competition between groups, social classes, or societies over power and economic resources and rewards.

Role conflict is the internal feeling of stress that comes from being pressured, frustrated, or torn in opposite directions in attempting to fulfill role obligations (Yorburg, 1993). The term "role strain" is sometimes used to describe one or two particular kinds of role conflict: conflict that arises from contradictory demands within a role, such as the need for a parent to love but also to punish children, and conflict between the incompatible demands of two different roles (work/family conflicts). The concept actually includes other sources of conflict, however. Most sources of role conflict increase in industrialized societies. This is a major reason why we cannot claim that sociocultural evolution results in greater happiness, satisfaction, or more widespread feelings of psychological well-being for most people in industrial or postindustrial societies.

We all experience **intrapsychic conflict** or contradictory psychological impulses, feelings, or needs (anger or love, independence or dependence, dominance or submission). These are personality characteristics that affect the way we play out our culturally defined roles. These conflicts are important because they affect the way we relate to others. We may want closeness, but need privacy. We may want to be needed, but also need freedom. We may value equality, but need to be in control.

In **relationship conflict** stress arises mainly because partners (couples, parents and children, friends, teachers and students, employers and employees) do not agree about mutual rights and obligations. In **situational conflict** feelings of frustration and stress have to do more with external circumstances (loss of a job, divorce, death of a family member, poverty) than with personality differences or differences in expectations in a relationship (Yorburg, 1993).

Sources of Role Conflict

Role conflict is an important concept for understanding social change because conflict often results in nonconformity to cultural norms. If enough people stop conforming to traditional role expectations, societies, cultures, roles, and personalities change. There are five major sources of role conflict. All become more widespread in postindustrial societies (Yorburg, 1993):

Demands of Competing Roles   Most studies of role conflict focus on situations in which an individual is torn between two roles that are contradictory in the demands they make. The employed mother experiences this kind of conflict (Spitze, 1988; Hochschild, 1989; Goldsmith, 1989). People have just so much time and energy, and they cannot be in two places at the same time. If her child is ill, a working mother may not be able to go to work. If she is at work, she cannot be active in her child's school activities. She will feel torn, guilty, and stressed as she inevitably disappoints children, teachers, and employers, one or all, at one time or another.

Career-oriented upper-income men and two-job (or three-job), moonlighting, lower-income fathers in the United States experience a similar conflict in juggling obligations between work and family (Kimmel and Messner, 1992). In one study of approximately 500 two-career couples in the Detroit metropolitan area, men listed "time for each other" as the major activity lacking in their married lives; women listed "doing household tasks" as their major stressor (Vannoy-Hiller and Philliber, 1989, p. 149).

Contradictions in the Role   Another source of role conflict is the contradictory demands built into the same role. The most frequent example of this type of role conflict is the discrepancy between exercising power and feeling affection or love in a relationship. Teachers and parents must discipline children, but they are also expected to have warm and affectionate relationships with these children. Disciplinary measures often arouse anger on the part of children and students, particularly when they are required to do what they do not want to do. Parents and teachers, on the other hand, can become enormously angry at a child's stubbornness, destructiveness, or irrationality. Power and love are incompatible needs, and love and anger are opposite and inconsistent feelings.

Teachers, particularly at the elementary school level, have an additional contradiction built into their role: they must relate to each child as a unique person, but at the same time they must evaluate the child's work and award grades according to impersonal academic standards. The fact that some students become "teacher's pets" points to the difficulty in reconciling these inconsistent demands. The classmates of teacher's pets usually question the teacher's ability to evaluate these students objectively.

Lack of Mutual Expectations   Conflict stemming from a lack of mutual expectations in relationships becomes widespread as roles change. Husbands and wives and unmarried partners in families frequently have this conflict (Lye and Biblarz, 1993). The employed wife may feel that the husband should share household and childrearing obligations more. Or the husband may disagree with the wife's desire to go out and earn independent income, although this source of conflict is fast disappearing in the United States today (Whyte, 1990). It is long gone in societies such as the former Soviet Union, Eastern European countries, and Scandinavia, where about 90 percent of women with dependent children are employed, compared to about 68 percent in the United States (Cherlin and Furstenberg, 1988; Statistical Abstract of the United States, 1992, Table 620).

This source of role conflict was rare in preindustrial societies. Economic and political conditions did not provide many alternatives to the traditional roles of men and women in these societies, and traditional norms were reinforced by the family, church, and local community. These were powerful controlling forces in agricultural societies.

Inadequate Resources   Another source of role conflict stems from a lack of adequate economic, intellectual, physical, or psychological resources to perform a role. Inadequate economic resources (food) was the major source of role conflict in preindustrial societies. In industrial societies, the unemployed father who cannot support his family has this type of conflict. The passive, unathletic, or highly emotional male in a society that defines masculinity in terms of aggressiveness, physical strength, and emotional unavailability and restraint will also feel this type of conflict (Pleck, 1992).

In postindustrial societies, the persistence of the traditional personality traits of men and women becomes a source of widespread role conflict. It is another example of cultural lag. An emphasis on male dominance, physical strength, and emotional reserve becomes a problem in societies where women earn independent income, are strong enough to operate machines and fight mechanized wars, and want companionship, friendship, warmth, and emotional support from their partners.

The traditional emphasis on male independence is another source of conflict, especially for middle-class young men. Many are at least partially economically dependent on their parents for increasing numbers of years, because the time required to finish their education and training takes longer. And those who take longest (Ph.D.'s in engineering, the natural sciences, mathematics, and computer sciences, for example) experienced a two-thirds increase in their unemployment rate from 1989 to 1992, according to the Bureau of Labor Statistics (Kilborn, 1993). Private companies have cut back on research, and Washington's determination to reduce the deficit has resulted in large-scale cuts in government spending on space and nonmilitary laboratory research.

Women who have been traditionally socialized to be passive, submissive, and dependent are poorly equipped to succeed in the competitive world of market economics. In postindustrial societies, almost all women are employed or self-employed during more years of their lives than ever before. And, increasingly, they are competing for higher-paying, more prestigious jobs. Traditional feminine socialization experiences are poor preparation for these new roles.

Traditional conceptions of female sexuality based on sexual repression, maintaining virginity, and the double standard—which allows sexual freedom for men but not for women—are also a source of conflict for many women, especially for those who are not religious. The traditional norms are inconsistent with current permissive attitudes toward sexual activity. Pressures from peers and the media reinforce the new sexual norms. Women still experience stronger disapproval than men for promiscuity and infidelity, however, and they are less likely to engage in this kind of behavior (Greeley, 1991a). They are also more likely than men to feel guilty about casual sex that is engaged in for pleasure only, without long-term regard for the sexual partner (Reiss and Lee, 1988).

Ambiguous or Absent Role Definitions   Another source of role conflict that becomes much more frequent in postindustrial societies is a result of very rapid social change and the absence or ambiguity of norms, anomie, in new or very different situations. The roles of unmarried middle-class couples who are living together and the roles of partners in gay or lesbian marriages are examples. Here, the statuses are new or are becoming more common, but they are not sufficiently recognized by the wider society so that expectations about behavior are generally agreed on.

In cohabitation relationships, the role of the female is less traditional than in a conventional marriage. Cohabiting partners report greater equality in their relationships and more sharing of housework. But the evidence indicates that people who enter these statuses bring previous norms with them. Research studies show that men in these relationships do no more housework than husbands in more traditional households (Buunk and van Driel, 1989). There is a contradiction between what they say and what they do, which points to some degree of conflict about expectations or wishes in these relationships.

Women in lesbian relationships often experience conflict in relating to other members of the community (Caldwell and Peplau, 1990; Peplau, 1991). This holds especially for lesbian partners raising children (usually from heterosexual previous relationships). At parent/teacher conferences that both partners attend, how is the partner introduced to those who do not know of the relationship?

Expectations between lesbian partners, however, are not usually a source of conflict. Conflicts over power are rare, since women are less likely than men to seek power in their relationships (Hegtvedt, Thompson, and Cook, 1993). Butch and femme roles are also rare. Roles are worked out and negotiated, since they depend on talent, taste, and interests rather than gender.

The feeling of frustration or conflict in these kinds of situations arises from having few or no cultural guidelines to define even the broad limits of rights and obligations in relationships. What are the obligations of grown children to a widowed parent living 1,500 miles away? Of friends to a divorced husband and his former wife? Of stepmothers and stepfathers to their new partner's children, when the other biological parent is still alive? This was a very unusual situation in agricultural societies, where divorce was rare and people who remarried were usually widows or widowers.

Some roles were defined very explicitly in agricultural societies, but are now ambiguous. Others have to be worked out on an individual trial-and-error basis, because they were rare or did not exist at all in agricultural societies. All promote frustration, conflict, and change.

Reducing Role Conflict

Since role conflict is experienced at the level of the individual, solutions to role conflict are also attempted at this level. But as pointed out earlier, if large numbers of people are experiencing role conflict and are engaging in similar kinds of behavior to reduce this conflict, cultural and subcultural role definitions ultimately change. This is seen most clearly in the new definitions of masculinity and femininity in the roles of men and women that are becoming more prevalent in industrialized societies, especially in the United States and Sweden (Popenoe, 1988).

More men are taking on roles that require nurturing qualities and emotional support. They are working in occupations such as nurse, social worker, and elementary schoolteacher that were previously sex typed as female. They are increasingly suing for and winning custody of their children. This is happening even in situations in which the children are very young and the wife has not been guilty of neglect, abuse, or abandonment.

More women, on the other hand, are entering top-level administrative positions in government and industry that require toughness and assertiveness. Furthermore, some women, mainly in the upper-middle class, are leaving marriages without their children so that they can be free to pursue a career.

Establishing a Hierarchy of Obligations   One way to try to reduce role conflict is to set up a hierarchy of obligations. We decide what is most important, somewhat important, and unimportant. And we do this on the basis of values. If an employed mother feels that her children come first, she will abide by this value in fulfilling obligations to her children rather than to her job when the two conflict. The agony of choice is reduced if she can follow this pattern consistently. Priorities are clearer and guilt and anxiety are somewhat diminished.

Compartmentalizing Role Obligations   Another technique is to set up a time schedule for fulfilling competing obligations—to compartmentalize them—so that they do not conflict as much. College professors usually have to fulfill two major obligations in their role. They must teach and they must publish, both of which can be very demanding. The strain of trying to do both can be eased if professors set up and follow a schedule: writing on weekends, during intersessions, and during summer vacations; or teaching mornings, writing afternoons, reading evenings (and struggling to keep awake).

One other relatively common and not earthshaking way to ease the strain of conflicting role obligations is to delegate some of the obligations of the role to others—to baby-sitters, housekeepers, administrative assistants, deputy chairpersons, or vice presidents, for example. However, this usually requires not only finding a dependable person who will assume some of the obligations of the role, but paying for the substitute as well. The poor delegate responsibilities to family members when they can; if they can't, the obligations do not get fulfilled.

None of the techniques just mentioned affects the wider society directly; but if large numbers of children are neglected because their employed mothers can't afford to pay for substitutes to take care of them, this can have serious consequences for the wider society. For the most part, however, these techniques for reducing role conflict simply ease the personal strain and frustration that people feel because of too many pressures.

Escaping the Field   Other techniques for reducing role conflict do have more obvious consequences for the wider society. If role conflict becomes very severe, the ultimate solution is to escape the field or vacate the status by quitting, deserting, running away, dropping out, abdicating, or getting a divorce. Most positions can be relinquished in this way in modern societies, because more alternatives are available than there were in agricultural societies. The statuses of parent and other ascribed positions—male, female, young, old, black, white—however, are difficult or impossible to leave. If enough people engage in escaping the field as a response to role conflict, wars are lost, governments are overturned, schools and churches are reformed, and family laws—those concerning divorce and child custody, for example—are changed.

Redefining the Role   Even more effective in promoting widespread and permanent social change in societies is another technique for coping with role conflict, redefining the role. The employed mother asks the father to share homemaking and child care obligations more, and the father complies. Fathers, however, get mixed messages because the role is in flux (Gibbs, 1993a). When fathers attend teacher/parent conferences or come with mothers to the pediatrician's office, they tend to be treated as "nonpersons." Managers still take male workers aside and warn them not to take paternity leave if they want to get ahead. "Househusbands," who stay home and take care of house and children while their wives go out to work, have difficulty

TABLE 4.1

Role Conflict

Definition: Role conflict is an internal feeling of stress (pressure, tension, anxiety, frustration, guilt) that results from contradictory requirements in the performance of roles.

Sources of Role Conflict	**Techniques for Reducing Role Conflict**
• Demands of competing roles (limited time and energy) • Contradictory demands built into the role (love and power) • Lack of mutual expectations about rights and obligations • Inadequate or inappropriate resources to perform the role • Ambiguous, changing, or absent role prescriptions	• Establishing a hierarchy of obligations (from most to least important, on the basis of values) • Compartmentalizing role activities (separating in time) • Delegating obligations (getting help from others) • Escaping the field (quitting the job, dropping out, divorce) • Redefining the role (communication, negotiation, compromise)

getting accepted and respected in the outside world. Fathers are not treated as equal partners in parenting in most places, even if they want to be.

Racial/ethnic minority populations are also trying to redefine their social status and roles. They are demanding more rights—more respect, power, and equality of opportunity—and government and industry are replying with affirmative action programs. But these changes take place very slowly, if at all, and not continuously. Depressions and recessions tend to reinforce or reinstate traditional role definitions. There are counterrevolutions in human relationships as well as in politics.

In redefining a role, members of a society who experience role conflict may choose new and nonconforming means for fulfilling their role obligations (Hage and Powers, 1992). Sometimes, these means are defined by the wider society as criminal, revolutionary, insane, peculiar, or simply unconventional or nontraditional. But they usually reflect widespread changing needs in the society, and if they work, they tend to become accepted in time (see Table 4.1).

URBAN VALUES AND MOBILITY

Values, as pointed out in the last chapter, can either hasten or delay social change. Certain values such as familism, ethnocentrism, religion, fatalism, and authoritarianism are strong in agricultural societies. These values slow down social change. They lock people into the past and into the security of traditional ways of doing things.

As societies shift from agriculture to manufacturing as the major means of producing resources, urban centers become more widespread and urban values become more prevalent. These values—individualism, rationalism, achievement, and egalitarianism—promote social change. They promote social change because they encourage people to discover, create, invent, take risks, and borrow ways of thinking, feeling, and doing from other societies. Why does this change in values occur? The next chapter contains a more detailed discussion of why and how values change in major types of societies. For now, we can simply note, once again, that economic resources and economic and educational opportunities increase in industrialized societies. They also become somewhat more equally distributed. In addition, mobility of all kinds increases. And as these things happen, the masses of people become more convinced of the possibility of controlling their destinies, at least to some extent. Education is the most important factor affecting the shift to urban values (Inkeles, 1983).

Types of Mobility

Three kinds of mobility increase as societies industrialize: geographic, social, and psychological. More people move geographically, from country to city, region to region, society to society. Technological advances in transportation accelerate the movement of populations in the search for economic opportunity or escape from political persecution or family conflicts.

Social mobility, the movement up or down from one social status to another in the social class system, also increases as societies become more complex. More and different types of jobs become available, and skills and educational requirements also become more specialized as societies industrialize. In postindustrial societies, the urban middle class becomes the predominant class.

As people move into a new social class, they tend to adopt different attitudes, values, and norms. In addition, as the masses of people become more literate and less isolated, **psychological mobility**, identification with models outside of the family or the local community and comparisons with reference groups to which we do not belong, also increases. At the level of family relationships, psychological mobility involves a moving away from emotional dependence on the family of origin, which is now known as separation or "breaking away" (see Figure 4.1).

Any kind of movement away from family and community diminishes their influence on behavior. For example, Los Angeles has the highest rate of black-white intermarriage in the United States. Two sociologists, trying to explain this fact, found that the high rates of intermarriage applied mainly to people who had migrated to Los Angeles as adults from racially tolerant communities in the United States or from a foreign country (Tucker and Mitchell-Kernan, 1990).

FIGURE 4.1

Three Types of Mobility

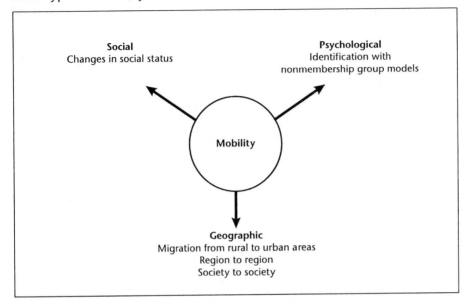

Industrialized societies are characterized not only by increased geographic mobility, but by heightened social and psychological mobility as well.

The movement away from the area in which they had grown up seemed to be a significant factor affecting couples' tendency to intermarry, since this diminished the control of their families and their community over their choice of a marital partner. Those who had grown up in Los Angeles, on the other hand, were not more likely to intermarry than residents of other locales.

Subcultural norms and social controls are also an important factor influencing black-white intermarriage rates, however. California has a larger number of migrants than other states. The subculture is more tolerant of intermarriage and other forms of nonconforming behavior. The South has also experienced high rates of in-migration in recent years, but its black-white intermarriage rates have not increased significantly.

Deviance

Deviant behavior is behavior that is strongly disapproved of by large numbers of people in a society. The label is usually applied to behavior that is defined as criminal. Invention and creativity can also be defined as deviant, however, since discovery and innovation require a rejection of conventional wisdom and norms. They require the desire and ability to transform existing knowledge and techniques into new forms and ideas. This, too, is nonconformity to norms, and this, too, is deviance, if the new forms and ideas are widely disapproved.

Some years ago, sociologist Robert K. Merton (1968) constructed a typology of the various ways in which individuals may be oriented toward culturally defined goals and culturally acceptable means for achieving these goals (see Table 4.2). Most people, however, adapt by conformity. They strive for material success, spiritual salvation, respect, power, wisdom, or whatever else their culture or subculture defines as the ultimate goal in life. And they use the means that are considered appropriate to achieving this goal: hard work, education, self-denial, prayer, exercise, or learning, for example.

Anomie

Sociocultural evolution and social change weaken cultural and subcultural norms, a social condition referred to earlier as *anomie*. The norms become weaker because they are inadequate, inappropriate, or contradictory. And since agreed-on norms are essential to social life, individuals and groups invent new norms to fit their new circumstances. Anomie is both a social condition and a personal experience. Individuals who experience anomie are less bound by social control. They are more susceptible to new and different behavior, attitudes, values, and norms. They are more likely to engage in *collective behavior*, which is defined in the next section, and in *deviance*, which is discussed in chapter 7. Anomie is a result of social change, but it is also a source of social change when large numbers of individuals make up new rules to live by.

In anomic situations, individuals are not bound by the norms that define either conventional goals or means. Often, this occurs when there is a discrepancy between culturally defined goals and the availability of means for achieving these goals.

If a society places a high value on material success, but does not provide opportunities for people to achieve this goal, deviant behavior is a possible consequence. Merton (1968) called this situation "structural strain" and outlined various deviant ways that people may adapt under these circumstances:

Innovation   Individuals may accept the goals, but engage in "innovation" at the means level, stealing, robbing, swindling, or bribing to achieve material success.

Ritualism   They may give up the goal that is difficult or unattainable and overdo the means—the straw-boss phenomenon in which the bureaucrat or

TABLE 4.2

Individual Ways of Adapting

	Culturally Approved Goals	*Culturally Approved Means*
Conformity	Accepts	Accepts
Innovation	Accepts	Rejects
Ritualism	Rejects	Accepts
Retreatism	Rejects	Rejects
Rebellion	Rejects/substitutes new goals	Rejects/substitutes new means

Source: Adapted with permission from Robert K. Merton, 1968, *Social Theory and Social Structure,* New York: Free Press, p. 194.

the inmate insists on slavish obedience to rules and regulations to the detriment of his or her clients or fellow inmates.

Retreatism When neither the goals nor the means are attainable or acceptable, people may withdraw completely: collectively into communes or convents, or individually into the isolated retreat of alcoholism, drug addiction, or mental illness.

Rebellion Finally, Merton identified "rebellion" as a deviant response in which both culturally approved goals and means are rejected and new goals and means are substituted. Radicals do this, but they are not retreatists. They may go underground, or they may eventually conform. Even if they must go into hiding, however, they do not usually give up their goals (McAdam, 1989).

Merton pointed out that criminal behavior is socially located, occurring most often among the poor, who cannot obtain the means to achieve material success because of discrimination or lack of economic and educational opportunities. In fact, all types of deviant behavior tend to be socially located. The frequency of specific kinds of criminal, bureaucratic, and retreatist behavior, as well as radicalism, varies according to class, age, ethnic origin, and urban or rural residence. Relatively few young people, for example, are bureaucratic; relatively few older people are radicals. Rural residents are more likely than city dwellers to conform to traditional norms.

Underlying anomic situations and many forms of deviant behavior is role conflict. Most often this conflict stems from inadequate or inappropriate economic, intellectual, emotional, or physical resources for performing culturally prescribed roles. Deviant behavior represents a redefinition of these roles by males and females, rich and poor, young and old, minorities and nonminorities. Means and ends become increasingly flexible in modern societies, deviant behavior becomes more frequent, and social change in the cultural sphere accelerates. Deviance is discussed further in chapter 7.

COLLECTIVE BEHAVIOR

What do fads, fashions, hijacking, graffiti writing, lynch mobs, rumors, riots, and revolutions have in common? They are all forms of what sociologists call collective behavior. **Collective behavior** is new and different behavior that spontaneously arises and quickly spreads among a large number of people in a society.

They are responding to new, different, and, often, temporary norms. The behavior spreads through direct contact, or indirectly through the media. Actor Clark Gable appears in a movie without an undershirt. A new fashion is born, and the men's underwear industry goes into a recession. A television program details the manufacture of a Molotov cocktail bomb, and a new home industry is created. Participants in new social movements are interviewed in newspapers, magazines, and television, and people around the world find new alternatives, solutions, goals, and means for carrying out these goals.

Collective behavior is most likely to occur when large numbers of people are experiencing a sense of fear, deprivation, insecurity, or boredom. In modern times it occurs most often under conditions of anomie in which traditional norms and social controls are weak or not applicable. It occurs most frequently among people who are least locked into the societies in which they live. In industrialized societies, adolescents, the urban poor, the unemployed, members of minority groups, and disaffected intellectuals are most likely to engage in collective behavior. For different reasons, these various categories of people tend to be outsiders, marginal to the centers of power, prestige, and wealth in a society.

Unforeseen disasters—fires, floods, earthquakes, blackouts, military invasions, tidal waves—also precipitate collective behavior. The ordinary norms of everyday life no longer work. People may panic. Cooperation, give-and-take, order, and predictability may disappear. Stability returns if leaders emerge quickly enough to take charge and establish new norms to cope with the situation. But, at least temporarily, it is a different kind of stability.

This type of collective behavior occurs in all societies. Most forms of collective behavior in technologically developed societies, however, do not occur in response to specific, temporary disasters. Changing public opinion, fads, fashions, and social movements are more general reactions involving greater numbers of people and a greater possibility of social change in the society in which they occur. The effects of fads and fashions may be superficial. But the effects of changes in public opinion and social movements can be extensive, at least in the long run.

There are always enabling circumstances that promote collective behavior. Social problems such as poverty and discrimination are examples. People may live with these conditions for centuries. But in technologically developing or developed societies, the traditional beliefs and values defining these conditions as inevitable or justifiable become weaker. People have more economic resources and opportunities. They are more educated and mobile geographically. They are more mobile psychologically. Reference groups expand, and expectations rise. The traditional social controls become less effective.

Large numbers of people may decide to revolt against authority. **Riots**, for example, are temporary revolts against authority. Or people may decide to join social movements to effect more permanent change in the society. Frequently, these actions are precipitated by a specific and traceable event or incident—a police killing in a ghetto, an arrest in a gay community, a book on the roles of women or men that becomes a national best-seller.

Riots and social movements are responses to perceived deprivation or a desire to see certain cherished beliefs, values, and norms preserved or enacted. Rumors, panics, mass hysteria, fads, and fashions are more often responses to fear, uncertainty, insecurity, or boredom. **Rumors** are information that may be true, false, or a combination of both. Usually of unknown origin, they spread spontaneously by word of mouth among large numbers of people. They arise in situations in which people feel fearful and believe that information from official sources—employers, government, or the mass media—is inadequate or false. Rumors are an element in many forms of collective behavior. **Panics** are disorganized, destructive actions that occur in situations of intense fear, such as the sudden outbreak of fire.

Mass hysteria is a more widespread and diffused type of free-floating fear or anxiety reaction in which behavior is based on a **delusion**, a false belief. Historically, the fear of poisons and epidemics triggered reactions of mass hysteria. In situations of mass hysteria, destructive behavior may be directed toward weaker minorities or outsiders not actually responsible for the problems of the society (witches, communists, or Jews, for example). The targets of mass hysteria are "scapegoats." Sometimes these less powerful out-groups are deliberately used by governments to divert attention from the real economic and political sources of the society's problems. The Nazis made Jews the scapegoats for the severe economic depression Germany experienced in the early 1930s, though Germany's depression was primarily a product of the worldwide depression that began in 1929. The witch-hunts during the McCarthy era in the United States occurred after the former Soviet Union developed the atomic bomb.

Fashions refer to current and usually temporary styles of dress, speech, belief, and behavior. Fashions do not exist in small, technologically simple societies. In these societies, individuals inherit their social status at

Focus on Social Issues

THE GOLDFISH-SWALLOWING FAD

[Fads and fashions arise frequently and tend to spread rapidly in modern societies as a result of advances in mass communication technology—especially movies, television, and personal computers. Fads and fashions are embraced very enthusiastically while they last, but do not usually become part of the culture or lead to widespread social change. The current shift in the U.S. diet to low- and nonfat foods as a means of reducing weight and improving health, however, offers an example of a fad that may become a cultural trend. Other fads, such as bra burning during the 1960s and "streaking," running nude through public places, in the 1970s, disappeared quickly. Another historical example of a fad that did not become cultural is the goldfish-swallowing craze. This fad arose on college campuses in the late 1930s, during the Depression, and spread from Massachusetts to Missouri, at a time when many parents were having trouble putting more conventional food on the table.]

A Harvard freshman was the first to swallow a live fish. . . . Three weeks later, an undergraduate at Franklin and Marshall in Lancaster, Pennsylvania, ate three goldfish. New records for goldfish consumption were then set almost daily. At the University of Pennsylvania, one intrepid soul swallowed 25; at the University of Michigan, 28; at Boston College, 29; at Northeastern University, 38; at MIT, 42; and at Clark University, 89 were devoured at one sitting. . . . But a pathologist with the U.S. Public Health Service cautioned that goldfish may contain tapeworms that could lodge in the intestines and cause anemia, and by the spring of 1939, the goldfish-gobbling craze had gone the way of the dance marathon.

—Jack Levin, *Sociological Snapshots,* 1993, Thousand Oaks, CA: Pine Forge Press

What Do You Think?

1. What are some examples of recent fads in the United States?
2. How did these fads spread?
3. Can you think of any particular fad that might become part of the culture? Why or why not?

birth. Everyone knows where everyone else is located socially. Status does not change, except on the basis of age. There is no status insecurity, since individuals do not compete for jobs or wealth. There is no need to indicate a changed social status by a change in dress, speech, or behavior. And there is no need to constantly affirm one's attractiveness, distinctiveness, or wealth by constantly changing one's outward appearance.

Fads are new forms of behavior that are temporary but very enthusiastically pursued while they last. Fads in toys (hula hoops) or sports (in-line skates) usually come and go without much comment. Fads in diet, health, and religion, however, may meet with disapproval on the grounds that they are harmful in some way to the self or to the society's beliefs or values. Fads, like other fashions, help people establish their identity when this is a problem. The young and the newly rich or near-rich are those most likely to participate in fads.

In complex, technologically developed societies, new issues are constantly arising and changes occurring. Changing attitudes or beliefs about these issues and events held by those members of a society who are concerned or affected by them is known as **public opinion.** In small, isolated, slowly changing societies, all people are usually concerned by the local, isolated events that occur. In more complex societies, interests diverge, particularly along economic, political, religious, and generational lines. Opinions about what is going on in a society also tend to diverge along these lines. It is possible to measure public opinion, to mobilize and attempt to influence public opinion by propaganda, to use public opinion to support or oppose public policy. To the extent that government leaders pay attention to public opinion, this opinion affects the direction of social change.

Many forms of collective behavior are defined as deviant (see chapter 7), at least initially. The new and different behavior may or may not take hold permanently. Whether it does depends, to some extent, on the effectiveness of attempts at social control by established authorities in the various institutional spheres—parents, presidents, priests, and provosts, for example. The socialist revolutions in China and Russia were successful, finally, when the central governments were too weakened by war with outsiders to effectively crush these internal social movements. Fascist political and social movements in Italy, Germany, and Spain were successful when the social democratic governments in these countries were weakened by the economic depression of the 1930s, but refused to counter force with force to destroy these movements.

Social movements, attempts by organized groups to hasten or resist change, are a form of collective behavior, but with certain special features. Unlike other forms of collective behavior, such as fashions or fads, social movements usually endure. And like all forms of collective behavior, they are important because if they are successful they change the culture, roles, relationships, and the distribution of power and resources in a society. Since the Industrial Revolution, social movements have been a major factor in promoting deliberate social change, particularly in the realm of politics.

Characteristics of Social Movements

Social movements differ in the amount of change they seek and the area of life in which they seek change. Their goals may be broad or narrow, seeking change in the entire society or only on one issue, such as the environment,

TABLE 4.3

Characteristics of Social Movements

• Organization—explicit statuses and roles	• Ideologies—symbols, slogans
• Communication	• Broad or narrow goals
• Values and norms	• Violent or nonviolent means

women's rights, or abortion. Movements may be revolutionary in that they seek radical or very deep and far-reaching change. Or they may seek specific and limited change in economic, political, religious, family, educational, recreational, or personal life (as Alcoholics Anonymous and other psychological self-help movements do).

Social movements are organized. In the early stages, revolutionary movements are usually (but not always) led by charismatic leaders. In time, successful social movements develop a structure (distinct parts that relate to each other in regular, recurring ways), with leaders, administrators, and followers. Role definitions and expectations evolve as the organization grows. Communication with members and potential recruits through meetings, rallies, and publications is essential to this growth. In the initial start-up stages, the availability of resources (financing, experienced organizers, communication facilities) is also essential for success (Zald and McCarthy, 1979), as is recruitment from different social classes and ethnic groups (Heckathorn, 1993). The beliefs, values, and norms of social movements are embodied in their ideologies. An **ideology** is a set of beliefs that justifies group interests and serves as a basis for organizing and acting, especially in political and economic life (Mannheim, 1936; Brinton, 1938). Ideologies are often condensed into slogans, such as "Liberty, Equality, Fraternity," "Bread, Land, and Peace," "Power to the People," "We Shall Overcome," "Protect Our Children," or "The Right to Life." Movements may also develop symbols: a burning cross, a clenched fist, a swastika, a hammer and sickle, or a sign representing peace, love, or gender. Ideologies, slogans, and symbols reinforce feelings of belonging and identity and serve as rallying points for members and new recruits (see Table 4.3).

Types of Social Movements

Except for movements that aim primarily at personal, psychological change, all social movements are ultimately political. They arise in opposition to established leaders, policies, or norms. They question the legitimacy of authority to a greater or lesser extent. They are classified as **regressive**,

conservative, **reform**, or **revolutionary** on the basis of their goals and the means they use to achieve these goals.

Regressive Movements   Some movements attempt to restore previously prevalent values, norms, or social conditions; in a sense, the object is to bring back the past (Buechler, 1990). Counterrevolutions are attempts to return to power by those who have lost power. In the United States, the John Birch Society has sought to restore political and economic conditions that existed in the past, before the crash of 1929. It has opposed the greater responsibility the federal government has taken since that time in managing the U.S. economy and redistributing income through taxation, welfare, and entitlement policies. The Ku Klux Klan has sought to turn back the clock on gains made by African Americans during the twentieth century. Regressive movements frequently use violence, secretly or openly, to achieve their goals. When these goals include restoring extreme political and economic inequality, they are usually labeled "reactionary" by opponents.

Utopian communal movements—especially those communes characterized by authoritarian social control, traditional gender roles, and rigidly binding religious or philosophical norms—are usually nonviolent and regressive in certain respects (Galanter, 1989). They may be in opposition to major societal values and norms, but they do not usually fight established authority. Instead, members withdraw, usually to rural areas, where they may attempt to re-create some aspects of life characteristic of technologically less advanced societies without interference from the wider society. Certain segments of the youth movement of the 1960s and various contemporary religious communes in the United States are examples of this type of movement.

Conservative Movements   These movements resist further change and attempt to maintain the status quo in specific areas of social life, usually by nonviolent means. In the United States today, a number of conservative movements have developed in opposition to women's rights, gay rights, and civil rights policies such as affirmative action.

Reform Movements   These movements aim at specific and limited change in existing institutions. They seek change usually through a minor redistribution of power and economic resources in the direction of greater equality or more protection for members of a society. The civil rights and women's movements are reform movements that seek greater economic and political equality for African Americans and women. The goals of the consumer movement are more limited. Consumer advocate Ralph Nader and his associates seek to curb the economic power of manufacturers and protect consumers from poor or unsafe products, false advertising, and unfair prices (see Table 4.4). The ecology and antinuclear movements seek to curb the power of government

TABLE 4.4

Organizations Founded by Ralph Nader and His Associates

Americans Concerned About Corporate Power	National Coalition for Nursing Home Reform
Aviation Consumer Action Project	National Coalition for Universities in the Public Interest
Capitol Hill News Service	National Insurance Consumer Organization
Center for Auto Safety	Ohio Public Interest Action Group
Center for Public Interest Law	Parents' Action Committee on Toys
Center for Science in the Public Interest	Pension Rights Center
Center for Study of Responsive Law	PROD
Bank Watch	Professionals for Auto Safety
Freedom of Information Clearinghouse	Public Citizen
Harvard Watch	Buyers Up
Housing Research Group	Citizen Action Group
Center for Women's Policy Studies	Congress Watch
Citizen Utility Boards	Critical Mass Energy Project
Citizens Against Rate Hikes	Health Research Group
Clean Water Action Project	Litigation Group
Clearinghouse on Professional Responsibility	Tax Reform Research Group
Congress Probe	Visitors' Center
Congress Project	Public Interest Research Group
Connecticut Citizen Earth Action Group	Retired Professionals Action Group
Corporate Accountability Research Group	Student Public Interest Research Groups Nationwide
Disability Rights Center	Telecommunications Research and Action Center
Equal Justice Foundation	Trial Lawyers for Public Justice
Essential Information	Voter Revolt
Fair Test	
FANS (Fight to Advance the Nation's Sports)	
The Military Audit Project	
Multinational Monitor	

Source: D. Bollier, *Citizen Action and Other Big Ideas: A History of Ralph Nader and the Modern Consumer Movement,* 1989, Washington, DC: Center for Responsive Law.

and industry in order to protect the public from environmental destruction and from toxic pollutants and radioactive substances.

Revolutionary Movements These movements are organized attempts to effect radical change (from the Latin "radix," meaning root) in the distribution of power and wealth in a society. A coup d'état is not a revolution, because in this type of situation there is simply an exchange of members of the same dominant class who are in official positions of power with those who are not. Wealth and power remain concentrated in the same social class and its supporters.

    Successful revolutions in agricultural and industrializing societies occur under the following conditions (Brinton, 1938; Russell, 1974; Skocpol,

1979; Goldstone, 1986; Taylor, 1988): (1) the central administrative and military forces of the government have been severely weakened by destructive wars with other countries (France in 1789, Russia in 1917, and China in 1911 and 1949, for example); (2) there is a widespread loss of belief in the legitimacy, or right to have power, of the government; (3) awareness of the unfair and unchanging concentration of wealth and power in the society is widespread, as are rising but unfulfilled expectations in a time of economic change; and (4) a segment of the population, usually the educated, urban middle class, comes forward with the skills and desire to lead a movement to redistribute power and wealth.

Even if all these conditions are present, however, a revolution may not occur or, if it does occur, it may not be successful. The shifting of the loyalty of the army to the leaders of the revolution appears to be another essential feature of successful revolutions (Russell, 1974). The tremendous superiority of the weapons and highly sophisticated surveillance equipment of modern industrial states may be a major reason for the rareness of successful revolutions in these societies.

If a revolution is successful, the new leaders must confront the problem of legitimating their power. This is a particularly serious problem for movements based on democratic values and norms, since certain apparently necessary preconditions of democracy—advanced economic development and mass literacy—have been absent in the agricultural societies in which successful revolutions have occurred. Power struggles between different factions in the leadership of successful revolutions frequently result in the murder or imprisonment of the leaders of more democratic or less forceful factions. This is the origin of the adage that revolutions devour their own children.

The new government may take on a totalitarian structure intolerant of any dissent (a political form that Russian Communist leader V. I. Lenin referred to as "democratic centralism"). Although this is theoretically a temporary exigency, necessary only until leaders need no longer question the loyalty of any segment of society, the transition to a nontotalitarian form can take a very long time, if it occurs at all. Examples are the shifting off-again, on-again policy of tolerating limited dissent in the People's Republic of China since 1949 and in the former Soviet Union for more than 70 years after the October Revolution of 1917.

In industrializing societies, the landowning class avoids revolution in a number of ways: (1) timely but limited reforms that redistribute a small amount of the society's economic resources to needier segments of the population; (2) the killing or imprisonment of potential or actual leaders of revolutionary movements; (3) **co-optation**, the bringing of potential revolutionary leaders into the political and economic fold by giving them jobs in the government; and (4) the directing of government policies, officially and unofficially, openly or behind the scenes.

Social change is speeded up greatly by the new leaders of successful revolutions who assume power. But even here there is a lag period before the new men (and sometimes women) of power can change systems of values and roles in the societies they now control. It usually takes a generation before the new values become part of the culture. Children, socialized in the schools to embrace the ideology of the successful revolution, become the mainstay of the new order.

Power and Social Change

Power, like values, can be used to promote social change as well as to prevent it. Those who have power usually also have personal and material resources to back up their ability to get what they want, especially against resistance. In the societies that are least developed technologically, personal qualities such as intelligence, resourcefulness, and physical and emotional strength and health are most important in determining power. In these societies there is little or no economic surplus. As societies begin to develop technologically, economic resources and economic inequality increase. Leaders whose power is based on the wealth their families have managed to accumulate become concerned not only with their personal safety, but also with the distribution of the economic surplus in the society and the maintenance of their privileges. Since social change involves both cultural change and a change in the social location and rewards of large numbers of people, political leaders usually resist change.

As societies industrialize, however, citizens slowly become more aware and less accepting of inequality, and social change accelerates. Social movements become global in their influence (Morris and Mueller, 1992). Instant worldwide telecommunication systems now carry the messages of scientists and movement leaders (on the environment, population growth, and famine, for example) to ever-widening global audiences.

Other factors that also promote wide-ranging social change in human societies include racial/ethnic conflicts, population growth, and changes in the physical environment. These topics are discussed in detail in later chapters.

Study Guide

REVIEW OBJECTIVES

After studying this chapter, you should be able to:

1. Define conflict and describe various ways in which conflict among groups or societies can lead to social change.
2. Describe the sources of role conflict and the major ways to reduce role conflict. Understand how role conflict at the microlevel may lead to social change at the macrolevel.
3. Discuss the reasons for the increase in anomie in industrial societies and the relationship between anomie and social change.
4. Describe three types of mobility and explain why mobility promotes nonconforming behavior, or deviance.
5. Define various kinds of collective behavior and distinguish between collective behavior that may lead to social change and collective behavior that does not.
6. Explain how power may be used to prevent or promote social change.

SUMMARY

1. Humans exchange or trade resources and rewards, cooperate and share, compete according to mutually agreed-upon rules, or engage in destructive conflict to obtain resources and rewards. Conflict between groups and societies leads to global change in modern times. Widespread role conflict is also a major source of social change, especially in postindustrial societies. Attempts to reduce role conflict by large numbers of people lead to cultural changes in values and norms and to widespread changes in roles and relationships.

2. Anomie also increases in postindustrial societies as certain norms become inadequate, inappropriate, or conflicting. In addition, new situations arise, or situations that were rare become common, and large numbers of individuals must find new rules by which to live. Geographic, social, and psychological mobility also weaken social control and promote greater nonconformity.

3. A weakening of social control promotes deviance and collective behavior. As sociocultural evolution proceeds, communication becomes instant and worldwide, drawing global recruits for collective behavior. People who are least locked into their societies—adolescents, young adults, the poor, the unemployed, minorities, and disaffected intellectuals—are most likely to engage in collective behavior.

4. The effects of fads and fashions are usually temporary and superficial. But the effects of public opinion and social movements can lead to widespread social change in values and in political and economic conditions.

5. Social movements are organized attempts to effect social change. They differ in the amount of change they seek, the areas of life in which they seek change, and the means they use to effect change.

6. Modern or urban values—individualism, rationalism, achievement, and egalitarianism—promote social change because they encourage people to take control of their lives and use the best information available to do this. Education is the most important factor affecting the shift to urban values. Urban values encourage invention, discovery, risk taking, and cultural diffusion.

7. The concepts of values and power are useful in explaining either social order or social change. Traditional values can prevent or slow the rate of social change. They usually lag behind developments in science, technology, and economics. And for this reason, they are often a major source of role conflict in rapidly changing societies. New values, on the other hand, spread throughout a society if they are more appropriate to changing economic and political conditions. And when new values spread, cultures and societies change dramatically.

8. Power can also delay or speed up social change. Political leaders whose power is based on wealth in societies in which there is an economic surplus usually try to prevent social change. They use their power to maintain their privileges and prevent redistribution of economic resources. They can maintain social stability, at least temporarily, through the use of force.

9. The power of leaders of successful social movements, particularly revolutions, can bring about widespread social change in all spheres of life. Here, too, preexisting traditional values may slow this change, however. Most revolutions are followed by counterrevolutions, eventually if not immediately.

GLOSSARY

Collective behavior: New and different behavior engaged in spontaneously by large numbers of people.

Competition: Efforts to obtain exclusive rewards or resources that are bound by explicit norms or rules.

Conservative social movements: Movements that attempt to prevent further change and maintain the status quo.

Cooperation: A common effort to obtain rewards or resources that are shared by all members of a group or a society.

Co-optation: Diffusion of potential dissent by bringing political activists into the government.

Delusion: A persistent false belief that may, in large groups, be the source of mass hysteria.

Deviant behavior: Behavior that violates important social norms and is disapproved of by a large number of people in a society.

Exchange: The trading of resources and rewards on the basis of differing needs in a relationship.

Fads: Temporary behavior that is very enthusiastically pursued by large numbers of people.

Fashions: Temporary styles of dress, speech, belief, and behavior.

Ideology: A set of beliefs that justifies group interests and serves as a basis for organizing and acting in basic areas of social life.

Intrapsychic conflict: Internal, psychological conflict that results from contradictory impulses, feelings, or needs.

Mass hysteria: A widespread anxiety reaction based on a false belief.

Panics: Disorganized destructive behavior that occurs in situations of intense fear.

Psychological mobility: Changes in values, interests, and identity that stem from identification with models outside of the family and local community.

Public opinion: The attitudes and beliefs of large numbers of people about issues and events that concern them at any particular point in time.

Reform social movements: Organized attempts to change existing political or economic circumstances in specific and limited ways, particularly through gradual redistribution of resources and opportunities in a society..

Regressive social movements: Movements that attempt to restore values, norms, or social conditions prevalent in a society in the past.

Relationship conflict: Stress that arises mainly because partners in a relationship do not agree about their rights and responsibilities.

Revolution: A sudden and basic redistribution of power, prestige, and economic resources in a society.

Revolutionary social movements: Attempts to effect radical change in the distribution of power and wealth in a society.

Riot: A temporary but violent and destructive outburst against authority by people who are in similar social locations, especially racial/ethnic and social class.

Role conflict: Feelings of stress that stem from being pressured, frustrated, or torn in opposite directions when fulfilling role obligations.

Rumors: Information, usually of unknown origin, that spreads spontaneously among people in a stressful, uncertain situation.

Situational conflict: Feelings of stress that arise from threatening or negative external circumstances, such as loss of a job or death of a family member.

Social change: Large-scale changes in culture and in the social location of individuals, groups, or societies.

Social conflict: Destructive efforts by societies, groups, and individuals to obtain exclusive material rewards (goods and services) and nonmaterial rewards (prestige and power).

Social mobility: Movement up or down from one social status to another in the social class system.

Social movements: Organized efforts to promote or resist social change.

PRACTICE TESTS

True ▪ False Test

___ 1. Cooperation among different groups in a society promotes mutual tolerance and understanding.

___ 2. The term "zero-sum game" is a concept that has to do with competition for resources.

___ 3. The "violent fringe" of Islamic fundamentalism is an example of a microlevel conflict.

___ 4. A strike held by a workers' union in a particular company can be characterized as a macrolevel conflict.

___ 5. Lack of mutual expectations is a frequent source of role conflict.

__ 6. Long-term social change renders some roles ambiguous or obsolete.

__ 7. Economic resources and opportunities are more plentiful in industrialized societies as compared to agricultural societies.

__ 8. Collective behavior tends to arise and spread slowly in a society.

__ 9. Alcoholics Anonymous is a well-known example of a social movement.

__ 10. Social and environmental conflicts and crises can promote extensive social change.

Multiple-Choice Test

__ 1. Which of the following choices could most accurately be described as a social change?
   a. charitable shipments of food, clothing, and medical supplies to people in countries in political crisis
   b. a shift in an individual's stance on abortion rights
   c. the dissolution of a long-time marriage
   d. the industrial revolution

__ 2. Conflicts between groups and between societies are known as occurring at the:
   a. distal level.
   b. reference group level.
   c. macrolevel.
   d. fundamental level.

__ 3. A businesswoman who wants to devote a lot of time to her children but is reluctant to work fewer hours at the office may be experiencing:
   a. role conflict.
   b. relationship conflict.
   c. situational conflict.
   d. intrapsychic conflict.

__ 4. The most drastic response to role conflict is to:
   a. take on more roles.
   b. somehow get out of the situation that engenders conflict.
   c. redefine the role.
   d. compartmentalize role obligations.

__ 5. Which of the following values has historically speeded up social change?
   a. familism
   b. ethnocentrism
   c. authoritarianism
   d. egalitarianism

___ 6. A change in status in the social class system is termed:
   a. social mobility.
   b. fatalism.
   c. psychological mobility.
   d. subcultural norms.

___ 7. A person who is experiencing structural strain may display any of the following adaptations *except:*
   a. ritualism.
   b. innovation.
   c. collective behavior.
   d. retreatism.

___ 8. Riots can be described as:
   a. based on rumor.
   b. temporary revolts.
   c. mass hysteria.
   d. panics.

___ 9. Which of the following phenomena is likely to be the most long-lasting in a society?
   a. social movements
   b. fads
   c. fashions
   d. public opinion

___ 10. Ross Perot's "United We Stand" political platform is an example of:
   a. a fashion.
   b. a social movement.
   c. public opinion.
   d. an ideology.

Matching Test

Match each concept with its definition, illustration, or explication below.

1.
___ (1) Social changes
___ (2) Individual changes
___ (3) Conflicts over rewards and resources
___ (4) Exchanges
___ (5) Competition

a. May cause cooperation or competition
b. Trading of resources and rewards
c. Large-scale shifts in social location
d. Efforts to obtain resources or rewards
e. Alterations in personal treatment

2.

___ (1) Internal source of stress
___ (2) Intrapersonal conflict
___ (3) External source of stress
___ (4) Stress between family members
___ (5) Contradictory demands within a
role

a. Situational conflict
b. Individual personality conflicts
c. Relationship conflict
d. Role conflict
e. Role strain

3.

___ (1) Priorities set based on values
___ (2) Time scheduled for fulfilling duties
___ (3) Increases as roles change
___ (4) Difficulty in fulfilling requirements
of multiple roles
___ (5) Often an offshoot of rapid social
change

a. Lack of mutual expectations
b. Compartmentalized role obligations
c. Ambiguous or absent role definitions
d. Hierarchy of obligations established
e. Demands of competing roles

4.

___ (1) Seek to maintain the status quo
___ (2) Spontaneous, widespread new
behavior
___ (3) Diffuse dissent
___ (4) Engage in a common effort
___ (5) Minimal and gradual redistribution

a. Conservative social movements
b. Reform
c. Collective behavior
d. Co-opt
e. Cooperate

5.

___ (1) Accepts goals, accepts means
___ (2) Rejects goals, accepts means
___ (3) Accepts goals, rejects means
___ (4) Substitutes new goals, substitutes
new means
___ (5) Rejects goals, rejects means

a. Rebellion
b. Conformity
c. Retreatism
d. Innovation
e. Ritualism

REVIEW QUESTIONS

1. Describe and give examples of four ways humans can interrelate in pursuing resources and rewards.
2. What are the major sources of role conflict? Give examples.
3. What are the major ways to reduce role conflict? Give examples.
4. Define and give examples of three types of mobility. How does mobility lead to social change?
5. Define what Merton called "structural strain," and describe how this may result in social change.

6. Which types of collective behavior become more frequent in industrial societies? Why?
7. What are the basic characteristics of social movements?
8. Distinguish among major types of social movements in terms of means and ends.
9. Under what conditions are revolutionary movements most likely to be successful?
10. How can values and power be used to promote or resist change?

APPLYING SOCIOLOGY

1. Describe an experience of role conflict you have had at home, school, work, or play. What is the source of the conflict, and how have you attempted to reduce it?
2. Have you or your family experienced geographic, social, or psychological mobility over your lifetime? How did this affect your values, interests, and behavior?
3. Describe behavior you have engaged in at one time or another that is defined by society as deviant. Can you explain this behavior from a sociological rather than a psychological point of view? (Use concepts such as anomie, reference group, group sanctions, and subcultural norms.)
4. Describe several examples of collective behavior that you have participated in recently, such as fashions, fads, rumor, or social movements.

PART II

Human Societies: Major Social Trends

The major types of human societies that appear during the course of sociocultural evolution vary significantly with respect to power, conflict, roles, and relationships in major areas of life. These societies are described in chapter 5, with special emphasis on economic changes that occur as scientific knowledge increases and technology becomes more efficient and effective. Major changes in values are also discussed, especially those that occur as societies make the shift from agriculture to machines as major productive techniques. Chapter 6 explores the trends toward increasing urbanization during the course of sociocultural evolution and toward the globalization of economic and political activities and identities in modern times. Global directions in population growth and control and the spread of environmental hazards are also described in this chapter, with an emphasis on possible future scenarios. As societies become increasingly complex and rates of social change accelerate, nonconformity increases and crime also becomes global. These trends are described in chapter 7, as are various theories that attempt to explain the reasons for increased nonconformity in modern times. The chapter concludes with a discussion of crime in the United States, with special emphasis on social class differences in the kinds of crime committed and reactions to these crimes by the criminal justice system. Historically, racial/ethnic minorities arise primarily as a result of migration and wars. During the course of sociocultural evolution, contact between societies increases, as does racial/ethnic minority formation. Chapter 8 explores various aspects of minority/dominant group relationships and conflicts, historically and around the world today, with a cross-cultural focus on women and older people as minorities, as well as on racial/ethnic minorities.

5

Human Societies

The story of human social life from the first appearance of hominids (about 4 million years ago) and the species *Homo sapiens* (about 100,000 years ago) has certain logical dividing points. These divisions are based on two major technological changes: the beginning of planting and the invention of machines to produce resources.

The beginning of planting (about 10,000 years ago) and the invention of machines (about 250 years ago) are often referred to as the "Agricultural Revolution" and the "Industrial Revolution." They were revolutions in the sense that they radically changed the human experience and human ways of life. Unlike modern political revolutions, however, they did not occur overnight.

We can classify most human societies on the basis of whether they have the techniques of planting food and producing goods by machines. When we do, we find that the basic social institutions in these societies—

144

families, economic life, government, education, and religion—have varied in certain typical ways.

In this chapter we focus on general, overall changes in the human experience as scientific knowledge accumulates and technology becomes increasingly complex and efficient in human societies. We also look at why certain values, called urban values, become more widespread, especially as societies industrialize. We see how and why occupations become increasingly specialized as societies become more complex. The origins of economic inequality and the current spread of global economic organizations in societies around the world are discussed in chapter 10. More specific changes in other major institutions as societies become more complex are also discussed in later chapters. Here we lay the groundwork for what is to come.

In the classification of human societies, herding and fishing societies do not fit into neat categories. We inevitably face this sort of problem when we attempt to categorize human beings and their social environments. Ultimately, each individual, group, and society is unique.

Most societies are now changing rapidly and are mixed in the way they obtain resources and adapt to their environments. Is present-day India, for example, primarily an agricultural or an industrial society? We classify societies according to how widely technological inventions or discoveries such as the plow, machines, electricity, or computers are in use. We also look at how a majority of a society's citizens obtain or produce economic resources. We focus on these particular aspects because they are given the greatest explanatory weight in the sociocultural evolution model.

India is an industrializing nation, but it is not yet industrial. A majority of India's citizens still earn their living by working the land. When most of India's workers are employed in manufacturing industries, India will be classified as an industrial society.

To avoid confusion, we use the present tense to describe all types of societies. Most of the simplest societies, however, no longer exist. Those that do exist have been greatly changed by contact with technologically more advanced societies and cultural diffusion. These societies are described in terms of their essential distinguishing features, as these existed in pure form, before contact with other societies. These descriptions are what Max Weber called **ideal-types,** definitions that contain the essence of what is being described in pure form (Weber, 1949 [1903–1917], pp. 90–92). Weber constructed ideal-typical definitions of such abstract concepts as Christianity, capitalism, and bureaucracy. Ideal-types are hypothetical constructions, not actual historical phenomena. They are created to serve as a theoretical standard against which reality can be compared. They are *not* "ideal" in the sense of what should or ought to be.

Here, we look at ideal-typical descriptions of major types of societies. It is important to be aware, however, that social reality is, and always has been, much more complex and complicated. Ideal-types are exaggerations of reality, because no one example of whatever is being defined contains all essential features in exactly the same form.

Socialism, for example, can be defined ideal-typically as an economic system in which income-producing property is publicly owned. Wealth and income are distributed equally among all citizens or on the basis of individual need. The government assumes responsibility for the health, education, and welfare of the population. The economy operates on the basis of central government planning (5-year plans, for example). It determines what is produced, how much is produced, and the price of whatever is produced. Cooperation is the basic value in economic relationships. And rank in the social structure is based on merit, not inheritance. **Capitalism,** on the other hand, emphasizes private ownership and operation of productive property, competition, prices based on supply and demand, private profit, free enterprise, and the acquisition of personal wealth.

These are ideal-typical definitions. No socialist or capitalist society in existence today (or ever, for that matter) has had all of the above features. But these definitions are useful as a standard, or yardstick, for classifying societies as more or less socialist or capitalist. Actually, most writers and scholars now use less loaded terms to refer to types of economies. Socialist economies are usually called planned economies and capitalist economies are called market economies.

We now also use the term **mixed economies.** This refers to market economies with large public as well as private sectors. These economies are also characterized by widespread government regulation over the operation of privately owned businesses and industries. In Sweden, for example, the government employs over 40 percent of the workforce (Wright and Cho, 1992). In the United States, this figure is 20 percent. Canada and Norway fall somewhere in between. Government regulation in mixed market economies includes the defining of safety standards, the setting of minimum wages, and the determining of environmental control practices and compulsory social insurance payments for workers.

TYPES OF HUMAN SOCIETIES

Anthropologists usually classify societies as hunting and gathering, horticultural, herding (or pastoral); agricultural (or agrarian); and industrial (Childe, 1951, 1964; Goldschmidt, 1959; Hoebel, 1966; Harris, 1980). Sociologists have added the terms preindustrial and postindustrial. Although they differ from each other in important ways, hunting and gathering and horticultural societies are usually classified together as *nonliterate societies* because they have no written language. We use the term nonliterate because it is more descriptive and less loaded than other terms that have been used in the past to refer to these types of societies—terms such as primitive, savage, uncivilized, barbarian, or backward.

Hunting and Gathering Societies

The first appearance of hominid species, from which *Homo sapiens* is the most recent to evolve, occurred approximately 4 million years ago, and perhaps even earlier (Pfeiffer, 1985). Physical anthropologists keep pushing back this date as new skeletal remains are discovered and as better techniques for dating these remains are invented. From the beginning of human social life until the technique of planting began to spread, sometime around 10,000 years ago, humans survived primarily by hunting wild animals and gathering wild vegetation. For over 99 percent of human history, men, women, and children lived in **hunting and gathering societies** (Lee and DeVore, 1968).

Tools and Weapons   In simple hunting and gathering societies, tools and weapons are constructed of stone and wood. Stone is used to cut meat, skin animals, scrape hides, and sharpen wooden tools and spears. Stone choppers and wooden spears are the basic weapons and tools in these societies. Technological advance is relatively slow.

Fire and human muscle power are the major sources of energy in simple hunting and gathering societies. Before the appearance of *Homo sapiens,* fire was probably used only after it had started from natural causes. Fire increased control over the natural environment by providing warmth, light, and protection against invaders of the camp or cave.

Advanced hunting and gathering societies appear after the evolution of modern humans, *Homo sapiens sapiens.* Bone is the major new raw material in widespread use to make weapons and tools in these societies. Advanced hunting and gathering societies understand the principle of the lever, which is used to construct spear-throwers, thereby doubling the distance a spear can travel. The effectiveness of the spear is also increased by using sharpened tips of bone rather than stone to penetrate targets.

The most important invention that increases the efficiency of weapons in advanced hunting and gathering societies, however, is the bow and arrow. Arrows travel much farther than spears and penetrate the target with greater force. Accuracy is also increased, because the target is sighted at eye level.

Tools in advanced hunting and gathering societies are much more varied than in simple ones. Inventions in widespread use include pins, needles with eyes, spoons, axes, hammers, shovels, grinding slabs, and pestles. Drawings, sculptures, and carvings are also common. These artifacts provide invaluable insights into the ways of life of extinct societies. Surviving art forms, especially drawings, provide important clues about religious and economic life. Art reveals the knowledge, attitudes, beliefs, and emotions of a people as well as more observable things such as their behavior, dress, housing, and food preferences.

Economic Life In hunting and gathering societies, members of the small band collect wild fruits, vegetables, and nuts, hunt animals, and sometimes fish. These economic resources are perishable, movable, and often unpredictable. Food cannot be stored, preserved, or accumulated for very long.

Of the basic types of human relationships—cooperation, exchange, competition, and conflict—cooperation and exchange are by far the most prevalent. Cooperation is important in societies in which hunting and fishing are group efforts. But independence and resourcefulness are also highly valued traits in this type of society. People are frequently on their own and they are taught to be self-reliant (Ellis, Lee, and Peterson, 1978; Ellis and Peterson, 1992). The sharing of the catch or kill is common. This is a way of spreading the risk so that no single family will have to suffer or do without after a reversal or a run of bad luck. Competition and conflict are minimal.

There is no accumulated **economic surplus**—more food or other goods than the society needs or can use—to compete for or fight over. Societies that have no surplus goods are called **subsistence economies.** The economic goods and services available are enough to provide mainly for the local population. There is usually little or no trade with other societies. Human muscle power and human skills are the only means of production.

Most hunting and gathering societies (about 90 percent) move frequently as local supplies of food or water are exhausted or as conflicts arise with neighboring bands. But population pressures are minimal, since hunting and gathering societies usually have between 20 and 40 people in them. And there is plenty of space to move on. Those who are fortunate enough to have located near permanent, rich sources of food such as fish and sea mammals or groves of nut trees move less often, or not at all. The band "owns" these resources, but they are collectively, not privately, owned.

More mobile bands do not own food resources, but they move in a familiar territory. Usually the rights of a band to a certain territory are respected by other bands. The advantage of moving in a definite territory is that seasonal changes are more predictable, trails are familiar to hunters, and the band is spared unnecessary insecurity.

Our idea of private property applies mainly to personal possessions in the more mobile hunting and gathering societies. The ownership of land that is soon to be abandoned is pointless. Personal property such as tools and weapons is easily and quickly constructed from plentiful materials and is not particularly distinctive or valuable. This property is usually given away after death, quite casually, to anyone who wants it. There are no domesticated animals to transport personal property. Moving this property would be a problem if it accumulated.

Work is divided up on the basis of age and sex. Women more often collect wild vegetation. They bear and nurse children, sometimes throughout the entire span of their short lives. They tend the hearth and nurse the

ADAPTATION IN STONE-AGE SOCIETY

Through the ages, humans have adapted to environmental conditions, such as climate, with remarkable resourcefulness. In arctic climates, stone-age hunters dressed in ways that maximized protection, despite a lack of established scientific knowledge about thermodynamics and sophisticated equipment to ease survival.

The clothes and tools of the 5,300-year-old naturally mummified frozen body found in 1991 by hikers in the Alps suggest he wore the equivalent of L.L. Bean cold-weather gear. The Alpine iceman knew how to dress for the cold. He wore several layers of garments to provide good insulation for feet, head, and body. His shoes were made of calfskin, filled with grass and held in place by an inner string "sock." Instead of a Swiss army knife and a propane lamp, however, he had a copper ax, a flint knife, and fire-starting equipment (flint flakes and fungus used for tinder) (Spindler, 1994).

What Do You Think?

1. What are some major advances in scientific knowledge that were unknown when your parents were growing up? When your grandparents were growing up?

2. What are some major technological advances that were unknown during your parents' childhood? Your grandparents' childhood?

3. How have these scientific and technological advances affected daily life in three generations of your family?

wounded, ill, and dying. Men more often hunt and fashion tools from stone, wood, or bone. But roles are flexible. Segregation of men and women in work or leisure activities is not extreme and some degree of role sharing is common (Yorburg, 1974). Both men and women are economic providers. Women sometimes join in hunting small animals. Men sometimes cook and care for young children (but not very young infants) (Nance, 1975).

Age is the other basis for assigning work in hunting and gathering societies (Simmons, 1945). Only people with exceptional health, strength, or luck survive to old age in these societies (and people are defined as old before the age of 50). Because survival to old age is rare, the aged are believed to be under the special protection of supernatural spirits (Keith, 1990). Quick reflexes and physical strength are essential in hunting and gathering societies. Older people who no longer have the strength or speed to hunt or forage for food are given work that is less demanding. They dress the kill, process hides, or help with young children.

Societies in which there are few available sources of energy other than human muscle power use the aged in physically less demanding but socially necessary tasks. Since there is no written language, the memories of old people are important resources for passing on traditions, legends, and folktales to the next generation.

The only specialized occupations are that of headman (political leader) and shaman (spiritual leader and healer). These occupations are not full time, however. Leaders usually do what everyone else does most of the time. They are present in more settled communities with stable and richer food supplies, and their status of headman or shaman is not hereditary. The rights and obligations of the headman or shaman cannot be passed on to children. Leaders are recruited on the basis of merit: personal qualities such as a privileged relationship with the spirit world, problem-solving ability (intelligence), or special talents or skills. These qualities must withstand the test of time, however. If they fail to perform satisfactorily, they lose their status and their influence.

Although there is no leisure class in hunting and gathering societies, several anthropologists have referred to these societies as the original affluent societies. But the affluence in these societies is in leisure time and not in material possessions or economic goods. It has been estimated that a workweek of no more than 20 hours was required to obtain sufficient food in the earliest hunting and gathering societies (Sahlins, 1972).

Organized group warfare is absent in the more mobile societies. Sexual rivalry and conflict are the most frequent reasons for fighting and feuding. Inequality is based primarily on individual differences in personality, health, strength, or intelligence. It is not based on economic differences, hereditary privileges, or the spoils of war. Slavery is practically unknown.

Social Change   The rate of social change in the more isolated hunting and gathering societies is unimaginably slow. The amount of knowledge and the technological level are so low that there is little that can be combined into new inventions except over very long periods of time, usually thousands of years. The pool of talent that can be drawn from for new inventions is also small because the population is small. It remains limited in size primarily because additional people cannot be supported by the economy. Death rates and birth rates are usually balanced, intentionally adjusted by practices such as infanticide and abortion when the balance is disturbed. Accidents, infectious diseases, and food shortages keep the population down. Most children in hunting and gathering societies do not survive to adulthood (see Table 5.1 on pp. 162–163).

Horticultural Societies

With the introduction of planting, human communities became much more varied and complex. Women probably made this discovery originally (Yorburg, 1974). They collected wild vegetation and very likely were the first to notice that stored or discarded vegetables sometimes took root and could be deliberately produced. Men, on the other hand, since they did the hunting, probably discovered the techniques for domesticating, or taming, wild animals.

Anthropologists usually trace the first appearance of **horticultural societies** to the Middle East, about 10,000 years ago, although there is some controversy about this. Horticulturalists (from the Latin *hortus,* or garden) rely primarily on plant cultivation for economic resources, but planted areas are small in size, like gardens, and not very productive.

Historically, **fishing societies** appeared earlier. These societies rely primarily on fishing as a means of subsistence. Nearly all fishing societies, except those in arctic areas, supplement their diet by gathering or hunting, but fishing is the basic economic activity. Fishing societies are slightly more advanced technologically than hunting and gathering societies. They are also larger in size, containing an average of about 60 people, and they are far more likely to have permanent settlements. This occurs because fish are a steadier and more dependable economic resource.

Fishing societies do not produce food deliberately, but fish reproduce much faster than land animals. They provide a more abundant and dependable food supply than is typical in hunting and gathering societies.

Herding societies appeared about the same time as horticultural societies. These engage in the herding of domesticated animals rather than planting as their most widespread economic activity. They do this because their geographic environment (desert, arctic, or mountainous areas) will not support planting (Lenski, 1988). But the environment does contain animals such as goats, sheep, camels, cattle, or reindeer that can be domesticated and used as a source of food or transportation. Herding societies are considered parallel to simple horticultural societies. Their technological level is similar, and in both types of societies, for the first time, food can be produced. This provides a more predictable food supply and makes possible the accumulation of an economic surplus, trade, and more population.

Archaeologists do not agree about whether and where else the independent discovery of plant cultivation took place in Europe, Asia, and the Americas (the New World). It now appears that the original inhabitants of the Americas came to the New World during the Ice Age. They traveled over a solid land bridge that connected Siberia and Alaska. At the end of the Ice Age, this land bridge was submerged as the ice melted and the oceans rose. The New World was cut off from the Old World several thousand years before horticulture appeared in the Middle East. Nevertheless, horticulture did arise in the New World, apparently as an independent discovery, and with remarkable similarities to the form it took in Old World cultures (Harris, 1980).

Horticultural societies in the Americas were not as successful in domesticating animals, nor were they as advanced in the use of harder metals such as copper, tin, or bronze as horticultural societies in the Old World.

But the Maya of Yucatan developed an ideographic system of writing, a calendar, and a numeral system that included the concept of zero–rare accomplishments for horticultural societies anywhere (Coe, 1987, 1993).

Archaeologists are still searching for more remains of extinct societies that would help answer questions about whether the appearance of horticulture, particularly in Asia, was a result of cultural diffusion or an independent discovery. What is clear, however, is that the basic technique of planting evolved very gradually and that people in different environments made unique contributions to this development. Depending on varying natural resources, different societies cultivated new and different varieties of plants and domesticated new and different kinds of animals.

Tools and Weapons The wooden hoe and digging stick are the basic tools used for planting in simple horticultural societies. Other important inventions in these societies are pottery, weaving, and leather working. Housing becomes more complex in horticultural societies, providing more space and greater protection against sun, rain, snow, heat, and cold. More permanent materials such as sun-dried clay are used to build houses, and special rooms or buildings may be constructed for specialized uses, such as religious or ceremonial activities. Protective walls around entire villages also appear. Soft metals such as gold are used in some simple horticultural societies, but mainly in ceremonial or craft objects.

Advanced horticultural societies, in contrast, are characterized by the widespread use of harder metals–copper, tin, or bronze–for making tools and weapons. This use of metals depends on a knowledge of smelting and casting. And this, in turn, requires a source of heat such as the pottery kiln that is much hotter than a wood-burning fire. We see, here, how inventions accumulate and build on one another. We also see, once again, how cumulative inventions increase effectiveness in coping with the environment. Metal tools and weapons are incomparably more efficient than stone, wood, or bone for piercing, digging, cutting, and scraping.

The increased efficiency of tools and weapons in advanced horticultural societies is accompanied by changes in the human as well as the non-human environment. Conflict, as a basic type of human relationship, becomes far more prevalent in these societies. Technological advances provide more resources, including people (slaves), to fight over and more effective weapons to fight with. The evidence of this change comes from archaeology. Excavated graves of adult males from extinct simple horticultural societies rarely contain weapons, nor do these communities contain walls or other types of defense. The graves and ruins of advanced horticultural societies, however, provide evidence of extensive warfare and slavery.

Economic Life The capacity to produce an economic surplus in horticultural societies has far-reaching consequences for social life. The population grows because the population in preindustrial societies increases as the food supply increases. Some horticultural societies have been able to support as many as 2,000 or 3,000 people. Settlements are also more permanent. Horticulturalists do not have the techniques of irrigation, fertilization, and crop rotation; nor do they have the plow. But even the simplest horticultural societies are usually able to work their land for several years before the soil becomes exhausted and the community must move on.

The division of labor in horticultural societies is still primarily on the basis of gender and age. Men usually clear the fields by slashing and burning trees and other wild vegetation. Women usually do the planting (in between the tree stumps and other debris). In societies where hunting is not a major economic activity, males perfect their skills as warriors and shift their aggressive energies and impulses to warfare. This, too, is a profitable economic activity. Population pressures are great, and the spoils of war (including livestock) are valuable and easily stolen and increase wealth much faster than planting vegetables.

Private property and social inequality are characteristic of horticultural societies. More stationary and affluent settlements permit the accumulation of greater quantities of heavier, bulkier, more elaborate, and more valuable possessions. Some families are more productive than others, initially perhaps because they happen to have produced more children. Children are an economic asset in societies that rely primarily on planting. They do household chores, till the fields, weave cloth, make pottery, help build houses, and help fight wars.

Some families become quite wealthy relative to others, and the accumulated wealth is passed on to their children from generation to generation. Wealth, in addition to personal qualities, becomes a basis for prestige and power in horticultural societies.

A small number of full-time specialized occupations arise. Since more food is produced than needed, some members of the society can be released from food production and can become specialists in food preparation (such as baking), crafts, and tool or weapon making. This promotes trade and commerce. Excess items made by full-time specialists can be traded for items in other societies in which different techniques or natural resources are in use. Simple horticultural societies have subsistence economies. Advanced horticultural societies actively engage in trade, usually in permanent market centers.

Economically, the desire to accumulate wealth, the inequality that this produces, and the conflict that is promoted are the most striking distinguishing features of horticultural societies in contrast to hunting and gathering societies. War is extremely common and slavery is more prevalent in horticultural societies than in any other type of society. Customs such as human sacrifice, cannibalism, and head-hunting, rare in human history, are found only in horticultural societies.

But horticulturists do not usually have the population or the communications and transportation technology to occupy conquered societies (see

FIGURE 5.1

Some Consequences of the Shift to Horticulture

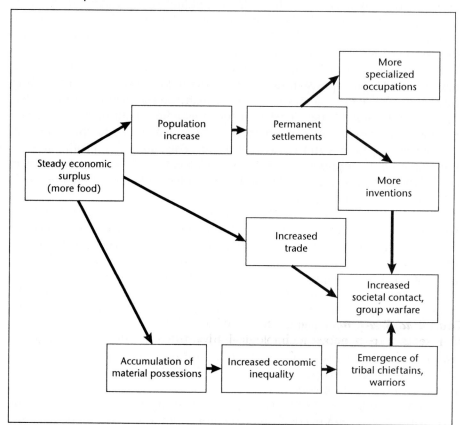

The discovery of planting led to widespread social change in all major areas of life.

Table 5.1 on pp. 162–163). They raid and plunder and return to home base. It is easier to take away movable resources, such as livestock and people, than to stay and attempt long-term control and exploitation over conquered peoples (Childe, 1964).

Agricultural Societies

With the invention of the plow about 6,000 years ago, the first **agricultural societies** (from the Latin *ager,* or field) appeared. Many sociocultural changes in horticultural societies are intensified in agricultural societies: (1) the size of populations, (2) the permanence of settlements, (3) the size of the economic surplus, (4) the number of full-time specialized occupations, (5) the degree of social inequality, and (6) the amount of trade. Three additional features that are found in only a handful of horticultural societies, in Central America or China, become widespread in agricultural societies: the use of a written language, the existence of permanent urban centers, and wars characterized by the occupation of conquered territories and permanent control over conquered peoples.

Wars in technologically less advanced societies, as mentioned earlier, do not usually involve settlement and continued exploitation of defeated societies. But developments in knowledge and technology in agricultural societies make empire building possible and profitable. With a written language, administrators can keep track of taxes, tributes, and tithes exacted from conquered societies. Better roads and better means of transportation on land and water improve the mobility of soldiers, government tax collectors, and political administrators.

A larger economic surplus (more food, especially) increases population and frees more people to become full-time professional soldiers and administrators. Greater population pressures and the greatly increased wealth of nations inspire systematic and sustained, organized, planned, and continuous exploitation of weaker societies by stronger, more powerful ones.

Tools and Weapons The invention of the plow in agricultural societies represents a tremendous technological advance over the hoe and digging stick. Much greater areas of land can be cultivated more effectively, and because the plow digs deeper, weeds can be buried and used to fertilize the soil. In addition, nutriments from deep within the soil can be brought back to the surface to continuously nourish new plants.

The use of manure to fertilize crops and the use of irrigation also promote stable, permanent land cultivation and stationary, permanent, and very large settlements. Another tremendously important discovery in agricultural societies is the use of oxen to pull the plow. Herding societies use the energy of horses, and, later, camels for transportation. In agricultural societies, however, animal power replaces human muscle power in the production of food. Later, the power of wind and water is also harnessed. Advanced agricultural societies are also characterized by an extensive use of iron for making tools and weapons. Other important inventions that occur as these societies develop technologically are gunpowder, the clock, the printing press, the spinning wheel, windmills, and water-powered mills.

The potential for scientific and technological advance is greatly intensified in agricultural societies. The number of people who can serve as a source of creativity and invention is vastly increased. The number of accumulated inventions and the amount of knowledge and accurate information about the environment are much greater. Contacts and communication between societies with different cultures also expand.

Nevertheless, technological advance actually slows down in advanced agricultural societies (Childe, 1951; Lenski, 1966; Lenski, Lenski, and Nolan, 1991). The incentive to discover or invent more efficient techniques for increasing productivity will not be great if the economic surplus is promptly and mercilessly seized by the military forces of the landowning aristocracy. And this is the typical situation in preindustrial agricultural societies. Peasants are reduced to a minimum subsistence level and the fruits of increased productivity end up in the hands of the ruling elites. Peasant revolts are frequent, but they are brutally suppressed and have rarely been successful until recent times.

The landowning class channels its creative energies into war and conquest as a way of increasing wealth. It does not contribute to technological development, since it defines working with the hands as degrading and unsuitable to the elevated status that members of this class have. It has little motivation or interest in scientific or technological advance. War is a quicker way to obtain the goods it seeks.

Economic Life   Social inequality becomes more extreme in agricultural societies. The greatly increased productivity of these societies provides more to distribute to the most powerful families and their economic dependents. It has been estimated that the landowning aristocracy, usually no more than 2 percent of the population in advanced agricultural societies, receives at least half of the national income (Lenski, 1966). It usually owns between one-half and three-quarters of the land in any specific society.

Most workers are in the **primary sector** in agricultural societies. They extract natural resources from land and sea. They work at farming, fishing, mining, or lumbering. Because peasants can produce so much more food than horticulturalists, many more people are released to become full-time specialists as administrators, soldiers, clergy, self-employed crafts workers, tool and weapon makers, and merchants.

Money economies begin to replace barter economies. In simple societies, people barter. They exchange services for goods, or goods they do not need or want for goods other people have. Taxes, rents, and wages are paid in grains such as barley or wheat, but grains are heavy and perishable. As techniques of metalworking improve in advanced agricultural societies, much more metal becomes available. Governments take control over the manufacture of standardized units of metal with agreed-upon value, and these metals are used increasingly to pay for goods and services.

Merchants can buy what they do not need or want (spices, metal tools and weapons, pottery and ornaments) to sell to others at a profit. Merchants, as buyers and sellers, increase demand and promote trade. They tend to locate near one another and near full-time crafts workers, in permanent urban trading centers.

Merchants are important in the large urban centers that develop in agricultural societies. The governing class, including religious leaders, also locates in these centers, since the settlements are usually surrounded by walls and provide greater protection. Merchants, crafts workers who own their own tools and shops, soldiers who have some authority over the common foot soldier, local government officials, and the lower levels of the clergy form a small but growing class in agricultural societies—the **middle class**.

Middle-class people are at the middle levels of society with respect to economic resources, power, or prestige. They own small amounts of income-producing property—land, shops, housing, tools—that they or other people use. They depend primarily on knowledge and communication skills in their work. They sell, keep records, manage, teach, heal, and pray.

The middle class functions largely in the service of the upper class. It helps channel the economic surplus from the poor to the rich (Lenski, 1966). It also helps the rich use up the economic surplus by providing them with luxury goods. An urban **working class** also arises in agricultural societies. The working class consists of people who are at the lowest levels of society with respect to economic resources, power, or prestige. They work with things rather than with people and communication skills. They usually do not own property, including the tools with which they work in small shops.

The middle class and the urban working class grow in number as societies industrialize. And insofar as these classes manage to appropriate more of the economic surplus for themselves, social inequality is somewhat reduced in industrialized societies. But the working and middle social classes are not large in agricultural societies, and the masses of people—the peasants—experience little change in their economic well-being. The advantages of technological advance and increased economic productivity are wiped out by the ruthless and efficient exploitation of the masses by the rich, as well as by increases in population.

In the aftermath of plagues, famines, floods, wars, and other disasters, the standard of living for peasants in agricultural societies is temporarily raised. This is a human example of the law of supply and demand. Peasants become more valuable when there are fewer of them to produce goods. But this relief soon disappears as the birth rate rises in keeping with better times. In fact, life for peasants in agricultural societies is typically poor, nasty, brutish, and short, to paraphrase seventeenth-century philosopher Thomas Hobbes.

Industrial Societies

The beginnings of the Industrial Revolution are usually traced to England in the mid-eighteenth century. At this time, new sources of power (notably steam) and machines, many of which had actually been invented earlier, rapidly came into greater use in the production of economic resources. By 1800, England became the first industrial nation in the

FIGURE 5.2

Some Consequences of the Shift to Agriculture

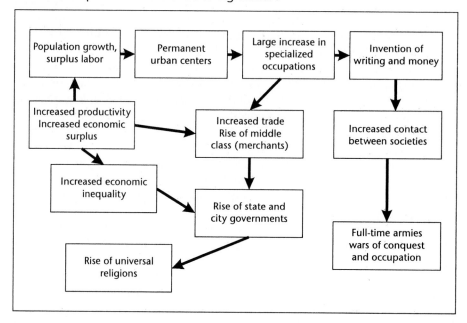

Two distinguishing features of agricultural societies are written languages and wars of conquest and occupation (colonialism).

world (Lenski, Lenski, and Nolan, 1991). A majority of its citizens were employed in the **secondary sector,** in the manufacture of machine-made goods rather than in agriculture. The United States did not reach this stage until the 1870s, after which it rapidly surpassed England in level of industrialization.

Creative energies that had been submerged for hundreds of years in agricultural societies, curbed by extreme exploitation and severe political repression, were unleashed during the early stages of the Industrial Revolution. Scientific research blossomed and technology benefited. In industrial societies, technology becomes a practical application of scientific research. In the early stages of industrialization, inventions are made by gifted, self-employed amateurs. In advanced industrial societies, most inventions are made by teams of research scientists working for large industrial firms.

The events, ideas, and values that led to the Industrial Revolution in England and continental Europe are subjects of much debate and controversy. To isolate even the most important causes is extremely difficult. The voyages of discovery and exploration that began in the fifteenth century in Europe were certainly one important factor (Tawney, 1926).

FIGURE 5.3

The Industrial Revolution in Europe: Underlying Conditions and Major
Developments

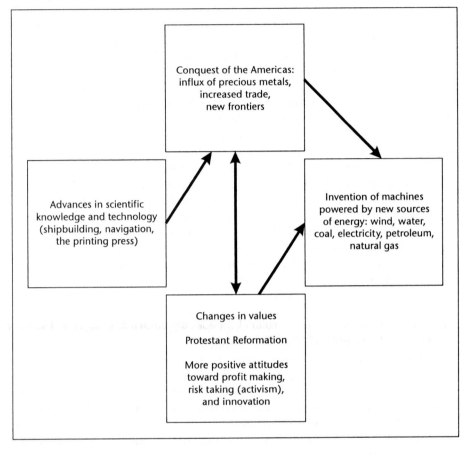

Increased economic resources from colonies and widespread changes in values were
major factors in the Industrial Revolution in Europe.

Travelers brought in material goods that were scarce or previously unknown. They also provided greater factual information about the shape of
the world. This, in turn, stimulated scientists to seek additional empirical
information about other aspects of the human environment and experience.

Colonization brought into Europe vast quantities of precious metals
(silver and gold), and the money economy was given a tremendous boost.
For the middle social classes, economic resources and opportunities were
greatly increased. This is important to bear in mind, because it is the middle
class, as businesspeople, research scientists, and leaders of social move-

ments, that becomes a major source of social change in industrializing and industrialized societies.

In the realm of values, the Protestant Reformation advanced the Industrial Revolution in Protestant countries (Weber, 1958 [1904]). The Protestant Reformation was a response to social conditions that had been changing in agricultural societies at least since the time of the Crusades. The Crusades opened up new culture contacts and trade routes. New material wants were created and urban centers increased in importance.

The doctrines of Protestantism as set forth by Martin Luther and John Calvin in the sixteenth century, shortly after the beginning of the voyages of discovery, provided a set of values and beliefs that eventually were adopted by urban merchants and craftsworkers. These values and beliefs reinforced and supported commercial interests and activities.

Luther identified honest work in one's calling as a way of serving God. He removed the stigma that the ancient Greeks and Romans attributed to work and the association of work with punishment and sin that had been the view of the medieval Roman Catholic Church. The Church had frowned on the accumulation of goods beyond what was necessary for existence. It had stigmatized the merchant and moneylender as thieves and parasites.

Calvin, on the other hand, regarded profit making as a respectable source of income, as respectable as wages or rents. Calvin's doctrine of predestination held that individuals were destined at birth for salvation or damnation. People could do nothing to change their fate. This led to constant and pressing anxiety on the part of the deeply religious about whether they were among the saved or the damned.

Material success, however, came to be interpreted as a sign that a person was favored by God and was destined to "dwell in God's house forever." It served as evidence that provided relief from a person's anxiety about his or her fate. Hard work, self-denial, and self-discipline were the means to bring about material success.

Certainly, the founders of Protestantism had no idea of the far-reaching latent consequences of their movement in promoting profit-making enterprises and industrialization. That there was such a relationship, at least in the West, is indicated by the fact that the first nations to industrialize were Protestant. But the enormous wealth shipped into these countries from their colonies was an important preexisting factor (Tawney, 1926). Japan, the first nation to industrialize in the East, experienced no great change in the religious sphere before industrializing. Japan was, however, a colonizing power.

The Protestant ethic was itself to some extent a response to changing economic conditions. The increased wealth and opportunities that colonialism brought stimulated inventiveness, risk taking in business, and competitiveness, particularly among the urban middle classes. Human societies began to take their great leap forward from agriculture to industrialization.

Technology Probably the most important technological invention that precipitated the Industrial Revolution was the steam engine. Advances in productivity and efficiency occurred first in textile industries. By the end of the eighteenth century, the steam engine was being applied widely in the manufacture of textiles in England.

Other additional sources of energy that came into widespread use during the eighteenth and nineteenth centuries were coal, natural gas, and, later, petroleum and electricity. The iron and coal industries also developed greatly during the early stages of the Industrial Revolution. By the mid-nineteenth century, the railroad industry had revolutionized transportation, followed by the development in the twentieth century of automobiles and airplanes. At the same time, the telephone, telegraph, radio, photography, and movies brought sweeping change in the realm of communications.

In industrial societies, machine power replaces human and animal power. In advanced industrial societies, machines begin to replace human brain power. Automation and computers are the major new inventions in this area. Atomic energy and solar energy are major new sources of power. In transportation, airplanes compete with automobiles, trucks, and railways as a faster, more efficient means of transporting people and things. Television supplements photography and movies, and visual communication allows people from all over the earth to become familiar with other societies' ways of life.

In this brief summary of the major scientific and technological advances in industrialized societies, the pattern described applies mainly to the West, especially England and the United States. It is important to recognize, however, that industrialization did not and does not need to assume this step-by-step pattern in all societies.

Many countries that are industrializing now are simultaneously importing the various technologies and skills that developed at different times in the West. They are building roads, railways, airports, telephones, and television stations, textile and steel industries, and nuclear reactors all at the same time. Technological evolution, especially in the later stages, allows agricultural societies that can and want to catch up to take giant steps toward industrialization, especially if they have valuable natural resources such as oil. We will return to this theme in chapter 10 when we look at contemporary global economies.

Economic Life The economic life of industrialized societies is characterized by vastly increased economic resources, a tremendous increase in the number and type of full-time specialized occupations, and somewhat decreased economic inequality. Social change is constant and very rapid. The economic and human costs of wars usually surpass the economic gains of military successes, and the deadliness of military weapons such as nuclear bombs creates the threat of world destruction.

TABLE 5.1

Types of Societies

Type of Society	Major Technological Advances	New Sources of Energy	Economic Characteristics
Simple hunting and gathering (hominids)	Use of stone, wood, choppers, spears.	Fire, human muscle power.	Hunting and gathering. No economic surplus. Little or no trading with other societies.
Advanced hunting and gathering (*Homo sapiens*)	Use of bone. Spear-throwers, bow and arrow, pins, bone needles with eyes, spoons, axes, saws, bone hammers, shovels, grinding slabs and pestles, mattocks. Sculpture, carving, drawing.		Division of labor on the basis of age and sex. No full-time specialized occupations. Little or no economic inequality.
Horticultural	Digging stick, hoe. Domestication of animals (herding). Pottery, leather working, weaving, use of metal (gold) in ceremonial objects.	Nonhuman animal power (for transportation).	Planting, tending of livestock. Small economic surplus. Some trade and commerce. Some full-time specialized occupations. Some economic inequality. Slavery infrequent.
Advanced horticultural	Use of metal (copper, tin, bronze) in weapons, tools. Technique of smelting.		Greater economic surplus. Permanent markets. More full-time specialized occupations. Greater economic inequality. Widespread slavery.

The standards of living and purchasing power of the working and middle classes rise in industrial societies, aided by mass production, social movements, political parties, labor organizations, and welfare state policies that benefit all social classes. New economic ideologies arise to justify the political and economic goals of all interest groups (Mannheim, 1936).

The two most widespread economic ideologies in industrializing and industrialized societies are capitalism and socialism. Economic inequality persists, however, regardless of the economic ideology of particular industrializing or industrial societies. Today, as China, Eastern Europe, and the former Soviet Union shift to market economies, a new breed of successful, ruthlessly materialistic private business owners arises. Their consumer excesses approach those of the newly rich in any country at any time (Bura-

Type of Society	Major Technological Advances	New Sources of Energy	Economic Characteristics
Agricultural	The plow, irrigation, fertilization, writing.	Nonhuman animal power (cattle, oxen) to pull plows.	Most workers in primary industries. Emergence of money as a medium of exchange. Emergence of a middle class. Full-time urban traders, merchants, and crafts workers. Extreme economic inequality.
Advanced agricultural	Iron, gunpowder, the clock, printing press, spinning wheel, windmills, water-powered mills.	Water power, wind power.	Money economy becomes more widespread. Small increase in middle class.
Industrial	Steam engine, flying shuttle, spinning machines, trains, vulcanization of rubber, automobiles, telegraph, telephone, aircraft.	Coal, petroleum, natural gas, electricity.	Most workers in secondary industries. Large increase in middle class. Full-time specialists in all occupations. Factories replace land as major economic resource. Capitalism, mixed economy, or socialism. Unemployment, underemployment. Economic inequality decreases somewhat.
Advanced industrial or postindustrial	Automation, computers, television.	Atomic energy, solar energy.	Most workers in tertiary industries. New middle class of salaried employees is the majority. Widespread employment of women.

woy and Krotov, 1992; Solomon, 1993). Inequality in the United States also grew considerably during the decade of the 1980s, according to reports on household income issued by researchers at the Federal Reserve and the Internal Revenue Service (Nasar, 1992b).

In industrial societies, a majority of workers manufacture machine-made food, shelter, and clothing. They work in factories rather than at home or in small shops. At first, they use natural materials to manufacture products. As technological development and population increase continue, however, the supply of natural materials decreases and the demand for goods increases. In advanced industrial societies, there is a shift toward synthetic foods, fibers, and building materials. Diet sodas, prefabricated houses, plastic furniture, and fake furs become widely available.

In advanced industrial or postindustrial societies, a majority of the workforce is employed in the **tertiary sector,** engaged in providing services rather than extracting natural resources or producing goods. In the working class, services involve waiting on others—preparing food for them, cleaning up after them, transporting them, and repairing their clothes, houses, and furnishings. Middle-class workers rely mainly on communication skills in doing their work. They manage, sell, distribute, teach, heal, advise, write letters, and keep records.

The middle social classes become the predominant class in postindustrial societies. Many of the sons and daughters of the old, self-employed, small property–owning middle class become the new middle class. They become salaried employees in large-scale government, industrial, and commercial organizations. Massive machinery, mass production, and mass consumption require massive organizations to manage, coordinate, and keep records in all highly industrialized societies.

In market economies, unemployment and underemployment become serious problems. In agricultural societies, most people work as long as they are physically able. Unemployment follows surges in population growth and is corrected by plagues and famines that wipe out surplus population. In industrial market economies, unemployment follows the ups and downs of the business cycle. In postindustrial market economies, those with the lowest level of skills and education have the highest rates of unemployment.

In market economies, in addition, vast numbers of people are employed in keeping up the demand for products in the selling, promoting, and advertising industries. Advanced market economies thrive on whetting consumer appetites through advertising, changing, or improving products, driving out most smaller competitors, fixing prices at artificially high levels, and making minimal reforms. The functional equivalent of nineteenth-century railroad, oil, and mining robber barons in postindustrial societies are financiers, speculators, and investors who live off capital rather than productive enterprise (Phillips, 1993).

Another important economic change that occurs in postindustrial societies is the widespread employment of women, particularly in the vastly expanded service occupations. Women in all societies have engaged in economically productive work in addition to bearing children (Yorburg, 1975). In agricultural societies, women typically tend domestic animals, plant gardens, make pots and baskets, and take in sewing and washing for extra income. In cities they take in boarders as well as sewing and washing. The important point is that they usually work in or near the home.

In the earliest industrializing societies, women usually went out to work in factories as young and unmarried workers or as married workers in a family unit. Wages were paid to the male head of the family. In more advanced industrial societies, women have earned independent income, but mainly as factory or domestic workers. Most women workers have been young and never married. The invention of the typewriter in the 1880s

TABLE 5.2

Consequences of the Industrial Revolution

From 1750 to the present, the following changes occurred as societies changed from agricultural to postindustrial forms:

- a great increase in estimated world population (from about 725 million to about 5.5 billion).
- a large decline in birth rates (one-third) and a three-fold increase in life expectancy.
- more stages in the life cycle: adolescence, youth, middle age, young-old, and over 85.
- a complete reversal in rural/urban population ratios—from 90 percent rural to 90 percent urban.
- an almost complete shift from family to nonfamily production of economic resources.
- far more specialization in occupations.
- mass production and speeded up automation.

- mass literacy and almost complete elimination of illiteracy.
- a shift from hereditary to elected political offices.
- the emergence of global political and economic institutions (the United Nations, the World Bank, the International Monetary Fund, the International Labor Organization).
- the development of global travel, communication, production facilities.
- the growth of global cultural patterns: dress, food, music, urban values.
- an increase in the possibility of world destruction by means of global environmental depletion and pollution and intercontinental weapons systems.

brought some middle-class women into the workforce, but they were also young and unmarried, for the most part. The primary change as societies become postindustrial is the greatly increased employment of middle-class and married women—with and without children. This is today a worldwide trend (Cherlin and Furstenberg, 1988; Blumberg, 1991).

FROM TRADITIONAL TO URBAN VALUES

Up to now we have focused primarily on external economic changes that occur as science and technology develop in human societies. Accompanying these changes have been certain basic shifts in the internal human experience.

We have seen how the internal experience of role conflict becomes more widespread and intense as societies industrialize. Another major change is in the realm of values—from traditional to modern. This too promotes role conflict. Differences in values between generations of a family may lead to a lack of mutual expectations between parents and their children (Yorburg, 1993). This conflict is especially pronounced among immigrants from rural villages of industrializing societies who settle in the large cities of postindustrial societies. Immigrant parents are more likely than their children to retain traditional values, such as familism, for example.

In industrial societies, the traditional values of fatalism, familism, authoritarianism, and religiousness compete with newer values emphasizing activism and achievement, individualism, egalitarianism, and rationalism (Yorburg, 1973; Inkeles and Smith, 1974; Inkeles, 1983).

The transition from what has been called traditional or agricultural values to modern or urban values is not complete, however, even in the most advanced industrial societies. There are exceptions and reversals. In the Middle East and the now-independent states of the former Soviet Union, for example, religious faith is increasing. In the conflict between traditional and urban values, most people are somewhere in the middle, and many are ambivalent or inconsistent in their feelings and behavior.

The overall direction of change is, nonetheless, maintained by increases in scientific knowledge and in the number of well-educated citizens in postindustrial societies. Technological developments in communication and transportation, changes in the economy, and increased population mobility of all kinds (geographic, social, and psychological) also play an important role in promoting this trend.

Rural areas in agricultural societies are characterized by certain typical values appropriate to rural conditions. The masses of people in preindustrial agricultural societies are born poor and die poor. For all but a handful, mainly middle-class residents of urban centers and a few especially talented peasants who may rise in the lower ranks of the army or church, opportunities to change one's economic position in life are nonexistent. As societies industrialize and economic resources and opportunities increase, however, urban values become more widespread (Yorburg, 1973; 1974).

Fatalism

The belief that one's overall status in life is preordained and one cannot and must not do anything to change one's destiny or fate, a doctrine known as **fatalism,** is widespread in agricultural societies. Most languages contain expressions that reflect this value: It is God's will; What will be, will be; That's life; It is written; Them's the breaks; That's the way the cookie crumbles.

Activism

As resources and, above all, real opportunities increase with technological and scientific development, fatalism declines. Middle-class individuals, as well as members of the working class who are in situations in which they can rise economically, shift to the value of **activism.** They take an active rather than a passive approach to their life circumstances. **Achievement**

motivation, the desire to compete successfully for rewards and resources, increases.

Those who value achievement set high economic, educational, political, or religious standards and work hard to attain their goals. They take risks and fight for what they want, and what they want is likely to change in advanced industrial societies. Modern language reflects this shift away from fatalism: Nothing ventured, nothing gained; There's always room at the top; We shall overcome.

Familism

In agricultural societies, the needs of the family as a group are considered more important than the needs of individual members, a value known as **familism.** The family is responsible for satisfying almost all human needs in such societies. It provides economic support and physical care, love, protection, education, identity, and meaning and purpose in life—at least ideally.

It is difficult for adults as well as children to survive outside a family group in agricultural societies. There are no commercial laundries or fast-food chains, few inns, and no apartment houses. Most unmarried adults or dependent children are forced to attach themselves to family groups as boarders, lodgers, servants, employees, apprentices, or poor relatives. The family is the economically productive unit in agricultural societies. On the land and in urban areas, the means of production are owned or controlled by families, usually led by the male head of the family. The fate of the individual is inseparable from the fate of the family, an all-important group.

Individualism

One value that becomes more important as societies industrialize is **individualism.** Family members increasingly go out to work in the nonfamily economy, in factories, stores, offices, and schools. They earn independent income and the family loses its absolute economic control over its individual members. The standard of living rises, opportunities grow, and individuals move away from their families in search of better jobs. They begin to attach more importance to their own needs and wishes when these conflict with family obligations.

The oldest child may not give up educational or other personal goals to support younger sisters and brothers or aged parents. Young people may choose their marriage partners, or live with partners without marrying, whether or not their parents approve. Young couples may decide not to have children because their careers are more important to them. Mothers may leave their children to pursue careers. Husbands may divorce their wives after many years of marriage. Personal satisfaction and gratification become more important and duty and family obligations somewhat less prominent as individualism becomes widespread.

Authoritarianism

As education increases and resources become somewhat more evenly distributed in industrialized societies, **authoritarianism,** the insistence on absolute and unquestioning obedience to fixed rules, declines. It declines in the relationship between citizen and ruler, employer and employee, husband and wife, and parent and child. The middle class grows and education becomes universal. Women achieve more equal levels of education and go out to work. Adult children may have more resources, education, and income than their middle-aged parents. Or children may end up with fewer of these resources than their parents, especially in the middle classes, as is often the case now in the United States (for the first time in its history) (Phillips, 1993; Newman, 1993). Opportunity and the need for talent and drive in technologically developed societies play havoc with traditional conceptions of the sanctity of inherited authority.

Achievement and personality (and luck) become more important and family, gender, birth order, and race become less important in determining identity, power, and destiny. Those in power become less powerful as dependents become less dependent. A male head of a household cannot exercise absolute control over his wife and children if they can leave to take jobs in the nonfamily economy. Elected government leaders become more sensitive to public opinion if they can be ousted from public office and deprived of power. Workers in industrialized societies with high unemployment rates experience serious limitations in their choices and alternatives. Still, they can change jobs more readily than could slaves, serfs, indentured servants, or apprentices in medieval societies.

Any insistence on absolute obedience to those in power is less feasible when people have more choices and alternatives. In elections in democratic industrial societies, negative campaigning—personal attacks on political opponents—highlights these alternatives. The policies of authoritarian governments in agricultural societies of ruling by decree, claiming the divine right of kings, or declaring "off with their heads" aim, by contrast, to secure categorical obedience.

Authoritarianism is also not possible in situations that are new or constantly changing. The rules become outdated or no longer apply. Where there are no rules, problem-solving ability, independence, and self-reliance become increasingly important (Ellis and Peterson, 1992).

Egalitarianism

The shift toward **egalitarianism** as a value in industrialized societies does not mean that all people in a society gain equal economic resources, prestige, or power. It means that opportunities to obtain economic rewards, power, and prestige come to be based, in principle, on personal qualifications such as intelligence, hard work, ambition, and confidence. They are not based on inherited statuses such as gender, racial/ethnic origin, and family membership. Privilege, power, and prestige are earned or achieved; they are not bestowed on the basis of birth.

In reality, inherited statuses continue to affect the outcome of individuals' lives in all societies, in spite of differences in level of industrialization or political and economic ideology. And meritocracies based on talent, drive, and hard work create a new kind of economic inequality. In *deindustrializing* economies, within postindustrial societies, manufacturing jobs decline as a result of increased automation and the export of manual jobs to other societies where labor costs are cheaper. This is a major reason for current economic difficulties in the United States, Germany, and Japan. In Japan, for example, Japanese-owned and -operated companies are exporting jobs to Taiwan, Indonesia, and Malaysia, where wages are much lower than in Japan. Those who have less training and cannot find manufacturing jobs become a permanent *underclass* in deindustrializing economies (Kaus, 1992).

Religiousness

All societies and peoples, at all times, have developed beliefs and practices having to do with the supernatural and sacred. **Religiousness** involves a belief in supernatural causation and control over human destiny and the events of daily life. This belief is based on faith rather than observable or scientific demonstration of cause and effect. Religiousness also usually implies an emphasis on spiritual, otherworldly rewards, although this is not a necessary feature of this value. Religious beliefs and practices represent a way of coping with human suffering and the unknown, uncertain, and seemingly uncontrollable.

Rationalism

As societies industrialize and scientific knowledge accumulates, human control over the environment increases tremendously and the realm of the unknown and uncertain contracts. As this occurs, humans come to value **rationalism** more. Rationalism involves a means-ends approach to solving life's problems. The means we choose to achieve our goals are logical. They have been tested and found to be the most efficient and effective means for achieving these goals.

Religiousness declines as a constraint over behavior as rationalism becomes more prevalent. Knowledge diminishes faith as a guide to action and human relationships. Ancient humans prayed to the gods to ensure safe passage across the seas. Modern humans invent radar. Parents of a sick child in traditional societies pray and make offerings to the church. In industrialized societies they take the child to a pediatrician. When prescription drugs can restore mental health, mental illness is less likely to be viewed as an invasion of the body by evil spirits.

Religiousness does not, by any means, disappear in advanced industrialized societies, however. Particularly in times of severe personal or societal crisis, it reappears with renewed force. In fact, this is happening now in many parts of the world—in Russia and Eastern Europe, for example. Furthermore, science cannot provide answers to the ultimate questions of human existence, nor can it provide guidance on moral issues and solace for human suffering.

The competition and conflict between science and religion characteristic of advanced agricultural and industrializing societies in the West diminish as science and technology continue to develop. In advanced industrial societies, pastoral counselors are trained in psychology. Most people go to doctors when they are ill, but many also pray for recovery and restoration.

Ethnocentrism

Another value prevalent in agricultural societies is ethnocentrism. This, as defined in chapter 3, is the tendency to judge one's own culture, society, group, and customs to be superior to all others. Ethnocentrism involves a fear of strangers and an inability to understand or accept out-group differences. It tends to decline as people from different racial or ethnic groups have more contact with one another, especially equal-status contact (as between middle-class blacks and whites in the United States, for example). This results directly from increasing migration to urban centers in technologically advanced societies. It also results indirectly from higher levels of education and exposure to diverse models of racial/ethnic and class origins, at a worldwide level, in the communications media.

Currently, in a period of enormous political upheavals (especially in Eastern Europe and Africa), ethnocentrism is on the rise. Severe economic frustration can precipitate open aggression toward outsiders, especially those that have been historical scapegoats in a particular society and culture. Cultural traditions of tolerance or intolerance toward particular minorities are, however, a major factor in determining how or whether this hostility breaks out.

Whatever the reality, the ideal culture in the United States has always emphasized **tolerance,** an acceptance and respect for group (racial/ethnic and religious) differences (Myrdal, 1944). The original English settlers, whose culture became the dominant one in the United States, came here,

after all, to escape religious persecution, as did many other European settlers. Today, the United States is experiencing serious economic difficulties,
and hostile behavior toward ethnic minorities has increased. But despite
inflated exposure in the news media, racist skinheads, the most openly
violent racist groups in the United States today, have only about 3,500 members nationwide, according to one recent survey (Applebome, 1993).

Cultural Relativism

The view that the practices of other cultures and groups should not be
judged by the standards of one's own culture or group is known as **cultural
relativism.** More people in democratic industrialized societies begin to
value tolerance as the standard of living rises and authoritarianism, particularly in the family, declines. People feel less aggressive if they are less frustrated economically. Furthermore, if children are permitted to express
aggression more freely as they grow up at home, as they are in most democratic industrial societies, they are less likely to repress and displace their
aggressive impulses onto outsiders (Fromm, 1941; Adorno et al., 1950).

As cultural relativism increases, people become more sophisticated.
They are less likely to experience culture shock and are more likely to be
tolerant of group and societal differences as long as these do not violate
basic human rights. They gain a live-and-let-live attitude toward human differences and an increased awareness that their own way of life is not necessarily the only good or required way to live. This promotes social change,
since other ways of life may be more readily accepted. Tolerant people are
less rigid and more open to new and different ways of thinking, feeling,
and acting. They are more flexible and adaptable. Contact and familiarity
may or may not breed contempt, but they do diminish the fear of strangers
and strange ways.

RISING EXPECTATIONS

Frontiers of different kinds expand as societies industrialize. The invention
of artificial sources of light (powered by gas, oil, or electricity) expands
the frontier of time through the evening hours, even as the frontiers of
space begin to contract (Melbin, 1978). People in industrialized societies
do not have to regulate their waking lives on the basis of sunset and sunrise.
They can sleep fewer hours, and with greatly increased machine productivity, they can work fewer hours. Leisure time expands, as does the value
placed on leisure time. Work declines and leisure increases as a major source
of satisfaction and meaning in life for more people.

Technological inventions in the realms of transportation and communication diminish physical and psychological isolation. Psychological fron-

tiers and horizons are extended as reference groups, identifications, hopes, and ambitions expand (in what we referred to as psychological mobility in chapter 4). In agricultural societies, people find it difficult to identify with groups or individuals outside their family or community. They have great difficulty imagining themselves living anywhere else or being anyone else. On interviews, in response to the question, "If you were king . . ." they can reply only, "But I could not be king" (Lerner, 1958, p. 50). Modern humans have no such difficulties. In fantasy, they can be almost anyone, live almost anywhere, and have almost anything.

Urban values and urban images spread as more people migrate to urban centers. This change in the internal human experience also occurs as modern technologies invade rural areas: first a road, then a bus, then electricity, radio, and finally, television and the world. With this invasion come increased educational and occupational opportunities, comparatively and in the long run, and **rising expectations.** More people want more than they already have, and they come to feel that they have a right to these resources and rewards.

White-collar crime (bribery, corruption, and fraud) committed by middle- and upper-class people in their work situations is related directly to the phenomenon of rising expectations. Poverty does not necessarily cause crime. People who are economically well off can also experience the anomie that Merton (1968) attributes to a discrepancy between culturally defined goals (wealth, fame, power) and legitimate means to achieve these goals. When ambition is boundless and legitimate accomplishments do not or cannot measure up, crime will occur among all classes.

In agricultural societies, the masses of people experience the frustrations of material deprivation—of poverty, disease, and untimely death. In industrialized societies, most people are better off materially, but they tend to experience the psychological deprivation of rising and unfulfilled expectations.

Another major change that occurs in the inner dimension of the human experience as societies industrialize is a rise in class consciousness. People become more aware of their economic interests and how these are being served or subverted by those who have political power in their societies. Marx was very critical of the "rural idiocy" of isolated and uneducated peasants who could not be mobilized for revolution because they had so little awareness of their economic situation in the wider context of the total society. But the historical record since Marx's time is clear. In fact, peasants can and have been mobilized by leaders of social movements. All segments of a society can be mobilized as advances in education, communication, and transportation promote migration and wipe out physical and psychological isolation everywhere.

Study Guide

REVIEW OBJECTIVES

After studying this chapter, you should be able to:

1. Classify major types of human societies.
2. Describe the basic differences in the amount of scientific information and type and efficiency of tools and weapons available in major types of societies.
3. Trace how sociocultural evolution affects economic life.
4. Explain why *specific* urban values—activism, individualism, egalitarianism, rationalism, and cultural relativism—become increasingly prevalent as societies industrialize.

SUMMARY

1. The Agricultural Revolution and the Industrial Revolution are the two major dividing points in classifying human societies.

2. As the trend toward sociocultural evolution continues in human societies, a majority of workers shift from hunting and gathering to producing food and machine-made goods and providing services.

3. Other basic economic changes include an increase in trade and commerce, growth of the economic surplus, and multiplication of the number and kind of full-time specialized occupations. Social inequality increases tremendously and then decreases somewhat.

4. Basic changes also occur in values and consciousness, especially as societies change from agricultural to industrial economies. Certain urban values—activism, individualism, egalitarianism, rationalism, and cultural relativism—become more widespread.

5. In the course of sociocultural evolution, people experience rising expectations. They become more aware of their economic interests. Material deprivation decreases, but psychological deprivation stemming from rising but unfulfilled expectations increases.

GLOSSARY

Achievement motivation: A strong need to compete successfully for resources, rewards, and recognition.

Activism: A belief in fighting to effect a change in one's life circumstances rather than passively accepting one's fate.

Agricultural societies: Literate societies in which the plow is used in planting.

Authoritarianism: An insistence on absolute and unquestioning obedience to fixed rules.

Capitalism: An economic system characterized by private ownership and operation of the means of production, competition, private profit, and the accumulation of personal wealth.

Cultural relativism: The belief we should not judge the ways of life of other cultures or societies by the standards of our own.

Economic surplus: The existence of more goods in a society than are needed to fulfill basic needs.

Egalitarianism: A belief that power, privilege, and prestige should be achieved on the basis of personal qualifications rather than inherited or ascribed statuses.

Familism: The view that the needs of the family as a group are more important than the personal needs of any individual member.

Fatalism: A belief that one must accept and not try to change one's life circumstances.

Fishing societies: Societies in which fishing is the basic economic activity.

Herding societies: Societies in which the tending of domesticated animals is the most important economic activity.

Horticultural societies: Nonliterate societies in which cultivated plants are the major economic resource and planting is the most widespread economic activity.

Hunting and gathering societies: Nonliterate societies in which the technique of planting is unknown and people live by hunting animals and gathering wild vegetation.

Ideal-type: A definition of a concept that includes only essential features in pure form.

Individualism: An emphasis on the needs and desires of the individual in preference to those of the group.

Middle class: People in the middle levels of society with respect to wealth and income, level of education, and occupa-

tional prestige; they work primarily with people and with communication skills.

Mixed economies: Market economies with a significant public sector (government employment) and varying degrees of government regulation over private businesses.

Primary sector: An economy or part of an economy that involves gathering or extracting raw materials from land and sea, through fishing, mining, forestry, or planting, for example.

Rationalism: A belief that the means used to achieve our goals should be logically chosen on the basis of scientifically verified knowledge and information.

Religiousness: A belief in the supernatural causation and control of human affairs and, usually, an emphasis on otherworldly rewards.

Rising expectations: The desire for more resources, rewards, and recognition than one has and a belief in everyone's right to have these things.

Secondary sector: That part of an economy that involves the manufacture of machine-made products from raw materials provided by others.

Socialism: An economic system characterized by public ownership of income-producing property, cooperation, and equal distribution of wealth and income or distribution on the basis of need.

Subsistence economy: An economy in which goods and services provide only for local needs and there is little or no trading with other societies.

Tertiary sector: That part of an economy that involves providing services rather than producing goods or extracting natural resources.

Tolerance: An acceptance and respect for human physical and cultural differences.

White-collar crime: Crimes committed in work situations by people in the middle and upper social classes of industrialized societies.

Working class: People having the lowest level of resources, prestige, or power in a society, who work primarily with things and with manual skills.

PRACTICE TESTS

True ▪ False Test

___ 1. The major sources of energy in simple hunting and gathering societies are fire and human muscle power.

___ 2. Extreme economic inequality is a characteristic that has been common to all societal forms throughout human history.

___ 3. Herding societies have existed since hominids first appeared on earth.

___ 4. Landowning classes have traditionally had little interest or motivation in scientific or technological advance.

___ 5. In the secondary sector, people work in the manufacture of machine-made goods rather than in agriculture.

___ 6. Industrializing countries experience cultural diffusion.

___ 7. Fatalism is a belief most characteristic among industrialized societies.

___ 8. Canada and the United States have authoritarian governments.

___ 9. Ethnocentrism presumably decreases with higher levels of education.

___ 10. Cultural relativism and authoritarianism are compatible.

Multiple-Choice Test

___ 1. *Homo sapiens* first appeared approximately:
   a. 10,000 years ago.
   b. 100,000 years ago.
   c. 1 million years ago.
   d. 4 million years ago.

___ 2. Which of the following terms describes the ideal-type of the United States?
   a. socialism
   b. capitalism
   c. American Revolution
   d. secular

___ 3. For most of human history, people have lived in societies that may be termed:
   a. hunting and gathering.

b. horticultural.

c. pastoral.

d. agrarian.

___ 4. Collectively, societies that have no surplus goods are known as:
   a. preindustrial.
   b. industrial.
   c. subsistence economies.
   d. command economies.

___ 5. The use of nonhuman animal power for transportation first appeared in:
   a. industrializing societies.
   b. horticultural societies.
   c. simple hunting and gathering societies.
   d. advanced hunting and gathering societies.

___ 6. In a horticultural society, a relatively sudden spurt in population growth and social conflict would most likely be attributable to the:
   a. institution of socialism.
   b. institution of democracy.
   c. ability to utilize harder metals such as copper and bronze.
   d. capacity to produce an economic surplus.

___ 7. The technological invention that brought about the development of the first agricultural societies was the:
   a. smelter.
   b. plow.
   c. ability to create fire.
   d. windmill.

___ 8. In barter societies, people:
   a. exchange services/goods.
   b. become more socially egalitarian.
   c. usually own property.
   d. rely on their communication skills.

___ 9. All of the following are common characteristics of industrialized societies *except:*
   a. vastly increased economic resources.
   b. a high level of occupational specialization.
   c. rapid and constant social change.
   d. increased economic inequality.

___ 10. In egalitarian societies, economic, political, and social opportunities are based on:
   a. inherited wealth.
   b. gender.

c. personal qualifications.

d. racial origin.

Matching Test

Match each concept with its definition, illustration, or explication below.

1.

__ (1) *Homo sapiens* appeared

__ (2) Industrial Revolution

__ (3) Hominids appeared

__ (4) Agricultural Revolution

__ (5) Invention of the plow

a. 250 years ago

b. 6,000 years ago

c. 10,000 years ago

d. 100,000 years ago

e. 4 million years ago

2.

__ (1) Hypothetical constructions

__ (2) Economic system

__ (3) Earliest societies

__ (4) Herding societies

__ (5) Simple hunting and gathering

a. Hunting and gathering

b. Pastoral

c. Ideal-types

d. Hominids

e. Socialism

3.

__ (1) Advanced agricultural

__ (2) Horticultural

__ (3) Agricultural

__ (4) Advanced hunting and gathering

__ (5) Advanced horticultural

a. Plow

b. Iron

c. Bow and arrow

d. Digging stick

e. Use of metal

4.

__ (1) Primary sector

__ (2) Secondary sector

__ (3) Tertiary sector

__ (4) Small economic surplus

__ (5) No economic surplus

a. Horticultural societies

b. Industrial societies

c. Hunting and gathering societies

d. Agricultural societies

e. Postindustrial societies

5.

__ (1) Activism

__ (2) Familism

__ (3) Rationalism

__ (4) Fatalism

__ (5) Ethnocentrism

a. Belief in destiny

b. Intolerance of "others"

c. Achievement motivation increases

d. Needs of the family

e. Logical goals

REVIEW QUESTIONS

1. What are the major types of human societies and approximately when, in human history, did they come into existence?
2. On what basis do we classify contemporary societies as agricultural, industrializing, industrial, or postindustrial?
3. What do hunting and gathering and horticultural societies have in common and how do they differ?
4. What are three major sociocultural changes that occur in agricultural societies? Why do they occur?
5. What are the major distinguishing sociocultural characteristics of industrial societies?
6. How did colonization and the values of the Protestant Reformation promote the Industrial Revolution in Europe?
7. What are the basic characteristics of socialism (planned economies), capitalism (market economies), and mixed economies? Give examples of each type of economy in contemporary societies.
8. How and why do postindustrial societies differ from industrial societies in terms of civilian employment in primary, secondary, and tertiary sectors of the economy?
9. What are the major value changes in industrial societies? Give examples of each.
10. Why do specific urban values become more widespread in industrial societies, especially activism, individualism, egalitarianism, and rationalism?
11. What does the concept of "rising expectations" help explain?

APPLYING SOCIOLOGY

1. Think of some technological inventions that have occurred during your lifetime. How have these inventions changed your life?
2. How would you rate your own values on a scale from traditional to urban? Look specifically at the following:
   a. your goals and expectations.
   b. the means that you use to achieve your goals.
   c. your relationships with family, friends, authority figures (teachers, employers, and parents).
3. Compare your values with those of your parents and, if possible, your grandparents. To what extent has there been a shift from traditional to urban values in three generations?
4. To what extent can you explain the role conflicts you experience in your relationships with family, friends, and authority figures in terms of differences that arise from traditional or urban values?

Urbanization, Population, Environment

One of the major trends in sociocultural evolution is the rise and spread of cities and city life. Social scientists, literary figures, and others who have thought and written about the city have often done so in love-hate terms. Cities are described as centers of opportunity, learning, commerce, creativity, entertainment, excitement, and freedom from traditional values and restraints. But cities are also identified with crisis, bankruptcy, crime, poverty, ghettos, riots, pollution, loneliness, anonymity, and impersonality. In fact, there is some truth in both of these portraits. Let us review for a moment how the different images of cities came about. We will then better understand the problems of cities today, as well as their possible future throughout the world.

179

SOCIOCULTURAL EVOLUTION AND URBANIZATION

The shift of populations from rural areas to cities and their surrounding areas is known as **urbanization**. **Cities** are relatively dense, permanent concentrations of people who engage in manufacturing or service activities rather than food production. By definition, cities cannot arise until after the invention of planting and the existence of a food surplus in human societies.

Preindustrial Cities

The oldest cities are known as **preindustrial cities** because they arose before the Industrial Revolution (Sjoberg, 1960). Most early preindustrial cities date back to between 5,000 to 6,000 years ago, although archaeologists date the city of Jericho to at least 10,000 years ago (Mellaart, 1964). In their original form, preindustrial cities were small, densely populated, and surrounded by walls, with narrow streets designed for traveling on foot. The centers contained palaces, temples and other religious buildings, and storage facilities for food. The main marketplace, operated by less-privileged citizens, was usually located outside the protection of the city walls. The earliest cities arose along trade routes, in areas where trade routes crossed, or near rivers and other bodies of water that could be used for transporting goods into and out of the city easily.

The first cities contained crafts workers, artists, and other specialized workers as well as soldiers, administrators, clergy, and the hereditary ruling elite and their servants (Childe, 1951; Sjoberg, 1960; Trigger, 1985). Soldiers were necessary to protect residents, goods, and supply and trade routes. Government administrators coordinated the activities of the military in providing protection and maintaining social control. They also supervised tax collection and the building of public works such as city walls, temples, and pyramids.

Religious beliefs provided support for the rule of the elite and their rights, privileges, and enormous wealth. In the earliest cities, religious leaders and political rulers were of the same class, often from the same family. Political rulers were sometimes considered the earthly incarnation of the gods, or at least their representatives in worldly pursuits. In these societies, state and church were fused, a phenomenon known as **theocracy.**

Temple priests in the Middle East invented writing about 5,000 years ago (Childe, 1951). Writing enabled the governing elite to keep track of taxes and debts owed and paid. Literacy was largely confined to the priestly class in the oldest cities, however, because writing was very complicated and time consuming to learn. It was considered an art form, and books were religious art objects.

The earliest cities were far more unstable and vulnerable than cities in the most advanced agricultural societies. They grew or declined in population and were sometimes destroyed by changing environmental conditions, plagues, or foreign invasion. Those cities that survived and grew in size were characterized by extreme segregation on the basis of occupational specialization. Guilds, the forerunners of modern labor unions, protected and controlled recruitment and rewards in the specialized occupations. Neither prices nor goods were standardized with respect to cost or quality.

Prices for the same products varied with the particular buyer and seller; prices were not marked. Handmade products varied in quality according to the varying skills of individual crafts workers. There was little concern about time, and work schedules were irregular. Contact with and information about the outside world was limited.

Industrial Cities

Cities as we know them today could not exist without certain advances in transportation, communication, food storage and preservation, and sanitation and public health. Widespread urbanization could not take place in human societies until the Industrial Revolution (Childe, 1951, 1964). Supporting huge non-food-producing populations adequately involves certain requirements: (1) a highly mechanized agriculture and a very large food surplus; (2) efficient and dependable techniques for transporting food by land, sea, and air; (3) a knowledge of canning, refrigeration, and the chemistry of food preservation; and (4) sufficient knowledge of the causes of disease and the techniques of sanitary sewage disposal to prevent devastating epidemics and plagues.

Industrial cities, by comparison with preindustrial cities, occupy larger geographic areas and contain a larger proportion of the society's population. Streets are wider, transportation is better, and communication is faster. Manufacturing, financing, and marketing operations overshadow political and religious institutions in most industrial cities. Trade and communication networks are worldwide. The middle class and the service sector increase. Working-class unions come into existence and slowly expand their base into the middle class.

In industrial societies, segregation is more often on the basis of class and ethnic origin than of occupational specialization. Products and prices are standardized. Time and the passage of time become very important (Melbin, 1978). Work schedules are regular. The masses are literate, use a standardized language in all regions of the society, and are exposed to the mass media (radio, movies, television, newspapers, books, and magazines).

TABLE 6.1

Preindustrial and Industrial Cities

	Preindustrial Cities	*Industrial Cities*
Cultural focus	Political, religious, commercial centers	Commercial, service, manufacturing centers
Physical configuration	Small, walled, densely populated	Large, sprawling, geographically expanding
Transportation and communication	Poor internal and external facilities	International facilities
Segregation of population	Mainly by occupation	Primarily on basis of race/ethnicity
Class structure	Rigid	Open; possible to move up or down
Size of middle class	Small	Large
Level of economic inequality	Extreme	Moderate by comparison to preindustrial cities
Economic resources, forms of wealth	Land the major economic resource (and form of wealth)	Factories the major means of production; money and securities (stocks, bonds) the major forms of wealth
Labor organizations	Workers organized into guilds	Some workers organized into national labor unions
Standardization	Products not standardized with respect to quality	Products standardized
Setting of prices	Bargaining for price	Prices standardized
Work schedules	Irregular, but long	Standardized
Level of literacy, media development	Widespread illiteracy	Mass literacy, mass media
Political and religious authority	Religious and political leadership fused	Religion and government separate institutions

URBANIZATION IN THE UNITED STATES

The tremendous increase in the rate and extent of urbanization in modern times has given rise to new concepts for classifying geographic areas on a scale from rural to urban. In the United States, the Bureau of the Census defines a city as any politically independent area with a population of 2,500 or more people. Recognizing that arbitrary numbers do not a city make, the bureau uses the concept of **Metropolitan Statistical Area (MSA)** or, more simply, metropolitan area for collecting data on urban life. MSAs are areas containing a central city of 50,000 or more, surrounded by a population linked to the city by communication and transportation networks and economic, recreational, or other service ties.

The areas surrounding central cities are known as **suburbs**. Approximately three-quarters of the population of the United States lives in an MSA, with slightly more living in suburban areas than in the central cities (Frey, 1990).

In postindustrial societies, many densely populated metropolitan areas have grown to such an extent that they have virtually merged with one another geographically to form a **megalopolis.** The most dramatic examples of this trend are the Ruhr Valley region in Germany and the section of the U.S. East Coast from Boston to Virginia.

In the past 200 years, the United States has experienced a major shift of its population from farms to cities. In 1790, when the first census was taken, 95 percent of the population lived on farms. In the 1990s, this figure has declined to 1.9 percent (*Statistical Abstract of the United States,* 1992, Table 1073). Farmers (2.4 percent of the civilian workforce in 1990) produce more than enough food to feed not only the urban population in the United States, but also urban populations in many other parts of the world. The U.S. government has paid farmers not to produce even more food at times when market conditions were unfavorable, so that prices and profit levels could be maintained.

Urban Growth and Change

Sociologists have attempted to construct models of urban growth based on human ecology. **Ecology** is the study of the relationship of living organisms to their environment. Human ecology, as applied to urban growth, refers to the movement of peoples and their interaction with both the natural environment and the technologically created environment, which includes roads, railroads, office buildings, and factories.

In ecological studies of lower animal forms, competition, natural selection, and interdependence are basic concepts. In human ecology, these and other concepts have been used to describe changing patterns of land use in and around cities that reflect relationships between humans and their urban environment. **Centralization** is the tendency for similar structures and activities to be concentrated in specialized areas or centers. Centralization is physically convenient, up to a point, and is good for business. In New York City, Wall Street, Madison Avenue, and Broadway are all examples of centralization.

In recent years, there has been a tendency for industry, stores, and offices to move out of central cities into less costly, less congested areas, a phenomenon known as **decentralization.** The most visible examples of it have been the decline of department stores in the central business districts of large cities and the rise of suburban shopping malls.

Segregation refers to the tendency for people of the same ethnic origins or religion to live near one another. Segregation is involuntary when it is a result of discrimination or poverty. It may also be voluntary, however, when affluent members of religious or ethnic minority groups choose to live in a segregated wealthy area, sometimes referred to as a "gilded ghetto." These groups live together because minority neighbors and reference groups share the same disadvantages with respect to tolerance or acceptance by the wider society. They avoid the slights and hurts that occur in interactions with those outside the group.

Harlem in New York City, the Watts section of Los Angeles, and the Black Belt in Chicago are well-known examples of involuntary segregation. The term **ghetto** was first used in American sociology by Louis Wirth (1928) to refer to segregated Jewish communities. The word is Italian and originally referred to the segregated Jewish quarter of Rome. Since the 1960s, the term has been used to refer to all segregated racial, ethnic, or religious communities within cities. Ghettos are not necessarily slums, and it is important to distinguish between the two. The Sugar Hill section of Harlem is a "gilded ghetto" within a ghetto.

A **slum** is an urban area characterized by very high rates of poverty and unemployment, overcrowding, and deteriorated housing and public facilities. The inhabitants of ghettos may be rich or poor; the inhabitants of slums are poor, or near-poor.

The terms **invasion** and **succession** have also been used by urban sociologists to describe neighborhood change in large cities. Invasion occurs when activities or people with new and different social and economic characteristics, such as ethnic origin or economic class level, enter a neighborhood for the first time. Succession refers to the total or almost total replacement of the original population and activities by the new population or newer types of activities.

Though the decline of neighborhoods as a result of invasion and succession usually receives more publicity, neighborhoods may also rise in prestige and property values as a result of unplanned trends in invasion and succession. The earlier, less well off inhabitants of Greenwich Village in New York City have been largely displaced by successful professionals, intellectuals, and business executives. A similar process has occurred in the Haight-Ashbury section of San Francisco and the Historic Hill section of Newport, Rhode Island. In Miami, Florida, slum areas have been converted into middle-class neighborhoods by middle-class Cuban refugees.

In the process known as **gentrification**, middle- or upper-class people invade slum areas to buy and rehabilitate decaying or abandoned houses.

They are urban homesteaders, pioneers in brick and cement jungles. Usually they have no children or are affluent enough to be able to send their children to private schools outside the slum area. Local residents in gentrifying neighborhoods do not oppose the invasion of the middle class. They are eventually forced to move, however, because they cannot afford the higher rents that result from rising land values and property taxes.

Since the 1980s, middle-class African Americans have in large numbers fled to the less prosperous suburbs surrounding large central cities (O'Hare et al., 1991). Usually, these suburbs are large satellite cities located on the borders of central cities; examples include Evanston, outside of Chicago, and New Rochelle, outside of New York City. They are not protected from invasion by any ecological barriers such as parks or highways.

The term gentrification was coined by the displaced English poor and working class to describe the takeover of their neighborhoods in London by well-off young professionals, the modern gentry. This trend has been going on in the major cities of Europe for some time. It is now becoming apparent in the United States in many larger, older cities.

The new elite of doctors, lawyers, architects, and business executives have brought with them stores and entertainment facilities. Boutiques, nightclubs, chic restaurants, sidewalk cafes, gourmet and natural food stores, bookstores, and shops offering antiques, art, crafts, and foreign imports cater to the needs of the new inhabitants. Mom-and-pop stores and soul food and take-out restaurants (and the customers who patronize these places) are departing.

Most of the new urban property owners are already residents of the city and are simply remaining in the city rather than investing in homes in the suburbs. There has not been a massive return to the city by middle-aged or older suburbanites whose children are grown; they are aging in place (Frey, 1990). The number of poor people, minorities, and older people being displaced by upper-middle-class whites varies in different cities. But there has been a significant invasion and succession of this kind, although it seems to be slowing in the United States in recent years.

Many of the young people coming into or remaining in the cities grew up in the suburbs. They reject what they perceive as the boredom, isolation, and homogeneity of the wealthier suburbs. They are the postwar baby boom generation, more likely to delay or forgo marriage, or be divorced. The city is more hospitable to singles.

Other factors have also contributed to the preference of younger people for the city. Co-ops, condominiums, and older brownstones located in decaying neighborhoods of large cities are usually a better buy than single-family homes in the suburbs. In addition, constantly increasing automobile traffic has made commuting more stressful and time consuming. The cost of gasoline and garage space has soared.

Finally, the problems of the cities have spread to the suburbs. The crime rate in suburban areas is now rising faster than in central cities. And many successful suburban professionals and business executives are sending their children to private schools in the suburbs to escape problems of drug abuse and violence that are becoming increasingly prevalent in suburban public schools.

Major retail stores, office buildings, and supermarkets are beginning to return to some central cities. Inexpensive farmland on the outskirts of expanding suburbs is becoming scarce, particularly in megalopolitan areas. But, values as well as economic factors underlie this return to the city. Affluent young people prefer the city for all activities, including shopping. They are good customers for retail goods such as clothing and household items.

Cities and Suburbs

The movement of the middle class back into the cities has been a mere trickle compared to the massive wave of middle-class flight from cities to suburbs. The return of the middle class may become highly significant in the future of cities, however, especially in cities that are deindustrializing and are increasingly specialized in recreational, commercial, or political activities. Some of these cities, most recently Miami, are attracting international settlers (Sassen and Portes, 1993). They are becoming high-income enclaves of the national and international hereditary rich, the newly rich (entertainment and sports celebrities), and international business and professional elites.

Low-income people, with low levels of skill and training, are fleeing to the bordering suburbs, following the lower-skilled jobs that are now more often located in these suburbs. These older, more diverse, and less affluent and politically active suburbs contain cheaper, deteriorating housing that can be broken up and converted into cheaper rentals for the newer, poorer arrivals. Competition for space, economics, and cultural values are the primary variables affecting urban ecological change. Economic factors are important in determining where people live, work, play, and invest. But values are also an important factor. Financially hard-pressed city governments will sometimes preserve tax-free historical parks and landmarks in high-rent areas despite a desperate need for income-producing structures. Members of second- and third-generation Italian American families will continue to live near one another in deteriorating city neighborhoods, even though they could afford to live elsewhere. Familism is an important value in this subculture (Squier and Quadagno, 1988).

Clearly, large cities cannot exist when the natural environment makes the construction or maintenance of transportation and communication facilities difficult. Jungles, deserts, polar regions, and mountainous areas usually do not have large cities. Cities have been located along trade routes and near bodies of water, as pointed out earlier. But urban growth is also affected by the necessity to skirt mountains, lakes, and marshes that cannot be drained and filled.

Many cities have lost population as they have been bypassed by major highways and railroads. Others have declined as industries and offices flee to other areas to escape high rents, high property taxes, local income taxes, congested streets, violent crime, or a combination of these conditions.

The tremendous growth of suburbs, especially since World War II, is one of the most striking features of urbanization in the United States. From the 1970s to the mid-1980s, the largest metropolitan areas experienced a decline in population, however. Here, again, technological advances and economics are basic factors that determine how many people and which people can leave the city for the suburbs—and move to even more rural urbanizing areas beyond them known as **exurbs**. For those who can afford a choice between city and suburb, values are also important.

With each major technological advance in transportation in the nineteenth and twentieth centuries, from the horse-drawn carriage to the electric trolley or streetcar, to subways, modern commuter trains, and mass-produced automobiles, cities expanded where they could, and suburban areas increased in population. Improvements in the techniques of road building, bridge and tunnel construction, and federally sponsored highways encouraged this trend.

In the United States after World War II, the shortage of housing in central cities, the postwar economic and baby booms, new techniques for building cheaper, mass-produced housing, and the ready availability of low-interest mortgages from the Federal Housing Authority and the Veterans Administration almost emptied the central cities of middle-class families with young children. Over the years, and especially from 1970 to the mid-1980s, many industries, stores, and offices followed the middle classes to the suburbs, skimming the taxpaying economic cream from the central cities (Frey, 1990). What is left now, largely, are the very rich, the masses of poor or working-class minorities, artists, students, writers, intellectuals, professionals, single people who work in the city, white ethnics (Italian Americans, for example), the aged, the downwardly mobile, the chronically unemployed, and the homeless.

Suburban residents frequently work or continue to use recreational and mass-transit facilities in the central cities, although many more are now commuting to work between suburbs rather than into central cities (Frey, 1990). They do not usually support the city with their taxes, although there are movements to change this in some areas of the country.

Economic and Political Problems of Cities

The changing economic and population base of central cities as business, industry, and the white middle class have left is a major reason for the economic problems of many large cities in the United States today. Reductions in federal spending on public housing and social services during the 1980s have added to the toll, especially as this has helped to create large homeless populations. Huge federal government cutbacks in subsidies for public works during the 1980s have led to serious decay in the **infrastructure**—the roads, bridges, tunnels, waterworks, and sewerage systems—of the largest cities (O'Hare, 1990).

The poor cannot pay adequate taxes to support the greater need they have for social services of all kinds. They cannot support the increased fire and police protection, medical care, day care, and welfare that multiproblem, impoverished populations require. Many migrants to large cities have arrived with few skills, usually from rural areas in the United States or from impoverished areas in other countries. They arrive in search of jobs and economic opportunity. But they are arriving at a time when unskilled and semiskilled jobs have greatly declined as industries and retail businesses have left the large central cities. The situation worsens in the face of recessions, middle-class tax revolts, and persistent trade deficits and national debt in the United States.

The political problems of large cities in the United States reinforce the economic problems of these cities. The emphasis on local government and the norm of "community control" fragments political decision making and prevents the regional cooperation and coordination necessary to solve problems that are regional in scope. It subverts **urban planning**—deliberate, rational attempts to direct and control urban change. Examples of central-city problems that are regional in their effects are congestion, crime, pollution, highway and mass-transit repairs, water supplies, and public utility failures.

Many older central cities are not even regarded as good places to visit (much less live in) anymore. Their centers are abandoned at night. Their slums are burned out, collapsing, and drug-, vice-, roach-, and rat-ridden. Their residents increasingly are victims of random violence (drug shootouts), carjackings, rapes, and murders. Their mayors apply for help to state legislatures, Congress, banks, and corporations, where they often make costly tax and aid compromises because they do not have more viable alternatives at the present time.

Urban Renewal

Urban renewal programs in the United States are an example of the invasion/succession process. They have been described as people-removal programs by minority urban leaders. Low-income people have been displaced by shopping and recreational centers, luxury apartment complexes, hotels, and office buildings that serve the middle and upper classes. The poor are driven to other blighted areas where their increased demand for housing increases their rent and their economic and psychological problems. Urban renewal has both beautified central cities and intensified the problems of the poor, particularly the minority poor.

Global Cities

Even as large industrial firms become increasingly global, or multinational, in their production operations, the headquarters of these firms tend to be increasingly centralized in what have been called **global cities** (Robertson, 1992; Sassen, 1993). New York, London, Frankfort, and Tokyo are global cities. As sites of commercial banks and investment firms, they are also centers of international finance (banking and securities trading), which grew three times as fast as world trade in the 1980s.

Global cities contain a concentration of high-tech business information services and experts in international law, accounting, and advertising to serve international corporations and investors. Global cities have long histories as banking, trading, and commercial centers. In the United States, New York, Chicago, San Francisco, and, now, Miami are among the cities defined as global or world cities (Sassen and Portes, 1993). In global cities around the world, the process of gentrification intensifies, as armies of high-income experts from postindustrial societies invade and take over local residential and commercial space. This is accompanied by increasing exclusion from jobs, housing, and other material comforts of low-income local populations, who do not have the skills and training to compete in the new market. Global cities are becoming like the earliest preindustrial walled cities that protected and insulated the richest and most-privileged members of their societies. But the new walls in global cities are made of money and high-tech skills, not stones and mortar.

The Future of Cities

If world population growth can be controlled in time, if the increased pollution of land, air, and water can be brought within tolerable limits in time, if the world supply of food and natural resources can be adequately maintained or supplemented in time, if atomic warfare and human destructiveness can be controlled effectively for all time, then scientific and technological development will be universal and the future will be urban. Farm workers will commute from urban areas to work on totally mechanized farms that will be operated like factories. Factories and information service industries will continue to spread out in all geographic areas, limited only by natural ecological barriers. And the gap between rural and urban areas in income, education, communication and recreational facilities, values, and material comforts, diminishing since the 1970s in the United States and other postindustrial societies, will disappear entirely.

The question is whether, when, and at whose expense these changes will occur. Which categories of people will have to suffer and for how long if industrialization and urbanization are to be accomplished throughout the world? The future of cities depends largely on the capacity and willingness of central governments in various societies to cooperate with each other, to plan rationally, to keep future human needs in mind, and to keep human greed for power and wealth sufficiently in check.

International planning and cooperation to promote industrialization in developing societies and restructuring in former socialist societies that are changing to market economies is growing, but is still inadequate. And awareness of the long-range dangers of overpopulation, famine, disease, environmental destruction, and large-scale conflict over scarce resources is dangerously inadequate.

The future of cities is intimately tied to the continuing spread of technological advances to the countryside and to developing countries. Technological advance is the great leveler. Even now, China, Hong Kong, South Korea, Singapore, and Taiwan are industrializing at a phenomenal pace (Greenhouse, 1993). But this process takes time. How much time depends very much on the willingness and ability of central governments in industrialized societies to help and to plan for the future, with an awareness of the long-range, international consequences of their short-range policies.

DEMOGRAPHY, ECONOMICS, AND VALUES

The human species has multiplied spectacularly in the past 250 years. Concern about the possible consequences of this growth for the quality and continuation of life on earth is increasing. Information about populations has become vital to planning for human needs now and in the future.

Social scientists who specialize in **demography** do statistical studies of human populations. They collect information about the size, rate and kind of growth, spatial distribution (urban and rural), and composition (age, ethnic origin, gender, religion) of populations in various societies. They provide data on **vital statistics**—birth, death, marriage, and divorce rates.

The **crude birth rate** is the number of live births per 1,000 people in a society in a particular year. The **fertility rate** is a more refined measure of the birth rate: the number of live births per 1,000 females from 15 to 44, the childbearing ages. The **total fertility rate** is the average number of children born per woman over a lifetime. The **death rate** is the number of deaths per 1,000 people in a given year.

Demographers also study **migration patterns.** Migration refers to both **immigration,** the movement of people *into* a society, and **emigration,** the movement of people *out of* a society. Internal migration is movement within a society from farms to cities, from cities to suburbs, from north to south, or the reverse. Population growth occurs when birth rates and immigration exceed death rates and emigration.

In the United States, demography is sometimes identified as a subfield of sociology because economic circumstances and values vary according to social location. Economics and values are basic factors in explaining demographic changes. If we want to explain and predict changes in human populations—in their size, geographic location, age, sex ratio, ethnic composition, and occupational and educational levels—we must locate these populations in physical, temporal, and cultural space.

Demographers study changes in birth rates, death rates, migration rates, and the consequences of these changes. They focus on the past or the present, on preindustrial, industrializing, and industrialized societies, and on urban and rural areas. They also study demographic changes among the classes, generations, racial/ethnic and religious groups. They then look primarily to changing economic factors and values to explain the demographic facts they record. Conflict theorists tend to place more weight on competition and changing economic opportunities; functionalists usually give more weight to values in their explanations of demographic change.

Generations, Economics, and Values

If we take one locating factor—age and generation—we can see clearly how changes in economic opportunities and values have affected birth, marriage, and divorce rates in the different generations in the United States. We can also see how changing demographic variables have affected economics.

The Depression Generation   All people born during the same period of time comprise what demographers call an **age cohort**. Age cohorts born in the United States during the Depression years were small in number (Elder, 1974). Primarily for economic reasons, the birth rate was lower than it had ever been. This generation came of age during the post–World War II era of economic prosperity. Unemployment was low. Jobs were readily available as the economy caught up with the demand for consumer products that was postponed during the war years. Competition from war-devastated European societies and Japan was limited.

There were fewer young adults to fill available jobs because of low birth rates during the Depression. Wages and salaries rose. Marriage and birth rates also rose sharply, promoted by economic affluence and the return of soldiers after the war. Housing was cheap and readily available. Mass-produced Levittown houses in Long Island, New York, were available for an easily financed $11,000 and a $100 down payment (Halberstam, 1993). The living was easy and the outlook was optimistic.

The Baby Boom Generation   The postwar baby boom from 1946 to 1964 produced the largest generation in the history of the United States (Bouvier and DeVita, 1991). It had a more difficult time, in certain respects, than the Depression-born generation. The baby boom generation generally experienced much less childhood poverty. But it also experienced far more overcrowding, understaffing (in schools, for example), and more extreme competition in achieving goals such as good grades, college admission, jobs, and promotions.

The older members of this generation, born between 1946 and 1954, shared in the economic affluence of the 1960s and early 1970s. The younger members of the generation, however, entered the job market at a time of recession and inflation. Their great number heightened youth unemployment and underemployment. Many young people took jobs for which they were overqualified. College graduates worked in clerical, sales, and blue-collar service and factory jobs. The greater demand for goods and services of this more populous generation, furthermore, reinforced inflationary trends in the 1970s and 1980s. Federal government cutbacks on social services in the 1980s diminished the availability of public service jobs.

Some demographers argue that per capita household income of baby boomers is actually higher than that of their parents, however, because of certain demographic adjustments they have made to lower earnings (Esterlin, Macdonald, and Macunovich, 1990). Baby boomers are more likely than their parents to have married late or remained unmarried, to have had few or no children, and to live in two-earner households.

The Current Young Adult Generation   Since 1960 the fertility rate in the United States has been declining more or less steadily, and it is now below replacement level (*Statistical Abstract of the United States,* 1992, Table 84; National Center for Health Statistics, 1993). Demographers define replacement level as the total fertility rate necessary for a generation to replace itself, excluding immigration and emigration. A similar trend toward below-replacement-level fertility has occurred in all postindustrial societies. A major reason for the declining fertility rate in these societies since the 1960s is the tremendous increase in the number of women in the labor force, especially married women (Cherlin and Furstenberg, 1988).

In postindustrial societies such as the United States, job expansion occurs mainly in clerical, sales, and other white-collar service occupations. Because of continuing sex segregation in many occupations, women are more likely than men to take lower-level service jobs when these jobs open up. The majority of women work primarily for economic reasons. They need and want the money they earn. They must help pay for the food they prepare. And women who work outside of the home usually value smaller families and have lower fertility rates than women who do not (Robey, Rutstein, and Morris, 1993).

Inflation and recurring recessions since 1973 and U.S. taxation policies in the 1980s, which hit the middle class hardest, have also promoted the increased employment of women. They created a greater need for two-income families. Purchasing power, measured in real wages (corrected for inflation) declined and continues to decline in the 1990s (Pollard, 1992). The greater economic independence of young women has been an important factor in the current tendency to delay marriage and childbearing, which also lowers the birth rate.

The young adult generation that is currently entering the labor market is not as easily labeled as the Depression and baby boom generations. Even though this generation is smaller in number because of lower birth rates in the 1970s (the "baby bust" or "birth dearth" years), its members are in competition with vast numbers of an older generation that got there first, are still relatively young, and are holding onto their jobs, if they can.

There are other major differences between today's 20- to 29-year-olds and those of approximately 20 years ago in the United States (Kalish, 1992). The economic climate—the enormous national debt and deficit, widespread layoffs in all sectors of the economy, slow economic growth—is far worse now. This generation is also much more ethnically diverse than previous generations. During the 1980s, about 8 million people immigrated to the United States legally (Gelfand and Yee, 1991). This is the second largest wave of immigration to the United States since the turn of the century. A majority of these immigrants were young adults.

Compared to the equivalent generation of 20 years ago, those currently in their 20s are also more likely to be college educated and single. They include more single mothers and more unmarried couples living together. A higher percentage are living at home (or with another relative) and are unemployed or underemployed (Newman, 1993). Members of this generation are earning less, in real wages, and they are less likely to own private homes.

Demographers tend to treat demographic variables such as changing birth and death rates as independent variables or basic causes. They are not. They are a reflection of more fundamental changes in economics, politics, and values, as well as of new scientific discoveries and technological advances. But demographic changes can be an important factor affecting the opportunities of different generations in a society at any given time.

DEMOGRAPHY AS A DISMAL SCIENCE

In recent years, some demographers and many social commentators, willingly or not, have become voices of future doom (Hardin, 1993; Brown, Kane, and Ayres, 1993). They record the enormous growth of human populations, they predict future growth as best they can, and they fear for the possible extinction of the human species. Their visions of a "standing room only" world, of poisoned or inadequate food, air, water, and energy supplies, and of uprisings by the famished against the overfed have spread and become part of the popular consciousness.

Malthus, Marx, Economics, and Values

This dismal vision has a long history in the social sciences. Thomas Robert Malthus (1766–1834), an economist, clergyman, and the father of 11 daughters, published his classic work *An Essay on the Principle of Population* (1798) not long after the beginning of the Industrial Revolution.

On the basis of a review of population changes in various societies in different stages of technological development, Malthus formulated the "principle of population": In the absence of any constraints, population increases geometrically, doubling every 25 years (1, 2, 4, 8, 16, etc.). The food supply, on the other hand, increases arithmetically (1, 2, 3, 4, 5, etc.) (Malthus, 1938 [1798], pp. 10–11). Population growth, therefore, outstrips the means of subsistence.

This "natural" tendency, according to Malthus, is curbed to some extent by "preventive checks" and "positive checks" (1938 [1798], pp. 12–19). Preventive checks are *voluntary* practices of "moral restraint" such as celibacy or delayed marriage (1938 [1798], pp. 259–261). As a clergyman, Malthus ruled out as immoral other voluntary restraints such as abortion, infanticide, and birth control. He could not even consider the possibility of voluntary sterilization, since the technique for this procedure was unknown in his time.

Positive checks are *involuntary* constraints on population growth that arise from "human misery," specifically the misery of war, disease, famine, and vice. Malthus regarded vice as a positive check insofar as it breaks up families and leads to illegitimacy and the neglect and death of children. Vice is voluntary, but its effects, usually, are involuntary.

In his overview of human societies, Malthus observed that positive checks become less prevalent in "civilized" societies. In the first edition of his work, he was doubtful that moral restraint, particularly among the poor, would increase sufficiently to compensate for the population growth that would occur as wars, disease, and famine continued to decline.

Malthus's essay went through seven editions, however, and toward the end of his life he became more optimistic about future population growth. He came to believe that moral restraint would spread, even among the urban poor in industrializing societies. As they become more educated, the poor in these societies would become more aware of how their "self-interest" would be better served by having smaller families (1938 [1798], pp. 259–261).

Karl Marx did not regard overpopulation as a cause of poverty. He blamed economic factors, principally the capitalist system of production, which exploits labor and promotes unemployment. He emphasized that un-controlled production for private profit cannot provide sufficient jobs for all, especially during the down phases of the business cycle. He also be-lieved that it was in the interest of capitalist economies to encourage surplus population, because this keeps the supply of labor up and the cost of labor down. Large populations also drive profits up by creating a greater demand for goods and services (Marx, 1906 [1867], pp. 689–710).

Marx believed that an economy in which human need was the basic standard for allocating jobs, goods, and services would eliminate the ne-cessity for population control. The original Marxian view has been modified in contemporary socialist societies. Shortly after the revolution in China, for example, Mao Zedong announced that "two hands can produce more food than one mouth can eat." Therefore, population control was unnecessary. It soon became apparent, however, that since not all hands produce food (city dwellers do not), and since there were many more mouths to feed in China than in other countries, it would be necessary to control population growth. China now has a more widespread program of contraception, sterilization, and abortion services than any other industrializing society and has reduced the birth rate to below replacement level (Haub, 1993).

The Soviet Union and other countries in Eastern Europe had fluctuat-ing population control policies between 1945 and 1990, depending on changing short-term military and labor needs. Since 1990, during a time of great upheaval and transition, Russia has experienced a sharp drop in its birth rate, as have some Eastern European societies.

Industrial democracies have also instituted population control pro-grams. Advances in technology have eliminated the need for huge armies of people in the fields and factories and on the battlefield. Values have changed, and many governments of industrial societies have assumed at least some of the responsibility for the health, education, and welfare of their citizens. The larger the population, the greater the cost of public serv-ices that must be provided. And welfare state services are costly to business and industry as well as to other sectors of industrial societies.

We now have much more information about population size and change in major types of societies than was available to Malthus and Marx. We also have many additional years of population change to analyze and explain. How have economic factors and values actually affected historical patterns of population change in various parts of the world? How have preventive and positive checks limited population growth, especially in the past 250 years?

SOCIOCULTURAL EVOLUTION AND POPULATION CHANGE

In nonliterate societies of the past, birth and death rates were very high. In hunting and gathering societies, life expectancy at birth was usually less than 30 years. Inadequate food supplies, disease, and accidents promoted premature aging and early death in most of these societies. Infant mortality rates were also very high. Frequently, 50 percent or more of the children born died within a year. Infanticide and abortion were widely practiced, especially if another child was born while the mother was still breast-feeding. There was no other source of food for young infants, no plastic bottles or packaged baby foods and formulas. A more stable food supply in horticultural societies promoted an increase in population, but birth and death rates remained high, and life expectancy continued to be low by modern standards.

In the earliest agricultural societies, population grew, but since most of the economic surplus was confiscated by the governing elite, this growth was limited (Lenski, 1966). The great frequency of wars, famine, and disease also kept population down. The first birth control devices were invented in these societies, as were practices such as celibacy and the legal limitation of the marriage rate, which also restricted population growth. Actually, the ancient world in Europe had safe, effective birth control techniques that were lost during the Middle Ages, another example of the effects of changing values (the shift to Christianity) on sociocultural evolution (Riddle, 1992).

Birth rates have always been very high in agricultural societies. Children are an economic asset and are highly valued as a source of cheap labor. Children work the fields and tend the herds. They do not have to be supported while they spend long years in school. They do not leave home to make their fortunes elsewhere. Like their parents, they are bound to the land. There is no retirement in agricultural societies, nor are there pensions or social security. In an economy in which machines have not replaced their labor, people keep working until they die. If parents get sick and cannot work, they rely on their children to support them. And the children do support their parents. Familism is a very strong value in agricultural societies.

In the absence of strong centralized governments and adequate police forces, the family in agricultural societies was in the past usually the only source of help for family members who experienced injury or injustice at the hands of others. The family protected its own. Blood revenge was family revenge. Concepts of femininity and masculinity were also tied to large numbers of children in agricultural societies. Children were visible proof of male virility (Lewis, 1959).

Inability to have children or failure to bear a son were the major reasons for divorcing a wife (and for higher rates of suicide among women) in Asia (Yorburg, 1974). A widow with a large number of older children was a good catch in agricultural societies. She brought willing workers with her into a new marriage.

The first dramatic spurt in population growth occurred in the West in the late eighteenth century after the beginning of the Industrial Revolu-

FIGURE 6.1

Projected World Population by Region, Central Scenario, 1990, 2030, and 2100

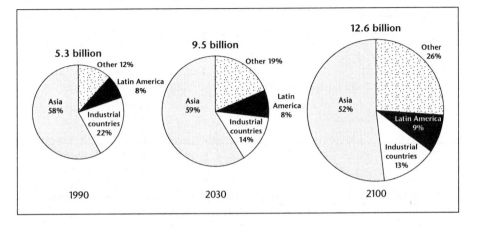

Sources: Population Reference Bureau, *Population Today,* 22(7) (July/August 1994), p. 3; Wolfgang Lutz, "The Future of World Population," *Population Bulletin* 49(1) (June 1994). Adapted by permission.

Societies that are now industrialized will decline as a proportion of world population over the next 100 years.

tion. Since then, the population of the earth has increased sixfold. At the present rate of growth (1.7 percent increase per year), world population, currently approximately 5.5 billion, is projected to reach 10.7 billion by 2030, almost double what it is now (Horiuchi, 1993). Ninety-five percent of this growth is expected to take place in the poorest and least technologically advanced countries of the world, which already have the youngest populations.

The initial dramatic increase in population after the Industrial Revolution occurred as advances in sanitation and food production reduced deaths from infectious diseases and starvation. Later, developments in scientific medicine also lowered deaths from infectious diseases, most dramatically after the invention of penicillin in 1928. Life expectancy increased sharply. Technological advances not only increased food supplies, but improvements in communication and transportation reduced the destructive effects of local famines. It became possible to ship food quickly to previously isolated areas. Wars as a check on population growth also declined as military technology improved and weapons became more costly and more complicated, as well as more deadly.

More recently, most checks on population growth have been voluntary, although they have applied methods of which Malthus would not have approved. Advances in medical science and technology have provided safe, simple, and effective contraceptive devices and have greatly simplified fe-

TABLE 6.2

The Demographic Transition

	Birth Rates	Death Rates	Type of Society
Stage 1	Very high	Very high	Agricultural
Stage 2	Very high	Lower than in stage 1	Industrializing
Stage 3	Low but fluctuating	Low and steady	Industrial

male as well as male sterilization procedures. Voluntary sterilization is now the world's most widely used contraceptive method.

The Demographic Transition

Demographers use the concept of the **demographic transition** to summarize the essential features of population change in Europe and North America since the Industrial Revolution. According to the demographic transition model, birth and death rates in the West have gone through three stages during the past 250 years (Chesnais, 1993).

Stage 1 existed before the Industrial Revolution. In this stage, birth and death rates were very high, averaging about 40 births and 40 deaths per 1,000 people per year. Population in most agricultural societies remained fairly stable because of this balanced ratio. Stage 2 occurred after the beginning of the Industrial Revolution. In this stage birth rates remained very high, but death rates began to decline. This occurred as initial advances in scientific knowledge (about sanitation) and technology (increased food supplies) reduced deaths from infectious diseases and starvation. As these involuntary population checks declined, population growth increased tremendously. It was this stage of population growth that concerned Malthus so much.

The birth rate began to decline slowly in stage 3 until a balance was reached between birth and death rates. The slowly declining birth rate in stage 3 was a result of changing values. This, in turn, was largely related to changing economic conditions and mass education, especially of women. At the same time, large numbers of children became less necessary to ensure the economic support of parents in their old age, since developments in sanitation and medicine enabled most children to survive into adulthood. More important, children became more of an economic burden than an economic asset in these urbanizing and industrializing societies.

Living quarters in urban centers were cramped. Education was costly. And there was less guarantee of an economic payoff from children in the form of support in old age. Children more frequently migrated to the cities in search of jobs and became less available to help and support their parents.

Contemporary industrialized societies are in stage 3 of the demographic transition (see Table 6.2). They are approaching **zero population growth**, stability in the size of their populations because of a balance between birth and death rates and immigration and emigration rates (Day, 1992). In the United States, death rates are low and steady, at about 10 per 1,000 people per year (National Center For Health Statistics, 1993). The total fertility rate in 1992 was 2.0, which is below replacement level because of a relatively high infant mortality rate among the poor. Even among women on welfare, the total fertility rate is below replacement level. Contrary to popular belief, the size of the average welfare family is declining (see Figure 6.2 on p. 200). The average number of children per mother is now 1.9. Birth rates of about 15 per 1,000 people are also low, but they have fluctuated slightly from generation to generation.

In democratic industrial societies, this fluctuation in birth rates relates primarily to changing values and economic and political conditions from one generation to the next (Esterlin et al., 1990). In the more authoritarian socialist societies (before the current shift to market economies), changes in birth rates were more influenced by government policy (Cherlin and Furstenberg, 1988). This seems to be changing. Russian society now has a birth rate of 10.7 per 1,000, but a death rate of 12.2 per 1,000 (*Population Today*, July/August 1993, p. 8). Russia and the Ukraine, among the most industrialized of the republics of the former Soviet Union, are now experiencing population decline.

Death rates level out and remain fairly steady in stage 3 because medical science conquers most infectious diseases (with the exception, now, of AIDS). Advances in life expectancy dwindle and life expectancy stabilizes, however, because new diseases usually come along to replace those that are conquered by medical advances. In addition, there are natural limits to life expectancy.

In 1900 the major causes of death in the United States were influenza and pneumonia. Life expectancy was 49.1 years. In 1993, the major causes of death in the United States were heart disease and cancer. Strokes and accidents were next in frequency. Influenza and pneumonia accounted for only a small number of all deaths.

Life expectancy in the United States is currently fairly stable at 75.5 years, with females outliving males by an average of about 7 years (U.S. Bureau of the Census, 1992, Table 103). AIDS is now the leading killer of black men aged 25 to 44 and the second-leading cause of death for white men in this age bracket (*New York Times,* September 1, 1993, p. A13).

FIGURE 6.2

The Total Fertility Rate of Women on Welfare

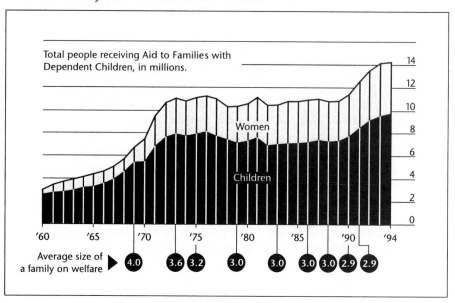

Source: *New York Times,* June 19, 1994, p. E4; based on figures from the House Ways and Means Committee, 1994. Used by permission.

The total fertility rate of women on welfare in the United States has been declining since the 1970s.

The Population Explosion

Most societies that are industrializing today in Asia, Africa, Latin America, and the Middle East are in stage 2 of the demographic transition. But there is a major difference between the experience of industrialization in these areas and the earlier experiences of Europe and North America (Chesnais, 1993). In contemporary industrializing societies, birth rates have remained very high, but death rates have been lowered much faster and more effectively. Medical and economic aid from technologically advanced societies is responsible for this rapid decline, although infectious diseases, parasites, and malnutrition continue to be the leading causes of death. Life expectancy is also suddenly much higher, although it is about 25 years lower on average than in industrialized societies.

The changes in values that led to a decline in the birth rate in the West took place over a period of more than 250 years, however. These values are not changing fast enough in present-day industrializing societies to keep pace with the abrupt decline in the death rate (Chesnais, 1993).

FIGURE 6.3

Life Expectancy for World Regions, 1994

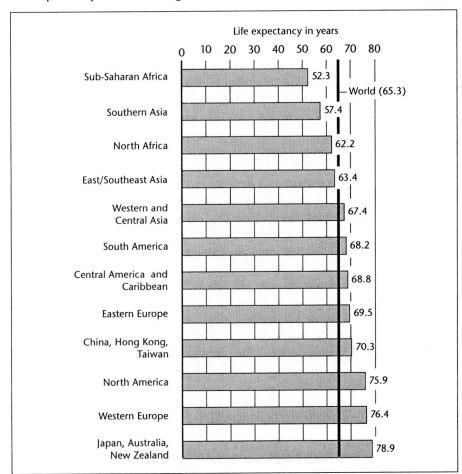

Source: Population Reference Bureau, *Population Bulletin 49*(1) (June 1994); based on figures from *1994 World Population Data Sheet.* Used by permission.

The geographic areas with the highest life expectancy levels generally have the lowest fertility rates, as shown in Figure 6.4 on page 202. Life expectancy figures are lower in North America than in other industrial societies, largely because of higher infant mortality rates in the United States.

The result is a cultural lag (by Western standards) that has resulted in extremely rapid population increases in these countries. Western demographers have referred to this increase as the **population explosion.**

Most societies that are now industrializing are experiencing severe problems because urbanization and population growth are proceeding faster

FIGURE 6.4

Total Fertility Rates for World Regions, 1994

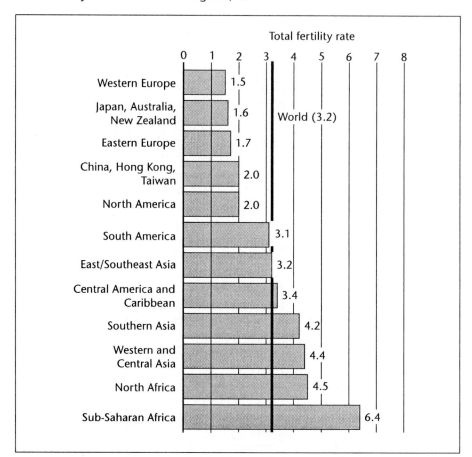

Source: Population Reference Bureau, *Population Bulletin 49*(1) (June 1994); based on figures from *1994 World Population Data Sheet.* Used by permission.

Total fertility rates vary widely in various parts of the world, depending very largely on differences in government policy and the persistence of traditional values. High fertility rates combined with lower life expectancies in industrializing societies result in populations that are "bottom heavy" with young people.

than technological advances in agriculture and industry. These societies, especially in Africa and the Middle East (with the exception of Israel), have experienced tremendous population growth. They have imported the medical advances of more technologically developed societies. At the same time, total fertility rates vary between 4 and 6 children per woman (Robey, Rutstein, and Morris, 1993). The agricultural and industrial sectors of these countries cannot as yet support this tremendous population growth. It is easier and cheaper to import antibiotics than it is to import tractors and manufacturing equipment and the knowledge of how to operate machines.

Most contemporary industrializing societies want to industrialize as quickly as possible. But the efforts of these societies are hampered by the necessity to divert much of their increasing agricultural resources into feeding their burgeoning populations. They do not have enough of a surplus to purchase the vast quantities of tools and machinery necessary to speed industrialization. Furthermore, much of the economic aid they receive from industrialized societies is used to build up military strength, or is diverted to secret bank accounts in other countries by corrupt authoritarian leaders.

Future Population Growth

Even if values change more quickly than expected and modern birth control devices are widely adopted, most currently industrializing societies will probably experience huge population increases in the near future. The population profiles of these societies are bottom heavy with young people. In most industrializing societies in Africa and the Middle East, approximately one-half of the population is under 20 (Horiuchi, 1993; Roudi, 1993; Omran and Roudi, 1993). When these young people reproduce, they will produce greater numbers of infants, even if they limit their families to two or three children. About one-third of married women in currently industrializing societies (not counting China) use contraceptives (Robey, Rutstein, and Morris, 1993).

In the Middle East, the total population is expected to double within the next 30 years, even if total fertility rates go down to half of current levels (Omram and Roudi, 1993). Women are achieving greater literacy, are marrying at a later age, and are more likely to be employed in the nonfamily economy in some countries. But there has also been an upsurge in Islamic fundamentalism in these societies, which is opposed to the changing status and roles of women. The changing condition of women will play a crucial part in the region's demographic future, as it will, for that matter, in other industrializing societies. Industrialized societies will continue to experience much slower population growth (Day, 1992). They have an aging population because life expectancy has been high and the birth rate low for some time. Fewer people are now entering the reproductive ages, and for those who do, family planning is far more widespread and acceptable than it used to be. The United States ranks 14th in the use of contraceptives among 29 of the more industrialized societies (Camp, 1992). This is believed to be one reason why adolescent pregnancy rates are higher in the United States than in other advanced industrial societies.

Predicting the future of global population growth is like taking an inkblot test: we each see what we want (or hope) to see. Sociobiologists tend to view human adaptation as a long-term evolutionary process with extinction as the inevitable result of the natural order of things. They believe extinction will come as a consequence of changes in the natural environment. Social scientists are more likely to emphasize the advantage of humans as inventive, tool-making animals over other animals in the long-term evolutionary struggle for survival. For this reason, social scientists tend to be more optimistic. They are more likely to assume that advances in science and technology will protect the environment and provide substitutes for necessary natural resources before they are depleted as world population doubles—and even beyond.

SOCIOCULTURAL EVOLUTION AND THE ENVIRONMENT

Scientific and technological developments in the past have been evaluated in terms of increased control over the environment. But as societies become highly industrialized and urbanized, the basic human challenge shifts from control over the environment to the preservation of that environment. Technological development has had many latent consequences. Larger concentrations of people and industries in metropolitan areas produce huge amounts of waste and a great drain on irreplaceable resources. We are now in a position to destroy our surroundings and ourselves by pollution, global ozone depletion and warming, exhaustion of nonrenewable natural resources, and destruction of our natural environment through soil erosion, deforestation, nuclear waste, and the poisoning of rivers, lakes, and oceans.

World population is increasing by about 100 million people a year (Horiuchi, 1993). At the same time, grain and beef production and supplies of fish and seafood are declining, the spread of irrigated land is declining, and the use of additional fertilizers in advanced industrial societies currently does little to raise output. Tens of millions of people in nonindustrialized societies live in poverty, misery, and starvation or near-starvation, and their numbers are growing.

Increasingly, they press against the borders of wealthier societies. Exclusion laws, additional guards, barbed wire, and guns are no solution to the problem. They do not work in the long run. Assisting poor countries with family planning and education (especially for women, who make up about three-quarters of the world's illiterate population) does work. Economic and technical aid to poorer countries that is used to increase economic productivity, fulfill basic human needs, and provide security in old age also works.

In the past, a major threat to continued human existence has been war and human conflict and destructiveness. But now, we must add the threats created by scientific and technological advances and population

Focus on Social Issues

THE LATENT FUNCTIONS OF TECHNOLOGICAL DEVELOPMENT

[Advances in scientific knowledge and technology have resulted in a number of unintended consequences that threaten the natural environment and the survival of the human species. Among these are increased population pressures, the depletion of natural resources, the poisoning of land, sea, and air by industrial products and by-products, and the possibility of world destruction by atomic weaponry. In 1989, an Exxon Corporation oil tanker ran aground and spilled millions of gallons of oil in Prince Edward Sound, with disastrous consequences for both wildlife and human life in the area.]

It is 9:32 last Thursday morning and Otter 76 is fighting for her life. She is pinned to a makeshift operating table in a clammy elementary school gym, lungs scored by petroleum poisons. She rattles and gasps, slow spasms rolling up in waves from her hind flippers to her bewiskered snout. She foams at the mouth and she excretes crude oil. It takes four men to hold her down. . . .

Otter 76 is one of hundreds of otters plucked from Prince Edward Sound since Exxon Corp.'s tanker, the *Exxon Valdez*, ran aground March 24 and smeared the sound's emerald waters with 10 million gallons of oil. Of those otters, only 134 made it alive into the improvised otter rescue center set up here in gym by a patchwork crew of top marine mammal experts, volunteer animal lovers, and hired hands. Their struggles to keep dying otters alive are desperate, touching, occasionally maybe even heroic.

—Charles McCoy, "Heartbreaking Fight Unfolds in Hospital for Valdez Otters," *Wall Street Journal,* January 20, 1989, p. A1

What Do You Think?

1. What are the major sources of global environmental pollution today?
2. What are possible solutions to this problem?
3. Do you think these solutions will come in time? Why or why not?

growth that the planet may not be able to sustain. Will scientists be able to invent additional sources of energy and techniques for preserving the air, soil, and water and supplementing the food supply soon enough? Will those who have political and economic power everywhere in the world agree to cooperate unselfishly in a rational, worldwide planning program? Will these leaders be able to control human destructiveness and maintain necessary levels of goods and services for vastly increasing numbers of better-educated people with higher expectations?

The answer is more a matter of personal optimism or pessimism than the possibilities of exact scientific prediction. Optimists have pointed to the leveling of population growth in the two largest societies in the world—India and China—as a hopeful sign for future population trends in other currently industrializing societies. In November 1993, 97 countries around the world signed an agreement to phase out the manufacture of industrial chemicals that deplete the earth's protective ozone layer. By August 1993, this destruction had slowed substantially and recovery in the ozone layer is expected to begin by the year 2000 (Stevens, 1993). For now, we can identify trends and possible solutions to population and environmental issues and, depending on our general outlook, expect the worst or live in hope.

Study Guide

REVIEW OBJECTIVES

After studying this chapter, you should be able to:

1. Explain how sociocultural evolution has affected city growth and city life.
2. Describe the basic concepts used by sociologists to describe and explain the shift from rural to urban life.
3. Examine the major trends and problems of urban life in the United States today.
4. Discuss the dysfunctions of urban renewal and why urban planning in the United States has failed to meet human needs and solve environmental problems.
5. Assess the possible future of cities, given the global trends in human social life that seem most likely to continue.
6. Describe some basic concepts used in the study of human populations.
7. Explain how technological advances have affected population growth in the West.
8. Analyze the reasons for the current population explosion in industrializing societies.
9. Discuss how sociocultural evolution affects the environment.

SUMMARY

1. Cities could not arise until after the invention of planting and the achievement of a food surplus. They could not grow and become widespread until technological and scientific advances occurred in the areas of transportation, communication, food storage

and preservation, sanitation, and public health.

2. Compared to preindustrial cities, industrial cities are larger, less isolated, more specialized in occupations, and segregated on the basis of class and ethnic origin rather than occupation. In advanced industrial societies, trade and communication become worldwide and service occupations predominate.

3. In the United States about three-quarters of the population lives in Metropolitan Statistical Areas. After World War II, the shortage of city housing, economic affluence, the high birth rate, mass-produced cheaper housing, and low-interest government mortgages attracted many families (middle and working class and white) to the suburbs. Retail stores, offices, and factories followed. The concentration of impoverished minorities and the aged in central cities increased. The tax base eroded as the need for social services increased.

4. In the 1990s the trend continues. Many of the largest central cities, especially in the North, are losing population. Middle-class white flight continues, but the poor (white and nonwhite) are also leaving in search of jobs or rents they can afford. Urban problems such as high crime rates and drug abuse are spreading to the suburbs.

5. At the same time, in a number of central cities in the United States (and Europe), upper-middle-class professionals and business executives are remaining and investing in city housing in larger numbers. Large retail stores and office buildings (but not factories) are returning. This may, eventually, even out the many differences between cities and suburbs in economic and political problems and in the quality of life. Certain cities, called global cities, contain a concentration of international banks and investment firms, offices of multinational corporations, and experts in law, advertising, accounting, and information firms that serve them.

6. Industrialization and urbanization could be universal in the future if certain threats to continued human existence are brought under control in time. These threats are overpopulation, famine, the exhaustion of natural resources, the destruction of the environment by pollution and erosion, and the destruction of the human population by nuclear warfare.

7. If these various problems are solved or kept under control, the future of all societies will be urban and industrial. Urban-rural differences in income, education, transportation, communication and recreational facilities, values, and material comforts will continue to diminish and, eventually, disappear. This will not occur, however, unless central governments everywhere agree to cooperate and plan to resolve world economic and environmental problems rationally, and soon.

8. Demography is the study of the size, distribution, and composition of populations in various societies. Demographers focus primarily on birth, death, marriage, divorce, and migration rates and factors such as economics and values that affect these rates.

9. Malthus was one of the first social thinkers to attempt to analyze population growth scientifically. He identified voluntary and involuntary checks on population growth and gave the greatest weight to values in explaining and predicting population trends. Marx and his followers gave more weight to economics. They did not view population growth as a problem, except insofar as capitalism is unable to support this growth.

10. In preindustrial societies, population grew very slowly with the shift from hunting and gathering, to horticultural, to agricultural economies. The demographic transition model refers to major changes in birth and

death rates in the West since the beginning of the Industrial Revolution.

11. The current population explosion in industrializing countries is a result of a large imbalance between persisting very high birth rates and a sharp drop in death rates as medical advances are imported from industrial societies.

12. The rate of world population growth in the future will depend on how quickly currently industrializing nations are able to complete the industrializing process and bring their birth rates into balance with their death rates. This, in turn, depends on education (especially of women), family planning, the population policies of leaders, the amount of technical and economic aid they receive from technologically advanced societies, their natural resources, and geographical location.

13. If current fertility rates continue, world population is expected to double by 2030. Almost all of this growth will take place in the poorest countries. Population increase and technological advances pose serious potential threats to the natural environment and the adequacy of food, water supplies, and other natural resources all over the world.

GLOSSARY

Age cohort: All people in a society born during the same period of time.

Centralization: The tendency for similar structures and activities to be concentrated in the same geographic areas of large cities.

Cities: Dense, permanent settlements of people who engage in manufacturing or service activities and do not produce food.

Crude birth rate: The number of live births per 1,000 people in a society in a given year.

Death rate: Number of deaths per 1,000 people in a society in a given year.

Decentralization: The tendency of people, structures, and functions to move out of cities to less congested or less expensive areas.

Demographic transition model: A three-stage model of population change in the West, including North America, since the Industrial Revolution.

Demography: The statistical study of the size, distribution, and composition of human populations.

Ecology: The study of the relationship between living organisms and their environment.

Emigration: Migration out of a society.

Exurb: An urbanizing rural area beyond the suburbs.

Fertility rate: The number of live births per 1,000 females aged 15 to 44 in a given year.

Gentrification: A trend toward the purchase and rehabilitation of decaying housing in poor neighborhoods by the white upper-middle and upper classes.

Ghetto: A segregated racial, ethnic, or religious community within a city.

Global cities: Cities that contain a concentration of international financial institutions, offices of multinational industrial firms, and high-tech business information services and experts.

Immigration: Migration into a society.

Industrial cities: Larger cities, segregated on the basis of class and ethnic origin, in which first manufacturing and then commercial and service activities predominate.

Infrastructure: Public facilities such as roads, bridges, tunnels, waterworks, and sewerage systems.

Invasion: The movement into a neighborhood of people and activities that differ from those that have been there before.

Megalopolis: Two or more metropolitan areas that have merged into one continuous urban tract.

Metropolitan Statistical Area (MSA): A central city of 50,000 or more people surrounded by suburbs.

Population explosion: The huge population increase occurring in most contemporary industrializing societies.

Preindustrial cities: Cities that arose before the Industrial Revolution.

Segregation: The separation and exclusion of minorities from certain activities and facilities.

Slum: An urban area characterized by very high rates of poverty and unemployment, overcrowding, and deteriorated housing and public facilities.

Suburbs: Politically independent areas surrounding and linked to cities by economic and other ties.

Succession: The successful establishment in an area of new and different types of people or activities.

Theocracy: A society in which the positions of political and religious leaders are combined and held by the same people.

Total fertility rate: The average number of children born to each woman in a society over her lifetime.

Urban planning: Deliberate attempts by governments to control, coordinate, and subsidize urban growth or change, to whatever extent political ideology and available public economic resources will allow.

Urbanization: The movement of populations from agricultural to urban areas.

Vital statistics: Measures of basic demographic variables such as birth, death, marriage, divorce, and migration rates.

Zero population growth: Stable population size as a result of a balance between birth rates and immigration, emigration, and death rates.

PRACTICE TESTS

True ▪ False Test

___ 1. The United States fits the definition of a "theocracy."
___ 2. Even in the earliest cities, the elite classes had enormous wealth.
___ 3. Industrial cities, as compared to preindustrial cities, have superior infrastructures.
___ 4. In the sociological sense, "ecology" refers exclusively to protection of the physical environment.
___ 5. Gentrification often results in rising land values.
___ 6. Urban renewal programs have not been without controversy.
___ 7. The low birth rates in the United States during the Depression affected the labor market in the post–World War II era.
___ 8. Marx considered overpopulation to be the major cause of poverty in human societies.
___ 9. In agricultural societies, birth rates are high.
___ 10. The Middle East is currently experiencing tremendous population growth and related social problems.

Multiple-Choice Test

___ 1. The oldest cities in human history are termed:
   a. theocracies.
   b. metropolitan areas.
   c. preindustrial cities.
   d. megalopolises.

___ 2. A cultural focus that is the same for both preindustrial and industrial cities is that they are:
   a. commercial centers.
   b. service centers.
   c. political centers.
   d. religious centers.

___ 3. The term "ghetto" was first applied to segregated U.S.:
   a. black communities.
   b. Jewish communities.
   c. Irish communities.
   d. Italian communities.

___ 4. Which of the following persons is most likely to become a new urban property owner in the United States?
   a. Vicki, 38, lives in a suburb only 5 miles from the city proper.
   b. Clarence, 47, plans to move to the suburbs when he has saved enough money.
   c. Andres, 29, has always lived in the city and considers suburban life dull.
   d. Mathilda and Harold, both nearing retirement age, have lived in the city for all of their married lives.

___ 5. Deliberate attempts to direct and control urban change constitute:
   a. urban planning.
   b. demography.
   c. queue theory.
   d. globalization.

___ 6. The movement of people into a society is most precisely called:
   a. emigration.
   b. vital statistics.
   c. migration.
   d. immigration.

___ 7. Which of the following is the largest generation in U.S. history?
   a. the turn-of-the-century immigrant population
   b. the Depression-born generation
   c. the baby boom generation
   d. the current young-adult population

___ 8. Which of the following theorists was most concerned with the effects of population growth?
   a. Malthus
   b. Marx
   c. Spencer
   d. Darwin

___ 9. In agricultural societies, the strongest unit, the most protective in society, is the:
   a. family.
   b. tribe.
   c. community.
   d. national government.

___ 10. In which global region is the total fertility rate the highest today?
   a. Central Asia
   b. Sub-Saharan Africa
   c. North Africa
   d. Western Europe

Matching Test

Match each concept with its definition, illustration, or explication below.

1.

___ (1) Megalopolis
___ (2) Theocracy
___ (3) Urbanization
___ (4) Suburb
___ (5) Preindustrial city

a. Shift from rural areas to cities
b. Large metropolitan areas merged
c. Before the Industrial Revolution
d. Fusion of church and state
e. Area surrounding the central city

2.

___ (1) Succession
___ (2) Ecology
___ (3) Decentralization
___ (4) Ghetto
___ (5) Gentrification

a. Rehabilitated slum areas
b. Interaction with the environment
c. Move into less congested areas
d. Segregated community within a city
e. Neighborhood change

3.

___ (1) Infrastructures
___ (2) Succession/invasion process
___ (3) Global cities
___ (4) Traffic control
___ (5) Community control

a. Urban renewal
b. Urban planning
c. Fragmented political decision making
d. Cutbacks leading to decay
e. Major financial centers

4.

__ (1) Total fertility rate

__ (2) Crude birth rate

__ (3) Migration

__ (4) Death rate

__ (5) Baby boomers

a. Age cohorts

b. Deaths per 1,000

c. Live births per 1,000

d. Average number of children per woman

e. Movement of peoples

5.

__ (1) Marx

__ (2) Agricultural societies

__ (3) Malthus

__ (4) Demographic transition

__ (5) Cultural lag

a. Principle of population

b. Capitalism encourages population surplus

c. Model of population growth

d. High birth rates

e. A cause of population growth

REVIEW QUESTIONS

1. What are four necessary preconditions of widespread urbanization in human societies?
2. Describe the basic differences between preindustrial and industrial cities.
3. What are the major ecological patterns in urban growth and change?
4. Discuss the major reasons for the economic and political problems of large cities in the United States today.
5. Identify and describe the basic characteristics of global cities.
6. Discuss the relationship among economic and political change, demographic change, and value changes, especially among succeeding generations in the United States.
7. How and why do population statistics change during the course of sociocultural evolution?
8. Is the demographic transition model likely to apply to currently industrializing societies? Why or why not?
9. How has sociocultural evolution affected the global environment? What are the major current issues concerning the future of this environment?

APPLYING SOCIOLOGY

1. Analyze how your community (city, suburb, or small town) has been affected by ecological changes (natural or technological) in your lifetime.
2. Contrast these changes with earlier ecological conditions in your area as recalled by your parents or other older residents.

3. To what extent did ecological factors such as size, location, architecture, transportation, or other facilities affect your choice of a college and your present housing?
4. To what extent did economic factors or values affect your choice of a college and housing?
5. Locate yourself socially by class, ethnic origin, age and generation, religion, and gender. How have these statuses affected your family size, your actual or expected age at marriage, and the number of children you have or expect to have?
6. How have demographic variables such as age at marriage, size of the nuclear family, age at death, and cause of death varied in your family in the past three generations?

7

Deviance

In all societies, some degree of order and predictability in human relationships is essential. There must be more cooperation than conflict and more agreement than disagreement about what is real, right, important, and desirable. Authoritarian governments or leaders may be able to force individuals to comply with their wishes, but they cannot do so indefinitely, at least in modern times (Kelman and Hamilton, 1988). Agreement is difficult to enforce in industrial societies, particularly when alternatives are available or conceivable.

To the extent that they think, feel, and behave in expected, predictable, and socially approved ways, people have been successfully socialized. They have internalized the norms, attitudes, values, and beliefs of their groups and their society, and they conform. In contrast, **deviance** is the violation of important norms that is strongly disapproved of by large numbers of people in a society. It refers to "conduct which the people of a group consider so dangerous or embarrassing or irritating that they bring special sanctions to bear against the persons who exhibit it" (Erikson, 1966, p. 6).

Actually, any violation of a norm is deviant. But sociologists have been more interested in nonconformity to the norms that are most closely linked

214

to the ultimate concerns of sociology, social stability and social change. We study social movements because successful social movements change norms, values, and expectations. These movements redefine who and what is good or bad and right or wrong in a society.

THE RELATIVITY OF DEVIANCE

It is important to be aware that definitions of what is deviant vary with time, place, and culture. Norms change, and in industrialized societies they change rapidly. In the course of sociocultural evolution, and especially as scientific knowledge accumulates, the visions of shamans come to be defined as hallucinations and former heretics may come to be regarded as geniuses who were ahead of their time. In patriarchal agricultural societies, the norms for female sexual behavior prescribed virginity at marriage, fidelity after marriage, and dutiful, joyless, sexual submission within marriage. In the United States in recent years, women who do not enjoy sex have come to be defined as psychologically disturbed (Singer, 1979; Komarovsky, 1985), and premarital genital sexual activity has become the norm (Reiss, 1993). A majority of young women in the United States are no longer virgins at the time they (first) marry.

Virginity at marriage, although no longer typical, is not defined as deviant, however, and certainly not in fundamentalist religious subcultures (Bendroth, 1993). Sexual infidelity in marriage is still regarded as deviant in the United States, but laws prohibiting adultery (still on the books in many states) are rarely enforced against consenting adults. Gay and lesbian sexual behavior is more accepted now than it was in the past. Homosexuality was once defined as a psychological disorder in the *Diagnostic and Statistical Manual of Mental Disorders* published by the American Psychiatric Association. In the third, revised edition of this manual, only those who are deeply troubled by their sexual orientation and want to change it are considered to have a psychological disorder (DSM-III, 1987, p. 296).

Drug addiction is strongly disapproved of, but most people are not aware that alcohol and tobacco are drugs. Drinking is not deviant, but drunkenness is. Smoking is now defined as deviant in some contexts. Laws restricting smoking in public places may eventually be extended to private places.

The Medicalization of Deviance

Developments in the medical sciences in industrialized societies, especially since World War II, have led to a tendency to define many forms of deviance as illness. Sociologists call this tendency the **medicalization** of deviance. The tendency now is to view increasing numbers of disapproved behaviors or conditions as involuntary. Drug addiction, alcoholism, and obesity are examples.

Critics of this trend have long pointed out that the medicalization model gives medical practitioners social control over strongly disapproved nonconformity (Zola, 1966; Szasz, 1974; Clark, 1988). It has also resulted in huge, profitable industries to treat these conditions. Nevertheless, the medicalization model does remove some of the stigma attached to these kinds of nonconformity. It also encourages people to take an active stance toward their problem and to do something about it—where this is possible. Furthermore, in the United States, self-help support groups are diminishing the role of the medical establishment in treating behavior disorders, however they are defined.

Some forms of antisocial behavior, such as compulsive stealing (kleptomania), are now defined as medical problems, especially if the offender is of middle- or upper-income status. Children who demonstrate behavioral problems in school are now more likely to be defined as hyperactive and in need of medication. In postindustrial societies, people are often treated as "sick" rather than punished as "bad," especially if they are middle class. Insanity is an accepted legal defense in the United States, even against murder—which does not mean it can be proved in most cases.

But deviance is not an entirely relative matter that always depends on who, what, and when, and on changing social circumstances. If there is an objective standard for cultural definitions of deviance, it rests on destructiveness to the self and others. Murder and suicide are disapproved of in all societies, except in certain cases, which, depending on the society, may range from homicide committed in self-defense, to "mercy killing," to suicide attacks in war, to socially sanctioned human sacrifice.

In the United States, the stigmatization of mentally ill individuals, particularly those considered "psychotic," often rests on a fear of their destructiveness. Most people who are diagnosed as psychotic, however, may be disruptive but are not destructive when their psychotic symptoms are kept under control with medication (Link, Andrews, and Cullen, 1992). Psychiatrists cannot predict violence in specific patients, however, and they are often wrong when they try.

That direct, observable, physical destructiveness to the self or others is a basic standard for making judgments about deviance is indicated by repeated surveys in the United States (Inciardi, 1993). The most widespread and strongest disapproval is directed at violent crimes against people, such as murder, rape, sexual abuse, kidnapping, and assault. Property crimes such as arson, burglary, and theft rank second.

There is much less agreement about condemning what sociologists once called "crimes without victims," such as alcoholism, drug addiction, gambling, prostitution, and suicide (Schur, 1965). In these cases, the deviant behavior may be viewed more sympathetically, as a product of an unhappy childhood in a multiproblem family or other extenuating circumstances. The victim is the self (and the family).

Destructiveness in these cases is self-destructiveness. But even destructiveness as a standard for defining deviance is relative, to some extent.

TABLE 7.1

Fear and Violence at School

		Urban	Suburban	Rural
Students who said they were victims at school	Violent crimes	8%	7%	7%
	Property crimes	2	2	1
Students who said they were afraid of attacks	At school	24	20	22
	To and from school	19	13	13
Students who said they avoided certain places at school out of fear		8	6	6
Students who said they had taken a weapon or other object to school for protection		3	2	1

Source: New York Times, April 21, 1993, p. B11. Based on a 1989 Justice Department survey of 10,000 students. Used by permission.

Violence—defined as physical aggression against others—appears to be the norm in a few nonliterate societies in which bravery, fortitude, and warfare are highly valued. Economic resources are scarce, and daily existence is usually extremely stressful in these societies. In preindustrial societies where cultural values and childrearing practices promote violence, it is the nonviolent person who is deviant (Edgerton, 1976; Levinson, 1989; Ross, 1993).

The United States Bureau of Justice Statistics releases annual reports on violent crime based on the National Crime Victimization Survey conducted by the Census Bureau. According to this survey, there has been a 50 percent increase in juvenile crimes (among 12- to 17-year-olds) since 1987 (*New York Times,* July 18, 1994, p. A16). The fear of violent crime affects students in suburban and rural schools as well as urban schools (see Table 7.1). The overall rate of violent crimes (rapes, robberies, and assaults), excluding murder, however, appears to have declined somewhat since 1981, which was the peak year in the United States.

Homicide and assault rates are much higher in the United States than in any other Western industrial democracy (Reiss and Roth, 1993). Senator Daniel Patrick Moynihan has argued that this kind of deviance is becoming the norm in the United States and calls for more "outrage" and less acceptance on the part of government and citizens (Moynihan, 1993). Actually, as noted earlier, public opinion polls in the United States indicate considerable concern over and fear of violence, especially in large cities (Smolowe, 1993). In a Gallup poll conducted in 1993, 43 percent of the adult population (compared to 36 percent in 1965) reported that they were afraid to walk alone at night in their neighborhoods (*Gallup Poll Monthly,* December 1993, p. 20).

A recurring theme in current research on violence in the United States is the claim that violent individuals are genetically or physically defective or deficient (Reiss and Roth, 1993). This is a complicated issue with a long history in the social sciences. We return to this question shortly, when we discuss biological theories of deviant behavior.

THEORIES OF DEVIANCE

Scientific attempts to explain deviance have given the greatest weight to biological, psychological, or sociological factors. Biological and psychological theories are most helpful in explaining why particular individuals are or become deviant—regardless of their social location. Sociological explanations are essential to an understanding of variations in the amount of deviance (rates), the kind of deviance (violent or nonviolent), and the reactions to deviance in various cultures and subcultures (social locations).

Biological Theories

Biological explanations of deviance assume the existence of defective genes, hereditary criminal instincts, or human nature in the form of inborn aggressive or destructive drives that result in deviant behavior. Defective genes are relevant to involuntary deviance insofar as they are responsible for hereditary physical or mental disability. Even here, however, the extent to which heredity is responsible for certain types of mental illness, for example, has not been established, and involuntary deviance may be disruptive but is usually nonviolent.

The relativity of definitions of deviance, depending so much on who, when, and where, does not support a criminal instinct theory of deviance. If specific criminal instincts existed and were more important than environmental factors, types of deviance would not vary in frequency from group to group and society to society, or from time to time in the same society, as they do.

Related attempts to trace criminal behavior to inherited physical traits, such as head shape or body type, have not been substantiated by reliable scientific research. Italian criminologist Cesare Lombroso (1836–1909) achieved fame in the early twentieth century with his claim that criminals are evolutionary misfits and throwbacks who possess the physical traits of lower animal forms—sloping foreheads, protruding jaws, excess body hair (Lombroso, 1911). Later studies, based on more refined measurements of representative samples of criminal and noncriminal populations, have not borne out Lombroso's claims.

In the 1940s, sociologist William H. Sheldon and his associates classified people into three body types: endomorphs, who are soft, fat, and round; mesomorphs, who are muscular, wiry, and athletic; and ectomorphs, who are thin, delicate, and weak. Based on a small sample of juvenile delinquents, Sheldon and his colleagues concluded that since mesomorphs predominated in their sample, this body type results in delinquency (Sheldon, Harte, and McDermott, 1949).

Other sociologists tested Sheldon's hypothesis. Edwin H. Sutherland, using different criteria for defining delinquency, found no significant differences in body types among delinquents and nondelinquents (Sutherland, 1951). But Sheldon and Eleanor Glueck (1956) did find a predominance of mesomorphs in their sample.

Delinquent behavior often requires strength, speed, and agility. Wiry, athletic young people are more likely to be delinquent because they would be better and more successful at it. But this does not mean that this body type causes delinquency. Most mesomorphs are not delinquent, nor are most delinquents mesomorphs, if unreported as well as officially reported cases of delinquency are included in the sample.

More difficult to refute by direct measurement and observation are the beliefs of the human nature theorists. **Human nature** refers to the common biological inheritance of humans everywhere that is assumed to determine specific behavior patterns. These biologically grounded theories trace deviance, particularly of the physically destructive type, to assumed innate, aggressive instincts or drives or to behavioral genes for complex traits, such as selfishness or altruism (Freud, 1961 [1923]; Wilson, 1978).

Freud was the most famous proponent of an innate, biological aggressive or destructive instinct that may result in deviant behavior. He viewed the personality as consisting of three parts: the unconscious "id" that is the seat of inborn libidinal (love) impulses and aggressive (hate) impulses; the largely conscious "ego" (except for defense mechanisms) that copes with reality and has learned to function in terms of the demands and needs of others as well as the self; and the "superego," or conscience, that stands guard over the selfish, impulsive id, which constantly threatens to break through the socialized ego (Freud, 1961 [1923]).

In Freud's words, the id operates according to the pleasure principle, the ego operates according to the reality principle, and the two are in constant conflict. A failure in the process of identification and internalization in relationships with caregivers during early childhood results in a faulty superego and the breaking through of destructive sexual and aggressive impulses.

Sociobiologist Edward O. Wilson (1975; 1978; 1993) provides a more recent example of a biologically grounded human nature theory. He assumes the existence of "behavioral genes," not only for such specific traits as aggression, territoriality, selfishness, fondling, and kissing. He also assumes a genetic (inherited) basis for more complex traits such as religiousness, same-sex sexual orientation, and schizophrenia.

Wilson's behavioral genes, like Freud's aggressive and libidinal instincts, are not as yet observable, measurable, verifiable, or predictable as genetic traits. That certain traits are adaptive, widespread, or even universal, does not prove that they are inborn. Humans face similar problems everywhere. They react with similar and often identical adaptive responses. But this does not make the behavior genetic and inevitable.

Theories of human nature of the pessimistic variety have conservative political implications. There is little that can be done to change humans or the societies in which they live if humans are born bad. This is the argument of the social Darwinists, except that, according to them, only the poor and nonwhites or non-Europeans are born bad, that is, unintelligent and incapable of conforming to middle- and upper-class standards of morality.

Arguing more generally and including all humans in his argument, Wilson claims that socialism as a system of political and economic reform contains scientifically inaccurate conceptions of human nature. In Wilson's view, a system based on sharing, cooperation, and internationalism could not work because humans are born selfish and tribalistic or ethnocentric (Wilson, 1978; 1993). Freud also gave more weight to biology than to social reform in determining the way things are and have to be:

> The Communists believe that they have found the path to deliverance from our evils. According to them, man is wholly good and is well-disposed to his neighbor; but the institution of private property has corrupted his nature. The ownership of private wealth gives the individual power, and with it the temptation to ill-treat his neighbor; while the man who is excluded from possession is bound to rebel in hostility against his oppressor. . . . [But] aggressiveness was not created by property. It reigned almost without limit in primitive times when property was very scarce. (Freud, 1961 [1930] pp. 112–113)

Freud's anthropology is inaccurate. Aggressiveness was not widespread in hunting and gathering societies, the type of society humans have lived in for 99 percent of their existence on earth. The evidence from zoology, anthropology, psychology, and physiology does not support the existence of a destructive instinct or behavioral genes for selfishness, tribalism, or territoriality in humans and their closest primate ancestors (Montagu, 1978).

Animals kill for survival—to satisfy hunger needs. They do not kill for pleasure, and only rarely because of jealousy or rivalry. Human definitions of what is necessary for survival may be irrational at times, but this is not evidence of a genetic predisposition. Territorial defense patterns in nonhumans are a means for protecting food and sexual privileges in animal groups. But territoriality usually involves threatening display rather than the killing of intruders. Furthermore, hominids and other close relatives of *Homo sa-*

piens did not and do not have the pattern of territoriality. And they are not usually belligerent except when provoked.

Physiologists have not been able to demonstrate the existence of chemical and physical changes in the body that indicate a spontaneous build-up of internal aggressive energy, similar to changes that occur in blood sugar levels as hunger builds up. Currently, there is no conclusive evidence of innate aggression. The available evidence suggests that aggression occurs primarily in response to an external attack or to situational frustration (Buss, 1994).

We have a vast body of data from the field of psychology indicating that aggression is frequently a response to **frustration**—defined as the blocking of immediate or long-range needs or goals. It also occurs as a defense against attack and as a means to achieve valued goals that cannot be obtained otherwise (Buss, 1978; 1994). If aggression is universal in human societies, it is because frustration is universal. Economic and political conditions affect the amount of frustration in a society, and the culture encourages or inhibits the expression of aggression. It also defines targets of aggression, such as strangers, minorities, and certain kinds of noncon-formists.

Biological explanations of deviance do have some bearing at the level of the individual, however. Here, they apply to certain kinds of involuntary deviance (hereditary defects and diseases) and to individual differences in temperament that have a genetic basis. Psychologists have contributed much to an understanding of temperamental differences among individuals. And this brings us to the topic of psychological explanations of deviance.

Psychological Theories

Psychologists look to temperament and experiences of emotional depriva-tion, especially in infancy and early childhood, for their explanations of deviance. Temperament refers to a genetic predisposition to react to the environment in a certain way. It consists of two major components: energy or activity level and emotionality (Buss, 1994). People with high energy levels are more active, assertive and restless, need less sleep, and have more difficulty relaxing than others. They may also be more uninhibited, impul-sive, and impatient.

People who are highly emotional react more intensely and sensitively to their environment and are less tolerant of frustration. They cry more during infancy, are more irritable and "difficult" during childhood, and are more moody as adults (Buss, 1978; 1994).

That individual differences in temperament are very likely to have a genetic basis is indicated by research on newborns and identical twins. Videotapes of newborn infants of the same social class (Escalona, 1968) show extreme individual differences in activity, sensitivity, and frustration tolerance. Social class might affect energy levels of newborns, since mothers who have poor diets and receive inadequate prenatal care give birth to more listless and lethargic babies. But if this possible variable is controlled by comparing only infants from the same social class, we find marked individual differences in temperament, regardless of ethnic origin or gender.

Studies of identical twins reared together and apart also support the hypothesis of a genetic component in temperament (Buss, 1994). Identical twins have identical sets of genes. Comparisons between pairs of identical twins who were separated at birth and grew up in different homes and pairs of fraternal twins who were similarly reared apart indicate a much higher degree of similarity in temperament between the separated identical twins than the separated fraternal twins. Temperament, incidentally, is more easily observed and measured than inherited intelligence. For this reason, studies of the inheritance of intelligence among identical twins, raised separately since birth, have been suspect.

Temperament is relevant to an explanation of deviance because individuals who are more active, emotional, and impulsive would presumably experience more frustration as a result of the social restraints imposed by others. But even here it is important to remember that groups and societies vary tremendously in the amount of conformity and control they impose and require. An individual's biological predisposition to break rules may be encouraged or suppressed, or may become irrelevant, depending on the culture or subculture and political and economic conditions in a society at a particular time.

Psychologists also focus on childhood emotional deprivation as a predisposing factor in deviance. This deprivation arises initially from rejection, neglect, too little or too much discipline and control, and harsh, brutal, or inconsistent treatment in relationships with parents or parent substitutes in infancy and early childhood (Ainsworth and Bowlsby, 1991). The so-called sociopath, for example, has no sense of morality, feels no guilt about behavior that is destructive to others, and is unable to form close, lasting ties with others (McCord and Tremblay, 1992). Studies of individuals with this type of personality indicate a failure to identify with parents or other childhood caregivers as a result of cruel and severe psychological abuse and physical punishment.

Not all instances of individual predisposition to deviance stem from a failure to identify with parents, however. Parents may themselves be deviant, or, as psychoanalysts pointed out long ago, children may be carrying out their parents' unconscious wishes in their destructive or nonconforming behavior (Eissler, 1949). Not all people who are deviant are psychologically disturbed, nor are all psychologically disturbed people deviant. For a more complete picture of the causes and consequences of strongly disapproved nonconforming behavior, we need to add a sociological dimension to the picture.

Sociological Theories

Sociological explanations of deviance have focused primarily on social location as this affects the learning and the reinforcement of specific kinds of deviant behavior and reactions to this behavior by those in positions of authority. These theories are useful in explaining different patterns of deviance in different subcultures—street crimes, teenage pregnancy, drug abuse, and prostitution among the poor; bribery, embezzlement, and tax fraud among the rich. Prostitution, for example, defined as contractual payment for sexual services, varies according to the social class of the participants. Generally, female street or house prostitutes service mainly working-class males, call girls service mainly middle-class males, and economically dependent mistresses service mainly upper-class males.

Anomie Theory   Merton's application of Durkheim's concept of anomie to deviant behavior, called "structural strain theory," is an attempt to explain why the rate of deviance generally increases in rapidly changing industrialized societies (see chapter 4). As a functionalist, Merton pointed to the disequilibrium, or imbalance, created in modern societies when socially approved goals—wealth, success, social esteem—cannot be achieved by many people who do not have the socially approved means for achieving these goals—a good education, a good job, the "right" social background, or the necessary amount of ambition and drive. This promotes anomie and nonconforming behavior.

Delinquency is criminal behavior on the part of young people, usually under age 16. Anomie theory has been used by a number of sociologists to explain the phenomenon of delinquent gangs in low-income neighborhoods. In a classic study, Albert Cohen (1955) observed that the delinquent male gang and its activities provide the prestige and social esteem that gang members are unable to obtain from respectable citizens in the wider society. Cohen pointed out that delinquent gang members in poverty areas are unsuccessful in school and at sports. They do not have the social background or educational means that most middle-class boys have for achieving acceptance, tolerance, approval, and success in the outside world.

Richard Cloward and Lloyd Ohlin (1960) carried this theory further by specifying three different types of delinquent gangs. The "criminal gang" steals and robs for economic gain. The "conflict gang" engages in gang warfare and territorial defense to achieve or maintain social status; the gang's activities do not bring economic rewards. The "retreatist gang" seeks escape through mind-altering drugs, from marijuana and heroin to alcohol.

These distinctions have historical validity, but they blur in more recent times in the United States. Newer research focuses on the increase in violence among *all* gangs in low-income areas, especially those areas with concentrations of racial/ethnic minorities (Hagedorn, 1988; Anderson, 1990; Moore, 1991; Padilla, 1992). Most sociologists relate this increased violence to the spread of drug use and drug dealing (primarily involving cocaine and crack), the ready availability of guns in the United States (compared to other industrial societies), and the decline in economic opportunity for inadequately skilled, poorly educated citizens in a deindustrializing economy.

Cultural Transmission Theory   Other sociologists have focused on deviant behavior as primarily a result of subcultural norms that are learned through the process of socialization in different subcultures in complex societies. In the 1920s, Clifford R. Shaw and Henry D. McKay (1929) found that street-crime rates remained high in certain neighborhoods of Chicago despite the fact that a succession of different ethnic minorities had occupied these neighborhoods.

Sociologist Edwin H. Sutherland (1939) used the concept of **cultural transmission** to describe how these patterns of deviant behavior are learned and passed down from generation to generation in the same neighborhood, same corporation, or same geographic region. He explained criminal behavior as a consequence of **differential association**–selective, intimate, personal contact with others who engage in behavior that is defined as criminal. The situation determines the type of crime committed. Automobile manufacturers, for example, do not violate pure food and drug laws, but meat-packing corporations might. According to Sutherland, whether or not any particular individual becomes a delinquent or a criminal depends on the frequency, duration, and intensity of the relationship with others who engage in delinquent or criminal behavior.

More recently, sociological research on gang violence has pointed to the spread of adolescent violence to Middle America, and across racial/ethnic and social class lines (Sullivan, 1989; Willis, 1990). The newer research on gang violence in low-income, minority neighborhoods now emphasizes the continuation of adolescent gang influences into adulthood, after prison terms are served, and beyond (Hagedorn, 1988; Moore, 1991). Some gang members, usually from psychologically stronger, more successful families, make it to the suburbs and a somewhat better future, economically; most do not (Williams, 1989; Hagan, 1991). For members of adolescent gangs, **recidivism**–a lifetime of repeated criminal behavior after an initial conviction–is more likely now than in the past.

Labeling Theory   Other sociologists have focused primarily on how societal definitions and reactions to deviant behavior create and reinforce this kind of behavior. According to the labeling perspective, a person or an act is deviant because certain people in a society successfully label it as such (Becker, 1964). "The deviant is one to whom that label has successfully been applied; deviant behavior is behavior that people so label" (Becker, 1963, p. 6). It is not an intrinsic quality of the act or the person. According to Howard S. Becker (1963, p. 147–163), the labelers are "crusading reform-

Focus on Social Issues

MOBILITY AND NONCONFORMITY

[From a sociological perspective, O. J. Simpson experienced all three of the kinds of mobility—social, psychological, and geographic—associated with an increased likelihood of nonconforming and unconventional behavior. The following excerpt focuses more on psychological factors as determinants of his behavior during a crisis, but both sociological and psychological factors must be taken into account in explaining his conduct and experiences during a sensational murder investigation and trial.]

In crisis, people condense into their essential selves. O. J. Simpson was, essentially, a great runner. This was how a bow-legged kid with rickets had escaped the slums where he was born, how a football superstar had become a national icon, always outrunning his obstacles. . . . "I'll tell you," he used to say, "my speed has always been my best weapon. So if I can't run away from

whatever it is, I don't need to be there." But there was never a run like last week's final play. . . . He wasn't really trying to escape. He just wanted his mother. He wanted to go home. He found his blocker in his faithful friend and longtime teammate Al Cowlings and together . . . they eluded the police who had come to take O. J. into custody on charges of first-degree murder.

Word of the flight soon went out, and the crowds were on their feet, cheering. Police picked up O. J.'s cellular-phone calls and began tracking the route of the Ford Bronco along the San Diego freeway. Reporters pursuing in helicopters overhead said that he had a gun to his head. . . . Downtown at headquarters, the SWAT teams and crisis negotiators sat like everyone else, following the route of the Bronco on television.

—Nancy Gibbs, "End of the Run," *Time,* June 27, 1994, pp. 29–35

What Do You Think?

1. How does this passage illustrate both a psychological and a sociological approach to explaining O. J. Simpson's initial flight from the police?

2. How would the experience of being arrested, charged, and defended against a charge of murder differ, typically, for a person who is not an upper-class celebrity? How might the verdict and the sentence differ, typically?

3. What role did the media play in the O. J. Simpson case? Do you believe their role was helpful or destructive to the defense? To the prosecution?

ers," "rule creators," and "moral entrepreneurs." High-income people with more power to resist stigmatized labels are able to avoid punishment and disgrace that less powerful people cannot avoid.

The question of who gets labeled deviant and who does the labeling becomes more important in modern societies, where practically everyone breaks some rules some of the time. At the macrolevel, labeling theorists have used the conflict model to explain why the same behavior—the behavior of a recluse or a hermit, for example—is defined as eccentric, or perhaps just a bit weird, when it occurs in the upper class, but is labeled mental illness when it occurs among the poor (Szasz, 1974).

The destructive activities of middle-class high school boys are labeled mischievous ("boys will be boys"). When the same type of activity (vandalism, truancy, fighting, drunkenness, or stealing) occurs among working-class boys, whose language, manners, and social origins are less impressive to teachers and principals, it is called delinquent (Chambliss, 1973).

At the microlevel, labeling theorists have used the symbolic interaction model to focus on the underlying meanings of public confrontations between accused or disabled people and their accusers or would-be benefactors. In a classic paper, sociologist Harold Garfinkel (1956) called this situation a "degradation ceremony." Imprisonment or admission to a mental institution, for example, involves a public and official declaration that an individual now occupies a deviant status. The doors close on the inmate. Clothes and other personal property are exchanged for uniforms, hospital gowns, and institutional property. Life becomes totally regulated, controlled, and restricted. And identity, self-esteem, and self-concept change forever (Goffman, 1961). The desire to avoid labeling and possible reinforcement of deviant behavior is the rationale underlying government policies that favor probation rather than imprisonment for younger, first-time offenders.

A public confrontation with authority figures such as parents, police, principals, or employers may result in a refusal to accept the label of deviant, especially by powerful people. The label sticks and becomes a self-fulfilling prophecy if it is accepted. Sociologist Edwin Lemert (1967) focused on this phenomenon in his classic distinction between primary deviance and secondary deviance. **Primary deviance** is the original behavior that resulted in the deviant label. **Secondary deviance** is behavior that follows labeling and is a response to the label.

A young, male, working-class high school student, for example, may be suspended from school for being a troublemaker in the classroom. (A middle-class boy would be sent to a psychiatrist.) With time on his hands, he becomes involved with a group of boys who were also suspended for similar reasons. Out of anger, boredom, and a desire for spending money, the group robs a neighborhood store. Caught, tried, convicted, and sent to a correctional facility, these boys develop self-concepts as criminals that become self-fulfilling prophecies.

Acting out in the classroom was the primary act of deviance. Confrontation and suspension was the degradation ceremony. Robbing a store was an act of secondary deviance that perpetuated the label and changed the boy's self-concept. Other examples of secondary deviance include a suicide attempt by an individual who has already been hospitalized and labeled mentally ill, and the muggings that drug addicts engage in to support their habit.

TABLE 7.2

Theories of Deviance—Basic Concepts

Biological Theories	Psychological Theories	Sociological Theories
Criminal instinct	Temperament	Anomie
Aggressive instinct	Emotional deprivation in	Structural strain
Genetic defect	early childhood	Cultural transmission
Human nature	Frustration/aggression	Differential association
		Labeling
		Primary deviance
		Secondary deviance

Limitations of Sociological Theories

Sociological theories cannot answer the question of why a specific individual becomes a nonconformist. Not everyone in situations where crimes may be committed becomes a criminal. Not everyone without socially approved means to achieve socially approved goals becomes deviant. Why does one brother become a priest and another a criminal? Why does one politician accept payoffs and another does not? Why does one person choose to associate with delinquent rather than nondelinquent friends?

Labeling theory cannot explain why certain individuals become deviant in the first place. It cannot account for secret deviance that no one observes or labels. But it does make a valuable contribution to an understanding of how power and social location, especially socioeconomic status, affect definitions of deviance, the persistence of deviance, and reactions to deviance. The answers to the question of why specific individuals become deviant lie in the realm of psychology and individual differences in personality and temperament. But sociologists (and anthropologists) have made valuable contributions to understanding group and societal differences in the frequency and types of nonconformity and reactions to nonconformity, now and in the past.

DEVIANCE AND SOCIOCULTURAL EVOLUTION

Deviance is universal. What varies is the kind of deviance, the amount of deviance, and reactions to deviance. People in all societies break rules. They murder, rape, cheat, steal, bully, and lie. But they do so more often in some societies than in others. If we are to understand why, we should look briefly at how deviant behavior and reactions to deviance have varied during the course of sociocultural evolution. This will provide some evidence on the question of how much weight to give to biological, psychological, and sociological variables in explaining deviance.

Hunting and Gathering Societies

In hunting and gathering societies, thievery is rare. There is nothing of value to steal other than food. Other types of nonconformity do occur, however, usually as a result of individual psychological differences. This nonconformity is linked closely to biological characteristics such as temperament (mood, energy level, reflexes, and frustration tolerance) and to mental or physical disability. Sanctions in hunting and gathering societies are informal—criticism, ridicule, avoidance, physical punishment, or exile from the band—and are enforced by all members of the band. There are no formal written laws or specialized law enforcement officials such as police, lawyers, or judges.

Resourcefulness is valued in these societies, as noted in chapter 5, and childrearing practices are not strict or authoritarian (Ellis and Peterson, 1992). But in such slowly changing, homogeneous societies, few choices or alternatives are available that could promote or encourage nonconformity.

Deviance in Horticultural Societies

In horticultural societies deviance is more frequent. There is usually an economic surplus to hoard or steal and there is inequality between families in prestige and in the distribution of power and property. Sanctions are informal, but individuals or families with more power may have more input in defining norms and enforcing sanctions. Deviance also becomes a subcultural as well as an individual phenomenon. The major subcultures in these societies are based on age or sex. Women as a group may secretly hoard food in a society in which food is scarce and the norms prescribe cooperation and sharing (Edgerton, 1976). Older men may refuse to turn over their power or extend their privileges to their grown sons as prescribed by the society's norms.

Deviance in Agricultural Societies

In agricultural societies, social change increases slightly, geographic mobility is more prevalent, and deviance is also more frequent. Formal sanctions and specialized, full-time law enforcement officials appear. But informal sanctions carried out by the community or members of the extended family continue to be the most important form of social control.

Subcultural deviance is enlarged to include not only subcultures based on age and gender but ethnic and class subcultures as well, particularly in urban centers. The uprooted poor in these centers, when they cannot work, turn to stealing, begging, prostitution, drunkenness, and assault. Individuals with physical or mental disabilities who lack family support must fend for themselves as best they can. Governments in agricultural societies do not assume responsibility for their care or support. Geographic mobility, especially from farms to cities, severs group ties and weakens the control of the family, local community, and neighborhood church.

The most prevalent forms of deviance in agricultural societies continue to be those that can be directly observed—crimes against property and people. Rebellions are short lived and local. Punishment for deviance is swift, inexpensive, direct, and brutal—torture, the severing of limbs (an eye for an eye), exposure, hanging.

The behavior of the landowning aristocracy, regardless of harmfulness and destructiveness to other members of the society, is not considered deviant. It is perceived as the right of this class to brutalize, starve, abuse, overwork, and otherwise exploit and suppress the poor and the weak. The poor are regarded as a breed apart, not quite human, and certainly without human rights (Pirenne, 1933; Lenski, 1966). Authoritarian military governments in Burma, Central America, and the Caribbean have ruled in a similar way in more recent times (Pierre-Pierre, 1994; Elliot, 1994; Shenon, 1994a).

Deviance in Industrial Societies

In industrializing societies, the middle class of manufacturers, bankers, merchants, and professionals expands. Competitiveness increases. Deviance is extended to occupational subcultures, as rules are bent and conflicts increase. The "robber barons," for example, were nineteenth-century capitalists in the United States who sometimes used illegal, openly violent methods such as strikebreaking to increase their wealth and power and to achieve and maintain their upper-class status (Josephson, 1934).

That the aristocratic, hereditary governing class should have unlimited power and privileges comes slowly into question in industrial societies and is eventually defined as deviant. This may occur gradually, as the middle class takes over the top official positions of power in a society and becomes the new upper class. Or it may occur rapidly, as a result of revolutions—usually led by urban middle-class people—as in Europe over the last five centuries (Tilly, 1993).

Formal sanctions and specialized law enforcement officials grow in number and importance in industrialized societies. Informal sanctions such as gossip or personal revenge may, however, persist in rural areas. In these areas, lawsuits may be defined as "unneighborly" (Ellikson, 1991, p. 60). In some industrial societies (the United States and Great Britain, for example), we are seeing a revival of nongovernment enforcers, such as vigilantes, neighborhood patrols, and private security forces to deal with increased youthful violence in low-income minority neighborhoods (Johnston, 1992).

The segregation of street criminals and the mentally ill in prisons and mental institutions becomes widespread in industrial societies. In the movement from industrializing to urban industrial societies, deviance increasingly takes the form of **white-collar crime**, secret and nonviolent deviance on the part of middle- and upper-class people in their occupational activities (Sutherland, 1983; Weisburd et al., 1991). Such crime—fraud, embezzlement, price fixing, fee splitting, misleading or false advertising, bribery, tax evasion—becomes more common as economic opportunity increases. The costs and consequences of this type of hidden crime are indirect and more difficult to observe and measure. The economic costs to the public of white-collar crime are greater than the costs of other crime (Weisburd et al., 1991). Offenders, however, are much more likely to be placed on probation, assigned to do community service, or given short sentences in hotel-like minimum security prisons (Wheeler, Mann, and Sarat, 1988).

As mobility of all kinds (geographic, psychological, and social) increases in industrial societies, group ties are severed and social control is weakened, especially when individuals reject their membership groups but are not members of the new groups they identify with. The concepts of relative deprivation and status inconsistency are crucial for understanding why mobility promotes nonconformity.

Earlier we saw that the feeling of being deprived depends on our reference groups, those we use as a standard of comparison in evaluating our life circumstances. The poor will feel very deprived if they aspire to the rewards and resources of the middle or upper classes and there is even the slightest possibility of rising in the class structure.

The feeling of being economically deprived is common in urban industrial societies, even though the standard of living for *most* people is actually much higher than in agricultural societies. Those who feel more deprived and frustrated are more likely to break rules, however, regardless of their objective circumstances. White-collar crime is not usually committed by the economically needy. It is committed more often by those whose ambition and horizons are open ended and unlimited. There is always someone, somewhere, who has more power, more prestige, or more money.

Status inconsistency is a discrepancy between ascribed and achieved statuses, or between the characteristics that determine social class standing (education, income, and occupational prestige). The concept is important because widespread status inconsistency in a society promotes social unrest and reform or revolutionary social movements. For example, people who rank high in wealth but low in prestige and power, such as wealthy, successful merchants before the French Revolution, or those who rank high in prestige but low in power and wealth, such as college professors or

TABLE 7.3

Deviance and Sociocultural Evolution

Trends	Underlying Conditions
Frequency: From rare to widespread	Intensified social change
Sanctions: From informal to formal	Greater economic opportunity; more life
Enforcers: From family and community to	choices
full-time specialists	More geographic, psychological, and social
Type: From observable and violent to	mobility
secret and nonviolent	Increased breaking of family, friendship,
Social Location: From individual, to age	and community ties
and sex subcultures, to class and	Increasing anomie
ethnic subcultures, to global structures	Expansion of reference groups
linked by international	Relative deprivation; rising expectations
telecommunication systems	Global telecommunication facilities

impoverished former aristocrats, are more likely to be in the forefront of social movements.

Karl Marx and Sigmund Freud, despite their educational and intellectual qualifications, had low prestige and were unable to obtain high-level professorships in Germany because of their religious origins. Fidel Castro was a lawyer, but he was born to an unmarried mother. Relative deprivation and status inconsistency promote nonconformity among outsiders who are not co-opted by dominant groups in a society.

In addition to mobility of all kinds and the breaking of group ties, very rapid social change is another underlying factor that promotes increased nonconformity in industrial societies. There may be no norms to cover some aspects of new situations, or the norms may no longer be appropriate to changing conditions, the situation Durkheim referred to as anomie. When norms are weak or absent, the effectiveness of social control declines and deviance becomes more prevalent. As societies urbanize and industrialize, deviance becomes more frequent in different segments of the population and increasingly involves secret, nonphysical, and indirectly destructive behavior (see Table 7.3).

DEVIANCE AND CRIME

Many sociologists who study deviance focus primarily on **crime,** deviant activity that is defined by governments as illegal. Crime may also include *failure* to act—to save a life, for example, in situations where a relationship is based on birth (parents and children) or legal contract (husbands and wives). In industrial democracies, laws are usually based on majority agreement about what is right or wrong, good or bad. When ideas change about what is right and good or wrong and bad, laws change. But there is often a lag between changing majority opinion and the law. Laws may be enacted or may continue to be enforced even when there is little consensus about them if they promote the interests of government leaders who have the power to make and enforce these laws. Or they may refuse to enact laws that a majority of people would like to see in place. An example is the failure to limit the terms of U.S. senators to 12 years, a measure that has long been supported by many voters.

Functions and Dysfunctions of Deviance

Durkheim (1938 [1895]) was the first of many sociologists with a functionalist perspective to emphasize shared values and beliefs as the basis for defining deviance and crime in a society. While most functionalists have focused on the negative effects of deviance, some have pointed to its positive functions in strengthening group norms and reinforcing group loyalties. Public punishment of offenders reaffirms group norms. Programs requiring high school students to visit prisons make young people aware of the consequences of criminal behavior. Conflict with outsiders helps unify insiders (Coser, 1956).

Durkheim also pointed to the usefulness of deviant groups or outsiders as a target for societal frustration (1938 [1895], pp. 65–73). In times of crisis, outsiders may provide an outlet for "moral outrage." In modern language, these individuals, ranging from racial/ethnic minorities to supposed witches, have sometimes served as scapegoats, diverting attention from the real threats or causes of misery in a society (Erikson, 1966).

Widespread nonconformity also serves to identify social problems. Violence and destructive mischief on the part of adolescents, for example, point to the need for programs to channel the energies of young people who are not successful in academic, work, or athletic activities into other, more constructive outlets (Jencks, 1992). For decades, sociologists have noted that members of violent gangs in low-income neighborhoods get recognition and prestige from their peers for their destructive behavior (Shaw and McKay, 1929; Cohen, 1955; Cloward and Ohlin, 1960; Chambliss, 1973; Hagedorn, 1988; Moore, 1991). This is an effective alternative for the respect and acceptance they do not receive from authority figures in the wider society—teachers, principals, and police officers—as well as other citizens.

In the 1990s, violent crime has been perceived in public opinion polls as the most serious social problem in the United States, with economic and health care problems in second and third place (Smolowe, 1993; *Gallup Poll Monthly,* March 1994, p. 28). Shooting sprees in suburban shopping malls, McDonald's restaurants, movie theaters, and trains have fostered the perception that no place is safe anymore. And, in fact, homicides and assaults in smaller cities and towns are creeping upward, while such incidents are declining slightly in the largest cities.

Functionalists have also pointed to the dysfunctions of deviance. The United States has the largest prison population in the entire world (Colvin, 1992; Inciardi, 1993). Government spending on controlling crime diverts resources from education, health care, and other needs of the larger population. Furthermore, widespread and increasingly random violence creates an atmosphere of fear and distrust that affects all human relationships. At the same time, in less violent arenas, publicized scams and pervasive rule bending in all areas of life in the United States reinforce this distrust.

Conflict Perspectives

Conflict theorists have focused on the social-class basis of crime and punishment—on how justice differs for people depending on their income and educational levels, their occupational prestige, and their power (Sutherland, 1983; Wheeler, Mann, and Sarat, 1988; Weisburd et al., 1991). In legal terms, crime is any activity defined by governments as harmful for which specific penalties and punishments are prescribed. But, as conflict theorists have long pointed out, it is the the most powerful groups in a society that define what is harmful, and they usually minimize or do not include their own harmful behavior in this definition (Chambliss and Mankoff, 1976; Zimring and Hawkins, 1992).

The rich are treated more leniently than the poor for the same offenses. This applies at every stage of the legal process: arrest, bail, trial, verdict, and sentencing, with punishment often involving a suspended sentence and/or community service instead of imprisonment or execution (Wheeler, Mann, and Sarat, 1988). No upper-class person in the United States has ever been executed for murder, despite convictions for murder in this class.

The poor are more likely than middle- and upper-class people to be arrested for loitering, vagrancy, drunkenness, fighting, and stealing. They are more likely to be detained in jail because they are unable to meet bail. They are more likely to be imprisoned because they cannot afford private lawyers or psychiatrists and have no influential relatives who will accept responsibility for them. They are less likely to be paroled because it is more difficult for them to prove that they are, or could be, respectable citizens.

Crime is widespread in all social classes; what vary are the opportunities and means to commit certain kinds of crime. The poor are more likely to commit street crimes; the rich commit corporate crimes. Direct physical violence such as mugging is more obvious and visible than crimes such as ignoring safety regulations, keeping two sets of books (on actual as well as reported income), infringements of patents, trademarks, and copyrights, restraint of trade, poisoning the environment, or price fixing. The public also exhibits greater agreement and awareness about the destructiveness of street crime as compared to white-collar crime. Are nuclear accidents a result of human error, or are they a result of irresponsible cost cutting and safety violations on the part of industries? Even nuclear physicists have disagreed about the answers to these questions in specific instances of nuclear accidents.

The true prevalence of crime in the United States is not revealed in official statistics. Self-report studies, in which people are asked on anonymous questionnaires to check off crimes and misdemeanors they have committed such as jaywalking, speeding, or illegal parking, indicate that illegal behavior is widespread. The major source of information about reported crime in the United States, the FBI's annual *Uniform Crime Reports,* includes the decisions of juvenile and criminal courts and reported violent crimes (such as murder, rape, robbery, and assault), larceny (embezzlement, forgery, and bad checks, for example), theft, prostitution, drug abuse, and gambling. But it excludes decisions by supervisory boards, regulatory commissions, and other administrative bodies such as the Internal Revenue Service. These agencies deal with cases of fraud, misrepresentation, and dishonesty on the part of higher-status people.

The results of victimization studies, in which people are asked whether they have reported the instances of mugging, vandalism, robbery, or assault that they have experienced, indicate something about the actual prevalence of crime in the United States. According to repeated surveys, more than 9 out of 10 people do not report these incidents to the police (Inciardi, 1993). Those surveyed most frequently give the following reasons for their failure to report crimes: (1) the police would not be able to help because they are inefficient, incompetent, or overwhelmed; (2) there is insufficient evidence; (3) the respondents do not want to press charges against the offender who is a relative, friend, or coworker; (4) they fear publicity or revenge by the offender; or (5) they do not want to take the time to testify in court (Inciardi, 1993).

The violation of important norms is widespread in the United States. Everyone violates laws at times, knowingly or unknowingly. What varies is who gets caught, what people are caught doing, and what happens to people after they are caught. This is directly related to socioeconomic status.

Furthermore, if the concept of crime is extended to behavior that causes the greatest harm to the greatest number, it should include murder, assault, and repression carried out by authoritarian military governments and law enforcement officials. These acts are committed against those that the officials define as political enemies (in war and peace) and against ethnic minorities, the powerless, and the poor. The crime in these instances is the violation of human rights and the failure to respond to basic human needs of citizens by government leaders (Zimring and Hawkins, 1992).

CRIME AND PUNISHMENT IN THE UNITED STATES

The latest developments in science and technology have resulted in faster identification and capture, although not in conviction, of criminals in the United States. Newer technologies are also changing the way convicted offenders are treated. Fingerprints, formerly matched by comparing smudgy fingerprint cards by hand, are now matched by computers that break down fingerprints into mathematical formulas and scan thousands of prints in an hour. DNA technology can match a bit of hair, blood, semen, or saliva to a suspect with almost 100 percent accuracy.

The criminal justice system is overwhelmed by the increased volume of cases, mainly from drug arrests since the "war on drugs" began in the 1980s (Inciardi, 1993). New antidrug laws increase penalties for drug-related crimes. More police have been assigned to drug enforcement, more arrests are being made of drug offenders, and prison populations are exploding (see Figure 7.1 on p. 236). Not only does the United States have the second-largest prison population (after Russia) in the entire world, but this population has quadrupled since 1973 (Clines, 1993, 1994). It now stands at 1.4 million.

Newer trends in law enforcement policy in the United States utilize the latest advances in automation and psychology. Intensive peer-group counseling led by teams of probation workers is being tried out for probationers with a history of violent behavior. In some cities, less violent probationers can now wear electronic ankle bracelets and report to machines equipped with voice-recognition technology.

In prisons, appointing inmates to administrative positions so that they develop a stake in maintaining order seems to help prevent prison riots (Colvin, 1992). When fellow inmates are in positions of authority, prisoners are more likely to take administrators as reference groups. Rehabilitation, a form of resocialization, may also be more likely. As labeling theorists have repeatedly documented, however, imprisonment typically provides further training in antisocial behavior and does not rehabilitate prisoners. It is the functional equivalent of going to graduate school and is strongly associated with future recidivism.

The increased presence of intravenous drug users and others at high risk for AIDS in prisons has resulted in the spread of the virus that causes AIDS among inmates (Inciardi, 1993). This has encouraged experimental prison-based drug treatment programs and more liberal release policies for those who are not drug offenders. Military-style boot camps for first offenders, federal subsidies to provide more police officers on the streets, more stringent gun control laws, and extension of the death penalty to include more types of killing are newer directions in public policy. Experts and government leaders, however, disagree about the deterrence or rehabilitation effects of most policies.

FIGURE 7.1

Crime and Punishment

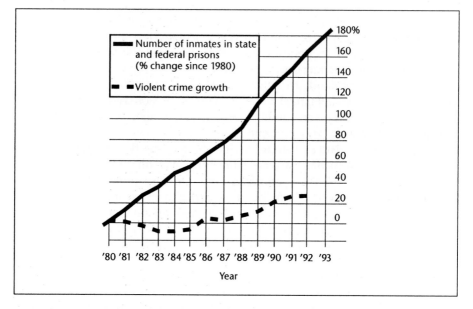

Source: Time, February 7, 1994, p. 58. Used by permission.

The number of inmates in state and federal prisons has grown more than five times as fast as the number of violent crimes, largely because of longer sentences for drug offenders.

According to Gallup polls, more than three-quarters of the U.S. population favors the death penalty (Gibbs, 1993b). The death penalty remains popular in most states (see Figure 7.2). Most criminologists, however, question the deterrence effect of capital punishment. Murders are usually impulsive, unplanned, and committed in the heat of uncontrollable rage. In these circumstances, rational consideration of possible long-term consequences is unlikely. Also, as noted earlier, the greatest increase in violent crimes is occurring among young people in gangs who are between 12 and 17 years old. They are more likely to think about dying on the streets today or tomorrow than by lethal injection sometime in the remote future.

The United States has had a stronger emphasis on individualism and greater geographic, social, and psychological mobility than other industrial democracies, and this has promoted extraordinary artistic creativity, individual achievement, and personal expression. U.S. popular culture is admired and imitated around the world. The other side of the coin, however, is unprecedented violence, unmatched in any other industrial democracy

FIGURE 7.2

Who Is Executed and Where

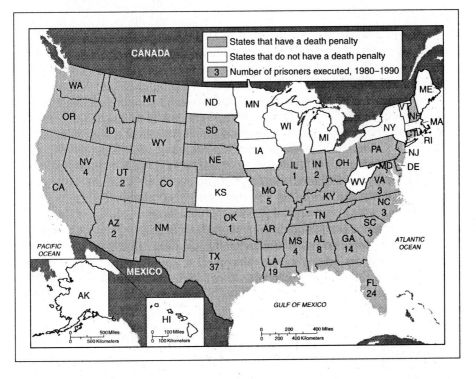

Sources: U.S. Bureau of Justice Statistics, *Capital Punishment 1991; Statistical Abstract of the United States,* 1992.

Most states now have a death penalty, though the number of prisoners executed has been small in most cases. The death penalty retains wide public support despite the lack of evidence to support its deterrent effect.

in the world. In the United States, even relatively poor adolescents have easy access to cars, drugs, and guns, a lethal combination in any society.

GLOBAL WHITE-COLLAR CRIME

The spread of multinational trading and investment firms, multinational industries, and secret, illegal, global political intervention by governments in modern times has elevated white-collar crime to previously unattainable heights. Intermittently, from the 1960s through the 1980s, for example, the CIA illegally financed thousands of armed mercenaries fighting secret wars, from Southeast Asia to Nicaragua (Hagan, 1994). During the 1970s and 1980s, the Bank of Credit and Commerce International (BCCI) laundered billions of drug-trafficking dollars illegally across national boundaries. The bank continued to operate for at least 10 years after its activities began to arouse the suspicion of the FBI and the Drug Enforcement Administration in the early 1980s. This is believed to be due to the huge number of powerful people in high and respectable places who were involved in BCCI's illegal operations (Hagan, 1994).

Illegal practices by multinational industries that have led to increased debt, deficits, diseases, and deaths around the world (especially in poorer societies) include (1) illegal price-fixing that increases the price of imported products, such as oil; (2) underpricing products sold to foreign subsidiaries, which are then resold for untaxed or lower-taxed capital gains profits; (3) "dumping" unsafe products on industrializing societies that have less restrictive safety laws, without revealing the known, dangerous side effects of these products; (4) testing risky new drugs on the poorest populations in industrializing societies, where informed consent is not required and the risk of lawsuits is minimal; and (5) bribing political officials to favor their products or relax regulatory laws (Hagan, 1994). The white-collar crimes of individuals working alone or in small groups in the past seem trifling compared to the organized, sophisticated, high-tech global crimes of modern times.

INVOLUNTARY DEVIANCE

That murderers, rapists, burglars, drug addicts, and prostitutes experience disapproval from large numbers of people is obvious. But some people occupy a disapproved status regardless of their behavior. They may or may not violate social norms, but they experience exclusion, stigma, and low social esteem in the wider society because of a physical or mental disability. Disabilities include visual impairment, hearing impairment, chronic illness, mental retardation, and mental illness (Sagarin, 1975). They are the subject of widespread negative stereotypes and experience prejudice and discrimination in education, housing, transportation, and employment. Former mental patients seem to experience even greater difficulty finding employment than physically disabled job applicants (Jones et al., 1991). If individuals with physical or mental disabilities were defined as a minority, they would constitute the second largest minority (36 million people) in the United States, after women (Meyerson, 1988).

People with disabilities have in common physical or psychological traits that are reacted to with disapproval, avoidance, distaste, or embarrassment. People with stigmatized traits may violate social norms, but if they do, it is because they *cannot* conform even if they want to, as in the case of autistic or severely disabled Down's syndrome children who are placed in regular classrooms and cannot participate in classroom activities in exactly the same way as other children. As sociologist Edward Sagarin (1975) observed, the nonconformity of these children is involuntary.

Like ethnic minorities, women, and others who have been excluded from full participation in mainstream activities and opportunities, people who are visually impaired, hearing impaired, and physically disabled have organized into social movements in the United States. Picketing by people in wheelchairs has worked very effectively to change rules defining the boundaries between the able and disabled. Wheelchair ramps and reserved parking spaces for disabled people are now commonplace in facilities used by the public.

The Rehabilitation Act of 1973 and the Education for All Handicapped Children Act of 1975 require business firms and schools that receive government contracts or funds to follow affirmative action and "inclusion" guidelines in hiring or admitting disabled workers and students. The Americans with Disabilities Act of 1990 helped remove some of the architectural and transportation barriers that made it difficult or impossible for many disabled people to commute to and enter workplaces. The deviant status persists, but the norms of access and acceptance are changing—to an extent.

Sociologist Talcott Parsons (1978) defined those who are sick and do not make every effort to get well as deviant. Actually, this is not a common type of deviance in the United States, where independence is a very strong value. To be unable to function and to be dependent on others for physical care is dreaded by most people, especially the elderly, who are more likely to be in this situation (Keith, 1990). In preindustrial societies, as well as modern-day Japan, for example, being physically taken care of in old age is defined as a *right* that elderly parents of adult children may expect. But in the individualistic United States, especially in the nonimmigrant, middle social classes, physical or mental disability in old age is more likely to be defined as a personal failure and a disgrace (Draper and Keith, 1992).

Study Guide

REVIEW OBJECTIVES

After studying this chapter, you should be able to:

1. Define deviance and describe the forms it takes.
2. Explain how definitions of deviance vary at different times and in different places (the relativity of deviance).
3. Describe biological, psychological, and sociological theories of deviance.
4. Examine variations in the frequency, type, and reactions to deviance during the course of sociocultural evolution.
5. Assess the global deviance of multinational corporations.
6. Describe the functions and dysfunctions of deviance.
7. Explain the relationship among social class, power, and deviant behavior.
8. Discuss recent trends in violence, law enforcement, and public policy in the United States.

SUMMARY

1. Deviance, from the point of view of the society, is a failure of socialization resulting in behavior that is strongly disapproved. Definitions of deviance vary with time, place, culture, and subculture.

2. Theories of deviance emphasize biological, psychological, or sociological factors in explaining deviance. Biological theories, insofar as they focus on defective genes, are useful in explaining involuntary deviance.

3. Psychological theories explain individual deviance. They emphasize individual differences in temperament and in relationships with caregivers during early childhood as a cause of deviant behavior.

4. Sociological theories use the concepts of anomie, cultural transmission, and labeling to explain differences in the rates and kinds of deviance in different groups and societies at different times. They also focus on

social location (social class, especially) in their research on reactions to deviance.

5. During the course of sociocultural evolution, deviance increases in frequency, becomes subcultural as well as individual, and, in industrial societies, is more often indirectly destructive, nonphysical, and secret or less easily observable. Formal sanctions and specialized law enforcement officials also become increasingly prevalent as societies industrialize. Global economies promote global white-collar crimes.

6. Crime is deviant activity that is defined as illegal by governments. It does not usually include harmful behavior on the part of governments that violate human rights and human needs.

7. The rich are treated more leniently than the poor at every stage of the legal process: arrest, detention or release on bail, trial, ver-

dict, and type of penalty imposed for the same crime. Crime is widespread in all classes, but opportunity to commit specific types of crime varies by class. The poor are more likely to commit street crimes; the rich are more likely to commit white-collar crimes in government, business, and industry.

8. Violent crime among the young has increased, the process of identifying criminals has improved, and the criminal justice system in the United States is increasingly unable to cope with the problem. Newer trends in law enforcement are controversial, with experts and politicians disagreeing about what works and does not work in detering crime and rehabilitating criminals.

9. Involuntary deviance involves individuals who are born with physical or mental traits that are disapproved of or who experience a disability that prevents conformity to norms.

GLOSSARY

Crime: Deviant activity that is defined as illegal by government authorities.

Cultural transmission: The learning of deviant behavior that is characteristic of particular geographic areas, societies, or groups.

Delinquency: Criminal behavior on the part of young people, primarily those under 16.

Deviance: Behavior or characteristics that violate important social norms and are strongly disapproved of by a large number of people in a society.

Differential association: Selective, intimate relationships with models whose behavior is defined as criminal.

Frustration: The blocking of immediate or long-term needs or goals.

Human nature: The common biological inheritance of humans that is assumed to determine specific behavior patterns.

Medicalization: The trend toward defining increasing numbers of nonconforming behaviors and conditions as illnesses.

Primary deviance: Behavior that results in being labeled deviant.

Recidivism: Repeated criminal acts by those who have been convicted of a crime.

Secondary deviance: Additional deviant behavior that is a response to being labeled deviant.

Status inconsistency: A discrepancy between two or more variables that determine a person's overall social status or prestige in a society.

Violence: Physical aggression against others.

White-collar crime: Secret and nonviolent crime committed by higher-status people, usually in their occupational activities.

PRACTICE TESTS

True ▪ False Test

___ 1. Strictly speaking, any violation of a social norm is deviant.

___ 2. Definitions of what is deviant have remained fairly consistent over time and across cultures.

___ 3. In the United States today, victimless crimes are generally judged more harshly than are violent crimes against people.

___ 4. Sociological studies have proven conclusively that the mesomorphic body type causes delinquency.

___ 5. Aggression often is a response to frustration in meeting one's immediate or long-range needs or goals.

___ 6. Another term for "cultural transmission" is "cultural diffusion."

___ 7. Deviance is more frequent in horticultural societies than in hunting and gathering societies.

___ 8. Crime is widespread in all social classes except the most elite.

___ 9. The change in the number of inmates in U.S. state and federal prisons since 1980 indicates that capital punishment is a strong deterrent to murder.

___ 10. People with disabilities are more likely than others to be involuntarily deviant.

Multiple-Choice Test

___ 1. In industrialized societies, developments in medical science have led to a tendency to define many forms of deviance as:
   a. germs.
   b. cancers.
   c. illness.
   d. cures.

___ 2. Stigmatization of people who are considered psychotic is a result of fear of their:
   a. destructiveness.
   b. passivity.
   c. emotional distance.
   d. pain.

___ 3. Involuntary deviance is usually:
   a. hereditary.
   b. nonviolent.
   c. abusive.
   d. due to mental retardation.

___ 4. Theories regarding human nature are based on:
   a. religion.
   b. economics.
   c. biology.
   d. environment.

__ 5. A researcher is attempting to explain deviance in a sample study. The subjects are described primarily in terms of their activity/energy levels and emotionality. The researcher is relying on:
  a. psychological theories.
  b. biological theories.
  c. sociological theories.
  d. criminological theories.

__ 6. Labeling theorists argue that deviant behavior is due to:
  a. family genetics.
  b. human nature.
  c. temperament.
  d. societal definitions and reactions.

__ 7. Deviance is primarily due to individual psychological differences in:
  a. multinational corporations.
  b. industrialized societies.
  c. hunting and gathering societies.
  d. anomic societies.

__ 8. The first sociologist with a functionalist perspective to emphasize shared values and beliefs as a basis for defining deviance and crime in a society was:
  a. Durkheim.
  b. Parsons.
  c. Merton.
  d. Marx.

__ 9. According to conflict theorists, which of the following persons is least likely to receive harsh punishment/penalties for a crime?
  a. a prostitute
  b. a factory worker
  c. a postal worker
  d. an accountant

__ 10. All of the following people have committed crimes for financial gain in the course of their work. Which is likely to have the most negative (e.g., widespread) impact as a result of these illegal activities?
  a. the owner of a Northeastern trucking company
  b. the mayor of a fairly large city
  c. an executive in an international chemical products company
  d. an official in a local trade union

Matching Test

Match each concept with its definition, illustration, or explication below.

1.

(1) Suicide
(2) Alcoholism
(3) Drunkenness
(4) Drinking
(5) Kleptomania

a. Self-victim
b. Not deviant
c. Medicalization model
d. Antisocial behavior
e. Deviant

2.

(1) Involuntary deviance
(2) Hereditary criminal instinct
(3) Frustration
(4) Human nature
(5) Temperament

a. Biological theories
b. Common biological inheritance
c. Psychological theories
d. Blocked goals
e. Usually nonviolent

3.

(1) Id
(2) Ego
(3) Superego
(4) Sociopathic
(5) Twin studies

a. No guilt
b. Genetic component
c. Unconscious
d. Conscience
e. Copes with reality

4.

(1) Freud
(2) Wilson
(3) Sheldon
(4) Merton
(5) Lombroso

a. Criminals are evolutionary throwbacks
b. Biologically grounded human nature theory
c. Structural strain
d. Proponent of destructive instinct
e. Body types

5.

(1) Delinquency
(2) Cultural transmission
(3) Differential association
(4) Recidivism
(5) Secondary deviance

a. Behavior passed generationally
b. Criminal behavior among the young
c. Response to being labeled deviant
d. Contact with criminals
e. Repeat offenses

REVIEW QUESTIONS

1. What is meant by the idea of "the relativity of deviance"? Give examples. Under what circumstances does this concept not apply?
2. How do various theories of deviance–biological, psychological, and sociological–help to explain deviant behavior? Give examples of the usefulness of each type of theory.
3. How do the frequency, type, sanctions, and kinds of deviance vary during the course of sociocultural evolution?
4. What are the underlying conditions that promote deviance?
5. What are some positive functions of deviance?
6. How do conflict theorists approach the study of deviance and crime?
7. What is meant by the medicalization of deviance? How does this promote conformity?
8. What disadvantages do disabled people share with other minorities in the United States?

APPLYING SOCIOLOGY

1. Make a list of all the types of behavior you have engaged in that are deviant or actually against the law, such as jaywalking, littering, truancy, shoplifting, or cheating on exams.
2. What sanctions did your parents and other authority figures in your life use to enforce conformity to norms?
3. Have you ever experienced a public confrontation with an authority figure that led to secondary deviance? How did your conception of yourself change as a result of this public confrontation?
4. Are any deviant patterns common and specific to your subculture?
5. How have your various statuses (class, gender, ethnic origin, age) affected confrontations you have had with principals, police, employers, or other authority figures?
6. Compare your experiences involving deviance with those of others you know, or know of, who occupy a different social status and were reacted to differently by authority figures.

8

Minorities

Violent conflict over material resources (land, jobs, money, and money-making enterprises) and nonmaterial resources (power and prestige) between minorities and dominant groups has been on the rise during the twentieth century. This kind of conflict has increased in frequency and intensity all over the world. It has taken different forms in different societies: the overthrowing of colonial governments, ethnic and tribal warfare, Protestant-Catholic, Hindu-Muslim, Christian-Muslim, and Jewish-Arab clashes. But the underlying basis is the same—economic frustration and the unequal distribution of power and economic resources in human societies. What are minorities, and why have their conflicts become so prominent in recent times?

CHARACTERISTICS OF MINORITIES

A **minority** is a large number of people "who, because of their physical or cultural characteristics, are singled out from others in the society in which they live for differential and unequal treatment" (Wirth, 1945, p. 347). Cultural differences may involve language, values, beliefs, and norms. Physical differences may involve visible characteristics such as skin color, the shape of the eyes, nose, and lips, hair texture, height, or physical disabilities. What defines a minority, however, is exclusion from full economic, political, religious, or recreational participation in the society. A minority may in fact be a numerical majority in a society. Indigenous populations in societies colonized by European countries in the past usually outnumbered their conquerors. In the United States today, women are a minority constituting 51 percent of the population.

In his classic definition of minorities, sociologist Louis Wirth also included recognition or awareness of "collective discrimination." A sense of sharing a common heritage or feelings of community or belonging together is typical of minorities. Minorities exist, however, even if they do not perceive themselves as such. Exclusion, domination, and inequality are the objective, defining variables. Increased awareness of minority status may lead to social movements and open confrontation, as in the current women's movement. It does not define the status, however.

Minority status is not usually voluntary. People are often born into the status. They are born female, African American, or Asian American, or they achieve minority status when they become old. And it is difficult, if not impossible, to change these ascribed statuses. Membership in a religious group that is a minority may be voluntary, however. Members of racial/ethnic minority groups tend to marry within their groups because of ethnic pride or because of opposition to intermarriage from other groups as well as their own.

Minorities have less power, and since power usually begets wealth, they very often have fewer economic resources as well. Dominant populations maintain their status by control of material goods—land, factories, money, and securities—as well as by prejudice, discrimination, segregation, and subordination. The term **prejudice** (from the Latin for "prejudgment") refers to internalized attitudes and beliefs that are usually negative stereotypes. Journalist Walter Lippmann, who coined the term "stereotype" in the 1920s, called them "pictures in our heads" (Lippmann, 1922). Stereotypes, as defined in chapter 2, are images of a particular group that are exaggerated and are applied indiscriminately to all members of the group. Stereotypes are not supported by empirical research.

The statement that there is less exclusion of African Americans from certain prestigious occupations in the United States today than there was 30 years ago is a generalization based on survey research evidence. The

FIGURE 8.1

Voting for a Black Presidential Candidate

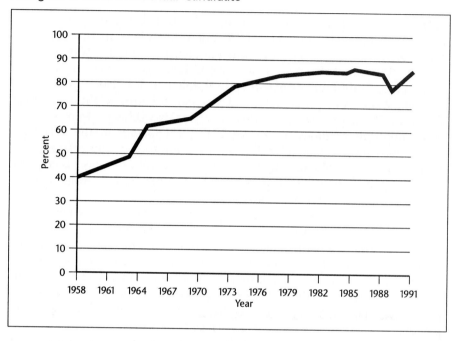

Sources: Surveys by the Gallup Organization, 1958–1969; National Opinion Research Center, University of Chicago, 1974–1991.

The question asked in this survey was: If your party nominated a well-qualified black man for president, would you vote for him? The percentage of people who answered "yes" is recorded on the graph above. This percentage has more than doubled since the late 1950s.

statement that African Americans are unintelligent or lazy is a stereotype. Stereotypes may be negative or positive and may be applied to dominant groups as well as minorities. Stereotypes are often used to justify differences in the power, wealth, and opportunities of different categories of people in a society.

Numerous surveys have reported a decline in prejudice in the United States since the beginning of the civil rights and women's movements in the 1960s up to the 1970s. In a Gallup poll conducted in 1963, nearly half (45 percent) of the whites polled said they would move if an African American family moved in next door (reported in American Institute of Public Opinion, 1978). Less than half (47 percent) would vote for a qualified African American for president. Twenty percent said they approved of interracial marriage.

FIGURE 8.2

Voting for a Female Presidential Candidate/Approving of Married Women in Business

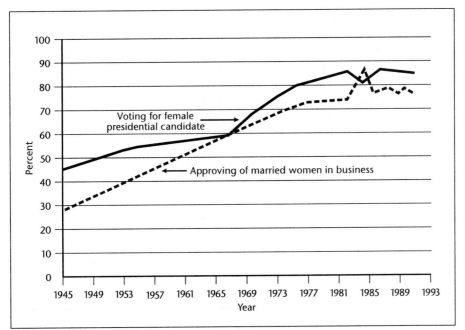

Sources: Female presidential candidate: Surveys by American Institute of Public Opinion (Gallup), 1937–1971; National Opinion Research Center, General Social Surveys, 1972–1989. Married women in business: Surveys by the Roper Organization for *Fortune,* 1945; American Institute of Public Opinion (Gallup), 1970; National Opinion Research Center, General Social Surveys, 1972–1991.

This graph shows the percentage of Americans who said they would vote for a female presidential candidate and the percentage who said they approved of married women earning money in business or industry. It points to a major change in values and attitudes toward women's roles over the past 50 years.

Fifteen years later, by 1978, only 4 percent of whites said they would move if an African American family became their neighbors. Over three-quarters of the population (77 percent) said they would vote for an African American for president (see Figure 8.1), and over one-third (36 percent) approved of intermarriage. A slightly lower percentage (76 percent) would vote for a qualified woman for president, but this, too, had risen from less than half (46 percent) in 1963 (American Institute of Public Opinion, 1978). By 1991, about 85 percent of voters would vote for an African American or a woman for president. These figures indicate dramatic change during this period of time, but the change may be exaggerated because of pressure felt by those polled to give socially acceptable responses.

More recently, however, attitudes toward minorities in the United States and other countries have hardened in response to widespread economic recession, increased economic hardship, and more militant confrontations between dominant and minority groups. In the United States this has taken the form of increasing opposition to new immigration. More than three quarters of the immigrants to the United States since 1960 have been nonwhite and/or non-European: Asians have constituted 22 percent of immigrants, Latinos 47 percent, and blacks, mainly from the Caribbean, 7 percent (Passel and Edmonston, 1992, Table 9). In polls taken in 1993, while 59 percent of respondents reported having felt in the past that immigration was good for this country, 60 percent now felt it was a "bad thing" (Morganthau, 1993, p. 19). And whereas 33 percent in 1963 felt that immigration levels should be decreased, 61 percent had this opinion in 1993 (Mydans, 1993, p. 16). The economic burden to taxpayers of providing needed social services to poorer or older immigrants in a time of economic downturn was the major reason given by those polled for their change in attitude.

Prejudice is internal and subjective. It consists of negative attitudes, beliefs, and perceptions. **Discrimination** refers to overt behavior that excludes minorities from wealth, power, opportunities, and activities. People who discriminate may or may not be prejudiced. They may discriminate because it is economically profitable to do so, even though they have no particular ill feelings about a minority (Merton, 1949). And people who are prejudiced may or may not discriminate. They may be prevented from acting on their attitudes and beliefs by law. But prejudice and discrimination usually go together.

Dominant groups also try to maintain their status and privileges by segregation. **Segregation** is a consequence of discrimination. It involves separation and exclusion from residential, commercial, occupational, recreational, educational, and religious facilities and activities. Segregation is usually involuntary because dominant groups enact and enforce norms of exclusion. But it may represent the desire of the outgroup to limit their social relationships to others who share the same disadvantages in the wider society, as in the gilded ghettos described in chapter 6. The degree of segregation of minorities is related to their degree of perceived physical difference (however mixed) from the dominant population.

In the United States, African Americans experience the most segregation (O'Hare, 1992a). Individuals of Latino origin are more likely to be living in segregated neighborhoods than Native Americans and Asian/Pacific Islanders, who have roughly the same level of segregation. The greater segregation of Latinos is usually attributed to their more recent arrival and the greater persistence of strong familistic values (O'Hare, 1992a). Any decline in economic opportunities in the wider society also tends to promote segregation because it diminishes chances for mobility and acceptance of minority populations (see Table 8.1).

TABLE 8.1

Characteristics of Minorities

• Physical and/or cultural distinctiveness • Involuntary membership (ascribed status) • Exclusion, segregation • Experiences of prejudice, discrimination	• Political and economic subordination, inequality • Friendship and marriage within the group • Consciousness of common heritage; feelings of belonging

ORIGINS OF RACIAL/ETHNIC MINORITIES

Minorities are classified according to whether the unequal treatment they experience is based primarily on perceived physical or cultural differences. Gender differences are physical, as are the differences that come with old age, but both are associated with changes in norms and values that usually vary along generational lines.

Race is an ambiguous concept. It refers to certain inherited physical traits that originally distinguished human populations thousands of years ago. Many of these physical differences are believed to have evolved as isolated inbreeding populations in different geographic areas adapted to different geographic environments. Dark skin, for example, filters out the ultraviolet rays of the sun, which, at high levels, increase the risk of skin cancer, though the body requires this sunlight to manufacture vitamin D. Dark skin is adaptive in tropical climates, but could increase the chances of vitamin D deficiency, rickets, and death in colder climates where there is less sun. According to this theory, lighter-skinned people were more likely to survive and therefore become prevalent in colder climates as a result of genetic change and natural selection. Darker-skinned people would be more likely to survive in equatorial or tropical climates.

Defining or classifying races is problematic, however, because migration, exploration, wars, slavery, and colonization have resulted in a great deal of contact and interbreeding among races, especially since the beginning of agriculture. Many human populations (such as Polynesians or Latinos) are so physically mixed that it is difficult or impossible to classify them as belonging to one or another race (O'Hare, 1992a; Lott, 1993).

In the past, the most common racial classification system divided the human species into three broad categories: Caucasoid (light skin, straight or wavy hair), Mongoloid (yellowish skin, skin fold over eye), and Negroid (dark skin, closely curled hair). Notice that these terms end with the suffix "oid," meaning "like."

Such racial classifications are based on ideal-types. Reality is more complex and often more confusing, as census takers quickly find out.

The Census Bureau does not recognize a separate "mixed race" category. (It does note that Hispanics/Latinos may be of any race.) But the high intermarriage rates of Latinos, Asians, and Native Americans with partners of different ethnic origin, coupled with their rapidly growing numbers, have led to a minor boomlet of children of mixed race or mixed ethnicity in the United States. In 1989, more than one-half of the children born to a Native American parent had a mother or father of different ethnic origin, as did one-third of the births to an Asian parent. Nearly one-third of the births to a Latino parent of any race also had a non-Latino mother or father (Kalish, 1992). Resistance by legislators to the inclusion of a "multiracial" category in the census centers on the possible necessity to redraw legislative districts that this might involve (Wright, 1994). Widespread reassessments of civil rights programs in housing, education, and employment might be necessary if more people are excluded from or included in other racial categories as a consequence of a new "multiracial" category.

In the United States, nearly every census has measured race differently. In 1790, when the first census was conducted, the population was divided into free white males, free white females, other persons (free blacks and "taxable Indians"—those who lived in or around white settlements), and slaves. In the nineteenth century, slaves were classified as black or mulatto. In the 1890 census, the mulatto category was further broken down into quadroons and octoroons. Currently, in classifying the population, the "one drop" rule prevails. This defines as black any person with even a single drop of "black blood" (Wright, 1994).

In the 1990 U.S. Census, when offered the choices of white, black, American Indian/Alaskan Native and Asian/Pacific Islander, 10 million people checked off "Other" (Barringer, 1993). Most were later identified by the Census Bureau as Hispanics.

The Office of Management and Budget periodically issues statistical directives that serve as the basis for racial classifications in the U.S. Census. Asian Indians were originally classified as nonwhite. Later, they were classified as white. Nonwhite status, however, now brings with it certain advantages, such as affirmative action directives, minority contracting privileges, and antidiscrimination laws. In the 1990 Census, Asian Indians were once again classified as nonwhite. The Association of Indians in America had successfully lobbied to have Asian Indians included in the Asian/Pacific Islander category in the 1990 Census (Barringer, 1993).

The important thing about race is the social definitions that societies give to the term. Racial purity is a myth that continues to exist for ideological rather than scientific reasons. Dominant groups often classify people racially on the basis of arbitrary and ambiguous traits. Nevertheless, perceived physical differences are often a more important reason than cultural differences for the persistence of prejudice, discrimination, and segregation against a particular category of people in a society. If a person is of mixed racial origins, which is more important in classifying that person—skin color, facial characteristics, or other features? Why should one physical trait be more significant than another in classifying people racially? Even more to the point, why has it seemed necessary or important to classify people racially? The answer to the last question is that ethnic origin is a basis for minority status and inequality. Governments concerned with the needs of their populations and willing to act on this concern must know who and how many people are minorities. They must know what their problems are, compared to the rest of the population. Classification has also served to identify targets of discrimination, however, as in Germany during the Nazi era.

Cultural definitions promote or diminish awareness of differences and affect evaluations of these differences. Dominant groups tend to associate inherited *physical* differences of various populations with inherited *mental* differences, such as intelligence and temperament. They justify their power over minorities and their exploitation and exclusion of these groups on racial grounds. This is a major reason why the concept of race has been so appealing to so many people historically.

Darker-skinned peoples such as the Moors or Tartars were colonizers. They were not regarded as intellectually or temperamentally inferior by their subjugated populations. Power and wealth affect reactions to and evaluations of physical differences. Racial minority status, like so many other phenomena in human societies, is a matter of time, place, and society. This is especially clear in the case of specific ethnic groups that are not classified as minorities on the basis of perceived physical differences. Greeks and Italians were not minorities when ancient Greece and the Roman Empire were colonizing societies. Both groups have been minorities in a number of societies, including the United States, since then, primarily on the basis of cultural rather than physical differences.

Ethnic minorities (from the Greek *ethnos,* meaning "nation") trace their ancestors to a particular country or continent. They may have distinctive physical traits, which is why we use the concept **racial/ethnic minority.** Often these have been blurred by centuries of migration and interbreeding, however, as in the case of the Jewish population. Jews have a feeling of common identity and cultural traditions that are shared by those who identify as Jews. But they have inhabited a great variety of countries. They are less likely than Arabs, who were less mobile geographically over the centuries, to have retained the physical traits originally associated with Semitic peoples from the Middle East (Allport, 1958).

The first ethnic minorities were slaves in the more advanced horticultural societies. Slavery continued to be a source of minority group formation until the later stages of the Industrial Revolution. It is now outlawed as a form of human domination in all industrial societies. But descendants of former slaves, if they are physically or culturally distinct, continue to experience exclusion in the societies in which they live.

By far the most frequent source of minority group formation in the past has been wars of conquest and occupation. This has sometimes resulted from the overrunning and annexation of neighboring societies and their populations. More frequently, however, minorities were formed as the result of colonization by distant societies.

In the twentieth century, two world wars, socialist revolutions in many parts of the world, the population explosion in industrializing societies, and the partitioning or breaking up of societies into new political units (as in the former Soviet Union) have resulted in massive movements of human populations. Economic hardship and natural disasters have been other major forces in the migration of populations and the creation of new minorities. The uprooted are usually minorities in the societies that receive them.

Religious conflicts have often disguised underlying economic conflicts—as in Lebanon and Northern Ireland today. In recent times, overpopulation has enhanced the economic deprivation experienced by the poor in industrializing societies. But barriers to immigration have become more stringent as the need for unskilled labor declines in postindustrial societies. For this reason, the creation of new minorities has slowed considerably. More often, now, minorities already in existence are struggling to achieve the power and political independence they once had and lost. The results, in the form of ethnic conflict, are all around us in Asia, Africa, Eastern Europe, the Middle East, and elsewhere.

Subcultural differences, such as language, religion, values, and norms, usually distinguish racial/ethnic minorities. Minorities may also have distinct patterns of dress, food preparation, music, art, leisure, and recreational preferences. In the United States in recent times, these differences have increasingly been viewed as positive rather than negative and have become less likely to prevent social mobility and acceptance in mainstream occupations. Fifty years ago, many movie stars, especially those who played romantic leads, adopted English names to conceal their minority origins. Today entertainers more often retain their family names, although many do not (see Table 8.2). The geographic distribution of minority groups in the United States remains uneven, with the Midwest having relatively few minority group members by comparison to the West and the South (see Figure 8.3 on p. 256).

THEORIES OF PREJUDICE AND RACIAL/ETHNIC CONFLICT

Prejudice, discrimination, and racial/ethnic conflict are closely tied to social location. They vary in intensity and frequency in different cultures and societies at different times. Explanations of who is prejudiced, why, and under what circumstances draw from a wide variety of theoretical perspectives. Researchers who use a sociocultural evolution model focus primarily

TABLE 8.2

Selected Entertainers' Original and Stage Names

Alphonso D'Abruzzo	Alan Alda
Allen Konigsberg	Woody Allen
Frederick Austerlitz	Fred Astaire
Betty Joan Perske	Lauren Bacall
Anthony Benedetto	Tony Bennett
Nicholas Coppola	Nicolas Cage
Cherilyn Sarkisian	Cher
Issur Danielovitch	Kirk Douglas
Robert Zimmerman	Bob Dylan
Sally Mahoney	Sally Field
Greta Gustafsson	Greta Garbo
Caryn Johnson	Whoopi Goldberg
Ehrich Weiss	Harry Houdini
Krishna Banji	Ben Kingsley
Eugene Orowitz	Michael Landon
Lee Yuen Kam	Bruce Lee
Georgios Panayiotou	George Michael
Carlos Ray	Chuck Norris
Winona Horowitz	Winona Ryder
Ramon Estevez	Martin Sheen
Annie Mae Bullock	Tina Turner

Source: The World Almanac and Book of Facts 1994, Mahwah, NJ: Funk & Wagnalls.

From the late nineteenth century, when Harry Houdini began performing, until today, U.S. entertainers have used stage names to conceal their ethnic origins.

on global, historical, and cross-cultural evidence in their explanations. They point to the effects of cultural (material and nonmaterial), economic, and political changes as human societies become more complex as factors in ethnic prejudice and conflict (Ross, 1993).

Conflict theorists have focused specifically on the competition between dominant and racial/ethnic minority groups over the unequal distribution of power and income and wealth in a society (Semyonov and Cohen, 1990; Beck and Tolnay, 1990; Bellanger and Pinnard, 1991). Functionalists have focused more on ethnocentrism, subcultural differences, and the learned cultural transmission of prejudiced beliefs and hostile behavior toward minorities (Merton, 1949; Prothro, 1952; Pettigrew, 1971). Psychologists have pointed to a greater personal need to hate outsiders on the part of particular personality types (Fromm, 1941; Adorno et al., 1950).

It is important to point out, once again, that these are not competing or mutually exclusive perspectives. There are no rigid boundaries between theoretical perspectives in modern times, anymore than there are rigid boundaries between societies, cultures, social classes, and life stages.

FIGURE 8.3

Racial/Ethnic Groups in the United States

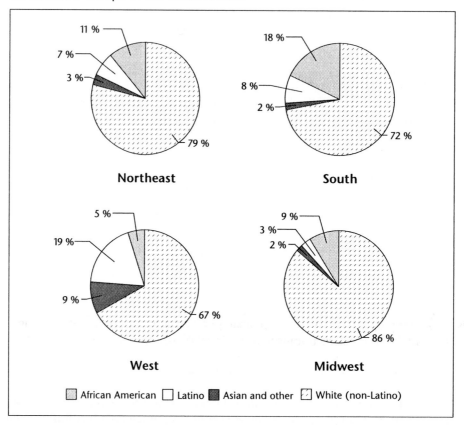

Source: *The United States Population Data Sheet,* 10th ed., Population Reference Bureau, Inc., 1991.

The most European American area of the United States is the Midwest, with 86 percent of its population descended mainly from British, Irish, German, Scandinavian, and Slavic people; whereas in the West, with relatively high percentages of Latinos and Asians, the European American majority drops to 67 percent. Despite large northern and western migrations of southern blacks, the South still has the highest percentage of African Americans.

Psychological Theories

Psychological explanations of prejudice have tended to relate hatred toward minorities to abusive, authoritarian, or rejecting parent/child relationships in childhood. Some years ago, Theodore Adorno and his colleagues (1950) conducted a massive series of surveys, interviews, and psychological tests to determine the psychological origins of prejudice. Questions centered on discipline experienced during childhood and attitudes toward minorities.

The researchers concluded that very strict, rigid, cold, and physically punishing childrearing practices produce authoritarian personalities. The **authoritarian personality**, according to these researchers, is characterized by extreme political and economic conservatism, ethnocentrism, and prejudice.

More specifically, researchers in this tradition describe authoritarian individuals as very conventional and conformist, sexually repressed, superstitious, submissive toward those who have more power, and bullying and sadistic toward those who have less power. Authoritarian individuals value power and toughness. They feel threatened by minorities, whom they view as dangerous. They avoid thinking about themselves, especially their motives and feelings. They view others in rigid, stereotyped terms.

Psychologists who use this model believe that children who are not permitted to express anger and hostility toward tyrannical parents or caregivers tend to deny this anger and displace it onto scapegoats. **Scapegoats** are less powerful people in a society who are held responsible for individual or social problems in the society.

According to scapegoat theory, the feelings of frustration and rage that humans cannot express toward brutal or rejecting parents, exploitative bosses, harsh teachers, or ineffective, unjust, or oppressive governments are displaced onto powerless minorities. Scapegoating may take the form of expulsion, imprisonment, lynching and other kinds of genocide, vandalism, or bullying. Those who scapegoat justify their actions by attributing to minorities destructive impulses of their own that they are not aware of—impulses to rape, murder, assault, cheat, steal, or lie. For example, white men have lynched black men on the grounds that they have raped or would like to rape white women. Historically, in reality, white men have been far more likely to rape black women than have black men to rape white women. And the real but repressed object of rage and hostility in the case of rape, according to scapegoat theory, is the frustrating, rejecting, abusive, or unavailable mother, father, or other caregiver during infancy and childhood.

Sociological Theories

Psychological theories, however valid, cannot alone explain differences in the frequency and intensity of racial and ethnic conflict at different times and places, or even at the same time in different parts of the same society. Sociologists have added an understanding of the importance of social location in time and in geographic and cultural space in explaining differences in the intensity of prejudice and discrimination and the frequency of ethnic conflict.

Cultural Transmission Adorno and his colleagues (1950) found that authoritarian personalities were not much more prevalent in the South than in the North during the 1950s. But reported prejudiced attitudes were more

Focus on Social Issues

ETHNIC CONFLICT IN AFRICA

[The fall of dictatorships and increased political freedom may unleash ethnic tensions that have long been suppressed by autocrats and their security forces. This is especially likely to happen when a ruling ethnic group is a numerical minority and fears losing its privileged position in a society. The result may be open conflict and violence or subtle subversion of newly installed democratic forms of government. The sudden death of a leader, democratic or autocratic, followed by an unanticipated political void, may also bring submerged ethnic conflicts to the surface. In Africa, despite national governments established by colonial powers, geographically based tribal identities and loyalties remain very strong and do not coincide with national political boundaries.]

Already the drive for political rights south of the Sahara has consigned the archetypal autocrat–the "president for life" who rules with a fly whisk and a squadron of secret police–to the same graveyard as apartheid, African socialism, and the ships that brought the first European colonizers 500 years ago. . . .

A rise in ethnic tension, while part of the worldwide explosion of claims of sovereignty and self-determination in the post–cold war era, is particularly dangerous in Africa, where the boundaries inherited from colonialism do not correspond to the areas inhabited by ethnic groups. . . . "[W]e have two civilizations here. The Western one on top, where everything is fine and differences are submerged in talk of national unity. And a parallel one underneath, an African one, where ethnic groups are the reality."

–John Darnton, "Africa Tries Democracy, Finding Hope and Peril," *New York Times,* June 21, 1994, pp. A1, A8

What Do You Think?

1. What other factors might be involved in the current worldwide increase in ethnic conflict, especially on other continents?
2. How might the focus of a functionalist, a conflict theorist, and a sociobiologist differ in explaining the contemporary increase in ethnic violence?
3. What do you see as a possible solution to this problem?

frequent in the South. Why? Sociologists and social psychologists have focused on the learning, or cultural transmission, of prejudiced attitudes from generation to generation in different geographic areas, social classes, and families (Merton, 1949; Prothro, 1952; Pettigrew, 1971). When models and reference groups have prejudiced attitudes, these attitudes are learned in childhood through the process of identifying with family, teachers, friends, and community members whom we admire and respect. This type of prejudice in nonauthoritarian individuals, however, is not based on a deep-seated psychological need to be hostile to outsiders. Presumably, it would be easier to change when individuals move to another area or experience a change in their cultural environment.

Conflict Theory   Cultural transmission theory alone cannot explain why prejudice is stronger in certain cultures or subcultures than in others. It cannot explain the origins of prejudice. More important, it cannot explain changes in prejudice and in ethnic conflict during different periods of time in a particular society. To answer these questions, the conflict model is helpful. Conflict theorists point to the unequal power of minorities and the desire by dominant groups to exploit and profit from them economically in explaining prejudice, discrimination, and racial/ethnic conflict (Hewitt, 1977; Semyonov and Cohen, 1990; Bellanger and Pinnard, 1991). Prejudiced beliefs provide the justification for the inequality, exclusion, and subordination of minorities.

Racial/Ethnic Violence   According to conflict theory, violence between minorities and dominant groups increases as subordinate groups lose what Karl Marx called their "false consciousness." The subordinate population stops believing in the ideologies that justify their subordination. This occurs primarily as a result of the higher level of education and income that even the poor attain as sociocultural evolution yields vastly increased economic resources in human societies. Social movements arise and are led by individuals who are experiencing change, often improvement, in their life circumstances. Seldom do those who are most miserable and downtrodden in a society have the energy or the insight to start social movements.

Conflict theorists also relate increased racial/ethnic violence to increased economic stress or political frustration in particular societies. Violence in a society can take the form of civil war, rioting, or **terrorism**—politically motivated violence directed against civilian populations. In a pioneering study of 19 societies with racial, religious, or ethnic minorities, three factors were most closely related to the occurrence of racial/ethnic violence: extreme economic inequality and deprivation, political repression, and demographic changes (Hewitt, 1977). The demographic changes involved large increases in the minority population and a relative decline in the dominant population.

When economic and political frustration rises in a society, hostility toward minorities also rises. This is happening currently in a great number of societies, including the United States, Great Britain, Germany, and Eastern European societies. Historically, the increasing public anti-Semitism and xenophobia in Germany that helped the Nazi Party come to power in 1933 coincided with a severe economic depression; Germans blamed the economic crisis on Jews and foreigners. In the United States, E. M. Beck and Stewart E. Tolnay (1990) studied reported incidents of lynching in the Deep South region of the United States during the years 1882–1930. They found that lynching was more frequent during the years when the price of cotton declined and inflation increased. Lynch mobs were most likely to be made up of economically marginal white farmers, furthermore. The declining importance of agriculture as the South began to industrialize and the decrease in the African American population as a result of migration to the North diminished the frequency of lynching after 1900.

POLICIES TOWARD MINORITIES

Governments have reacted to minorities in two basic ways, depending on the usefulness and profitability of maintaining the minority status in the particular society. In some cases, they have tried to eliminate minorities, either by expulsion or extermination, or, alternatively, by total absorption. In other cases, they have attempted to maintain that status by continued exclusion and domination.

Extermination and Expulsion Policies

The most extreme way to eliminate minorities is to kill off as many members as possible. The native populations of South Africa, the United States, and Hawaii, as well as the Jews and Gypsies during the Nazi era in Germany, have been victims of genocidal policies.

Expulsion also removes unwanted, unnecessary, but sometimes economically advantaged minorities. In the United States, Native Americans were driven from their rich tribal lands onto desolate and barren reservations. More recently, as former colonies around the world have achieved independence, minority commercial peoples such as the Chinese in Vietnam and Asian Indians in Uganda, who had achieved a certain degree of economic success, mainly as shopkeepers, have been expelled. The property of these peoples was confiscated by leaders of the original native populations who achieved dominant status once again in these societies.

Assimilation and Acculturation Policies

Minorities can also be eliminated by absorbing them into the dominant population—a process known as **assimilation.** Assimilation, as the term is defined here, involves a complete loss of distinct racial/ethnic identity. Up to now at least, it has not been possible to find a human society of any size and complexity in which assimilation has resulted in a complete merging of racial/ethnic minorities with the dominant groups in a society. Children of mixed parentage are labeled Colored in South Africa; Mestizo in Mexico; and Cafuso, Mazambo, Preto, or Escuro in Brazil. They continue to maintain a distinct identity and to experience varying degrees of exclusion and inequality.

In the United States today, Native American and Japanese American women have the highest intermarriage rates among minority group women.

In Los Angeles County in 1989, 40.6 percent of Japanese American women married outside their ethnic background, as did over one-half (53.7 percent) of Native American women (Tucker and Mitchell-Kernan, 1990). In contrast, although the intermarriage rate of African Americans has doubled in recent years, it remains at less than 3 percent (U.S. Bureau of the Census, 1992, Table 55).

Acculturation is the learning of the language, values, norms, and skills necessary for social mobility in a particular society. Different minority populations do not acculturate to the same degree or in the same length of time. According to dozens of studies of immigrant acculturation, certain conditions help or hinder the acculturation of specific minorities (Yorburg, 1973, 1974, 1983).

Physical and Cultural Differences   The degree of cultural and physical distinctiveness from the dominant population is an important factor in determining the extent of acculturation and the speed with which it takes place. In the United States, white, English-speaking, Protestant immigrants have historically acculturated (and assimilated) most rapidly. We rarely refer to people as English, Scottish, or Welsh Americans. We do have a concept of Irish Americans, however. Irish and English immigrants have similar physical characteristics and speak the same language. But most Irish immigrants, unlike English immigrants, have been Catholic rather than Protestant. This makes Irish immigrants that much different, culturally, from the dominant groups in the United States, who are often labeled WASPs (White Anglo-Saxon Protestants).

Latino immigrants to the United States from Central and South America and the Caribbean have generally shared the same language, religion, and certain other norms and customs. But Cuban Americans who fled Cuba after the revolution of 1959 have acculturated more quickly than Mexican Americans (Portes, 1993). Most Mexican American immigrants are poor and from rural areas with strong traditional values. The initial Cuban immigration was largely middle class and urban in origin. The modern values of rationalism and achievement that Cuban immigrants brought with them were closer to the dominant values in the United States today. The Cuban immigrants also arrived, usually, with more education and money to help give them a start in the new society.

Physical difference from the dominant population is also important in affecting rates of acculturation of various minorities. Racial differences are usually more visible than cultural differences. African Americans, who are among the oldest immigrants to the United States, continue to experience a higher degree of exclusion than other, more recent immigrant minorities, whose physical differences are usually less obvious.

Latino immigrants to the United States have a higher median family income and lower rates of poverty than African Americans (U.S. Bureau of the Census, 1993). African American poverty is usually linked to the increasing number of unmarried women who head families in that subculture. But African American married couples have also experienced an increase in poverty in recent years (Pear, 1993a).

Attitudes and Costs   The willingness of minorities to acculturate also affects their rate of acculturation. Cultural pluralism does not necessarily slow the process of acculturation, since social mobility does not require the loss of group distinctiveness in more tolerant social climates. On the other hand, the strong familistic values of Mexican American immigrants to the United States from rural areas in Mexico tend to slow acculturation (Skerry, 1993). Children of Mexican immigrants are less willing to accept scholarships at distant colleges or better jobs in far-off cities because they do not want to leave their families. Families are a highly valued source of emotional support in this subculture.

The attitudes toward acculturation of newer legal immigrants to the United States, especially those from Latin and Central America, differ significantly from European immigrants in the past. In New York City, slightly over half of the legal immigrants who find it difficult or impossible to return home for visits—political refugees and immigrants from distant societies—become citizens after the 5-year waiting period (Sontag, 1993). These are mainly from the former Soviet Union (with 53 percent of emigrés becoming citizens after 5 years) and from China (with 56 percent becoming citizens at that time).

By contrast, less than a third of the legal immigrants from Central and South America and the Caribbean have become citizens even after 10 years in the United States. In part this is because they retain their national identity and are reluctant to give it up. Some entertain the hope of returning home when they have saved enough money or accumulated enough material goods. Fear of the citizenship exam, which contains civics questions that even many native-born citizens would find difficult to answer, is another reason for remaining in political limbo.

In the first large-scale study of the children of immigrants to the United States in over 50 years, sociologist Alejandro Portes (1993) compared attitudes of these children with those of second-generation European American children earlier in the twentieth century. The study was based on 5,000 interviews with eighth- and ninth-grade children of Haitian and Cuban immigrants (mainly in Miami) and Mexican, Filipino, and Vietnamese immigrants (mainly in San Diego).

The most striking difference from previous generations is the much stronger pride the children of the more recent immigrants feel about their parents' cultural traditions and ethnic identities. While most are bilingual, they prefer English and speak it more fluently than their parents' native language. And most share the dream of social mobility through education. Fifty or more years ago, however, the children of European immigrants found more entry-level unskilled and semiskilled jobs, especially in industry.

Members of this generation will find their initial prospects for advancement more limited.

As for the attitudes of dominant groups, equal status contact with minorities of the same social class promotes acceptance and respect. Integrated housing and schools work best in neighborhoods where minorities and dominant groups are of the same social class. Also, discrimination on the part of dominant groups becomes more costly in industrial welfare state societies, since it results in higher health care, welfare, and law enforcement costs to governments and taxpayers.

In industrial democracies, a large base of unskilled labor is unnecessary, and governments take over the costs of health, education, and welfare, to a greater or lesser extent. Discrimination promotes poverty and increases the costs to the dominant groups of providing remedial services of all kinds to the poor. The cost of maintaining those incarcerated in prison, the majority of whom are from lower-income groups, becomes prohibitive.

Economic and Political Conditions Another important factor in acculturation is economic and political conditions in a society at the time of arrival. At the time of the civil rights and women's movements, economic conditions in the United States were favorable to acculturation. This changed with the downturn in the business cycle beginning in the early 1970s and the continuing loss of working-class jobs that require little education and technical skills.

Discrimination not only becomes increasingly costly, economically, in industrial societies, it also results in greater psychic costs to the dominant population. Guilt, pessimism, and demoralization are more likely when there is a split between cultural ideals of tolerance and equality and actual behavioral norms of hostility and discrimination toward minorities. Swedish sociologist Gunnar Myrdal (1944) referred to this contradiction as "the American dilemma" in his famous study of racial/ethnic relations in the United States in the 1940s. In more recent times, the situation has become much more psychologically distressing to dominant and minority populations alike. Economic and family changes (unemployment, the increase in single-parent households), drugs, guns, shattered expectations, and materialism have greatly intensified violence among poorer minorities. And the fear and outrage of better-situated members of the society have grown proportionately (Rubin, 1992).

Ample job opportunities and good educational facilities promote acculturation for two reasons. Competition and hostility between minorities and the lower socioeconomic levels of the dominant population are diminished. Also, greater numbers of minority populations are able to rise into the middle class. European immigrants to New York City around the turn of the twentieth century, for example, had much less difficulty acculturating than the non-European immigrants who are arriving now. For almost 125 years, professional training at night at free city colleges had provided a

TABLE 8.3

Factors Affecting Rates of Acculturation

• Degree of physical and cultural difference from the dominant population in a society • Willingness of minorities to acculturate • Attitudes and beliefs of the dominant population (prejudices and stereotypes) • Costs of discrimination compared to the advantages of exclusion	• Educational and economic opportunities available in the society • Degree of contact with or isolation from the dominant population • Nearness to country of origin • Age at immigration, recency of arrival, and gender

pathway to security and acceptance for countless numbers of ambitious but impoverished European immigrants or their children. Many industries today have fled the city, city schools have serious academic and disciplinary problems, and free higher education is no longer available at the City University of New York.

The experience of Mexican American immigrants to the United States illustrates clearly the importance of the availability of economic and educational opportunities in affecting rates of acculturation. Mexican Americans who have settled in rural areas of Texas, Arizona, New Mexico, and California and who are employed as agricultural workers maintain their traditional culture virtually intact (Tienda and Wilson, 1992; Portes, 1993). They encounter high levels of discrimination. Mexican Americans who settle in these areas have significantly lower median levels of income and education, are more likely to live in segregated barrios, and have much lower rates of intermarriage than Mexican Americans who settle in Los Angeles (Skerry, 1993).

Contact and Isolation   Contact with the dominant culture and population promotes acculturation if the minority identifies with dominant groups and internalizes their cultural patterns. Indirect contact through movies and television is a very influential source of acculturation in contemporary industrializing and industrial societies. Direct contact is even more important. Immigrants who settle in ethnically mixed neighborhoods acculturate more rapidly than those who settle in ethnic ghettos. An immigrant woman who works as a domestic in an upper-middle- or upper-class household will acculturate more quickly than a woman who works in a factory with other immigrants from her native country. The factory worker will have less need to learn the language, dress, and other aspects of the new culture.

Closeness to Home   Immigration to a society that is close to the country of origin slows acculturation in the new society. Ethnic subcultural patterns are reinforced by frequent visits to the homeland. This is true, for example, of French Canadian immigrants living in northern Maine and Puerto Rican immigrants in New York City (Tienda and Wilson, 1992). They retain their original language and customs more easily. In contrast, Cuban immigrants, who until recently were not permitted to return to Cuba, experienced an additional push toward acculturation for this reason.

Age, Recency of Arrival, and Gender   For the individual, age at immigration, recency of arrival, and gender are also important factors affecting acculturation. In the United States, adult legal immigrants are permitted to sponsor members of their immediate families—parents, brothers, sisters, and children. The majority of parents sponsored are between the ages of 55 and 65 when they arrive (Gelfand and Yee, 1991). Outside contacts and employment are unlikely because of difficulty with the language and anxiety about using public transportation. Immigrant women of this age, especially those from more traditional, patriarchal societies, are even more likely than men to be isolated and homebound. They usually provide child care, cooking, and housekeeping for their adult children who work outside the home (Yee, 1992).

Cultural pluralism is one current ideal for racial/ethnic relations in the United States. In part, this reflects the strong value of individualism in the United States and the current tendency to equate assimilation with conformity and homogenization. In part, this appears to be a reaction by third-generation European Americans who now feel that their immigrant grandparents rejected their cultural heritage too hastily (Danzger, 1989). And, in part, this is probably a response by ethnic minorities generally to the emphasis on raising levels of pride, self-esteem, and self-image of African Americans and women in the current civil rights and women's movements.

It is important to understand that in the United States cultural pluralism refers to a tolerance and acceptance of differences in customs and physical appearance. But at the deeper level of values, the experiences of urbanization, education, and social mobility into the middle class continue to weaken the traditional values of immigrant ethnic minorities, especially among those who have migrated from rural areas of more traditional societies.

WOMEN AS A MINORITY

Women have only recently come to regard themselves as a minority and not all women (or men) agree with this judgment. Women have all the characteristics of a minority, however, except for the practice of in-group marriage. (Lesbian marriages are relatively uncommon.) The physical distinctiveness of women, despite unisex trends in dress, has been the basis of prejudice, discrimination, and segregation in many spheres of life. Sex is an ascribed characteristic. We discussed women's economic roles in non-literate and agricultural societies in chapter 5. In urban industrializing societies, women's economically productive role at first declines (Blumberg, 1991). In the cities, women rarely spin thread, weave blankets, sew clothes, plant vegetable gardens, or tend chickens and pigs. They buy these products in stores. Their consumer role increases, especially in the middle class, as does the economic burden on men as sole providers. Poorer women usually continue to do factory or domestic work after they have children, mainly in the "informal economy" (taking in washing, ironing, and sewing) (Sanchez, 1993).

Prejudice and Discrimination

In recent decades, married women all over the world, with or without children, have increasingly shared the provider role, and discrimination against employed women has gradually declined (Blankenship, 1993). In the United States, the passage of Title VII civil rights legislation in 1964 gradually became the basis for challenging many kinds of inequality experienced by women at work. Stereotyped images in the media and in elementary and secondary textbooks portraying women in traditional roles at home and on the job have also declined, especially over the past 20 years (Clark, Lennon, and Morris, 1993).

Husbands' attitudes toward working wives have also changed. In the United States, only about 15 percent of all families with children are supported by a male only (Wilkie, 1993). The rest are supported by two earners or by single mothers, three-quarters of whom are divorced. Given the decline in real purchasing power and the need for women's earnings in the middle as well as the working classes, it is not surprising that men are now more likely to approve of their wives' employment. Attitudes have tended to lag behind changing economic realities, however, especially among older white men and among immigrant men from rural areas of more traditional societies (Wilkie, 1993).

Husbands whose wives are employed report greater marital satisfaction and less psychological stress than husbands in the same social class whose wives are full-time homemakers (Spitze, 1988; Whyte, 1990). Only if the husband does not want the wife to work or she herself does not want to work does her employment increase marital stress and dissatisfaction.

Women experience more segregation in occupations than any other minority. This segregation occurs in all societies. Women are overwhelmingly concentrated in domestic service jobs, factory work (usually involving food preparation or the manufacture of textiles or clothing), office work, retail selling, and preschool and elementary school teaching.

In the United States, between 1980 and 1990, the percentage of women in the professions almost doubled, and women now outnumber men in professional occupations (Pollard and Tordella, 1993). Almost two-thirds

(65 percent), however, are in traditional female professions, working as teachers, social workers, nurses, and librarians. Only one in four lawyers, one in five doctors, and one in eight dentists are women.

Surprisingly, sex-typed segregation in occupations is greater in Sweden, with ideals of equal opportunity, than in Japan, where patriarchal traditions emphasizing male dominance are stronger (Charles, 1992). Sweden has a much larger welfare state service sector than Japan. College-educated women in Sweden have more jobs available in predominantly female occupations such as teaching and social work than their counterparts in Japan, where women are more likely to be employed in nonsegregated occupations because traditional women's jobs are less available. Once again we see how cultural ideals conflict with economic realities.

In the United States, women who are employed full time currently earn about 70 percent of the average salary of male full-time workers (England, 1992). Married women who are employed contribute about 40 percent, on the average, to their family income, in part because they tend to shift to part-time work after the birth of a child. Married African American women earn about 90 percent as much has their husbands. As the last to be hired in occupations that were formerly not open to them, women have been the first to be fired in the current job squeeze. They lack seniority or tenure.

Many working mothers in the United States seek out lower-level or part-time jobs in service industries where they can have more flexible hours. As mentioned earlier, among married women who have preschool children and whose husbands are present, over half (56.8 percent) are employed (*Statistical Abstract of the United States, 1992,* Table 621). And this is the fastest-growing category of women workers in the United States today. At the same time, government-sponsored facilities for child care in the United States are less adequate than in most other industrial societies (Hayes, Palmer, and Zaslow, 1990). Women with family responsibilities are excluded from many high-level jobs that require travel and long hours. In the working class, in situations where wives work part time (as waitresses or cashiers, for example), fathers are the most frequent tenders of their children. They manage this by working different shifts.

Women, especially those who are older (over 75) and widowed or are young single mothers supporting children, are very likely to be poor. The size of both groups is increasing dramatically in the United States today. Sociologists have referred to this trend in the United States as the "feminization of poverty."

Ironically, highly educated, middle-class women with children in poor, currently industrializing societies are freer to pursue higher-level jobs than women with children in the United States (Kandiyoti, 1987). The extended family is more available to provide help. There are also more poor, uneducated women available to provide inexpensive, full-time housework and child care. In the United States, less than 2 percent of married couples with children employ domestic help—usually part time (Goldscheider and Waite, 1991). Governments in poor, industrializing societies do not provide child

TABLE 8.4

Women and Blacks in Congress, 1939–1994

| Year | Women | | | | Blacks | | | |
| | House | | Senate | | House | | Senate | |
	Dem.	Rep.	Dem.	Rep.	Dem.	Rep.	Dem.	Rep.
1994	36	12	5	2	38	1	1	0
1991	20	9	1	1	24	1	0	0
1989	14	11	1	1	24	0	0	0
1979	11	5	1	1	16	0	0	0
1969	6	4	0	1	9	0	0	1
1959	9	8	0	1	3	0	0	0
1949	5	4	0	1	2	0	0	0
1939	4	4	1	0	1	0	0	0

Source: *Congressional Quarterly Weekly Reports* for appropriate years.

care services, and husbands are even less likely to help with child care and housework than in industrial societies (Sanchez, 1993).

Even in the United States, however, across all family types, mothers with children present do between two-thirds and nine-tenths of the routine household work (Demo and Acock, 1993). Fathers do more than younger children, although adolescent girls usually take over from fathers. Employed married mothers and single mothers spend less time on household chores, the former apparently because time pressures force them to lower their standards, the latter because they have less housework to do when a partner is not present (Demo and Acock, 1993).

In the United States, women are a 53-percent majority of the voting age population. They are as likely to vote as men, but they hold few elective offices. There have been only 9 women state governors in the United States (as of 1994). The 103rd Congress included 7 women senators (out of a total of 100) and 48 women in the House of Representatives (out of a total of 435). Two out of nine Supreme Court justices are women. These numbers, however, are expected to increase dramatically in the near future. The end of the cold war has shifted political issues away from national security (an area of accepted "male" expertise) to domestic issues. Women are presumed to be more knowledgeable and competent in areas such as health care, education, and welfare reform. Both political parties are now scrambling to nominate women for political office.

Norway has an extraordinary presence of women in government. Norway is a prosperous, largely ethnically homogeneous society with a strong cultural heritage emphasizing economic equality. As Norway's economy became global, however, real power shifted from national politics to the private sector power of multinational corporations and Norwegian men followed. This is an age-old pattern. In the nineteenth century, women began to fill elementary school and secretarial positions after these occupations were vacated by men.

In the economic sphere, in the United States, women have made great inroads in lower-level professions and business executive positions, but no Fortune 500 company has ever had a woman chief executive officer. Males also dominate top leadership roles in all religious faiths, with the exception of the Christian Science church, which was founded by a woman. Women may be saints, they may be prophets, they may be evangelists. But for the most part, they do not hold the highest-level positions of power and authority in the major religious denominations in the United States.

Since the 1970s, women have been ordained as clergy in the Lutheran, Episcopalian, and Reform and Conservative branches of Judaism. In the Roman Catholic church, women may not be ordained, but for many decades nuns have been given professional training to provide for the social service and educational needs of the Catholic population. In the past, this served the latent function of providing a subsidized route to upward mobility for many lower-income women who would otherwise be excluded from professional occupations (Ebaugh, 1993). Today, given changing attitudes and greater possibilities for women's mobility in secular sectors, convents in the United States have been experiencing a decline in new recruits.

Extreme differences between men and women in education, economic and political opportunities, and family roles are declining in many parts of the world. But they persist, even in the most advanced industrial democracies (see Table 8.5 on p. 270).

Global Women's Movements

The current women's movement is international. Issues such as economic independence and equal pay, educational and political equality, adequate child care, and prevention of violence against women are shared by various women's movements, within and across societies (Margolis, 1993). There are differences that divide, however. Political and religious opponents in industrializing societies that were once colonies tend to view the Western women's movement as a new form of cultural "contagion" from the West (Kandiyoti, 1987). Other opponents of the women's movement in industrializing societies have argued that class is more important than gender in determining women's lot (Katzenstein and Mueller, 1987). And still others argue that feminists undervalue the economic and psychological importance of women's traditional roles in subsistence agriculture, child care, and housework (Lazreg, 1988).

As agricultural societies industrialize, however, women are propelled into the nonfamily economy (Bloom and Brender, 1993). This subverts the traditional roles of women, regardless of class, country, or religion and what-

TABLE 8.5

Persisting Gender Differences

In contrast to men, women in their work/family roles:

- continue to assume major responsibility for household chores and childrearing, regardless of hours and type of employment.
- have higher expectations for closeness, communication, emotional support before marriage; report greater disillusionment after marriage.
- experience greater distress and guilt over problems of husbands, children, parents, in-laws, and other family members; men are more likely to deny problems.
- are more likely to seek help from therapists; are more willing to talk about feelings in therapy.
- experience more extreme shifts in family roles than men—in and out of jobs and caregiving obligations to young and old.

- become more assertive in old age (after children are grown); men become more emotionally expressive.
- are more likely to divorce at highest income and educational levels (graduate degrees); the wealthiest, best educated males are more likely to stay married or to remarry after a divorce.
- experience greater economic difficulties after a divorce; men report more loneliness after a divorce.
- have greater difficulties as stepparents in remarriages (stepmother image; conflicts with biological mother over loyalty, discipline, authority over stepchildren).
- earn about 70 percent of what men earn in full-time employment; are concentrated in lower-paying specialties within an occupation—known as "mommy tracks" in large business and professional firms.

---

ever the costs or benefits of these roles are, or have been, to men, women, and societies.

Globally, certain conditions are associated with stronger women's movements in societies that have been surveyed: (1) higher levels of industrialization and urbanization; (2) economic growth and expanding educational and occupational opportunities for women as well as men; and (3) democratic rather than authoritarian governments. In societies that are experiencing widespread poverty and economic decline or recession, women's movements do not thrive (Margolis, 1993).

OLDER PEOPLE AS A MINORITY

Older people, as the term is used here, refers to those who are over 65—those legally defined as senior citizens in the United States. Are older people a minority? Do they experience domination, exclusion, and inequality? They do not if they are physically and mentally healthy—and most are. At any one point in time, only about 5 percent of the older population in the United States is in a nursing home, has Alzheimer's disease, or lives in segregated adult housing (usually by choice, however) (Atchley, 1994).

Older people may not be perceived as a minority. Age is an advantage in seeking and holding public office, since it is associated with wisdom, sound judgment based on years of practical experience and accumulated knowledge (Baltes, 1993). Authoritarian societies, such as China, are often controlled by older men who will not relinquish their power and cannot be voted out of office. This has been common in economically stratified authoritarian societies throughout human history.

Economically, in the United States, older people (except for widows over 75) are now less likely to be living in poverty than children. Most (about 60 percent) own their own small homes (purchased in the boom years after World War II).

Older people who experience domination, abuse, and other indignities sensationalized in the media are few in number. They are usually poor, severely incapacitated, and unable to get the long-term care they need, or have a history of strained relationships with their families (Finkelhor and Pillemer, 1988; Wolf and McCarthy, 1991). Furthermore, children are (and have been) far more likely than older people to be victims of physical abuse in families and random or intentional violence on the streets (deMause, 1974, 1991; Straus and Gelles, 1990; Atchley, 1994).

Why, then, do we include older people in a chapter on minorities? We classify older people as a minority because they experience unequal treatment on the basis of an ascribed physical characteristic—age. They are discriminated against in employment. They are the subject of widespread negative stereotypes and, like other minorities, they have organized to further their economic interests.

The United States is a youth-oriented society. Older people have been negatively stereotyped in a variety of ways that depict them as "burdensome" and "distressful" to their families and to society. Given their increasing numbers and longer life expectancies, they are being scapegoated in the news media for the growing "burden" they place on a troubled and inadequate health care system (see, for example, Beck, 1993).

The call is to "ration" scarce, expensive life-saving procedures in favor of the young, who, if cured, have more life left to live (Samuelson, 1993). People over 65 are accused of having a greedy and "insatiable" desire to live as long as possible and, in many cases, longer than necessary, right, or proper (Callahan, 1993).

Stereotypes, Burdens, and Reality

Let us look first at stereotypes about older people that do not have immediate policy implications. In the United States, certain beliefs about older people are widespread: (1) their productivity at work declines, (2) their intelligence and creativity decline, (3) their sexuality disappears, (4) they become increasingly cranky and irritable, and (5) they make unreasonable demands on family members. None of these beliefs is supported by social scientific research.

Overall economic productivity need not decline as people age. A review of over 150 studies of factory workers 55 or older indicates that loyalty to employers, job turnover, absenteeism, and injuries on the job were less frequent among older workers than among younger workers (Doering, Rhodes, and Schuster, 1983). Speed in producing products declines with advancing age, as reflexes slow down, but motivation, a slower but steadier effort, seems to compensate for this decline among older workers.

A decline in overall intelligence and creativity also does not occur among healthy older people, even for those who are over 80 or 90 (Schaie, 1990; Willis et al., 1992). Cultural expectations about aging may affect memory in older people more than has been appreciated by researchers in the past. Psychologists Becca Levy and Ellen Langer tested performance on four memory tasks among younger people (age 15 to 30) and older people (age 59 to 91) in Beijing, China, and in the United States (1994). Older Chinese outperformed older subjects tested in the United States, and their memory scores did not statistically differ from those of younger Chinese. They also reported more positive attitudes toward aging than older subjects in the United States. Negative stereotypes in the United States about memory loss in old age may become self-fulfilling prophesies.

Among gifted older people, there seems to be a resurgence of creativity and productivity—what one researcher has called the swan-song phenomenon (Simonton, 1990). Sexuality also does not decline among healthy older people who have had continuous, satisfying sexual relationships in middle age (Weg, 1990).

The popular image of older people as typically "cranky," "irritable," and "demanding" is another unsupported stereotype. Personality does not change dramatically in old age (Kogan, 1990; Silver, 1992). Certain individual personality tendencies—depression, compulsiveness, selfishness—tend to become intensified in old age, but these are not new or different for individual older people or typical of older people, generally (Atchley, 1989; Belsky, 1990; Fiske and Chiriboga, 1990).

Older people are also widely believed to be an economic burden to their middle-aged children. In the United States, about 18 percent of parents over 65 live with a middle-aged child (Aquilino, 1990). In most of these situations, however, the home that is shared is the *parent's* home. The middle-aged child moves in with the older parent, usually for economic reasons, after a divorce or loss of a job. Only 5 percent of parents over 65 move into an adult child's household.

It is well known that adolescents fight to establish their independence. What is less well known is that older people fight to maintain their independence, especially among those over 85, who become increasingly frail physically (Horowitz, Silverstone, and Reinhardt, 1991; Draper and Keith, 1992).

Most older parents in the United States are not a financial burden to their children. According to the evidence from national surveys, until parents are 85 or older, more financial help goes from parents to their nearest or neediest grown child than the other way around (Hoyert, 1991). The amount of help parents and their adult children give to each other depends on family histories, income and wealth, geographic closeness, health, age, and the marital status (married, divorced, widowed, or never married) of the adult child and the parent (Eggebeen, 1992).

Family patterns of closeness and support that were typical *within* each generation are passed on in the relationship *between* generations, regardless of social circumstances (Hoyert, 1991). Most parents in the United States (about three-quarters) maintain positive and satisfying friendship relationships with their adult children, and most adult children feel positive about their relationship with their aging parents (Bengtson and Roberts, 1991). Adult children who received consistent love, support, acceptance, and encouragement from their parents when they needed it return this care. They do so willingly when the time comes and the need arises, even though caregiving may result in severe role conflict, especially for full-time employed middle-aged daughters (Gerstel and Gallagher, 1993).

Scientists, philosophers, and journalists increasingly write about the war between the generations. They point to the increased economic well-being of older people as a result of Social Security and other entitlements, which they claim comes at the expense of children and taxpayers. In fact, the poverty rate among older people who live alone (mainly widowed women over 75) is about the same as that of children (Butler, 1993). Since 1992, higher-income older people have been paying higher taxes on their entitlements. Repeated national polls and surveys indicate that most people of all ages want the old to keep their entitlements, or even have them increased. They approve of including long-term care in the national health care program.

The belief that older people have an "insatiable" desire to prolong their lives is a myth. Those who are very old (especially over 85) do not typically fear death (Bould, Sanborn, and Reiff, 1989; Atchley, 1994). They do not cling to life whatever the cost to themselves, their families, or their society. Their reference groups are family members and friends who have already died, usually at a younger age. They go gently and with dignity—if they are allowed to.

Hospices, where terminally ill people die with medication to relieve pain and without medical procedures to prolong life, are spreading throughout the country. Living wills, requesting that no extraordinary measures be taken to prolong life for the terminally ill, are also becoming increasingly popular. Newer generations of nonimmigrant older people are healthier and will be less of a drain on health care costs in the future.

Those who are more educated and skilled typically continue to work as much and as long as they can. According to the evidence from longitu-

TABLE 8.6

Stereotypes about Older People

Stereotype	Fact
Older people experience a decline in intelligence and creativity.	Among older people in good health, there is no significant decline in intelligence and creativity, even for those in their 80s and 90s.
Older people are less productive on their jobs.	Older people may work more slowly, but they also work steadily, with less absenteeism, greater job satisfaction, and greater loyalty to employers than younger employees exhibit.
Sexuality disappears for older people.	Sexual interest and activity generally decrease but continue to exist, particularly for those who are in good health.
Women experience a decline in well-being after menopause.	Post-menopausal decline in well-being is not typical, let alone necessary or inevitable.
Older people are a financial burden to their children.	Up to age 85 and older, parents help children economically more than children help their parents, according to national surveys.
Older people are cranky, irritable, and demanding.	Among healthy individuals, there are no major changes in personality with advancing age.

dinal studies that follow the *same* individuals as they age, most highly educated older men do not retire unless they are fired, lose their jobs because of a mandatory retirement policy, or become physically or mentally incapacitated (Elder and Pavalko, 1993). Yet prejudices continue to exist that older men and women are "crocks," "greedy geezers," or "vegetables." These outdated stereotypes are a current example of cultural lag in the United States (Crews, 1993). Other industrial democracies do not scapegoat their oldest people for their economic problems to the same extent.

Doctors and hospitals in the United States routinely prescribe unnecessary, costly tests and seek to prolong the lives of terminally ill individuals even when this causes needless pain and suffering. Such practices are motivated largely by the fear of malpractice suits. In reality, patients or their families infrequently win malpractice suits against doctors or reap "astronomical" rewards. However, the United States is the most litigious society in the world. Bringing suit has become a cultural pattern with negative consequences for health care and health insurance costs. This, too, is not the fault of older people.

Surgeons will not perform a hip replacement on a frail 92-year-old woman (who may die soon after the operation), and hospitals will not keep infants alive who are born with only a brain stem if they do not fear malpractice suits. It should be noted, however, that there are other and perhaps more important reasons for prolonging the lives of terminally ill patients of any age and with any physical condition. State laws require these procedures in the absence of living wills. Furthermore, expensive tests and procedures that are possibly unnecessary may be ordered, especially in for-profit hospitals, if payment is ensured. It is often difficult to objectively determine which tests and procedures are, in fact, necessary or desirable in the treatment and possible cure of specific medical problems.

The Social Status of Older People

As sociocultural evolution has proceeded in human history, the overall prestige of the oldest people in human societies has varied, but not greatly. Differences in their social status depend on differences in economic and political conditions and cultural values in specific societies. Generally, their social status is lower in the simplest societies where living conditions are extremely difficult. It is also lower, generally, in most complex societies. It is higher in horticultural and agricultural societies, especially if older people maintain control over their property (Keith, 1990).

In hunting and gathering societies that are characterized by the harshest climates and most severe economic hardships, the oldest members typically experience a decline in social status as their health and strength decline. They have greater difficulty functioning in harsh environments when they become frail, and they are often expected to voluntarily depart from a world they can no longer keep up with comfortably and with dignity (Keith, 1990). Assisted suicide for incapacitated or terminally ill old people is an age-old practice.

On the other hand, the knowledge and wisdom of older people are highly valued in nonliterate societies (Simmons, 1945). Their accumulated lifelong experiences continue to be useful and relevant in societies that do not change much. And they are essential as teachers who pass on oral traditions and folklore in societies that do not have a written literature.

Anthropologists usually explain the decline in the social status of older citizens in postindustrial societies in terms of their diminished usefulness in maintaining these societies. Their labor is not as needed and their skills are more likely to be out of date in a society that is rapidly changing and increasingly technologically advanced. Within the present generation of older people, for example, computer literacy is not widespread. In general, however, personal attributes and control over property diminish the decline in social status for specific individuals.

The status of older citizens is highest in economically stratified horticultural and agricultural societies that practice religions involving ancestor worship. Cultural values such as authoritarianism and familism that prescribe respect for authority and for older people are also important. Globally, these values continue to be strongest in East Asian societies such as China and Japan. But they are declining somewhat among younger generations in these societies.

Historically and throughout the world today, individual differences in wealth, intelligence, psychological strength, and physical and mental health have counterbalanced the effects of culture and economic and political conditions in determining the overall social status of older people. Extreme disability, however, is accompanied by a loss in social status in all societies.

Study Guide

REVIEW OBJECTIVES

After studying this chapter, you should be able to:

1. Define what minorities are.
2. Describe how minorities came into existence.
3. Examine the basic perspectives of conflict and functionalist theorists in the study of racial/ethnic relations.
4. Explain how and why minorities have been preserved in some societies and eliminated in others.
5. List the factors affecting rates of acculturation of various racial/ethnic minorities in a society.
6. Describe newer trends in minority/dominant population relationships in the United States today.
7. Give the latest available social scientific information about the minority status and treatment of women and people over 65 in the United States today.

SUMMARY

1. Minority groups are physically and/or culturally distinct from dominant groups. They usually have less prestige and power and fewer economic resources, and experience prejudice, discrimination, exclusion, and inequality in major areas of life.

2. Race and sex are physical bases for minority status, although race is an increasingly ambiguous concept. These forms of physical difference are based on ascribed characteristics. Ethnic subcultural distinctiveness,

by contrast, is based on shared cultural traits that can change and disappear.

3. Women have all the characteristics of minority group status except in-group marriage. They experience prejudice, discrimination, and segregation, especially in the economic and political spheres, on the basis of their biological, ascribed status as females.

4. Psychological theories of prejudice focus on particular types of parent-child relationships in explaining individual differences in prejudice and tendencies to scapegoat minorities. Sociological theories focus on the learning or cultural transmission of prejudice in various social locations. Conflict theorists have focused more specifically on the economic gains that dominant groups experience as a result of prejudice and discrimination. They relate changes in the frequency and intensity of racial and ethnic prejudice and conflict between dominant and minority groups to changes in economic and political conditions in societies during various periods of time.

5. Historically, racial and ethnic groups became minorities usually as a result of wars in which other societies were raided for slaves, annexed, or colonized and occupied. Migration resulting from natural disasters, economic hardship, and political or religious persecution also created minorities in certain societies.

6. Dominant groups have usually reacted to minorities in two ways. First, they have attempted to eliminate minority groups by extermination, expulsion, or assimilation. Second, when racial/ethnic origin or gender is the basis of minority status, dominant groups have sought to maintain that status by continued exclusion and subjugation when it is more profitable to do so. In industrial democracies, exclusion and inequality become increasingly dysfunctional economically.

7. Factors affecting rates of acculturation of immigrant minorities include (1) the degree of physical or cultural difference from the dominant population, (2) minority and dominant population attitudes toward acculturation, (3) the costs of discrimination, (4) the availability of economic and educational opportunities in a society, (5) the degree of contact with or isolation from dominant groups, (6) nearness to country of origin, (7) recency of immigration, (8) gender, and (9) age at arrival (for individuals).

8. In the United States, African Americans, Latinos, and Native Americans experience the greatest degree of discrimination and exclusion. All experienced some economic and political gains in the late 1960s and early 1970s, but they have experienced an even greater decline in economic gains than nonminorities since the 1980s.

9. By comparison to European immigrants in the past, recent immigrants to the United States have placed greater emphasis on racial and ethnic pride and cultural pluralism. Poorer immigrants are not acculturating as quickly as more educated immigrants, nor will they go as far, probably, because of the permanent decline in entry-level unskilled and semiskilled jobs in the United States.

10. Globally, women's movements have been stronger and women's status higher in societies that have achieved a higher level of sociocultural evolution, have more available economic and educational opportunities, and have democratic rather than authoritarian governments.

11. People over 65 in the United States constitute a minority because of widespread discrimination in employment, negative stereotypes about them, and the tendency to hold them responsible for current economic stresses and health care problems in the society.

GLOSSARY

Acculturation: The learning of the language, values, norms, and skills necessary for social mobility in a particular society.

Assimilation: The complete loss of racial and/or ethnic identity by means of acculturation and intermarriage.

Authoritarian personality: A person who ranks high on tests of political and economic conservatism, ethnocentrism, and prejudice.

Discrimination: Behavior that excludes minorities from wealth, power, opportunities, and activities.

Prejudice: Rigid and exaggerated negative images and beliefs about culturally or physically distinct people in a society.

Race: A population that shares certain distinct physical characteristics.

Racial/ethnic minorities: Categories of people who trace their ancestry to particular countries or continents, share similar physical and/or cultural traits, and experience unequal treatment in a society.

Scapegoats: Less powerful people in a group or a society who are wrongly blamed for the problems of the group or the society.

Segregation: Separation and exclusion of a minority from residential, commercial, occupational, recreational, educational, or religious facilities and activities.

Terrorism: Politically motivated violence directed against civilian populations.

PRACTICE TESTS

True ▪ False Test

___ 1. Today there is less exclusion of African Americans from certain prestigious occupations in the United States than was the case a generation ago.

___ 2. Discrimination always accompanies prejudice.

___ 3. Different societies may give different social definitions to the term "race."

___ 4. Many factors may play a role in prejudice, discrimination, and racial/ethnic conflict.

___ 5. Cultural transmission theory alone can explain why prejudice is stronger in certain cultures than in others.

___ 6. Only in Brazil has assimilation resulted in a complete merging of racial/ethnic minorities with the dominant social group.

___ 7. Upward social mobility requires the loss of group distinctiveness.

___ 8. Discrimination is economically as well as psychologically costly.

___ 9. Women are more likely than men to be poor.

___ 10. In the United States today, older people are less likely than children to be living in poverty.

Multiple-Choice Test

___ 1. In which of the following eras has violent conflict over material and nonmaterial resources been most frequent and most intense?
   a. the thirteenth century
   b. the seventeenth century
   c. the nineteenth century
   d. the twentieth century

___ 2. Discrimination:
   a. occurs only in the mind.
   b. occurs openly.
   c. is inclusive of minorities.
   d. rarely involves prejudice.

___ 3. Defining or classifying "race" is so difficult because:
   a. the act of even considering race is intrinsically prejudiced.
   b. certain terms such as "Hispanic" and "black" have fallen out of favor in the United States.
   c. many human populations are physically very mixed.
   d. scholars fear alienating certain racial groups.

___ 4. The term "ethnic minorities" derives from a Greek work meaning:
   a. color.
   b. family.
   c. religion.
   d. nation.

___ 5. All of the following traits characterize the authoritarian personality *except:*
   a. politically conservative.
   b. sexually promiscuous.
   c. ethnocentric.
   d. prejudiced.

___ 6. Which of the following is an example of cultural transmission of prejudice?
   a. Josie grew up in a family renowned for its historic hatred of blacks.
   b. Cornelia has harbored a profound dislike and distrust of Germans since she lived through World War II.
   c. Vilma has learned prejudice against Asian people while at college.
   d. Nelson has felt hostile toward white people since he was among the first African Americans to be integrated into a white high school.

___ 7. The Nazis' genocide against the Jews and Gypsies is an example of:
   a. acculturation policies.
   b. assimilation policies.
   c. extermination policies.
   d. expulsion policies.

___ 8. Which of the following conditions or results is not associated with acculturation?
   a. an economy in recession
   b. good educational facilities
   c. lowered competition between minorities and the lower socio-economic levels of the dominant population
   d. willingness to acculturate

___ 9. Which of the following people is most likely to be a woman?
   a. a lawyer
   b. a dentist
   c. a social worker
   d. a doctor

___ 10. Which of the following is a fact as opposed to a stereotype?
   a. Older people lose their sexual interest.
   b. Women experience a decline in well-being after menopause.
   c. Older people are often cranky and irritable.
   d. Older people make good employees.

Matching Test

Match each concept with its definition, illustration, or explication below.

1.
(1) Segregation
(2) Prejudice
(3) Race
(4) Minority
(5) Scapegoat

   a. Negative beliefs and images
   b. Group excluded from full societal participation
   c. Separation, exclusion
   d. A person or group wrongly blamed
   e. A population with distinct physical characteristics

2.
(1) Lippmann
(2) Adorno and colleagues
(3) Porto
(4) Myrdal
(5) Wirth

   a. Coined the word "stereotype"
   b. Provided the classic definition of "minorities"
   c. Studies of children of immigrants
   d. Defined "the American dilemma"
   e. Examined psychological origins of prejudice

3.
(1) Consequence of discrimination
(2) Ambiguous concept
(3) Created by slavery
(4) Identity retained despite migration and interbreeding
(5) Largely due to cultural transmission

a. Race
b. Jews
c. Segregation
d. Prejudice in the South
e. First ethnic minorities

4.
(1) Terrorism
(2) Rising hostility toward minorities
(3) Assimilation
(4) Expulsion
(5) Acculturation

a. Associated with economic and political frustration
b. Removal of minorities
c. Absorbed into the dominant culture
d. Politically motivated violence
e. Eases social mobility

5.
(1) Cultural pluralism
(2) Authoritarian
(3) Discriminate
(4) Racial/ethnic minorities
(5) Intermarriage

a. Highly prejudiced/ethnocentric
b. Exclude minorities from opportunities
c. Share physical and/or cultural traits
d. Promotes assimilation
e. Current U.S. ideal

REVIEW QUESTIONS

1. What are the characteristics of minorities? How do they originate in various societies?
2. What are the problems in defining and classifying races?
3. How do psychologists explain prejudice?
4. What is the difference between assimilation and acculturation, and why is this distinction important?
5. How can the different factors affecting rates of acculturation be illustrated by comparing the experiences of various minorities in the contemporary United States?
6. What have been some of the consequences of the widespread employment of married women of all social classes in postindustrial societies?
7. How do the work/family roles of women differ, typically, from that of men?
8. Globally, what conditions are associated with stronger women's movements in societies that have been surveyed?
9. What are some of the stereotypes about older people that have been disproved by social scientific research?

APPLYING SOCIOLOGY

1. What physical or cultural characteristics (values, personality traits, customs, and patterns of dress or speech, for instance) do you have that stem from statuses that you were born with (gender, racial/ethnic origin, social class, etc.)?
2. Do you know people who seem to have authoritarian personality traits? What kind of relationship do they have with their parents?
3. If your attitudes toward minority groups, or toward being in a minority group, are different from those of your parents, how would you explain this difference?
4. Think of various minorities in the United States today. Do you have "pictures in your head" about these minorities that might be stereotypes?
5. What images come to your mind when you think of the word "American"? How much of this could be a projection of your own self-image? How much of this reflects a feeling of being an outsider? Why is either image true for you?

Major Institutions

Activities in major areas of human social life focus on the satisfaction of basic human needs. These activities become increasingly separate and specialized during the course of sociocultural evolution. In chapter 9, major changes in family functions, forms, and roles and relationships, historically and in various parts of the world today, are described, and possible reasons for these changes are discussed. Chapter 10 surveys changes in the distribution of goods and services in human societies, with special emphasis on trends in inequality in major types of societies, historically, and in the United States today, especially as compared with other societies. The changing nature of work as a result of the spread of computer technology and global, electronic telecommunication systems is also explored. The focus in chapter 11 is on major trends in the functions of government during the course of sociocultural evolution, with special emphasis on the conditions necessary for the existence of democratic forms of government. Formal education becomes increasingly essential to adaptation as societies become more complex. Chapter 12 describes major historical trends in education, with a special focus on differences in social class and minority educational achievement. Explanations for these differences in achievement, globally and in the United States today, are also explored. Historical and contemporary changes in religious beliefs and practices are described in chapter 13. Religion is surveyed as a source of new values, as well as traditional values.

9

Families

In times of rapid social change and severe economic and political crisis, the decline and fall of the family becomes a favorite preoccupation of those who question traditional arrangements (Popenoe, 1993; Stacy, 1993). This was as true in ancient Greece and Rome as it is in the United

States today. Two recent network television broadcasts on the family were subtitled "An Endangered Species?" and "A Vanishing Ideal?"

The questioning is appropriate. Families as they existed in traditional societies are endangered, and certain traditional family ideals and expectations are vanishing—probably forever. But the current problems faced by families in the United States and elsewhere stem from scientific, technological, and economic changes, along with certain government policies and global events. They are not caused by fundamental defects in family groups. Ultimately for biological reasons and more immediately for psychological and sociological reasons, no other type of group could replace the family for all members of a society for very long. Neither the society nor its citizens would survive.

BIOLOGICAL, PSYCHOLOGICAL, AND SOCIOLOGICAL BASES

Family groups provide care for the biologically very dependent human young, help control sexual rivalry in human societies, and provide emotional support for young and old. It has been argued, quite convincingly at times, that the basic functions of families could be performed better by other kinds of groups. This is, up to a point, true. In industrial societies, governments have taken increasing responsibility for many of the traditional functions of the family—protection, health care, economic support. In such societies, experts know more than parents about many things. Doctors, nurses, and nutritionists know more about health care than most parents do. Teachers know more about reading, writing, and arithmetic. Lawyers know more about legal rights and protection. Clergy know more about religious ritual. Psychologists and social workers know more about emotional problems and mental illness.

Why, then, do all societies have family groups? Why has no society successfully eliminated the family as a group for bearing and rearing children?

The answer is that it is not possible to do so on a large scale. Why? Substitute groups—nurseries, schools, dormitories—would have to be organized along bureaucratic lines in order to take on the functions of the family, especially in urban industrial societies with large populations. And bureaucracies are impersonal by definition.

Efficiency and predictability are basic values in bureaucracies. Emotions interfere with smooth functioning. But emotions are the basis of family relationships. Teachers, nurses, doctors, and other caregivers, by contrast, tend to limit their emotional involvement with those they serve. Such caregivers may, in addition, change jobs, breaking ties and moving on. The stability, security, and depth of emotional support that are at least possible in family groups are impossible in bureaucratically organized large groups. For good reason, the family is the only major institution that has not been transformed into a bureaucratic organization as societies have become increasingly complex.

WHAT IS A FAMILY?

Finding a definition of the family that includes all types of family groups in all kinds of societies is not easy. For this reason, we defined a family in chapter 3 as a relatively enduring group based on marriage, birth, adoption, or mutual definition (as in unmarried-partner families). Membership in a family includes a feeling of belonging to the group, a deep, personal, emotional involvement with the group, and an identity that is defined by the group.

Certain types of family groups have not traditionally been sanctioned by law or religion, such as never-married women and their children, unmarried couples with children, or gay and lesbian families. If people *define* themselves as a family, however, they *are* a family (Marciano and Sussman, 1991). We cannot ignore nontraditional family groups, especially now that they are increasing rapidly in many societies and becoming the norm in some. In Sweden, for example, unmarried parents with children now outnumber married parents with children (Ahlberg and DeVita, 1992, Table 5, p. 23).

In the United States today, nearly one out of four never-married women aged 18 to 44 are mothers (Bachu, 1993; National Center for Health Statistics, 1993). This rate has increased by almost 60 percent over the past decade. Almost half of all children under 18 in the United States live in a single-parent household at some time when they are growing up (Bumpass, 1990). Over one-half of African American children are born to unmarried mothers. Are these mothers and their children not families? Are gay couples who live together and share expenses and support not families? Obituaries for gay men in some newspapers now routinely list companions as survivors, together with mothers, fathers, sisters, and brothers.

SOCIOCULTURAL EVOLUTION AND FAMILY LIFE

Family relationships have exhibited certain typical variations in human societies during the course of sociocultural evolution. When we look at the overall picture from the beginnings of human history up to the present, however, a rather startling picture emerges. Despite enormous differences in cultures and conditions, family relationships in the simplest (hunting and gathering) and most complex (postindustrial) societies exhibit similar patterns, although these patterns emerge for different reasons in each type of society (Yorburg, 1973, 1983, 1993). Because of these remarkable similarities, we will discuss family life in the simplest and the most complex societies together, although we will first discuss an important difference between the two types of societies. We will also examine the different patterns in horticultural and agricultural societies.

Family Functions

Before considering the similarities between families in the simplest societies and those in the most complex societies, it is important to recognize an aspect of family life—family functions—in which the simplest and most complex societies differ. In general, families provide physical care, socialization, protection, and emotional support. As societies become increasingly complex, however, these family functions come to be shared by trained experts—teachers, doctors, lawyers, police, therapists. But families do not entirely lose these functions in industrial and postindustrial societies. What they lose is their monopoly over providing for their members' needs as societies become increasingly complex.

Family Forms

Family groups are either nuclear or extended in form. A **nuclear family** consists of parents and their children—the immediate family—whether or not they share the same household. An **extended family** is made up of several nuclear families, or parts of nuclear families, that are in daily, or almost daily, contact. They may live in the same household, or they may live upstairs, downstairs, down the street, or around the corner. The most important variables in determining whether or not families are extended are the amount of contact, authority (control, advice, and influence in decision making), economic help, and emotional support exchanged between nuclear families and their relatives (Yorburg, 1975). In both hunting and gathering societies and postindustrial societies, nuclear families are the prevalent family form.

Hunting and Gathering Societies   Life expectancy is short in hunting and gathering societies, and three generations rarely survive to form extended families. Young people usually marry outside of the small band because the choice of partners within the band is very limited. Most bands are too poor to support large, extended families, which are also not practical when the band is constantly on the move in search of food. In such large families, the chances that some member will be ill or unable to keep up are multiplied.

Industrial and Postindustrial Societies   In the most complex societies, the practice of moving away from the family to take a new job is a major factor in the breakup of extended families. Psychological conflicts between the generations are another important factor, as family members choose to escape these conflicts by moving away; this is much easier in industrial societies than it was in preindustrial societies. Social mobility up, down, and away from the social class of parents or siblings also breaks up extended families. Social mobility usually results in a move to a new neighborhood, as well as changes in interests and ways of life. Family members may have relatively little in common or be unable to keep up economically with socially mobile relatives. A religious or ethnic intermarriage that is disapproved of by relatives may also serve to weaken extended family ties.

In industrial societies, extended families own common economic resources (such as land, livestock, or a family business). They work together and they exchange goods and services daily. They eat together, bring up children together, spend their free time together. Socialization, physical care, emotional support, advice, and protection are provided almost completely by the extended family network. In industrial societies, this form is most prevalent among the poor, where younger generations are economically dependent on an older parent or parents, or among the very rich, where the oldest living member does not turn over property or control. However, extended families in which the oldest living member has complete economic control and power over younger generations are rare (except in English murder mystery novels).

At the other extreme, the isolated nuclear family lives at a significant geographic distance from other relatives. It may maintain indirect contact by telephone and letters. Visiting is infrequent, limited usually to ceremonial occasions such as weddings, major anniversaries, and funerals. The isolated nuclear family is completely self-sufficient economically and receives no help of any kind from other relatives. Emotional support, advice, and protection are provided by friends and paid experts (bankers, lawyers, psychotherapists). These specialists and distant models in the mass media are more important than the extended family in the socialization of children and adult members of the nuclear family. The extended family has no authority or influence on decisions made in the isolated nuclear family. This family form is most common within the upper-middle class and the new upper class (newly rich and/or famous).

Most families are somewhere between these two extremes with respect to contact, economic independence, emotional support, authority, and protection. Some are closer to the pure extended form. In the semi-extended family, members of nuclear families earn independent incomes in the nonfamily economy—in factories, stores, and offices. But there is daily contact and exchange of help. Relatives are most important in providing emotional support and advice. And they are very influential in decisions that are made by the nuclear family. This family form is prevalent among the working classes, the poor, and impoverished recent immigrants to industrial societies.

TABLE 9.1

Family Forms: Contact, Authority, Economic Dependence, Emotional Support

	Truly Extended	*Semi-Extended*	*Semi-Nuclear*	*Isolated Nuclear*
Frequency of Contact	Daily contact.	Daily contact.	Regular visiting, weekly usually, but no daily contact.	Infrequent visits on ceremonial occasions.
Authority and Influence of Family Members	Oldest members exert strict authority over younger gener-ations.	Nuclear family authority, but influence of relatives on nuclear family decisions is strong.	Influence of relatives on nuclear family decisions is weak.	Relatives exert no influence on nuclear family decisions.
Economic Dependence	Complete economic interdependence of related nuclear families.	Economic independence of nuclear family, but daily exchange of goods and services with relatives.	Largely self-sufficient nuclear family. Help from relatives in emergencies.	Nuclear family is completely self-sufficient economically. No help from relatives.
Emotional Support	Complete emotional interdependence.	Relatives most important in providing emotional support, protection, socialization. Some reliance on outsiders.	Nuclear family reliance on relatives for emotional support is weak, but not absent.	Nuclear family and a variety of outsiders provide socialization, emotional support, and protection.

Source: Adapted from Betty Yorburg, "The Nuclear and the Extended Family: An Area of Conceptual Confusion," 1975, *Journal of Comparative Family Studies 6*, pp. 1–14.

Other families are closer to the isolated nuclear form. Semi-nuclear families are economically independent. They get help from relatives, but only during emergencies such as family illness, divorce, or the loss of a job. They see one another regularly but do not live near enough to be in daily contact. Relatives are important in recreational activities, however. They visit and entertain each other, usually on weekends. But they exert little influence on nuclear family decisions, such as whether or where to move, how to spend family income, how to discipline children, and how to spend leisure or vacation time (see Table 9.1). This family form is widespread among middle-income groups in industrial societies.

Horticultural and Agricultural Societies   In tribal horticultural and herding societies, a form of the extended family known as **polygamy** is a widespread cultural ideal. This involves the marriage of one man to more than one woman—**polygyny**. Or one woman is married to several men (usually brothers)–**polyandry**. Polyandry is rare and occurs in the poorest herding societies, where women do not plant or herd animals. It takes more than one man to support a woman and her children in these societies. In polygynous societies, women usually perform a major role in producing economic resources (planting). Only the wealthiest families can afford polygamy, however, and a majority of families throughout history have practiced **monogamy.** In this family form, one woman is married to one man (at any particular time).

In agricultural societies, extended families are the ideal. But frequently, as in simpler societies, three generations do not survive to share the same household or live near each other for very long. Brothers, sisters, cousins, aunts, and uncles are usually close by to provide daily help, care, and support, however. Daily contact and exchange of goods and services are the most important factors in defining an extended family. Historians have sometimes defined away the extended family by insisting that three generations must live in a *single* household to qualify in this category.

Extended families, in fact, were not widespread in agricultural societies and are probably more common in the United States today. According to national surveys, between 1969 and 1989 about one-third of middle-aged white women and two-thirds of black women lived in extended three-generation family households "for at least a part of their middle years" (Beck and Beck, 1989, p. 147). Doubling and tripling up of nuclear families in the same apartment or house are frequent among poorer minorities and among new immigrants to the United States, at least when they first arrive.

Premarital Sexual Behavior

All cultures have attempted to control the sexual activity of married women and men outside of marriage. Adultery, a sexual relationship between a married person and a partner who is not the spouse, can be destructive to family stability. But the sexual activities of young, never-married people are free and relatively unrestricted in the simplest and the most complex societies. In all societies, economic factors significantly affect cultural norms about sexuality. But biological factors are more important in hunting and gathering societies than in other societal forms. Developments in medicine, science, and technology, by contrast, become increasingly important in postindustrial societies.

Hunting and Gathering Societies In hunting and gathering societies, families live at a subsistence level. There is no surplus food or other goods to trade. Families do not differ in wealth and possessions. The mating activities of children are not crucial to the economic future of the family line. Also, premarital pregnancy is rare for biological reasons. Women are usually not fertile until from 1 to 3 years after they start menstruating; in hunting and gathering societies, most children are married at puberty or even earlier. Furthermore, puberty occurs later, on the average, in such societies than it does in postindustrial societies. Children have more balanced diets, receive better health care, and physically mature more quickly as societies become more complex.

Industrial and Postindustrial Societies   Economic changes and developments in medicine, science, and technology promote freer sexual behavior in postindustrial societies, especially for women and for the middle social classes. Children leave family farms and businesses to work for outsiders in business and industry. Especially in the later stages of industrialization, they earn independent incomes that are not turned over to parents.

Education, personality, and luck become increasingly important in determining the economic fate of children, except among the very rich and the very poor. Governments assume some of the responsibility for the welfare of older people and poorer people. Working- and middle-class parents have little or no property to leave their children. They educate their children as best they can, and they rely on pensions, savings, and Social Security for support in their old age.

Parents have less control over their independently employed children. And since they themselves can expect to be less dependent on these children, they become less concerned, although certainly not unconcerned, about the sexual behavior and marital choices of their children. The mating behavior of children becomes less crucial to the economic future of the family (D'Emilio and Freedman, 1988).

Developments in science and technology diminish control over sexual behavior in other ways. Industrialization uproots people and encourages the movement to cities, where family, religious, and community control over nonconforming behavior, including sexual behavior, is weaker. The shorter workweek in later stages of industrialization provides more leisure time for dating and sexual activity.

The Sexual Revolution   The term **sexual revolution** refers to a time of rapid and widespread change toward more liberal sexual attitudes and freer sexual behavior. This happened just before, during, and after World War I (1914–1918) in the United States and Europe (Reiss and Lee, 1988; Whyte, 1990). It did not start during the 1960s, as is widely believed. The *public* morality during the period from about 1910 to 1929 required virginity before marriage and faithfulness after marriage. The *private* morality was different, especially for those who were planning to marry anyway. In the 1960s, the private morality went public—people became more open about their sexual behavior. But major changes in sexual behavior had occurred decades earlier.

Medical and scientific developments around the turn of the century providing more effective birth control techniques and better control over sexually transmitted diseases eased fears and also promoted greater sexual

FIGURE 9.1

Sexual Activity of Teenagers

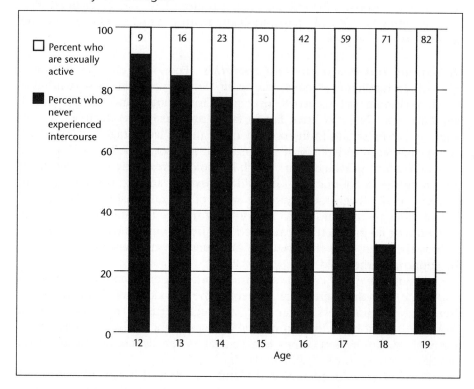

Source: The Alan Guttmacher Institute, *Sex and America's Teenagers,* 1994, p. 19. Used by permission.

More than 8 out of 10 women in the United States are sexually active by age 19.

liberalism, which continued until the advent of AIDS. The automobile and mass transit took young people out of farmhouses and crowded urban apartments. Dating in public places, away from the watchful eyes of mothers and fathers, replaced courtship in private parlors and porches. Commercial, nonfamily entertainment (movies, bars, and nightclubs) replaced barn raisings, hoedowns, and church suppers, which had been family activities. The growth of hotels and motels increased the availability of private meeting places for sexual activity. From its beginnings, the pattern of premarital sexual freedom spread gradually and continuously in the United States and Europe, especially among the middle classes.

Reports of AIDS cases, beginning in 1981 in the United States, have done little to slow the trend toward having more than one sexual partner during a single year among unmarried heterosexual men aged 20 to 39 (Klepinger et al., 1993). In contrast, most gay men, about 70 percent, are now faithful to their partners. Gay men are now much less likely to have multiple partners during a single year than before the threat of AIDS (Billy et al., 1993). The men who are at the highest risk of becoming infected with the human immunodeficiency virus (HIV), intravenous drug users and those who engage in sex with many partners, however, increase the risk by being less likely to use condoms than those who are at lower risk (Dolcini et al., 1993).

The threat of AIDS may be a major reason for what sociologist Andrew Greeley (1991a) has called a "fidelity epidemic" among married men and women in the United States. His study was based on questions about sexual behavior asked by the National Opinion Research Center in its annual General Social Surveys between 1972 and 1989. Greeley found that "96 percent of all married Americans had only one partner in the previous year [their husband or wife]" (p. 11). Furthermore, "Ninety percent of the respondents (91 percent of the women and 89 percent of the men) say that they have had only one sexual partner for the duration of their marriage" (p. 26).

A later study, using 1990 General Social Survey data, found that only 3.3 percent of currently married men and women reported having had more than one sexual partner in the previous year (Anderson and Dahlberg, 1992). The results are quite consistent. Even if as many as one-fourth of the respondents were untruthful, married people are apparently much more faithful to one another than portrayals in the media and popular beliefs would indicate.

About 90 percent of men and 80 percent of women in the United States are not virgins when they marry for the first time. By age 19, a total of 8 out of 10 U.S. teenagers are sexually active (Alan Guttmacher Institute, 1994) (see Figure 9.1). Those who are virgins at marriage are usually deeply religious people. The **double standard** that allows sexual freedom to men but not to women has declined considerably. But it has not disappeared. Women continue to have fewer sexual partners over their lifetimes than men (Anderson and Dahlberg, 1992). Unmarried women are less likely than men to have more than one partner in any one year (the figures are 18 percent for men versus 9 percent for women). They are less likely than men to engage in casual sex; about 1 percent of women do in a given year, whereas 7 percent of men do (Greeley, 1991a; Anderson and Dahlberg, 1992). And women are judged more harshly than men when they do engage in casual sex (see Table 9.2 on p. 296).

Horticultural and Agricultural Societies In horticultural societies, a mixed pattern existed. In Samoa, for example, the common people were free to have sexual intercourse with whomever they pleased before marriage. But princesses were guarded carefully and were expected to be virgins when they married (Mead, 1928). A similar pattern has marked herding societies. In agricultural societies, differences in wealth, power, and prestige among families become more extreme as the economic surplus increases.

TABLE 9.2

The Sexual Revolution

Definition: A widespread change toward more liberal sexual attitudes and freer sexual behavior in the United States and Europe

Who: Mainly the middle class; mainly women

When: Before, during, and after World War I (1914–1918)

Why:

- Developments in medicine and science that provided more effective contraception and better control over sexually transmitted diseases
- Technological developments that created more factory and service jobs (secretarial, selling) that drew workers from the farms to cities
- Inventions of the automobile, mass transit, and dating

- More leisure time
- Replacement of family recreation (church suppers, hoedowns, and barn raisings) by commercial, nonfamily entertainment (movies, bars, nightclubs, social clubs)
- Spread of motels and hotels, increased availability of private meeting places for sexual activity

---

Control over the sexual behavior of the young, particularly females in the wealthiest families, becomes more repressive. Biological paternity becomes very important in patriarchal societies because of the emphasis on family lineage and the inheritance of property in the family line. And the double standard prevails.

Marital Choice

Choice of marital partners, like premarital sexual behavior, is freest in the simplest and the most complex societies. Women as well as men have control over economic resources in these societies. In families with two earners in postindustrial societies, the economic status of the partner that a woman chooses is less important than in other societies for the economic future of the woman, her children, and her family. And there is less interference and pressure from the family to make a "good" match. A teacher married to a teacher can have combined earnings that will almost equal those of a male doctor or successful businessman who in the past would have been the sole support of his family. Women who control economic resources are freer to choose mates on the basis of personality, qualities of the relationship (closeness, respect, acceptance, emotional support), and personal preference rather than economic practicality.

Historically, love and marriage have not gone together like a horse and carriage (Yorburg, 1974). This was particularly true in horticultural and agricultural societies, where marriages were usually arranged by parents, who bargained and traded to make the best deal possible economically—for the family. In societies in which women had important economically productive roles, the bride's parents usually received a bride price to repay them for the loss of a valuable worker. In societies in which women's economic role was less important and the production of as many children as possible was women's major economic contribution to the family, the husband's parents usually received a dowry. Love interfered with this strictly practical business arrangement and was viewed as deviant, tragic, or a nuisance.

Gender Differences Currently, in postindustrial societies, the changing economic roles of women and changing attitudes of men and women have had a profound effect on who marries whom, why, and when. The slow but steady increase in the number of women in higher-level occupations in service economies delays marriage. Training for these jobs takes more time, and both women and men in the middle social classes often strive to complete this training before marrying. They may live together without marrying, but they are less likely to marry at an early age. Men who are working class or poor and cannot find working-class jobs that pay adequately are also delaying marriage (Landale and Tolnay, 1991). School dropouts are the most likely to enter into living-together relationships (Bumpass and Sweet, 1989).

Traditionally, women and men have had different priorities in their search for someone to marry. In the past, women have been more likely to value ambition, industriousness, and the potential earning power of their suitors in choosing a marital partner. They have tended to marry men who are slightly older, richer, and more educated than themselves (Bernard, 1982). Men have tended to place more emphasis on youth, good looks, and physical attraction in making their choices. And richer, more educated men have had the greatest success in finding younger, more attractive women (Kenrick and Trost, 1989).

A cross-cultural study by psychologist David Buss (1990) indicates the persistence of this gender difference in marital choice; Buss surveyed 33 industrializing and industrial societies located on six continents and five islands. In postindustrial societies, however, this pattern is beginning to change. Marriages are more likely to be between status equals—in age, education, and potential or actual earnings (Schoen and Weinick, 1993). In fact, many highly educated women with high earning capacity are now marrying down with respect to education, income, and age—though the men they choose are generally no more than 2 to 3 years younger (Whyte, 1990). This is especially true in the African American subculture. A large difference in education in favor of the woman, however, makes it more likely that the marriage will end in divorce (Bumpass, Martin, and Sweet, 1991).

Movies and women's magazines reflect this reversal of the traditional pattern in their depictions of romantic attachments between female professionals and male construction workers or storekeepers. The media are not usually in the forefront of cultural change. They need to appeal to a mass market in order to sell their products. But they do tend to reflect what is going on in a society, especially changing values and norms.

Liking, friendship, confiding, and emotional closeness and support become very important in choosing a partner in postindustrial societies. Good looks are important at first meetings. They strongly affect who approaches whom at a party or anywhere else where people meet for the first time. Men who consider themselves unattractive usually do not approach women whom they perceive to be very attractive unless they have other assets to offer—high income, high social status, power, intelligence, understanding, kindness (Hatfield and Sprecher, 1986). Partners' looks are generally less important to women, older people, and men and women who have had a chance to get to know each other over a long period of time—at school or at work, for example.

In the most technologically advanced societies, various other approaches to meeting potential partners have evolved. The emphasis is on common interests and values and similarities in personality rather than on physical attractiveness. Participants use the latest developments in telecommunications. On college campuses, users of BITNET's Relay Network and similar systems communicate visually via words and symbols on their computer screens.

Sociologist David J. Hanson (1993) has interviewed a number of people who met on Relay and are now living together, engaged, or married. Exchanging messages on computer screens gives people who are shy or insecure about their physical appearance a better chance to connect with others on the basis of personality and interests, sight unseen. Successful romantic relationships typically progress from casual chatting to long conversations on the system. This is followed by an exchange of letters and photographs, telephone conversations, and then, finally, face-to-face meetings.

Older unmarried adults, usually in their 30s and 40s, use a variety of commercial methods for selecting dates—personal ads, matchmaking consultants, video dating, and computer matching. Dating services are sometimes class ranked, age graded, and/or ethnically segregated. Some employ the latest technologies, such as personal computers, modems, fax machines, videotapes, audiocassettes, and teleconferencing to arrange dates for clients. Computer matching, based on filling out personality questionnaires, is not particularly successful in leading to marriage, however (Woll and Young, 1989). Matching often brings together people who like the same things, but not each other. Love has its rational and logical aspects. But its mysterious aspects tend to evade computers, cameras, questionnaires, and consultants.

In finding a partner, the great majority of people make choices of which their parents would approve. They choose partners who are similar in personality, social background, physical attractiveness, intelligence, number of siblings, height, weight—even eye color (Buss, 1985). Life experiences, values, and expectations are similar. This makes it easier for people to talk to each other initially and to understand and support each other in the long run. Opposites may attract, but incompatibilities repel, as patience eventually wears thin.

Husband-Wife Relationships

Within the limits set by sex differences in average size and strength, husbands and wives have the most egalitarian relationships in hunting and gathering societies and postindustrial societies. Egalitarianism here does not mean that both partners have absolutely equal power to make any family decisions that must be made. This could result in a stalemate. In egalitarian family relationships, power is not arbitrarily assigned on the basis of gender or age. It is based on the varying resources and interests of those involved. Power shifts according to changing circumstances and specific decisions that must be made. Actually, power is more likely to be irrelevant in most situations that arise in egalitarian households—in two-career families, for example (Vannoy-Hiller and Philliber, 1989).

Resources and Power Women have more control over economic resources in the simplest and in the most complex societies. These resources increase their power. In industrial societies, married women who are gainfully employed have more power. The longer they have worked and the higher the prestige and income of their occupations relative to those of their husbands, the more power they typically have.

But we cannot mechanically and automatically translate the economic resources of husband and wife into power. Other noneconomic resources also affect power in families. Differences between husband and wife in personal resources, such as intelligence, education, mental health, physical health, and psychological strength (confidence and self-esteem), also affect power in specific families. There may be a difference between husband and wife in the degree of commitment each has to the relationship. The one who loves more gives, and gives in, more. In sociology, this has long been known as "the principle of least interest" (Waller, 1951, pp. 190–192). Women in living-together relationships with men, for example, tend to be more committed to—more interested in maintaining—the relationship than their partners. Those who are more committed are less likely to exercise power on the basis of their superior resources (DeMaris and MacDonald, 1993). Guilt, gratitude, and/or sympathy for a partner (who may be facing unemployment or illness, for example) are other reasons why people

FIGURE 9.2

Percentage of Household Chores Done by Mothers with Husband Present

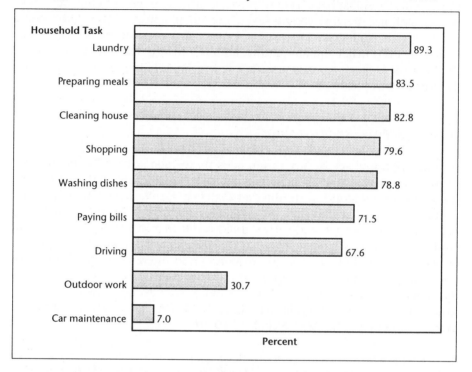

Source: Adapted by permission from David H. Demo and Alan C. Acock, "Family Diversity and the Division of Domestic Labor: How Much Have Things Really Changed?" *Family Relations 42* (1993), p. 325.

Mothers with husbands present do from two-thirds to nine-tenths of the routine daily chores in their households in the United States.

do not exercise power when they could, or even when they should (Hochschild, 1989).

Male dominance is most extreme in herding and agricultural societies. The complete and absolute power of the male in societies and families is known as **patriarchy**. **Matriarchy**—rule by women as a class—is not the primary power arrangement in any society, and matriarchy is not very common in individual families. Those matriarchal families that do exist in industrial societies are usually matriarchal by default, because the husband or the father has died, deserted, or become incapacitated. In agricultural societies, the power of the deceased patriarch passes to the eldest son rather than to the surviving wife.

The strength of preexisting patriarchal traditions in a particular society also affects the amount of power wives gain by obtaining control over independent economic resources. Patriarchal traditions have not been as strong or rigid in the United States, which has no medieval legacy, as they have been in Europe and Asia. Women were in short supply in colonial times in the United States and were highly valued from the beginning. It is no accident that the women's movements of the nineteenth and twentieth centuries originated in the United States.

Gender Roles Women and men are most likely to share in child care, homemaking, economic production, and recreational roles and activities in the simplest and the most complex societies. Extreme physical and psychological separation of the sexes in these areas, by contrast, is characteristic of horticultural, herding, and agricultural societies.

Women do the gathering of wild fruits, nuts, and vegetables in hunting and gathering societies, as we noted earlier. In most of these groups, except in arctic areas, gathering rather than hunting provides the major part of the food supply, although meat is more highly valued (Lee and DeVore, 1968). In industrial and postindustrial societies, the latter especially, almost all women, including married women, are employed at some time during their lives. Economic role sharing promotes sharing by husband and wife in domestic chores and child care, especially when female relatives in the extended family are not available to help.

Married women with children continue to perform most household chores with little participation from their husbands. Husbands spend more time on car maintenance and outside work, such as lawn mowing (see Figure 9.2). Married fathers whose wives work outside the home, however, are increasingly more likely to provide primary care for their preschool children than grandparents are (see Figure 9.3 on p. 302).

As a reflection of the increasing importance of egalitarianism in middle-class families, most married women in the United States feel that companionship is the most important aspect of marriage, more important than economic support or the opportunity to have children (Goode, 1993). Modern, middle-class husbands and wives, unlike their ancestors in agricultural societies, value doing things together. They eat, sleep, walk, talk, and plan together. They communicate love, hate, fears, joys, dreams, fantasies, and realities more freely. They do more touching, kissing, hugging, and joking than was typical in agricultural societies.

This happens as husband and wife become more equal in status and the husband-wife tie becomes more important than the parent-child tie. Younger, more educated, more mobile working-class husbands and wives are approaching the middle class in their declining emphasis on authoritarianism.

Parent-Child Relationships

Some years ago, psychologist Diana Baumrind (1968, 1980) classified parent-child relationships in a way that researchers still find useful. She iden-

FIGURE 9.3

Primary Care Providers for Preschool Children While Mothers Work, 1991

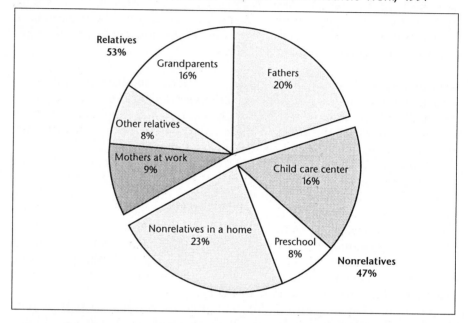

Note: Includes all children under age 5 whose mothers are employed. "Preschool" includes children in kindergarten programs.

Source: Martin O'Connell, "Where's Papa? Fathers' Role in Child Care," *Population Trends and Public Policy,* no. 20 (September 1993), p. 3; data from U.S. Bureau of the Census, Survey of Income and Program Participation, 1992.

Fathers are now more likely than grandparents to be caring for preschool children while their wives are at work.

tified three types of **parenting styles**—authoritarian, permissive, and authoritative. The three types of parent-child relationships differ with respect to (1) expression of emotion, which may typically be reserved or warm; (2) type of rules, which may range from rigid to flexible; (3) style of discipline, which may employ physical or psychological punishment; and (4) emphasis of values, which may be on strict obedience or on independence, self-reliance, and self-control.

Authoritarian parents insist on strict obedience to rules that require no explanation. Fathers, especially, express little warmth and affection toward their children. The parents' needs and desires come first. If children ask why they cannot have something, such as a chocolate bar, they are told "Because I say so." Children are physically punished if they disobey or express anger against a parent. Parents assume that children cannot be trusted to obey and conform unless they fear being slapped, spanked, or beaten.

Focus on Social Issues

PSYCHOLOGICALLY CORRECT PARENTING

[In postindustrial societies, advances in scientific knowledge in many fields, especially psychology, medicine, and nutrition, cut into the traditional monopoly of families in providing for the intellectual, emotional, and physical care of children. Experts increasingly share these functions with parents. Parents who seek out expert advice, however, may have great difficulty choosing among competing childrearing techniques, some of which turn out to be fads with little lasting scientific significance.]

Beth Tulipan was trading shop talk with a fellow mother when the mother made this modern-day confession: "I almost said it," she told Mrs. Tulipan. "I almost said, Because I said so . . ." Other modern offenses against small children include being negative, criticizing, screaming, threatening, spanking, bribing or uttering any of the following phrases: "You're too big a boy to cry"; "It's on your plate, finish it"; "Don't be sad"; "You don't hate your sister, you love her." . . . "It's like being politically correct—only you have to be psychologically correct in your parenting," says Mrs. Tulipan, of Hinsdale, Ill. . . .

It has never been easy being a parent, but today's parents have it rough. They face not only the traditional problems—biting, whining, and hitting, for example—but also a veritable tower of Babel of expert advice on childrearing. Earlier generations of middle-class mothers learned from one another as they passed time on park benches or front porches. Today, the next-door neighbor has been replaced by thousands of books, magazines, seminars, newspaper columns, videocassettes, and early childhood experts, advising parents on every facet of raising children.

—Cynthia Crossen, "Kids Acting Up? Don't Yell; Validate Their Tiny Feelings," *Wall Street Journal*, December 10, 1991, p. A1

What Do You Think?

1. Why has "psychologically correct" parenting become a source of concern in the United States today?
2. Do all social classes and ethnic groups experience this concern equally? Why or why not?
3. Why does democratic childrearing become more prevalent in industrial societies?

Permissive parents express a great deal of warmth and affection toward their children. They frequently hug, touch, hold, kiss, tickle, or scratch their children. They try to explain their rules, and they are frequently challenged when they do. In refusing to allow a child to have a chocolate bar, for example, they may explain that it is bad for the child's teeth, will spoil lunch or dinner, or will cause an allergic reaction. Physical punishment is never used. Children are sent to their room or deprived of privileges, such as watching television, playing with friends, staying up late, or having a special treat. The emphasis is on rewards for good behavior, and bad behavior may, within limits, be ignored in the hope that it will go away.

Permissive parents who are not confident, however, have trouble saying no and being firm (LeMasters and DeFrain, 1989). This results in endless arguments, a lack of rules, or inconsistent rules or discipline. Parents give up rather than compromise. And children tend to grow up with little self-control or discipline and with the feeling that their parents do not care.

The current formula for bringing up children in middle-class households in industrial societies is "strictness with affection" or **authoritative childrearing** (Baumrind, 1968, 1980). Others use the term **democratic childrearing** to refer to this parenting style (Spock, 1989). Authoritative parents are firm and set clear limits. They are in control and take their own needs and wishes into account in making rules. Children share in decision making, but "[parents] give their children firm, clear leadership and ask for cooperation and politeness in return" (Spock, 1989, p. 145). Democratic parents encourage curiosity by answering questions and allow their children to express anger. Children who are disciplined in this way are, as adults, more likely to have a high degree of confidence, self-reliance, and cheerfulness and to view their parents as friends.

Social Location and Childrearing

Democratic childrearing patterns are most prevalent in hunting and gathering and among the middle and upper social classes in industrial and post-industrial societies (Ellis and Petersen, 1992). Authoritarian parent-child relationships (especially father-child relationships) are typical in agricultural societies and among the working class and poor in industrial societies. This conclusion was supported in a classic cross-national study of fathers' disciplining practices by sociologist Melvin L. Kohn (1969).

He explained this in terms of parental values and the personality traits that are most useful to adults in these societies and social classes. Most adults in agricultural societies and in the working classes of industrial societies have little control over their lives. Factory workers punch time clocks and have a half-hour for lunch, for example; business executives do not punch time clocks and can take 2-hour lunches. Later research studies support Kohn's conclusions (Bradley, Caldwell, and Rock, 1988; McLoyd, 1990; Jay Belsky, 1990).

Independence, resourcefulness, self-reliance, and self- control are valuable traits in situations where there are opportunities to change your life circumstances—when you must take risks, plan ahead, or undergo long years of training and delay rewards. Independence is frustrating and useless, by contrast, in authoritarian life and work situations.

(Continued on page 306)

TABLE 9.3

Sociocultural Evolution and Family Life

	Hunting and Gathering	Horticultural	Agricultural	Industrial and postindustrial
Family Functions	All-inclusive: physical care, intellectual development, emotional support	All-inclusive	Some sharing with experts, specialists	Sharing with experts, specialists in all spheres, including emotional support Emotional support becomes most important
Family Structures (Forms)	Nuclear	Extended	Extended and semi-extended	Nuclear and semi-nuclear
Premarital Sexual Activity	Unrestricted	Mixed, depending on social status Higher status females restricted	Restricted, double standard for all females	Unrestricted, except for the deeply religious
Marital Choice	Personal preference, free choice, personal qualities	Arranged by family, social background most important	Arranged by family on basis of social status	Romantic love, personal preference, personal qualities, shared interests and values most important
Husband-Wife Relationships				
Power	Egalitarian	Varies depending on social status	Authoritarian	Egalitarian. Senior partner/junior partner roles
Gender Roles	Work and leisure activities shared	Separate work and leisure activities	Physically and emotionally separate	Shared leisure activities, two-earner households, shared childcare, less sharing of household chores
Communication	High, talking, confiding, joking	Mixed, depending on social status	Low	High, closeness, sharing, companionship, friendship most highly valued
Parent-Child Relationships	Permissive	Mixed, depending on social status	Authoritarian	Permissive/Authoritative (democratic)

When life is hazardous and unpredictable, when there is little control over one's immediate environment, or when social change is very rapid and technological advances threaten human survival, parents are more democratic. They are also more democratic when economic opportunities increase. Children must be independent, resourceful, and self-reliant to survive and succeed. To teach children to obey rules without questioning is unrealistic when rules are constantly changing, contradictory, or simply nonexistent.

Parents everywhere reflect their worldviews and life circumstances in the way they bring up their children. If parents must obey strict authorities and if there is little hope of social mobility or changing economic circumstances for their children, parents will bring up their children to obey strict rules. If opportunities and choices exist, particularly at work, and if independent judgment is important because rules are more flexible or entirely absent, parents will emphasize self-reliance, independence, and flexibility.

Actually, authoritarian childrearing practices were never as dominant in the United States, with its open frontier and the belief in the American dream, even before industrialization, as they have been in other agricultural societies. Foreign travelers to the United States have long commented on what they perceive as the rudeness of American children and their lack of discipline and proper respect for elders.

ALTERNATIVE FAMILY FORMS

Since the 1960s, several alternatives to traditional family groups have been growing rapidly in the United States and other postindustrial societies. Living together in a sexual relationship without marrying (usually called **cohabitation** by sociologists) has become an extension of the dating relationship for many young, never-married people. There are also living-together couple and family households involving individuals who have previously been married and may have children from a previous marriage. Another increasingly common alternative to the traditional family group is the household headed by a single parent.

Heterosexual Living-Together Relationships

In the United States, heterosexual living-together couples are more likely than married couples to be urban, living in the Northeast or the Far West, not religious, unconventional in their behavior, and untraditional in their values (Buunk and van Driel, 1989; Schoen and Weinick, 1993). Compared with married couples who are similar in other respects, they are more likely to have parents who are divorced, to describe their parents' marriages as unhappy, and to have poor relationships with their parents.

Living-together relationships have spread to the middle classes largely as a result of more liberal sexual attitudes and the availability of better contraceptive techniques. Other factors that have promoted this global trend include (1) the extended period of adolescence in postindustrial societies, where training for adult occupations takes longer; (2) the decline in available jobs for less educated, less skilled workers, which also delays marriage; (3) higher psychological expectations in marriage, which, in principle, necessitate that partners know one another well before making a permanent commitment; and (4) the high divorce rate, which may reinforce a psychological fear of commitment.

Duration   While the number of living-together households continues to increase, the rate of increase has slowed (Thornton, 1989). Almost two-thirds of those who remarried in the 1980s set up housekeeping with their spouses beforehand. Forty percent of all living-together relationships end within a year (Bumpass and Sweet, 1989). The couple either marries or splits up. Only 1 in 10 living-together couples stays together without marrying for more than 5 years. The partners are most often older, divorced people who do not want to take a chance on marriage again. Such living-together couples also include much older widowed women who may lose benefits if they remarry, or older, wealthy, unmarried women and men whose middle-aged children resent sharing an estate with a new stepparent and exert strong pressure on their parents to remain unmarried.

Class, Ethnic, and Gender Differences   High school dropouts are the group most likely to enter a living-together relationship before the age of 25; nearly one-half do (Bumpass and Sweet, 1989). By comparison, about one-third of all high school graduates enter this kind of relationship before the age of 25, and less than one-fourth of all college graduates fall into this category. There seems to be a recent turnabout in the willingness of younger, college-educated women to cohabit, however. Research studies and publicity in the media about the possible exploitative aspects of this kind of relationship for women may be a factor here.

In surveys, living-together couples are more likely than married couples to report egalitarian values. While cohabiting women spend less time than married women on housework, their partners do not spend more time than husbands on these chores (Buunk and van Driel, 1989). Apparently, housekeeping standards are lower in living-together households.

African Americans, who are about three times more likely than whites to be poor, are also three times more likely to live together without marrying (Bumpass and Sweet, 1989). Historically, however, this was not always the case. In Philadelphia between the years 1880 and 1925, African American family households were almost as likely as white households to consist of married couples (Furstenberg, Hershberg, and Modell, 1975). Unemployment rates were low and males were easily able to find work in an economy that needed their labor.

Divorce Rates   Surprisingly, divorce rates for those who lived together before marrying are higher than for those who did not (Bumpass and Sweet, 1989). This is true in all societies that have been surveyed, including Sweden, Denmark, and many societies in Western Europe (Bennett, Blanc, and Bloom, 1988). One would expect that living together before marrying would give couples a chance to work out potential conflicts—over finances, household chores, sexual problems, contacts with friends and family, and incompatible needs for closeness, privacy, independence, or togetherness. We would expect the couple to avoid marriage if they were unable to make the necessary compromises and concessions while living together.

Why then do couples who have lived together have a higher divorce rate after they marry? We don't really know. One possible reason is that those who live together may be less conventional (DeMaris and MacDonald, 1993). Not being deeply religious or traditional, they would be more tolerant in their attitudes toward divorce. Also, for younger people, living together is really an extension of the dating relationship, and partners in such relationships tend to be more considerate and tolerant and less demanding. They may tolerate certain behavior before they marry (such as infidelity, addictions, selfishness, or irresponsibility) that they are unwilling to tolerate after marriage. Marriage changes expectations. It may be easier to start afresh than to try to change what is established but is no longer acceptable in a relationship.

Same-Sex Living-Together Relationships

Legally, same-sex couples are single and experience the same legal disadvantages as heterosexual living-together couples. In the event of a breakup, if one partner has more financial resources or has contributed more to the accumulation of property, there is no legal presumption in favor of a 50-50 split. If children are involved, gay or lesbian parents who are not biologically related to a child have no recourse to court-ordered visitation rights (Johnson, 1994). On the other hand, Vermont recently became the first state to extend health benefits to the nonmarried same-sex or heterosexual partners of state employees. And more than a dozen cities in the United States now extend these benefits to nonmarried partners of municipal employees, regardless of sexual orientation.

Gay and lesbian couples do not usually conform to popular stereotypes in their speech, behavior, body language, or roles (Harry, 1988). Roles depend more on skills, tastes, and interests than on traditional gender-role prescriptions (Peplau, 1991). Traditional gender socialization, however, does tend to carry over, to some extent. Since women have generally been less likely to value power in their close relationships, a majority of lesbian couples report "equal power" in their relationships (Caldwell and Peplau, 1990, p. 214). In the past, lesbian couples were also more likely than gay male couples to value long-term commitment and sexual fidelity. More recently, however, gay men have been almost as likely as lesbian women to report monogamy in their partner relationships (Billy et al., 1993). This is probably largely a response to the AIDS epidemic.

Same-sex couples experience far greater disapproval from family, community, and church than nonmarried heterosexual couples. They are more likely to voluntarily segregate themselves geographically. Gay and lesbian communities are often located in areas surrounding private colleges in larger cities (Heyl, 1989). In these neighborhoods, same-sex couples find newspapers, bookstores, restaurants, clothing stores, therapists, lawyers, doctors, dentists, and others who cater primarily to their interests and needs. They find new reference groups and approval, acceptance, and reassurance from like-minded people.

Gay rights organizations and the Metropolitan Community Church, an interdenominational church for lesbians and gays, sponsor lectures, picnics, dances, and other social events that keep members from feeling isolated. Economically, however, especially in meccas such as San Francisco, a large-scale influx of gays and lesbians usually results in high rates of unemployment and underemployment for this particular wave of migrants from less hospitable places.

Single Parents

Eight out of 10 single-parent households in the United States are headed by women. A majority of these women receive no child support from the divorced, separated, or never-married fathers of their children (Kissman and Allen, 1993; King, 1994). These families are three times more likely to be living in poverty than families where a father is present. And the situation faced by many single parents of sole responsibility for the care of children is unique.

In no known nonliterate or agricultural society were mothers ever the exclusive caretakers of young children, or even of infants. In three-quarters of these societies, they were not even "principally involved" after infancy (Crano and Aronoff, 1978). The community or the extended family was there, and currently in the United States, the extended family continues to be there among the poor. This is especially true among the African American poor and among more recent Asian and Latino immigrants to the United States (Peterson, 1993; Jayakody, Chatters, and Taylor, 1993). But middle-class single parents, mainly divorced women, are much more likely to be on their own.

Some of the reasons for the increase in nonmarital births in industrial societies are known: (1) more teenagers are starting sexual activity earlier; (2) a majority, especially in the United States, know little or nothing about the facts of reproduction and do not use contraception; and (3) the great majority of parents in the United States are unwilling or unable to discuss sex with their children (Ahlberg and DeVita, 1992).

Among older, unmarried, high-income professional and business women and women in the arts, having a child before it is too late is a major reason for nonmarital births (Bachu, 1993). The highest rates of nonmarital births occur in the rural South, not in high-poverty areas in large cities in the North or Midwest, as is commonly believed (Rooks, 1993).

In the African American subculture, according to the National Survey of Families and Households, women prefer to be married, ideally (Bulcroft and Bulcroft, 1993). For many women over 20, however, this becomes less of a real goal. As a group, these women have the highest percentage of nonmarital births in the United States. They gradually lower their expectations with respect to marriage in response to several factors: (1) a very high black male unemployment rate, (2) relatively low educational levels and earnings of black males who are employed, and (3) a much lower survival rate into adulthood for black males than for other groups. The sex ratio of marriageable men to women in the African American subculture is extremely unbalanced. "For every three black unmarried women in their 20s, there is roughly only one unmarried man with earnings above the poverty threshold" (Lichter et al., 1992, p. 797).

African American males, at the same time, are less willing than white males to get married. Their economic future is less secure. In adulthood, many continue to be attached to male peers whom they have known since adolescence. They see no special benefits in getting married (South, 1993).

The higher rate of single parenthood among African Americans in the United States is also attributed by some sociologists and historians to differences in subcultural values (Ruggles, 1994). These higher rates are traced to experiences of African Americans under slavery and the survival of (polygynous) African cultural values among African Americans today.

Effects on Children To a large extent, the effects of single parenting on children depend on social location. In the United States, studies in the 1950s and 1960s were based primarily on children who were in therapy or in correctional institutions. These studies traced the behavior problems of these children to neglect or harsh, inconsistent discipline by harassed single mothers. Since the early 1970s, however, research has shifted to large-scale surveys and focused on the effects of low income and widespread poverty among families headed by single mothers (McLanahan and Booth, 1989).

According to these national surveys, children raised in mother-only families, compared to those in two-parent households, (1) are more likely to experience short- and long-term economic and psychological disadvan-

TABLE 9.4

Effects of Single Parenting on Children

Changing Focus in Research Studies:

1950s, 1960s: psychological effects

1970s to present: effects of poverty

Current Survey Research Results:

Children in mother-only families exhibit the following characteristics regardless of income and ethnic origin:

- They are more likely than those in two-parent families to experience short- and long-term economic deprivation.
- They achieve lower levels of education, with boys more negatively affected than girls; they are more likely to drop out of high school; in the middle class, they are less likely to attend college.

- In the case of girls, they have a greater risk of becoming single mothers than for girls in two-parent families.
- They are more likely to marry early, to have children early, and to get divorced.
- They are more likely to be arrested for committing crimes, and to be addicted to drugs and alcohol.

tages, (2) achieve lower levels of education and are more likely to drop out of school, (3) are more likely to commit antisocial acts and to be addicted to drugs and alcohol. Boys are more negatively affected, academically, than girls (Biblarz and Raftery, 1993). Girls are more likely to become single parents in adulthood as a result of nonmarital pregnancy or divorce. Both boys and girls are more likely to marry early, have children early, and divorce.

These effects are widespread in mother-only families, regardless of income and racial/ethnic origin. They are more frequent, however, among impoverished, minority single-parent families. It is difficult to separate out the relative importance of social circumstances, psychological factors such as maternal depression, and values in determining these outcomes. But even in the highest-risk situations of poverty and high-crime neighborhoods, we find individual children who are cheerful and confident and who function well at school and at home. Again, we are dealing with probabilities, not inevitabilities (see Table 9.4).

DIVORCE AND REMARRIAGE

Divorce rates have generally been higher in societies in which women's social status has been higher and their economic role more independent (Yorburg, 1974; Pearson and Hendrix, 1979; Goode, 1993). In horticultural **patrilineal societies** that trace descent through the male line, divorce rates have been low. **Matrilineal societies**—in which descent is traced through the female line—have had higher divorce rates. Women in these societies have been the major producers of food and have had higher social status. In agricultural societies, rates have usually been low. When marital choice is based on personal preference, when marital happiness and the tie between husband and wife are given great importance, and when women as well as men have alternatives, divorce rates have been higher.

Cross-Cultural Differences in Divorce Rates

Divorce rates tend to rise with the level of sociocultural evolution. But divorce rates were higher in certain agricultural societies such as Japan, Egypt, and Algeria in the late nineteenth century than they are in the United States today (Goode, 1993). And Japan, at least at the present time, has low divorce rates, despite a high level of industrialization. Nevertheless, if we take into account all causes of nuclear family breakdown, such as death of a spouse and desertion as well as divorce, more families are remaining intact today, and for longer periods of time, than ever before (Kain, 1990).

Generally, divorce rates rise in industrial societies for several reasons. Women have a greater possibility of supporting themselves in jobs other than as domestic servants or factory workers. Men can buy cooked food, laundering, clothing, and other goods and services that wives or female relatives provided in agricultural societies. Urbanization and geographic, social, and psychological mobility weaken the control of family, church, and community. And, finally, modern expectations in marriage for constant love, happiness, companionship, and mutual fulfillment are far more difficult to achieve than the traditional goals of economic cooperation and the gratification of physical needs that historically bound husbands and wives.

The United States has the highest divorce rate of all industrial societies (Ahlburg and DeVita, 1992). This is usually attributed to high and often unrealistic expectations of marriage in the United States, as compared to other societies (Glenn, 1990). Married people in other societies are better able to distinguish between personal and marital sources of unhappiness. A widespread myth in the United States is that a good marriage satisfies all basic needs, provides a person's major identity, and cures all feelings of loneliness and despair (Crosby, 1991). No single relationship can do all that.

Another cultural myth in the United States that promotes disillusionment after marriage is that a partner's basic personality can be changed by true love and friendly persuasion. Basic personality does *not* change as a result of a marriage ritual. A partner who is violent in a dating relationship, for example, will be violent after marriage (Straus and Gelles, 1990). The same is true of partners who are selfish, irresponsible, or lacking in ambition.

Still another myth, widely reported in the media, is that 50 percent of all marriages end in divorce. It is important to expose this misconception, since it can become a self-fulfilling prophecy. Journalists arrive at the 50 percent figure by comparing the number of marriages with the number of divorces in the same year. The couples who are getting married and those who are getting divorced in a particular year, however, are not the same people. The only valid way to determine the actual divorce potential of married couples during any particular period of time is to follow the same couples through the years and count the actual number of divorces and separations after a certain number of years. We now have at least one national study that has done just that.

Sociologist Theodore N. Greenstein (1990) examined data from a national sample of 5,159 women who got married in 1968 and were interviewed almost yearly over a period of 15 years. He found that 20.5 percent were separated or divorced from their husbands by the end of that time. Since most divorces occur within the first 7 years of marriage, this is probably a more accurate predictor of divorce in the United States.

Another study by sociologist Norval D. Glenn reached an almost identical conclusion. Glenn analyzed data on households from the General Social Survey conducted yearly by the National Opinion Research Center. He focused on the years from 1973 to 1988 and concluded that almost a fifth of marriages ended in separation or divorce over a period of 9 to 29 years from the date of marriage (Glenn, 1993). To predict that one out of five marriages will end in separation or divorce is more realistic than the one out of two predictions that have become a cliché in the media. We need more longitudinal studies on this topic, but recent divorce rate trends in the United States seem to support this more optimistic figure.

Trends in Divorce Rates

The divorce rate in the United States increased considerably during the 1960s and 1970s, especially among the middle classes and among families with small children (Ahlburg and DeVita, 1992). In 1977, however, the divorce rate began to level off and has declined very slightly since then.

Many of the reasons for the increase, leveling off, and beginning decline in the divorce rate are understood (Cherlin, 1992; Yorburg, 1993). Duty, obligation, and self-sacrifice, reinforced by religion and family pressure, have declined as standards for maintaining marriages. Increased economic pressures since recurring worldwide recessions began in the early 1970s have intensified marital problems. High or low income and wealth are important factors in stabilizing or destroying marriages. In the United States, the higher the class, the lower the divorce rate. The poor have the highest separation and legal divorce rates, often with the help of legal aid services (Bumpass, Martin, and Sweet, 1991).

Women have more economic alternatives, despite economic downturns, and are encouraged by the women's movement to take these alternatives. Both sexes are freer to enjoy sex without marrying. More liberal no-fault divorce laws that do not require proof of guilt (of adultery, cruelty, and so on) have spread gradually throughout the United States. Divorces are much easier and cheaper to get.

The leveling off and slight decline of the divorce rate are related to the decline in the marriage rate, the increase in living-together relationships, and the rise in the average age at marriage. The older people are at first marriage, the less likely they are to experience economic stress. They are also less likely to experience dramatic changes in values, interests, goals, and accomplishments. And they are less likely to grow apart than they would from those they might have married when they were very young.

Teenage marriages in the United States have twice the separation rate of marriages entered into after the age of 22 (Martin and Bumpass, 1989). And marriages among people in their early twenties are far more likely to end in divorce than marriages begun by those in their middle and late twenties (Ahrons, 1994). This has led to the concept of the "starter marriage," which, like a "starter house," is shed when a family outgrows it. These youthful marriages and early divorces receive little public notice since they do not usually involve children and the accumulation of large amounts of property. They do, however, involve incompatibilities in personality, interests, and values that become more apparent and less tolerable as partners mature.

Remarriage

The remarriage rate in the United States has been going down since the late 1960s (Ganong and Coleman, 1994). This decline is due, in part, to increased economic uncertainties since the 1970s. Divorced men paying child support are less likely to be able to assume financial responsibility for a second family, even in two-earner families. The declining divorce rate is another reason for the trend toward fewer remarriages. Still, close to one-half of all new marriages in recent years have involved at least one partner who was previously married (Bumpass, Martin, and Sweet, 1991). People remarry at about the same rate as they did during the nineteenth century in the United States. The big difference, however, is that now about 90 percent are divorced from their partners in first marriages. Up until the 1920s, those who remarried were far more likely to be widowed than divorced (Ihinger-Tallman and Pasley, 1987).

College-educated women and men are more likely than high school graduates or dropouts to remarry (Greenstein, 1990). Among whites, about three-quarters of divorced people remarry, as compared with about one-

FIGURE 9.4

Changing Shares of Household Types

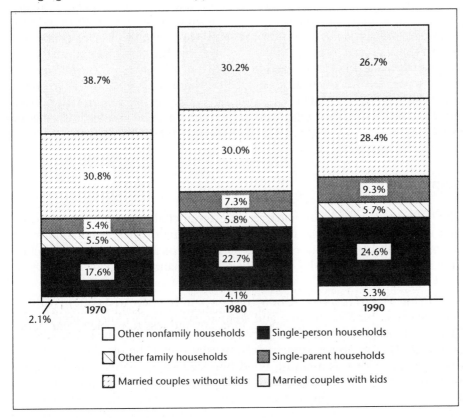

Sources: American Demographics; 1970, 1980, and 1990 censuses.

Since 1970, the percentage of households consisting of traditional families (married couples with children) has been declining steadily.

fourth of African Americans and one-half of Latinos. Rates of remarriage in the South, the Midwest, and the Far West are higher than in the Northeast.

Remarriages have a higher divorce rate (about 10 percent higher in most studies) than first marriages (Booth and Edwards, 1992). Stability, however, depends a great deal on the age at first and second marriage. Those who remarry between the ages of 25 to 44 have lower divorce rates than those who were younger when they first married and then remarried (Ganong and Coleman, 1994).

Reported marital satisfaction in remarriages does not differ significantly from first marriages (Glenn, 1990). Why, then, do remarriages have higher divorce rates? This is usually explained in terms of greater differences in social background in second marriages, personality difficulties, or values.

Partners in second marriages are more likely to differ in age, religion, and social origins, factors that are associated with higher divorce rates (Ganong and Coleman, 1994). Passionate love is not given as a reason for remarrying as often as more "practical" reasons. People in second marriages are, at the same time, less likely to choose a mismatch in the personality of their partners. As for values, divorce does not seem as ominous to someone who has been through it before. There are fewer "stayers" in second marriages—fewer people who value commitment above more individual or personal considerations (Martin and Bumpass, 1989).

Stepfamilies

The households created by remarriages often include stepchildren, children of a spouse from a former marriage. While many of these stepfamilies are strong and stable, they also exhibit certain typical problems. (Schwebel, Fine, and Renner, 1991; Hill, 1992; Beer, 1992; Ganong and Coleman, 1994):

Unwilling Participants   A new, instant family is created, often without adequate time for the children and stepparents to get to know, accept, and like one another. Except when previous households were characterized by severe conflict or abuse, stepchildren usually prefer the old life to the new one. Where there was a strong bond between single parent and child, especially mother and daughter, it is disrupted by the new stepparent. Children who resent a stepparent are a major source of stress in remarriages, especially for stepmothers, who generally have more responsibility for the daily care and discipline of children in the household than do stepfathers.

Ex-partner and In-law Intrusions   Since the great majority of remarriages follow a divorce rather than the death of a husband or wife, the biological parent is now very likely to be a presence in the new relationship. Conflicts over finances and the disciplining of children, especially, are widespread. Usually, grandparents of a first marriage exert their claim to maintain contact with their grandchildren. Boundaries, privacy, and independence are more difficult to maintain in remarriages.

Role Conflict   Family members in first marriages usually know what is expected of them. In remarriages involving children, there are few cultural guidelines that define responsibilities and obligations. Conflicts usually center on lack of mutual expectations with regard to discipline, finances, and marital versus parental obligations. Stepparents may be required to cope with the competing needs of stepchildren, new biological children, and noncustodial biological children. These conflicts are intensified when time and money are scarce.

FUTURE FAMILIES

Families will survive because of the basic human need for stable, enduring, emotional support—in childhood certainly, but in adulthood as well. Some individuals thrive on solitude (Storr, 1988). Most do not. Certain observable trends—the rising social status of women, freer premarital sex, greater emphasis on equal partnership and sharing between husband and wives, the growth of alternatives to marriage, fewer children, and more democratic childrearing practices—are likely to continue in all industrial societies (Ahlburg and DeVita, 1992). The underlying political and economic conditions that have promoted these trends are likely to continue. Role conflict and increases in single-parent households are also likely to continue, as will poverty in the United States, at least for now.

Certain family stresses are expected to increase around the world. The global aging of human populations brings with it concerns about health care and caregiving in all societies. Adult daughters, the primary caregivers to older parents, are more likely to be employed in the nonfamily economy in industrial societies and are less available for caregiving. This is a major source of role conflict among middle-aged women, regardless of the love they may feel for their parents (Gerstel and Gallagher, 1993).

Another trend, especially in the United States, is the growth of minority populations (Ahlberg and DeVita, 1992). By the year 2000, one in three school-age children in the United States will be of minority ethnic origin (compared with one in four today). Child poverty rates are between two and three times higher among minorities than among the rest of the population, and these poverty rates are slowly but steadily increasing in the United States (O'Hare, 1992a). This will have important consequences for the stresses and potential accomplishments of future generations of children and adults in the United States.

Homelessness among family groups is also increasing in the United States, although the public is not aware of the extent of the problem. Homeless families are less visible than single adults with mental, drug, or alcohol problems. They are not on park benches or in cardboard homes on the street. According to a national survey sponsored by the United States Conference of Mayors, 43 percent of the homeless population in 1993 were families—single mothers and their children, mainly—and their numbers had increased 30 percent since 1992 (*New York Times,* December 22, 1993, p. A18).

A significant number are working poor. Most of these families have borrowed money, doubled up with relatives and friends, left older children with relatives, left town to look for work, and used free clinics and soup kitchens. Whatever they do, they are unable to afford a home of their own.

Many of the problems of families in the United States compared to others reflect government policies that differ from those in other industrial societies (Hofferth and Deich, 1994). Day-care facilities are especially inadequate in the United States, as are prenatal, postnatal, and health insurance programs. Other industrial democracies are far ahead in providing these services, as well as family allowances (direct payments to families for each child they have), preferential housing for families with children, job training and retraining, better elementary school education, and free higher education.

In the United States, individual state governments differ in their political philosophies. States that spend more on social services have lower rates of divorce, suicide, and births to unmarried teenagers (Zimmerman, 1992). These are all indicators of family well-being. States with political philosophies that are more committed to the good of all of the people provide more generously for social programs, regardless of their financial problems and circumstances. They value families, as well as family values.

Study Guide

REVIEW OBJECTIVES

After studying this chapter, you should be able to:

1. Give some reasons why family groups are universal.
2. Describe how and why family functions and forms, premarital sexual behavior, marital choice, and husband-wife and parent-child relationships have changed during the course of sociocultural evolution.
3. Define the characteristics of heterosexual and same-sex living-together relationships and single-parent families as alternative family forms.
4. Describe demographic patterns in living-together relationships with respect to geographic location; duration; class, ethnic, and gender differences; and divorce rates for those who marry.
5. List possible reasons for the recent, slight decline in divorce rates in the United States and the decades-long increase that preceded this decline.
6. Assess the probable future of families worldwide, especially with respect to marital and parental roles, power, and role conflict.

SUMMARY

1. Family groups are found in all societies because of the need to ensure physical care of the very dependent human young, control sexual rivalry, and provide a stable source of emotional support for children and adults. In urban industrial societies, substitute bureaucratic groups would be unable to perform the function of providing secure and stable long-term emotional support for the young.

2. During the course of sociocultural evolution, families have lost their monopoly in fulfilling needs such as physical care, socialization, protection, and emotional support. These functions are shared increasingly with teachers, doctors, lawyers, therapists, and other experts.

3. The simplest and most complex societies share family group patterns such as a nuclear family structure, free premarital sexual relationships, free marital choice, egalitarian husband-wife relationships, and democratic parent-child relationships. Historical changes in the amount, distribution, and control over economic resources and developments in science and technology are important variables in explaining these patterns.

4. Alternatives to marriage, such as living together without marrying, reached a peak in the 1980s for middle-class people and have been leveling off for this class since then. Living-together arrangements, except for those that involve older people, are usually viewed as temporary, and, in fact, they

are. Only 10 percent of these arrangements last more than 5 years, and those that do are usually among older people who were previously divorced or widowed and have no intention of remarrying.

5. Living together is an extension of the dating relationship made possible by more liberal sexual attitudes and more effective contraceptive techniques. Partners in living-together relationships are usually less committed and are less likely to come from similar social backgrounds than husbands and wives. If they marry, they are more likely to divorce than couples who did not live together before marrying.

6. Most single parents are divorced, especially in the middle class. A majority of the women who are single parents receive no child support from the fathers of their children, and the families that these women head are three times more likely to be living in poverty than families where the father is present.

7. Divorce rates in the United States, the highest in the world, have leveled off in recent years and are now declining slightly. The later median age at first marriage, the decline in the marriage rate, and more realistic expectations in marriage are among the factors that explain this trend.

8. The rate of change in family relationships appears to be slowing in postindustrial societies. Future trends will be strongly influenced by government policies.

GLOSSARY

Authoritarian childrearing (parenting): An adult-centered parenting style characterized by strict obedience to nonnegotiable rules that are not explained or justified. This parenting style is typical in agricultural societies and among more traditional segments of industrial societies. Also called **democratic childrearing.**

Authoritative childrearing: A parenting style characterized by consistent, strict but democratic discipline, warmth, and affection that is typical in the middle social classes in industrial societies. Also called **democratic childrearing**.

Cohabitation: Unmarried, living-together sexual relationships.

Double standard: The social norm that allows sexual freedom to men but not to women.

Extended family: Two or more nuclear families or parts of nuclear families that live in daily contact and are economically and psychologically interdependent.

Matriarchy: Rule or dominance by females in a society or family.

Matrilineal societies: Societies in which the female line is most important in descent and inheritance of property.

Monogamy: Marriage limiting partners to one husband and one wife.

Nuclear family: Parents and their children; the immediate family.

Parenting styles: Parent-child relationships that vary with respect to expression of emotion, discipline, flexibility of rules, and emphasis on obedience versus self-reliance. These vary, typically, in different types of societies and in different social classes in the United States today.

Patriarchy: Complete and absolute power of males in societies and families.

Patrilineal societies: Societies in which the male line is most significant in descent and inheritance of property.

Permissive childrearing: A child-centered parenting style characterized by very flexible rules.

Polyandry: Marriages involving one wife with several husbands.

Polygamy: Marriages involving one husband or wife with more than one spouse.

Polygyny: Marriages involving one husband with several wives.

Sexual revolution: A time of rapid change in sexual values, attitudes, and behavior that occurred in the middle social classes in the United States and Europe before, during, and after World War I.

PRACTICE TESTS

True ▪ False Test

___ 1. Some people believe that the functions of families would be better performed by other groups in society.

___ 2. Extended families disappear in industrial and postindustrial societies.

___ 3. Only the more complex types of societies attempt to control the sexual activity of married women and men outside of marriage.

___ 4. Arranged marriages are most common in societies in which women control economic resources.

___ 5. Gender roles shift from societal type to societal type (e.g., agricultural to postindustrial).

___ 6. Couples who cohabitate are more likely to have poor relationships with their parents than are couples who are married.

___ 7. The increase in reported monogamy among gay men is most likely an adherence to traditional values.

__ 8. Male children in mother-only families achieve lower levels of education than boys in two-parent families.

__ 9. The divorce rate in the United States has decreased slightly since the late 1970s.

__ 10. The institutions of postindustrial societies will likely eliminate the need for families.

Multiple-Choice Test

__ 1. As they existed in traditional societies, families are:
   a. endangered.
   b. consistent in form if not appearance.
   c. extinct.
   d. increasing.

__ 2. Bureaucracies, by definition, cannot provide individuals with:
   a. efficiency.
   b. predictability.
   c. emotional involvement.
   d. routine.

__ 3. Families in hunting and gathering societies differ fundamentally from families in postindustrial societies in that they:
   a. give emotional support to their members.
   b. have a monopoly over providing for their members' needs.
   c. socialize their members.
   d. protect their members.

__ 4. Polygyny and polyandry are forms of:
   a. monogamy.
   b. religions.
   c. isolated nuclear families.
   d. polygamy.

__ 5. The so-called sexual revolution in the United States:
   a. began before World War I.
   b. began during the 1960s.
   c. never really occurred.
   d. reversed itself with the spread of AIDS.

__ 6. Love and friendship are most likely to be valued characteristics of marriages in:
   a. hunting and gathering societies.
   b. horticultural societies.
   c. agricultural societies.
   d. postindustrial societies.

___ 7. Rule by women as a class is termed:
   a. matriarchy.
   b. polyandry.
   c. patriarchy.
   d. polygamy.

___ 8. Which of the following conditions is not considered an incentive to cohabitation?
   a. declines in available jobs for less-skilled workers
   b. higher psychological expectations in marriage
   c. shorter periods of adolescence
   d. high divorce rates

___ 9. Which industrialized country has the highest divorce rate?
   a. the United States
   b. Japan
   c. Sweden
   d. Britain

___ 10. Which of the following are problems that are typical of stepfamilies?
   a. unwilling participants
   b. lack of cultural values
   c. ex-partner and in-law intrusions
   d. role conflict

Matching Test

Match each concept with its definition, illustration, or explication below.

1.
(1) Kindergarten
(2) Cohabiting
(3) Polyandry
(4) Isolated nuclear family
(5) Monogamy

a. Self-defined family
b. Substitute family group
c. One spouse
d. More than one husband at once
e. Infrequent family visits

2.
(1) Family
(2) Isolated nuclear
(3) Semi-nuclear
(4) Semi-extended
(5) Truly extended

a. Daily contact
b. Relatives exert no influence on nuclear family decisions
c. Nuclear family authority, but relatives' influence is strong
d. Support/reference group
e. Largely self-sufficient

3.
(1) Hunting and gathering societies
(2) Industrial societies
(3) Postindustrial societies
(4) Horticultural societies
(5) Agricultural societies

a. Mixed sexual patterns
b. Wealth differentials, sexual controls strengthen
c. Marriage at puberty
d. Freest sexual behavior
e. Workweek shortens, time for sexual activities increases

4.
(1) Nuclear family
(2) Polygamy
(3) Extended family
(4) Matriarchy
(5) Patriarchy

a. Nuclear family form
b. Several nuclear families
c. Male controlled
d. Mother, father, children
e. Female dominated

5.
(1) Double standard
(2) Cohabitation
(3) Sexual revolution
(4) Gender roles
(5) Husband-wife relationships

a. Sexual restrictions/expectations
b. Vary per society norms
c. Male vs. female activities/functions
d. Liberalization of sexual attitudes and behavior
e. Living together, unmarried

REVIEW QUESTIONS

1. What is a family, and why are family groups unlikely to disappear in human societies?
2. How and why have family functions varied during the course of sociocultural evolution?
3. How and why have family forms varied in major types of societies?
4. Why are premarital sexual behavior, marital choice, and husband-wife and parent-child relationships similar in the simplest and the most complex human societies?
5. Why has the pattern of living together in a sexual relationship without marrying increased among the middle social classes in postindustrial societies?
6. In what ways are same-sex and heterosexual relationships similar and dissimilar?
7. What are some of the reasons for the increase in nonmarital births in industrialized societies?
8. According to recent national surveys, what are the effects on children of all social classes and racial/ethnic origins of growing up in single-parent households?

9. Historically, how and why have divorce rates varied? Why do they generally increase in industrialized societies?
10. Which of the current trends in family roles and demographics are likely to continue? Why?

APPLYING SOCIOLOGY

1. How would you classify your family on a scale from truly extended to isolated nuclear?
2. Who had the authority in your parental home? Why? Did this change during the years? If so, why did it change?
3. What changes in role sharing, if any, have occurred in your family in three generations? How would you explain these changes?
4. How did the social class location of your family affect your family's values, structure, functioning, and relationships?

10

Economies and Inequality

We have seen that changes in the amount and distribution of goods and services in major types of societies have profoundly affected human social life. During the course of sociocultural evolution, economic inequality arises, reaches its most extreme level, and then becomes relatively less extreme (Lenski, 1966; Lenski, Lenski, and Nolan, 1991). Since horticultural societies first appeared about 10,000 years ago, economic inequality has been a major factor in determining differences in the quality of life for families and individuals. How do we explain the continued existence of economic inequality?

THEORIES OF ECONOMIC INEQUALITY

Theories of inequality attempt to explain the origins and persistence of economic inequality; ideologies, by contrast, seek to justify inequality. In the field of sociology, the structural functional model, the conflict model, and the sociocultural evolution model are used to focus on different aspects of inequality. Functionalists stress the necessity, inevitability, and positive consequences of economic inequality. They point to the consistent ranking of certain occupations as more prestigious and worthwhile than others, and the widespread agreement in values that this demonstrates. They stress evo-

325

lution rather than revolution in their theories of social change and economic inequality. But they give relatively little weight to developments in scientific knowledge and technology and to power as factors that may explain social change and inequality (Moore, 1960; Parsons, 1977).

In a classic statement of functionalist theory, sociologists Kingsley Davis and Wilbert E. Moore (1945) argued that unequal economic rewards in human societies are functional for maintaining societies. These differences in average income and wealth, they asserted, motivate talented members of complex societies to prepare for more difficult occupations that require lengthy training, such as physician, college professor, or research scientist.

Melvin Tumin (1953) was among the first of many sociologists to criticize this theory for insufficiently noting that economic rewards are not necessarily based on talent or hard work. Inheritance and ascribed characteristics such as gender and racial/ethnic origin interfere with equality of opportunity. And those receiving the greatest rewards, the hereditary upper class, often contribute little that is important or functional in maintaining the societies in which they live.

Conflict and sociocultural evolutionary theories of economic inequality have followed Marx and Engels in giving primary weight to scientific and technological advances as factors affecting the amount, kind, and distribution of available economic resources. Contemporary conflict and evolutionary theorists have been able to employ much more accurate information from anthropology and history than was available in the time of Marx and Engels. And contemporary theorists take into account developments that Marx and Engels did not foresee: (1) the enormous growth of the public sector in both democratic and authoritarian governments; (2) the spread of mixed economies in all societies, with market and publicly owned productive enterprises often existing side-by-side in the same society; and (3) the enormous increase in middle-class service jobs in information-based postindustrial economies.

Like Marx and Engels, modern conflict theorists concentrate on class conflict and differences in opportunity that depend on class origins (Mills, 1959; Coser, 1956; Dahrendorf, 1959; Lenski, 1966; Domhoff, 1990). They also emphasize the dysfunctional aspects of economic inequality—the suffering, competition, and destructive conflicts that stem from past and present efforts of powerful elites to maintain their wealth and privileges.

Conflict theorists focus on the roles of power and social origins as well as talent and effort in influencing the economic rewards that individuals receive. They examine the ways in which ideology and government policy operate to serve the interests of the wealthiest members of various societies. They usually deny that a classless society is possible or avoid the question of classless society entirely.

There is some validity to the functionalist position that unequal rewards are necessary in complex societies. Although such rewards may motivate people to choose more difficult jobs, however, the economic rewards in certain occupations do not match the years of training invested. Truck drivers, for example, usually earn more than elementary school teachers, who spend many more years learning the skills necessary for their work.

Contemporary conflict theorists have been more likely to focus on the unfairness of the *degree* of economic inequality among members of a society, especially in market economy societies, than on economic inequality per se. In 1989, chief executives in the United States earned 120 times the wages of the average U.S. worker (compared to about 35 times as much in the mid-1970s). In the former Soviet Union, by contrast, plant directors earned 5 or 6 times as much as workers (Naser, 1992a). The figures for the United States, furthermore, do not include stock options and other not-so-obvious fringe benefits of being an executive at a large corporation, benefits that also have monetary value. "In no other advanced industrial nation is the income gap so wide between managers and professionals and production workers" (Reich, 1993, p. A19). Conflict theorists have argued that the enormous differences between the poor and near-poor and the very rich (especially those who are not particularly talented or productive) are unnecessary, unfair, inhumane, and unjustifiable.

Because of the increasing complexity of advanced industrial societies and the hidden ways in which government policy comes to be indirectly influenced, modern conflict theorists have a more complicated task (Domhoff, 1990). But conflict theorists have been growing in number in recent years (Horowitz, 1993), especially as economic inequality has become more extreme. The accelerated concentration of wealth within a small upper social class is a global trend. It is currently visible not only in Great Britain and Germany, for example, but also in authoritarian revolutionary socialist societies (such as China and the former Soviet Union) that started out more equal than others (Burawoy and Krotov, 1992; Walder, 1992; Brauchli, 1993).

SOCIOCULTURAL EVOLUTION AND ECONOMIC INEQUALITY

Humans are evaluating animals. In every society, they rank each other on a scale from high to low in prestige, depending on their cultural values and economic and political conditions. In most societies, furthermore, there is fairly general agreement about where people belong on this scale.

In hunting and gathering societies, age and gender are the major bases for categorizing individuals and for assigning overall prestige in the society. Within these categories, however, individuals differ in esteem, respect, and influence. This is based on personal qualities such as strength, bravery, resourcefulness (ability to solve problems), and temperament. Power differences between families and between individuals (excluding the shaman and headman) are minimal, nor are there differences in property. There is no extra food or material goods to hoard or fight over. Power and property, therefore, do not determine overall prestige of families or individuals in these societies.

In horticultural and agricultural societies, the basis for evaluating and ranking humans expands to include property, power, and ancestry. The family becomes the unit that is ranked. Individuals are ranked as members of a family, and this rank does not change, typically, over the course of a person's life.

Economic inequality first arises in horticultural societies, because these societies can produce more food and other goods than are needed for people to survive and function adequately. Some families accumulate more of these assets than others, initially perhaps because of the contributions of a larger number of children or more resourceful, hardworking children. This accumulated property is inherited by succeeding generations of family groups, and inequality continues along family lines.

In urban industrialized societies, ancestry declines somewhat in importance in determining individuals' destinies, although it continues to be very significant. It provides a start in life, and this start usually has long-term consequences. Except for members of the hereditary upper class, most people today must run as fast as they can to stay in the same economic place as their parents.

In chapter 2 we introduced the distinction between economic and social class. Social class as the term is used here refers to overall rank, or social status, in a prestige hierarchy. The advantage in using this term is that it allows us to rank people in all societies, including hunting and gathering societies, where differences in wealth and power are minimal. Social class rank, or overall social status, is based on ascribed *and* achieved characteristics: on ancestry, gender, power, property and income, education, and occupational prestige.

Marx defined economic class in terms of a group's ownership or nonownership of the means of production (land, businesses, and equipment). In advanced market economies, the distinction between owners and nonowners blurs. Where corporations and stockholders are the typical form of productive enterprise, the definition of economic class should include management of or control over, as well as ownership of, productive property. Managers, however, usually own stock in the corporations they manage. In fact, a number of larger U.S. corporations are now requiring their managers to buy stock in the companies they manage (Rowland, 1993). The assumption behind this trend is that ownership motivates managers to work harder.

Weber, like Marx, defined class economically—in terms of differences among individuals in a society according to the economic resources they possess. Economic resources in industrial market economies consist of property (corporate stocks, bonds, or real estate, for example) and income (earnings from wages, salaries, and investments). How much people have of both determines their economic rank in a society. And this determines what Weber called their "life chances" (1946 [1914]).

But Weber also described two other ways of ranking people—according to differences in the amount of authority and prestige they possess. He defined **authority** as legitimate or official power. Examples of authority include the power of hereditary kings and elected officials. **Prestige**, or "social honor," is based on social origins (ancestry) and "lifestyle." Lifestyle consists of how people earn their money (occupation or other sources of income), what they buy (such as house type and furnishings), and whom they know (friends, associates, and individuals known through club memberships).

Both Weber and Marx captured important aspects of inequality in the ranking of human beings in societies. If we apply the sociocultural evolution model to this problem, we come up with a way of combining their ideas that applies to all individuals in all societies. We do this by ranking people in terms of prestige. For ranking people in industrial societies, we use the concept of social class. This refers to overall prestige, or social status (respect and esteem), as determined by ascribed and achieved characteristics and by lifestyle and life chances.

Ascribed characteristics, such as family origin, racial/ethnic ancestry, and gender, strongly affect overall prestige and how far we can go in the social class structure (Hauser and Sewell, 1986; Corcoran et al., 1990; Mayer, 1991). Even in the most advanced industrial societies, merit is hedged by social background, as well as luck.

In more complex societies, the achieved aspects of social class position include income and property, level of education, and occupational prestige. Most people in the United States and in other industrial societies agree about the prestige of various occupations. And this agreement has been fairly consistent in the United States since attempts to measure occupational prestige were begun by the National Opinion Research Center almost 50 years ago. As we noted in chapter 1, the major standard used by the public in ranking occupations is responsibility for the public welfare. The amount of education required and typical earnings are also important in ranking occupations.

The social class location of individuals and families is one of the most important facts social scientists can determine about them. It affects not only the quality of life but the length of life as well. People in the higher social classes in the United States today travel more, read more, have more education, and are more likely to vote. They also have more friends and entertain them more, receive more mail, and join more organizations. Social class affects attitudes, values and behavior, happiness, self-confidence and self-esteem, alienation and prejudice, the type and extent of mental and physical illness, and the kind and amount of role conflict.

Generally, social class location affects patterns of thinking, feeling, and behaving as well as patterns of speech, dress, and recreation. Ultimately many of these traits are psychological. But their extent or frequency among members of a society is strongly related to social class location (see Table 10.1).

TABLE 10.1

The Significance of Social Class

According to nationwide surveys, higher positions in the social class structure (excluding the old upper class, on which little survey data is available) are associated with the following characteristics:

- higher self-esteem and greater psychological and economic security.
- better physical and mental health, lower rates of acute and chronic illness, and longer life.
- less likelihood of being institutionalized for mental illness, physical illness, or crimes against family or society.
- healthier diets, more exercise, less smoking, and less obesity.
- lower birth and divorce rates.

- later, more flexible life transitions—older age at first marriage, parenthood, grandparenthood, retirement; greater likelihood of changing careers, returning for education, remarriage, starting new families at older age (among men).
- greater marital and work satisfaction and less likelihood of retiring.
- more reading, traveling, letter writing, friends, and social and volunteer activities.
- looking, feeling, and acting younger than one's chronological age.

SOCIAL STRATIFICATION

The **social stratification** systems of human societies are the ranked layers or strata of members of these societies. Historically, the ranked categories or **strata** (from the Latin *stratum,* meaning "layer") that have distinguished members of a society in terms of prestige have had different names.

In more complex literate societies, these layers are called **castes** if position or social status is ascribed (hereditary), unchangeable, and sanctioned by religion. In medieval agricultural societies, the ranked layers were called **estates**. The social status of nobles, commoners, serfs, and slaves was sanctioned by law and extremely difficult to change. Downward mobility occurred when population increased and there was an oversupply of peasants to work the land. Upward mobility was possible for a handful of urban merchants or especially talented peasants, but this was rare. As industrializing and industrialized societies become more complex in terms of scientific knowledge, technology, statuses, and roles, the layers or strata that develop are called **classes**.

Climbing the social status ladder in class societies is theoretically possible for anyone. Ideally, effort, training, and talent or merit are the keys to success. Social status is not guaranteed by birth. Position can change over the course of a lifetime. There are no certainties in class systems, except perhaps for those whose families have been at the very top or very bottom for more than one generation. Even here, however, good or bad luck may provide a passport, up or down, for those who are uniquely fortunate or unfortunate.

Social Mobility

The movement from one status to another in the social class or social stratification system is known as **social mobility**. Mobility may be "vertical"
up or down the social class structure, or it may be "horizontal"—from one
position to another within the same social class level (from secretary to
bookkeeper, for example). In the past, when fewer middle-class women
were employed, the amount of vertical social mobility in a society was
usually measured by comparing the occupational prestige of males at two
different points in their lives. Social scientists also measured intergenerational mobility from one class to another, within families, by comparing
the occupations of fathers and sons.

Measures of intergenerational social mobility are an attempt to determine how open different societies have been in providing opportunities
for moving up in the social class structure. Industrial societies are more
open than agricultural societies because technological advance creates more
middle-level, nonmanual service occupations. The movement of large categories of people up or down in social class because of changes in the
occupational structure is called **structural mobility**. People move up or
down because the total number of working- or middle-class jobs in a society
increases or decreases. In the United States at the turn of the century, for
example, most women employed in the nonfamily economy were factory
workers or domestics. As men left middle-class secretarial and elementary
school teaching jobs for better ones, and more of these jobs became available, large numbers of women entered middle-class occupations. Today, as
the number of factory jobs declines, many unemployed men lose their social
status as members of the upper working class and become poor or near-
poor.

Movement from the working class into the lower levels of the middle
class does not differ much from one industrial society to another, in those
that have been studied (Hauser and Grusky, 1988). In a classic comparative
study conducted by sociologists Peter Blau and Otis Dudley Duncan (1978
[1967]), approximately one-third of the sons of working-class fathers in
various industrialized market economy societies, including the United States,
made it into the middle class, usually at the lower levels. In the United
States, this situation has not changed much over the centuries.

Moving from the working class to higher class levels is difficult in all
industrial societies. No society has a truly open class system. Because of
the inheritance of property and the inheritance of occupations along family
lines (nepotism), equality of opportunity has not existed since plant cultivation was first invented and an economic surplus was first created. Not
even revolutionary socialist societies that have attempted to do away with
class distinctions have had true equality of opportunity. University entrance
in these societies was and is limited largely to urban students from the
middle levels of society.

In the United States, the most important factor in determining occupational mobility has been family background. Ethnic origin, family size (number of siblings), the educational background, occupation, and income of the father, and the educational background of the mother have been more important than school performance and test scores in determining whether individuals decide to go to college (Corcoran et al., 1990).

In the past, the United States has had more movement from the lower levels to the higher levels of the middle class than other industrialized societies because college admissions have been more open. A far greater percentage of high school graduates enroll in universities (about 30 percent) than in other industrializing and industrial societies, including the former Soviet Union and the People's Republic of China (where about 5 percent enroll in universities). But off- and on-again worldwide recessions since 1973 and much greater competition for higher-level jobs have resulted, at least temporarily, in widespread underemployment and downward mobility for the most recent U.S. college graduates (Kaus, 1992; Phillips, 1993; Newman, 1993).

Multinational corporations have moved many manufacturing jobs from the United States to industrializing societies, and automation has eliminated increasing numbers of lower-level jobs, as we noted earlier. At the same time, the higher-level jobs of business executives and professionals in service industries have also declined in number because of the increased trend toward the merging and acquiring of smaller companies by large corporations in the United States (DiPrete, 1993). The taking over of smaller publishing, advertising, or food companies, for example, usually means that duplicate staff (editors, account executives, or market researchers, for example) will be fired.

Status Inconsistency

In complex, rapidly changing societies, individuals become increasingly likely to experience a discrepancy or inequality between their ascribed and their achieved statuses or among their occupational prestige, their level of education, and their income. We call this status inconsistency, a term introduced in chapter 7 (see p. 230). Impoverished aristocrats, minorities who have achieved high standing in business or the professions, and college professors, who rank high in occupational prestige and education but relatively low in income, are examples of status inconsistency. This concept is important because widespread status inconsistency in a society can lead to social unrest.

Members of racial/ethnic or religious minorities who experience a contradiction between the respective prestige of their ascribed and achieved statuses tend to become active in reform or revolutionary social movements. Many highly successful African American professionals today feel a great deal of resentment toward colleagues who do not accept them socially (Whitaker, 1993; Cose, 1993). Their high achieved status is inconsistent with their lack of social acceptance by peers (and subordinates) whose racial/ethnic status is perceived as higher.

As we noted in chapter 7, members of the hereditary upper classes who experience downward mobility with respect to wealth through loss of their ancestral lands, factories, or securities may become active in conservative or regressive social movements. College professors, who rank very high on level of education and occupational prestige but relatively low on income (an example of discrepancy among several achieved characteristics), are often in the forefront of reform social movements.

The Persistence of Inequality

How does inequality first arise in human societies, and, even more important, why has inequality persisted? Why is there not more equality, especially in revolutionary socialist societies, but also in market economy societies? The first part of this question was answered earlier. Inequality in the distribution of material goods and rewards in human societies arises initially as a result of differences among families in family members' personal qualities (strength, intelligence, and drive) and in levels of fertility. Large extended families, especially polygamous families, have more productive workers, are able to accumulate more wealth and property, and can fill more positions of power and authority in their society.

Inequality is maintained by (1) family or military *force,* in situations where the power and wealth of families and government leaders are not considered legitimate; (2) *ideologies*—beliefs or doctrines, such as the principle of the divine right of kings, that justify dominant group interests and inequality; and (3) the *inheritance* of property and occupations from one generation to the next in particular families.

Inequality persists because governments protect and do not redistribute the great wealth that is concentrated in the hands of a very small upper stratum. It persists historically, because both the powerful and the powerless, the rich and the poor, usually accept the ideologies of the dominant elites in particular societies.

Ideologies have played a tremendously important role in maintaining social inequality. As Marx pointed out, the ruling ideas of any age are the ideas of the ruling class. According to Marx, the poor and powerless have believed in the ideologies of the dominant class because of their false consciousness—their lack of awareness of their class interests.

In the United States, the shared belief of rich and poor in equality of opportunity—the basis of the American dream—has probably been the single most important factor in preventing more widespread reform and redistribution of national wealth, which failed to occur even during the Depression and the New Deal era (Yorburg, 1969). The high unemployment rates of the Depression era were brought down by the increased demand for products during and after World War II and not by New Deal reform policies and ideologies.

Religious ideas of divine will justified the power and privilege of rulers in agricultural societies. The poor suffered and looked to otherworldly rewards. Death was the great and only leveler in this world. In industrializing and industrial societies, social Darwinism has justified the inequalities of colonialism and unregulated capitalism. Additional slogans such as "free enterprise" and "equal opportunity" in market economies have also been very effective in keeping people in their place.

The idea of a classless society—equal and unranked, politically and economically—has served a similar function in revolutionary socialist societies. Revolution resulted in elimination of the tremendous concentrations of wealth that had characterized czarist Russia and pre-Communist China. But the inheritance of privilege and influence within certain families, if not the inheritance of enormous wealth, was in time reinstated. According to Mao Zedong:

> Humanity, left to its own, does not reestablish capitalism, but it does reestablish inequality. The forces tending toward the creation of new classes are powerful. (*New York Times,* September 10, 1975)

The difficulties of market economies (boom-and-bust business cycles) are rivaled by a basic problem faced by societies that aim for equality. Families are irreplaceable in providing for basic emotional needs in large, urban industrial societies, as we have seen. At the same time, families favor their own members, regardless of prevailing economic and political ideologies.

GLOBAL ECONOMIC INEQUALITY

While the relative inequality of citizens in industrial societies has declined because of huge increases in productivity, the gap between industrial and industrializing societies has widened over the past 250 years. Currently, industrializing societies are located primarily in South and Central America, the Caribbean, southern and eastern Asia, the Middle East, and Africa. These societies contain over three-quarters of the world's population. While most of them have experienced some betterment in their material well-being, progress in this direction has been unexpectedly slow (see Figure 10.1). At the same time, however, the gradual decline in illiteracy and exposure to movies and television have raised expectations that cannot be fulfilled, except by a very small elite.

Wars, internal violence, famine, and disease are spreading, except in a handful of these societies. China, South Korea, Singapore, Taiwan, and other East and Southeast Asian societies are successfully making the transition to industrial market economies, and they are doing so very rapidly.

FIGURE 10.1

Global Economic Inequality

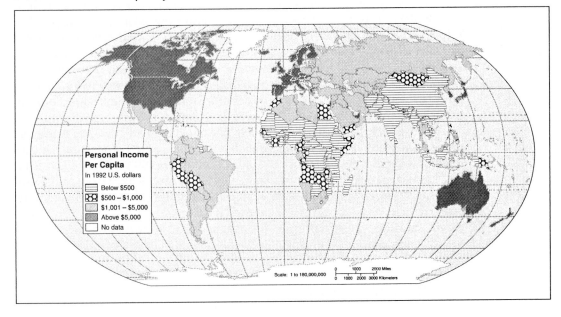

Source: *The World Almanac and Book of Facts 1993,* Mahwah, NJ: Funk & Wagnalls.

The gap between industrialized societies and industrializing societies, particularly those in Africa and southern and eastern Asia, remains wide.

Singapore, in fact, can now be classified as postindustrial. India, a democratic industrializing society, lags behind (Kristof, 1993). A Chinese woman is almost twice as likely to be literate as an Indian woman. Life expectancy in China is 69 years. In India it is 60 years. The infant mortality rate in India is double that of China.

Why has this process been so uneven in different countries, all of which have imported the techniques and technologies, medicines, and foods of more advanced industrial societies? The failure to control population increases in poorer societies is certainly a major factor. As noted in chapter 6 (see p. 200), currently industrializing societies are in stage 2 of the demographic transition. Death rates have declined much faster than birth rates. Children are still viewed by parents as a source of cheap labor and support in old age. Epidemics and famines do not restore the balance between population, work, and food supplies as effectively as they did in agricultural societies.

In contemporary industrializing societies, surplus children leave the increasingly subdivided and exhausted land as soon as they are able and flood into the large cities. They look for jobs that do not exist or are in very short supply. They live in shantytowns that expand faster than the inner core of these cities. It is in these inner areas that the elites live, surrounded by beggars and protected by walls, bodyguards, dogs, and guns.

Education is a major factor in determining the economic and political future of citizens in industrializing societies, as it is for citizens in industrial societies (Inkeles and Smith, 1974; Inkeles, 1983). Education is more important than any other factor in eliminating the cultural lag between industrialization and traditional values, especially fatalism. The societies that are industrializing most rapidly and successfully today have emphasized educating their younger people and bringing population growth under control.

The poorest industrializing societies (such as Bangladesh and Egypt) have the highest illiteracy rates. But illiteracy is slowly being wiped out in many industrializing societies (Bloom and Brender, 1993). Foreign aid from industrial societies, whether for humanitarian or political reasons, is lost on societies run by corrupt military leaders who preempt much of this aid for personal gain. These military governments are grounded on force, propaganda, and the susceptibility to propaganda that is promoted by a lack of formal education.

INEQUALITY IN THE UNITED STATES

The U.S. government attempts to redistribute goods and services and to relieve extreme economic inequality by cash payments and subsidies to the poor, disabled, unemployed, ill (through Medicaid and Medicare), and older people (through Social Security). Social Security benefits are paid for, in part, by contributions from employers and employees. Government payments to the needy are financed by taxes. But the amounts paid out in this way to lower-income people, and the cost of these payments to the U.S. taxpayers, are far less than the amounts paid out in the form of subsidies and tax remissions to various kinds of businesses. And billions of dollars of potential tax income are lost to the government because of unreported legal or illegal income, tax frauds, tax shelters, and tax loopholes that benefit mainly the rich and very rich.

Unlike income taxes, which are more or less progressive (the rate of taxation going up as income goes up), many taxes are flat taxes. Everyone pays at the same rate, regardless of wealth or income. Sales taxes and taxes on liquor, cigarettes, gasoline, and certain food items, however, take a higher proportion of working-class and middle-class incomes than of upper-class incomes. In addition, the rich pay no taxes on interest earned from state and municipal bonds.

The tax system in the United States has not effectively served to redistribute wealth. In fact, economic inequality has increased dramatically since the 1960s, especially during the 1980s (Nasar, 1992a). This is indicated in official federal statistics, even though these statistics do not reveal

FIGURE 10.2

Share of Total Net Worth of U.S. Families

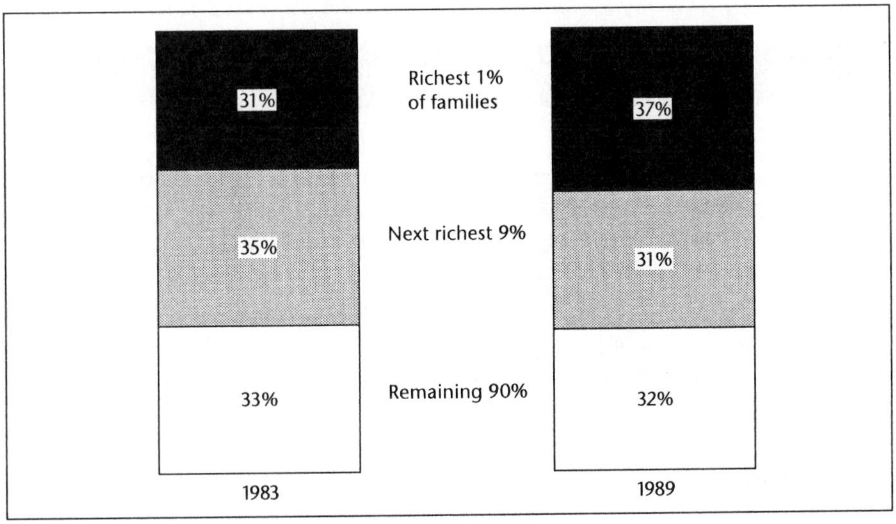

Sources: New York Times, based on Federal Reserve data. Used by permission.

Wealth continues to be very unequally distributed in the United States.

hidden wealth and income–in Swiss or Caribbean bank accounts, for example–disproportionately held by the rich. The IRS compiles data on the concentration of wealth in the United States from the reported value of wealth holders' estates.

In 1983, the top 1 percent of the population owned 31.6 percent of the total national wealth, consisting of real estate, corporate stock, bonds, cash savings, trust funds, life insurance, and other forms of wealth. By 1989, according to Federal Reserve figures, the upper 1 percent of the population owned 37 percent of the national wealth (see Figure 10.2), and the total worth of the top 1 percent (approximately 800,000 households) was greater than that of the bottom 90 percent (about 84 million households). Their tax rate had been reduced from more than 35 percent in 1977 to less than 27 percent in 1989 (Krugman, 1992; Nasar, 1992a) (see Figure 10.3 on p. 338). This tax rate was 70 percent during the New Deal era. By 1989, according to the Federal Reserve's triennial Survey of Consumer Finances published in 1992, the top 1 percent of the population owned 49 percent of all publicly held stock, 78 percent of bonds and trusts, 62 percent of business assets, and 45 percent of commercial real estate (see Figure 10.4 on p. 339).

(Continued on page 339)

FIGURE 10.3

Income Gains of U.S. Families, 1977–1989

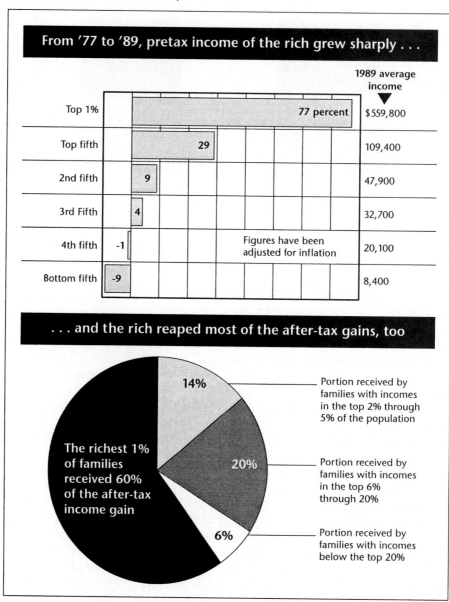

Sources: *New York Times;* based on data from the Congressional Budget Office and Paul Krugman of the Massachusetts Institute of Technology. Used by permission.

The top 1 percent of the population experienced the greatest increase in income in the years 1977–1989.

FIGURE 10.4

Share of Assets Owned by Families in Each Part of the Wealth Spectrum in 1989

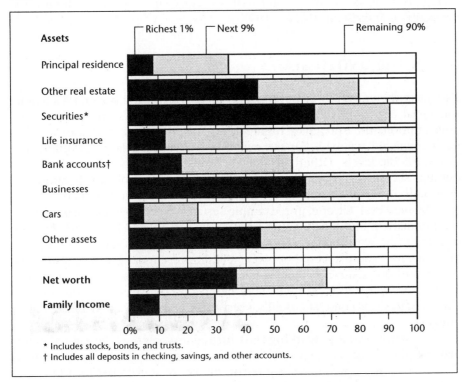

Sources: "Who Owns What," *New York Times*; based on data from a 1989 Federal Reserve survey.

The top 1 percent of the population owns almost two-thirds of the stocks, bonds, and trusts in the United States.

In the early 1990s, some of those in the highest income group, such as stock market and real estate speculators, experienced a reversal of fortune. Despite some losses in total wealth, however, there has been little decline in accumulated wealth and property among these newly rich individuals. The wealthiest citizens now employ highly sophisticated tax and estate-planning experts to ensure that their wealth will be protected, regardless of their occupational and income ups and downs.

In democratic industrial societies, prestige is more equally distributed than in agricultural societies, particularly at the middle levels. Authority is also more equally distributed, especially at local levels. But extreme economic inequality persists. The standard of living (per capita income and access to goods and services) is higher at *all* levels in industrialized societies, because technological advances and mass production greatly increase the total wealth of nations. The economic pie is much larger. But the size of the slice going to the top 1 percent of the population in the United States, as well as in other industrial societies such as Great Britain and Germany, is increasing (Nasar, 1992a).

SOCIAL CLASSES IN THE UNITED STATES

Except at the extremes of poverty and great wealth, the boundaries among the social classes in the United States tend to blur. Mass production, mass consumption, the spread of higher levels of education, and the belief in egalitarianism have made for somewhat less obvious social class differences at the middle levels. Other present-day industrial societies, as well as agricultural societies throughout history, have been more obviously stratified, especially in terms of outward symbols such as dress and speech.

In medieval Europe, for example, estates were clear-cut segments of the population, and membership was rigidly symbolized by dress. The type of dress to be worn by members of different estates was sanctioned by law. Peasants, for example, could not wear silk. In present-day Europe, distinctive patterns of dress survive, though without legal sanctions. European manual workers are likely to wear their work clothes on the streets; workers in the United States, by contrast, usually keep their work clothes in lockers after hours.

Similarly, whereas working-class men and women in the United States may employ some class-specific patterns of speech, Cockney English in Great Britain is a much more distinctive marker of social class location. And at higher socioeconomic levels in the United States, neither speech nor dress clearly distinguishes upper-middle- and upper-class people. Income and wealth, however, do.

Nevertheless, the various social classes in the United States differ visibly in their possession of the things money can buy, including health and prolonged life, as well as in their values. According to an analysis of over 13,000 death certificates by researchers at the National Center for Health Statistics, the death rate from 1960 to 1988 among families with a household income of $9,000 was more than three times higher than that of families with an income of over $25,000 (Pear, 1993b). This difference in death rates had doubled over a period of 20 years, furthermore. A similar disparity exists in Great Britain, incidentally, despite its National Health Care Plan.

Mortality rates reflect health habits such as exercise, low-fat diets, and smoking. But they also reflect deaths from violence, accidents, and job-related injuries and diseases, which are more widespread among the poor.

Most sociologists follow the pioneering work of anthropologist W. Lloyd Warner and sociologist Paul Lunt (1941) in locating six social classes in the United States. People in these six social classes typically differ in

TABLE 10.2

Typical Occupational Positions in Different Social Classes

OLD UPPER CLASS: Top positions in business, industry, government.	UPPER WORKING CLASS: Manual work, skilled or semiskilled. Operatives; retail sales (cashiers); low-paid craftspeople; steadily employed service workers (domestics, taxi drivers).
NEW UPPER CLASS: Top positions in business, industry, government, professions, entertainment, sports.	
UPPER MIDDLE CLASS: Near but not at the top of various occupational hierarchies requiring communication skills. Higher-level professionals; middle management; medium-size business owners.	LOWER WORKING CLASS (POOR): Unskilled manual work, underemployed (part-time) or unemployed. Occasional service workers; laborers; clericals.
LOWER MIDDLE CLASS: Higher-paid clerical, nonretail sales (sales reps), lower-level management (foremen, office managers), semiprofessions (case workers, parole officers), self-employed craftspeople, small storekeepers or small farm owners.	

Source: Adapted from Dennis Gilbert and Joseph A. Kahl, *The American Class Structure*, 1993, Belmont, CA: Wadsworth.

ancestry, values, and lifestyle, as well as income, education, and occupational prestige.

Warner divided the three broad strata in the United States—upper, middle, and lower—into upper and lower levels: the upper and lower upper class, the upper and lower middle class, and the upper and lower lower class.

This way of referring to the various social class strata is awkward and confusing. Also, most people in the United States dislike the term "lower class" and prefer the term "working class" to refer to the lower levels of the class structure. For these reasons, the terms "old upper and new upper class," "upper middle and lower middle class," and "upper working and lower working class" (or poor) are used here in describing the six major social classes in the United States.

Occupation is the most valid indicator of social class location. It is closely associated with income and education, the two other easily measurable determinants of social class location. Income alone can be misleading as an indicator of class, as mentioned earlier, since many manual workers earn higher incomes than clerical and sales workers, who are middle class in values and lifestyle.

Since most people live in families, the family is the unit that is usually ranked in determining social class location. Dependent children are classified with their parents until they complete their education and become employed independently. But how do we rank a family in which the father is a manual laborer and the mother is a secretary or salesperson? Is the family working class or middle class?

In the past, the husband's occupation, income, and education were used by sociologists to determine the social class location of families. In the present-day United States, however, most families are two-earner households. Furthermore, about one-third of the wives of male manual laborers in this country are in middle-class occupations. These women identify with the middle class (Simpson, Stark, and Jackson, 1988).

The wife's occupation and social status are now recognized as being important in the social class location of families. For purposes of predicting family values and behavior more accurately (whether children will go to college, for example, or husband and wife will share leisure-time activities), families should be classified according to the most prestigious occupation of any adult member of the household, male or female. If the wife of a male factory worker has a middle-class occupation, the family is more likely to be middle class in lifestyle. If a wealthy heiress marries a ski instructor, the couple's lifestyle will be upper class, unless the heiress is disinherited by her family.

About 2 percent of the U.S. population is upper class by birth or achievement. This class is relatively stable in size. The upper middle class, consisting of about 10 percent of the population, had been growing rapidly until the recession in 1990–1991. In industrialized societies with rationally planned and expanding economies, the increased need for expert middle managers in business and industry and for expert professionals creates additional jobs at the upper-middle-class level. It is the lower middle class, encompassing about 43 percent of the population, however, that has been growing the most rapidly, as businesses engaged in distributing, selling, advertising, and communicating have increased and manufacturing jobs have declined.

The working class, about 30 percent of the population, has been declining in number and influence as semiskilled and unskilled jobs have continued to be automated out of existence or sent abroad. The poor, or lower working class, increased in size during the 1980s and early 1990s and in 1992 made up about 14.5 percent of the population (Pear, 1993a; Gilbert and Kahl, 1993) (see Figure 10.5).

The Old Upper Class

The two levels of the upper class differ in the length of time the families have been wealthy. The old upper class, people like the Rockefellers, Du Ponts, Fords, Roosevelts, Astors, and Vanderbilts, have inherited their wealth from family members who are no longer alive. Members of the new upper

FIGURE 10.5

Poverty in the United States

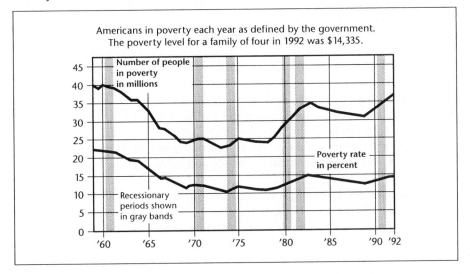

Americans in poverty each year as defined by the government. The poverty level for a family of four in 1992 was $14,335.

Number of people in poverty in millions

Poverty rate in percent

Recessionary periods shown in gray bands

Source: "Poverty in the United States," *New York Times,* October 5, 1993, p. A20; data from Census Bureau, National Bureau of Economic Research. Reprinted with permission.

The percentage of families living in poverty has been increasing recently, but it is not as high as it was in 1960.

class represent the first generation in their families to be rich—and, sometimes, famous. Since those in the old upper class do not usually answer questionnaires or grant interviews to sociologists, it is difficult to obtain objective information about them. Profiles of old-upper-class people in magazines, newspapers, books, and movies are not necessarily representative of all members of this class. Much of our information about the values, social life, and world outlook of the old upper class comes from members of this class who have written about what they have directly experienced or observed (Baltzell, 1991).

Social scientists have usually been limited to secondary sources such as the *Social Register, Who's Who in America,* Bureau of the Census publications on income and wealth in the United States, and published membership lists and accounts of activities of upper-class schools, resorts, private clubs, and political or economic organizations.

What, then, do we know about the values and behavior of this class that social scientists, journalists, and members themselves would probably agree about? As in the working class, the old upper class consists of traditional and modern segments. The older generations are more traditional, familistic, authoritarian, and ethnocentric. Their models are Anglo-Saxon

Protestant ancestors who established the family fortune in land ownership before the Civil War and in business and liquid capital (money, stocks, bonds) after the Civil War. Values associated with the Protestant ethic—thrift, self-control, emotional reserve, physical endurance, and the work ethic—are strong in this part of the old upper class.

Familism is indicated in naming practices such as passing on the first name of the member who founded the family fortune to succeeding generations (with the suffixes Jr., II, III, or IV following the name). The mother's maiden name may also be used as the first or middle name of children. Extended family closeness is preserved by spending leisure time together on family compounds or on lengthy and frequent joint vacations. Family rituals such as debutante balls, formal engagements, large weddings, christenings, and Thanksgiving and Christmas gatherings of the entire clan are extremely important in this class.

Ethnocentrism is strong, but not necessarily because of fear, threat, or lack of information about out-groups. The primary motive in avoiding outsiders is to preserve the family from intermarriage with the middle classes or ethnic minority groups. This is an age-old practice of the hereditary upper class in economically stratified societies. Currently, it is maintained by exclusive clubs, resorts, and schools that restrict membership to this class.

Authoritarianism in the family is reinforced by separation and emotional reserve. This is indicated by the custom of maintaining separate bedrooms for husband and wife. Parents are separated from their children, who are cared for by servants, regardless of whether the parents are at home or away. Children are usually sent to boarding schools when they are old enough.

The old upper class is changing, as are all social classes in the United States. Technological advance and increased mobility affect the classes differently, however. Large national and international corporations absorb the family businesses of the hereditary rich. Heirs may retain ownership of large blocks of stock, or they may shift their assets to other corporations and investments. They may remain as executives in the merged companies, but often they do not. Local community roots are weakened for this class as their geographic base in land or business shifts. Geographic mobility for the hereditary rich is international in scope and much more frequent than in other classes. The availability of high-speed, charter jet transport since World War II has extended their social networks to almost all parts of the world.

Authoritarianism and ethnocentrism have declined among younger generations of the old upper class. Children in this class have more options than in the past, when they were bound to family enterprises and were totally dependent economically. Ethnocentrism declines somewhat as contact with other classes increases. Prestigious schools and colleges expand their recruitment to include very talented scholarship students, usually from the middle classes. More complex technologies and economies require a wider base of talent than the old upper class alone can provide. And the newly rich and near-rich aristocracy of talent push on and into old-upper-class havens and retreats, slowly but more surely than in the past.

The New Upper Class

Members of the new upper class are self-made men and women who have risen, usually from middle-class origins, to the very top positions in business, government, the professions, entertainment, and sports. In the past, they would have served the old upper class, but they would not have been permitted to socialize and intermarry with the hereditary wealthy. In modern times, talented entertainers (often more wealthy than the old upper class) are invited to eat dinner with this class. During the Middle Ages, they entertained the aristocracy during or after dinner. In industrialized societies, skill and talent, particularly of the kind that has resulted in national or international fame and vast wealth, are more highly valued.

Members of the new elite of talent in the United States are more likely than the old upper class to engage in what sociologist Thorstein Veblen called **conspicuous consumption**. The new upper class buys to impress. It buys obviously costly diamonds, art, furs, cars, mansions, and other material possessions that are far in excess of what is necessary for physical comfort. Veblen wrote highly critical and often bitter descriptions of business, the class structure, and higher education in the United States. He explained conspicuous consumption in terms of the need for prestige:

> In order to gain and hold the esteem of men, it is not sufficient merely to possess wealth or power. The wealth or power must be put in evidence, for esteem is awarded only on evidence. (1953 [1899], p. 42)

The old upper class does not need to play this particular game. The members of this class were born wealthy, and prestige, respect, and influence come naturally. Members of the new upper class value achievement and hard work very highly, since this is the basis of their wealth, recognition, and acceptance. But the toll is heavy, as indicated by frantic leisure activities and the frequent reliance on psychotherapists, medications, and drugs in this class.

Familism is not strong in the new upper class, because the members of this class have been very mobile socially, geographically, and psychologically. Families are more likely to be isolated nuclear in structure. There is a great gap between the members of the new upper class and the extended families (and former friends) that they have left behind.

Nuclear family relationships reflect the middle-class origins of most members of this class. Marital relationships are more egalitarian and less formal and reserved than in the more traditional old upper class. Parent-child relationships are more spontaneous, more democratic, and more emotionally intense and involved. Divorce rates are higher than in the old upper class. Married women in the new upper class are more likely to be employed gainfully than their old-upper-class counterparts, who still generally play the role of full-time companion, absentee household manager, and fund-raiser for favorite charities (Ostrander, 1984; Daniels, 1988).

Generally, many of the differences in family life, values, and behavior that set the old upper class apart from the new are disappearing, especially among younger, more modern members of the old upper class. All classes are responding to the same changing conditions that bring about a decline in the traditional values in industrialized societies. Among these changing conditions are greater mobility of all kinds, more knowledge and education, greater economic independence from the family, and more choices and alternatives, economically and personally.

The Upper Middle Class

Upper-middle-class men and women are businesspeople, public servants, professionals, athletes, and entertainers who are successful but not at the top in their various occupations. Most are college graduates; many have graduate training. They have high incomes and, usually, substantial savings or property, but they are not multimillionaires and, therefore, not upper class. They have careers, not jobs. And they are very invested in these careers and the work ethic. Exceptional talent, hard work, and drive may result in wealth, national recognition, and movement into the new upper class for at least some members of this stratum.

Members of the upper middle class are able to exercise a high degree of control over their work situations, since freedom at work increases directly with the prestige of an occupation. Doctors and business executives work long hours, but they can exercise more initiative in their work situations than automobile mechanics and retail clerks.

Upper-middle-class people are usually very geographically mobile. The isolated nuclear family is not uncommon in this class, since members are frequently transferred by their corporations or pursue new and better job opportunities in faraway places. The two-career family is becoming increasingly common (about two-thirds of the wives of higher professionals are employed). Commuter marriages, in which husband and wife maintain separate residences part of the week because they work in different cities, is an upper-middle-class and new-upper-class pattern that is also becoming more common (Bunker et al., 1992).

Many of the values and activities of the upper middle class are similar to those of the new upper class. But there is an enormous difference between the two strata in income and wealth. A clearer picture of the upper middle class is available, since the members of this class are more willing to be studied and to write about themselves. Journalists, social scientists, and social critics are often upper middle class, and they have a tendency to project their own experiences onto the entire society. Several clichés and stereotypes about life in the United States, such as the "generation gap" and the "midlife crisis" of middle-aged males, are actually more characteristic of this class than of other social classes.

Surveys based on more representative samples of people in the United States indicate that most adult children and their parents feel their basic values are quite similar, as mentioned earlier (Rossi and Rossi, 1990; Bengtston and Roberts, 1991). The midlife crisis, an abrupt and dramatic decline in morale among middle-aged males who have failed to realize their ambitions, does not occur in the working class (Rubin, 1992). Men in this class have never expected to conquer the world, and they do not experience profound disappointment as life goes by. Identity crises are far more prevalent among people in their 20s and 30s who cannot find meaningful work in the United States today.

Egalitarianism in husband-wife relationships is an important value in the upper middle class, especially among two-career couples. Power and the amount of role sharing in the home depend far more on particular interests and time available than on rigid gender role definitions and conceptions. Studies of successful two-career marriages (those with high reported marital satisfaction) indicate that "the exercise of power as an expression of domination or subordination is not a part of these relationships" (Vannoy-Hiller and Philliber, 1989, p. 145).

Rationalism is also an important value, especially among the highly educated. Upper-middle-class people are likely to be caught up in the latest ideas and fashions in human relationships. Many are engaged in an endless search for the newest scientific (and sometimes not-so-scientific) formula for successful childrearing, greater personal happiness ("growth"), and better homes and gardens. Communication and intimacy are their latest catchwords in judging and improving personal relationships.

Conspicuous consumption is more frequent among upper-middle-class businesspeople than among professionals, whose prestige is built into their degrees. It is mainly the artistic, creative, and intellectual segments of the upper middle class who have bought and rehabilitated deteriorating property in urban renewal areas and warehouse districts in recent years. They avoid the more obvious symbols of class standing. But they furnish their homes with the latest in original design furniture, if they can afford it, or with genuine antiques, if they identify with the old upper class.

The Lower Middle Class

Lower-middle-class people work at the less prestigious and less-well-paying jobs that require communication skills. In addition to clerical and sales workers, this socioeconomic category also includes small property owners (farmers and storekeepers), lower-level professionals (teachers and nurses), and lower-level management. In these jobs, knowledge and communication skills are more important than tools, equipment, and machines. Secretaries work with machines but continue to use communication skills that have not yet been taken over by computers. Salespeople use persuasive ideas and a knowledge of their products in their jobs.

People in this class have usually completed high school, but most do not have 4-year college degrees, although they may have degrees earned at trade schools or community colleges. They have lower incomes, less savings, and less mobility than the upper middle class, with which they identify. They are in between the working and upper middle classes in the adoption of urban values. They value achievement highly, but ambition is centered on their children. Parents are usually prevented from rising in the class structure because of limited education. But often they exert strong pressures and make extreme sacrifices to help their children move into the upper middle class.

Ethnocentrism and familism are stronger in the lower middle class than in the upper middle class. The semi-nuclear family structure is most prevalent. Members of the lower middle class are not usually in daily contact with relatives, but they are more likely to live within easy visiting distance and see each other regularly than is typical of the upper middle class.

Parent-child relationships are less authoritarian in this group than in the working class. Physical punishment is not a technique frequently used for disciplining children. But permissiveness is tempered by stricter limits than are typical in the more affluent and individualistic upper middle class (LeMasters and DeFrain, 1989).

Real and effective egalitarianism and role sharing in the home are more prevalent in the lower middle class than in the working class and among older members of the upper middle class. Traditional gender role conceptions are less rigid than in the working class. Female relatives (such as grandmothers, aunts, and married sisters) are less likely to be available on a daily basis to help out and maintain role segregation between husbands and wives. Personal and economic resources of husband and wife are usually more equal than in the upper middle class. Husbands have less time-consuming jobs, and there is less money available to delegate household responsibilities to paid help. For these reasons, they actually help out more around the home than upper-middle-class husbands (Demo and Acock, 1993).

Upper-middle-class social scientists have had difficulty depicting the lower middle class objectively and sympathetically. Profiles of this class have usually emphasized their conformity, political conservatism, exaggerated respectability, thrift, and petty striving. But members of the lower middle class perform important functions as the most active and dedicated rank-and-file members and workers in church, service, and political organizations in the United States. Most employed members of this class are not unionized, however. Their purchasing power has declined significantly, and their life-style has been threatened severely in recent years by recurring recessions in the United States.

The Upper Working Class

The upper working class consists of people working for wages in skilled or semiskilled occupations. Skilled jobs require vocational training, long apprenticeships, or extensive on-the-job training. Semiskilled jobs, like most factory work, usually require only a few days of on-the-job training. Both categories of workers are more likely to be unionized than white-collar work-ers. Although they have more security and self-esteem than unskilled work-ers, skilled and semiskilled workers have less control over their lives and jobs than white-collar workers. Manual workers' limited education, lack of savings, and traditional values make them more vulnerable to the uncertain-ties and unpredictabilities of modern life.

The percentage of male high school dropouts in this group is high, but not as high as among the poor. Wives often have more education than their husbands and work at more prestigious jobs, since females are less likely than males to drop out of high school. Authority in the home appears to be patriarchal, but women in this class have very real authority in most day-to-day decision making—by default if for no other reason.

In this class, other traditional values remain strong, particularly among older members. Familism is important. The semi-extended family provides essential economic and psychological help. It is more important than ex-perts, friends, clubs, or formal organizations as a source of emotional sup-port, advice, and leisure-time activities.

Religious beliefs are strong, especially among women, but churchgoing is less frequent than in the middle class. Joining clubs or other associations, except for labor unions and certain patriotic organizations, is not frequent in this class. Participation in clubs or organizations is minimal and marginal.

Ethnocentrism is also strong, reinforced by lower levels of education, less mobility, and less contact with strange people, places, and things. Ex-posure to the mass media could possibly dispel some false beliefs about out-groups. But exposure to television and print in this class is limited largely to entertainment and sports rather than informational programs and articles.

Since most manual jobs (like most lower-level white-collar jobs) are dull, routine, and dead-end, work has less meaning than family and leisure activities. **Alienation**—a feeling of powerlessness, separation, and detach-ment from one's work (and the world)—is widespread. Upper-working-class employees are more likely than middle-class employees to say they would not make the same occupational choice if they were to start over again. Wages, purchasing power, and jobs have been declining since the 1980s, and growing numbers within the working class are employed as temporary workers, part-time workers, and workers on contract (DiPrete, 1993).

The paycheck is not adequate for conspicuous consumption, which would be pointless in any case, since the worker's economic status is usually obvious. But new purchases provide temporary relief from frustrations at home and work. Upper-working-class men and women are very vulnerable to the temptations of the "buy now, pay later" credit card economy. They buy the top of the line on the assumption that you get what you pay for. They are unlikely to subscribe to magazines that test and give information about consumer products.

As in the other social classes, younger members of the upper working class are less traditional in their values than older members. They have a higher level of education and are more geographically mobile, often moving into the suburbs. They are also more likely to be separated from their extended family, and the extended family loses some of its previous influence and importance. Younger members are more egalitarian, less fatalistic (although quite pessimistic in recent times), and more knowledgeable and rational in coping with the demands of everyday life.

The Lower Working Class (The Poor)

In the United States, the lower working class or poor are those who do not have enough money to maintain an adequate standard of living as defined by the federal government. In 1992, a family of four was classified as poor if it had a cash income of less than $14,335 (Pear, 1993a). Of these families, 40 percent had members who worked during the year, and 9.2 percent of these family members had full-time year-round jobs. According to O'Hare (1992b), the highest rates of poverty are in the rural South (and Southwest)—in Mississippi, Louisiana, West Virginia, and New Mexico. Forty percent of all poor people live in the South, which had the highest increase in poverty rates in 1992.

Official poverty levels are adjusted each year to reflect changes in the Consumer Price Index. But the figure is the same nationwide, despite wide variations in the cost of living in different parts of the country. Between 1981 and 1991, poverty in the United States increased, became more concentrated geographically (in areas where over 40 percent of the population is classified as poor), and involved increasing numbers of children (22 percent of children under 18 in 1993) (Pear, 1993a).

Many of the poor are recent migrants from the countryside or impoverished immigrants from other countries. But unlike previous generations of migrants, they arrive at a time when automation has eliminated many of

(Continued on page 352)

TABLE 10.3

Social Classes in the United States

Social Class	Percentage of Population (Approximate)	Wealth and Income	Family	Education	Religion	Politics	Recreation
Old Upper Class	0.5%	Hereditary wealth, highest income, multimil-lionaires	Extended, semi-extend-ed, high birthrate	Liberal arts at prestigious colleges	Church-goers, Episcopalian	Conservative	Frequent, lavishly expensive, sexually integrated traveling and entertaining, sponsorship of the arts
New Upper Class	1.5%	Achieved wealth, highest income, multimil-lionaires	Isolated nuclear, semi-nuclear, moderate or low birthrate	Varied, depending on occupation	Frequent change of church preference	Conserva-tive or independent	Patterned after the old upper class
Upper Middle Class	10%	High income, property, savings	Isolated nuclear or semi-nuclear, low birthrate	4-year college, professional training	Frequent change of church affiliation	Liberal or independent	Independent travel, entertaining friends
Lower Middle Class	43%	Moderate income, small savings, little or no property	Semi-nuclear, low birthrate	High school; some college graduates	Most frequent churchgoers	Conserva-tive	Group travel, television, visiting relatives
Working Class	30%	Moderate income, little savings, little or no property	Semi-extend-ed or semi-nuclear, moderate birthrate	High school; some high school dropouts	Religious faith strong, churchgoing moderate	Economically liberal, conservative on civil rights issues	Television, visiting relatives, sex-segre-gated leisure activities
Poor	15%	No savings, income inadequate to purchase essential goods and services	Extended or semi-extend-ed, high birthrate	Largest percentage of high school dropouts, widespread functional illiteracy	Religious faith very strong, particularly among women; churchgoing infrequent	Alienated, apathetic, nonvoting	Television, visiting relatives

the unskilled jobs in laundries, restaurants, hotel basements, and nonunionized factories and hospitals that were available in the past.

The traditional values—fatalism, religiousness, ethnocentrism, authoritarianism, and familism—are strongest among newer immigrants who are poor. They are the most recently uprooted from agricultural environments and rural ways of life. The urban values are visible to them, but their objective life circumstances prevent the adoption of these values. Familism, for example, is reinforced by a desperate need for help that is not available except from the family (Taylor, 1988). Authoritarianism persists when parents feel absolutely powerless except at home. Religious faith remains very strong when uncertainty, injustice, calamity, and crisis are daily experiences. Fatalism is reinforced by unemployment and never-ending stress and blows from a harsh, hostile, and uncontrollable outside world (see Table 10.3).

Gender Differences in Poverty

Women in the United States are much more likely to be poor than are men (Casper, McLanahan, and Garfinkel, 1994). This gender gap is equally marked among African Americans and whites, although the percentages of both men and women living in poverty are much higher in the African American subculture. In cross-national statistical studies of industrial societies, two factors seem to be most important in determining the higher rates of poverty among women: the percent of women employed and the rate of parenthood (including single parenthood). Other significant but less important factors are marital status, education, and age (Casper, McLanahan, and Garfinkel, 1994). Cultural values, government policy, and religion are also important, especially in countries where poverty-rate differences between women and men are minimal.

Poverty rates of men and women differ most in the United States; they are much less in Canada, Australia, the United Kingdom, and West Germany; and they differ almost not at all in Italy, the Netherlands, and Sweden (Casper, McLanahan, and Garfinkel, 1994). Only in Sweden is the poverty rate for men actually higher, but only by 1 percent. Women in Sweden are almost as likely as men to be in the labor force. The Swedish government promotes gender equality in employment through heavily subsidized day care programs and liberal parental and sick leave policies.

The Netherlands has a low marriage rate and a relatively low rate of female employment. State welfare policies, however, provide a high income floor, beneath which no Dutch citizen, male or female, is allowed to fall. Italian men and women have very high rates of marriage. The poverty rate is high in Italy, but since men and women are more likely to be married, they are more likely to share the same standard of living. The Roman Catholic Church continues to be effective in discouraging divorce and nonmarital childbearing.

THE CHANGING NATURE OF WORK

In industrial societies, workplaces grow larger, work tasks grow smaller, and feelings of alienation become widespread among the least skilled, least hopeful members of society. People who are alienated feel powerless and out of the mainstream. Marx traced alienation to a loss of control over the conditions and products of one's work. In agricultural societies, craftsworkers labored at their own pace, used their own tools, set their own standards, and sold their own products. Factory workers in industrial societies do none of this. Dissatisfaction with work is high, but most workers in the United States would continue to work even if they did not have to.

Certain factors are associated with higher worker satisfaction in the United States: (1) security, which is more important now than high wages; (2) interesting tasks; (3) opportunity to learn new skills and develop individual potential; (4) opportunity to participate in improving the work situation, productivity, and the product; and (5) respectful treatment (Kohn, 1993). These are more important in increasing productivity than simply offering rewards or monetary incentives to motivate workers.

Younger, more educated workers in the United States, reared in less authoritarian households, are not as tolerant as older workers of rigid supervision on the job. They are also less tolerant of boredom and routine than older workers. Employers are responding with programs to increase workers' responsibility in determining work conditions and improving productivity. Increasingly, workers in teams alternate responsibility for production, quality control, materials, personnel, and safety.

The new manual worker operating automated machines in postindustrial societies has "clean hands," while traditional manual laborers swell the ranks of the unemployed or underemployed (Salgado, 1993). The old world lives on—in agriculture, mining, manufacturing, transportation, and construction—but it is much reduced. The factories that remain in postindustrial societies are still noisy, dirty, and sometimes dangerous. But just as the Industrial Revolution wiped out many earlier trades and crafts, many traditional workers are now being replaced by the automated intelligence of modern industrial technology.

The new worker needs to "get smart" (Reich, 1993)—to learn the new problem-solving skills needed in computerized, high-tech global economies. This requires retraining for displaced workers and lifetime learning, or intellectual retooling, in the workplace for all workers at all levels. The pace of scientific and technological advance and sociocultural evolution in postindustrial societies has quickened beyond almost all expectations.

The Virtual Workplace

In his classic work *The Division of Labor in Society* (1933 [1893]), Émile Durkheim described a major change in the nature of work and human connectedness ("solidarity") as societies industrialize. In preindustrial societies, people felt a bond with one another based on similarities in their work activities and in their "beliefs, traditions, and collective practices" (p. 84). He called this kind of connectedness **mechanical solidarity**, signifying something automatic and unself-conscious.

In industrial societies, work activities become increasingly specialized, individualism increasingly pronounced, and dependence on others with different skills increasingly essential. Durkheim called this kind of linking among individuals (and societies), based on rational awareness and deliberate choice, **organic solidarity**. Writing more than 100 years ago, Durkheim anticipated a "European society" founded on economic specialization and cooperation and practical necessity that would go beyond national borders and identities (p. 405). Durkheim's vision is, in fact, becoming a reality, but in a way he could not have imagined. In postindustrial societies, a new kind of linking, a new kind of solidarity, and a new reality emerge. In the popular language, this interactive space has been labeled **virtual reality**, because it is a computer-constructed reality. Examples are a workplace, a battlefield, the insides of a human body (used for training surgeons), or an automobile (used for training mechanics) with which individuals can interact. This leads to a new and different kind of solidarity in postindustrial societies. We can call this **virtual solidarity**–a feeling of community, bondedness, or togetherness that is cemented by electronic links.

Increasingly, we live and work in a virtual world, connected by personal computers, modems, faxes, direct-link telephone lines, cellular phones, videophones, and beepers. The videophone image on the computer screen is the virtual equivalent of the conference room (and the water cooler). It is used by those who work at home but need to connect with a team or a supervisor, or who feel the need to duplicate the informal, face-to-face camaraderie of the office (Calem, 1993; Patton, 1993).

The basic raw material in this virtual world is information (Gilder, 1991; Reich, 1991; Toffler and Toffler, 1993). We buy it and sell it, manufacture it, and trade it. The new electronic infrastructures are data- and media-jammed superhighways with access to world data banks and global telecommunication networks. With this development has come a new cottage industry, the virtual workplace, in which increasing numbers of white-collar workers become **telecommuters.** They interact with their firms via computerized and telephonic links from their offices at home or from nearby satellite offices set up by their firms.

According to Link Resources, a market research firm, about 39 million people in the United States worked at home in 1992, an increase of 20 percent from 1991 (Calem, 1993). Of these, about 6.6 million were tele-

Focus on Social Issues

PUBLIC AND PRIVATE

[Honesty and directness in communicating with others are now cultural norms in the United States. The sphere of the private is no longer sacred. Silent thoughts, fears, and the most intimate forbidden experiences are now routinely exposed to others–family, friends, strangers. Pretense and shame are outmoded. "Tell it like it is" and "Let it all hang out"–slogans of the student movements of the 1960s–are now cliches in human relationships. The merging of the public and the private is underwritten by the highly competitive market economy. Whatever sells, improves ratings, and increases recognition, royalties, readers, and viewers is the standard. Reality sells.]

In the past, novels alone seemed capable of giving us intimate knowledge of strangers' lives; today that role tends to be filled, however deceptively, by confessional talk shows, . . . autobiographies, . . . 24-hour news coverage and the proliferation of tabloid television. As we are exposed to more and more bizarre stories in the news (a woman cutting off her husband's penis, a president accused of asking a woman to perform oral sex), as the old rules of civility break down, it also becomes increasingly difficult for the fiction writer to satirize or even dramatize social conflicts. . . . As Mark Twain once remarked, "Truth is stranger than Fiction, but it is because Fiction is obliged to stick to possibilities; Truth isn't."

–Michiko Kakutani, "With Reality Reeling, Pity the Poor Realist," *New York Times*, June 22, 1994, pp. C13, C18

What Do You Think?

1. How might the economic factor affect the increase in the amount of information available about the private lives of strangers in postindustrial societies?

2. How might politics and a strong need for power on the part of particular leaders affect this trend?

3. How might changing values play a role?

commuters employed by businesses and government agencies. About 23.8 million were self-employed, as consultants, small-business owners, contract workers, and typists. And about 8.6 million took extra work home from the office to do after hours. Large corporations such as Sears, Bankers Trust, and American Express have now established telecommuting programs, and others are joining them daily.

Employers cite a number of advantages to telecommuting: (1) greater employee productivity, due to fewer interruptions by coworkers, less absenteeism, lower turnover rates, and higher morale; (2) lower overhead expense for office and parking spaces; and (3) fewer air quality problems with environmental agencies, who are requiring corporations employing more than 200 people to cut back on employee automobile commuting 25 percent by 1996.

Employees point to savings in time and in money for transportation, business clothes, and lunches. They also appreciate having more time to spend with family, especially young children. Complaints have centered on (1) the need for self-discipline in structuring their time and work; (2) feelings of isolation; (3) interruptions by neighbors, children, phone calls; and (4) inadequate supervision.

Telecommuting is not for everyone. It works best in service occupations that do not require spending a great deal of time with clients and colleagues. Limiting it to two or three days a week also seems to work best. Since telecommuting is also well suited to part-time contract and consulting work, there is always the possibility that it will be used to cut back on full-time jobs in occupations where there is a current oversupply of available workers, however. Some employees fear that the virtual workplace may lead to a virtual workforce.

Study Guide

REVIEW OBJECTIVES

After studying this chapter, you should be able to:

1. Describe the differences among functionalist, conflict, and sociocultural evolution theorists in explaining the origin and extent of economic inequality in human societies.
2. Give examples of different kinds of status inconsistency, and explain why this concept is important.
3. Discuss present-day trends in global inequality.
4. Describe the differing lifestyles and life chances of the various social classes in the United States today.
5. Examine changes in the nature of work in postindustrial societies.

SUMMARY

1. In explaining economic inequality, structural functionalists have emphasized the necessity of unequal economic rewards to motivate people to perform more difficult functions in society. Conflict theorists have focused on the dysfunctional aspects of inequality and on the use of power and ideology by dominant groups to obtain and maintain their wealth and privileges. Sociocultural evolution theorists focus on developments in scientific knowledge and technology as these affect inequality.

2. The gap in the quality of life between rich and poor diminishes as societies become industrialized because of the enormous increase in the amount of resources produced. But the gap in the standard of living between rich and poor nations has been increasing in recent times.

3. According to government statistics, the concentration of wealth among the upper 1 percent of the U.S. population increased enormously during the 1980s and early 1990s.

4. All societies are stratified in terms of the relative prestige of individuals and families. Overall prestige in industrializing and industrial societies is based on both ascribed characteristics and achieved characteristics, such as education, income, and occupation. In these societies, movement up or down in the social class structure is possible, but most people do not move much either way.

5. There are six major social strata in the United States: the old upper class, the new upper class, the upper middle class, the lower middle class, the working class, and the poor, or lower working class.

6. Members of the old and new upper class have the greatest wealth and highest income and occupy the top positions in business and industry, government, the professions, the arts, entertainment, and sports.

7. Middle-class people work mainly with communication skills. Upper-middle-class people are highly successful in various occupational spheres, but even the most successful lack the vast wealth characteristics of the upper class.

8. Members of the lower middle class work with communication skills in clerical and sales fields, lower-level management and professions, and public service, or they own small businesses and farms.

9. Members of the working class work primarily with their hands. They use tools and equipment to carry out skilled or semi-skilled jobs. The poor do not have enough income to maintain an adequate standard of living. During the 1980s, the poor increased in number, especially among immigrants and children under 18, and became much more likely to live in areas of concentrated poverty.

10. Developments in telecommunication systems in postindustrial societies have made possible a new type of work situation in which employees receive and supply information from home offices.

GLOSSARY

Alienation: Separation and emotional detachment from one's work and the world. It is characterized by feelings of helplessness and powerlessness.

Authority: Power that is regarded as legitimate, right, and proper in certain widely recognized statuses, such as royalty in monarchies and popularly elected government officials in democracies.

Castes: Ranked layers in a social stratification system in which membership is established by birth, cannot be changed, and is sanctioned by religion.

Classes: Ranked layers of people who receive similar rewards and possess similar privileges in a society. Position in class structures can be achieved or lost and is not sanctioned by law or religion.

Conspicuous consumption: The purchase of costly, unnecessary goods to confirm one's social status.

Estates: Ranked layers in a social stratification system in which position is based on birth and is sanctioned by law.

Influence: Informal, unofficial, and sometimes hidden power over people and events.

Mechanical solidarity: Cooperative relationships based on feelings of similarity and belonging together.

Organic solidarity: Cooperative relationships based on increasing vocational specialization and the interdependence that this makes necessary as societies industrialize.

Prestige: The amount of respect accorded to a widely recognized status in a society.

Social mobility: Movement from one status to another in the social class or social stratification system.

Social stratification: A system of ranking of people in layers or strata above and below each other with respect to varying criteria.

Strata: The layers that make up a social stratification system.

Structural mobility: Movement up or down in social class by large numbers of people because of changes in the occupational structure, such as the number of working- or middle-class jobs available.

Telecommuters: Employees who work at home or near home and receive or transmit information to their firms by means of PCs and modems, faxes, direct telephone links, cellular phones, videophones, and beepers.

Virtual reality: A computer-constructed, duplicate reality with which individuals can interact.

Virtual solidarity: A feeling of community and cooperative relationships based on and cemented by electronic links.

PRACTICE TESTS

True ▪ False Test

___ 1. The sociologist Melvin Tumin was one of the first to criticize functionalist theory, arguing that it did not adequately note that economic rewards are not necessarily based on talent or hard work.

___ 2. Even in industrialized societies, one's ancestry is very important in determining one's destiny.

___ 3. Social stratification is minimal in postindustrial societies.

___ 4. An individual's ascribed and achieved statuses can differ significantly.

___ 5. Economic inequality has decreased in the United States since the 1950s.

___ 6. The boundaries between the social classes in the United States are profound at all levels.

__ 7. The upper class in the United States is relatively stable in size (about 2 percent of the population).

__ 8. Familism is one of the most strongly held values in the new upper class.

__ 9. Newer immigrants who are poor are likely to retain the traditional values–familism, religiousness, and so on–that are characteristic of agricultural societies.

__ 10. Telecommuting works best in service occupations that require close contact with clients and colleagues.

Multiple-Choice Test

__ 1. Most modern conflict theorists do not believe that:
   a. a classless society is possible.
   b. social origins play a role in influencing the economic rewards that people receive.
   c. government policy serves the interests of the wealthiest members of society.
   d. enormous differences between the very poor and the very rich are unfair.

__ 2. In hunting and gathering societies, in broad terms, people are categorized based on their:
   a. material wealth.
   b. property.
   c. age and gender.
   d. ancestry.

__ 3. Economic inequality first arises in:
   a. hunting and gathering societies.
   b. agricultural societies.
   c. horticultural societies.
   d. industrializing societies.

__ 4. In medieval agricultural societies, the ranked layers of members of society were called:
   a. castes.
   b. classes.
   c. strata.
   d. estates.

__ 5. Inequalities in societies are maintained by all of the following *except:*
   a. ideologies.
   b. the lower classes' rejection of the ideologies of the dominant elites.
   c. force.
   d. inheritance of property and occupations.

__ 6. Membership in estates was rigidly symbolized by:
   a. hair color.
   b. the wearing of a mark on the forehead.
   c. speech patterns.
   d. dress.

__ 7. Which is not a characteristic of upper-middle- class people?
   a. geographic mobility
   b. a high degree of control over work
   c. rigid gender role definitions
   d. egalitarianism in husband-wife relationships

__ 8. Feelings of alienation are most likely among the:
   a. upper working class.
   b. upper middle class.
   c. lower middle class.
   d. new upper class.

__ 9. *The Division of Labor in Society,* which describes a major change in the nature of work and human connectedness, was written by:
   a. Durkheim
   b. Marx
   c. Weber
   d. Merton

__ 10. The linking between individuals based on rational awareness and deliberate choice is termed:
   a. mechanical solidarity.
   b. virtual reality.
   c. organic solidarity.
   d. virtual solidarity.

Matching Test

Match each concept with its definition, illustration, or explication below.

1.

(1) Kingsley Davis and Wilbert E. Moore
(2) Theories of inequality
(3) Melvin Tumin
(4) Functionalists
(5) Ideologies

a. Attempt to explain the origins and persistence of economic inequality
b. Seek to justify inequality
c. Classic statement of functionalist theory
d. Criticized functionalist theory
e. Stress necessity of economic inequality

2.

(1) Marx
(2) Sociocultural evolution model
(3) Social classes
(4) Castes
(5) Weber

a. Life chances
b. Ranking approach for all societies
c. Means of production
d. Strata in industrialized country
e. Layers in more complex literate society

3.

(1) Social mobility
(2) Social stratification
(3) Structural mobility
(4) Status inconsistency
(5) Ideologies

a. Justifications
b. Movement of between strata
c. Discrepancy between ascribed and achieved statuses
d. Occupational structure-related movement
e. Ranked layers

4.

(1) Old upper class
(2) Upper working class
(3) New upper class
(4) Lower middle class
(5) Upper middle class

a. Top positions in business and government
b. Lower-level management
c. Skilled or semiskilled manual work
d. Top positions in professions and entertainment
e. Higher-level professionals

5.

(1) W. Lloyd Warner
(2) Classes
(3) Income and education
(4) Lower class
(5) Occupation

a. Social strata in the United States
b. Most valid indicator of social class location
c. Divided U.S. social classes into three broad strata
d. Easily measurable indicators
e. Working class

REVIEW QUESTIONS

1. What are some major differences in functionalist and conflict perspectives on economic inequality?
2. How did Marx and Weber define the concept of class, and how can their views be reconciled to take into account stratification in all types of societies?
3. How does social mobility relate to structural mobility? Give examples.
4. How does economic inequality arise in human societies, and what are three major reasons why it persists?
5. What are the major factors in the current increase in global economic inequality between industrial and industrializing societies?
6. What factors are associated with higher worker satisfaction in the United States today?
7. How does virtual reality differ from traditional ways of working, learning, and belonging?
8. What are the advantages and disadvantages of telecommuting, from the points of view of employers and employees?

APPLYING SOCIOLOGY

1. How has your social class location or that of your parents affected the following aspects of your life:
   a. your parents' childrearing practices?
   b. your values on a scale from traditional to urban?
   c. your political attitudes and behavior?
   d. your religious attitudes and practices?
   e. your educational experiences and goals?
   f. your patterns of dress and speech?
   g. your leisure activities now and in the past?
2. Do you feel other locating factors such as ethnic origin have been more important than social class in affecting your attitudes and behavior?
3. What would you do with the extra time if your day were extended to 26 hours? Ask others this question and see if you get different typical responses from individuals in different age, generation, and occupational categories. How would you explain these differences?

11

Power and Politics

Power—who has it and what is done with it—does not become a problem in human societies until it becomes tied to differences in wealth. This cannot occur until sociocultural evolution creates an economic surplus that is unequally distributed. And the relationship between power and wealth does not usually become a matter of widespread challenge and controversy until societies begin to industrialize.

SOME BASIC CONCEPTS

Max Weber (1946 [1919]) defined **politics** as efforts to share power or influence the distribution of power either among states (particularly nation-states) or among various groups (such as political parties and interest groups) within a state. In other words, politics is the struggle to obtain or maintain power by individuals and groups. For Weber, the **state** is a human community that successfully exercises a monopoly over the legitimate use of physical force in a certain territory. **Government** is the concrete, visible

363

instrument of the state. Governments function to protect citizens against internal and external threat. They also control the distribution of economic resources in societies with an economic surplus. Historically, governments have been authoritarian, democratic, or mixed—containing elements of both types of political power.

Authoritarian leaders have absolute power that cannot be challenged, except by other members of the governing elite. The people they govern have no voice in choosing them, have no legal right to protest against them publicly (by assembly or in the media), and cannot remove them from power. Authoritarian leaders usually rule for life. They are succeeded by heirs (usually sons) or by a new leader appointed by the dominant elite. Authoritarian governments may be monarchies, dictatorships, oligarchies, military juntas, or colonial administrations.

Democratic governments are usually found in industrial societies. They are characterized by (1) multiparty contested elections; (2) laws and written regulations specifying how officials are to be elected, the limits of their power, and the length of their terms in service; and (3) the right of citizens to express opposition to and remove those in power (Lipset, 1994).

Political relationships, in which unequal levels of power are a major aspect of the relationship, occur in all kinds of groups and in all spheres in life. Examples are the power of husbands over wives (or wives over husbands), parents over children, teachers over students, employers over employees, and clergy over parishioners. In this chapter, we focus primarily on the power of leaders and rulers of societies and states, both historically and in the present world.

FUNCTIONALIST AND CONFLICT PERSPECTIVES

Functionalists view the modern state as performing certain functions that are necessary to maintain the stability of societies: (1) enforcing laws that protect citizens from destructive behavior by other citizens in the society; (2) mediating disputes between opposing interest groups (the classes, religions, regions, racial/ethnic groups, young and old, men and women, and so on); (3) subsidizing citizens in need and planning for the future needs of all citizens; (4) representing the society in cooperative relationships with other societies (through alliances, trade agreements, and international organizations); and (5) defending the state in competition and conflicts with other states.

In the past, conflict theorists have focused primarily on class conflict, especially to the extent that it promotes social change. They have also examined the role of the state in supporting the economic and political interests of dominant groups in human societies. More recently, conflict theorists have focused on other sources of conflict, not all of which have economic implications. In the United States, as noted in chapter 2, conflicts over issues such as abortion, sex education, gay and lesbian rights, and gun control do not have a clear economic basis. Policy decisions on these issues, however, do reflect and promote social change.

TYPES OF AUTHORITY

People obey those who are in power in some cases because they want to, and in others because they have to. They obey willingly if they believe those with power have the right to exercise that power. Weber, as we saw in the last chapter, defined authority as legitimate power. The authority is tied to a widely recognized position or status in a society, regardless of who occupies that position at any particular time. Weber distinguished authority from power, which is based purely on force or coercion. By contrast, police may exercise force, but their authority to do so is usually regarded as legitimate. This is an important distinction, because governments rise or fall in the long run depending on whether the people they govern believe they are legitimate.

When revolutions occur, the authority of established governments is no longer regarded as legitimate. Successful revolutionaries who become the leaders of new states try to legitimate their power among all segments of the population. They may inform and educate their subjects, or they may manipulate and propagandize them about public issues or concerns. They may glorify their accomplishments and create cults of personality around themselves, as did Lenin in the Soviet Union and Mao Zedong in the People's Republic of China. To legitimate their rule, these leaders may establish new monarchies, as they did in Iran in 1925 and in Jordan in 1946. Or they may draw up written constitutions to give legal sanction to their rule, as they did in India in 1948, Egypt in 1922, the Soviet Union in 1922, and Russia in 1993. They may also use a combination of these techniques to establish their legitimacy.

Weber (1946 [1914]) distinguished among three basic kinds of legitimate power, or types of authority: traditional, charismatic, and legal-rational.

Traditional Authority

Leaders whose authority is based on the sanctity of tradition inherit their power at birth, although there may be competing claims by other relatives, and these leaders do not exercise their power until the incumbent ruler dies. The **traditional authority** of these leaders is justified by beliefs and ancient customs handed down from the past. Tribal chiefs in horticultural societies, sheikhs in herding societies, and emperors, kings, and queens in agricultural societies have ruled on the basis of tradition. Their right to rule may be viewed as sacred, especially in societies where they are regarded as head of the established state religion or God's representative on earth. They are bound by custom, ceremony, and ritual, but they do not rule on the basis of written regulations and laws that they are required to follow. They may be tyrannical, incompetent, or incapacitated, but they cannot be removed from office by popular will as long as they are alive.

The most important administrative positions on the staff of leaders who rule on the basis of traditional authority are usually filled by members of their clan or family, who qualify on the basis of blood relationship rather than technical training. Personal loyalty is reinforced by family ties and economic interdependence. The king and members of his administrative staff have the widest possible scope in exercising unlimited, arbitrary, and authoritarian power over subjects. Under ordinary circumstances, **succession**—the turning over of authority to a new leader—is not a problem. The oldest son usually inherits the authority of his father.

Monarchies in most contemporary industrial democracies, such as Japan, the United Kingdom, and Norway, are called constitutional monarchies. Their power is largely symbolic. They are not directly involved in policy making. Their function is to promote solidarity among subjects by reinforcing pride in a common national identity, despite widely differing class interests or ethnic identities. They are no longer regarded as the personification or the representative on earth of a supreme being, but they may be head of the state church and "keeper of the faith," as the monarch is in the United Kingdom. A few traditional monarchies continue to exist, mainly in the Middle East. Kuwait and Saudi Arabia, for example, are ruled by nuclear royal families and relatives in their extended families who exercise absolute, authoritarian power over their subjects.

Charismatic Authority

Charismatic authority is based on a belief in "a certain quality of an individual personality by virtue of which he is set apart from ordinary men and treated as endowed with supernatural, superhuman, or at least specifically exceptional powers or qualities" (Weber, 1946 [1914], p. 358). The authority of charismatic leaders lies in their personalities, not in a widely recognized legitimate or customary position or status. Shamans in nonliterate societies and certain leaders of religious or political movements in agricultural and industrial societies, such as Joan of Arc, Lenin, Mahatma Gandhi, and Malcolm X, are examples of charismatic leaders.

As originally conceived by Weber, charismatic leaders arise in times of crisis. They do not usually hold official positions in church or state. They are sometimes revolutionaries. Their power is based on faith, hero worship, and absolute trust. Loyalty to the leader is fueled by the intense suffering, despair, passions, and hopes of followers. The administrative staffs of charismatic leaders are not relatives or hired officials. They are disciples and followers whose loyalty is based on faith rather than blood relationship or economic reward. Followers are mobilized and inspired by a belief in their leader's promise of religious or economic salvation.

Charismatic leaders are not bound by custom or by written laws and regulations. The authority of charismatic leaders lasts only as long as belief in their magical powers lasts. If they fail to provide the promised salvation or fall off their moral pedestal, they very quickly lose their authority, as, for example, did U.S. televangelists Jim Bakker and Jimmy Swaggart.

Since the powers of charismatic leaders are not transferable, hereditary, customary, or routine, succession has been a serious problem in the governments and religious sects and cults that they have established. The deaths of such revolutionary leaders as Lenin, Gandhi, and Mao were followed by intense and destructive power struggles and major changes in government policies. This is the origin of the adage that revolutions devour their children. Charismatic leaders are usually reluctant to groom others to take over, because their power is based on their uniqueness, and they encourage the belief that they are irreplaceable.

Legal-Rational Authority

Authority that is bound by explicit laws, rules, and regulations that define the conditions and limits of power, at least in principle, is called **legal-rational authority**. This type of authority is most prevalent in industrial societies. Leaders such as presidents and prime ministers are elected or appointed rationally on the basis of merit and according to law. They are assisted by bureaucratic organizations staffed by administrators who are ranked in a hierarchy with respect to authority. Administrators are hired on the basis of technical competence, as certified by examinations or diplomas. They work full time, at a fixed salary, and are promoted on the basis of seniority, achievement, or both.

The strictly defined authority of leaders with legal-rational authority resides in the office rather than in the person who occupies that office at any particular time. The loyalty of bureaucratic administrators is to the system rather than to the temporary occupant of a leadership position. And succession is also regulated by explicit laws and procedures.

In postindustrial societies, talent, knowledge, and experience determine the authority of legal-rational leaders. Expertise is the basis on which they are elected (and reelected), and they use their expertise to determine and carry out their policies. Political campaigns are run by specially trained, highly experienced professional consultants, aided by pollsters and media experts. Elected officials recruit experienced administrators and social and natural scientists from universities, research institutions, and think tanks. Experts are appointed to temporary positions as advisers at the top of various government bureaucracies. Their scientific knowledge and experience

TABLE 11.1

Types of Authority

	Basis of Legitimacy	Leadership Status	Succession
Traditional	Customs, religious beliefs	Ascribed	Based on birth
Charismatic	Belief in the extraordinary personal qualities of the leader	Acquired	Problematic
Legal-rational	Legal elections, expertise of elected officials	Acquired	Prescribed by law

in the public and private sectors—in government and the economy—become indispensable to the task of governing. Their **expert authority** is based on outstanding talent, training, experience, and drive.

POWER AND SOCIOCULTURAL EVOLUTION

Three aspects of power and politics vary, typically, over the course of sociocultural evolution: (1) the *sources* of political power—why and how it comes about; (2) its *justifications*—the beliefs and ideologies that support it; and (3) its *distribution*—who exercises it.

Hunting and Gathering Societies

Personal resources such as physical strength, intelligence, resourcefulness, and bravery were the bases of power in hunting and gathering societies and throughout most of human history. Proof of exceptional abilities commanded respect and obedience from the group. Age also commanded respect, but this, too, was on the basis of personal qualities—the wisdom and accumulation of experience and knowledge that come with time. Also, in hunting and gathering societies, only exceptional people managed to survive to old age.

Shamans, or medicine men, and headmen in hunting and gathering societies had charismatic authority that was not transferable or hereditary. Their power was temporary, lasting only as long as they could prove their superior skills or ability. Headmen did not have exclusive rights to weapons or the use of force, since all male members of these societies knew how to make and use the simple weapons that were known.

Horticultural Societies

With the invention of horticulture, the basis of power shifted to the possession of other resources in addition to personal qualities. Economic resources such as wives, children, domestic animals, and ornaments became important in determining power. In simple horticultural societies, the headman and shaman were sometimes the same person. The head of the largest and most well off family sometimes became a tribal chief, with authority over more than one village. This authority was not usually exercised, however, except during a time of crisis. Physical force was rarely used by those in power. As in hunting and gathering societies, chiefs and their families did not have exclusive ownership of weapons that they could use to control the rest of the society. The personal qualities of tribal leaders, particularly military skill, continued to be important.

In advanced horticultural societies, the power of leading families increased as wealth increased. These families used their wealth to support and protect nonrelatives who joined them, worked for them, and fought for them. They also increased their size by purchasing more wives, who produced more sons and warriors. The power of the kings and nobility became hereditary and enforceable, regardless of personal qualities. Ideologies developed to justify the continuing rule of dominant families and the payment of tribute to these families by weaker and poorer families.

The beginnings of the state, as Weber defined it, appear in certain advanced horticultural societies, such as China (Mair, 1962; Service, 1975). The invention of bronze and its use in weapons in advanced horticultural China was a major factor in the defeat of simple horticultural societies by the Chinese warrior nobility. The use of this metal in weapons and ceremonial objects was monopolized by the nobility.

Generally, the nobility in advanced horticultural societies required the payment of taxes from conquered societies, but they usually allowed defeated peoples to retain their lands and leaders. There was no need to develop a large governmental apparatus or a very extensive military organization to control populations that were nearby. The power of governments in horticultural societies was usually based on **autocracy**, or rule by a single individual. Power was concentrated in the hands of a hereditary chief or king.

Agricultural Societies

The earliest agricultural societies engaged in empire building in faraway places. Technological developments in transportation and communications made this possible. Distant conquered territories were more likely to be settled and governed by the victors. Full-time government officials and state bureaucracies multiplied. Administrators directed the large-scale activities of widely scattered tax collectors and the military.

When one tax collector was collecting taxes from 10 families, the tax collector could easily keep track of who was paid up and who was not. When 1,000 tax collectors were collecting taxes from 1,000,000 people, however, an administrator back at headquarters became essential to prevent loss, waste, duplication, or chaos. Administrators kept records, coordinated activities, and provided necessary supplies to workers. Government administrators in agricultural societies were usually members of the nobility.

Full-time military positions also multiplied in agricultural societies. Fighting and conquering became too much for the aristocracy alone to handle. Kings established full-time professional armies. At the same time, technological advances led to more costly and complicated weaponry. The ruling families and their dependents monopolized the use of these more efficient and effective weapons. Power and political relationships became highly coercive and authoritarian.

Government in the earliest agricultural societies was either an autocracy or an **oligarchy**—rule by the few (from the Greek *oligos,* or few). Usually, this meant rule by a handful of aristocratic families who had absolute power. In the feudal era in Europe, and in certain advanced horticultural societies, a king could not control remote regions of the country, particularly those isolated by geographic barriers such as lakes or mountains. Local power was largely in the hands of hereditary feudal lords who owned the surrounding lands. These lords paid taxes to the king and fought under him in times of war, but were otherwise quite independent and very powerful.

In modern times, oligarchy persists in currently industrializing societies that are ruled by a small number of landowning families or a military junta that represents and shares their interests. Military juntas are conservative or regressive military leaders who seize power illegally by means of a **coup d'état**. The military leaders of a coup do not attempt revolutionary economic reforms that would redistribute wealth in the societies they govern. They maintain power by military force after overthrowing other military groups or legally elected governments, as they did in Haiti in 1991 after the election of President Jean-Bertrand Aristide, for example.

Some industrializing agricultural societies approach a form of government known as totalitarianism. **Totalitarian governments** are authoritarian, but they intrude into all aspects of social life—the economy, education, the family, religion, recreation—including the most private. The government dictates private as well as public morality (Berger, 1986). It trains secret police forces who have the power to arrest, punish, torture, and kill dissenters. The news media and the universities are censored and controlled by the central government. **Propaganda**—distorted information or disinformation used by leaders to mold the opinions of followers, subjects, and citizens—is pervasive. Dissenting messages (and messengers) are destroyed by force (see Table 11.2).

Totalitarian governments operate most effectively in industrialized societies. Advances in technology gradually eliminate the isolation and local

TABLE 11.2

Democratic, Authoritarian, and Totalitarian Governments

	Democratic Governments	Authoritarian Governments	Totalitarian Governments
Free elections	Yes	No	No
Right to dissent—free speech, press, assembly	Yes	No	No
Sphere recognized as legitimately "private"	Yes	Yes	No

independence of rural populations. To control people totally, one must be able to reach them. Roads and modern developments in transportation and surveillance equipment make this much easier in industrialized societies. Totalitarian governments in industrializing societies have a more difficult time, especially in tropical countries. Guerrillas can take cover in dense jungles and can sometimes defeat government forces who are armed with superior weapons.

Totalitarian governments may be led by a **dictator**—one person with absolute governmental power. Unlike the power of kings and queens, however, the autocratic power of dictators is not hereditary. But, like other autocrats, they cannot be removed from office by legal means. Current examples of dictators in industrializing agricultural societies include Muammar al-Qaddafi in Libya and Saddam Hussein in Iraq.

Industrial and Postindustrial Societies

The spread of democracy, or rule by the people (from the Greek *demos*, meaning people), in the West is closely associated with the Industrial Revolution and its consequences. In Europe the number of urban, middle-class merchants increased tremendously as a result of explorations and the import of raw materials from colonies in the Americas, Africa, and Asia. Over the centuries, the concentration of wealth gradually shifted from the landowning nobility to the cities.

The success of the Protestant Reformation in the sixteenth century had demonstrated the possibility of successfully protesting against and defeating rigid, authoritarian rule in the sphere of religion. The invention and spread of machine technology expanded business enterprises and increased the size of the middle class still more.

Industrialization required government protection of incoming and outgoing goods over wider territories. Feudal and tribal systems (in industrializing

TABLE 11.3

Authority and Sociocultural Evolution

Society	Sources of Authority	Justifications	Distribution of Authority
Hunting and Gathering	Age; gender; personal qualities	Proven ability; religious beliefs	Diffused; temporary; not hereditary
Horticultural	Birth; economic resources	Tradition; religious beliefs	Somewhat diffused; permanent; hereditary
Agricultural	Birth; economic resources	Tradition; religious beliefs	Autocratic or oligarchic; permanent; hereditary
Industrial, Democratic	Personal qualities; economic resources	Elections; expert qualifications (merit)	Somewhat diffused; temporary; not hereditary

horticultural societies) were gradually replaced by **nation-states**—legally constituted central governments that provide protection of people and facilitate trade and commerce over wide geographic areas (Skocpol, 1979).

In the process, and as a result of economic conflicts and political compromises, weaker societies were absorbed by stronger ones, and artificial states were created out of territorially distinct and culturally diverse ethnic groups. Many of these states are just now beginning to come apart—in Eastern Europe, for example.

Industrial technology requires a higher level of skills and education among all strata of the population. Educated, more informed people are less likely to accept arbitrary authoritarian rule. The growth of urban centers in European industrializing societies promoted urban values, weakened fatalism, and increased class consciousness among people with similar economic interests. They were in closer contact with one another than were isolated, illiterate peasants in agricultural regions.

The middle class led successful challenges to the oligarchic rule of the landed aristocracy in country after country in the West, as science and technology advanced and belief in the ideology of the divine right to rule declined. Wealth continued to be the basis of power, but the source of this wealth shifted increasingly from land to business enterprise.

Democracy

Going back to the city-states of ancient Greece, democracy was the historic ideal in urban centers. Democracy was a rare form of government, however, before the Industrial Revolution. In fact, pure democracy has never existed in large societies. Even in the democracies of the Greek city-states and in the small towns of the New England colonies, women, indentured servants, men who did not own property, and the young—a majority of the members of society—did not have the vote. In an ideal democratic society, all segments of the population would have equal input in selecting and electing candidates and determining government policy.

In small towns and villages, *direct democracy* is possible—all eligible citizens can vote on all the policies that affect them. In large, complex societies, this becomes impractical. Here, voters elect *representatives* to serve in legislatures or parliaments. The hope is that representatives will make political decisions that further the interests of those who elected them. If they do not, they can be voted out of office. Routine decision making is left to these representatives, while major issues are sometimes put to a popular vote in a *referendum*.

In *parliamentary systems,* voters elect representatives from slates of candidates listed by party, and a variety of parties generally win seats in parliament. Heads of government, usually called prime ministers, are chosen by the majority party in parliament. They are not elected directly by the public. If no party wins a majority of the seats in parliament, a coalition government is formed. Two or more parties join together and elect a prime minister. They usually vote as a block on specific issues. If they cannot agree, or if they lose a referendum on a major issue, new elections are called. In any event, the ruling party or coalition is legally required to call elections after a certain period of time—after 5 years, for example, in the United Kingdom.

Parliamentary democracies are often found in combination with constitutional monarchies, as in the United Kingdom, Sweden, Denmark, Norway, the Netherlands, and several smaller European countries. Newer democracies, such as Israel and other states that were formerly colonies of European powers, usually have parliamentary systems without a constitutional monarchy.

Representative democracy in the United States differs from the parliamentary system in that presidents are elected directly, by popular vote. It is quite possible for the president and a majority of the legislature to be of different parties, as has been the case in the United States most of the time over the past 4 decades. The president and legislators in Congress serve for fixed terms and cannot be removed from office because of wins or losses on specific issues until the next election. A majority popular vote, even a majority of one, carries an entire congressional district. It is for this reason that third parties in the United States have little chance of winning in national elections (Amy, 1993). They cannot muster a majority of the votes in enough congressional districts.

Despite coalitions that cross party lines and the difficulty of pinning down the two parties' positions on some issues, these parties are generally seen as representing distinct interest groups. The Republican Party is usually identified with the interests of upper-income citizens and conservative public policies. The Democratic Party is regarded as more likely to represent

FIGURE 11.1

Foundations of Effective Democracy

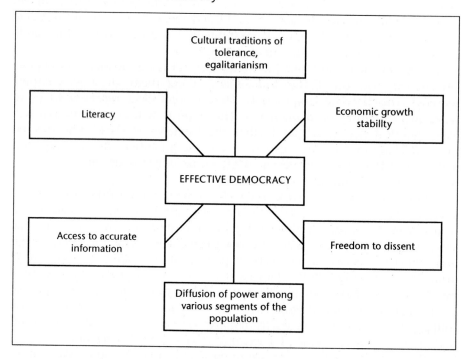

Source: Seymour Martin Lipset, "The Social Requisites of Democracy Revisited," *American Sociological Review* 59 (1994), pp. 1–22.

The conditions of effective democracy are closely related and tend to occur together in societies that have strong democratic governments.

the interests of lower-income citizens and egalitarian economic reforms. It is usually more lenient on law and order issues because of its stronger commitment to racial/ethnic minority interests.

The two dominant parties sometimes appeal to, and actually represent the economic interests of, only a minority of the electorate. Multiple parties in parliamentary democracies are more likely to represent distinct, and conflicting, economic interests in the society, and generally there is greater class consciousness in these societies (DeMott, 1990).

Political scientist Douglas J. Amy (1993) is among those who argue the case for proportional representation in the United States. Candidates would take seats in legislatures according to the proportion of votes their parties receive—provided this is more than 3 to 5 percent. There would then be many more parties and many more interests represented in government. However, the problems with this type of system are that (1) multiparty coalitions tend to be unstable, (2) a small party whose support is needed to swing a vote on an issue may achieve more power than its numbers justify, and (3) the system discourages compromise and agreement. Furthermore, converting to this type of system at the national level would require amending the U.S. Constitution.

The Foundations of Democracy   Certain conditions seem to be necessary for the existence of effective democratic governments: (1) a stable industrial economy; (2) cultural traditions of egalitarianism; (3) a literate population and a large, urban, educated middle class; (4) the freedom to voice dissent; (5) access to accurate information; and (6) a diffusion of power among various segments of the population (Lipset, 1994). All of these are interrelated, but the first three are basic—especially in times of crisis.

During the worldwide depression of the 1930s, countries with strong egalitarian cultural traditions, such as the United States and the Scandinavian countries, instituted major economic reforms. Countries with strong authoritarian traditions shifted to virulently nationalistic, totalitarian governments headed by fascist dictators, as in Germany, Italy, and Spain. In 1993, during economic crises in Germany and Italy and economic upheaval in Russia as it shifted to a market economy, fascist candidates showed unanticipated strength at the polls (Stent, 1993). Egalitarian cultural traditions, economic development, and economic stability are all basic to democratic government (Lipset, 1994).

The Future of Democracy   Most of the world's populations do not live under democratic governments. Democracies are found primarily in Europe and in societies colonized in the past by Western European countries—in North and South America, Australia, and India, for example. Some industrializing societies hold periodic, ritual, uncontested elections that have no real effect on the actual authoritarian distribution of power in the society. Other societies previously dominated by dictatorships, such as Taiwan, South Korea, Spain, and Chile, have moved in a more democratic direction.

Educated citizens in postindustrial economies need and want a free flow of all kinds of information. A major problem is posed, however, by the enormous quantity and complexity of the information needed to make rational policy decisions in large, postindustrial societies. The increased reliance on experts in these societies brings with it a built-in danger of default by citizens and oligarchy based on exclusive, expert knowledge (see Table 11.3 on p. 373).

The Iron Law of Oligarchy

A tendency toward oligarchy appears to be inevitable in all large-scale organizations, and perhaps also in all large, technologically advanced societies. Writing in the period before World War I, Robert Michels (1949 [1915]), a

German economist and statistician, called this tendency "the iron law of oligarchy." He based his theory on a study of social democratic parties and trade union movements in Europe. Michels pointed to the lack of desire for power among rank-and-file members of organizations (and among the masses of people in larger societies) as an important factor in the tendency toward oligarchy.

Leaders, on the other hand, have a very strong need for power. They go to great lengths to preserve and increase their power once they have it. They compromise with and join the enemies that they cannot overpower, ensuring that they will retain their own power. They avoid risks and abandon policies that might threaten their position. And above all, they become, in Michels's words, "technically indispensable" to their organizations because of their highly developed, specialized skills, especially in administration and public relations.

Michels's observations on the tendency toward oligarchy in trade unions, political parties, and governments also apply to contemporary postindustrial societies, but with some very important differences. Skill in public relations becomes even more important in democratic postindustrial societies, when the media and the public have instant access to public (and often private) events. Television exposes the facial expressions, emotions, and personalities of political leaders in a way that written and spoken words might have concealed in the past. Impression management becomes transparent; character flaws are more difficult to conceal. In the United States, personality often outweighs issues in determining votes (Burnham, 1987).

The technical indispensability of leaders becomes especially evident in advanced industrialized societies, in which public policy issues become extraordinarily complex. Increasingly, it takes highly trained, very skilled specialists to understand them and to carry them out. The dependence of government on experts supports a trend toward oligarchy founded on specialized knowledge. Talent, knowledge, training, and experience, the basis of expert authority, become scarce commodities.

Leaders who do not possess this authority themselves must know where to get it and how to use it. In the United States, President Clinton selected the most important members of his cabinet in 1993 on the basis of their expertise in banking and finance, administration, medicine, law, and education, with talent, training, and merit outweighing wealth and ancestry. These choices were based on the need for specialists with recognized competence to deal with extremely complex issues—the budget, trade deficit and debt reduction, health care, and ethnic conflict, for example. For the first time, white Anglo-Saxon Protestant males from the old upper class were a small minority among cabinet appointees. Lower-middle-class and even working-class origins did not disqualify potential appointees, nor the president himself, for that matter.

The second reason for the trend toward oligarchy that Michels observed, a disinterest in power by people at the lower levels of the organizations he studied, also needs updating. Ordinary citizens may not have as strong a need for power as political leaders do, as Michels recognized. But levels of education are generally higher in postindustrial societies than in other societies. College-educated people, especially, are better informed about public issues, less likely to be persuaded by propaganda, and more likely to think critically about current events (Hyman, Wright, and Reed, 1975). Education, especially in the liberal arts, is designed to "liberate" the mind and promote critical thinking (Chomsky, 1988; McLaren and Lankshear, 1992; Macedo, 1993).

Citizens in democratic industrial societies may delegate their power to elected officials, but they still feel they have a right to influence government policy. Ever more sophisticated daily, weekly, monthly, and yearly polls make the will of the people known to those who would listen. Currently, the White House receives more than 10,000 letters a day from U.S. citizens.

Responding to a constantly expanding daily diet of printed and electronic news images and commentary, citizens in the United States have transformed the *right* to criticize into an obsessive *need* to criticize, especially in a time of increased economic stress (Graff, 1993). Leaders in all areas of life—government, family, education, religion, business, and the professions—wear their crowns less easily now than they once did.

The news media, furthermore, do not have the uncritical acceptance and steamroller effect often attributed to them. Family and friends filter the visual and verbal messages of the media in what sociologists have called a *two-step flow of communication* (Katz and Lazarsfeld, 1955; Katz, 1957; Turner and Killian, 1987). Word of mouth is more important than the reviews of television and newspaper critics in determining the popularity of movies, for example. The public trusts the opinions of family and friends more than those expressed in the media.

Since the 1960s, journalists have shifted their style of reporting on politics and political candidates from the purely descriptive to the interpretive. They express a point of view in their analyses, but the opinions expressed are now more often critical and possibly more distorted than in the past.

Nevertheless, negativism and sensationalism pall, after a while, and the public tends to discount much of what they see and hear from journalists (Patterson, 1993). In polls conducted after the 1992 elections, the public gave the news media the lowest rating of any source of information about candidates and issues. They ranked reporters lower than the candidates, talk shows, debates, and even televised political ads and political consultants as a trustworthy source of information about campaign issues (Patterson, 1993).

THE NEW STATELESSNESS

In postindustrial societies, increasing numbers of people do not identify themselves according to their national citizenship. Families and individuals

Focus on Social Issues

DEMOCRACY IN ACTION

[Social change does not occur at the same pace in all areas of life. Western cultural patterns of dress, such as blue jeans, jackets, and ties, and food and drink preferences, such as fast food and Coca Cola, diffuse more easily than democratic forms of government.]

In the precious shade of a gnarled Combretum tree, two dozen Ju/wa Bushmen, squatting in the dust like baseball catchers, pass around metal pipes stuffed with tobacco and talk about forming a government. . . . "The white man has spoken for us too often. We must have a government to speak for ourselves. . . . We must organize, we must make out own laws." . . . As Namibia gets its independence from South Africa later this year, the Bushmen fear their [land] will be grabbed by covetous trophy hunters, conservationists, and cattle ranchers. . . .

Those gathered under the gnarled tree don't at all fit the image of Bushmen popularized in the film "The Gods Must Be Crazy"—bow-and-arrow hunters dressed only in loincloth and beads and so out of touch with the modern world that a Coca-Cola bottle is a mystery. These Bushmen are fully clothed; some wear ties and jackets for the occasion. They smoke Winstons and Benson & Hedges (in addition to the metal pipes). Crushed Coke cans litter Bushmanland as they do other parts of the world. Bushmen still hunt, but mainly to supplement their farming and cattle raising.

[A]n old man named Xashe . . . is wearing a U.N. tee shirt pledging "free and fair" elections for Namibia, but he confesses to not knowing what an election—free, fair, or otherwise—is.

—Roger Thurow, "For the Bushmen, It's Not the Gods That Must Be Crazy," *Wall Street Journal,* July 13, 1989, p. A1

What Do You Think?

1. What does this quote illustrate about social change and cultural lag?
2. Why do social scientists conclude that mass education and literacy are a major underlying condition of effective democracy?
3. What are some other underlying conditions that appear to be important in maintaining democratic forms of government?

who have multinational residences, bank accounts, and reference groups feel less allegiance to their country of origin, especially if they are not involved in politics. Young, college-educated Europeans travel frequently and are less nationalistic than previous generations, as noted in chapter 4 (Riding, 1993).

Highly trained, globally connected professionals with an international market for their financial and technical talents also live in a stateless world and are constantly on the move. The United States both exports and imports more high-tech talent than any other country in the world.

In addition, soldiers of fortune, mercenaries who were usually military officers in their country of origin, are stateless in their loyalties and identities. They roam the globe, selling their expertise to any military or paramilitary group intent on maintaining or overthrowing local state power.

Cooperation and Conflict

As economic markets and networks become increasingly international, political power also becomes global. The CEOs of multinational banks are welcomed like heads of state when they visit debtor nations. The passage of the North American Free Trade Agreement (NAFTA) and the expected ratification of the General Agreement on Tariffs and Trade (GATT) will not only affect the price of plums in Peoria. The agreements are expected to increase the political and economic interdependence of all nations, large and small.

GATT, signed by 117 countries, will cut protective tariffs on goods by about one-third, on the average. It is expected to stimulate business and investment activity by opening new markets and encouraging member nations to specialize in producing whatever goods they can make most efficiently. The consequences of these accords are not yet clear, and there is strong disagreement about this even among experts (Passell, 1993).

Certainly, there is historical precedent for optimism. In the nineteenth century, when England removed tariffs on wheat imported from central Europe and North America, the economy shifted to a greater emphasis on manufacturing, and England soon became the richest country in the world. But this took place at the expense of English farmers, who were pauperized and uprooted from farms, family, and friends as they moved to the cities to take jobs in factories, where they worked under abysmal conditions.

Currently, displaced factory workers in industrialized societies that have exported jobs turn to low-paying service jobs, unemployment insurance, or welfare (called the dole in the United Kingdom). By contrast, industrializing societies that export more goods, and keep population growth under control, are improving their standard of living at an extraordinary pace. China, South Korea, Taiwan, and Singapore are several examples.

The Organization for Economic Cooperation and Development (OECD) estimates that the combination of reduced tariffs and more generous import quotas will increase world income by $270 billion annually by the turn of the century (Passell, 1993). If this happens, national borders and nationalism will continue to weaken, at least in countries that profit from the agreements.

Force and Conflict

Political independence rests on the ability of national governments to withstand internal and external threat. Weber emphasized that a state must successfully monopolize the use of force within its borders (1946 [1919]). This force is legitimate when it is used to control crime, but not dissent, within the state and to defend against attacks by other states. The government monopoly over the use of force is threatened when citizens legally bear arms of their own, however, as they do in the United States.

More important, the development of multinational corporations and, now, well-armed multinational criminal organizations poses a real threat to the monopoly over the use of force by governments—especially in newer and weaker states. Strong governments and multinational corporations have long protected themselves against threats to their economic and political interests in weaker, currently industrializing states by subsidizing government or revolutionary forces, military or paramilitary, within these states (Weiner, 1993). For decades, U.S.-based multinational corporations have, with government assistance, been instrumental in the overthrow of governments unsympathetic to their economic interests—in Iran, Chile, and Guatemala, to name but a few well-documented examples.

Multinational criminal organizations are also stateless. The term *mafia,* which originally referred to organized crime groups in Italy, is now an international term found in most of the world's languages. This is because the new, stateless mafia groups are global in their operations, linked by sophisticated, high-speed telecommunications networks (*Newsweek,* November 23, 1993, pp. 16–27).

Unlike traditional mafia figures, the new men of criminal power—drug lords, weapons merchants, prostitution purveyors—are usually college educated and technically highly skilled. These individuals, whose wealth sometimes reaches into the billions, are unleashed by global advances in technological development and driven by boundless greed. They attend international conferences, clad in conservative business suits and cloaked in the latest security devices. They can intercept radio signals when they are in the air and use encrypted cellular phones to prevent the tracing of telephone calls on the ground or in the air. Within seconds, they can launder billions of dollars by electronic transfers to major financial centers in Europe, Asia, and the United States.

Weaker states, especially in Eastern Europe, the former Soviet Union, and newly industrializing societies in Central America and Asia, are especially vulnerable to the exploits of these crime lords. Newer, less secure governments are too weak and unstable to combat heavily armed mafia members.

Now that the cold war is over, intelligence agencies around the globe are shifting their emphasis from tracking down spies to capturing international criminals. All over the world, the export of raw materials is falling into criminal hands, as is actual political control over governments of small nations—from Central America to the Pacific Ocean.

There is some reason for optimism about the future, however. We should bear in mind that ruthless and unlimited greed is a poor basis for cooperation among groups who have the same goals—in this case, money and power. We are now seeing a type of international cooperation among organized criminal groups that was unknown among traditional competing mafia groups headed by local neighborhood or village families. But if demand for what they have to offer should decline, competing global criminal organizations will turn on each other—as their forebears have done in the past.

The demand for the mafias' goods and services is declining dramatically in postindustrial societies that have solved the problem of poverty within their borders. Even in the United States, by 1993, cocaine use had declined more than 75 percent from its peak in 1985 (Califano, 1993). Marijuana use was at its lowest level in 20 years. There seems to be a slight reversal of this trend more recently. Addiction patterns vary according to social location, however. For the most part, declines in cocaine and marijuana use in the United States have occurred among the more educated middle-class population. Poverty has increased in the United States in recent years. Addiction to self-destructive drugs, including alcohol and tobacco, continues to be highest among the lowest-income segments of the population, who tend to experience the highest levels of environmental stress. And the United States is still the biggest market in the world for addictive drugs.

POWER IN THE UNITED STATES

For decades, a controversy has raged between social scientists who hold two very different theoretical models of political power in the United States.

Democratic Pluralism

In the first model, **democratic pluralism**, power and influence are seen as fragmented and dispersed among many organized groups in the United States (Dahl, 1961, 1982). These groups represent categories of the population that have different economic and political interests. Interest groups—corporate, small business, labor, religious, regional, racial/ethnic, women's, environmental, and consumer organizations—are viewed as competing against one another in determining specific government policies (Pampel and Williamson, 1988).

All interest groups, it is argued, have *some* power, none has *complete* power, and each can at least exercise a veto that will delay or prevent public policy decisions that threaten their interests.

A recent example of the power of various interest groups is the delay in health care reform in the United States, despite initial widespread public demand for prompt action. The delay was accomplished by intense lobbying, massive advertising, and the provision of questionable if not false information to the public. Doctors, insurance and pharmaceutical companies, and privately owned hospitals, nursing homes, and health maintenance organizations spent massive amounts of money to delay or prevent reform. According to figures released by the Federal Election Commission, contributions to the campaign funds of members of Congress, especially those who sit on committees that consider health care reform legislation, by the American Medical Association and by other interested parties increased some 30 percent during the first 10 months of 1993 (Lewis, 1993). By mid-1994, these interest groups had contributed $26 million to the campaign funds of members of Congress (Clymer, Pear, and Toner, 1994).

The democratic pluralism model, like the model of cultural pluralism, assumes equality of opportunity, if not of results, in the competition for economic resources and political power among the various social classes and racial/ethnic groups in the United States today.

Since the 1930s, some social scientists have argued that wealth, particularly corporate wealth, and political power do not go hand in hand in the United States (Burnham, 1961; Dahl, 1961, 1982). They have maintained that corporations are now owned by thousands upon thousands of individual stockholders. They have argued that the shift from family-owned businesses to a corporate economy has dispersed business ownership away from the old upper class and has resulted in a **managerial revolution**, or takeover by a new business elite (Burnham, 1961). The new corporate managers, they argue, come from a broader base of social class origins and have different and competing interests, depending on the particular business or industry they are in. This balances things out and prevents power from being too concentrated in any particular social class (Dahl, 1961, 1982).

The Power Elite

A very different model of wealth and power in the United States is the **power elite** or dominant class model. Sociologist C. Wright Mills popularized the concept of the power elite in the late 1950s. He identified members of this elite as those at the top in government, business, and military bureaucracies in the United States. He defined the **military-industrial complex** as consisting of top people in the military and in corporations—chiefs of staff at the Pentagon and CEOs in defense industries, for example—who share an interest in promoting large military expenditures. He argued that the individuals at the tops of these hierarchies are of the same social class—the inner and "higher circles" of the old upper class—and are involved in overlapping corporate directorships and social cliques that attend the same private schools, belong to the same exclusive social clubs, intermarry, and work and think "if not together at least alike" (1959, p. 11).

Mills focused primarily on the political activities of those who are in formal, official positions of authority in the United States. Sociologist G. William Domhoff provided evidence of the social activities and informal political influence of the "leadership arm" of the upper social classes—

mainly directors of banks and the largest corporations (Domhoff, 1967, 1983, 1990). He concluded that they exert strong influence on government policy, regardless of whether they occupy official positions of authority in government or the military at any particular time.

Other sociologists have continued to argue for and document the existence and effective political influence of this small and, in C. Wright Mills's words, "inner group" of people who have tremendous wealth and economic power. As self-made, extraordinarily ambitious and successful individuals, or as members of large, old upper-class, elite extended families, they own a disproportionate amount of stock and bonds in major American corporations (Mintz and Schwartz, 1985; Dye, 1990; Bartlett and Steele, 1992). They consist of less than 1 percent of the population in the United States. And they maintain frequent and close contact with one another.

Many of these individuals, as documented by power-elite sociologists, are major owners or directors of more than one of the largest U.S. corporations. They are disproportionately active in and occupy top administrative positions in local, state, and federal government agencies, advisory committees, and business associations (Useem, 1984). They are business leaders with a very broad vision, however. Because of their multiple and often diverse business affiliations, they are able to rise above the frequent secondary conflicts in the business sector—between large corporations and small business firms, financial institutions and manufacturing industries, oil and military industries, and so on. They promote their special interests by exerting strong influence on government leaders, government policy, and the election of political candidates.

They have done this, according to Domhoff (1967, 1983, 1990), by (1) lobbying; (2) providing self-serving advice and distorted information to government leaders and agencies; (3) engaging in bribery and gift giving; (4) promising and giving high-level jobs in business to government employees; (5) financing sympathetic or expedient political candidates, legally and illegally; (6) co-opting upwardly mobile professors and other experts who are fellow members of advisory committees and councils and who are then appointed to top government posts; and, (7) occasionally, by accepting these posts themselves (Bartlett and Steele, 1992).

Domhoff reviewed much of the research on the effectiveness of competing interest groups in determining government policy in the United States from the 1930s through the 1980s. He documented the defeats and victories of three major coalitions—multinational corporate interest groups, small-business groups, and labor/liberal groups. His review indicates that, on contested issues, corporate interest groups almost always win.

In the past, during periods of severe economic crisis or racial/ethnic conflict, corporate interests supported the labor/liberal coalition in opposition to the very conservative small-business coalition. This was how labor/liberal victories—on the Social Security Act and the National Labor Relations Act, for example—were actually won in the 1930s (Gilbert and

Howe, 1991). Corporate groups agreed to concessions to restore stability to a society in crisis—concessions that were gradually modified later in favor of business interests.

Why do large corporations and small-business interests almost always win? Domhoff gives three reasons: (1) they have more money than the labor/liberal coalition, (2) they are more cohesive and less divided (on issues such as civil rights versus law and order, for example), and (3) they have more access to government officials.

What was the situation in 1993, given the end of the cold war, the election of a Democratic president, and a serious economic crisis? Despite some well-publicized cutbacks in military spending; a small, compromise increase in taxes on higher incomes; and the passage of a much-reduced job training program and a college loan program, funds for the continuation of the Strategic Defense Initiative (Star Wars) were included in the federal budget for 1994. Most experts doubt that this project could stop a full-scale nuclear attack. And it will cost billions of additional taxpayers' dollars in research and development to find out.

Plans to finance a new aircraft carrier at a cost of $5 billion, to buy additional F-22 Stealth fighters (to defend against future Russian fighters that in fact will not be built), and to raise Pentagon salaries by $2.5 billion per year for 5 years were not canceled. At the same time, the budget for financing mass transit and highway repairs, early education programs, job training, and energy and scientific research was cut by more than half in 1993 (*New York Times,* December 27, 1993, p. A16). In New York City, where families make up 75 percent of the homeless, an estimated 38,000 people a month were being turned away from emergency food shelters that had run out of food (*New York Times,* December 22, 1993, p. A18). And during this same period, a costly humanitarian military operation to save starving people in Somalia was being funded, with questionable success. In the United States, the military-industrial complex is alive, if not altogether well.

The strong influence and high standing of the military, in fact, is indicated in repeated public opinion polls conducted in the United States since 1973. While the public would not endorse an undemocratic military takeover of the United States government, they have more confidence in the military than in any other occupational category. While organized religion outranked the military in the 1970s, since 1985, the polls have indicated a higher level of public confidence in the military than in organized religion and the police (*Gallup Poll Monthly,* No. 343, April 1994). In 1994, Congress and the criminal justice system ranked at the bottom in terms of public confidence (see Table 11.4).

Specific and dramatic examples of the hidden influence and political activities of the multinational corporations and other interest groups in the United States have been repeatedly exposed in the press by investigative reporters, the muckrakers of modern times. And, once again, as they did at the turn of the century, policy-oriented sociologists have backed up the

TABLE 11.4

Confidence in U.S. Institutions—1994

	Great Deal	Quite a Lot	Some	Very Little	None	No Opinion
The military	30%	34%	26%	8%	•	2%
The church or organized religion	29	25	29	14	2	1
The police	22	32	33	11	1	1
The U.S. Supreme Court	18	24	38	16	1	3
The presidency	16	22	34	24	3	1
Television news	15	20	37	25	2	1
The medical system	14	22	38	24	2	2
Public schools	14	20	40	23	2	1
Banks	12	23	46	17	•	2
Newspapers	11	18	42	26	2	1
Organized labor	11	15	41	28	3	2
Big business	9	17	42	28	2	2
Congress	7	11	48	29	3	2
The criminal justice system	6	9	35	44	5	1

• Less than 0.5%

Source: *The Gallup Poll Monthly,* April 1994. Based on a nationwide Gallup survey.

muckrakers with their patient, less dramatic, but often ingenious empirical studies of the less obvious political activities and the very real political influence of organized interest groups in the United States.

Advocates of the power elite model argue that the democratic pluralism model does not accurately reflect political relationships and government policies in the United States today. They contend that democratic pluralism cannot exist in a situation in which upper- and upper-middle-class business, professional, and military leaders disproportionately influence government policy at all levels. It cannot exist, they reason, when the great majority of employees in the working and lower middle classes are not represented by labor unions or by other organized interest groups that have political power. The working class, especially factory workers, has lost much of whatever political power it once had. Even labor unions are increasingly oligarchic and powerless to promote the interests of their rapidly shrinking memberships.

Contemporary power elite advocates also argue that the upper middle class has the advantage of such business and professional associations as the National Federation of Independent Business, the American Medical Association, and the American Bar Association. These well-funded associations have political action committees (PACs) that advertise, make political contributions to candidates, and otherwise protect the interests of this class. The largest category of people in the United States, however, the lower middle class, does not have this kind of political influence.

Those who reject the democratic pluralism model also point to the fact that the poor are not represented at all by people from their own social class at the national level. The poor, furthermore, are the least likely to vote in a society where voter turnout in national elections is lower than in most other industrial and postindustrial societies (Burnham, 1987). It is actually lower than national surveys in the United States indicate, because people do not like to admit that they did not vote. They give the socially desirable response when asked if they voted (Presser and Traugott, 1992).

Functionalists have emphasized the role of governments in maintaining order and planning and coordinating the distribution of goods and services to citizens. This governments do, to a greater or lesser extent in various societies. But governments have also functioned at all times and in all societies since technological advances created an economic surplus to maintain the power and wealth of dominant members and their families, as conflict theorists have pointed out (Lenski, 1966).

In industrial societies, democracy and egalitarianism have been basic motivating values and major rallying slogans of the educated, urban, middle classes that have led most organized reform and revolutionary movements, especially in Europe (Lipset, 1959; Tilly, 1993). Of all the urban values, egalitarianism has proven the most difficult to achieve, with rationalism a close second. As for the future, "the prospects for social change didn't look very good at the end of the 20s or 50s either. No one foresaw the New Deal and no one expected a massive civil rights movement. If history teaches us anything, it is that no one can predict the future" (Domhoff, 1990, p. 285).

Study Guide

REVIEW OBJECTIVES

After studying this chapter, you should be able to:

1. Explain how and why political attitudes, values, and relationships change during the course of sociocultural evolution.
2. Describe how justifications for power have changed historically.
3. List the effects of economic globalization on power and politics in countries that are in different stages of technological evolution.
4. Explain the relationship between wealth and power in the United States today.

SUMMARY

1. The power of rulers and leaders of societies, states, and social movements has varied historically along three dimensions: the bases of power, justifications for power, and distribution of power.

2. Power in hunting and gathering societies was based on age, sex, and personal qualities. The power of headmen was charismatic, diffuse, and temporary; it was not hereditary.

3. In horticultural societies, the possession of economic resources becomes an additional basis of power. Religious beliefs as well as personal merit justify the power of tribal chiefs, and power becomes more concentrated, permanent, and hereditary.

4. In agricultural societies, economic resources become the primary basis of political power. Tradition and religious beliefs justify the power of rulers. Power becomes very concentrated and authoritarian, as well as permanent and hereditary.

5. In industrial societies, once again, personal qualities, as well as economic resources, become important in determining political power. Power is justified on the grounds of personal merit and is exercised according to legal-rational guidelines that define its conditions and limits. Political power remains concentrated in the hands of the dominant economic classes, officially or unofficially, but the power of specific government leaders is temporary and is not hereditary.

6. A new statelessness arises in global economies. Economic interests, identifications, and reference groups become increasingly international. Newer and weaker states, such as small, currently industrializing nations, have greater difficulty maintaining their political autonomy, given their great economic dependence. Increased nationalism and ethnic conflict are frequent responses to severe economic stress in industrializing and industrial societies.

7. Increasingly, studies of political power and influence in the United States have indicated that politically active members of the old and new upper class who hold interlocking directorships in the largest banks and corporations have enormous influence on government policy and the political process at all levels—local, state, and national.

GLOSSARY

Authoritarian governments: Governments in which leaders have permanent power that cannot be challenged or limited.

Autocracy: Rule by a single individual.

Charismatic authority: Legitimate power based on a belief in the extraordinary qualities of a leader.

Coup d'état: A violent replacement of government leaders with other leaders, usually from the same social stratum.

Democractic governments: Governments in which citizens collectively participate in decision making, either directly or, indirectly, through elected representatives.

Democratic pluralism: A model of political power in which all classes and ethnic groups are viewed as equally capable of affecting government policy and the political process.

Dictator: An autocrat whose power is not hereditary but who cannot be removed from office by legal means.

Expert authority: Authority based on training and expertise in a particular area of scientific knowledge or applied skills.

Government: The visible, functioning apparatus of the state.

Legal-rational authority: Legitimate power based on merit and limited by legal rules and regulations.

Managerial revolution: The theoretical takeover of corporations by managers who do not own the firms that employ them, creating a new and more broadly based business elite.

Military-industrial complex: An informal alliance of military leaders and corporate executives based upon shared political and economic interests.

Nation-states: Legally constituted central governments that provide protection for people and regulate trade and commerce over a wide geographic area.

Oligarchy: Rule by a small number of individuals or families.

Politics: The struggle to obtain or maintain power by individuals and groups in a society.

Power elite: A model of power in which top leaders in business, government, and the military are seen as the dominant political force in the United States.

Propaganda: Distorted information or disinformation used by leaders to mold the opinions of followers, subjects, and citizens.

State: A society that has a monopoly over the legitimate use of force in its territory.

Succession: In governments, the turning over of authority to a new leader.

Totalitarian governments: A form of government in which leaders exercise total control over all aspects of the lives of citizens.

Traditional authority: Legitimate power based on ancient custom and tradition.

PRACTICE TESTS

True ▪ False Test

__ 1. Functionalists view the modern state as detrimental to social stability.

__ 2. In the traditional authority form of legitimate power, leadership is inherited.

___ 3. The civil rights leader Martin Luther King Jr. is an example of a charismatic leader.

___ 4. The beginnings of the "state," as Weber defined it, first appeared in advanced horticultural societies.

___ 5. The spread of democracy is closely associated with the Industrial Revolution.

___ 6. Higher levels of education are likely to correlate with individuals' greater interest in holding power in a society.

___ 7. Political independence rests on the ability of a national government to withstand internal as well as external threat.

___ 8. The democratic pluralism model assumes that people have equal opportunity to acquire economic resources and political power.

___ 9. C. Wright Mills includes the military industrial complex in the membership of the power elite in the United States.

___ 10. Advocates of the power elite model are likely to agree with the conclusions of the democratic pluralism model.

Multiple-Choice Test

___ 1. Power becomes a problem in societies when it is tied to differences in:
a. wealth.
b. religion.
c. family structure.
d. socioeconomic form.

___ 2. Weber's definition of "authority" asserts that it is:
a. socioeconomic class.
b. education level.
c. family structure.
d. legitimate power.

___ 3. Nepotism is most likely in societies where authority is:
a. held by a democratically elected legislative body.
b. charismatic.
c. traditional.
d. legal-rational.

___ 4. The three aspects of power and politics that typically vary over the course of sociocultural evolution include all of the following *except:*
a. desirability.
b. sources.
c. justifications.
d. distribution.

__ 5. Rule by the few is termed:
   a. democracy.
   b. oligarchy.
   c. meritocracy.
   d. coup d'état.

__ 6. Michels's iron law of oligarchy states that a tendency toward oligarchy is:
   a. inevitable in all large-scale organizations and, perhaps, technologically advanced societies.
   b. most likely where religious belief is weakest.
   c. strongest when the desire for power is high among rank-and-file members of organizations/masses of people in society.
   d. diminished in industrial and postindustrial societies.

__ 7. According to the two-step flow of communication, which of the following is (are) most influential?
   a. the media
   b. word of mouth
   c. the U.S. president's press secretary
   d. U.S. senators

__ 8. The phrase "the new statelessness" refers to:
   a. the increase in births to unmarried women.
   b. the possibility of world governance by the United Nations.
   c. the growth of the power of multinational corporations.
   d. people's increasing lack of identification with their national citizenship.

__ 9. According to principles of democratic pluralism, interest groups in the United States:
   a. all have some, but none has complete, power.
   b. are too weak to have much impact.
   c. hold too much power over the federal government.
   d. do not represent "the people."

__ 10. The power elite consists of _____ of the population of the United States.
   a. less than 1 percent
   b. about 10 percent
   c. nearly 20 percent
   d. close to 40 percent

Matching Test

Match each concept with its definition, illustration, or explication below.

1.
___ (1) Power
___ (2) Government
___ (3) Autocracy
___ (4) Mixed government
___ (5) Oligarchy

a. Rule by a single person
b. The visible, functioning state apparatus
c. Elements of authoritarian and democratic
d. The struggle to obtain or maintain power
e. Rule by a few

2.
___ (1) Max Weber
___ (2) Mao Zedong
___ (3) Douglas J. Amy
___ (4) Robert Michels
___ (5) C. Wright Mills

a. Political concepts and definitions
b. Power elite model
c. Chinese leader
d. Discussions of oligarchy
e. Advocates proportional representation

3.
___ (1) Functionalists
___ (2) Dictator
___ (3) Traditional authority
___ (4) Charismatic
___ (5) Legal-rational

a. Inherited power
b. Personality based
c. View the state as a social stabilizer
d. Rule driven
e. Authoritarian rule

4.
___ (1) Distribution
___ (2) Horticultural societies
___ (3) Hunting and gathering societies
___ (4) Industrial societies
___ (5) Agricultural societies

a. Autocratic rule
b. Nation-states
c. Power by personal qualities
d. The exercise of power
e. Bureaucracies multiplied

5.
___ (1) Representatives
___ (2) Direct democracy
___ (3) Parliamentary system
___ (4) Referendum
___ (5) Oligarchy

a. Candidates slated by party
b. Popular vote on issues
c. Tendency in trade unions
d. Large, complex societies
e. Small towns and villages

REVIEW QUESTIONS

1. What are the basic distinctions between authoritarian and democratic governments?
2. What are the major differences in the focus of functionalists and conflict theorists on governments, power, and politics?
3. Discuss Weber's classification of types of authority, giving examples of each type.
4. How do power and politics vary, typically, during the course of sociocultural evolution, especially with respect to sources, justifications, and distribution?
5. What conditions appear to be necessary for the existence of effective democratic governments?
6. What is oligarchy, and why does it arise in large-scale organizations in technologically advanced societies? Give examples in government in the United States today.
7. What trends, in education and access to information, for example, work against the trend toward oligarchy?
8. What is "the new statelessness," and why does it arise? Give examples.
9. What are the pros and cons in the argument about the existence of democratic pluralism or a power elite in the United States today?

APPLYING SOCIOLOGY

1. Are your political values similar to or different from those of your parents? How would you explain this?
2. To what extent do you feel your political opinions on specific issues and your voting behavior are influenced by the media, particular candidates, family, or friends? That is, does the two-step flow of communication apply to you?
3. With regard to rights and obligations, what are your beliefs about the role of government and the role of citizens in the United States?
4. How does your voting behavior relate to the discussion of democracy in this chapter?
5. Which of the two models of political power, elitist or pluralist, do you think applies to the way political issues are resolved in your community?
6. How does your perception of community power relate to your political party preference (if you have one) and your political values?

12

Education

Who should be educated, how, to what extent, and for what purpose? The answers to these questions have become increasingly controversial in recent years, especially in the United States. **Education** is the intentional teaching of the knowledge, skills, attitudes, values, and norms considered necessary to function in various widely recognized statuses in a society. It is a part of the broader process of socialization that all people experience as they grow up to be human, as this is defined by their society. But education, unlike other aspects of socialization, is always deliberate and conscious.

In simpler times, the means and goals of education seemed obvious. Now education, like the family, economics, politics, and religion, is viewed as an institution in crisis.

393

FUNCTIONALIST AND CONFLICT PERSPECTIVES

Ultimately, education functions to fulfill certain needs of societies—to pass on the basic knowledge, skills, and values of the culture; to select and train young people for adult occupational roles; and, at the higher levels in industrial societies, to promote research and the creation of new knowledge and skills.

The Functionalist Model

In the field of sociology, functionalists have focused on these goals. They usually assume that the basic need of societies for educated citizens is met by rational means and that merit—ability and hard work—has been the most important factor in determining occupational achievement (Parsons, 1959; Clark, 1962). Given the standards of rationalism and merit, educational policy determines (1) who will be educated; (2) how they will be taught, with an emphasis on memorizing facts or on learning how to learn; (3) how long they will be in school, from elementary through secondary to higher education; and (4) what the educational goal will be, whether narrow occupational training, liberal arts, or both.

Until the mid-1960s, the functionalist assumption that rationalism and merit are the basic standards for education and achievement in industrial societies was widely accepted (see, for example, Clark, 1962). Occupational statuses are regarded by functionalists as achieved, not ascribed. Students, they argue, are selected, encouraged or discouraged, and classified according to their abilities. These are measured by rationally constructed, objective tests of intelligence, knowledge, and achievement. **Tracking**, according to functionalists, is a rational means for separating and grouping students according to their merit, as measured by these tests. This, functionalists argue, enhances the efficiency of the educational process.

As knowledge accumulates and expands in rapidly changing postindustrial societies, educational institutions grow and adapt to these societies' changing needs. All people must be educated for longer periods of time, and, particularly at higher levels, education must promote flexibility, creativity, and critical thought (McLaren and Lankshear, 1992; Macedo, 1993). Beyond the memorization of discrete facts, such as multiplication tables, spelling, punctuation, and rules of grammar, the emphasis on understanding and on general principles of learning increases (Perkins, 1992; McLaren and Lankshear, 1992; Hurn, 1993). Students with this grounding are better able to cope with the possibility of intellectual retooling in later life, as their specific skills and knowledge become outdated.

According to functionalist theorists, opportunity is open and equal in expert societies, because these societies need all the talent they can get.

And talent, discipline, and hard work rather than power, contacts, birth, and ancestry determine who succeeds, how, and to what extent.

Functionalists also stress another vital need that education fulfills in industrial societies. Education promotes agreement or consensus about such values as cooperation, tolerance, egalitarianism, democracy, and patriotism. They contend that education humanizes citizens, diminishes ethnocentrism, and moderates the unbounded greed and authoritarianism displayed by rulers and employers in agricultural societies.

Writing in the early years of the twentieth century, Émile Durkheim (1956 [1922]) pointed to the public schools as crucial agencies for restoring a moral order that was being destroyed by industrialization and urbanization. He noted that education had liberated the masses of humans in agricultural societies from the narrow prejudices and parochial concerns of family and local communities. It had turned villagers and townspeople into citizens of nation-states. But it had also led to increased anomie and a decline in moral consensus. Durkheim and the functionalist theorists who followed him felt that it was the mission of education to restore this consensus.

Durkheim's goal seems more elusive than ever in contemporary, ethnically heterogeneous societies. But in the United States, compulsory, universal education was able, at least in the past, to turn millions of heterogeneous immigrants into more or less homogeneous citizens. Public elementary schools and comprehensive high schools, which offered both vocational training and college preparation courses, drilled grammatical English, U.S. history, the American dream, and the American way into all students. Acculturation was an important latent function of education. Mass education continues to have this effect in the United States, despite increases in minority ethnic pride among more recent, non-European immigrants and the new standard of multiculturalism (Portes, 1993).

As the economy has shifted from manufacturing, based on blue-collar jobs and working with things, toward service, based on white-collar jobs and working with people, school curricula, particularly in middle-class neighborhoods, have changed to meet these newer societal needs. Increasingly, schools have emphasized "life adjustment" and "personal growth"— qualities not required in the spinning mills or on the assembly line. These qualities, along with the general skills necessary for intellectual retooling, become functional in constantly changing and increasingly complex social situations.

The Conflict Model

In the United States, the continuing problems of poverty and unemployment, extreme economic inequality, racial/ethnic conflict, and revelations about deceit and corruption in high places have encouraged social scientists

Focus on Social Issues

SEPARATE AND UNEQUAL

[The United States is the only society in which public funding of primary and secondary education does not come entirely from national governments. Local community control and financing of education has led to wide discrepancies in per-pupil expenditures on education, especially between more affluent suburbs and impoverished ethnically segregated communities. One particularly impoverished community is East St. Louis, which is 98 percent African American. Since the following passage was written, the condition of East St. Louis schools has led to a takeover of the city school district by the state of Illinois.]

Fiscal shortages have forced the layoff of 1,170 of the city's 1,400 employees in the last 12 years. The city, which is often unable to buy heating fuel or toilet paper for the city hall, recently announced that it might have to cashier all but 10 percent of its remaining workforce of 230.... Last year the city lost its city hall in a court judgement to a creditor. East St. Louis is mortgaged into the next century but has the highest property-tax rate in the state....

A teacher at an elementary school in East St. Louis has only one full-color workbook for her class. She photocopies workbook pages for her children, but the copies can't be made in color and the lessons call for color recognition by the children.

A history teacher at the Martin Luther King School has 110 students in four classes—but only 26 books. Some of the books are missing the first hundred pages. ... As things stand, the city spends approximately half as much each year on every pupil as the state's top-spending districts.

–Jonathan Kozol, 1991, *Savage Inequalities,* New York: Crown, pp. 8, 37, 38

What Do You Think?

1. How might a functionalist explain the situation described in the above quote? A conflict theorist? A social Darwinist?

2. Describe recent changes in school integration policies. What are some possible reasons for this change?

3. How can we explain the fact that students in the United States usually score lower on tests of academic achievement, compared to other industrial and postindustrial societies?

and others to take a more disenchanted view of society and all its institutions, including education. In recent years, the more skeptical insights and research conclusions of conflict theorists have corrected some of the more idealistic assumptions of functionalist theory.

Conflict theorists have rewritten the history of education, documenting the role of schools in promoting the needs of the wealthier social classes rather than the needs of the society as a whole. They have focused on education as it tends to reinforce and perpetuate class differences and inequality (Bowles and Gintis, 1976; Meyer, 1977; Collins, 1979; Kozol, 1991). Studies of educational policies in other industrial societies indicate that the dominant classes, by and large, succeed in passing on their privileged status to their children. Workers' and teachers' organizations have attempted to democratize educational opportunities and diminish social class differences in educational achievement, but these differences remain (Bidwell and Friedkin, 1988).

According to conflict theorists, schools have operated to convince students, parents, and the public that educators employ rational techniques for sorting, sifting, and separating the most talented students from the less talented and untalented. But the evidence indicates that class origin and ascribed characteristics generally have been and continue to be more important than merit and indicators of merit, such as test scores and grades, in determining the amount of education, adult jobs, and adult incomes of various segments of the population (Bidwell and Friedkin, 1988; Hurn, 1993).

Conflict theorists argue that while those who are at or near the top occupationally do not usually lack talent and drive, social class factors play a major role in opportunities for achievement. In the United States, middle-class high school students are more likely to be placed in a college preparatory track than students from lower social strata who have similar ability, as measured by test scores and grades (Alexander, Cook, and McDill, 1978; Gamoran and Mare, 1989; Gamoran, 1992). Students with average measured abilities from higher-status families are also more likely to go to college than students with high abilities from poorer families.

Middle- and upper-class students are more likely to enter college, and they are more likely to graduate from college (U.S. Department of Commerce, 1993). Upper-class children are sent to elite private schools because this is a traditional feature of upper-class socialization. Middle-class children who have poor grades and low test scores are also sent to elite private schools, when at all possible, to avoid downward mobility (Lewis and Wanner, 1979). Sanctions are gentler and teacher recommendations are kinder in elite, secular, private schools.

In the United States, grade point averages and achievement test scores, regardless of the level or kind of schooling, are not highly correlated with future occupational achievement and income level (Rosenbaum and Kariya, 1991). In other societies, however, high scores on college entrance tests and graduation from an elite university are essential for high-level occupational achievement (Psacharopoulos and Velez, 1993). Academic achievement and economic success are highly correlated. But in all societies that have been studied, social class, along with racial/ethnic origin and gender, are better predictors of social mobility and economic destiny than academic performance (Hauser and Sewell, 1986; Bidwell and Friedkin, 1988; Garnier, Hage, and Fuller, 1989; Benovat et al., 1991) (see Table 12.1).

TABLE 12.1

Theoretical Perspectives on Education

	Functionalist Model	*Conflict Model*
Goals	Transmission of culture, knowledge, skills, norms, values necessary to maintain the society.	Maintain the power, privileges of dominant groups.
Means	Rational selection and training of qualified people on the basis of merit.	Class-differentiated education, transmission of ideology of the dominant groups.
Consequences	Adult occupation and income achieved primarily on the basis of ability and drive.	Adult occupation and income achieved primarily on the basis of inheritance and ascribed characteristics (ancestry, gender, racial/ethnic origin).

The Latent Functions of Education

Functionalists have focused on certain latent functions of schools. These are functions that were perhaps not originally intended, recognized, or acknowledged by those who controlled the expansion and content of schooling in industrializing societies. Even now, some latent functions remain unacknowledged in industrial societies. We have already mentioned the role of schools in the acculturation of immigrants to the dominant values of the new societies they enter. Schools have also served an important function as substitute caretakers for children, especially in later stages of industrialization, as extended families have dispersed and as mothers are increasingly employed outside the home.

In societies in which families become less effective in dictating the marital choices of their children, high schools and colleges have enabled eligible marital partners to meet. This is a latent function particularly of the more elite fraternity and sorority organizations on college campuses in the United States. Most of these organizations are ethnically exclusive and class ranked, although somewhat less so than in the past. The wealthier fraternities and sororities are supported and controlled by alumni who are mainly interested in seeing that their children and other children of the same social class and ethnic origins will meet, become friendly with, and marry people from the same or very similar social backgrounds. Parents in industrial and postindustrial societies continue to try to influence their children's marital choices in whatever way they can.

Schools also serve the latent function of easing the process of separation from parents. Schools reinforce the establishment of psychological independence from parents and provide a source of peer support of this goal, unsettling as this may be at times for parents. Schools also provide a setting for learning the social skills and cooperative values necessary to function in team work settings in adult occupational roles. All of these functions are necessary for psychological maturity and employment in industrial and postindustrial societies.

The Hidden Curriculum   Conflict theorists are more likely to emphasize other, less benign latent functions of schools. Specifically, they point to the generally unrecognized role of education in teaching different values, work habits, and expectations to students from different social class backgrounds. This has been labeled the **hidden curriculum** (Jackson, 1968). The hidden curriculum is functional, because students from different social origins have different occupational futures. But it is a latent function of education—largely unrecognized, if not unintended.

In the beginning stages of industrialization, universal compulsory education spread because the children of farmers had to be taught to live by the clock rather than the seasons, sunrises, and sunsets (Bowles and Gintis, 1976). Reading, writing, and arithmetic were not, for the most part, needed to operate the simple machinery of the time. Instead, mass education was necessary to teach future factory workers punctuality, obedience, and dependability.

In modern times, schools function to keep the more numerous young people out of the labor market in economies that cannot use their work. Conflict theorists also contend that schools serve the latent function of reinforcing and perpetuating economic inequality through testing, tracking, and counseling practices that discourage minorities and the poor. Such practices effectively blame students, rather than curriculums or policies, for academic failure (Hurn, 1993).

Schools in all geographic areas of the United States attempt, more or less successfully, to teach the values of patriotism, democracy, and egalitarianism. But in poorer school districts, in the vocational tracks in comprehensive high schools, and in community colleges, teachers' colleges, and commuter universities, greater stress is placed on punctuality, discipline, good work habits, respect for authority, and obedience to authority—again, with varying degrees of success (Bowles and Gintis, 1976; Hurn, 1993). These qualities are necessary and functional for workers, and for their employers, at the lower levels of the occupational hierarchy. But neither teachers nor students are consciously aware of this latent function of schools that serve lower-income students.

In contrast, schools that serve students from the middle and upper classes are more likely to stress flexibility, creativity, and resourcefulness. In the late 1960s and 1970s, innovations such as child-centered, unstructured **open classrooms,** and schools were introduced with great enthusiasm in the United States (Kohl, 1969; Silberman, 1969; Graubard, 1972; Barth, 1972; Miller, Kohn, and Schooler, 1986). Usually located in well-to-do suburban communities, these school settings emphasized less restriction on movement; desks and chairs were not nailed down, for example. Teachers were less authoritarian and rigid in the way they used equipment, in assignments, and in the pace and grading of academic performance. They encouraged student interaction on team projects and offered a greater choice of alternative learning activities.

Independence, self-reliance, innovation, and the ability to think critically are qualities that are functional in the higher-level professional and business occupations that these students were and continue to be more likely to enter (Miller, Kohn, and Schooler, 1986). Again, this is a latent function of this kind of educational setting that is not usually recognized by administrators and educators.

Since the 1980s, in response to widespread concern by educators, social critics, and the public about declining academic performance and test scores, teaching has shifted back to more traditional and structured teaching techniques (Armbruster, 1977; Ravitch, 1983). Nevertheless, overall trends in the United States have been in the directions of (1) less authoritarianism, (2) more innovative teaching, (3) more relevant curricula, (4) less tracking and ability grouping, and (5) more student choice in what they will learn and how they will learn it (Hurn, 1993). These trends are more functional in a multicultural society, where rules and regulations are constantly changing and resourcefulness and self-reliance are increasingly important for all members of society, regardless of class, ethnic origin, gender, or age.

Although schools teach many necessary skills, the specialized skills of countless occupations are acquired in on-the-job worker and executive training programs rather than in schools. These programs are usually more up to date than high school, trade school, and college undergraduate business courses. Much of what is taught in colleges has little relevance to specific adult occupational roles and the economy. To be able to quote Shakespeare or to argue philosophical questions has little practical value. Nevertheless, liberal arts undergraduate degrees are preferred by many employers in the United States. A return to an increased emphasis on a liberal arts core curriculum in 4-year undergraduate colleges in the United States is a reflection of this fact.

Critical Thinking   In the past, encouraging critical thinking has not been regarded as a legitimate function of schooling at the elementary and secondary levels. Instead, it has been a latent function of education at the precollege level to reinforce such traditional cultural beliefs as equal opportunity, free enterprise, and democratic pluralism—especially through courses in U.S. history, government, and economics.

Regardless of the content of these courses, however, the cultural ideology has not been successfully internalized by adults in the United States, three-quarters of whom end their formal education after high school. On repeated public opinion polls over the years, a large majority of the public has agreed with the statement that the rich get richer while the poor get poorer (*Gallup Poll Monthly,* No. 343, April 1994). Most are dissatisfied with the behavior of top business and political leaders. And most feel powerless to affect government policy. In response to this prevalent trend in public thinking, high schools have increasingly since the 1960s been offering interpretations of U.S. history and government that focus on the real rather than the ideal (FitzGerald, 1979).

At the college level, by contrast, teaching critical thinking has been a manifest rather than a latent function. Since the 1960s, studies of the changes in college students during their 4 years of undergraduate work indicate that they tend to become less rigid and authoritarian, less prejudiced, less conventional, and more open to new experiences and ideas (Trent and Medzger, 1968). The effects of higher education, furthermore, are permanent. College graduates at every age level, including those over 65 and long out of school, generally have greater knowledge—about national and foreign affairs, about history, literature, and the latest scientific discoveries, and about people, places, and events—than those who have less education (Hyman, Wright, and Reed, 1975). While advances in critical thinking skills are especially pronounced among college graduates, education at all levels has a lasting and enduring effect on values and on awareness of self and society.

As mentioned in chapter 5, in industrializing societies, level of education achieved is the single most important factor affecting the adoption of modern, urban values by individuals, regardless of whether they live in rural or urban areas. Sociologists Alex Inkeles and David Smith (1974) found that educated males in the six industrializing societies they surveyed were more open to new ideas, less bound by custom and tradition, less authoritarian, and better able to identify and empathize with people outside their local communities than were uneducated males.

Schools, Social Stability, and Social Change

The functionalist and conflict perspectives offer complementary and equally valuable interpretations of certain changes in schools and schooling, especially in Western industrial societies during the past 100 years. Proponents of both theoretical models, however, have tended to assume that schools play a greater role in promoting social stability or social change than the evidence indicates. Schools cannot transmit a moral unity that does not exist in a society. There are few values and norms that are universal and permanent in rapidly changing, complex industrial societies.

Schools did not create and cannot solve the problem of social inequality in human societies. Nonetheless, the ongoing controversy in the United States between functionalist and conflict theorists persists. Functionalists are more likely to argue for reforms in schools that would avoid additional expenditures of tax funds. They argue for changes in the attitudes, values, and expectations of communities, families, and students. Together with the establishment of higher standards (more academic course requirements) and more accountability in the schools, these changes are seen as the solution to inequality in educational results (Coleman and Hoffer, 1987). Conflict theorists are more likely to argue for a reordering of taxing and spending priorities at the national level to break the cycle of inherited disadvantage, especially among low-income students (Kozol, 1991; Jencks, 1992; Hurn, 1993).

The evidence indicates that *both* approaches will be necessary to resolve persisting problems of educational inequality in the United States. Partially in response to charges that the Scholastic Aptitude Test (SAT) was racially and culturally biased, the Educational Testing Service renamed it the Scholastic Assessment Test in 1993. In fact, scores on the SAT by women and minority students are highly correlated with the number of academic courses—courses in English, social sciences, history, foreign languages, natural sciences, and mathematics—these students have taken in high school (De Witt, 1993). Mexican American and African American students who report taking the fewest academic courses are among the lowest scorers. On the other hand, according to accumulating evidence, increased expenditures on compensatory education (such as Head Start) for poor, minority students have saved taxpayers millions of dollars (Zigler and Styfco, 1993). Early-childhood-intervention programs are among the least costly means of redressing inequalities.

EDUCATION AND SOCIOCULTURAL EVOLUTION

Historically, education has varied in the amount and kind of information that is taught, the degree of formal organization of schooling, specialization in the information that is taught, and the identity of students and teachers. These variations, in turn, have paralleled the accumulation of scientific knowledge and adaptive technical skills during the course of sociocultural evolution.

Education in Nonliterate Societies

In nonliterate societies, the family and the entire band or tribe taught and trained the young. Teaching consisted almost entirely of **informal education** (Spindler, 1963; Lenski, Lenski, and Nolan, 1991). There were no permanent, separate, and distinct statuses of teacher or student. Children learned by doing and playing and by directly observing, imitating, and helping adults. Adult activities such as hunting, gathering, planting, homemaking, childrearing, worshipping, and playing were clearly visible to all members of the society, including the children.

The only distinctly marked-off aspect of education occurred during the period when young people passed from childhood to adulthood. Initiation rites, or what anthropologists call rites of passage, took place at this time (van Gennep, 1960). For the young, this coincided with puberty. Puberty is a physiological developmental stage characterized by the onset of menstruation in females and the capacity to ejaculate in males. The secondary sex characteristics of breast development in females, voice changes in males, and body hair changes in both sexes also develop at this time. In nonliterate societies, the role of the student in initiation rites was temporary and was based on age and gender. The role of teacher was also temporary and part time. It was limited to conducting specific ceremonial rituals and teaching secret folklore, usually to males.

There was little role conflict, confusion, or disagreement about the values, attitudes, and norms that were taught informally to children in nonliterate societies. The emphasis was on encouraging self-reliance and independence rather than obedience and unthinking conformity (Ellis, Lee, and Peterson, 1978; Ellis and Peterson, 1992). Societies were not economically stratified, and children did not need training in obedience, since they were not going to grow up to obey authoritarian parents, rulers, or employers.

Social mobility was unknown. Children performed the same occupational roles as their parents did. Social change was also practically unknown. Skills did not become outdated, and there were fewer skills to learn than in more complex societies. Families and the community, therefore, were quite capable of teaching children all of the skills they would need to function successfully as adults. Almost all children of the same sex were educated equally. There were few differences in the amount and kind of training given to the young (Spindler, 1963).

Education in Agricultural Societies

In the earliest agricultural societies, the family and community continued to be the primary sources of informal education for the masses of the population. But **formal education** evolved for the few, with candidates for the priesthood and a few other members of the aristocracy as full-time students and male priests as full-time teachers. Instruction emphasized moral training and the cultivation of learning for the sake of learning, as well as literacy and other practical skills. In urban centers, children were often apprenticed outside the family for instruction in trades and crafts. In rural areas, priests sometimes selected a few promising peasant children for instruction in simple literacy, religious faith, and obedience to higher authorities, both religious and secular.

Education in Industrial Societies

The Industrial Revolution in the West was accompanied by a gradual but vast expansion in schools, teachers, and students—a trend that has accelerated tremendously during the past 100 years (Garnier, Hage, and Fuller, 1989; Hurn, 1993). Industrialization and urbanization uprooted farmers' children, destroyed many existing occupations, and created many new occupations. Families and village and tribal communities could no longer teach their children the many new and different skills required in an industrial economy. Farmers and blacksmiths could not teach their sons and daughters to be factory workers or clerks.

Basic literacy—reading, writing, and arithmetic—became essential for all citizens, even in the least-skilled occupations. Secular schools grew in number, as did the number of secular teachers. Female teachers gradually replaced males, mainly at the lower levels of education. Free and compulsory education became universal for children of all social origins in industrializing as well as industrial societies (Benovat et al., 1991).

The expansion of universal, compulsory public education in the West (and, eventually, to currently industrializing societies) has had enormous consequences for the experience of growing up in human societies. More children are segregated from their families for increasingly long periods of time to learn more demanding and specialized knowledge and skills. Adolescence, the period between puberty and the assumption of full-time adult occupational roles, did not exist as a stage in life or even as a word in the language of agricultural societies. Most children in these societies went directly into adult work roles at or before puberty, and sometimes long before.

In industrial societies, children are no longer able to directly observe most adult occupational roles, nor does much of the training that children receive relate directly to the performance of these roles. Youth subcultures develop that have territorial bases—at schools, playgrounds, and campuses—and distinctive language and dress patterns. The marginal status of adolescents as neither children nor adults renders them prone to collective behavior, vulnerable to fashions and fads and a tendency to join social movements. Marginal people who are in transit from one status to another (or who are members of low-income minorities) are less locked into dominant conventions and customs. The peer group becomes a very powerful source of taste, values, and norms in adolescent (and minority-group) subcultures.

Adult occupational status cannot be absolutely guaranteed by the family, except at the very top and very bottom of the social class structure—at the extremes of the very poor and the very rich. At the middle levels, the family does what it can, and it does a great deal. But many of the sons of

TABLE 12.2

Education and Sociocultural Evolution

	Nonliterate Societies	*Agricultural Societies*	*Industrial Societies*
Organization	Informal	Formal	Formal
Content	General	Specialized	Highly specialized
Teachers	Family, community	Priests, upper-class males	Middle-class males and females
Students	All members of the society	Some members of the aristocracy	All members of the society

upper-middle-class businesspeople and professionals in the United States have been downwardly mobile (usually to the lower middle class) in recent years (DiPrete and Grusky, 1991). Competition for good jobs and desirable marital partners and the question "What will I be when I grow up?" did not exist for most young people in agricultural societies. They became what their parents were.

EDUCATION IN CROSS-NATIONAL PERSPECTIVE

Compared to educational systems in other contemporary societies—industrializing, industrial, and postindustrial—that of the United States generally is more open at all levels. Tracking is declining in practice and usually does not begin until the later grades in comprehensive middle or high schools. **Ability grouping**—separating students in the same classroom according to ability—is now out of fashion in most elementary schools. The latest recommendations from the Department of Education emphasize raising academic requirements and standards for all students, regardless of ability (U.S. Department of Education, 1993b). This policy is based on research indicating that tracking tends to create rigid caste systems in many schools. Also, low-achieving students are less likely to drop out if they are placed in mixed-ability classes.

In the United States, elementary and junior high or middle schools have the same basic curriculum, and all schools contain students with the entire range of abilities. Japan has similar policies with respect to school structuring at elementary and junior high levels, but academic standards are far more demanding, and students work much harder than in the United States (Vogel, 1980; Rosenbaum and Kariya, 1991).

Compared to other industrial societies, with the exception of Japan, the United States has a higher level of participation in higher education; 58 percent of all 1992 high school graduates enrolled in some form of higher education, including trade schools, as of 1993 (U.S. Department of Commerce, 1993). Most students in European societies complete their high school education at age 16 (Hurn, 1993). In the United States, students who leave high school at age 16 (with a few exceptions) are defined as school dropouts and are less well prepared academically than their European counterparts. Colleges in the United States are not free, but students are freer to choose their colleges. They are freer to transfer from one college to another. And they are freer to leave and return to college at any time.

European schools are more likely to separate students with different abilities, as judged by teachers, at an early age, although these practices are changing in some countries, including the United Kingdom, France, and the Netherlands (Garnier, Hage, and Fuller, 1989; Benovat et al., 1991; Kreft, 1993; Dronkers, 1993). Students usually attend secondary schools with highly specialized curricula emphasizing either vocational or academic subjects, but not both. This is one reason why high school students in the United States do not fare well compared to students in other industrial societies on cross-national achievement tests in math or science (U.S. Department of Education, 1993b). They are competing against students in European societies who have specialized and concentrated on math and science longer and more intensively (Hurn, 1993). In the United States, students taking the tests come from a much broader range in social class origins, which also tends to lower average scores.

Since university admission is much more selective in Europe, students who want to attend universities work harder. Their education is far more focused, demanding, and structured. Students do not take such elective courses as driver education or creative writing. European and Asian students must prepare for national exams given to students at age 16 or 18. Results determine whether or not they will be among the select few who attend elite universities.

Students in the United States have much more flexibility about college entrance (unless they are aiming for Harvard, Princeton, or Yale) and tend to be more relaxed about homework and college preparation. And the link between the prestige of the college or university attended and future occupational achievement is much weaker in the United States.

Compared with students in other industrial societies, students in the United States test relatively poorly on national as well as international tests. They have a less rigorous curriculum, read fewer demanding books, watch more television, do far less homework, and enter the workforce or postsecondary school less well prepared (U.S. Department of Education, 1993b).

Given more choices in the courses they take, low-income students are more likely to choose academically less demanding courses, even though this has negative effects on their test scores (Lee, 1993). Furthermore, there has long been a streak of anti-intellectualism in the culture of the United States. In the past, intellectuals, especially from elite universities in the Northeast, were called "eggheads." Currently, in many comprehensive public high schools in the United States, high-achieving students are ridiculed as "nerds" and "dweebs" (Richardson, 1993).

As a culture, the United States has tended to value brawn and beauty more than brains. Many high-achieving students do not want to be identified as very smart, just as women in elite colleges, before the women's movement, sometimes "played dumb" in order to be popular with the opposite sex (Komarovsky, 1985, 1988).

Textbooks have declined in difficulty by two grade levels over the past 20 years (Coleman and Hoffer, 1987; U.S. Department of Education, 1993b). Few if any texts are aimed at above-average students. The result is a shortage of high-achieving graduates in science and mathematics. This is currently less of a problem, however, because of severe cutbacks in the hiring of Ph.D.'s by research firms and universities in the United States.

Nevertheless, there is a positive side to this comparative picture. In the United States today, more people remain in school longer, or return to school as older adults, than in any other industrial society. Concepts in the language such as "underachiever" and "late bloomer" reflect the fact that students in the United States have a greater chance to overcome unfair early track placements or recoup early academic failures than in other industrial societies.

In Japan and Hong Kong, the announcement of university entrance test scores is followed by a wave of suicides by students who fail to qualify. There are few second chances. In other societies, major career changes in adulthood or middle age are almost impossible.

Currently Industrializing Societies

Most industrializing societies have adopted the values and goals of universal education for all children (Benovat et al., 1991). This is widely accepted as essential for citizens in societies that are attempting to industrialize. A major problem in poorer industrializing societies is a lack of adequate funds to promote the goal of universal education, however. Schools are severely overcrowded, understaffed, and undersupplied.

Studies of education in industrializing societies provide some instructive insights into the effects of changing government policies and economic opportunities on the educational achievements of students. In industrializing societies that were formerly colonies, indigenous populations who achieve power have made significant gains in education as a result of preferred treatment by their governments. In Malaysia, for example, only a single generation after independence, Malays have achieved higher educational and occupational status than the Chinese and Indian segments of the population, which previously outranked them (Pong, 1993). Expectations are the crucial variable here. If people believe they have increased opportunities, they will be motivated to train for these opportunities (McCelland, 1961).

Gender Differences

Another example of the relationship between perceived opportunity and educational achievement is the cross-national decline in gender differences in math scores. This has occurred in societies where access to higher education and high-level service sector employment for women is more equal or has increased dramatically (Baker and Jones, 1993). In the United States, girls have consistently scored lower than boys on the math portion of the Scholastic Assessment Test (De Witt, 1993).

The reasons given by most teachers and researchers for these score differences are that (1) girls taking the test are more likely than boys to come from lower-income, less-educated households; (2) girls are socialized to regard themselves as less capable in math and are more likely to avoid taking advanced math courses in high school; (3) in classrooms, boys tend to dominate discussions and are given more time by teachers.

On an eighth-grade mathematics test, however, differences between boys and girls in the United States are *not* significant and in fact have been declining for over a decade (American Association of University Women, 1992). A cross-national comparison of performances on this test by 77,000 boys and girls in 19 countries indicates that girls had almost the same scores as boys in most countries (Baker and Jones, 1993). They had lower scores in countries where they are less likely to go to college and have fewer high-level job opportunities. In societies that were the most egalitarian in these respects (Belgium, Finland, Hungary, and Thailand), girls did slightly better than boys on the math test.

The researchers also found that high expectations and real equality of opportunity increased the amount of encouragement and support girls received from their parents and teachers. This is crucial for high achievement in any area of study, for any category of students, anywhere in the world (Coleman and Hoffer, 1987; U.S. Department of Education, 1993b).

EDUCATION IN THE UNITED STATES

Formal education is the major way to achieve upward social mobility in industrial societies. Since not everyone can achieve this mobility, schools become major battlegrounds for parents who want to pass on their privileged status to their children and for those who do not want to pass on their low status to their children. This conflict is quite serious in the United States, where strong cultural ideals of egalitarianism and democracy contradict the trend toward increasing economic inequality, especially among minority populations.

The Persistence of Social Class Differences

Since World War II, there has been an enormous expansion of higher education in the United States and, to a lesser degree, in many Western European countries. The underlying reason has been a belief that opening up educational opportunities, especially for poor and working-class students, would greatly increase their chances to compete for professional and managerial jobs (Hurn, 1993).

In the United States in the 1960s and 1970s, increases in scholarships, student loans, and other forms of financial aid made it much easier for lower-income students to attend college. More flexible admissions policies and special remedial programs were adopted to enable students with inadequate preparation for college to catch up (Ravitch, 1983). Community colleges experienced the greatest growth, enrolling more than half of all entering freshman college students in the United States (Monk-Turner, 1988). Low-income students, women, African Americans and Latinos are more likely to enroll in community colleges than in 4-year colleges and universities (Monk-Turner, 1990). In the 1980s and early 1990s, however, budget cutbacks and tuition increases have disproportionately affected the chances of working-class and minority students to attend college.

A latent, unintended function of more liberal educational policies has been to promote the opportunities of middle-class students more than those of poor or working-class students (Hurn, 1993). In terms of access to professional and managerial jobs, poor and working-class students have made few, if any, gains. African Americans have fared somewhat better (K. Wilson, 1979). Women from poor and working-class origins have done better than men with the same origins in postsecondary vocational training programs (Lewis, Hearn, and Zilbert, 1993; Boylan, 1993).

There are now more better-paying jobs available for women graduates of community colleges—in social services and in health care professions such as dental hygiene or lab technician, for example. Also, women are less likely to drop out of community colleges and are more likely than men to transfer from community colleges into professional programs in teaching and nursing at 4-year colleges (Monk-Turner, 1990). The masses of young women, as well as men, from lower-income families who have attended college have not, however, moved up to higher-level managerial or professional occupations.

The Rise in Credentialism

Aside from a shortage in managerial and professional jobs, what has happened as college education has expanded is that qualifications for all occupations have expanded. Some increases in knowledge and training are essential. They are a response to developments in science and technology and huge advances in information in postindustrial societies. Others are arbitrary and unnecessary. The increased importance placed on formal qualifications such as degrees and the inflation of degree requirements for specific occupations is called **credentialism** (Collins, 1979; Boylan, 1993).

The gap in high school graduation rates between low-income and middle-class students has been greatly reduced. But the value of a high school diploma as a ticket to higher-status jobs has also declined a great deal. Recent increases in the length of training and in degree requirements for certain occupations, such as an M.A. or Ph.D. in nursing, social work, accounting, and engineering, reflect a desire for greater prestige or higher income. They do not reflect actual increases in knowledge that must be mastered by specific individuals as developments in science and technology continue to bombard the intellect and the senses (Collins, 1979; Boylan, 1993). Increased specialization within a field of study, rather than more years of training and more degrees, is the rational response to the vast expansion in knowledge that is occurring in postindustrial societies.

Especially since the 1970s, when a huge increase in the number of students attending college took place in the United States, college degrees, as well as the dollar, have been devalued by inflation. Increasingly, graduate or professional degrees are required for jobs that could previously have been filled by those with B.A. degrees (Hurn, 1993). Even if poor and working-class students catch up in their rates of college graduation, they will not be ahead in the competition for high-level jobs. Many of these jobs now require graduate or professional degrees, such as M.B.A.'s for managerial jobs in business and master's degrees for elementary school teaching.

Another factor that promotes credentialism is the contraction of middle-management jobs in service industries. Employers are inundated with job applications for every opening that exists. They have tended to cope with this situation by raising the requirements for the positions offered. Many of these requirements are irrelevant to job performance, such as Ph.D.'s for nonacademic university staff and M.B.A.'s for midlevel communications managers.

The Persistence of Racial/Ethnic Differences

A major challenge in contemporary U.S. education is to improve the academic skills and performance of low-income minority students. To what extent can educational policies and reforms accomplish this goal? If racial/ethnic differences in academic achievement could be narrowed or eliminated, would there then be less inequality? Or would we simply have a system in which everyone has an equal chance to be unequal? We have better answers to the first question than to the second.

Trends in Educational Policies

Among the educational policies that aim to improve the academic skills of low-income minority students are (1) increasing school expenditures on teachers and equipment, especially in poor neighborhoods, (2) providing more compensatory early education, (3) integrating schools, (4) setting much higher academic standards, and (5) changing teachers' expectations.

Increasing School Expenditures   In 1983, the federal government re-leased a landmark 65-page report on education called *A Nation at Risk*. It marked the beginning of an effort to improve schooling in the United States that continues today. The study was conducted by the National Commission on Excellence in Education, which consisted of public school teachers and principals, school board members, university professors and presidents, a former governor, and professional educational consultants. Basically, the commission found that the effectiveness of education in the United States as measured by achievement tests had deteriorated seriously since the 1950s and 1960s.

Some of the commission's recommendations to improve achievement have been carried out by schools throughout the United States (Griffith, Frase, and Ralph, 1989). The length of the school year has been increased in many states. Compensatory preschool, after-school, and summer-school programs have increased in number. Curriculums have been made more demanding, especially in math and science. Permanent teacher licensing now more often requires a master's degree. And competency testing for experienced as well as new teachers is becoming more widespread. Since 1983, teachers' salaries have increased nationwide by an average of 22 per-cent over the rate of inflation (Celis, 1993a).

The results, however, have been mixed and disappointing. Student scores on the SAT and other standardized tests, while no longer declining, have not shown spectacular improvement (De Witt, 1993). Since 1976, when the Educational Testing Service first began reporting SAT racial/ethnic breakdowns, the median scores of African Americans have increased by 34 points in math and 21 points on the verbal portion. Verbal scores for whites have gone down 1 point and math scores have gone up 7 points since 1976. The gap is closing, but it is still quite large.

In explaining the persistence of black/white differences in achievement, conflict theorists point to spending increases that have benefited suburbs and smaller towns and cities while bypassing the largest cities with the greatest,

FIGURE 12.1

Average Starting Salaries of Public School Teachers Compared with Salaries in Private Industry

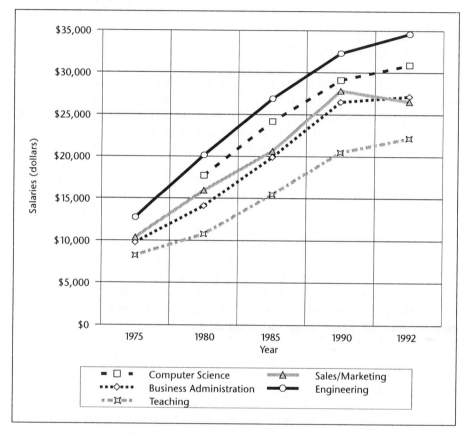

Source: Northwestern University Placement Center, *The Northwestern Lindquist-Endicott Report.*

Teachers' salaries have increased since 1975, but the gap between teachers' salaries and salaries in private industry has also increased since that time.

and still growing, concentrations of low-income minority students (Hurn, 1993). State legislatures share the expense of funding education with local communities. But most state legislatures favor suburbs and smaller communities in their allocations. And the largest cities often have a lower tax base to fund the education of their much needier students. The increases in single-parent families and in poverty rates have compounded the problem, as have middle-class tax revolts and recurring economic recessions.

Functionalists give more weight to parent and student attitudes and values and to student motivation and work habits in explaining the lower achievement scores of low-income minority students (Bidwell and Friedkin, 1988). After the passage of the 1964 Civil Rights Act, Congress commissioned a team of sociologists headed by James S. Coleman (1966) to undertake a survey of the relationship between school resources—including expenditures per pupil, class size, age of buildings, number of books in the library, and laboratory facilities—and student academic achievement. The study was the first large-scale application of social science survey research techniques to education.

The researchers found that although a majority of black students, 84 percent, scored lower than whites on tests of achievement, the differences in the facilities of predominantly black, working-class schools and predominantly white, middle-class schools were not great enough to account for these differences (Coleman, 1966). They concluded that social class factors such as family attitudes and values were more important than school resources in affecting the relative academic performance of black and white students.

Black students, largely from poor families, did not do as well as white students from homes that were working class and middle class. These white students were better prepared and motivated to cope with the demands of formal education. There were more books in their homes, in which parents also read to their children more often, and their attitudes toward school and learning were more positive. The familiar litany of poverty and its current correlates—homelessness, domestic violence, drug addiction, AIDS, gunfire, teenage pregnancy, and parental burnout and neglect—are bound to affect student functioning negatively.

Other researchers reached similar conclusions (Jencks et al., 1972). But although they concluded that school resources generally did not make a difference, the Coleman report and the studies that followed did find that extreme differences in school resources did make a difference in the achievement scores of minority students. In the most impoverished school districts in the largest cities, grossly inadequate, overcrowded, and unsafe facilities clearly do make a difference (Kozol, 1991).

Setting Higher Standards   Later research results have indicated which characteristics of particular schools seem to make the most difference, for students in the same social class. These studies have compared more successful and less successful schools, as measured by achievement test scores of students, in the same poor neighborhoods. They have found that certain factors that are less tangible than lab facilities and library books and have less to do with family background are most important in affecting student performance in specific schools in low-income areas: (1) strong leadership by principals; (2) clearly stated and understood teaching objectives; (3) safe, orderly, and attractive school buildings; and, above all, (4) high expectations and more demanding academic standards for all students (U.S. Department of Education, 1987; Coleman, Coleman, Hoffer, and Kilgore, 1982; Coleman and Hoffer, 1987; Jencks, 1992; Coleman, 1993).

This has led to the resurgence of a 1920s educational movement in the United States known as "outcome-based" education (Judson, 1994). This movement has the support of federal and state governments, leaders in business and industry, and many professional educators. The basic features of outcome-based education are (1) the setting of high academic standards for all students; (2) the elimination of letter grades, ability grouping, and tracking; (3) control over budget and curriculum by teachers and administrators; (4) teacher testing, retraining, and stiffer tenure requirements; (5) expansion of Head Start and other preschool programs; (6) and the use of computer technology for teaching in all schools—in low-income as well as high-income areas.

Instead of letter grades, students receive written reports on their progress. Graduation is not based on earning a specific number of course credits but on tests that prove the student has acquired the skills required for college admission or employment in skilled occupations.

Business leaders support the program because changes in the world economy are driving down wages for some unskilled factory jobs and eliminating many others in the United States. To compete with countries like Japan and Germany, with better-educated workforces, the United States must increase productivity. One way to do this is to increase the skills of workers (Eisler, 1994). The National Alliance of Business, a group of 3,000 enterprises concerned with worker training issues, estimates that U.S. businesses lose $25 to $30 billion a year because of the inadequate reading and math skills of workers (Celis, 1993c). This results in lost productivity, costly errors in products, and unnecessary industrial accidents.

Outcome-based education is opposed by some conservatives because it involves additional spending for more computers and preschool programs, especially in low-income neighborhoods. It is opposed by high-income parents because their children do quite well in existing programs. They fear that cooperative learning, in which all children progress together, without ability grouping or tracking, will hold back their children and "dumb down" curriculums (Judson, 1994). Advocates of outcome-based education claim that high-income parents are more concerned that the programs will increase competition from the working class for elite college placement and professional and managerial jobs. Religious fundamentalists oppose the movement primarily because it will give more authority over budget and curriculum to teachers, administrators, and state commissions of education rather than to local school boards, where the fundamentalists have more influence.

Early Intervention Programs   The pioneering work by social scientists on the importance of early learning experiences for later intellectual development and school achievement inspired early intervention, compensatory educational programs such as Project Head Start (Zigler and Styfco, 1993). These programs were begun in the United States in the mid-1960s. They were designed to compensate low-income minority children between the ages of 3 and 5 for inadequacies in their preparation to fulfill formal school requirements.

The initial results of these programs were disappointing, given the high expectations of those who sponsored them. Most programs offered a summer or a year of training to 4-year-old children. Child development experts characterized these initial efforts as too little, too late (Hunt, 1975). Head Start programs that begin with 3-year-old children and continue for a longer period of time have been more successful in improving the future academic performance of students (Zigler and Styfco, 1993).

Despite both the disillusioning results of original evaluation studies and more conservative attitudes toward domestic spending during the 1980s and early 1990s, government spending on Head Start programs increased. Later researchers found that children who participated in Head Start programs were less likely to repeat grades in later years or need special classes, which cost about four times more per student than regular classes (Consortium for Longitudinal Studies, 1979, 1983). Head Start programs include medical, dental, and family counseling referrals when necessary, as well as preparation for formal schooling. The children's self-image, test scores, physical health, and family relationships improve. Parents become more involved and invested in their children's educational experiences as a result of early intervention (Zigler, 1993).

In one follow-up study of young adults 16 to 21 years old who had participated in preschool programs in the early 1960s, one-third were enrolled in college or were steadily employed in skilled jobs (Deutsch et al., 1979). Less than 10 percent of the young adults in the control group, who had attended the same grade schools but had not participated in preschool training, had similar jobs or were enrolled in higher education programs. Other studies have found that participants in Head Start programs have lower rates of unemployment, teenage pregnancy, and delinquency (Brown, 1978, 1985).

School Integration In an attempt to improve the school achievement of African American students, the integration of schools in the United States was mandated by the Supreme Court in 1964. The Coleman Report (1966) was among the first to conclude that integration improves the academic performance of black students and does not diminish the achievements of white students. African American students from poorer neighborhoods benefit from attending middle-class schools, where standards and teacher expectations are higher. Students develop better study habits, more positive attitudes toward learning and school, and set higher academic goals for themselves. Other research supported the Coleman Report findings (Willie, 1978). A review of over 100 studies on the effects of integration confirmed

TABLE 12.3

Effects of Integration on Achievement of Minority Students

• Gradual increase in test scores after 2 years • Greatest gains in predominantly white schools • More effective if begun in early grades • More gains in the South than in the North	• Greater advances in math than in reading • Greater gains for students from middle-class rather than poor families • Greater likelihood of going to college • Greater likelihood of being employed in professional and managerial positions as adults

the conclusion that the test scores of black students increase, while the scores of white students are unaffected by school integration (Crain and Mahard, 1979).

Other investigators have found that the achievement test scores of African Americans rise more in predominately white schools than in integrated schools in which blacks continue to be a numerical majority. The increase in test scores occurs gradually, after at least 2 years. Age at which integration occurs is critical. African American students benefit most if integration occurs in the first three grades of elementary school. Advances have been greater in math than in reading scores. And in the absence of early compensatory programs, poor students gain less from attending integrated schools than do middle-class black students (K. Wilson, 1979).

The busing of students from one neighborhood to another as a means of desegregating schools has met with strong opposition from white parents whose children are affected, especially in the largest cities. Busing does not confront the basic problem, which is segregated housing (O'Hare and Usdansky, 1992). Furthermore, schools that are integrated have a tendency to become segregated again, as a consequence of "white flight,"—again, especially in the largest cities (F. Wilson, 1985). This flight, to the suburbs or to private religious or secular schools, usually begins when the black population of an integrated school reaches about one-third of the total student body (Giles, 1978). It occurs sooner if the entering African American students are poor and later if they are middle class (Giles, 1978).

Racial composition, however, is not the most important variable affecting the interracial climates of desegregating schools. Relationships between black and white students are less hostile when desegregation is slower and voluntary, reflecting gradual changes in the neighborhood, and when the entering African American students are from homes that are working or middle class rather than poor (see Table 12.3).

After three decades of costly and difficult efforts to integrate schools, the percentage of black and Latino students in segregated schools—those with more than 50 percent minority enrollment—is rising (see Figure 12.2 on page 418). A national survey conducted by the Harvard University School of Education found that two-thirds of all African American students and three-quarters of all Latino students were enrolled in segregated schools in 1991–1992, the highest percentage since 1968 (Celis, 1993b). Asian students were not included in the survey. The researchers point to the following reasons for the regression: (1) cutbacks in federal funding of busing and other integration programs during the 1980s and early 1990s; (2) increased rates of poverty, especially among minorities; (3) the greater concentration of minorities in neighborhoods with high rates of poverty; and (4) higher birth rates among minorities, especially among the Latino population.

In the United States today, school integration has become a lower priority than raising academic standards in the schools that minority students do attend. This is especially true at the college level. Separatism is increasing among all minorities—including women. Applications to women's colleges are soaring, as are applications to colleges run by and for African Americans. About one-third of African American college students attend predominantly black colleges (Harvey and Williams, 1989). Students report that they receive more encouragement and support from African American faculty. And they are more likely to remain in college and to graduate from college. "Separate but equal" as a standard for educating minorities is once again gaining support in the United States. But now its supporters are more likely to be minority students and their leaders rather than dominant groups.

Changing Teachers' Expectations   Research studies of student-teacher interaction in classrooms indicate that teachers in low-income, segregated, large-city schools tend to have low expectations about the achievement potential of their students (Brophy, 1983; Alexander, Entwistle, and Thompson, 1987; Kozol, 1991). Low expectations tend to become self-fulfilling prophecies (Nolen and Haladyna, 1990). Ability grouping and tracking reinforce low expectations for both teachers and students, which is a major reason why these practices are in decline in the United States (Veves, 1989; Weaver, 1990).

The current emphasis on setting high standards for all students stems from overwhelming evidence that if teachers demand less from their students, students will learn less (Hallinen and Sorenson, 1985). Students in Catholic high schools, including minority students, test higher than public school students on achievement tests (Coleman and Hoffer, 1987). Catholic high schools are less likely to use tracking systems. Even when they do track students, academic requirements do not differ much between college preparatory and vocational tracks (Gamoran, 1992). Assignments are more demanding and expectations are higher for all students. This results in the higher performance of all students in these schools.

It is now accepted among many social scientists that the lower test scores of low-income minority students do not reflect average differences

(Continued on page 419)

FIGURE 12.2

Assessing Schools and Diversity

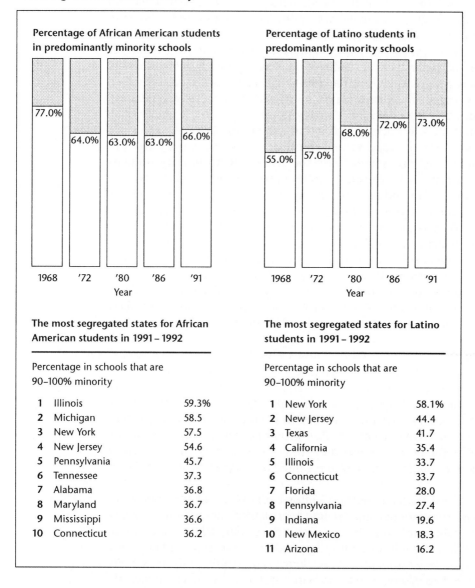

The most segregated states for African American students in 1991–1992

Percentage in schools that are 90–100% minority

1	Illinois	59.3%
2	Michigan	58.5
3	New York	57.5
4	New Jersey	54.6
5	Pennsylvania	45.7
6	Tennessee	37.3
7	Alabama	36.8
8	Maryland	36.7
9	Mississippi	36.6
10	Connecticut	36.2

The most segregated states for Latino students in 1991–1992

Percentage in schools that are 90–100% minority

1	New York	58.1%
2	New Jersey	44.4
3	Texas	41.7
4	California	35.4
5	Illinois	33.7
6	Connecticut	33.7
7	Florida	28.0
8	Pennsylvania	27.4
9	Indiana	19.6
10	New Mexico	18.3
11	Arizona	16.2

Source: Harvard University School of Education; *The New York Times,* December 14, 1993, p. B6. Used by permission.

The percentage of African American and Latino students in predominantly minority schools has increased in recent years; here, predominantly minority refers to schools in which 50–100% of the pupils are African American, Asian, American Indian, and/or Latino.

in native ability among different categories of the population (Elliot, 1988; Weinberg, 1989). Average test scores of large categories of people are too modifiable by environmental influences to reflect hereditary differences. Tests of ability are culture bound. They reflect white middle-class experience and the language of the white middle-class people who construct these tests (Miller-Jones, 1989). Test takers from different social class and racial/ethnic backgrounds may not understand the questions in the way the test writers intended. Also, test scores among ethnic minorities, including intelligence test scores, can be raised significantly by teaching test-taking skills (Frierson, 1989).

Furthermore, there are different kinds of intelligence, not all of which can be measured by standardized intelligence tests (Gardner, 1983). Creativity, for example, is not highly correlated with IQ scores. Standardized achievement test scores do predict academic performance, however, and they do affect the expectations of teachers about the future success or failure of particular students.

The extent to which test scores and student performance can be improved by imposing more demanding requirements is becoming increasingly recognized and applied in the United States. Compensatory efforts beginning in early childhood preschool programs also have long-term and cost-efficient benefits—for students, their families, the community, and the society.

Adult Education

If current trends in the United States continue, by the year 2000 there will be far more women than men, far more older students than traditional college-age students, and far more part-time than full-time students enrolled in college programs (U.S. Department of Commerce, 1993). Adult education for those who left school at one point or another in their lives is a major growth industry in the United States (Levine, 1993). Enrollments are booming, particularly in community colleges. But 4-year colleges and universities are also hurriedly expanding their off-campus programs. They are attempting to compensate for the decline in student applications to 4-year colleges and universities stemming from the decline in the birth rate in the United States since 1964.

Adults return to school for vocational or recreational reasons. They go because they want to catch up with new developments in their fields. They go because they want better jobs or higher salaries. Women who left paid employment to care for young children go back because they need fresh training for reentry into the workforce. Increasingly, older as well as younger men and women take adult education courses because they value education as an absolute good, regardless of practical considerations. Others may be do-it-yourself hobbyists who need technical help with their projects.

TABLE 12.4

Participation in Adult Education: 1990–1991

| | | | PARTICIPANTS IN ADULT EDUCATION | | | | | |
| | Adult popu-lation (1,000) | Number taking adult ed. courses (1,000) | Percent of total | Reason for taking course (percent)[1] | | | | |
Characteristic				Personal/ social	Advance on the job	Train for a new job	Improve basic skills	Complete degree or diploma
Sex:								
Male	82,154	25,923	32	24	67	8	1	13
Female	99,646	31,469	32	35	54	10	1	14
Age:								
17 to 24 years old	21,688	7,125	33	30	38	18	4	29
25 to 34 years old	47,244	17,530	37	25	63	12	1	14
35 to 44 years old	38,565	17,083	44	27	66	8	1	12
45 to 54 years old	25,375	8,107	32	29	70	6	1	7
55 to 64 years old	19,967	4,516	23	35	61	5	1	5
65 years old and over	28,960	3,031	10	73	22	4	–	3
Race/ethnicity:								
White[2]	143,144	47,401	33	30	62	8	1	13
Black[2]	20,141	4,586	23	30	53	14	3	13
Hispanic	13,804	4,032	29	31	48	16	4	12
Other races[2]	4,711	1,371	29	32	51	8	2	17
Educational attainment:								
Up to 8th grade	10,163	735	7	56	16	5	7	14
9th to 11th grade	17,581	2,520	14	30	43	13	3	16
Twelfth grade	67,129	15,077	22	31	55	13	2	9
Vocational school after high school	6,994	2,219	32	28	68	6	–	10
Some college	36,823	14,488	39	33	53	10	1	19
Associate's degree	5,034	2,461	49	22	71	7	1	15
Bachelor's or higher	38,076	19,891	52	28	70	6	–	11
Labor force status:								
Employed	115,620	47,143	41	24	68	9	1	13
Unemployed	9,820	2,099	21	27	29	27	2	25
Not in the labor force	56,361	8,149	14	64	17	10	2	11
Income:								
Under $10,000	27,504	3,843	14	37	34	16	3	14
$10,001 to $15,000	15,465	3,178	21	31	48	16	2	15
$15,001 to $20,000	16,117	3,308	21	32	50	13	2	16
$20,001 to $25,000	16,092	4,063	25	32	56	11	1	14
$25,001 to $30,000	17,973	5,445	30	33	53	14	2	15
$30,001 to $40,000	26,110	9,043	35	30	64	10	1	13
$40,001 to $50,000	21,303	9,313	44	29	64	6	1	12
$50,001 to $75,000	24,540	11,235	46	28	67	6	1	12
More than $75,000	16,695	7,963	48	27	66	6	1	10

– Represents or rounds to zero. [1]Reason for taking at least one course. Includes duplication. [2]Non-Hispanic. [3]For the currently employed.

Source: U.S. National Center for Education Statistics, *Adult Education Profile for 1990-91*; and unpublished data.

Still others may be lonely and looking for friends or marital partners. Or they may be seeking rational techniques for solving interpersonal problems.

Worker Retraining   Programs designed to upgrade the skills of industrial workers are becoming increasingly common in the United States today (Eisler, 1994). A higher level of education is required to communicate in the teams now used in manufacturing. Teamwork involves rotating responsibility for production control, costs, safety, materials, and personnel, as discussed in chapter 10. Higher math and reading skills are required to understand instructions and operate more sophisticated equipment in postindustrial societies. In world economies, greater efficiency and higher productivity are the major advantage that industries in postindustrial societies have in competition with lower-paid workers in industrializing societies.

In the United States, according to the National Association of Manufacturers, about one-half of the smaller companies and nearly three-quarters of the larger ones are sponsoring worker education programs—on company time and at company expense (Eisler, 1994). Much of this training is remedial education in basic math and reading. In the mid-1980s, the Motorola Company started a training program in new production methods, but many trainees could not comprehend or complete the course. Motorola then administered a reading test, which many workers failed. Those employees had to be taught basic reading skills. The company had a similar experience in setting up communication workshops. Since the workers came from 40 different countries, the company began to offer classes in English as a Second Language. In the 6 years between 1987 and 1993, production per employee doubled, the number of product defects fell from 6,000 per million units to 30, and the company saved over $3 billion (Eisler, 1993).

Noncampus College Programs   Off-campus or noncampus college programs leading to undergraduate or graduate degrees are burgeoning all over the United States. Classes are held at churches and community centers, at employees' work sites, or, with the aid of computers, in individual students' homes. They may be subject to fewer regulations by accrediting agencies than are traditional degree programs (Levine, 1993). The majority of the teachers in off-campus programs are part-time instructors who have little or no contact with the departments that sponsor their courses. Such programs usually offer fewer courses and options in fulfilling degree requirements. Admission standards are frequently more flexible, and graduate programs may not require theses or comprehensive examinations. Support services such as office staffs, libraries, career counseling, and job placement tend to be inadequate or absent.

Despite the drawbacks, thousands of people in the United States are pursuing their second chance in noncampus degree programs. They usually have heavy economic and family obligations. Women and minority students are overrepresented in these programs. Students taking graduate degrees may have had work experience that overqualifies them for at least some of the training offered. But they require the degree as a passport to promotion or salary increases. Off-campus degree students usually go at night or on weekends, near their homes or workplaces. Or they work independently at home and do not attend regular classes. They are more disciplined, having already made many of the decisions that distract younger students. And they earn higher grades than younger students.

Education for all, for as long as possible, appears to be the formula for the future in postindustrial societies. The extension of education up and down the life cycle, from infancy through old age, is beginning to parallel the historical expansion of formal education down and throughout the social class structure as societies industrialized. Developments in science and technology provide new things to learn, more time to learn, and better ways to learn more.

Study Guide

REVIEW OBJECTIVES

After studying this chapter, you should be able to:

1. Describe how education differs from the more general process of socialization.
2. Explain how functionalists and conflict theorists have differed in their interpretations of the goals and consequences of education and solutions to educational issues.
3. Describe how education varies in content, structure, and distribution in major types of societies.
4. Discuss current basic differences between education in the United States and in other industrial and industrializing societies.
5. Describe current issues and problems of education in the United States.
6. List special features of adult education in the United States today.

SUMMARY

1. Education is a part of the more general process of socialization. It is the conscious, deliberate, and intentional teaching of the knowledge, skills, attitudes, values, and norms that are considered essential for adult functioning in a society.

2. Functionalist explanations of the means, ends, and consequences of education focus

on schools as transmitters of the knowledge, skills, values, and norms necessary for the maintenance of a society. They view education as a rational process for selecting the most qualified people to fulfill adult occupational roles. They view achievement as primarily a consequence of merit, or ability and drive.

3. Conflict theorists focus on education as a means for maintaining and promoting the power and wealth of wealthier segments of societies. They view education as a means for reinforcing social class differences. They give more weight to social class origins and ascribed characteristics than to merit in explaining adult economic and occupational achievement.

4. In nonliterate societies, education was informal and unspecialized. All members of the family and community taught children approximately the same things. Formal education developed in agricultural societies. Full-time teachers (male priests) taught full-time students (the aristocracy) specialized knowledge in separate facilities (temples, schools, and universities). In industrial societies, learning becomes highly specialized. Members of all classes are educated, but to a different extent and in different ways. Teaching becomes primarily a secular, middle-class profession first for males, and then for females.

5. Compared to other industrial societies, education in the United States is more open and less elitist. Course requirements, especially in academic subjects, are less stringent in public schools. Students do less homework and do not perform as well on cross-national tests. Research on industrializing societies indicates that women and ethnic minorities dramatically improve their performance in school and on tests when they have more educational and occupational opportunities.

6. Controversies over educational policy in the United States center primarily on ways to diminish social class and racial/ethnic differences in academic performance and occupational achievement and how to improve declining literacy skills among almost all segments of the population. Setting high standards and providing a more demanding curriculum improve the school performance of all students, but especially those from low-income backgrounds.

7. Adult educational programs are booming in the United States. They are growing at a much faster rate than traditional programs. Students of all ages and social backgrounds enroll for vocational or recreational reasons. Literacy, basic skills, and computer skills programs are spreading in the workplace and community colleges. Women, working-class, and minority students are disproportionately represented in vocationally oriented programs, as are older people in recreational programs.

GLOSSARY

Ability grouping: Separation of students in the same classroom according to differences in test scores.

Credentialism: The increased importance placed on formal qualifications, such as degrees, and the inflation of degree requirements for specific occupations.

Education: The deliberate, conscious, and intentional teaching of the knowledge, skills, values, and norms of a culture.

Formal education: Teaching done in a school with recognized and distinct full-time statuses such as administrators, teachers, and students.

Hidden curriculum: The unrecognized role of schools in teaching different values, work habits, and expectations to students from different social class backgrounds.

Informal education: General training for adult roles provided by family and community.

Open classrooms: Child-centered educational environments in which there is less regimentation and greater flexibility in learning activities.

Tracking: The placement of students in separate, specialized classes on the basis of scores on tests of ability and achievement or teachers' judgments about students' abilities.

PRACTICE TESTS

True ▪ False Test

__ 1. Functionalists support the practice of tracking in the educational process.

__ 2. According to conflict theorists, the major determinant of a child's opportunities for educational achievement are academic ability and IQ.

__ 3. Socialization of students is an important function—albeit latent—of schools.

__ 4. Critical thinking is a legitimate function of schooling at the elementary and secondary levels.

__ 5. In hunting and gathering societies, education was almost entirely informal.

__ 6. Ability grouping has become more common in the United States as its positive impact on SAT scores and other academic measures has begun to be felt.

__ 7. Most textbooks are aimed at above-average students.

__ 8. While the gap between the SAT scores of blacks and whites in the United States has narrowed, it is still large.

__ 9. School desegregation is most successful when carried out quickly.

__ 10. Adult education is a large and growing "industry" in the United States.

Multiple-Choice Test

__ 1. Unlike other aspects of socialization, education:
   a. occurs naturally.
   b. is withheld from poor people.
   c. is not experienced by all people as they grow up.
   d. occurs deliberately and consciously.

___ 2. As compared to functionalist theory regarding education, the general tenor of conflict theory is:
  a. less well informed.
  b. more negative.
  c. more unrealistic.
  d. less aware of multiculturalism.

___ 3. The hidden curriculum is considered a latent function of education in that:
  a. teaching different values, habits, and expectations to people from different social origins is largely unrecognized, if not unintended.
  b. students from different social origins have different occupational futures.
  c. the purpose of education is to teach children those things that their parents are not capable of.
  d. it serves as a social leveler.

___ 4. Historically, education has varied in all of the following ways *except* in:
  a. the degree of formal organization of schooling.
  b. the kind of information that is taught.
  c. the degree of its role in creating and maintaining social inequality.
  d. specialization in the information that is taught.

___ 5. It is likely that formal education first appeared in:
  a. hunting and gathering societies.
  b. horticultural societies.
  c. agricultural societies.
  d. industrializing societies.

___ 6. Separating students in the same classroom according to ability is known as:
  a. ability grouping.
  b. formal religion.
  c. mainstreaming.
  d. credentialism.

___ 7. Which of the following groups is least likely to attend a community college as opposed to a 4-year university?
  a. African Americans
  b. middle-class young adults
  c. Latinos
  d. women

___ 8. Which of the following jobs is probably least likely to have a high rate of credentialism?
  a. college liberal arts professor
  b. nurse practitioner

    c. high school counselor

    d. Wall Street stockbroker

__ 9. *A Nation at Risk* was a report that raised the alarm about schooling in:

    a. Japan.

    b. Russia.

    c. the United States.

    d. South Africa.

__ 10. Which of the following is most likely to be part of a worker retraining program?

    a. Project Head Start

    b. SAT coaching

    c. early intervention

    d. remedial education in math and reading

Matching Test

Match each concept with its definition, illustration, or explication below.

1.

__ (1) Tracking

__ (2) Functionalist model

__ (3) Durkheim

__ (4) Education

__ (5) Conflict model

a. Standards of rationalism and merit

b. Merit-based grouping

c. Reinforcement of class differences

d. Intentional teaching

e. Schools as crucial agencies

2.

__ (1) Academic achievement

__ (2) Social class

__ (3) Latent function

__ (4) Hidden curriculum

__ (5) Lower-level education tracks

a. Somewhat correlated with economic success

b. Predictor of economic destiny

c. College as marital meeting ground

d. Teaches different values

e. Focus on discipline

3.

__ (1) Critical thinking

__ (2) Schools

__ (3) Alex Inkeles and David Smith

__ (4) Educational Testing Service

__ (5) Intervention programs

a. Education broadens

b. Means of redressing inequalities

c. Scholastic Assessment Test

d. Manifest function in college

e. Limited transmission of moral unity

4.
_ (1) Informal education
_ (2) Rite of passage
_ (3) Formal education for the few
_ (4) Basic literacy critical
_ (5) Universal, compulsory education

a. Marked-off aspect of education
b. Industrial societies
c. Large impact on family
d. Nonliterate societies
e. Agricultural societies

5.
_ (1) Ability grouping
_ (2) Industrial societies
_ (3) Separating by ability
_ (4) Outcome-based education
_ (5) Credentialism

a. Most likely in European schools
b. Highly specialized education
c. Perpetuates social class differences
d. 1920s educational movement
e. Diminishing in the United States

REVIEW QUESTIONS

1. What are the basic differences between functionalist and conflict perspectives on the goals, means, and consequences of education?
2. What are some latent functions of education, especially in educating students from different social classes?
3. How does education vary during the course of sociocultural evolution with respect to organization, content, teachers, and students?
4. How does education in the United States compare with educational systems in other contemporary societies—industrializing, industrial, and postindustrial?
5. How do cross-national studies illuminate gender differences in achievement in the United States?
6. In what ways do social class differences in education persist in the United States in terms of content, performance, and achievement?
7. What is credentialism? Why does it increase, and what are its consequences?
8. What are some of the basic issues in explaining differences in racial/ethnic school achievement? Focus especially on school expenditures, standards, and student and family values.
9. How do early intervention and school integration programs affect minority academic achievement?
10. What are the major trends in adult education in the United States today, especially those that involve worker retraining and off-campus college programs?

APPLYING SOCIOLOGY

1. To what extent and how have the expectations of your parents and teachers affected your academic performance in school and your future occupational goals?

2. Have your scores on standardized tests of ability and achievement been consistent with your grades and admission to college? If not, why not?

3. How has knowledge of your scores on standardized tests affected your feelings about yourself and your abilities?

4. Were you tracked in school, and, if so, were there social class, racial/ethnic, or gender differences among those who were placed in the different tracks in your school or schools? Do you feel your placement was entirely or largely on the basis of merit?

5. To what extent did your teachers emphasize ideal values—egalitarianism, democracy, patriotism? To what extent did your teachers encourage critical, independent thought? How would you relate this to your social class origins, as indicated by the occupations, education, and income of your parent(s) or guardian(s)?

6. How would you rate your schools on a scale from authoritarian and teacher centered to flexible and child centered? Again, how did this relate to your social class origins and to that of other students in your school?

13

Religion

Religion is a uniquely human experience. It requires language and the capacity to think about, worry about, and fear the past, the present, the future, and the unknown. It reflects the human need to cope not only with clear and present concerns but also with ultimate questions and meanings.

SOME BASIC CONCEPTS

Sociologists have studied religion as a cultural, subcultural, or temporary group phenomenon that is tied to social location. **Religion** may be defined as a shared set of beliefs and practices oriented toward the sacred and the supernatural. It unites believers into a moral community (Durkheim, 1951 [1912]; Otto, 1958). The **sacred** is anything material or nonmaterial, human or nonhuman, that is elevated above the ordinary and mundane. It is viewed with awe, reverence, mystery, and, sometimes, fear. Religious beliefs define

429

what is sacred. The **supernatural** is a parallel reality for believers—a reality that is based on faith. It does not require observation by the senses, nor does it require empirical proof that it exists.

Rituals are activities oriented toward the supernatural. Rituals are as varied as the beliefs they represent and the purposes they serve. Rituals may involve scarring, burning, animal sacrifice, immersion, kneeling, bowing, lighting candles, prayer, fasting, or ritual meals such as Holy Communion or the Passover Seder. Rituals may be relatively unstructured, emotional, and spontaneous. Or they may be formal, impersonal, and rigidly prescribed. They may mark a major status transition that requires emotional support and reinforcement from the community, such as birth, puberty, marriage, death—and now even divorce. Some Protestant churches, for example, have initiated rituals for divorced families to mark the transition into their new status. Rituals may express love, gratitude, praise, fear, or guilt. Rituals promote commitment to religious faith. They may be performed in private. But when they are performed with a group, they reinforce feelings of community with others who share the same religious beliefs.

Religious beliefs also prescribe and sanction relations with other human beings. They have been a major source of ethics and social control in human societies. Religious beliefs restrain impulse and reinforce conscience. They define and sanction rights and obligations in human relationships. The moral and ethical aspects of religious beliefs were once considered a major distinction between religion and superstition, which was defined as a belief in magic (Weber, 1963 [1922]; Malinowski, 1948).

Magic is also oriented toward the supernatural and the unknown. But Western scholars have distinguished magic from religion in several ways that are now believed to be more ethnocentric than accurate. Until recently it was believed that magic, as opposed to religion, involved the use of sacred objects intended to coerce supernatural forces or spirits into granting specific, concrete, immediate requests. Examples would include success in achieving a particular goal, recovery from an illness, revenge, or the defeat of enemies.

Magic was not believed to unite believers into a moral community. However, recent research has shown that believers and practitioners of magic often *are* united into moral communities. These groups have the same prohibitions against lying, stealing, incest, and murder that most (other) religions have, for example. Magical religions include Wicca, the revival of witchcraft that has occurred in the United States and the United Kingdom (Starhawk, 1979, 1982). They also include all varieties of African-derived religions that are practiced in the Americas: Santaria in Spanish-speaking areas, especially in the Caribbean and the United States (Canizares, 1992); Voodoo in Haiti, New Orleans, and New York (Brown, 1991); Yoruba in the United States; Candomble in Brazil; and Shango in Trinidad (Curry, 1991; Murphy, 1993).

Social scientists are now aware that both magic and religious ritual may or may not be oriented toward specific goals (Starhawk, 1979, 1982;

Neitz, 1988, 1990; Curry, 1991; Brown, 1991; Canizares, 1992). Prayer, for example, may express thanksgiving or humbly request forgiveness, or it may plead for a specific goal (Weber, 1963 [1922]; Malinowski, 1948). And a Wiccan magical ritual may be performed to honor the seasons, or to give thanks, or to heal a specific woman from the trauma of rape, for example (Starhawk, 1979). It is true that religious rituals are not usually coercive. But the ritual of exorcism, which is still practiced, albeit rarely, in the Roman Catholic Church and in many Protestant churches, can be extremely coercive.

In the past, religion has often operated to legitimate and protect the privileges of dominant groups, especially in those societies that have had **state religions**. These are religions supported by the government and claiming all citizens as members.

RELIGION AND SOCIOCULTURAL EVOLUTION

Religious beliefs and practices are found in all societies. As societies become more complex, major religions, originally associated with specific continents, tend to become global in their influence and membership.

Hunting and Gathering Societies

Religion in hunting and gathering societies was based on a belief in abstract, supernatural forces that intervene for good or evil in daily life, a concept similar to the idea of luck (Swanson, 1960; Lenski, Lenski, and Nolan, 1991). These forces could be anywhere or everywhere—in sticks, stones, plants, animals, people, the wind, or the rain—depending on group definitions. When these forces were endowed with human motives and emotions, they were called **spirits**. The belief that material objects or other natural phenomena possess spirits is known as **animism**.

The only important religious status in hunting and gathering societies was that of the shaman. The shaman used magical techniques to promote fertility, success in the hunt, and other desirable outcomes. Rarely did hunting and gathering societies have a concept of a Supreme Being, Force, or Creator. When they did, this Being was usually viewed as remote, powerless, and unconcerned with day-to-day human affairs.

Horticultural Societies

In horticultural societies, extended families organized into clans were typical. Ancestor worship was more common in these societies than in any other type of society. The family, including both its dead and living members, was dominant, rather than the awesome and all-powerful God or gods of more technologically advanced societies.

Totems—sacred plants, animals, or other objects—represented particular clans in horticultural societies. They were worshiped as symbols of the clan (Swanson, 1960). Ancestors were a very effective source of social control. Unlike living members of the society, ancestors were everywhere. They saw everything, at all times. It was not possible to hide from them or escape their surveillance.

In advanced horticultural societies, the ruling family was sometimes headed by a king who was regarded as divine or thought to possess supernatural powers. In these societies, belief in a Supreme Being became more widespread. Again, this Being was not usually concerned with daily affairs or with human morality. Religious rituals multiplied and became more elaborate. Religious beliefs explained economic inequalities among families. They motivated people to produce more than they could consume and to turn over this surplus to ruling families. Sacrifices and offerings of a portion of the economic surplus to full-time priests in exchange for religious services or blessings also became widespread.

Agricultural and Herding Societies

In agricultural societies (and in herding or pastoral societies), belief in a Supreme Being who has power to intervene in everyday life and is concerned with human morality becomes common. **Theistic religions**, centering on a belief in a powerful God or gods, are prevalent. In *monotheistic* religions, this God is the only and all-powerful God. In *polytheistic* religions, there is usually a single most powerful God who shares authority with other gods possessing narrower spheres of influences—as among the ancient Greeks and Romans. **Theologies**—doctrines that provide meaningful explanations of life and death, human origins and destiny, happiness and suffering, success and failure, and good and evil—become more elaborate than they were in earlier and simpler societies (Berger, 1969).

Ancestor worship declines in agricultural societies, with a few exceptions such as preindustrial China, Japan, and ancient Rome. During the period when Rome was the ruler of most of the lands of the Mediterranean, many religions existed side by side, in addition to the officially sanctioned cult of the emperor. These religions included Judaism; early Christianity; the worship of Mithra, a Persian god; and mystery religions—secret societies that worshiped various foreign gods.

Improved transportation, the spread of trade relations, empire building, and the desire to impose a uniform morality and uniform sanctions on culturally diverse conquered peoples all help to account for the spread of Judaism, Christianity, Islam, and Buddhism (Lenski, Lenski, and Nolan, 1991). **Universal religions**, or world religions, are faiths and communities of believers that transcend geographic boundaries. Older ethnic religions such as Hinduism in India, Confucianism in China, and Shintoism in Japan survived the spread of universal religions. Now, however, they too are transcending national and ethnic boundaries. The International Society for Krishna Consciousness (Hare Krishna), which came to the United States in the 1960s, has adherents in many parts of the world (Jacobs, 1989).

The spread of monotheistic religions, with their active, all-powerful, personal, male God, is closely associated with the development of patriarchy and the subordination of women in Europe and the Middle East (Yorburg, 1974; Schmidt, 1989). This is seen most clearly in the monotheism of herding societies, such as ancient Israel. Herding societies generally were very likely to worship a powerful Supreme Being. In these societies, warfare over lands and livestock was constant. Males were highly valued in their military and economic roles. Women's economic roles were less significant than in horticultural societies; women did not tend the herds. Power differences between women and men were extreme. As a general principle the statuses and roles of women and men in the home and the wider society have always been mirrored in religious beliefs and practices (Neal, 1979; Schmidt, 1989).

The pastoral and agricultural origins of Judaism and Christianity are evident in the religious language of the Bible and the worship services in churches and synagogues. Urban worshipers who have never been on farm hear such phrases as "The Lord is my shepherd," "Thy rod and thy staff shall comfort me," "the Lamb of God," and "separating the wheat and the tares." People in democratic societies all over the world call God "Lord" and "King." Some religious leaders have suggested that this kind of language interferes with people's understanding of the religious message. Recently, translations of the Bible have been introduced to reflect today's usage of English and the urban environment.

In the earliest advanced agricultural societies, church and state, like other institutions, became increasingly separate. Both continued to be upper-class institutions. Kings were thought to rule by the grace of God. **Theocracies**, in which high priests ruled by divine right, were rare, however. The church, wealthy by virtue of large land grants and tax exemptions from the governing class, shared and promoted the interests of this class. Rulers supported the belief in the divine sanctity of social inequality. The common people, however, developed and maintained their own forms of religiousness. In southern France, for example, one such form became so widespread and powerful that the Roman Catholic Church called it the Albigensian Heresy. Armies were sent into the area to force the people to return to the Church. Prisoners were taken back to Rome and tried.

Industrial Societies

As societies began to industrialize in the West, developments in science and technology greatly diminished the sphere of the unknown and the uncontrollable. These advances have seriously undermined the self-evident, absolute truths of Western religions. As scientific knowledge has spread, the world has become increasingly "demystified and disenchanted" (Weber, 1946, p. 139). The realm of the unknown, the mysterious, and the awesome has narrowed considerably—but not entirely disappeared.

In industrial societies, religion cedes some of its authority over social life to other institutions, a process known as **secularization** (Wallis and Bruce, 1992). The secularization model, in which rationalism replaces faith and religion loses influence in industrial societies, was dominant for many years in social scientific thinking. Some sociologists continue to support the idea that secularization is inevitable in industrial societies (Lechner, 1991; Wallis and Bruce, 1992; Wilson, 1992). But others are now challenging this notion (Bruce, 1992). They do not see religion as losing influence in the modern world (Stark and Bainbridge, 1985, 1987; Finke and Stark, 1988, 1989, 1992; Laurence, 1990; Crippen, 1992; Brown, 1992). These sociologists give two reasons for the worldwide resurgence in religious belief: (1) worldwide economic and political crisis and (2) the failure of alternative political and psychological movements to provide their participants with meaning and purpose. The global resurgence of religion is discussed in greater detail later in this chapter.

RELIGION AND SOCIAL STABILITY

Durkheim and other functionalists have long emphasized that religion has served to maintain social stability through the heightening of feelings of community and moral unity among those who share similar beliefs. Religious doctrines have reinforced the most important universal taboos in human societies, those against incest and murder. These doctrines have provided sacred legitimacy to norms that attempt to curb human competitiveness and destructiveness. These have been the obvious, manifest consequences of religious belief, especially for small, homogeneous, slowly changing societies.

The reinforcement of a common moral vision through religion can exist even in a country like the United States, which was founded on the principle of the separation of church and state. In the United States, religious ritual plays a role in major political events, such as conventions and inaugurals. It is important in legal functions, such as judicial procedures of courtroom testimony and the swearing in of jurors and new citizens. Almost all public events, in fact, are sanctified by prayer and an affirmation of the United States as one nation under God.

The use of religious ritual and belief to reinforce patriotism and sanctify important public events has been called the "civil religion" in the United States (Bellah, 1967). The civil religion legitimates political authority, just as state religions did in the past. It sanctifies political ideals, the past history, and the future destiny of the United States. But the civil religion in the United States is not identified with any particular faith or religious doctrine. It is based only on a belief in God.

In recent years, state religions have returned to political power in the Middle East. Islamic law is treated as the law of the land in a number of countries, including Iraq, Iran, and Saudi Arabia. Thieves can be punished by having their hands chopped off in the public square, a penalty spelled out in the Koran. Women must appear in public veiled and are forbidden to drive. All political and social functions stop for prayer. Similarly, in Israel, public buses do not run on the Sabbath.

In most democratic societies, religious affiliation is voluntary. In multicultural societies, the norms and values of a particular religion may be at odds with those of the dominant culture. For example, some Muslims in France, who are mainly North African immigrants, disapprove of educating their daughters, especially at higher levels. Muslim girls who have worn *foulards,* traditional head scarves, have been threatened with expulsion for violating the French school dress code.

In the United States, conflict between the norms of religious groups and the secular culture has led to the proliferation of religious private schools in the United States, especially conservative Christian schools (Peshkin, 1986; Parsons, 1987; Rose, 1988; Wagner, 1990). The rituals of some religious groups violate community norms. In Florida, a religious group had to go to the Supreme Court in *Church of the Lukumi Babalu Aye v. City of Hialeah* to win the right to perform animal sacrifices. In India, although the government has made both the dowry and the caste systems illegal, these religiously grounded traditions persist (Gargan, 1993).

RELIGION AND SOCIAL CHANGE

Religious movements have also been influential in challenging governments and changing societies. Religious political movements have been revolutionary, reform-oriented, conservative, or regressive. In fact, Karl Marx's claim that religious beliefs divert attention from economic suffering and deter revolutionary or radical political action needs updating in an era of global telecommunication and rising expectations. Marx pointed to the "illusory happiness" that religious faith provides. He and other theorists in this tradition have given great weight to the role of religion in promoting fatalism and spiritualism and an orientation toward otherworldly rewards. This role, they have argued, slows social change by dulling feelings of economic deprivation and the desire to fight for greater economic and political equality in this world.

But Marx also believed that Christian "chiliastic dream visions"—the belief in Christ's return to earth to reign during the millennium—could conceivably be translated into radical, secular political action (Marx and Engels,

1955b). The original band of Christians, for example, was inspired by the example of the prophets of the Old Testament to oppose the Roman ruling class. The Social Gospel, a late-nineteenth-century Protestant movement in the United States, supported reform that would strengthen the rights of the poor (Hopkins, 1940; White and Hopkins, 1976). Many clergymen were active in the U.S. civil rights movement.

A recent movement called **liberation theology** combines Marxist economic analysis with Catholic theology to work for radical reform. The movement began in Latin America in the late 1960s and has spread to Asia and Africa. Its goals are liberation from all forms of oppression—social, economic, racial, sexual, environmental, and religious. In each country where the liberation theology movement exists, however, its concerns differ depending on local conditions. Its theology is thus indigenous, or of the people (Levine, 1986, 1992; Ferm, 1986a, 1986b). Liberation theology is oriented toward an "option for the poor" and listening to the "voice of the voiceless" (Gutierrez 1984, pp. 125–160; Ferm, 1986a, pp. 32–34; Ferm, 1986b, pp. 22–63). Liberation theology has also appealed to women in industrializing horticultural societies (Fabella and Oduyoye, 1989) and to some religious feminists in the United States (Welsh, 1985).

Intensive case studies of liberation theology church activities among the poor reveal major role changes among once-isolated, defeated, lost individuals living in the slums, shantytowns, and hamlets of Colombia and Venezuela, for example (Levine, 1992). Self-esteem, confidence, solidarity, and initiative blossom. Studies of the "mountain religion" of Appalachia indicate that even the deeply religious are not fatalistic in modern times. They are very much aware of their problems and are seeking rational, this-worldly means for bettering their economic condition (Batteau, 1983; McCauley, forthcoming 1995).

Liberation theology is not without its critics (Novak, 1986; Nash, 1988; McGovern, 1989). The major criticism directed toward these beliefs is that they oppose private enterprise. Critics claim that liberation theology discourages activities that can make an economy grow. They feel that liberation theology comes too close to advocating the kind of economy that has failed in the former Soviet Union and Eastern Europe. Conservative Christian critics of liberation theology, by contrast, use their own theology to support the market economy and free enterprise in the United States (Opitz, 1981; Nash, 1983, 1988). Established religious organizations in the United States—including Catholic and Jewish groups and the more affluent Protestant denominations—have generally favored liberal economic reform. They have not advocated a radical economic restructuring of the economy or the government of the United States, however. The role of these organizations has been mainly reactive—that of supporters but not initiators of social change.

Prominent and wealthy Christians played an active role in the U.S. abolitionist movement in the early nineteenth century, although some theologians took a proslavery position (Bendroth, 1993). The abolitionists opposed slavery primarily on moral rather than economic grounds. Despite the wranglings of the theologians, the slaves themselves identified with the liberation themes of the Bible. They especially found meaning in the story of Moses leading the Israelites out of Egypt. Many slaves escaped and worked to help others escape via the underground railroad.

The Social Gospel movement was essentially a northern, urban movement that accepted biblical principles as guidelines for personal behavior and social life. The movement supported fair treatment for industrial workers and encouraged churches to engage in social action and to advocate public health measures. Leaders of the Social Gospel movement were also involved with improving the lives of African American citizens in the South (Hopkins, 1940; White and Hopkins, 1976).

Socialism has represented a related movement. Since the Society of Christian Socialists was founded in 1889, there has been a small but vocal minority of Christian Socialists in the United States (White and Hopkins, 1976). In the 1930s, a handful of Protestant ministers, members of the Fellowship of Socialist Christians, actively fought for more radical economic reforms than those achieved by the New Deal under President Franklin Delano Roosevelt. Norman Thomas, the leader of the Socialist Party of America for over 40 years, had been a Presbyterian minister before becoming a political activist (Yorburg, 1969).

Radical activist Protestant ministers have been a small but highly visible minority in reform social movements in the United States. Often they have held administrative or university positions, where they have been less subject than parish clergy to control by a more conservative congregation (Yorburg, 1969; Quinley, 1974). Although attention is usually focused on ordained ministers, it is important to be aware of the Christian laypeople who have been active in promoting Christian Socialist causes (Cort, 1988).

Although the religious history of the American civil rights movement is still being written, the record reveals a clear pattern. Its leadership in the African American community—from Martin Luther King Jr. to Malcolm X to Jesse Jackson—and its rank-and-file activists have primarily been people of faith (Paris, 1985; Branch, 1988; Lincoln and Mamiya, 1990). The idea that political activists are less likely to belong to religious organizations or to report themselves as deeply religious (Marx, 1967; Schuman and Hatchett, 1974) is no longer true. When King was assassinated, he was not involved in the fight against segregation. He was leading the "Poor People's March," which questioned the economic system and sought political solutions to the problem of poverty.

For the most part, the African American religious community has supported liberal economic reforms. It has placed its faith in moral persuasion to achieve equality of opportunity. An interesting development is the growing opposition to the welfare system among African Americans. This opposition is most prominent among African American Muslims, but also to a lesser extent among Christian groups. They argue that welfare creates dependency and that it emasculates the African American male by removing his economic role in the household.

Grassroots conservative and regressive religious political action groups have proliferated in the United States over the last 15 years (Wills, 1990; Watt, 1991). These include Concerned Women for America ("Lobbying from Your Kitchen Table"), the Christian Coalition (founded by Pat Robertson), the Pro-Life Action League, Operation Rescue, and Morality in Media. The presence of these groups in the United States demonstrates that concern for social change does not belong to any one side of the political spectrum.

The recent economic situation has also spurred the growth of religious hate groups in the United States. Groups like Christian Identity, which is incorporated as a church, preach white power and racial separatism. Their writings advocate violence against African Americans, Jews, and nonminorities who sympathize with minorities. These groups are ideologically related to the Skinheads, Neo-Nazis, and the Ku Klux Klan. While there are many pseudoreligious hate groups in the United States, most are small in number. Members are recruited through personal contact, computer bulletin boards, and even through public access television (Aho, 1990).

RELIGION AND SOCIAL CLASS

Historically, in the West, an offense against rulers was an offense against God. Religious movements such as the Crusades had a strong economic component—in that case, the opening of trade routes to the East. More important, they also had strong social class components, such as the need to divert peasant unrest caused by population increases and unemployment. This diversion function was also served by church-supported witch-hunts from the fifteenth to the seventeenth centuries. One psychological objective of witch-hunts was to shift blame for the economic crises of that time away from the dominant class and onto witches and other heretics (Erikson, 1966).

In the past, new religious denominations or sects were not founded or supported by members of the dominant class. In the 1920s, theologian H. Richard Niebuhr (1957 [1929]) did a classic study of Christian religious organizations in the United States. He concluded that sociological factors such as social class, urban or rural residence, racial/ethnic origin, and immigrant status were more important than religious doctrine in dividing major religions in the United States into denominations or sects.

Denominations are large, formal, religious organizations that are not state religions. They are well established, with formally trained clergy and other officials. They do not claim the status of a state religion and may, at times, be in opposition to the state. The United States has been called a "denominational society" because it does not have a state religion, such as the Anglican Church in England, and because of the great number and

THE APPEAL OF FUNDAMENTALIST RELIGIONS

[For someone who has moved away from family, community, and church, joining a fundamentalist church (see p. 444) can provide a much needed anchor. It offers a total way of life, an identity, and close emotional bonds to others.]

Les Newman, very much a middle-class American, has found a home in the church, one that allows him to take a critical view of the environing society. He says that "American society is becoming very self-oriented or very individual-oriented: what's in it for me, how much do I get out of it, am I getting everything I'm entitled to in my life? It is tearing down a lot that is right about the country. People don't look at the repercussions of their individual actions outside of themselves." For this evangelical Baptist, reared in the South, just graduated from a well-known business school, and now working as an executive in the Califor-

nia suburbs, . . . "[i]t is precisely because self-made individuals don't appreciate their need for God that they don't appreciate their need for other people.". . . He experiences both needs in the active life of his church congregation. Its members aren't "the standard go-to-church-Sunday-morning people" who practice "a ritual as opposed to a lifestyle." Church for this believer . . . "isn't just a place, it's a family" that has given him the closest friends he has. Despite leaving home, moving to California, and entering the competitive world of business, he has found a new family-like anchor for his life, a new bond to other people through the shared celebration of a "personal relationship with Jesus Christ."

–Robert N. Bellah et al., *Habits of the Heart*, 1985, Berkeley: University of California Press, pp. 155–56

What Do You Think?

1. What are the factors, including social and geographic mobility, that promoted the appeal of the evangelical Baptist church for Les Newman?

2. What are some of the universal characteristics of fundamentalist religions?

3. List some possible reasons for the current worldwide increase in the appeal of fundamentalist religions.

variety of established religious organizations that it does have (Greeley, 1972). Denominations, as Niebuhr noted, are class ranked, as are sects.

Sects are smaller, initially less formal religious groups characterized by a strict interpretation of theological beliefs, emotionally expressive ritual, adult conversion, lay clergy, and exacting personal ethics (Pope, 1942).

Niebuhr's thesis held up well until recently. He could not have foreseen two changes in the late twentieth century: (1) all social classes, even the upper class, now seek emotional satisfaction from their religious beliefs (Roof, 1993); and (2) mainline denominations have liberalized their politics and theology in the last 30 years. These trends have created changes in the traditional social class structure of American Protestantism. They have also caused changes in the worship styles of many denominational churches. In addition, there have been some recent schisms, or splits, of more conservative congregations from mainline denominations. These have created smaller but equally formal denominations. One such new denomination is the Presbyterian Church of America, which split some 20 years ago from what is now the Presbyterian Church USA. The Episcopal Church has also had some defections.

This conservative/liberal split in American religion cuts across social classes. Sociologist Robert Wuthnow called his 1989 book on this split *The Struggle to Define America's Soul.* Another sociologist, James Davison Hunter, entitled his 1991 book *Culture Wars.* Both authors focus on the same phenomenon. People in the United States are divided over issues such as (1) abortion; (2) the curriculum in the public schools, especially sex education; (3) the role of women in marriage and the church; and (4) pornography. These issues have polarized individual congregations. The same middle-class church, for example, could have some members who are involved in Operation Rescue—picketing abortion clinics—and others who support Planned Parenthood and are members of the Religious Coalition on Abortion Rights. In these activities, each side has members from varied social classes.

Sects, as Niebuhr observed, have in the past attracted members of the lower social strata who were uncomfortable with the practices of the established denominations. Often they were excluded from mainline membership because of their social class, race, or foreign origins. As they experienced social mobility and sects began to attract more middle-class members, the newer sects moderated their religious doctrines in the direction of greater liberalism. They approached the size, formality, and class composition of the large denominations. This, in turn, led to new spin-off sects for worshipers who remained at the bottom socially.

Historically, Christianity was originally a sect of Judaism that recruited its members from among the poor. Protestantism was initially a sectarian movement away from the Roman Catholic Church, with strong support among the peasants and the rising middle classes. In the United States, Christian Scientists and Mormons were once regional Protestant sects; they have now achieved wealth and the status of denominations. Jehovah's Witnesses, Seventh-Day Adventists, and the Assembly of God are also no longer considered sects.

Sectarian groups traditionally absorbed people who were poor, unemployed, drug addicted, mentally ill, or prisoners. They provided their members with identity, direction, and values that were, ultimately, in keeping with the requirements of the outside world. They still serve this function, but they also attract more middle-class members now. For example, sects such as the Black Muslims, now called the Nation of Islam, provided a bridge for nonconforming, isolated, economically marginal people into respectable statuses in the wider society (Lincoln, 1961). For many African Americans it still does. The Nation of Islam and other Muslim groups, however, now also attract members of the middle class.

As we have seen, sects are subdivisions of dominant, traditional religions in a society. **Cults**, in contrast, are defined by some sociologists, and in the popular usage, as small, rigidly authoritarian, and totally controlling religious groups. They are close-knit groups whose beliefs and practices represent a radical break with the dominant, traditional religions. Currently, researchers are more likely to use the term **new religious movements (NRMs)** to refer to cults. New religious movement is preferred because it is a nonjudgmental, catch-all term to describe the religious movements that first came to public notice in the West in the 1960s and 1970s (Lofland, 1966; Beckford, 1985).

Religious denominations and sects in the United States continue to be differentiated on the basis of the social class membership of their members, but less so than in the past (Roof, 1979; Roof and McKinney, 1987). Average differences in family income, education, and occupational prestige among white Protestants, Catholics, and Jews have narrowed considerably since nationwide surveys on this topic were begun in the 1940s, but the basic pattern persists (Gilbert and Kahl, 1993). Episcopalians, the predominant religious affiliation of members of the old upper class in the United States, rank first in measures of income and education. They have the highest percentage of college graduates and the highest median income of any religious category in the United States. Jews, Presbyterians, Lutherans, Methodists, Catholics, Mormons, and Baptists follow, in descending order (Gallup and Castelli, 1989).

In the United States, religious affiliation tends to validate social status. In the past, families and individuals who were upwardly mobile shifted their membership to more prestigious denominations where they could worship with their new status equals (Newport, 1979). Now it is not uncommon for their denominations to move up with them, especially in the South and among evangelical Christians (Ammerman, 1990). It is still true that those who are downwardly mobile or in personal crisis may seek out a new denomination, sect, or congregation. They may either undergo a religious conversion or make a deeper commitment to their own religious tradition (Heirich, 1978).

New conservative evangelical churches, however, like the Vineyard Fellowship and the Willow Creek Church, and traditionally upscale congregations like First Baptist in Dallas, now attract upwardly mobile converts or upwardly mobile members of lower-status evangelical congregations (Warner, 1988, 1990, 1991; Ammerman, 1990; Davidman, 1991; Kaufman, 1991).

The traditional stratification of denominations is starting to blur for two reasons: (1) many sectarian groups such as Seventh-Day Adventists and

Southern Baptists have changed with the upward mobility of their members, and (2) there has been much more recruitment of high-income members to the more rigorous religious groups that traditionally sought only low-income members. But average socioeconomic differences among members of various denominations in the United States persist (Gallup and Castelli, 1989).

Perhaps the most important factor to remember in attempting to understand the relationship between religion and social class in the United States is that the dominant class continues to be largely Protestant, primarily Episcopalian, but also Presbyterian or United Church of Christ. Individuals of these religions are predominant in the directorships of the 500 largest corporations in the United States (Burck, 1976; Baltzell, 1987 [1964], 1991). Despite some well-publicized changes in this pattern, Catholics continue to be underrepresented and Jews virtually absent from top positions in the largest and wealthiest corporations in the United States.

The question for the future is probably not whether the dominant class will be Protestant, but what sort of Protestants will dominate. Will they be members of liberal mainline denominations, or members of evangelical/conservative denominations? If religious conservatives gain ascendancy, will they include members who are minorities?

RELIGION IN THE UNITED STATES

As in the relationship between religion and social class, a look at religion in the United States today raises other questions that cannot yet be answered.

Mainline Protestantism

Research indicates that a major reason for the decline of mainline religions in the United States is the fact that the baby boomers (born between 1946 and 1964) are not returning to church (Johnson et al., 1993; Roof, 1993). In previous generations, young adults tended to drop out of church at about age 18. But they returned to church in their mid- to late twenties after marrying, and especially after becoming parents.

The baby boomers have not followed this pattern. Many have postponed marriage and childbirth until their late thirties and early forties. Many are still single and without children. Only a small percentage of this generation, including those who have married and become parents, are in the pews in mainline churches. The mainline churches are not replacing the members that they are losing to old age and death (Roof and McKinney, 1987; Roof, 1993; Woodward, 1993a). Will mainline groups continue to decline in numbers, or has this decline leveled off?

FIGURE 13.1

Religious Preference in the United States

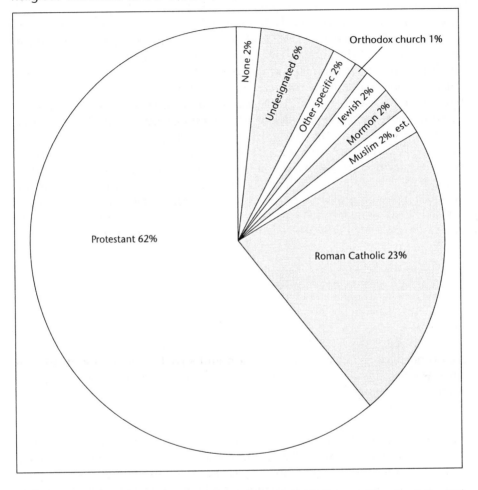

Source: Ari L. Goldman, 1993, "Portrait of Religions in U.S. Holds Dozens of Surprises," *New York Times* (April 10): A1, A18; *Gallup Poll Monthly,* 1994 (April): p. 29.

The percentage of Roman Catholics in the United States has grown slightly because of the large influx of immigrants from Catholic countries in Central and South America. Protestants, however, continue to constitute the majority in the United States.

Evangelical or Conservative Protestantism

Pentecostal Christians are Protestants who believe in what they call Baptism of the Holy Spirit, or speaking in tongues. Pentecostal Christians are **Evangelical Christians**. Evangelical, or conservative, Christians can be defined as those who (1) have made an individual decision for Christ, (2) believe that only this belief will lead to salvation, and (3) feel the need and responsibility to share their faith with others, that is, to evangelize. Christian fundamentalists are evangelicals, but not all evangelicals are fundamentalists.

Evangelical churches are growing, in part because they are attracting more members of the baby boom generation (Ammerman, 1987, 1990; Roof and McKinney, 1987; Johnson et al., 1993). Not only have more evangelical baby boomers come back to active participation in their church, but they have come back younger and with larger families than previous generations. Some of the fastest-growing evangelical congregations in the United States are populated mainly by baby boomers—some of whom were raised in mainline churches. Will evangelical denominations and congregations continue to grow in numbers? The real question for the future is whether the evangelical churches will retain the baby boomers' children as members when these children reach adulthood. Or will these young people find their parents' religion too rigorous and move toward mainline denominations, as their grandparents and great-grandparents did from the 1920s to the 1950s?

Fundamentalism

In the United States, the term **fundamentalism** was first used to refer to a movement in Protestantism that required strict adherence to biblical doctrines. Forms of fundamentalism may, however, be found in almost any religion. Fundamentalist groups have charismatic, authoritarian, male leaders, and they provide a primary source of communal and personal identity for believers. Such faiths are very demanding, requiring total acceptance and absolute compliance to doctrine. Believers view outsiders as hostile, and they punish their enemies. They maintain rigid boundaries to avoid contact with nonbelievers. They seek to extend the religious sphere to encompass all aspects of life—including government and education as well as the family. They are selectively traditional or modern, depending on the usefulness of various tools such as computers or technologies such as television in furthering their beliefs (Marty and Appleby, 1991). This description is an ideal-typical one; not every fundamentalist group will display all of these characteristics, but most display many (see Table 13.1).

Will the militancy of fundamentalisms cause them to break down because of infighting? This has been the historical pattern among more militant social movements. Or will these movements continue to grow, fight secularization, and become dominant in various societies, especially those that are currently industrializing (Misztal and Shupe, 1992)? In the United States, both Christian and Jewish fundamentalism are growing. Christian fundamentalists have become more visible because of their

TABLE 13.1

Characteristics of Fundamentalist Religious Groups

1. These groups arise or become more powerful in times of economic and political crisis, actual or perceived.	6. They seek to extend the religious sphere to all areas of life—government, education, family, economy, science, health, leisure.
2. They are the primary source of communal and personal identity for believers.	7. Believers look to a crisis at the end of time. They will have a special place in the new world (utopia) to come.
3. They practice what is defined as a pure form of their religion.	8. They use modern propaganda methods and technologies to advance their cause—public relations, news media, television, computers, bureaucratic organization.
4. They are led by charismatic, authoritarian leaders; require total commitment and obedience to all aspects of religious doctrine.	
5. They maintain rigid boundaries, defined by place, diet, dress, to avoid pollution by outsiders; name and punish their enemies.	

Source: Martin E. Marty and R. Scott Appleby, eds., 1993, *Fundamentalisms and the State,* Chicago: University of Chicago Press, pp. 817–35.

increasing affluence and sophisticated use of the media—especially television (Frankl, 1987; Schultze, 1991). The growth of Jewish fundamentalism in the United States is occurring because of increased recruitment and a higher birth rate. Again, the question is whether the new generation will continue in the faith of their parents.

Pentecostalism

Many new Pentecostal Christians in the United States are former Roman Catholics. This is especially true of Latino Americans. Pentecostal churches are growing rapidly all across the United States, however, and not just among Latinos.

Polls have indicated that Pentecostals in the United States are among the most conservative of all religious people. Ninety-five percent of Pentecostals, as compared to 61 percent of Catholics, feel that abortion is morally wrong. Eighty-nine percent of Pentecostals and 63 percent of Catholics believe that the Christian faith has all the answers to leading a successful life (Barna, 1992). As Pentecostals continue to grow in number and economic power, to what extent will they influence the dominant culture in the United States?

Roman Catholicism

The percentage of Roman Catholics in the United States is increasing because of the large influx of Latino immigrants. The disagreements that Roman Catholics have with their church are also increasing.

In one poll, 36 percent of Catholics disagreed with the statement, "Abortion is morally wrong" (Barna, 1992, p. 250). In a poll conducted by the Princeton Survey Research Associates for *Newsweek* (Woodward, 1993b), 41 percent stated that the church's position on abortion was too conservative. In the same poll, 62 percent disagreed with the church on birth control, and 46 percent rejected the official position on women's role in society. In 1974, only 29 percent had agreed that women should be ordained to the priesthood, but in 1993, 62 percent agreed. In 1974, 53 percent thought that married men should be ordained, but in 1993, 71 percent supported the ordination of married men (Woodward, 1993b). We see here a pattern of increasing disagreement with church policy. The question, then, is will the percentage of American Roman Catholics continue to grow in the United States? Or will the defections of Latinos from the Roman Catholic Church to Pentecostal churches in Latin America be mirrored in the United States, where the liberation theology movement is not an effective counterforce to prevent these defections?

Judaism

Judaism in the United States is undergoing the same kinds of changes as Protestantism. The main liberal branch, Reform Judaism, is not growing. Fundamentalist, or Orthodox, branches are recruiting more members, but total numbers are quite small. Widespread defections, intermarriage, and a low birthrate have greatly curtailed the number of people in the United States who consider themselves Jews, to a current level of 2.7 percent of the population (Grossman, 1993). Jewish religious leaders view these demographic trends as a crisis. About 52 percent of the marriages of baby-boom Jews are intermarriages. Two-thirds of the children of these marriages do not consider themselves Jewish (Grossman, 1993).

Islam

The Islamic population of the United States has been estimated by a recent poll as 0.5 percent of the population—about 1,250,000 people (Kosmin, 1991). Because this was a telephone poll conducted in English, there is a strong possibility that Muslims have been undercounted. Other estimates have gone as high as 2 percent, or about 5 million people (Goldman, 1991). Muslims include immigrants from all over the world. Islam is also growing in the African American community. An estimated 40 percent of all Muslims in the United States are of African descent—African immigrants and African

Americans. On the bases of immigration, conversion, and large families, it seems likely that Islam will grow rapidly in the future.

Eastern Religions and New Religious Movements

Eastern religions have been practiced in the United States for at least 100 years, although their adherents remain very small in number. Most members of traditional Eastern religions—Buddhism, Hinduism, and Taoism—are immigrants. Buddhists are the largest group, with an estimated 1 million members. The Hindu population is estimated at 0.5 million (Kosmin, 1991). It is very difficult to count adherents to these religions, because their small numbers do not show up in national polls. Also, many people who practice religions such as Wicca (witchcraft) and Santaria are unwilling to share this information with others. Other practitioners may be involved with some form of meditation in addition to professing membership in a traditional group. Polls in the United States will not pick this up. People are usually asked only about their religious identification, not about their practices. In the future we will be learning more about these religions as people become more open about their nonmainstream religious activities.

Women in Religion

There has been much debate about the status and role of women in various institutional spheres, including religion, over the last 30 years. In the mainline denominations such as Presbyterians, Methodists, Episcopalians, Reform and Conservative Jews, debates have centered on the ordination of women. Once some women were ordained, or, failing that, began functioning as pastors, researchers focused on the roles of the new women clergy (Nesbitt, 1993; Baer, 1993; Wallace, 1992, 1993; Davidman and Greil, 1993; Simon et al., 1993).

In the more conservative denominations, ordination has not been as important an issue as changes in gender roles, as women have left the home to seek employment. No matter what their religion, married women usually work outside the home in industrial societies. Biblical injunctions thought to call for the subordination of women have had to be reinterpreted (Ammerman, 1987; Klatch, 1987; Hunter, 1987; Rose, 1987, 1988; Bendroth, 1984, 1993; Stacey, 1990; DeBerg, 1990; Brereton, 1990; Wagner, 1990). The Islamic community (Haddad and Findly, 1985) and the Orthodox Jewish community (Kaufman, 1991; Davidman, 1991; Davidman and Greil, 1993) are also examining the ways in which traditional religious doctrine about women's roles can be applied in industrial societies.

Sociologists who have studied women's roles in the more conservative groups have sought to understand the appeal to women of organizations that deny the equality of the genders. Many researchers have come away with a more complex understanding of how, in some ways, women are protected in conservative groups. For example, women who convert to Islam claim that being veiled gives them protection against being harassed by men (Haddad and Findly, 1985). Orthodox Jewish women speak of how their religion honors women as women, and how the ritual monthly bath, the mikvah, draws women together in a special community of their own (Davidman and Greil, 1993). Fundamentalist Christian women speak of how respectful their husbands became after conversion, knowing that they would have to answer to God for the proper treatment of their wives and children (Wagner, 1990).

Women in Eastern religions in the United States have had limited roles, and numerous abuses of women have been reported in studies of cults (Jacobs, 1989; Gargan, 1993). These abuses have included beatings of disobedient wives by their husbands and sexual exploitation of women by movement leaders. Even when there are no outright abuses, the limitations placed on married life by such groups have often prompted defections (Jacobs, 1989).

Many nontraditional religious movements such as Christian Science and various spiritualist groups were founded and led by women. These movements gave women a freedom and power they had not had in mainline religious organizations. As the movements grew and became more respectable, however, men took over the leadership positions from women (Braude, 1989; Baer, 1993). A question now is whether this will also happen in groups like Santaria, Candomble, and Voodoo, in which women have a strong presence.

Because of this tendency for men to become the leaders, new religious groups are forming that are restricted to women only. Most of these intentionally reject male-dominated forms of religion. Examples are "Women Church" in Roman Catholicism (Trebbi, 1990) and women's spirituality groups focused on the female aspects of God as personified in the Goddess (Jacobs, 1990; Spretnak, 1982). Although it is impossible to estimate the numbers of women involved in various kinds of women's spiritual groups, they are being taken very seriously by the denominations. Pope John Paul II, for example, in his 1993 visit to the United States warned U.S. bishops about the growth of feminist nature worship (Cowell, 1993).

It is likely in the future that women's roles in religious organizations will continue to be a topic of concern within these organizations. In conservative groups there will be continued negotiation between religiously prescribed roles and the economic needs of modern families. In liberal groups there will be a continued effort to realize the equality they espouse. It is also likely that women-only, women-centered spirituality groups will continue to increase. In the United States, equality and cultural pluralism are cultural ideals; for the present, increasing inequality and separatism are the reality.

THE GLOBAL RESURGENCE IN RELIGIOUS BELIEF

As noted earlier in the chapter, socialists point to a worldwide resurgence of religion in modern-day industrial and postindustrial societies. They believe that the two factors underlying this trend are widespread economic and political crises and disenchantment with secular alternatives to religion.

Worldwide Economic Crisis

Global economic and political stresses are associated with the worldwide resurgence of religious faith and observance, especially among fundamentalist groups. Now fundamentalism is being used as a concept that applies globally (Roof, 1993; Marty and Appleby, 1991).

Research indicates that new fundamentalist groups arise and existing groups become stronger during periods of economic crisis (Marty and Appleby, 1991). Christian fundamentalism is spreading in North and South America (Marsden, 1987; Frankl, 1987; Harrell, 1987a, 1987b; Lawrence, 1989; Capps, 1990; Cohen, 1990; Lechner, 1990; Hunter, 1991; Ammerman, 1991). Jewish fundamentalism is also on the rise (Davidman, 1991; Kaufman, 1991; Landau, 1993). Islamic fundamentalism is growing in Pakistan, Malaysia, the Sunni Arab world, and Iran (Marty and Appleby, 1991). Hindu and Sikh fundamentalists are gaining strength in India. Sri Lanka and Thailand are experiencing a revival of Buddhism. New religious movements are spreading in Japan, as is Confucianism in industrial East Asia.

Fundamentalist Muslims control several Middle Eastern countries. Sunni Islam is active in transforming society in Egypt and the Sudan (Voll, 1991). Shi'ite Islam rules in Iraq and Iran. India is also experiencing a rise of Hindu fundamentalists who are supporting the idea of a Hindu state (Gold, 1991). In Latin America, scholars find it hard to draw a hard-and-fast line between evangelicals and fundamentalists (Deiros, 1991). What is significant is that a continent that has been essentially Roman Catholic is experiencing a huge growth in conservative Protestantism. Protestantism and Catholicism are competing for active members. This competition has made both sides more sensitive to the needs of the Latin American people.

The Decline in Secular Movements

A second reason given for the worldwide resurgence of religion is the decline in alternative secular movements. These political and psychological movements have been considered the functional equivalents of religion, because they have had similar functions and served similar purposes to those of religion. Secular social movements, such as socialism and psychological

FIGURE 13.2

Personal Importance of Religion in the United States

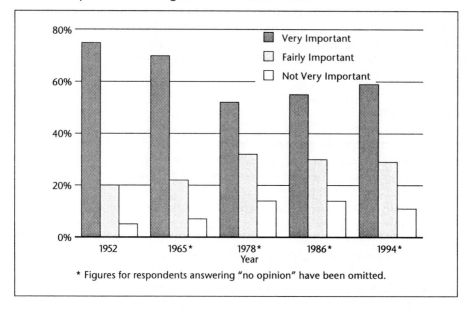

* Figures for respondents answering "no opinion" have been omitted.

Source: The Gallup Poll Monthly, April 1994, p. 3. Based on nationwide survey data.

The percentage of people in the United States for whom religion is very important has increased since 1978, but is lower than it was in 1952.

insight therapies, may not provide answers to ultimate questions of meaning and purpose in life. But these movements have attempted to provide guidelines for the good society or the good life. Believers have used socialist or psychological principles to provide standards for thinking, feeling, and behaving.

Socialism in industrial and industrializing societies was an attempt to solve the problem of economic inequality. But socialist societies could not solve the problem of inefficient production. Nor have free market economies solved the problem of imbalanced supply and demand. The vastly increased productivity of postindustrial societies has been accompanied by increased unemployment and a decline in purchasing power for all social classes except the upper class—at least at present. Who is to buy the more efficiently produced products in postindustrial market economies? The problems remain, regardless of type of society.

Psychological movements in industrial and postindustrial societies have also attempted to provide a worldview, direction, commitment, and community. The bases of these movements are shared beliefs in psychological principles. Professional insight therapies such as individual psychoanalysis

FIGURE 13.3

Frequency of Attendance of Church/Synagogue in 1994

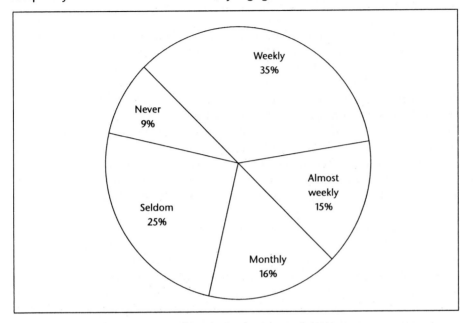

Source: The Gallup Poll Monthly, April 1994, p. 29. Based on nationwide survey data.

Church attendance in the United States has declined since the 1950s, but remains higher than church attendance in European postindustrial societies.

and its group-oriented spin-offs, such as Erhard Seminars Training (EST), the Sullivanians, and Lifespring, are in decline. But group self-help solutions are flourishing in the United States. The emphasis in these groups, whether religious, spiritual, or psychologically oriented, is on lay rather than professional leadership. Bible studies in people's homes, prayer groups, and the whole range of "Anonymous" groups—such as Alcoholics Anonymous, Narcotics Anonymous, and Overeaters Anonymous—are examples.

Although the beliefs and practices of these movements are, for the most part, not based on the realm of the holy or sacred, such political and psychological movements can provide satisfactions similar to those of religion. Belief and participation can bring relief from isolation, anger, anxiety, guilt, and grief. The movements provide identity and community, norms, values, and ideals.

Religious beliefs in the United States are stronger than in other industrialized societies and have remained remarkably stable over the past 20 years (Gallup, 1990; Warner, 1993). On national surveys, the great majority of adults in the United States (about 95 percent) say they believe in the existence of God, and most (about 70 percent) report that they believe in life after death. These are far higher percentages than in Western European countries (Gallup, 1990) (see Figure 13.3).

Psychological movements have been stronger in the United States than in other industrial societies, but competing, all-encompassing political ideologies, such as socialism, have been weaker. Furthermore, the United States has never had a state religion, identified with the dominant social class and subsidized by the government, in which membership is taken for granted. In the United States, which currently has almost 300 established denominations and sects, clergy have always had to compete for funds and members. They have had to personalize their appeal as much as possible to maintain or increase their membership. But at the same time, larger membership size and greater financial success bring bureaucracy, impersonality, and dissatisfaction among members with the remoteness of the religious experience. In industrial societies, this contradiction is built into the religious experience.

The sphere of the sacred, however, is a province that remains exclusive to religion. This sphere is now growing in significance as threat, terror, and sudden crises of all kinds become common worldwide (Robbins and Anthony, 1979, 1981, 1991; Wuthnow, 1989, 1992, 1993; Hunter, 1991).

The failure of secular social movements has left many people—entire societies—with no answers. In the United States, with a supermarket of religions and spiritual practices to choose from, people are choosing more freely than ever before. The traditionalist assumption of the first half of the twentieth century that people will remain in the religion of their parents no longer holds true. In the United States, there was always some exchange of members among various Protestant denominations (Bibby and Brinkerhoff, 1973, 1983). There were also conversions because of interfaith marriages. But the increased moving from religion to religion by individuals that has occurred in the last 30 years is unprecedented, even in the United States (Bellah et al., 1985; Roof and McKinney, 1987; Roof, 1993).

The popularity of Eastern religions grew in the late 1960s and 1970s. The United States and Western Europe experienced the arrival of the Unification Church, the "Moonies," from Korea at about the same time (Barker, 1984; Beckford, 1985; Bromley, 1988). Some of the new religious movements of all kinds that grew in the decade from 1965 to 1975 declined in the 10 years that followed. But others quickly took their place. Leaders of conventional and unconventional religious movements rose and fell, sometimes in scandal.

Globally, moderate mainline religions are declining, while conservative ones are growing (Bromley, 1988; Jacobs, 1989; Marty and Appleby, 1991). Conservative Christian groups, especially Pentecostal churches, are gaining adherents among all segments of the population. These groups expect members to convert before joining and to be highly committed. Among African Americans, Islam is thriving. Groups newer to the United

States that emphasize racial pride, such as Rastafarians, Children of the Sun, and African-derived religions, are also increasing in membership (Curry, 1991).

The United States, along with the rest of the world, has seen two major trends in religion over the last 30 years. Traditional mainline religions have been in crisis, a crisis to which they have responded in various ways. At the same time, increasing numbers of people as individuals are actively seeking the divine in an almost unlimited religious marketplace (Berger, 1969; Finke and Stark, 1992; Roof, 1993).

Study Guide

REVIEW OBJECTIVES

After studying this chapter, you should be able to:

1. Explain the meaning of basic concepts in the sociological study of religion.
2. Describe how religious beliefs and practice change during the course of sociocultural evolution.
3. Describe recent trends in religious belief and practice in the United States and worldwide.
4. List the characteristics of new religious movements and their probable future.

SUMMARY

1. Sociologists focus on religion as a cultural, subcultural, or temporary group phenomenon. They generally explain the universality of religion in terms of the functions that it performs for individuals, groups, and societies.

2. In hunting and gathering societies, religious beliefs centered on forces or spirits that had the power to intervene in daily life. Ancestor worship was widespread in horticultural societies. Religious beliefs explained economic inequality and justified turning over the economic surplus to ruling families. In herding and agricultural societies, theistic religions became widespread. Monotheism was the invention of constantly battling herding societies, and it reflected the extreme differences in the power, prestige, and economic roles of women and men in these societies.

3. In industrial societies, scientific knowledge diminishes the influence of religion in

daily life, but it cannot provide answers to ultimate questions of human existence. Political and psychological movements may fulfill similar needs for members by providing norms, values, commitment, community, and relief from anxiety, guilt, and suffering.

4. Worldwide economic and political stresses and the decline of alternative political movements such as socialism are considered to be major reasons for the global resurgence of fundamentalist religions.

5. Religion promotes social order by reinforcing commitment to group norms, values, and the existing social structure. In multicultural industrial societies, however, religious differences may be a basis of heightened ethnic conflict.

6. Historically, religious beliefs have reinforced social inequality. In an era of global telecommunication networks and rising expectations, new religious movements may hasten economic and political reform and social change, however. In the past, religious movements more often focused on otherworldly rewards and goals.

7. The economic factor has been a basic historical factor in the formation of religious sects and denominations. Religious groups in the United States are class ranked, although less so than in the past. Many lower-status sects have become denominations as the social status of their members increased. Also, single-issue differences in opinion, for example, on abortion, divide congregations and promote cross-class cooperation among various religious groups.

8. The fact that religious beliefs are stronger in the United States, relative to other industrial and postindustrial societies, is usually explained by the absence of a state religion. Competition among the many denominations and sects is believed to enhance the personal appeal of the religious experience. Also, while psychological and self-help movements have been strongest in the United States, sociopolitical movements that provide alternative, secular models for the good society have not been strong.

9. The status and role of women in religious groups have become increasingly controversial in the United States. Some women are responding by forming their own, separate religious groups.

GLOSSARY

Animism: The belief that material objects and/or natural phenomena possess spirits.

Cults: In the past, a concept variously applied to religious groups with nontraditional religious beliefs, loosely organized religious groups that may evolve into sects, and groups that share a single magical belief. This term has been supplanted by the term **new religious movements**. The term cult is now usually applied only to groups that have a single, authoritarian, charismatic leader.

Denominations: Large, formal religious organizations that are not state religions.

Evangelical Christians: Conservative Christians who have made a decision to follow literally the teachings of Jesus Christ and who attempt to convert others to their faith.

Fundamentalism: Religious movements advocating strict adherence to original religious teachings. They are found in almost every religion.

Liberation theology: A movement in industrializing societies that advocates radical political reform on the basis of Marxist economic analysis and Roman Catholic theology.

Magic: Practices that seek to coerce supernatural forces into granting immediate goals.

New religious movements (NRMs): a sociohistorically less judgmental term than cults for nontraditional religious beliefs or loosely organized religious groups that may evolve into sects.

Pentecostal Christians: Protestants who believe in the Baptism of the Holy Spirit, or speaking in tongues. They are evangelical Christians.

Religion: A shared set of beliefs and practices oriented toward the sacred and supernatural that unites believers into a moral community.

Rituals: Activities oriented toward relations between humans and the supernatural.

Sacred: Anything that is elevated above the ordinary and is regarded with awe, reverence, mystery, and, sometimes, fear.

Sects: Religious groups characterized by emotionally expressive rituals, conversion, strict interpretation of theological doctrine, and strong emphasis on personal morality. The term sect is usually limited to groups formed by people who have left established religious groups for a more rigorous religious life.

Secularization: A decline in the role of religious beliefs in guiding daily activities.

Spirits: Supernatural forces with human qualities of motivation and emotion.

State religions: Religions supported by a national government and claiming all citizens as members.

Supernatural: A realm or reality that does not require empirical observation or verification of its existence for believers.

Theistic religions: Religions that center on belief in the existence of a powerful God or gods.

Theocracies: Societies in which high priests rule by divine right.

Theologies: Religious beliefs that provide meaningful explanations of the major questions of human existence.

Totems: Sacred symbols that are representative of a clan.

Universal religions: Religions whose membership transcends societal and geographic boundaries.

PRACTICE TESTS

True ▪ False Test

___ 1. The practice of religion is found among all human as well as "lower" animal groups.

___ 2. Animists are people who devoutly believe in a state religion.

___ 3. In the secularization model, rationalism replaces faith and religion loses influence in industrial societies.

___ 4. Established religious organizations in the United States have always been initiators of social change.

___ 5. Originally, Christianity was a sect of Judaism.

___ 6. People who profess fundamentalism adhere strictly to biblical doctrines.

___ 7. Liberation theology is already a major force in the United States.

___ 8. Historically, women have had roles equal to those of men in organized religious organizations.

___ 9. Protestantism is the state religion of the United States.

___ 10. Traditional major religions throughout the world have been undergoing crisis and seeking ways to respond to crisis.

Multiple-Choice Test

___ 1. "Rituals" are defined as:
   a. a parallel reality for believers based on faith.
   b. activities oriented toward the supernatural.
   c. consistent from society to society.
   d. anything material or nonmaterial, human or nonhuman, that is elevated above the ordinary and the mundane.

___ 2. The only important religious status in hunting and gathering societies was held by the:
   a. sherpa.
   b. totem.
   c. family patriarch.
   d. shaman.

___ 3. The ancient Greeks could be described as:
   a. monotheistic.
   b. liberation theologists.
   c. polytheistic.
   d. agnostics.

___ 4. Ancestor worship is most common in:
   a. hunting and gathering societies.
   b. horticultural societies.
   c. agricultural societies.
   d. industrializing societies.

___ 5. Liberation theology may be said to be "indigenous" because it:
   a. exists only among ethnic or racial groups that are native to an area.
   b. is animistic.
   c. has as its goals liberation from all forms of oppression.
   d. adapts its concerns to local conditions.

___ 6. The primary economic component that is associated with the Crusades is:
   a. movement away from agriculturalism.
   b. the opening of trade routes to the East.
   c. the Industrial Revolution.
   d. economic losses due to the plague.

__ 7. Which of the following terms is preferred to "cults" because it is less value-laden?
   a. new religious movements
   b. Pentecostalism
   c. simple theocracies
   d. alternative religions

__ 8. Evangelical Protestantism owes its current growth largely to the:
   a. "twentysomething" generation.
   b. baby boomers.
   c. influx of Latino immigrants into the United States.
   d. elderly.

__ 9. Which of the following religions has the fewest adherents today in the United States?
   a. Buddhism.
   b. Hinduism.
   c. Taoism.
   d. Wicca.

__ 10. New fundamentalist religious groups as well as existing religions strengthen during periods of:
   a. economic growth.
   b. social stability.
   c. economic crisis.
   d. increase in secular movements.

Matching Test

Match each concept with its definition, illustration, or explication below.

1.
__ (1) Supernatural
__ (2) Sacred
__ (3) Magic
__ (4) Ritual
__ (5) Religion

a. Revered
b. Activity oriented toward the supernatural
c. Parallel reality for believers
d. Shared set of beliefs
e. Seeks to coerce supernatural forces

2.
__ (1) Hunting and gathering societies
__ (2) Horticultural societies
__ (3) Agricultural societies
__ (4) Herding societies
__ (5) Industrial societies

a. Shaman
b. Totem
c. Secularization
d. Monotheistic
e. Ancestor worship declines

3.
_ (1) Durkheim's theories
_ (2) Karl Marx
_ (3) Social Gospel movement
_ (4) Liberation theology
_ (5) Society of Christian Socialists

a. Biblical guidelines for behavior
b. Marxist economic analysis, Catholic theology
c. Apply best to agricultural societies
d. Nonfatalistic
e. Illusory happiness of religion

4.
_ (1) Crusades
_ (2) Offense against rulers
_ (3) Concerned Women for America
_ (4) African American religious community
_ (5) Martin Luther King Jr.

a. Grassroots conservative
b. Faith in moral persuasion
c. Applied also to gods
d. Poor People's March
e. Religious movement

5.
_ (1) Denominations
_ (2) Sects
_ (3) Niebuhr's thesis
_ (4) Abortion issue
_ (5) Cults

a. Classic study of U.S. Christian religious organizations
b. Conservative/liberal split
c. Totally controlling religious groups
d. Strict interpretation of theological beliefs
e. Formal religious organizations

REVIEW QUESTIONS

1. What were the basic views of Marx, Durkheim, and Weber on religion, and how did they differ?
2. How do magic and religion differ?
3. How do religious beliefs and practices vary in major kinds of societies?
4. What are the characteristics of fundamentalisms, and why are they on the rise globally?
5. How does religion promote social stability, and how does it promote social change, especially in recent times?
6. Historically in the United States, how did membership in a denomination or sect reflect social class origins? How is this changing in the United States today?
7. What are the major religious groups in the United States today? How and why are they changing in terms of recruitment and prospects for the future?
8. In the United States, what are some of the basic issues in the role of women in religion?
9. What is likely to be the role of women in religious organizations in the future?

APPLYING SOCIOLOGY

1. How have your various statuses—gender, racial/ethnic origin, age and generation, urban-rural residence—affected your religious beliefs and practices?
2. How do your opinions about religion compare with those of your parents and the general public in the United States? How would you explain similarities or differences?
3. How have your religious beliefs, practices, and affiliation changed, if at all, since you were a child? How would you explain this change, or lack of change? Use especially concepts of mobility—geographic, social, psychological—reference groups, and socialization.

Epilogue

What are some of the basic insights that sociologists have contributed to an understanding of changing human realities from the beginning of human history? Perhaps the most important contribution we have made is the insight that location in time and in geographic and cultural space is a crucial determinant of how people think, feel, and typically behave.

Many things that appear to be inevitable in human social life—organized group warfare and widespread human destructiveness, extreme economic inequality, great differences in the power of political and religious leaders and followers, women and men, parents and children, employers and workers, and teachers and students—are a matter of time and place. They are socially located. These conditions were absent or minimal for more than 99 percent of human history.

Over time, developments in science and technology brought more knowledge and control over the environment, more economic resources, more opportunity—and more inequality. Conflict and greed increased in human societies, not so much because of scarce resources, but because of the unequal distribution of the greater amount of resources that became available.

Over the centuries, the enormous increase in scientific knowledge has made possible more rational solutions to human problems. But values intervene. And values usually change more slowly than changes in science and technology. Religious values and beliefs, for example, have functioned as a very powerful source of social control in all societies. They have had a profound effect on the rate and direction of social change in specific societies.

In industrial societies, major institutions outside of the family—the economy, government, education, and religion—become more separate, formal, and specialized in their activities. They become bureaucratized. Traditional values (especially fatalism and authoritarianism, but also, and to a lesser extent, familism and religiousness) decline as economic opportunities and personal resources (especially education) increase. For individuals, formal education is the major factor in the movement away from traditional values in modern societies. The effects of higher education, the ability to think critically and resist propaganda, are enduring and permanent.

Families, whatever their current stresses and challenges and however they have changed as societies become more complex, are not likely to disappear in the future. They will survive because of the biologically grounded human need for a stable, enduring source of love and psychological support. They will survive because of the need to control sexual rivalry and conflict in human societies. And they will survive because no other type of group can provide totally dependent newborn infants with the intellectual, emotional, and physical care they need. In densely populated societies, substitute groups become bureaucratized, and bureaucracy, by definition, is impersonal; emotions interfere with efficiency. Furthermore, a careful look into the misery of family life among the masses of ordinary people in agricultural societies tells us that whatever the problems of contemporary families are, we should not long for the good old days that never really were.

As societies become more complex, social change accelerates and traditional role definitions, especially those of male and female, become outmoded. In modern societies, women need to be more assertive in work situations outside of the home and men need to be more emotionally available inside the home. Needs change and roles change. Values may help or hinder, but values change too, sooner or later.

Anomie and role conflict, from all sources and in all major spheres of life, also increase as societies become more complex. Mobility—geographic, social, and psychological—becomes widespread in modern societies. Church, family, and community ties weaken and nonconformity increases.

Most citizens in modern societies are less materially deprived than in agricultural societies. But identifications and comparisons with those who have more increase. Expectations rise and feelings of deprivation become relative—weaker or stronger, depending on whom we identify with—regardless of the objective social situation. Social movements proliferate in industrializing and industrial societies. These movements are not led by those who are most deprived, objectively, but usually by educated middle-class leaders.

As citizens become more educated, especially in postindustrial societies, old meanings and old justifications for human suffering lose their hold over the masses of people. Inequality is better understood and less well tolerated. Human destructiveness persists because human frustration and unfulfilled needs persist. The great importance of the economic factor in war and peace, power and submission, racial/ethnic conflict, family conflict, gender role conceptions, educational achievement, and religious experience becomes increasingly clear. We cannot ignore the economic factor and we had best not minimize it if we are to understand where we have been, where we are going, and where we can hope to go, as individuals and as members of the world community of human beings. Governments become more sensitive to the needs of citizens as the urban middle classes expand in more complex societies. Aristocracies, in which leaders derive their power from the inherited ownership of land, factories, or liquid capital, compete for political power with meritocracies. In meritocracies, leaders obtain power by achievement. Their power is based on personal qualities such as drive, talent, training, experience, and scientific knowledge. This was the dream of the founder of sociology, Auguste Comte—a once-impossible dream that seems, at last, to be coming true.

B. Y.

Glossary

Ability grouping: Separation of students in the same classroom according to differences in test scores. **405**

Acculturation: The learning of the language, values, norms, and skills necessary for social mobility in a particular society. **261**

Achieved status: A position in a group or society we attain because of choice or effort. **85**

Achievement motivation: A strong need to compete successfully for resources, rewards, and recognition. **166**

Activism: A belief in fighting to effect a change in one's life circumstances rather than passively accepting one's fate. **166**

Age cohort: All people in a society born during the same period of time. **191**

Agricultural societies: Literate societies in which the plow is used in planting. **154**

Alienation: Separation and emotional detachment from one's work and the world. It is characterized by feelings of helplessness and powerlessness. **349**

Altruistic suicide: Suicide that is motivated by a very strong commitment to a group and its goals. **12**

Animism: The belief that material objects and/or natural phenomena possess spirits. **431**

Anomic suicide: Suicide that stems from rapid social change and the breakdown of the norms that previously controlled people. **11**

Anomie: A social condition in which norms are weak or absent and do not control people. **11**

Applied sociology: The use of sociological research and knowledge to achieve practical goals. **21**

Artifacts: Things that are made or used in a society. **77**

Ascribed status: A position in a group or society that is based on birth and cannot usually be changed. **85**

Assimilation: The complete loss of racial and/or ethnic identity by means of acculturation and intermarriage. **260**

Authoritarian childrearing (parenting): An adult-centered parenting style characterized by strict obedience to nonnegotiable rules that are not explained or justified. This parenting style is typical in agricultural societies and among more traditional segments of industrial societies. **302**

Authoritarian governments: Governments in which leaders have permanent power that cannot be challenged or limited. **364**

Authoritarian personality: A person who ranks high on tests of political and economic conservatism, ethnocentrism, and prejudice. **256**

Authoritarianism: An insistence on absolute and unquestioning obedience to fixed rules. **168**

Authoritative childrearing (parenting): A parenting style characterized by consistent, strict but democratic discipline, warmth, and affection that is typical in the middle social classes in industrial societies. Also called **democratic childrearing. 304**

Authority: Power that is regarded as legitimate, right, and proper in certain widely recognized statuses, such as royalty in monarchies and popularly elected government officials in democracies. **329**

Autocracy: Rule by a single individual. **369**

Bureaucracy: A complex administrative organization that coordinates the activities of large numbers of people in carrying out large-scale tasks. **6, 100**

Capitalism: An economic system characterized by private ownership and operation of productive property, competition, private profit, and the accumulation of personal wealth. **146**

Case study: Intensive observation of a single example, or small sample, of a much larger category of social groups or situations. **58**

Castes: Ranked layers in a social stratification system in which membership is established by birth, cannot be changed, and is sanctioned by religion. **330**

Centralization: The tendency for similar structures and activities to be concentrated in the same geographic areas of large cities. **183**

Charismatic authority: Legitimate power based on a belief in the extraordinary qualities of a leader. **366**

Cities: Dense, permanent settlements of people who engage in manufacturing or service activities and do not produce food. **180**

Class conflict: The struggle over economic resources by members of different economic classes. **8**

Class consciousness: Awareness of how the economic interests of one's class are being served, or not being served, in a society. **34**

Classes: Ranked layers of people who receive similar rewards and possess similar privileges in a society. Position in class structures can be achieved or lost and is not sanctioned by law or religion. **330**

Cohabitation: Unmarried, living-together sexual relationships. **305**

Collective behavior: New and different behavior engaged in spontaneously by large numbers of people. **126**

Competition: Efforts to obtain exclusive rewards or resources that are bound by explicit norms or rules. **113**

Complexity: In the sociocultural evolution model, a trend toward increasing differentiation of parts and functions in the material and nonmaterial cultures of human societies. **44**

Concepts: Abstract terms or phrases that classify or characterize various aspects of reality. **32**

Conflict: A situation of opposing or contradictory needs, impulses, feelings, or desires within an individual or between people, groups, or societies. **47**

Conflict model: A theoretical model in which economics and conflict are given the greatest weight as explanatory factors. **47**

Consensus: The sharing of common values and interests in a society. **46**

Conservative social movements: Movements that attempt to prevent further change and maintain the status quo. **131**

Conspicuous consumption: The purchase of costly, unnecessarily goods to confirm one's social status. **345**

Control group: A group, as similar to an experimental group as possible, that does not experience a change. **60**

Cooperation: A common effort to obtain rewards or resources that are shared by all members of a group or a society. **112**

Co-optation: Diffusion of potential dissent by bringing political activists into the government. **133**

Counterculture: A subculture containing norms and values that conflict with certain basic values of the dominant culture. **82**

Coup d'état: A violent replacement of government leaders with other leaders, usually from the same social stratum. **370**

Credentialism: The increased importance placed on formal qualifications, such as degrees, and the inflation of degree requirements for specific occupations. **410**

Crime: Deviant activity that is defined as illegal by government authorities. **231**

Crude birth rate: The number of live births per 1,000 people in a society in a given year. **190**

Cults: In the past, a concept variously applied to religious groups with nontraditional religious beliefs, loosely organized religious groups that may evolve into sects, and groups that share a single magical belief. This term has been supplanted by the term **new religious movements**. The term cult is now usually applied only to groups that have a single, authoritarian, charismatic leader. **441**

Cultural diffusion: The spread of knowledge, values, skills, and material products from one society to another. **38**

Cultural lag: The tendency for the material culture (applied science and technology) to change faster than the nonmaterial culture (values, attitudes, and beliefs). **44**

Cultural pluralism: A cultural ideal precribing coexistence and mutual tolerance of all ethnic groups in a society. **81–82**

Cultural relativism: The belief we should not judge the ways of life of other cultures or societies by the standards of our own. **171**

Cultural transmission: The learning of deviant behavior that is characteristic of particular geographic areas, societies, or groups. **224**

Cultural universals: Ways of life found in every known society. **36**

Culture: The total social heritage attached to a society that is learned, shared by most people, and transmitted from generation to generation. **76**

Culture shock: The feeling of bewilderment experienced by people who enter a new and unfamiliar society or group with a different culture or subculture. **80**

Death rate: Number of deaths per 1,000 people in a society in a given year. **190**

Decentralization: The tendency of people, structures, and functions to move out of cities to less congested or less expensive areas. **184**

Delinquency: Criminal behavior on the part of young people, primarily those under 16. **223**

Delusion: A persistent false belief that may, in large groups, be the source of mass hysteria. **127**

Democratic governments: Governments in which citizens collectively participate in decision making, either directly or, indirectly, through elected representatives. **364**

Democratic pluralism: A model of political power in which all classes and ethnic groups are viewed as equally capable of affecting government policy and the political process. **381**

Demographic transition model: A three-stage model of population change in the West, including North America, since the Industrial Revolution. **198**

Demography: The statistical study of the size, distribution, and composition of human populations. **190**

Denominations: Large, formal religious organizations that are not state religions. **438**

Dependent variables: Conditions that are the consequence of other factors or conditions. **56**

Deviance: Behavior or characteristics that violate important social norms and are strongly disapproved of by a large number of people in a society. **123, 214**

Deviant behavior: *See* **Deviance.**

Dictator: An autocrat whose power is not hereditary but who cannot be removed from office by legal means. **371**

Differential association: Selective, intimate relationships with models whose behavior is defined as criminal. **224**

Discovery: A sudden awareness of something in the environment that already exists. **44**

Discrimination: Behavior that excludes minorities from wealth, power, opportunities, and activities. **250**

Dramaturgical model: A focus on the fictions that people create to be accepted or maintain a favorable impression. **52**

Dysfunctions: The negative consequences of a condition or an action for the maintenance of a group or society. **46**

Ecology: The study of the relationship between living organisms and their environment. **183**

Economic class: Rank in society determined by possession of economic resources (property and income); category of people sharing the same rank. **8**

Economic surplus: The existence of more goods in a society than are needed to fulfill basic needs. **148**

Education: The deliberate, conscious, and intentional teaching of the knowledge, skills, values, and norms of a culture. **393**

Efficiency: In technological evolution, increasing effectiveness in achieving goals in shorter periods of time using higher levels of skills. **43**

Egalitarianism: A belief that power, privilege, and prestige should be achieved on the basis of personal qualifications rather than inherited or ascribed statuses. **168**

Egoistic suicide: Suicide that stems from a lack of strong group ties. **11**

Emigration: Migration out of a society. **190**

Estates: Ranked layers in a social stratification system in which position is based on birth and is sanctioned by law. **330**

Ethnocentrism: The belief that our own groups and culture are the center of the universe and superior to all others. **80**

Ethnomethodology: The study of the taken-for-granted techniques used within various groups in coping with typical, everyday life situations. **51**

Evaluation research: Follow-up studies that measure the effectiveness of social programs. **21**

Evangelical Christians: Conservative Christians who have made a decision to follow literally the teachings of Jesus Christ and who attempt to convert others to their faith. **443**

Evolution: In the technological sphere, step-by-step improvements in efficiency, effectiveness, and complexity. **43**

Exchange: The trading of resources and rewards on the basis of differing needs in a relationship. **112**

Experimental group: A group that experiences a change under controlled conditions. **60**

Expert authority: Authority based on training and expertise in a particular area of scientific knowledge or applied skills. **368**

Extended family: Two or more nuclear families or parts of nuclear families that live in daily contact and are economically and psychologically interdependent. **289**

Exurb: An urbanizing rural area beyond the suburbs. **187**

Facts: Information, data, and evidence, based on observation, that can be checked or verified by others. **52**

Fads: Temporary behavior that is very enthusiastically pursued by large numbers of people. **128**

Familism: The view that the needs of the family as a group are more important than the personal needs of any individual member. **83, 167**

Family: A group related by blood descent, marriage, adoption, or mutual definition (such as unmarried-couple households with children). **72**

Fashions: Temporary styles of dress, speech, belief, and behavior. **127**

Fatalism: A belief that one must accept and not try to change one's life circumstances. **166**

Fertility rate: The number of live births per 1,000 females 15 to 44 in a given year. **190**

Fishing societies: Societies in which fishing is the basic economic activity. **151**

Folkways: Norms such as customs and manners that are not crucial for group survival and are not enforced by severe sanctions. **75**

Formal education: Teaching done in a school with recognized and distinct full-time statuses such as administrators, teachers, and students. **403**

Frustration: The blocking of immediate or long-term needs or goals. **221**

Function: The positive consequences a condition or an action has for maintaining a group or society. **46**

Fundamentalism: Religious movements advocating strict adherence to original religious teachings. They are found in almost every religion. **444**

Generalization: A statement about people, places, things, or events based on research evidence. **53**

Gentrification: A trend toward the purchase and rehabilitation of decaying housing in poor neighborhoods by the white upper-middle and upper classes. **184**

Ghetto: A segregated racial, ethnic, or religious community within a city. **184**

Global cities: Cities that contain a concentration of international financial institutions, offices of multinational industrial firms, and high-tech business information services and experts. **189**

Government: The visible, functioning apparatus of the state. **363**

Group: Two or more people involved in a recurring social relationship. **84**

Herding societies: Societies in which the tending of domesticated animals is the most important economic activity. **151**

Hidden curriculum: The unrecognized role of schools in teaching different values, work habits, and expectations to students from different social class backgrounds. **399**

Horticultural societies: Nonliterate societies in which cultivated plants are the major economic resource and planting is the most widespread economic activity. **151**

Human nature: The common biological inheritance of humans that is assumed to determine specific behavior patterns. **219**

Hunting and gathering societies: Nonliterate societies in which the technique of planting is unknown and people live by hunting animals and gathering wild vegetation. **147**

Hypothesis: A statement of an expected relationship between two or more variables or conditions. **56**

Ideal-type: A definition of a concept that includes only essential features in pure form. **145**

Identification: The act of imagining oneself in another person's place. **92**

Ideology: A set of beliefs that justifies group interests and serves as a basis for organizing and acting in basic areas of social life. **130**

Immigration: Migration into a society. **190**

Incest taboo: Prohibition on sexual relationships between close relatives in the immediate family. **36**

Independent variables: Factors or conditions that result in certain other conditions. **56**

Individualism: An emphasis on the needs and desires of the individual in preference to those of the group. **167**

Industrial cities: Larger cities, segregated on the basis of class and ethnic origin, in which first manufacturing and then commercial and service activities predominate. **181**

Influence: Informal, unofficial, and sometimes hidden power over people and events. **330**

Informal education: General training for adult roles provided by family and community. **402**

Infrastructure: Public facilities such as roads, bridges, tunnels, waterworks, and sewage systems. **188**

Instincts: Inborn biological tendencies to behave in certain very specific ways. **78**

Institutions: Major areas of social life in which activities are directed toward the satisfaction of basic human needs. **89**

Interactionist model: A focus on the learning and performing of roles within groups. **50**

Internalization: The process by which the norms, values, and beliefs of others become a part of our personality. **92**

Intrapsychic conflict: Internal, psychological conflict that results from contradictory impulses, feelings, or needs. **115**

Invasion: The movement into a neighborhood of people and activities that differ from those that have been there before. **184**

Invention: The deliberate creation of something new from existing elements in the culture. **44**

Language: System of arbitrary written or oral symbols whose meaning is agreed on by two or more people. **35, 79**

Latent functions: The consequences of a condition or action that are not intended or obvious. **46**

Laws: Norms that are written out and enacted by legislators in complex societies. **76**

Legal-rational authority: Legitimate power based on merit and limited by legal rules and regulations. **367**

Liberation theology: A movement in industrializing societies that advocates radical political reform on the basis of Marxist economic analysis and Roman Catholic theology. **436**

Looking-glass self: A self-image we develop that mirrors the judgments of those whom we relate to and who are important to us. **91**

Magic: Practices that seek to coerce supernatural forces into granting immediate goals. **430**

Managerial revolution: The theoretical takeover of corporations by managers who do not own the firms that employ them, creating a new and more broadly based business elite. **382**

Manifest functions: The consequences of a condition or an action that are intended and recognized. **46**

Market research: Surveys of the buying habits of the public and tests of consumer reaction to proposed new products or changes in products. **21**

Marriage: A socially sanctioned sexual relationship requiring some degree of permanence and faithfulness. **36**

Mass hysteria: A widespread anxiety reaction based on a false belief. **127**

Matriarchy: Rule or dominance by females in a society or family. **300**

Matrilineal societies: Societies in which the female line is most important in descent and inheritance of property. **312**

Mechanical solidarity: Cooperative relationships based on feelings of similarity and belonging together. **354**

Medicalization: The trend toward defining increasing numbers of nonconforming behaviors and conditions as illnesses. **215**

Megalopolis: Two or more metropolitan areas that have merged into one continuous urban tract. **183**

Meritocracy: A system of power and authority in a society organized on the basis of merit—training, talent, and drive. **101**

Metropolitan Statistical Area (MSA): A central city of 50,000 or more people surrounded by suburbs. **183**

Middle class: People in the middle levels of society with respect to wealth and income, level of education, and occupational prestige; they work primarily with people and with communication skills. **157**

Midlife crisis: A period of severe stress and acting out that is believed to occur in highly ambitious middle-aged men who fear aging or are dissatisfied with their lives. **99**

Migration: The movement of people into or out of a society. **190**

Military-industrial complex: An informal alliance of military leaders and corporate executives, based on shared interests, that is held to influence government policy. **382**

Minority: A large number of people singled out for unequal treatment in a society on the basis of physical or cultural characteristics. **247**

Mixed economies: Market economies with a significant public sector (government employment) and varying degrees of government regulation over private businesses. **146**

Model: A perspective or orientation toward reality made up of interrelated concepts. **32**

Monogamy: Marriage limiting partners to one husband and one wife. **292**

Mores: Norms that have intense feelings of right and wrong attached to them. **75**

Nation-states: Legally constituted central governments that provide protection for people and regulate trade and commerce over a wide geographic area. **372**

Natural experiments: The comparison of societies with different social conditions to determine the effects of the presence or absence of these conditions on whatever it is we are investigating. This is also called the comparative historical method, or, more simply, cross-cultural research. **10**

Nepotism: The inheritance of jobs within family lines. **85**

Networks: The total number of direct and indirect contacts we have with other people. **84**

New religious movements (NRMs): a sociohistorically less judgmental term than cults for nontraditional religious beliefs or loosely organized religious groups that may evolve into sects. **441**

Norms: Rules we learn that guide thinking, feeling, and behaving in typical situations. **75**

Nuclear family: Parents and their children; the immediate family. **289**

Oligarchy: Rule by a small number of individuals or families. **370**

Open classrooms: Child-centered educational environments in which there is less regimentation and greater flexibility in learning activities. **409**

Organic solidarity: Cooperative relationships based on increasing vocational specialization and the interdependence that this makes necessary as societies industrialize. **354**

Panics: Disorganized destructive behavior that occurs in situations of intense fear. **127**

Parenting styles: Parent-child relationships that vary with respect to expression of emotion, discipline, flexibility of rules, and emphasis on obedience versus self-reliance. These vary, typically, in different types of societies and in different social classes in the United States today. **302**

Participant observation: A research technique in which investigators assume a status and play a role in the group they are studying. **59**

Patriarchy: Complete and absolute power of males in societies and families. **300**

Patrilineal societies: Societies in which the male line is most significant in descent and inheritance of property. **311**

Pentecostal Christians: Protestants who believe in the Baptism of the Holy Spirit, or speaking in tongues. They are evangelical Christians. **443**

Permissive childrearing (parenting): A child-centered parenting style characterized by very flexible rules. **303**

Politics: The struggle to obtain or maintain power by individuals and groups in a society. **363**

Polyandry: Marriages involving one wife with several husbands. **292**

Polygamy: Marriages involving one husband or wife with more than one spouse. **291**

Polygyny: Marriages involving one husband with several wives. **291**

Population explosion: The huge population increase occurring in most contemporary industrializing societies. **201**

Positivism: The application of the methods of the natural sciences to the study of societies and social relationships. **7**

Postindustrial societies: Societies in which a majority of the labor force works in service occupations. **73**

Power: The ability to get what you want despite resistance. **47**

Power elite: A model of power in which top leaders in business, government, and the military are seen as the dominant political force in the United States. **382**

Preindustrial cities: Cities that arose before the Industrial Revolution. **180**

Preindustrial societies: Societies in which a majority of workers extract raw materials from land and sea by farming, fishing, and mining. **73**

Prejudice: Rigid and exaggerated negative images and beliefs about culturally or physically distinct people in a society. **247**

Prestige: The amount of respect accorded to a widely recognized status in a society. **329**

Primary deviance: Behavior that results in being labeled deviant. **226**

Primary sector: An economy or part of an economy that involves gathering or extracting raw materials from land and sea, through fishing, mining, forestry, or planting, for example. **156**

Propaganda: Distorted information or disinformation used by leaders to mold the opinions of followers, subjects, and citizens. **370**

Psychological mobility: Changes in values, interests, and identity that stem from identification with models outside of the family and local community. **122**

Public opinion: The attitudes and beliefs of large numbers of people about issues and events that concern them at any particular point in time. **129**

Pygmalion effect: Doing and becoming what other people expect you to do and become. **91**

Race: A population that shares certain distinct physical characteristics. **251**

Racial/ethnic minority: A category of people who trace their ancestry to particular countries or continents, share similar physical and/or cultural traits, and experience unequal treatment in a society. **253**

Rational social action: A choice of means that are logically the most efficient and effective for achieving desired ends. **13**

Rationalism: A belief that the means used to achieve our goals should be logically chosen on the basis of scientifically verified knowledge and information. **169**

Recidivism: Repeated criminal acts by those who have been convicted of a crime. **224**

Reference groups: Groups that we identify with and compare ourselves with. **93**

Reform social movements: Organized attempts to change existing political or economic circumstances in specific and limited ways, particularly through gradual redistribution of resources and opportunities in a society. **131**

Regressive social movements: Movements that attempt to restore values, norms, or social conditions prevalent in a society in the past. **130–131**

Relationship conflict: Stress that arises mainly because partners in a relationship do not agree about their rights and responsibilities. **115**

Relative deprivation: The idea that the subjective feeling of being deprived is relative and depends on whom we compare ourselves with. **93**

Religion: A shared set of beliefs and practices oriented toward the sacred and supernatural that unites believers into a moral community. **429**

Religiousness: A belief in the supernatural causation and control of human affairs and, usually, an emphasis on otherworldly rewards. **169**

Resocialization: The learning of a new role that requires the rejection of certain previous values, beliefs, and behaviors. **95**

Resources: Characteristics or possessions valued in a society because they promote survival, reduce stress, or gratify needs and desires. **47**

Revolution: A sudden and basic redistribution of power, prestige, and economic resources in a society. **8, 112**

Revolutionary social movements: Attempts to effect radical change in the distribution of power and wealth in a society. **132**

Riot: A temporary but violent and destructive outburst against authority by people who are in similar social locations, especially racial/ethnic and social class. **127**

Rising expectations: The desire for more resources, rewards, and recognition than one has and a belief in everyone's right to have these things. **172**

Rituals: Activities oriented toward relations between humans and the supernatural. **430**

Role conflict: Feelings of stress that stem from being pressured, frustrated, or torn in opposite directions when fulfilling role obligations. **115**

Roles: Scripts people follow as occupants of a particular status. Roles include beliefs about rights and obligations. **49, 85**

Rumors: Information, usually of unknown origin, that spreads spontaneously among people in a stressful, uncertain situation. **127**

Sacred: Anything that is elevated above the ordinary and is regarded with awe, reverence, mystery, and, sometimes, fear. **429**

Sample: In survey research, a smaller number of people chosen to represent a larger population. **56**

Sanctions: The rewards and punishments used by groups and individuals to enforce conformity to norms. **88**

Scapegoats: Less powerful people in a group or a society who are wrongly blamed for the problems of the group or the society. **257**

Scientific method: A series of steps that researchers follow in accumulating accurate and verifiable knowledge. **53**

Secondary deviance: Additional deviant behavior that is a response to being labeled deviant. **226**

Secondary sector: That part of an economy that involves the manufacture of machine-made products from raw materials provided by others. **158**

Sects: Religious groups characterized by emotionally expressive rituals, conversion, strict interpretation of theological doctrine, and strong emphasis on personal morality. The term sect is usually limited to groups formed by people who have left established religious groups for a more rigorous religious life. **439**

Secularization: A decline in the role of religious beliefs in guiding daily activities. **434**

Segregation: Separation and exclusion of a minority from residential, commercial, occupational, recreational, educational, or religious facilities and activities. **184, 250**

Self-fulfilling prophecies: Doing or becoming what others predict you will do or become, regardless of social circumstances. **91**

Sexual revolution: A time of rapid change in sexual values, attitudes, and behavior that occurred in the middle social classes in the United States and Europe before, during, and after World War I. **293**

Signs: Symbols such as cues or gestures that refer mainly to present conditions. **80**

Situational conflict: Feelings of stress that arise from threatening or negative external circumstances, such as loss of a job or death of a family member. **115**

Slum: An urban area characterized by very high rates of poverty and unemployment, overcrowding, and deteriorated housing and public facilities. **184**

Social change: Large-scale changes in culture and in the social location of individuals, groups, or societies. **112**

Social class: A large category of people who share a similar rank in a prestige hierarchy. Rank is based on property and income, education, occupation, ancestry, and gender. Also known as **social status**. **34**

Social conflict: Destructive efforts by societies, groups, and individuals to obtain exclusive material rewards (goods and services) and non-material rewards (prestige and power). **113**

Social control: The use of sanctions (rewards and punishments) to enforce conformity to group and societal norms. **88**

Social Darwinism: The application of Darwin's theory of biological evolution to explain inequality between different societies and among various categories of people in the same society. **9**

Social facts: Rules that exist outside of individuals and have a controlling force over them. They define right and wrong behavior, thought, and emotion within groups, communities, and societies. **10**

Social location: Location within a particular society or major category of people in a society at a particular time. **3**

Social mobility: Movement from one status to another in the social class or social stratification system. **122, 331**

Social movements: Organized efforts to promote or resist social change. **129**

Social status: A ranked position in the total society. **34, 87**

Social stratification: A system of ranking of people in layers or strata above and below each other with respect to varying criteria. **330**

Socialism: An economic system characterized by public ownership of income-producing property, cooperation, and equal distribution of wealth and income or distribution on the basis of need. **146**

Socialization: The process by which individuals learn to function in their groups and societies. **49, 90**

Society: A number of people who occupy a specific territory, share a common culture and identity, and are, or would like to be, politically independent. **73**

Sociobiology: A model in which complex personality dispositions such as aggression, selfishness, tribalism, and male dominance are believed to be genetically determined. **36**

Sociocultural evolution model: A theoretical model in which developments in science, technology, and economics are given the greatest weight as explanatory variables. **43**

Sociology: The study of the typical ways of thinking, feeling, and behaving of people who are similarly located in time and in physical and cultural space. **2**

Sociology of knowledge: The investigation of how location in time and social space affects the knowledge that is sought and the interpretation of this knowledge. **53**

Spirits: Supernatural forces with human qualities of motivation and emotion. **431**

State: A society that has a monopoly over the legitimate use of force in its territory. **363**

State religions: Religions supported by a national government and claiming all citizens as members. **431**

Status: A widely recognized position in a group or society. **49**

Status inconsistency: A discrepancy between two or more variables that determine a person's overall social status or prestige in a society. **230**

Stereotype: An exaggerated or untrue belief that is applied to an entire category of people. **53**

Strata: The layers that make up a social stratification system. **330**

Structural mobility: Movement up or down in social class by large numbers of people because of changes in the occupational structure, such as the number of working- or middle-class jobs available. **331**

Structural-functional model: A theoretical model in which social structure, values, and the tendency toward social stability are given the greatest weight as explanatory factors. **45**

Structure: Parts of a bounded whole (a cell, a group, or a society) that are related in a recurring, interdependent way. **46**

Subculture: Customs and traditions of particular segments of a society that differ in certain ways from those of the wider society. **81**

Subsistence economy: An economy in which goods and services provide only for local needs and there is little or no trading with other societies. **148**

Suburbs: Politically independent areas surrounding and linked to cities by economic and other ties. **183**

Succession: The successful establishment in an area of new and different types of people or activities; in governments, the turning over of authority to a new leader. **184, 366**

Supernatural: A realm or reality that does not require empirical observation or verification of its existence for believers. **430**

Survey research: The study of large numbers of people, using personal interviews or mailed questionnaires. **56**

Symbolic interaction model: A focus on perceptions and performance of roles as these are based on the use of mutually understood symbols, especially language, gestures, and cues (body language). **50**

Symbols: Concrete things that stand for more complex or abstract phenomena. **79**

Taboos: Norms that define prohibited behavior. **75**

Technology: Tools, weapons, and the skills necessary to operate these objects. **43**

Telecommuters: Employees who work at home or near home and receive or transmit information to their firms by means of PCs and modems, faxes, direct telephone links, cellular phones, videophones, and beepers. **354**

Temperament: Levels of emotional intensity, energy, and activity within individuals that are biologically grounded. **37**

Terrorism: Politically motivated violence directed against civilian populations. **259**

Tertiary sector: That part of an economy that involves providing services rather than producing goods or extracting natural resources. **164**

Theistic religions: Religions that center on belief in the existence of a powerful God or gods. **432**

Theocracy: A society in which the positions of political and religious leaders are combined and held by the same people; a society in which high priests rule by divine right. **180, 433**

Theologies: Religious beliefs that provide meaningful explanations of the major questions of human existence. **432**

Theory: A statement of the relationship between variables that explains why certain conditions exist or how they came about. **30**

Tolerance: An acceptance and respect for human physical and cultural differences. **170**

Total fertility rate: The average number of children born to each woman in a society over her lifetime. **190**

Total institution: A place in which people are confined and are under total control of the authorities. **95**

Totalitarian governments: A form of government in which leaders exercise total control over all aspects of the lives of citizens. **370**

Totems: Sacred symbols that are representative of a clan. **432**

Tracking: The placement of students in separate, specialized classes on the basis of scores on tests of ability and achievement or teachers' judgments about students' abilities. **394**

Traditional authority: Legitimate power based on ancient custom and tradition. **365**

Traditional values: Values that have been part of a culture for many generations. **82**

Universal religions: Religions whose membership transcends societal and geographic boundaries. **432**

Urban planning: Deliberate attempts by governments to control, coordinate, and subsidize urban growth or change, to whatever extent political ideology and available public economic resources will allow. **188**

Urbanization: The movement of populations from agricultural to urban areas. **180**

Value free: The principle that research techniques, observations, and conclusions must not be distorted by the investigator's values. **12**

Values: Beliefs about what is good, right, desirable, or important. **39**

Variable: Characteristics that vary in degree or type. **31**

***Verstehen* method:** A qualitative method of sociological research involving identification and empathy with subjects. **12**

Violence: Physical aggression against others. **217**

Virtual reality: A computer-constructed, duplicate reality with which individuals can interact. **354**

Virtual solidarity: A feeling of community and cooperative relationships based on and cemented by electronic links. **354**

Vital statistics: Measures of basic demographic variables such as birth, death, marriage, divorce, and migration rates. **190**

White-collar crime: Secret and nonviolent crime committed by people in the middle and upper social classes of industrial societies, usually in their occupational activities. **172, 230**

Working class: People having the lowest level of resources, prestige, or power in a society, who work primarily with things and with manual skills. **157**

Zero population growth: Stable population size as a result of a balance between birth rates and immigration, emigration, and death rates. **198**

Answers to Practice Tests

CHAPTER 1

True ▪ False Test

1. F   5. F   8. F
2. F   6. T   9. F
3. T   7. T   10. T
4. F

Multiple-Choice Test

1. c   5. d   8. b
2. a   6. a   9. b
3. d   7. c   10. b
4. a

Matching Test

1. (1)a, (2)e, (3)a, (4)b, (5)d
2. (1)e, (2)d, (3)a, (4)b, (5)c
3. (1)d, (2)a, (3)c, (4)e, (5)b
4. (1)e, (2)a, (3)d, (4)c, (5)b
5. (1)c, (2)a, (3)e, (4)b, (5)d

CHAPTER 2

True ▪ False Test

1. F   5. F   8. F
2. F   6. T   9. F
3. T   7. T   10. F
4. T

Multiple-Choice Test

1. d   5. b   8. c
2. d   6. a   9. a
3. a   7. b   10. b
4. a

Matching Test

1. (1)d, (2)a, (3)e, (4)b, (5)c
2. (1)a, (2)d, (3)c, (4)e, (5)b
3. (1)b, (2)a, (3)d, (4)e, (5)c
4. (1)d, (2)e, (3)b, (4)c, (5)a
5. (1)a, (2)e, (3)b, (4)c, (5)d

CHAPTER 3

True ▪ False Test

1. F   5. T   8. T
2. F   6. T   9. F
3. F   7. F   10. F
4. T

Multiple-Choice Test

1. b   5. d   8. b
2. a   6. a   9. d
3. d   7. c   10. a
4. c

Matching Test

1. (1)b, (2)c, (3)e, (4)d, (5)a
2. (1)b, (2)a, (3)e, (4)d, (5)c
3. (1)e, (2)b, (3)a, (4)d, (5)c
4. (1)b, (2)a, (3)e, (4)c, (5)d
5. (1)e, (2)a, (3)d, (4)b, (5)c

CHAPTER 4

True ▪ False Test

1. T   5. T   8. F
2. T   6. T   9. T
3. F   7. T   10. T
4. F

Multiple-Choice Test

1. d   5. d   8. b
2. c   6. a   9. a
3. a   7. c   10. d
4. b

Matching Test

1. (1)c, (2)e, (3)a, (4)b, (5)d
2. (1)d, (2)b, (3)a, (4)c, (5)e
3. (1)d, (2)b, (3)a, (4)e, (5)c
4. (1)a, (2)c, (3)d, (4)e, (5)b
5. (1)b, (2)e, (3)d, (4)a, (5)c

CHAPTER 5

True ▪ False Test

1. T   5. T   8. F
2. F   6. T   9. T
3. F   7. F   10. F
4. T

Multiple-Choice Test

1. b   5. b   8. a
2. b   6. d   9. d
3. a   7. b   10. c
4. c

Matching Test

1. (1)d, (2)a, (3)e, (4)c, (5)b
2. (1)c, (2)e, (3)a, (4)b, (5)d
3. (1)b, (2)d, (3)a, (4)c, (5)c
4. (1)d, (2)b, (3)e, (4)a, (5)c
5. (1)c, (2)d, (3)e, (4)a, (5)b

CHAPTER 6

True ▪ False Test

1. F   5. T   8. F
2. T   6. T   9. T
3. T   7. T   10. T
4. F

Multiple-Choice Test

1. c   5. a   8. a
2. a   6. d   9. a
3. b   7. c   10. b
4. c

Matching Test

1. (1)b, (2)d, (3)a, (4)e, (5)c
2. (1)e, (2)b, (3)c, (4)d, (5)a
3. (1)d, (2)a, (3)e, (4)b, (5)c
4. (1)d, (2)c, (3)e, (4)b, (5)a
5. (1)b, (2)d, (3)a, (4)c, (5)e

CHAPTER 7

True ▪ False Test

1. T	5. T	8. F
2. F	6. F	9. F
3. F	7. T	10. T
4. F		

Multiple-Choice Test

1. c	5. a	8. a
2. a	6. d	9. d
3. b	7. c	10. c
4. c		

Matching Test

1. (1)a, (2)c, (3)e, (4)b, (5)d
2. (1)e, (2)a, (3)d, (4)b, (5)c
3. (1)c, (2)e, (3)d, (4)a, (5)b
4. (1)d, (2)b, (3)e, (4)c, (5)a
5. (1)b, (2)a, (3)d, (4)e, (5)c

CHAPTER 8

True ▪ False Test

1. T	5. F	8. T
2. F	6. F	9. T
3. T	7. F	10. T
4. T		

Multiple-Choice Test

1. d	5. b	8. a
2. b	6. a	9. c
3. c	7. c	10. d
4. d		

Matching Test

1. (1)c, (2)a, (3)e, (4)b, (5)d
2. (1)a, (2)e, (3)c, (4)d, (5)b
3. (1)c, (2)a, (3)e, (4)b, (5)d
4. (1)d, (2)a, (3)c, (4)b, (5)e
5. (1)e, (2)a, (3)b, (4)c, (5)d

CHAPTER 9

True ▪ False Test

1. T	5. T	8. T
2. F	6. T	9. T
3. F	7. F	10. F
4. F		

Multiple-Choice Test

1. a	5. a	8. c
2. c	6. d	9. a
3. b	7. a	10. b
4. d		

Matching Test

1. (1)b, (2)a, (3)d, (4)e, (5)c
2. (1)d, (2)b, (3)e, (4)c, (5)a
3. (1)c, (2)e, (3)d, (4)a, (5)b
4. (1)d, (2)a, (3)b, (4)e, (5)c
5. (1)a, (2)e, (3)d, (4)c, (5)b

CHAPTER 10

True ▪ False Test

1. T	5. F	8. F
2. T	6. F	9. T
3. F	7. T	10. F
4. T		

Multiple-Choice Test

1. a   5. b   8. a
2. c   6. d   9. a
3. c   7. c   10. c
4. d

Matching Test

1. (1)c, (2)a, (3)d, (4)e, (5)b
2. (1)c, (2)b, (3)d, (4)e, (5)a
3. (1)b, (2)e, (3)d, (4)c, (5)a
4. (1)a, (2)c, (3)d, (4)b, (5)e
5. (1)c, (2)a, (3)d, (4)e, (5)c

CHAPTER 11

True ▪ False Test

1. F   5. T   8. T
2. T   6. T   9. T
3. T   7. T   10. F
4. T

Multiple-Choice Test

1. a   5. b   8. d
2. d   6. a   9. a
3. c   7. b   10. a
4. a

Matching Test

1. (1)d, (2)b, (3)a, (4)c, (5)e
2. (1)a, (2)c, (3)e, (4)d, (5)b
3. (1)c, (2)e, (3)a, (4)b, (5)d
4. (1)d, (2)a, (3)c, (4)b, (5)c
5. (1)d, (2)e, (3)a, (4)b, (5)c

CHAPTER 12

True ▪ False Test

1. T   5. T   8. T
2. F   6. F   9. F
3. T   7. F   10. T
4. T

Multiple-Choice Test

1. d   5. c   8. d
2. b   6. d   9. c
3. a   7. b   10. d
4. c

Matching Test

1. (1)b, (2)a, (3)e, (4)d, (5)c
2. (1)a, (2)b, (3)c, (4)d, (5)e
3. (1)d, (2)e, (3)a, (4)c, (5)b
4. (1)d, (2)a, (3)e, (4)b, (5)c
5. (1)e, (2)b, (3)a, (4)d, (5)c

CHAPTER 13

True ▪ False Test

1. F   5. T   8. F
2. F   6. T   9. F
3. T   7. F   10. T
4. F

Multiple-Choice Test

1. b   5. d   8. b
2. d   6. b   9. d
3. c   7. a   10. c
4. b

Matching Test

1. (1)c, (2)a, (3)e, (4)b, (5)d
2. (1)a, (2)b, (3)e, (4)d, (5)c
3. (1)c, (2)e, (3)a, (4)b, (5)d
4. (1)e, (2)c, (3)a, (4)b, (5)d
5. (1)e, (2)d, (3)a, (4)b, (5)c

References

Adorno, Theodore W., Else Frankel-Brunswik, Daniel J. Levinson, and R. Nevitt Sanford. 1950. *The Authoritarian Personality*. New York: Wiley.

Ahlburg, Dennis A. and Carol J. DeVita. 1992. "New Realities of the American Family." *Population Bulletin 47*. Washington, DC: Population Reference Bureau.

Aho, James. 1990. *The Politics of Righteousness: Idaho Christian Patriotism*. Seattle: University of Washington Press.

Ahrons, Constance. 1994. *The Good Divorce*. New York: HarperCollins.

Ainsworth, Mary D. and John Bowlby. 1991. "An Ethological Approach to Personality Development." *American Psychologist* 46: 333-41.

Aldous, Joan. 1990. "Family Development and the Life Course: Two Perspectives." *Journal of Marriage and the Family* 52: 571-83.

Alexander, Karl L., Martha Cook, and Edward L. McDill. 1978. "Curriculum Tracking and Educational Stratification: Some Further Evidence." *American Sociological Review* 43: 43-66.

Alexander, Karl L., Doris R. Entwistle, and Maxine S. Thompson. 1987. "School Performance, Status Relations, and the Structure of Sentiment: Bringing the Teachers Back In." *American Sociological Review* 52: 47-66.

Allport, Gordon. 1958. *The Nature of Prejudice*. Garden City, NY: Doubleday.

Altman, Lawrence K. 1993. "Medical Schools Gaining an Unexpected Popularity." *New York Times* (May 18): A1, A19.

Alwin, Duane F. 1990. "Cohort Replacement and Changes in Parental Socialization Values." *Journal of Marriage and the Family* 52: 347-60.

American Association of University Women. 1992. *How Schools Shortchange Girls*. Washington, DC: American Association of University Women Educational Foundation.

American Institute of Public Opinion. 1978. *Gallup Opinion Index*, Report No. 160: 21-4.

American Sociological Association. 1993. "Employment, Enrollment, and Membership Trends." Unpublished report.

Ammerman, Nancy. 1987. *Bible Believers: Fundamentalists in the Modern World*. New Brunswick, NJ: Rutgers University Press.

_____. 1990. *Baptist Battles: Social Change and Religious Conflict in the Southern Baptist Convention*. New Brunswick, NJ: Rutgers University Press.

_____. 1991. "North American Protestant Fundamentalism." Pp. 1-65 in *Fundamentalisms Observed*, edited by Martin E. Marty and R. Scott Appleby. Chicago: University of Chicago Press.

Amy, Douglas J. 1993. *Real Choices/Real Voices: The Case For Proportional Representation Elections in the United States*. New York: Columbia University Press.

Anderson, Elijah. 1990. *Streetwise: Race, Class, and Change in an Urban Community*. Chicago: University of Chicago Press.

Anderson, J. E. and L. L. Dahlberg. 1992. "High-Risk Sexual Behavior in the General Population: Results from a National Survey." *Sexually Transmitted Diseases* 19: 320-25.

Applebome, Peter. 1993. "Skinhead Violence Grows, Experts Say." *New York Times* (July 18): A18.

Aquilino, William S. 1990. "The Likelihood of Parent-Adult Child Coresidence." *Journal of Marriage and the Family* 52: 405-19.

Archer, Dane and Rosemary Gartner. 1984. *Violence and Crime in Cross-National Perspective*. New Haven: Yale University Press.

Armbruster, Frank. 1977. *Our Children's Crippled Future*. New York: Quadrangle Books.

Atchley, Robert C. 1989. "A Continuity Theory of Normal Aging." *Gerontologist* 29: 183-194.

Atchley, Robert C. 1994. *Social Forces and Aging,* 7th ed. Belmont, CA: Wadsworth.

Bachu, Amara. 1993. "Fertility of American Women: June 1992." *Current Population Reports* P20-470 (June).

Baer, Hans. 1993. "The Limited Empowerment of Women in Black Spiritualist Churches: An Alternative Vehicle to Religious Leadership." *Sociology of Religion* 54: 65-82.

Bailey, Michael. 1991. "A Genetic Study of Sexual Orientation." *Archives of General Psychiatry* 48: 1089-96.

Baker, David P. and Deborah Perkins Jones. 1993. "Creating Gender Equality: Cross-National Gender Stratification and Mathematical Performance." *Sociology of Education* 66: 91-103.

Baltes, Paul B. 1993. "The Aging Mind: Potential and Limits." *Gerontologist* 33: 580-94.

Baltzell, E. Digby. 1987 [1964]. *The Protestant Establishment: Aristocracy and Caste in America.* New Haven: Yale University Press.

_____. 1991. *The Protestant Establishment Revisited.* New Brunswick, NJ: Transaction Publishers.

Barker, Eileen V. 1984. *The Making of a Moonie: Choice or Brainwashing?* Cambridge, MA: Basil Blackwell.

Barna, George. 1992. *The Barna Report: 1992-1993.* Ventura, CA: Regal Books.

Barringer, Felicity. 1993. "Ethnic Pride Confounds the Census." *New York Times* (June 7): A3.

Barth, Roland. 1972. *Open Education and the American School.* New York: Schocken.

Bartlett, Donald L. and James B. Steele. 1992. *America: What Went Wrong?* Kansas City, MO: Andrews & McMeel.

Batteau, Allen, ed. 1983. *Appalachia and America: Autonomy and Regional Dependence.* Lexington: University Press of Kentucky.

Baumrind, Diana. 1968. "Authoritarian versus Authoritative Parental Control." *Adolescence* 3: 255-72.

_____. 1980. "New Directions in Socialization Research." *American Psychologist* 35: 639-52.

Beck, E. M. and Stewart E. Tolnay. 1990. "The Killing Fields of the Deep South: The Market for Cotton and the Lynching of Blacks, 1882-1930." *American Sociological Review* 55: 526-39.

Beck, Melinda. 1993. "The Gray Nineties." *Newsweek* (October 4): 65-6.

Beck, Rubye W. and Scott H. Beck. 1989. "The Incidence of Extended Households among Middle-Aged Black and White Women." *Journal of Family Issues* 10: 147-68.

Becker, Howard S. 1963. *Outsiders: Studies in the Sociology of Deviance.* New York: Free Press.

_____, ed. 1964. *The Other Side: Perspectives on Deviance.* New York: Free Press.

Beckford, James A. 1985. *Cult Controversies: The Societal Response to the New Religious Movements.* London and New York: Tavistock Publications.

_____. 1989. *Religion and Advanced Industrial Society.* London: Unwin Hyman.

Beer, William R. 1992. *American Stepfamilies.* New Brunswick, NJ: Transaction Publishers.

Bell, Daniel. 1973. *The Coming of Post-Industrial Society: A Venture in Social Forecasting.* New York: Basic Books.

Bellah, Robert N. 1967. "Civil Religion in America." *Daedalus* 96 (Winter): 1-21.

Bellah, Robert, Richard Madsen, Ann Swidler, and Steven Tipton. 1985. *Habits of the Heart: Individualism and Commitment in American Life.* Berkeley: University of California Press.

Bellanger, Sarah and Maurice Pinnard. 1991. "Ethnic Movements and the Competition Model: Some Missing Links." *American Sociological Review* 56: 446-57.

Bellant, Russ. 1991a. *Old Nazis, the New Right, and the Republican Party,* 3rd ed. Boston, MA: South End Press.

_____. 1991b. *The Coors Connection: How Coors Family Philanthropy Undermines Democratic Pluralism,* 2nd ed. Boston: South End Press.

Belsky, Janet K. 1990. *The Psychology of Aging.* Pacific Grove, CA: Brooks/Cole.

Belsky, Jay. 1990. "Parental and Nonparental Child Care and Children's Socioemotional Development: A Decade in Review." *Journal of Marriage and the Family* 52: 885-903.

Bendroth, Margaret. 1984. "The Search for 'Women's Role' in American Evangelicalism, 1930-1980." In *Evangelicalism in Modern America,* edited by George Marsden.

_____. 1993. *Fundamentalism and Gender: 1875 to the Present.* New Haven: Yale University Press.

Bengtston, Vern and Robert E. L. Roberts. 1991. "Intergenerational Solidarity in Aging Families: An Example of Formal Theory Construction." *Journal of Marriage and the Family* 53: 856-70.

Bennet, James. 1993. "Retirees Figure Big in Detroit Math." *New York Times* (September 14): D1, D5.

Bennett, Neil G., Ann Klimas Blanc, and David E. Bloom. 1988. "Commitment and the Modern Union: Assessing the Link between Premarital Cohabitation and Subsequent Marital Stability." *Journal of Marriage and the Family* 50: 127–38.

Benovat, Aaron, Yun-Kyung Cha, David Kamens, John W. Meyer, and Suk-Ying Wong. 1991. "Knowledge for the Masses: World Models and National Curricula, 1920–1986." *American Sociological Review* 56: 85–100.

Berger, Peter L. 1969. *The Sacred Canopy: Elements of a Sociological Theory of Religion.* New York: Doubleday.

———. 1986. *The Capitalist Revolution.* New York: Basic Books.

Bernard, Jessie. 1982. *The Future of Marriage,* 2nd ed. New Haven: Yale University Press.

Bibby, Reginald W. and Merlin Brinkerhoff. 1973. "The Circulation of the Saints: A Study of People Who Join Conservative Churches." *Journal for the Scientific Study of Religion* 12: 273–83.

———. 1983. "The Circulation of the Saints Revisited: A Longitudinal Look at Conservative Church Growth." *Journal for the Scientific Study of Religion* 22: 153–62.

Biblarz, Timothy J. and Adrian E. Raftery. 1993. "The Effects of Family Disruption on Social Mobility." *American Sociological Review* 58: 97–109.

Bidwell, Charles E. and Noah E. Friedkin. 1988. "The Sociology of Education." Pp. 449–71 in *Handbook of Sociology,* edited by Neil A. Smelser. Newbury Park, CA: Sage Publications.

Billy, John O. G., Koray Tanfer, William R. Grady, and Daniel Klepinger. 1993. "The Sexual Behavior of Men in the United States." *Family Planning Perspectives* 25: 52–60.

Blankenship, Kim M. 1993. "Bringing Gender and Race Back In: U.S. Employment Discrimination Policy." *Gender and Society* 7: 204–26.

Blau, Judith R., Kent Redding, and Kenneth C. Land. 1993. "Ethnocultural Cleavages and the Growth of Church Membership in the United States, 1860–1930." *Sociological Forum* 8: 609–638.

Blau, Peter and Otis Dudley Duncan. 1978 [1967]. *The American Occupational Structure,* rev. ed. New York: Free Press.

Blee, Kathleen M. 1991. *Women of the Klan: Racism and Gender in the 1920s.* Berkeley: University of California Press.

Bloom, David E. and Adi Brender. 1993. "Labor and the Emerging World Economy." *Population Bulletin 48.* Washington, DC: Population Reference Bureau.

Bloom, Harold. 1992. *The American Religion: The Emergence of the Post-Christian Nation.* New York: Simon & Schuster.

Blumberg, Rae Lesser, ed. 1991. *Gender, Family, and Economy: The Triple Overlap.* Newbury Park, CA: Sage Publications.

Blumer, Herbert. 1969. *Symbolic Interaction: Perspective and Method.* Englewood Cliffs, NJ: Prentice Hall.

Booth, Alan and John Edwards. 1992. "Starting Over: Why Remarriages Are More Unstable." *Journal of Family Issues* 13: 179–94.

Bould, Sally, Beverly Sanborn, and Laura Reiff. 1989. *Eighty-Five Plus.* Belmont, CA: Wadsworth.

Bouvier, Leon F. and Carol J. DeVita. 1991. "The Baby Boom-Entering Midlife." *Population Bulletin* 46 (November): 1–35.

Bowlby, John. 1953. "Some Pathological Processes Set in Train by Early Mother-Child Separation." *Journal of Mental Science* 2: 265–272.

———. 1958. "The Nature of the Child's Tie to Its Mother." *International Journal of Psychoanalysis* 39: 350–73.

Bowles, Samuel and Herbert Gintis. 1976. *Schooling in Capitalist America.* New York: Basic Books.

Boyer, Paul. 1992. *When Time Shall Be No More: Prophetic Belief in Modern American Culture.* Cambridge, MA: Belknap Press of Harvard University Press.

Boylan, Ross D. 1993. "The Effect of the Number of Diplomas on Their Value." *Sociology of Education* 66: 206–21.

Bradley, Robert H., Bettye M. Caldwell, and Stephen L. Rock. 1988. "Home Environment and School Performance: A Ten-Year Follow-up and Examination of Three Models of Environmental Action." *Child Development* 59: 277–88.

Branch, Taylor. 1988. *Parting of the Waters: America in the King Years, 1954–1963.* New York: Simon & Schuster.

Brauchli, Marcus W. 1993. "Chaotic Change: Free Enterprise in China Becomes a Free-For-All." *Wall Street Journal* (August 26): A1, A5.

Braude, Ann. 1989. *Radical Spirits: Spiritualism and Women's Rights in Nineteenth-Century America.* Boston: Beacon Press.

Brereton, Virginia Lieson. 1990. *Training God's Army: The American Bible School, 1880–1940.* Bloomington: Indiana University Press.

———. 1991. *From Sin to Salvation: Stories of Women's Conversions, 1800 to the Present.* Bloomington: Indiana University Press.

Brinton, Crane. 1938. *An Anatomy of Revolution.* New York: Vintage.

Bromley, David G., ed. 1988. *Falling from the Faith: The Causes, Course and Consequences of Religious Apostasy.* Beverley Hills, CA: Sage Publications.

Brophy, Jere E. 1983. "Research on the Self-Fulfilling Prophecy." *Journal of Educational Psychology* 75: 631–61.

Brown, Bernard. 1978. *Found: Long-Term Gains from Early Intervention.* Boulder, CO: Westview Press.

Brown, Bernard. 1985. "Head Start: How Research Changed Public Policy." *Young Children* 40: 9–13.

Brown, Karen McCarthy. 1991. *Mama Lola: A Voudou Priestess in Brooklyn.* Berkeley: University of California Press.

Brown, Lester R., Hal Kane, and Ed Ayres. 1993. *Vital Signs 1993: The Trends That Are Shaping Our Future.* New York: W. W. Norton.

Buechler, Stephen M. 1990. *Women's Movements in the United States.* New Brunswick, NJ: Rutgers University Press.

Bulcroft, Richard A. and Kris A. Bulcroft. 1993. "Race Differences in Attitudinal and Motivational Factors in the Decision to Marry." *Journal of Marriage and the Family* 55: 338–55.

Bumpass, Larry L. 1990. "What's Happening to the Family? Interactions between Demographic and Institutional Change." *Demography* 27: 485–95.

Bumpass, Larry L. and James A. Sweet. 1989. "National Estimates of Cohabitation." *Demography* 26: 615–25.

Bumpass, Larry L., James A. Sweet, and Theresa Castro Martin. 1990. "Changing Patterns of Remarriage." *Journal of Marriage and the Family* 52: 747–56.

Bumpass, Larry L., Teresa Castro Martin, and James A. Sweet. 1991. "The Impact of Family Background and Early Marital Factors on Marital Disruption." *Journal of Family Issues* 12: 22–42.

Bunker, Barbara B., Josephine M. Zubeck, Virginia J. Vanderslice, and Robert W. Rice. 1992. "Quality of Life in Dual-Career Families: Commuting Versus Single-Residence Couples." *Journal of Marriage and the Family* 54: 399–407.

Burawoy, Michael and Pavel Krotov. 1992. "The Soviet Transition from Socialism to Capitalism: Worker Control and Economic Bargaining in the Wood Industry." *American Sociological Review* 57: 16–38.

Burck, C. G. 1976. "Group Profile of the Fortune 500 Chief Executive." *Fortune* 93: 172–77.

Burnham, James. 1961. *The Managerial Revolution.* New York: John Day.

Burnham, Walter Dean. 1987. "The Turnout Problem." Pp. 97–133 in *Elections American Style,* edited by James Reichley. Washington, DC: Brookings Institution.

Burt, Martha R. 1992. *Over the Edge: The Growth of Homelessness in the 1980s.* New York: Russell Sage Foundation.

Buss, Arnold H. 1978. *Psychology: Behavior in Perspective.* New York: John Wiley.

———. 1994. *Personality.* Boston: Allyn & Bacon.

Buss, David. 1985. "Human Mate Selection." *American Scientist* 73: 47–51.

———. 1990. "International Preferences in Selecting Mates: A Study of 37 Cultures." *Journal of Cross-Cultural Psychology* 21: 5–47.

Butler, Robert N. 1993. "Dispelling Ageism: The Cross-Cutting Intervention." *Generations* (Spring/Summer): 75–82.

Butterworth, Nicholas. 1993. "Move Over Perot." *New York Newsday* (July 14): 52.

Button, Graham. 1991. *Ethnomethodology and the Human Sciences.* New York: Cambridge University Press.

Buunk, Bram D. and Barry van Driel. 1989. *Variant Lifestyles and Relationships.* Newbury Park, CA: Sage Publications.

Caldwell, Mayta A. and Letitia Anne Peplau. 1990. "The Balance of Power in Lesbian Relationships." Pp. 204–215 in *Perspectives on the Family: History, Class, and Feminism,* edited by Christopher Carlson. Belmont, CA: Wadsworth.

Calem, Robert E. 1993. "Tales From the 'Telecommuting' Front. Listen. You Might Be Next." *New York Times* (April 18): A1, A6.

Califano, Joseph A., Jr. 1993. "Battle Lines in the War on Drugs." *New York Times* (December 15): A27.

Callahan, Daniel. 1993. "Our Fear of Dying." *Newsweek* (October 4): 67.

Camp, Sharon L., ed. 1992. *World Access to Birth Control: 1992 Report on World Progress Towards Population Stabilization.* Washington, DC: Population Crisis Committee.

Canizares, Raul. 1992. *Walking With the Night: The Afro-Cuban World of Santaria.* Rochester, VT: Inner Traditions.

Capps, Walter H. 1990. *The New Religious Right: Piety, Patriotism and Politics.* Columbia: University of South Carolina Press.

Carpenter, Joel. 1980. "Fundamentalist Institutions and the Rise of Conservative Protestantism, 1929-1942." *Church History* 49 (March): 62-75.

Casper, Lynne M., Sarah H. McLanahan, and Irwin Garfinkle. 1994. "The Gender-Poverty Gap: What Can We Learn from Other Countries?" *American Sociological Review* 59: 594-605.

Celis, William, III. 1993a. "10 Years After a Scathing Report, Schools Show Uneven Progress." *New York Times* (April 28): A19.

_____. 1993b. "Study Finds Rising Concentration of Black and Hispanic Students." *New York Times* (December 14): A1, B6.

_____. 1993c. "Study Says Half of Adults in U.S. Can't Read or Handle Arithmatic." *New York Times* (September 19): A1, A22.

Chambliss, William J. 1973. "The Saints and the Roughnecks." *Society* 11 (November/December): 24-31.

Chambliss, William J. and William Mankoff, eds. 1976. *Whose Law, What Order?* New York: John Wiley.

Charles, Maria. 1992. "Cross-National Variations in Occupational Sex Segregation." *American Sociological Review* 57: 483-502.

Cherlin, Andrew J. 1992. *Marriage, Divorce, Remarriage,* rev. ed. Cambridge, MA: Harvard University Press.

Cherlin, Andrew J. and Frank Furstenberg Jr. 1988. "The Changing European Family." *Journal of Family Issues* 9: 291-97.

Chesnais, Jean-Claude. 1993. *The Demographic Transition: Stages, Patterns, and Economic Implications,* translated by Elizabeth and Philip Kreager. New York: Oxford University Press.

Childe, V. Gordon. 1951. *Man Makes Himself.* New York: Mentor.

_____. 1964. *What Happened in History,* rev. ed. Baltimore: Penguin.

Chilman, Catherine S. 1991. "Working Poor Families: Trends, Causes, Effects, and Suggested Policies." *Family Relations* 40: 141-98.

Chomsky, Noam. 1988. *Language and Politics.* New York: Black Rose Books.

Clark, Burton. 1962. *Educating the Expert Society.* New York: Intext.

_____. 1978. "Academic Differentiation in National Systems of Higher Education." *Comparative Education Review* 22: 242-58.

Clark, Candace. 1988. "Sickness and Social Control." Pp. 471-91 in *Social Interaction: Readings in Sociology,* 3rd ed., edited by Candace Clark and Howard Robby. New York: St. Martin's Press.

Clark, Roger, Rachel Lennon, and Leanna Morris. 1993. "Of Caldecotts and Kings: Gendered Images in Recent American Children's Books by Black and Non-Black Illustrators." *Gender and Society* 7: 227-45.

Clines, Francis X. 1993. "Some New Yorkers on Probation Will Begin Reporting to Machines." *New York Times* (May 24): A1, B3.

Cloward, Richard and Lloyd Ohlin. 1960. *Delinquency and Opportunity.* New York: Free Press.

Clymer, Adam, Robert Pear, and Robin Toner. 1994. "For Health Care, Time Was a Killer." *New York Times* (August 29): A1, A12, A13.

Coe, Michael. 1987. *The Maya.* New York: Thames & Hudson.

_____. 1993. *Breaking the Maya Code.* New York: Thames & Hudson.

Cohen, Albert K. 1955. *Delinquent Boys: The Culture of the Gang.* New York: Free Press.

Cohen, Norman J., ed. 1990. *The Fundamentalist Phenomenon: A View from Within, A Response from Without.* Grands Rapids, MI: William B. Eerdmans.

Coleman, James S. 1993. "The Rational Reconstruction of Society." *American Sociological Review* 58: 1-15.

Coleman, James S., Ernest Q. Campbell, Carol J. Hobson, James McPartland, Alexander Mood, Frederick D. Weinfeld, and Robert L. York. 1966. *Equality of Educational Opportunity.* Washington, DC: U.S. Government Printing Office.

Coleman, James S. and Thomas Hoffer. 1987. *Public and Private Schools: The Impact of Communities.* New York: Basic Books.

Coleman, James S., Thomas Hoffer, and Sally Kilgore. 1982. *High School Achievement: Public,*

Private, and Catholic Schools Compared. New York: Basic Books.

Collins, Randall. 1979. *The Credential Society.* New York: Academic Press.

Colvin, Mark. 1992. *The Penitentiary in Crisis: From Accomodation to Riot in New Mexico.* Albany: State University of New York Press.

Comte, Auguste. 1915 [1830–1842]. *The Positive Philosophy,* translated by Harriet Martineau. London: George Bell & Sons.

Consortium for Longitudinal Studies. 1979. *Lasting Effects after Preschool: Summary Report.* Washington, DC: U.S. Department of Health, Education, and Welfare.

_____. 1983. *As the Twig Is Bent: Lasting Effects of Preschool Programs.* Hillsdale, NJ: Erlbaum.

Cooley, Charles Horton. 1909. *Social Organization.* New York: Scribner's.

_____. 1964 [1902]. *Human Nature and the Social Order.* New York: Scribner's.

Coontz, Stephanie. 1992. *The Way We Never Were: American Families and the Nostalgia Trap.* New York: Basic Books.

Corcoran, Mary, Roger Gordon, Deborah Laren, and Gary Solon. 1990. "Effects of Family and Community Background on Economic Status." *American Economic Review* 80: 362–66.

Cort, John. 1988. *Christian Socialism.* Maryknoll, NY: Orbis Books.

Cose, Ellis. 1993. *The Rage of a Privileged Class.* New York: HarperCollins.

Coser, Louis A. 1956. *The Functions of Social Conflict.* New York: Free Press.

Cowell, Alan. 1993. "Pope Issues Censure of 'Nature Worship' among U.S. Women. *New York Times.* (July 3): 1, 4.

Crain, Robert R. and Rita E. Mahard. 1979. "Desegregation and Black Achievement: A Review of the Research." Pp. 704–40 in *Policy Studies Review Annual,* edited by Robert H. Haveman and B. Bruce Zellner. Beverly Hills, CA: Sage Publications.

Crano, William D. and Joel Aronoff. 1978. "A Cross-Cultural Study of Expressive and Instrumental Role Complementarity." *American Sociological Review* 43: 463–71.

Crews, Douglas E. 1993. "Cultural Lags in Social Perceptions of the Aged." *Generations* (Spring/Summer): 29–34.

Crippen, Timothy. 1992. "Further Notes on Religious Transformation." *Social Forces* 71:1 (September): 219–23.

Crosby, John. 1991. *Illusion and Disillusion: The Self in Love and Marriage,* 4th ed. Belmont, CA: Wadsworth.

Curry, Mary Elaine. 1991. *Making the Gods in New York: The Yoruba Religion in the Black Community.* Unpublished dissertation. Graduate Center of the City University of New York.

Dahl, Robert A. 1961. *Who Governs?* New Haven: Yale University Press.

_____. 1982. *Dilemmas of Pluralist Democracy: Autonomy Versus Control.* New Haven: Yale University Press.

Dahrendorf, Ralf. 1959. *Class and Class Conflict in Industrial Society.* Palo Alto, CA: Stanford University Press.

Daniels, Arlene Kaplan. 1988. *Invisible Careers: Women Civic Leaders from the Volunteer World.* Chicago: University of Chicago Press.

Danzger, M. Herbert. 1989. *Returning to Tradition.* New Haven: Yale University Press.

Darnton, John. 1993. "Western Europe Is Ending Its Welcome to Immigrants." *New York Times* (August 10): A1, A8.

Davidman, Lynn. 1991. *Tradition in a Rootless World: Women Turn to Orthodox Judaism.* Berkeley: University of California Press.

Davidman, Lynn and Arthur L. Greil. 1993. "Gender and the Experience of Conversion: The Case of "Returnees" to Orthodox Judaism." *Sociology of Religion* 54: 83–100.

Davis, Kingsley and Wilbert E. Moore. 1945. "Some Principles of Stratification." *American Sociological Review* 10: 242–49.

Day, Kathleen. 1993. *S&L Hell: The People and the Politics behind the $1 Trillion Savings and Loan Scandal.* New York: W. W. Norton.

Day, Lincoln H. 1992. *The Future of Low-Birthrate Populations.* London and New York: Routledge.

De Witt, Karen. 1993. "SAT Scores Improve for 2d Consecutive Year." *New York Times* (August 19): A16.

DeBerg, Betty A. 1990. *Ungodly Women: Gender and the First Wave of American Fundamentalism.* Minneapolis: Fortress Press.

Deiros, Pablo A. 1991. "Protestant Fundamentalism in Latin America." Pp. 142–196 in *Fundamentalisms Observed,* edited by Martin E. Marty and R. Scott Appleby. Chicago: University of Chicago Press.

DeMaris, Alfred and William MacDonald. 1993. "Premarital Cohabitation and Marital Instability: A Test of the Unconventionality Hypothesis." *Journal of Marriage and the Family* 55: 399–407.

deMause, Lloyd, ed. 1974. *The History of Childhood.* New York: Psychohistory Press.

_____. 1991. "The Universality of Incest." *Journal of Psychohistory* 19: 123–164.

Demerath, N. J., III, and Rhy H. Williams. 1992. *A Bridging of Faiths: Religion and Politics in a New England City.* Princeton: Princeton University Press.

D'Emilio, John and Estelle B. Freedman. 1988. *Intimate Matters.* New York: Harper & Row.

Demo, David H. and Alan C. Acock. 1993. "Family Diversity and the Division of Domestic Labor: How Much Have Things Really Changed?" *Family Relations* 42: 323–31.

DeMott, Benjamin. 1990. *The Imperial Middle: Why Americans Can't Think Straight about Class.* New York: William Morrow.

DeParle, Jason. 1993. "Big Rise in Births Outside of Wedlock." *New York Times* (July 14): A1, A14.

Deutch, Martin et al. 1979. *Social Class, Race, and Psychological Development,* 2nd ed. New York: Irvington.

Diaz-Stevens, Anna Maria. 1993a. *Oxcart Catholicism on Fifth Avenue: The Impact of the Puerto Rican Migration upon the Archdiocese of New York.* South Bend, IN: Notre Dame University Press.

_____. 1993b. "Institutional Change in the Ministry: A Model for Interpreting Church Reponse to Puerto Rican Migration to the United States." Paper presented at the annual meeting of the Society for the Scientific Study of Religion, October 29, 1993.

DiPrete, Thomas A. 1993. "Industrial Restructuring and the Mobility Response." *American Sociological Review* 58: 74–96.

DiPrete, Thomas A. and David B. Grusky. 1991. "Structure and Trend in the Process of Stratification for Men and Women." *American Journal of Sociology* 96: 107–43.

Doering, Mildred, Susan R. Rhodes, and Michael Schuster. 1983. *The Aging Worker: Research and Recommendations.* Newbury Park, CA: Sage Publications.

Dolcini, M. Margaret, Joseph A. Catania, Thomas J. Coates, Ron Stall, Esther S. Hudes, John H. Gagnon and Lance M. Pollack. 1993. "Demographic Characteristics of Heterosexuals with Multiple Partners: The National AIDS Behavioral Surveys." *Family Planning Perspectives* 25: 208–14.

Domhoff, G. William. 1967. *Who Rules America?* Englewood Cliffs, NJ: Prentice Hall.

_____. 1983. *Who Rules America Now? A View for the Eighties.* Englewood Cliffs, NJ: Prentice Hall.

_____. 1990. *The Power Elite and the State.* New York: Aldine de Gruyter.

Draper, Patricia and Jennie Keith. 1992. "Cutural Contexts of Care: Family Caregiving for Elderly in America and Africa." *Journal of Aging Studies* 6: 113–34.

Dronkers, Jaap. 1993. "Educational Reform in the Netherlands: Did It Change the Impact of Parental Occupation and Education?" *Sociology of Education* 66: 262–77.

DSM-III. *Diagnostic and Statistical Manual of Mental Disorders,* 3rd ed. 1987. American Psychiatric Association.

Durkheim, Émile. 1933 [1893]. *The Division of Labor in Society,* translated by George Simpson. New York: Macmillan.

_____. 1938 [1895]. *The Rules of the Sociological Method,* 8th ed., translated by George E. G. Catlin. Chicago: University of Chicago Press.

_____. 1947 [1912]. *Elementary Forms of the Religious Life.* New York: Free Press.

_____. 1951 [1897]. *Suicide: A Study in Sociology,* translated by John A. Spaulding and George Simpson. Glencoe, IL: Free Press.

_____. 1951 [1912]. *Elementary Forms of the Religious Life,* translated by Joseph Ward Swain. Glencoe, IL: Free Press.

_____. 1956 [1922]. *Education and Society.* Glencoe, IL: Free Press.

Dye, Thomas R. 1990. *Who's Running America? The Reagan Years.* Englewood Cliffs, NJ: Prentice Hall.

Ebaugh, Helen Rose Fuchs. 1977. *Out of the Cloister: A Study of Organizational Dilemmas.* Austin, TX: University of Texas Press.

_____. 1993a. "Patriarchal Bargains and Latent Avenues of Social Mobility: Nuns in the Roman Catholic Church." *Gender and Society* 7: 400–14.

_____. 1993b. *Women in the Vanishing Cloister: Organizational Decline in Catholic Religious Orders.* New Brunswick, NJ: Rutgers University Press.

Edgerton, Robert B. 1976. *Deviance: A Cross-Cultural Perspective.* Menlo Park, CA: Cummings.

Eggebeen, David J. 1992. "Family Structure and Intergenerational Exchanges." *Research on Aging* 14: 427–47.

Eisler, Gary K. 1993. "Industry's New School-house." *Education Life* (January 9): 22-3.

Eissler, Kurt R., ed. 1949. *Searchlight on Delinquency.* New York: International Universities Press.

Elder, Glen H., Jr. 1974. *Children of the Great Depression.* Chicago: University of Chicago Press.

_____. 1992. "Life Course." Pp. 1120-30 in *The Encyclopedia of Sociology,* edited by Edgar and Marie Borgatta. New York: Macmillan.

Elder, Glen H., Jr. and Eliza K. Pavalko. 1993. "Work Careers in Men's Later Years: Transitions, Trajectories, and Historical Change." *Journal of Gerontology: Social Sciences* 48: S180-91.

Ellickson, Robert C. 1991. *Order without Law: How Neighbors Settle Disputes.* Cambridge, MA: Harvard University Press.

Elliot, Michael. 1994. "The Case for Kind Colonialism." *Newsweek* (July 18): 44.

Elliot, Roger. 1988. "Tests, Abilities, Race, and Conflict." *Intelligence* 12: 333-50.

Ellis, Godfrey J., Gary R. Lee, and Larry R. Peterson. 1978. "Supervision and Conformity: A Cross-Cultural Analysis of Parental Socialization Values." *American Journal of Sociology* 84: 386-408.

Ellis, Godfrey J. and Larry R. Peterson. 1992. "Socialization Values and Parental Control Techniques: A Cross-Cultural Analysis of Child Rearing." *Journal of Comparative Family Studies* 23: 39-54.

England, Paula. 1992. *Comparable Worth.* Hawthorne, NY: Aldine de Gruyter.

Epstein, Cynthia Fuchs. 1988. *Deceptive Distinctions.* New York: Russell Sage Foundation.

Entwisle, Doris and Karl L. Alexander. 1992. "Summer Setback: Race, Poverty, School Composition, and Achievement." *American Sociological Review* 57: 72-84.

Erikson, Erik H. 1963. *Childhood and Society.* 2nd ed. New York: W. W. Norton.

_____. 1982. *The Life Cycle Completed: A Review.* New York: W. W. Norton.

Erikson, Kai T. 1966. *Wayward Puritans.* New York: Wiley.

Escalona, Sibylle K. 1968. *The Roots of Individuality.* Chicago: Aldine.

Esterlin, Richard A. 1987. *Birth and Fortune.* Chicago: University of Chicago Press.

Esterlin, Richard A., Christine Macdonald, and Diane J. Macunovich. 1990. "Retirement Prospects of the Baby Boom Generation: A Different Perspective." *Gerontologist* 30: 783-86.

Fabella, Virginia and Mercy Amba Oduyoye. 1989. *With Passion and Compassion: Third World Women Doing Theology.* Maryknoll, NY: Orbis Books.

Featherstone, Joseph. 1971. *Schools Where Chidren Learn.* New York: Liveright.

Feeney, Judith A. and Patricia Noller. 1990. "Attachment Style as a Predictor of Adult Romantic Relationships." *Journal of Personality and Social Psycholgy* 58: 281-91.

Ferm, Deane William. 1986a. *Third World Liberation Theologies: An Introductory Survey.* Maryknoll, NY: Orbis Books.

_____. 1986b. *Third World Liberation Theologies: A Reader.* Maryknoll, NY: Orbis Books.

Ferree, Myra M, 1991. "The Gender Division of Labor in Two-Earner Marriages: Dimensions of Variability and Change." *Journal of Family Issues* 12: 158-80.

Finke, Roger and Rodney Stark. 1988. "Religious Economies and Sacred Canopies: Religious Mobilization in American Cities, 1906." *American Sociological Review* 53 (February): 41-49.

_____. 1989. "Evaluating the Evidence: Religious Economies and Sacred Canopies." *American Sociological Review* 54 (December): 1054-1056.

_____. 1992. *The Churching of America, 1776-1990: Winners and Losers in Our Religious Economy.* New Brunswick, NJ: Rutgers University Press.

Finkelhor, David and Karl Pillemer. 1988. "Elder Abuse: Its Relationships to Other Forms of Domestic Violence." Pp. 244-54 in Gerald T. Hotaling, David Finkelhor, John T. Kirpatrick, Murray A. Strauss, eds. *Family Abuse and Its Consequences.* Newbury Park, CA: Sage Publications.

Fischer, Claude S. 1991. "Gender and the Residential Telephone: 1890-1940." Pp. 128-147 in *The Family Experience,* edited by Mark Hutter. New York: Macmillan.

Fiske, Marjorie and David A. Chiriboga. 1990. *Change and Continuity in Adult Life.* San Francisco: Jossey-Bass.

Fitzgerald, Francis. 1979. *America Revised: History Textbooks in the Twentieth Century.* Boston: Little, Brown.

Frankl, Razelle. 1987. *Televangelism: The Marketing of Popular Religion.* Carbondale/Edwardsville: Southern Illinois University Press.

Freedman, Samuel G. 1993. *Upon This Rock: The Miracles of a Black Church.* New York: HarperCollins.

Freud, Sigmund. 1961 [1923]. "The Ego and the Id." *The Standard Edition,* vol. 19, translated and edited by James Strachey. London: Hogarth Press.

_____. 1961 [1930]. "Civilization and Its Discontents." *The Standard Edition,* vol. 21, translated and edited by James Strachey. London: Hogarth Press.

Frey, William H. 1990. "Metropolitan America: Beyond the Transition." *Population Bulletin 45.* Washington, DC: Population Reference Bureau.

Frierson, Henry T. 1989. "The Impact of Testing Skills Intervention upon Black Nursing Students' Licensure Examination Performance." *Journal of Negro Education* 58: 82–91.

Fromm, Eric. 1941. *Escape from Freedom.* New York: Holt, Rinehart Winston.

Fuchs, Victor R. 1988. *Women's Quest for Economic Equality.* Cambridge, MA: Harvard University Press.

Furstenberg, Frank F., Jr., Theodore Hershberg, and John Modell. 1975. "The Origins of the Famale-Headed Black Family: The Impact of the Urban Experience." *Journal of Interdisciplinary History* 5: 211–233.

Galanter, Marc. 1989. *Cults: Faith, Healing, and Coercion.* New York: Oxford University Press.

Gallup, George, Jr. 1990. *Religion in America.* Princeton: Princeton Religion Research Center.

Gallup, George, Jr. and Jim Castelli. 1989. *The People's Religion: American Faith in the 1990s.* New York: Macmillan.

Gamoran, Adam. 1993. "The Variable Effects of High School Tracking." *American Sociological Review* 57: 812–28.

Gamoran, Allan and Robert D. Mare. 1989. "Secondary School Tracking and Educational Inequality: Compensation, Reinforcement, or Neutrality?" *American Journal of Sociology* 95: 1146–83.

Ganong, Lawrence and Marilyn Coleman. 1994. *Remarried Family Relationships.* Thousand Oaks, CA: Sage Publications.

Gardner, Howard. 1983. *Frames of Mind: The Theory of Multiple Intelligences.* New York: Basic Books.

Garfinkel, Harold. 1956. "Conditions of Successful Degradation Ceremonies." *American Journal of Sociology* 61: 420–24.

Garfinkel, Harold. 1967. *Studies in Ethnomethodology.* Englewood Cliffs, NJ: Prentice Hall.

Gargan, Edward A. 1993. "For Many Brides in India, a Dowry Buys Death." *New York Times* (December 30): A4.

Garnier, Maurice, Jerals Hage, and Bruce Fuller. 1989. "The Strong State, Social Class, and Controlled School Expansion in France, 1881–1775." *American Journal of Sociology* 95: 279–306.

Gelfand, Donald and Barbara W. K. Yee. 1991. "Influence of Immigration, Migration, and Acculturation on the Fabric of Aging in America." *Generations* (Fall/Winter): 7–14.

Gerstel, Naomi and Sally K. Gallagher. 1993. "Kinkeeping and Distress: Gender, Recipients of Care, and Work-Family Conflict." *Journal of Marriage and the Family* 55: 598–607.

Gibbs, Nancy R. 1993a. "Bringing Up Father." *Time* (June 28): 53–8.

_____. 1993b. "Laying Down the Law." *Time* (August 23): 23–6.

Gilbert, Dennis and Joseph A. Kahl. 1993. *The American Class Structure.* Belmont, CA: Wadsworth.

Gilbert, Jess and Carlyn Howe. 1991. "Beyond State vs. Society: Theories of the State and New Deal Agriculture." *American Sociological Review* 56: 204–220.

Gilder, George. 1991. *Microcosm.* New York: Simon & Schuster.

Giles, Michael W. 1978. "White Enrollment Stability." *American Sociological Review* 43: 848–64.

Glassman, Ronald M., William H. Swatos Jr., and Paul R. Rosen. 1987. *Bureaucracy against Democracy and Socialism.* Westport, CT: Greenwood Press.

Glenn, Norval D. 1990. "Quantitive Research on Marital Quality in the 1980s: A Critical Review." *Journal of Marriage and the Family* 52: 818–31.

_____. 1991. "The Recent Trend in Marital Success in the United States." *Journal of Marriage and the Family* 53: 26–70.

_____. 1993. "The News Is Bad, But Not Quite as Bad as First Reported." *Journal of Marriage and the Family* 55: 242–3.

Gleuck, Sheldon and Eleanor Glueck. 1956. *Physique and Delinquency.* New York: Harper & Row.

Goetting, Ann. 1990. "Patterns of Support among In-Laws in the United States." *Journal of Family Issues* 11: 67–90.

Goffman, Erving. 1959. *The Presentation of Self in Everyday Life.* New York: Doubleday.

_____. 1961. *Asylums.* Garden City, NY: Anchor.

_____. 1963. *Stigma: Notes on the Management of Spoiled Identity.* Englewood Cliffs, NJ: Prentice Hall.

_____. 1967. *Interaction Ritual.* New York: Anchor.

Gold, Daniel. 1991. "Organized Hinduisms: From Vedic Truth to Hindu Nation." Pp. 531–593 in *Fundamentalisms Observed,* edited by Martin E. Marty and R. Scott Appleby. Chicago: University of Chicago Press.

Goldberg, Stephen. 1993. *Why Men Rule.* Chicago: Open Court Press.

Goldman, Ari L. 1993. "Portrait of Religion in U.S. Holds Dozens of Surprises." *New York Times* (April 10): A1, A18.

Goldscheider, Frances and Calvin Goldscheider. 1994. "Leaving and Returning Home in the 20th Century." *Population Bulletin* 48 (March): 1–36.

Goldscheider, Frances K. and L. J. Waite. 1991. *New Families, No Families?* Berkeley: University of California Press.

Goldschmidt, Walter. 1959. *Man's Way: A Preface to the Understanding of Human Society.* New York: Holt, Rinehart & Winston.

Goldsmith, Elizabeth B. 1989. *Work and Family.* Newbury Park, CA: Sage Publications.

Goldstone, Jack A., ed. 1986. *Revolutions.* New York: Harcourt Brace Jovanovich.

Goode, William J. 1993. *World Changes in Divorce Patterns.* New Haven: Yale University Press.

Graff, Henry F. 1993. "In the Van of History." *Newsweek* (May 3): 39.

Graubard, Allen. 1972. *Free the Children.* New York: Pantheon.

Greeley, Andrew M. 1972. *The Denominational Society: A Sociological Approach to Religion in American.* Glenview, IL: Scott Foresman.

_____. 1979a. "The Sociology of American Catholics." *Annual Review of Sociology* 5: 91–111.

_____. 1979b. *Crisis in the Church: A Study of American Religion.* Chicago: Thomas More Press.

_____. 1991a. *Faithful Attraction: Discovering Intimacy, Love, Fidelity in American Marriage.* New York: Tom Doherty Associates.

_____. 1991b. "The Demography of American Catholics: 1965–1990." In Helen Rose Ebaugh, ed., *Vatican II and U.S. Catholicism, Volume 2: Religion and the Social Order,* pp. 37–58. Greenwich: JAI Press.

Green, Richard. 1993. *Sexual Science and the Law.* Cambridge, MA: Harvard University Press.

Greenhouse, Stephen. 1993. "Third World Economic Gains Give a Lift to U.S. Exporters." *New York Times* (August 19): A1,D3.

Greenstein, Theodore N. 1990. "Marital Disruption and the Employment of Married Women." *Journal of Marriage and the Family* 52: 657–76.

_____. 1993. "Maternal Employment and Child Behavioral Outcomes." *Journal of Family Issues* 14: 323–51.

Griffith, Jeanne E., Mary J. Frase, and John H. Ralph. 1989. "American Education: The Challenge of Change." *Population Bulletin 44.* Washington, DC: Population Reference Bureau.

Grossman, Lawrence. 1993. "Jewish Communal Affairs." Pp. 169–91 in *American Jewish Yearbook,* edited by David Singer and Ruth R. Seldin. New York and Philadelphia: American Jewish Committee and Jewish Publication Society.

Grun, Bernard. 1991. *Timetables of History,* 3rd ed. New York: Simon & Schuster.

Guth, James. 1993. "Secular Scholars and the Religious Right." *Chronicle of Higher Education* 7 (April): B3, B5.

Gutierrez, Gustavo. 1984. *A Theology of Liberation.* Maryknoll, NY: Orbis Books.

Hadaway, C. Kirk, Penny Long Marler, and Mark Chaves. 1993. "What the Polls Don't Show: A Closer Look at U.S. Church Attendance." *American Sociological Review* 58: 741–52.

Haddad, Yvonne Yazbeck, and Allison Banks Findly, eds. 1985. *Women, Religion and Social Change.* Albany: State University of New York Press.

Hagan, John. 1991. "Destiny and Drift: Subcultural Preferences, Status Attainments and the Risks and Rewards of Youth." *American Sociological Review* 56: 567–82.

_____. 1994. *Crime and Disrepute.* Thousand Oaks, CA: Pine Forge Press.

Hage, Jerald and Charles H. Powers. 1992. *Post-Industrial Lives: Roles and Relationships in the 21st Century.* Newbury Park, CA: Sage Publications.

Hagedorn, John M. 1988. *People and Folks: Gangs, Crime, and the Underclass in a Rustbelt City.* Chicago: Lakeview Press.

Hailman, Jack P. 1969. "How an Instinct Is Learned." *Scientific American* 12: 98-106.

Halaby, Charles N. and David L. Weakliem. 1993. "Ownership and Authority in the Earnings Function: Nontested Tests of Alternative Specifications." *American Sociological Review* 58: 16-30.

Halberstam, David. 1993. *The Fifties.* New York: Villard.

Hall, Edward T. 1959. *The Silent Language.* New York: Doubleday.

Hallinen, M. and Aage B. Sorenson. 1985. "Ability Grouping and Student Friendships." *American Educational Research Journal* 22: 485-99.

Hamer, Dean H., Stella Hu, Victoria L. Magnuson, Nan Hu, Angela M. L. Pattatucci. 1993. "A Linkage between DNA Markers on the X Chromosome and Male Sexual Orientation." *Science* 261 (July 16): 321-27.

Hammond, Phillip E. 1992. *Religion and Personal Autonomy: The Third Disestablishment in America.* Columbia: University of South Carolina Press.

Handel, Gerald and Gail G. Whitechurch, eds. 1994. *The Psychosocial Interior of the Family,* 4th ed. Hawthorne, NY: Aldine de Gruyter.

Handy, Robert T. 1960. "The American Religious Depression, 1925-1935." *Church History* 29:3-16.

_____. 1984. *A Christian America: Protestant Hopes and Historical Realities,* 2nd ed. New York: Oxford University Press.

_____. 1991. *Undermined Establishment: Church-State Relations in America, 1880-1920.* Princeton: Princeton University Press.

Hanson, David J. 1993. Personal communication.

Hardin, Garrett. 1993. *Living within Limits: Ecology, Economics, and Population Taboos.* New York: Oxford University Press.

Harlow, Harry F. and Margaret K. Harlow. 1962. "Social Deprivation in Monkeys." *Scientific American* 5: 136-46.

Harrell, David Edwin Jr. 1978. *All Things are Possible: The Healing and Charismatic Revivals in Modern America.* Bloomington: University of Indiana Press.

_____. ed. 1981. *Varieties of Southern Evangelicalism.* Macon, GA: Mercer University Press.

_____. 1987a. *Oral Roberts: An American Life.* New York: Harper & Row.

_____. 1987b. *Pat Robertson: A Personal, Political and Religious Portrait.* New York: Harper & Row.

Harris, Marvin. 1980. *Culture, People, Nature,* 3rd ed. New York: Harper & Row.

Hart, Stephen. 1992. *What Does the Lord Require? How American Christians Think About Economic Justice.* New York: Oxford University Press.

Harvey, William B. and Lea B. Williams. 1989. "Historically Black Colleges: Models for Increasing Minority Representation." *Education and Urban Society* 21: 328-40.

Hatfield, Elaine and Susan Sprecher. 1986. *Mirror, Mirror: The Importance of Looks in Everyday Life.* New York: SUNY Press.

Haub, Carl. 1993. "China's Fertility Drop Lowers World Growth Rate." *Population Today* 21 (June): 1.

Hauser, Robert M. and David B. Grusky. 1988. "Cross-National Variation in Occupational Distributions, Relative Mobility Chances, and Intergenerational Shifts in Occupational Distributions." *American Sociological Review* 53: 723-41.

Hauser, Robert M. and William H. Sewell. 1986. "Family Effects in Simple Models of Education, Occupational Status, and Earnings: Findings from the Wisconsin and Kalamazoo Studies." *Journal of Labor Economics* 4: S83-S115.

Hayes, Cheryl D., John L. Palmer, and Martha J. Zaslow, eds. 1990. *Who Cares for America's Children?* Washington, DC: National Academy Press.

Heckathorn, Douglas D. 1993. "Collective Action and Group Heterogeneity." *American Sociological Review* 58: 329-50.

Heirich, Max. 1978. "Change of Heart: A Test of Some Widely Held Theories about Religious Conversions." *American Journal of Sociology* 83: 653-680.

Hegtvedt, Karen A., Elaine A. Thompson, and Karen S. Cook. 1993. "Power and Equity: What Counts in Attributions for Exchange Outcomes?" *Social Psychology Quarterly* 56: 100-19.

Henneberger, Melinda. 1993. "For Some, Rituals of Abuse Replace Youthful Courtship." *New York Times* (July 11): A3, L33.

Hewitt, Christopher. 1977. "Majorities and Minorities: A Comparative Survey of Ethnic Violence." *Annals of the Academy of Political and Social Science* 433: 150-60.

Heyl, Barbara Sherman. 1989. "Homosexuality: A Social Phenomenon." Pp. 321-49 in Kathleen McKinney and Susan Sprecher, eds. *Human*

Sexuality: The Societal and Interpersonal Context. Norwood, NJ: Ablex.

Hilbert, Richard A. 1992. *Ethnomethodology and the Contemporary Condition of Inquiry.* Chapel Hill: University of North Carolina Press.

Hill, Martha S. 1992. "The Role of Economic Resources and Remarriage in Financial Assistance for Children of Divorce." *Journal of Family Issues* 13: 158-78.

Hochschild, Arlie. 1983. *The Managed Heart: Commercialization of Human Feeling.* Berkeley: University of California Press.

Hochschild, Arlie, with Ann Machung. 1989. *The Second Shift.* New York: Viking.

Hoebel, E. Adamson. 1966. *Anthropology,* 3rd ed. New York: McGraw-Hill.

Hofferth, Sandra L. and Sharon Gennis Deich. 1994. "Recent U.S. Child Care and Family Legislation in Comparative Perspective." *Journal of Family Issues* 15: 424-48.

Hoffman, S. D., E. M. Foster, and F. F. Furstenberg Jr. 1993. "Reevaluating the Costs of Teenage Childbearing." *Demography* 30: 1-13.

Honan, William H. 1994. "New Pressures on the University." *Education Life* (January 9): 16-18.

Hopkins, C. Howard. 1940. *The Rise of the Social Gospel in American Protestantism: 1865–1915.* New Haven: Yale University Press.

Horiuchi, Shiro. 1993. "World Population Growth Rate." *Population Today* 21 (June): 6.

Horowitz, Amy, Barbara M. Silverstone, and Joann P. Reinhardt. 1991. "A Conceptual and Empirical Exploration of Personal Autonomy Issues within Family Caregiving Relationships." *Gerontologist* 31: 23-31.

Horowitz, Irving Louis. 1993. *The Decomposition of Sociology.* New York: Oxford University Press.

Hoyert, Donna L. 1991. "Financial and Household Exchanges between Generations." *Research on Aging* 13: 205-25.

Hubbard, Ruth and Elijah Wald. 1993. *Exploding the Gene Myth.* Cambridge, MA: Harvard University Press.

Hunt, J. McVicker. 1975. "Reflections on a Decade of Early Education." *Journal of Abnormal Child Psychology* 3: 275-330.

Hunter, James Davison. 1983. *American Evangelicalism: Conservation Religion and the Quandary of Modernity.* New Brunswick, NJ: Rutgers University Press.

_____. 1987. *Evangelicalism: The Coming Generation.* Chicago: University of Chicago Press.

_____. 1991. *Culture Wars: The Struggle to Define America.* New York: Basic Books.

Hunter, Ski and Martin Sundel, eds. 1989. *Midlife Myths.* Newbury Park, CA: Sage Publications.

Hurn, Christopher J. 1993. *The Limits and Possibilities of Schooling,* 3rd ed. Boston: Allyn & Bacon.

Hyman, Herbert A. and Eleanor D. Singer, eds. 1968. *Readings in Reference Group Theory.* Glencoe, IL: Free Press.

Hyman, Herbert H., Charles H. Wright, and John S. Reed. 1975. *The Enduring Effects of Education.* Chicago: University of Chicago Press.

Ihinger-Tallman, Marilyn and Kay Pasley. 1987. *Remarriage.* Newbury Park, CA: Sage Publications.

Inciardi, James A. 1933. *Criminal Justice.* 4th ed. New York: Harcourt Brace Jovanovich.

Inkeles, Alex. 1983. *Exploring Individual Modernity.* New York: Columbia University Press.

Inkeles, Alex and David H. Smith. 1974. *Becoming Modern: Individual Change in Six Developing Countries.* Cambridge, MA: Harvard University Press.

Jackson, Philip W. 1968. *Life in Classrooms.* New York: Holt, Rinehart & Winston.

Jacobs, Janet Liebman. 1989. *Divine Disenchantment: Deconverting from New Religions.* Bloomington: Indiana University Press.

_____. 1990. "Women-Centered Healing Rites: A Study of Alienation and Reintegration." Chap. 19 in *In Gods We Trust: New Patterns of Religious Pluralism in America.* 2nd ed. New Brunswick, NJ: Transaction Publishers.

Jayakody, Rukmalie, Linda M. Chatters, and Robert Joseph Taylor. 1993. "Family Support to Single and Married African American Mothers: The Provision of Financial, Emotional, and Child Care Assistance." *Journal of Marriage and the Family* 55: 261-76.

Jelen, Ted. 1991. *The Political Mobilization of Religious Beliefs.* Westport, CT: Praeger.

Jencks, Christopher. 1979. *Who Gets Ahead: The Determinants of Economic Success in America.* New York: Basic Books.

_____. 1992. *Rethinking Social Policy: Race, Poverty, and the Underclass.* Cambridge, MA: Harvard University Press.

Jencks, Christopher, Marshall Smith, Henry Ackland, Mary Jo Bane, David Cohen, Herbert Gintis, Barbara Heyns, and Stephen Michelson. 1972. *Inequality: A Reassessment of the Effect of Family and Schooling in America.* New York: Basic Books.

Johnson, Benton, Dean R. Hoge, and Donald A. Luidens. 1993. "Mainline Churches: The Real Reason for Decline." *First Things* 31 (March): 13–18.

Johnson, Kirk. 1994. "Gay Divorce: Few Markers in This Realm." *New York Times* (August 12): A20.

Johnston, Les. 1992. *The Rebirth of Private Policing.* London: Routledge.

Jones, Brian J., et al. 1991. "A Survey of Fortune 500 Corporate Policies Concerning the Psychiatrically Handicapped." *Journal of Rehabilitation* 57 (October–December): 31–35.

Jones, Calvin, M. Clark, G. Mooney, H. McWilliams, L. Crawford, B. Stephenson, and R. Tourangeau. 1983. *High School and Beyond: 1980 Sophomore Cohort, First Follow-up (1982), Data File User's Manual.* Washington, DC: National Center for Education Statistics.

Josephson, Matthew. 1934. *The Robber Barons: The Great American Capitalists (1861–1901).* New York: Harcourt Brace Jovanovich.

Judson, George. 1994. "Bid to Revise Education Is Fought in Connecticut." *New York Times* (January 9): A21, A27.

Kain, Edward L. 1990. *The Myth of Family Decline.* Lexington, MA: Lexington Books.

Kalish, Susan. 1992. "Twentysomething Group Evades Easy Labels." *Population Today* 20 (November): 1–2.

———. 1993. "Population Experts Debate Impact of Immigration, Longevity's Limits, Population-Environment Links, and More." *Population Today* 21 (May): 1.

Kandiyoti, Deniz A. 1987. "Emancipated But Unliberated? Reflections on the Turkish Case." *Feminist Studies* 13: 317–38.

Kantor, Rosabeth Moss. 1977. *Men and Women of the Corporation.* New York: Basic Books.

Kaplan, Helen Singer. 1979. *Disorders of Sexual Desire.* New York: Brunner/Mazel.

Katz, Elihu. 1957. "The Two-Step Flow of Communication: An Up-to-Date Report on a Hypothesis." *Public Opinion Quarterly* 21: 61–78.

Katz, Elihu and Paul F. Lazarsfeld. 1955. *Personal Influence.* New York: Free Press.

Katzenstein, Mary Fainsod and Carol McClurg Mueller. 1987. *The Women's Movements of the United States and Western Europe.* Philadelphia: Temple University Press.

Kaufman, Debra Renee. 1991. *Rachel's Daughters: Newly Orthodox Jewish Women.* New Brunswick, NJ: Rutgers University Press.

Kaus, Mickey. 1992. *The End of Equality.* New York: Basic Books.

Keith, Jennie. 1990. "Age in Social and Cultural Context: Anthropological Perspectives." Pp. 91–111 in *Handbook of Aging and the Social Sciences,* edited by Robert H. Binstock and Linda K. George. New York: Academic Press.

Kelman, Herbert C. and V. Lee Hamilton. 1988. *Crimes of Obedience.* New Haven: Yale University Press.

Kemper, Theodore D. and Randall Collins. 1990. "Dimensions of Microinteraction." *American Journal of Sociology* 96: 32–68.

Keniston, Kenneth. 1970 "Youth: A 'New' Stage in Life." *American Scholar* 16: 586–95.

Kenrick, Douglas T. and Melanie R. Trost. 1989. "A Reproductive Exchange Model of Heterosexual Relationships." Pp. 92–118 in *Close Relationships,* edited by Clyde Hendrick. Newbury Park, CA: Sage Publications.

Kilborn, Peter T. 1993. "The Ph.D.'s Are Here, But the Lab Isn't Hiring." *New York Times* (July 18): A3.

Kimmel, Michael S. and Michael A. Messner, eds. 1992. *Men's Lives.* New York: Macmillan.

King, Valerie. 1994. "Nonresident Father Involvement and Child Well-Being: Can Dads Make a Difference?" *Journal of Family Issues* 15: 78–96.

Kirsh, Irwin, Ann Jungeblut, Lynn Jenkins, and Andrew Kolstad. 1993. "Adult Literacy in America: A First Look at the Results of the National Literacy Survey." Washington, DC: U.S. Department of Education.

Kishor, Sunita. 1993. "Gender and Child Mortality in India." *American Sociological Review* 57: 247–65.

Kissman, Kris and Jo Ann Allen. 1993. *Single-Parent Families.* Newbury Park, CA: Sage Publications.

Klatch, Rebecca. 1987. *Women of the New Right.* Philadelphia: Temple University Press.

Kleck, Gary. 1991. *Point Blank: Guns and Violence in America.* New York: Aldine de Gruyter.

Klepinger, Daniel H., John O. G. Billy, Koray Tanfer, William R. Grady. 1993. "Perceptions of AIDS Risk and Severity and Their Association with Risk-Related Behavior among U.S. Men." *Family Planning Perspectives* 25: 74–82.

Kogan, Nathan. 1990. "Personality and Aging." Pp. 330–46 in *Handbook of the Psychology of Aging,* 3rd ed., edited by James E. Birren and K. Warner Schaie. San Diego: Academic Press.

Kohl, Herbert. 1969. *The Open Classroom.* New York: New York Review of Books.

Kohn, Alfie. 1993. *Punished by Rewards: The Trouble with Gold Stars, Incentive Plans, A's, Praise and Other Bribes.* Boston: Houghton Mifflin.

Kohn, Melvin L. 1959. "Social Class and Parental Values." *American Journal of Sociology* 63: 337-51.

———. 1969. *Class and Conformity: A Study of Values.* Homewood, IL: Dorsey Press.

Kohn, Melvin L., Atsushi Naoi, Carrie Schoenbach, Carmi Schooler, and Kazimierz M. Slomczynski. 1990. "Position in the Class Structure and Psychological Functioning in the United States, Japan, and Poland." *American Journal of Sociology* 95: 964-1008.

Komarovsky, Mirra. 1985. *Women in College.* New York: Basic Books.

———. 1988. "The New Feminist Scholarship: Precursors and Polemics." *Journal of Marriage and the Family* 50: 585-94.

Kosmin, Barry A. with Seymour P. Lachman. 1991. *The National Survey of Religious Identification, 1989-1990.* Research report, The Graduate School and University Center of the City University of New York.

Kozol, Jonathan. 1991. *Savage Inequalities.* New York: Crown.

Kreft, Ita G. G. 1993. "Using Multilevel Analysis to Assess School Effectiveness: A Study of Dutch Secondary Schools." *Sociology of Education* 66: 104-129.

Kristof, Nicholas D. 1993. "Riddle of China: Repression and Prosperity Can Coexist." *New York Times* (September 9): A1, A10.

Kroeber, Alfred and Clyde Kluckhohn. 1963. *Culture: A Critical Review of Concepts and Definitions.* New York: Vintage.

Krugman, Paul. 1992. *The Age of Diminished Expectations.* Cambridge, MA: MIT Press.

Landale, Nancy S. and Stewart E. Tolnay. 1991. "Group Differences in Economic Opportunity and the Timing of Marriage." *American Sociological Review* 56: 33-45.

Landau, David. 1993. *Piety and Power: The World of Jewish Fundamentalism.* New York: Hill & Wang.

Lawrence, Bruce B. 1989. *Defenders of God: The Fundamentalist Revolt against the Modern Age.* San Francisco: Harper & Row.

Lazerwitz, Bernard and Michael Harrison. 1979. "American Jewish Denominations: A Social and Religious Profile." *American Sociological Review* 44: 656-66.

Lazreg, Marnia. 1988. "Feminism and Difference: The Perils of Writing as a Woman on Women in Algeria." *Feminist Studies* 14: 81-107.

Lechner, Frank. 1990. "Fundamentalism Revisited." Pp. 77-98 in *In Gods We Trust: New Patterns of American Religious Pluralism,* 2nd ed., edited by Robbins Thomas and Dick Anthony. New Brunswick, NJ: Transaction Publishers.

———. 1991. "The Case Against Secularization: A Rebuttal." *Social Forces* 69:4 (June): 1103-19.

Lederer, William J. and Eugene Burdick. 1958. *The Ugly American.* New York: W. W. Norton.

Lee, Richard B. and Irven DeVore, eds. 1968. *Man the Hunter.* Chicago: Aldine.

Lee, Valerie E. 1993. "Educational Choice: The Stratifying Effects of Selecting Schools and Courses." *Educational Policy* 7: 125-48.

LeMasters, E. E. and John DeFrain. 1989. *Parents in Contemporary America.* 5th ed. Belmont, CA: Wadsworth.

Lemert, Charles. 1979. "Science, Religion and Secularization." *Sociological Quarterly* 20: 445-461.

Lemert, Edwin M. 1967. *Human Deviance, Social Problems, and Social Control.* Englewood Cliffs, NJ: Prentice Hall.

Lenski, Gerhard. 1961. *The Religious Factor.* Garden City, NY: Doubleday.

———. 1966. *Power and Privilege.* New York: McGraw-Hill.

———. 1988. "Rethinking Macrosociological Theory." *American Sociological Review* 53: 163-71.

Lenski, Gerhard and Jean Lenski. 1978. *Human Societies.* 3rd ed. New York: McGraw-Hill.

Lenski, Gerhard, Jean Lenski, and Patrick Nolan. 1991. *Human Societies.* 6th ed. New York: McGraw-Hill.

Lerner, Daniel. 1958. *The Passing of Traditional Society.* New York: Free Press.

Lerner, Jacqueline V. 1993. *Employed Mothers and Their Families.* Newbury Park, CA: Sage Publications.

Levine, Daniel H., ed. 1986. *Religion and Politics in Latin America.* Chapel Hill: University of North Carolina Press.

———. 1992. *Popular Voices in Latin American Catholicism.* Princeton: Princeton University Press.

Levine, Daniel S. 1993. "Adult Students, Adult Needs." *Education Life* (April 4): 33-34.

Levinson, Daniel J. 1978. *The Seasons of a Man's Life*. New York: Alfred A. Knopf.

Levinson, David. 1989. *Family Violence in Cross-Cultural Perspective*. Newbury Park, CA: Sage Publications.

Levy, Becca and Ellen Langer. 1994. "Aging Free from Stereotypes: Successful Memory in China and among the American Deaf." *Journal of Personality and Social Psychology* 66: 989-97.

Lewis, Darrell R., James C. Hearn, Eric E. Zilbert. 1993. "Efficiency and Equity Effects of Vocationally Focused Postsecondary Education." *Sociology of Education* 66: 188-205.

Lewis, Lionel S. and Richard A. Wanner. 1979. "Private Schooling and the Status Attainment Process." *Sociology of Education* 52: 99-112.

Lewis, Neil A. 1993. "Medical Industry Showers Congress with Lobby Money." *New York Times* (December 13): A1, B9.

Lewis, Oscar. 1959. *Five Families*. New York: Basic Books.

Lichter, Daniel T., Diane K. McLaughlin, George Kephart, and David J. Landry. 1992. "Race and the Retreat from Marriage: A Shortage of Marriageable Men?" *American Sociological Review* 57: 781-99.

Lincoln, C. Eric. 1961. *The Black Muslim in America*. Boston: Beacon Press.

Lincoln, C. Eric and Lawrence Mamiya. 1990. *The Black Church in the African American Experience*. Durham, NC: Duke University Press.

Link, Bruce G., Howard Andrews, and Francis T. Cullen. 1992. "The Violent and Illegal Behavior of Mental Patients Reconsidered." *American Sociological Review* 57: 275-92.

Linton, Ralph. 1936. *The Study of Man*. Englewood Cliffs, NJ: Prentice Hall.

Lipmann, Walter. 1922. *Public Opinion*. New York: Macmillan.

Lipset, Seymour Martin. 1959. *Political Man*. New York: Doubleday.

_____. 1994. "The Social Requisites of Democracy Revisited." *American Sociological Review* 59: 1-22.

Lofland, John. 1966. *Doomsday Cult*. Englewood Cliffs, NJ: Prentice Hall.

Lombroso, Cesare. 1911. *Crime: Its Causes and Remedies*. Boston: Little, Brown.

Lott, Juanita Tamayo. 1993. "Do United States Racial/Ethnic Categories Still Fit?" *Population Today* (January): 6, 9.

Lye, Diane N. and Timothy J. Biblarz. 1993. "The Effects of Attitudes toward Family Life and Gender Roles on Marital Satisfaction." *Journal of Family Issues* 14: 157-88.

Macedo, Donaldo P. 1993. "Literacy for Stupefication: The Pedogogy of Big Lies." *Harvard Educational Review* 63: 183-206.

Mair, Lucy. 1962. *Primitive Government*. Baltimore: Penguin.

Malinowski, Bronislaw. 1948. *Magic, Science and Religion*. Garden City, NY: Doubleday.

Malthus, Thomas R. 1938 [1798]. *An Essay on the Principle of Population*. London: J. M. Dent.

Mannheim, Karl. 1936. *Ideology and Utopia*. New York: Harcourt Brace.

_____. 1952 [1928]. *Essays on the Sociology of Knowledge*. New York: Oxford University Press.

Marciano, Teresa D. and Marvin B. Sussman, eds. 1991. *Wider Families: New Traditional Family Forms*. New York: Haworth Press.

Margolis, Diane Rothbard. 1993. "Women's Movements around the World: Cross-Cultural Comparisons." *Gender and Society* 7: 379-99.

Marsden, George M. 1980. *Fundamentalism and American Culture: The Shaping of Twentieth-Century Evangelicalism, 1870-1925*. New York: Oxford University Press.

_____, ed. 1984. *Evangelicalism and Modern America*. Grand Rapids, MI: William B. Eerdmans.

_____. 1987. *Reforming Fundamentalism: Fuller Seminary and the New Evangelicalism*. Grand Rapids, MI: William B. Eerdmans.

_____. 1991. *Understanding Fundamentalism and Evangelicalism*. Grand Rapids, MI: William B. Eerdmans.

Marsden, Peter. 1992. *Sociological Methodology*, vol. 22. Cambridge, MA: Basil Blackwell.

Martin, Theresa Castro and Larry L. Bumpass. 1989. "Recent Trends in Marital Disruption." *Demography* 26: 37-51.

Martinson, Brian C. and Lawrence L. Wu. 1992. "Parent Histories: Patterns of Change in Early Life." *Journal of Family Issues* 13: 351-77.

Marty, Martin. 1976. *A Nation of Believers*. Chicago: The University of Chicago Press.

_____. 1986. *Modern American Religion: The Irony of It All*, vol. 1. Chicago: University of Chicago Press.

_____. 1991. *Modern American Religion: The Noise of Conflict*, vol. 2. Chicago: University of Chicago Press.

Marty, Martin and R. Scott Appleby. 1991. "Conclusion: An Interim Report on a Hypothetical Family." Pp. 814-842 in *Fundamentalisms Observed,* edited by Martin Marty and R. Scott Appleby. Chicago: University of Chicago Press.

Marx, Gary T. 1967. "Religion: Opiate or Inspiration of Civil Rights Militancy among Negroes?" *American Sociological Review* 32: 64-73.

Marx, Karl. 1906 [1867]. *Das Capital,* 3rd ed., translated by Samuel Moore and Edward Aveling. New York: Charles H. Kerr.

_____. 1964. *The Economic and Philosophical Manuscripts of 1844.* New York: International Publishers.

_____. 1964 [1844]. *Selected Writings in Sociology and Social Philosophy,* translated and edited by T. B. Bottomore and Maximilien Rubel. New York: McGraw-Hill.

Marx, Karl and Frederick Engels. 1955 [1848]. *The Communist Manifesto.* Englewood Cliffs, NJ: Prentice Hall.

_____. 1955. *On Religion.* Moscow: Foreign Language Publishing.

Matsueda, Ross L., Rosemary Gartner, Irving Piliavin, and Michael Polakowski. 1992. "The Prestige of Criminal and Conventional Occupations." *American Sociological Review* 57: 752-70.

Mayer, Susan E. 1991. "How Much Does a High School's Racial and Economic Mix Affect Graduation and Teenage Fertility Rates?" in *The Urban Underclass,* edited by Christopher Jenks and Paul Peterson. Washington, DC: Brookings Institution.

Mayseless, Ofra. 1991. "Adult Attachment Patterns and Courtship Violence." *Family Relations* 40: 21-8.

McAdam, Doug. 1989. "The Biographical Consequences of Activism." *American Sociological Review* 54: 744-60.

McCauley, Deborah Vansau. 1995 forthcoming. *Appalachian Mountain Religion: A History.* Urbana: University of Illinois Press.

McClelland, David. 1961. *The Achieving Society.* New York: Free Press.

McClelland, David. 1975. *The Power Motive.* New York: Free Press.

McCord, Joan and Richard E. Tremblay, eds. 1992. *Preventing Antisocial Behavior: Interventions from Birth through Adolescence.* New York: Guilford Press.

McGovern, Arthur F. 1989. *Liberation Theology and Its Critics: Toward an Assessment.* Maryknoll, NY: Orbis Books.

McLanahan, Sara S. and Karen Booth. 1989. "Mother-Only Families: Problems, Prospects, and Politics." *Journal of Marriage and the Family* 51: 557-79.

McLaren, P. and C. Lankshear. 1992. *Critical Literacy.* Albany: State University of New York Press.

McLoyd, Vonnie. 1990. "The Declining Fortunes of Slack Children: Psychological Distress, Parenting, and Socioemotional Development in the Context of Economic Hardship." *Child Development* 61: 311-46.

Mead, George Herbert. 1934. *Mind, Self, and Society,* edited by Charles W. Morris. Chicago: University of Chicago Press.

Mead, Margaret. 1928. *Coming of Age in Samoa.* New York: William Morrow.

_____. 1935. *Sex and Temperament in Three Primitive Societies.* New York: William Morrow.

_____. 1949. *Male and Female.* New York: William Morrow.

Melbin, Murray. 1978. "Night as Frontier." *American Sociological Review* 43: 3-22.

Mellaart, James. 1964. "A Neolithic City in Turkey." *Scientific American* (April): 94-106.

Merton, Robert. 1949. "Discrimination and the American Creed." Pp. 120-29 in *Discrimination and National Welfare,* edited by Robert M. McIver. New York: Harper & Row.

Merton, Robert. 1968. *Social Theory and Social Structure,* rev. ed. New York: Free Press.

Merton, Robert K. and Alice S. Kitt. 1950. "Contributions to the Theory of Reference Group Behavior." Pp. 40-105 in *Continuities in Social Research: Studies in the Scope and Method of "The American Soldier,"* edited by Robert K. Merton and Paul F. Lazarsfeld. Glencoe, IL: Free Press.

Meyer, John W. 1977. "The Effects of Education as an Institution." *American Journal of Sociology* 83: 55-77.

Meyerson, Lee. 1988. "The Social Psychology of Physical Disability: 1948 and 1988." *Journal of Social Issues* 44: 173-88.

Michels, Robert. 1949 [1915]. *Political Parties,* translated by Eden and Cedar Paul. Glencoe,IL: Free Press.

Miller, Karen A., Melvin L. Kohn, and Carmi Schooler. 1986. "Educational Self-Direction and Personality." *American Sociological Review* 51: 372-90.

Miller-Jones, Dalton. 1989. "Culture and Testing." *American Psychologist* 44: 360-66.

Mills, C. Wright. 1959. *The Power Elite.* New York: Oxford University Press.

Mintz, Beth and Michael Schwartz. 1985. *The Power Structure of American Business.* Chicago: University of Chicago Press.

Misztal, Bronislaw and Anson Shupe. 1992. *The Revival of Religious Fundamentalism in the East and West.* Westport, CT: Praeger.

Monk-Turner, Elizabeth. 1988. "Educational Differentiation and Status Attainment: The Community College Controversy." *Sociological Focus* 21: 141-52.

_____. 1990. "The Occupational Achievements of Community College and Four-Year College Entrants." *American Sociological Review* 55: 719-25.

Montagu, Ashley, ed. 1978. *Man and Aggression.* New York: Oxford University Press.

_____. 1986. *Touching: The Human Significance of the Skin.* New York: Columbia University Press.

Moore, Burness E. and Bernard D. Fine. 1990. *A Glossary of Psychoanalytic Terms and Concepts,* 2nd ed. New York: American Psychoanalytic Association.

Moore, Joan W. 1991. *Going Down to the Barrio: Homeboys and Homegirls in Change.* Philadelphia: Temple University Press.

Moore, R. Lawrence. 1986. *Religious Outsiders and the Making of Americans.* New York: Oxford University Press.

Moore, Wilbert E. 1960. "A Reconsideration of Theories of Social Change." *American Sociological Review* 25: 810-18.

Morganthau, Tom. 1993. "America: Still a Melting Pot?" *Newsweek* (August 9): 16-25.

Morris, Aldon D. and Carol McClurg Mueller, eds. 1992. *Frontiers in Social Movement Theory.* New Haven: Yale University Press.

Moynihan, Patrick. 1993. "Defining Deviancy Down." *American Scholar* 63: 17-30.

Murphy, Joseph M. 1993. *Working the Spirit: Ceremonies of the African Diaspora.* Boston: Beacon Press.

Mydans, Seth. 1993. "Poll Finds Tide of Immigration Brings Hostility." *New York Times* (June 27): 1, 16.

Myerson, Adam. 1991. "Building the New Establishment: Edwin J. Feuler on Heritage and the Conservative Movement." *Policy Review* 58 (Fall): 6-17.

Myrdal, Gunnar. 1944. *An American Dilemma: The Negro Problem and American Democracy.* New York: Harper & Row.

Naisbett, John and Patricia Aburdene. 1989. *Megatrends 2000.* New York: William Morrow.

Nance, John. 1975. *The Gentle Tasaday: A Stone Age People in the Philippine Rain Forest.* New York: Harcourt Brace Jovanovich.

Nasar, Sylvia. 1992a. "The 1980's: A Very Good Time for the Very Rich." *New York Times* (March 5): A1, D24.

Nasar, Sylvia. 1992b. "Fed Gives New Evidence of 80's Gains by Richest." *New York Times* (April 21): A1.

Nash, Ronald C. 1988. *Poverty and Wealth: The Christian Debate Over Capitalism.* Westchester, IL: Crossway Books.

Nash, Ronald H. 1983. *Social Justice and the Christian Church.* Milford, MI: Mott Media.

National Center For Health Statistics. 1993. "Births, Marriages, Divorces, and Deaths for 1992." *Monthly Vital Statistics Report* 41 (12) (May 19). Washington, DC: U.S. Government Printing Office.

National Commission on Excellence in Education. 1983. "A Nation at Risk: The Imperative for Educational Reform." Washington, DC: U.S. Government Printing Office.

Neal, Marie Agusta. 1979. "Women in Religious Symbolism and Organization," Chap. 9 in *Religious Change and Continuity,* edited by Harry M. Johnson. San Francisco: Jossey-Bass.

Neitz, Mary Jo. 1990. "In Goddess We Trust," Chap. 9 in *In Gods We Trust: New Patterns of Religious Pluralism in America.* 2nd ed. New Brunswick, NJ: Transaction Publishers.

Nesbitt, Paula D. 1993. "Dual Ordination Tracks: Differential Benefits and Costs for Men and Women Clergy." *Sociology of Religion* 54: 13-30.

Neugarten, Bernice A. and Dale A. Neugarten. 1987. "The Changing Meanings of Age." *Psychology Today* (May): 29-33.

Neugarten, Bernice L. 1974. "Age Groups in American Society and the Rise of the Young-Old." *Annals of the American Academy of Political and Social Science* 415: 187-98.

Newman, Katherine. 1993. *Declining Fortunes: The Withering of the American Dream.* New York: Basic Books.

Newport, Frank. 1979. "The Religious Switcher in the United States." *American Sociological Review* 44: 528-552.

Ng, Sik Hung and James J. Bradac. 1993. *Power in Language.* Newbury Park, CA: Sage Publications.

Niebuhr, H. Richard. 1957 [1929]. *The Social Sources of Denominationalism.* New York: New American Library.

Nisbett, Richard E. 1993. "Violence and U.S. Regional Culture." *American Psychologist* 48: 441–47.

Noble, Barbara Presley. 1993. "Women Pay More for Success." *New York Times* (July 4): A25.

Nolen, Susan Bobbit and Thomas M. Haladyna. 1990. "Personal and Environmental Influences on Students' Beliefs about Effective Study Strategies." *Contemporary Educational Psychology* 15: 116–30.

Noll, Mark A., ed. 1990. *Religion and American Politics: From the Colonial Period to the 1980s.* New York: Oxford University Press.

Novak, Michael. 1986. *Will It Liberate? Questions for Liberation Theology.* New York: Paulist Press.

O'Connell, Martin. 1993. "Where's Papa? Fathers' Role in Child Care." *Population Trends and Public Policy* 20 (September): 1–20.

Ogburn, William F. 1922. *Social Change.* New York: Viking.

O'Hare, William P. 1990. *America in the 21st Century: Infrastructure Needs.* Washington, DC: Population Reference Bureau.

———. 1992a. "America's Minorities–The Demographics of Diversity." *Population Bulletin* 47 (December): 1–47.

———. 1992b. "Can the Underclass Concept Be Applied to Rural Areas?" Washington, DC: Population Reference Bureau.

O'Hare, William P. and Judy C. Felt. 1991. "Asian Americans: America's Fastest-Growing Minority." Washington, DC: Population Reference Bureau.

O'Hare, William P., Kelvin M. Pollard, Taynia L. Mann, and Mary M. Kent. 1991. *African Americans in the 1990s.* Washington, DC: Population Reference Bureau.

O'Hare, William P. and Margaret L. Usdansky. 1992. "What the 1990 Census Tells Us about Segregation in 25 Large Metros." *Population Today* (September): 6–10.

Omran, Abdel and Farzaneh Roudi. 1993. "The Middle East Population Puzzle." *Population Bulletin* 49. Washington, DC: Population Reference Bureau.

Opitz, Edmund. 1981. "Perspectives on Religion and Capitalism." *Freeman* (December): 732–43.

Ostling, Richard N. 1992. "The Second Reformation: Admission to the Priesthood Is Just One Issue as Feminism Rapidly Emerges as the Most Vexing Thorn for Christianity." *Time* (November 23): 53–58.

Ostrander, Susan. 1984. *Women of the Upper Class.* Philadelphia: Temple University Press.

Otto, Rudolph. 1958. *The Idea of the Holy.* New York: Oxford University Press.

Padilla, Felix M. 1992. *The Gang as an American Enterprise.* New Brunswick, NJ: Rutgers University Press.

Pampel, Fred and John B. Williamson. 1988. "Welfare Spending in Advanced Industrial Democracies: 1950-1980." *American Journal of Sociology* 93: 1424–56.

Parkinson, C. Northcote. 1957. *Parkinson's Law.* Boston: Houghton Mifflin.

Paris, Peter. 1987. *The Social Teaching of the Black Churches.* Philadelphia: Fortress Press.

Parsons, Talcott. 1959. "The School Class as a Social System: Some of Its Functions in American Society." *Harvard Educational Review* 29: 297–318.

———. 1977. *The Evolution of Societies.* Englewood Cliffs, NJ: Prentice Hall.

———. 1978. *Action Theory and the Human Condition.* New York: Free Press.

Passel, Jeffrey and Barry Edmonston. 1992. "Immigration and Race: Recent Trends in Immigration to the U.S." Washington, DC: Urban Institute.

Passell, Peter. 1993. "U.S. and Europe Clear the Way for a World Accord on Trade, Setting Aside Major Disputes." *New York Times* (December 15): A1, D18.

Patterson, Thomas E. 1993. *Out of Order.* New York: Alfred A. Knopf.

Patton, Phil. 1993. "The Virtual Office Becomes Reality." *New York Times* (October 28): C1, C6.

Pear, Robert. 1993a. "Poverty in U.S. Grew Faster Than Population Last Year." *New York Times* (October 6): A20.

Pear, Robert. 1993b. "Big Health Gap, Tied to Income, Is Found in U.S." *New York Times* (July 8): A1, B10.

Pearson, Willie, Jr. and Lewellyn Hendrix. 1979. "Divorce and the Status of Women." *Journal of Marriage and the Family* 41: 375–85.

Peplau, Letitia Anne. 1991. "Lesbian and Gay Relationships." Pp. 177–199 in *Homosexuality,* edited by John C. Gonsiorek and James D. Weinrich. Newbury Park, CA: Sage Publications.

Perkins, David. 1992. *Smart Schools: From Training Memories to Educating Minds.* New York: Free Press.

Perry-Jenkins and Ann C. Crouter. 1990. "Men's Provider Role Attitudes." *Journal of Family Issues* 11: 136-56.

Peter, Lawrence J. and Raymond Hull. 1969. *The Peter Principle.* New York: William Morrow.

Peterson, Jean Treloggen. 1993. "Generalized Extended Family Exchange: A Case from the Philippines." *Journal of Marriage and the Family* 55: 570-84.

Peterson, Richard R. and Kathleen Gerson. 1992. "Determinents of Responsibility for Child Care Arrangements in Two-Earner Families." *Journal of Marriage and the Family* 54: 527-36.

Pettigrew, Thomas F. 1971. *Racially Separate or Together?* New York: McGraw-Hill.

Pfaff, William. 1993. *The Wrath of Nations.* New York: Simon & Schuster.

Pfeiffer, John E. 1985. *The Emergence of Man,* 4th ed. New York: Harper & Row.

Phillips, Kevin. 1993. *Boiling Point: Republicans, Democrats, and the Decline of Middle-Class Prosperity.* New York: Random House.

Pierre-Pierre, Gary. 1994. "Haiti Orders Out Foreign Monitors of Human Rights." *New York Times* (July 12): A1, A9.

Pirenne, Henri. 1933. *Economic and Social History of Medieval Europe.* New York: Harvest Books.

Pizzo, Stephen P. and Paul Muolo. 1993. "Take the Money and Run." *New York Times Magazine* (May 9): 26, 56.

Pleck, Joseph H. 1992. "Prisoners of Manliness." Pp. 98-107 in *Men's Lives,* edited by Michael S. Kimmel and Michael A. Messner. New York: Macmillan.

Pollard, Kelvin. 1992. "Income Down, Poverty Up." *Population Today* 20 (November): 5.

Pollard, Kelvin and Stephen Tordella. 1993. "Women Making Gains among Professionals." *Population Today* 21 (October): 1-2.

Pong, Suet-ling. 1993. "Preferential Policies and Secondary School Attainment in Peninsular Malaysia." *Sociology of Education* 66: 245-61.

Pope, Liston. 1942. *Millhands and Preachers.* New Haven: Yale University Press.

Popenoe, David. 1988. *Disturbing the Nest.* Chicago: Aldine de Gruyter.

———. 1993. "American Family Decline, 1960-1990." *Journal of Marrriage and the Family* 55: 527-55.

Portes, Alejandro and Min Zhou. 1993. "The New Second Generation: Segmented Assimilation and Its Variants." *Annals of the American Academy of Political and Social Sciences* 530 (November): 74-96.

Presser, Harriet B. 1993. "The Housework Gender Gap." *Population Today* 21 (July/August): 5.

Presser, Stanley and Michael Traugott. 1992. "Little White Lies and Social Science Models." *Public Opinion Quarterly* 56: 77-86.

Princeton Religious Research Center. 1978. *The Unchurched American.* Princeton: Gallup Organization.

Princeton Religious Research Center. 1979. *Religion in America, 1979-1980.* Princeton: Gallup Organization.

Prothro, E. Terry. 1952. "Ethnocentrism and Anti-Negro Attitudes in the Deep South." *Journal of Abnormal and Social Psychology* 47: 105-08.

Psacharopoulos, George and Eduardo Velez. 1993. "Educational Quality and Labor Market Outcomes: Evidence from Bogota, Columbia." *Sociology of Education* 66: 130-45.

Quinley, Harold. 1974. *The Prophetic Clergy: Social Activism among Protestant Ministers.* New York: Wiley.

Ravitch, Diane. 1983. *The Troubled Crusade: American Education, 1945-1980.* New York: Basic Books.

Raymond, Eric S. 1993. *The New Hacker's Dictionary.* Cambridge, MA: MIT Press.

Reich, Robert B. 1991. *The Work of Nations.* New York: Alfred A. Knopf.

———. 1993. "Workers of the World, Get Smart." *New York Times* (July 20): A19.

Reiss, Albert J., Jr. and Jeffrey A. Roth, eds. 1993. *Understanding and Preventing Violence.* Washington, DC: National Academy Press.

Reiss, Ira L. 1993. "The Future of Sex Research and the Meaning of Science." *The Journal of Sex Research* 40: 3-11.

Reiss, Ira L. and Gary R. Lee. 1988. *Family Systems in America.* New York: Holt, Rinehart & Winston.

Ribuffo, Leo P. 1983. *The Old Christian Right: The Protestant Far Right from the Great Depression to the Cold War.* Philadelphia: Temple University Press.

———. 1992. *Right, Center, Left: Essays in American History.* New Brunswick, NJ: Rutgers University Press.

_____. 1993. "God and Contemporary Politics." *Journal of American History* 79 (March): 1515–33.

Ricci, David M. 1993. *The Transformation of American Politics.* New Haven: Yale University Press.

Richardson, Lynda. 1993. "Public Schools Are Failing the Brightest Students, a Federal Study Says." *New York Times* (November 5): A23.

Riddle, John M. 1992. *Contraception and Abortion from the Ancient World to the Resaissance.* Cambridge, MA: Harvard University Press.

Riding, Alan. 1993. "In a Time of Shared Hardship, the Young Embrace Europe." *New York Times* (August 12): A1.

Rimer, Sara. 1993. "Felons and Farmers Lock Arms in the Flood." *New York Times* (July 29): A1, D23.

Robbins, Thomas, Dick Anthony and Thomas Curtis. 1975. "Youth Culture Religious Movements: Evaluating the Integrative Hypothesis." *Sociological Quarterly* 16: 48–64.

Robbins, Thomas and Dick Anthony. 1979. "Sociology of Contemporary Religious Movements." *Annual Review of Sociology* 5: 75–89.

Robbins, Thomas and Dick Anthony, eds. 1981. *In Gods We Trust: New Patterns of Religious Pluralism in America.* New Brunswick, NJ: Transaction Publishers.

Robbins, Thomas, and Dick Anthony. 1991. *In Gods We Trust: New Patterns of Religious Pluralism in America,* 2nd ed. New Brunswick, NJ: Transaction Publishers.

Robertson, Roland. 1992. *Globalization: Social Theory and Global Culture.* Newbury Park, CA: Sage Publications.

Robey, Bryant, Shea O. Rutstein, and Leo Morris. 1993. "The Reproductive Revolution: New Findings." *Population Reports,* Series M, no. 11. Baltimore: The Johns Hopkins University Press.

Rolison, Gary L. 1992. "Black, Single Female Headed Family Formation in Large U.S. Cities." *Sociological Quarterly* 33: 473–81.

Romanelli, Elaine. 1991. The Evolution of New Organizational Forms. *Annual Review of Sociogy* 17: 79–103.

Roof, Wade Clark. 1979. "Socioeconomic Differentials among White Socioreligious Groups in the United States." *Social Forces* 58: 280–289.

Roof, Wade Clark. 1993. *A Generation of Seekers: The Spiritual Journeys of the Baby Boom Generation.* San Francisco: Harper San Francisco.

Roof, Wade Clark and William McKinney. 1987. *American Mainline Religion: Its Changing Shape and Future.* New Brunswick, NJ: Rutgers University Press.

Rooks, Ronika N. 1993. "Motherhood Growing More Common Among Never-Married Women." *Population Today* 21 (11): 4.

Rose, Susan. 1987. "Women Warriors: The Negotiation of Gender Roles in an Evangelical Community." *Sociological Analysis* 48: 244–258.

_____. 1988. *Keeping Them Out of the Hands of Satan: Evangelical Schooling in America.* New York: Routledge.

Rosenbaum, James E. and Takehiko Kariya. 1991. "Do School Achievements Affect the Early Jobs of High School Graduates in the United States and Japan?" *Sociology of Education* 64: 78–95.

Ross, Marc Howard. 1993. *The Culture of Conflict.* New Haven: Yale University Press.

Rossi, Alice S. and Peter H. Rossi. 1990. *Of Human Bonding.* Hawthorne, NY: Aldine de Gruyter

Roudi, Nazy. 1993. "Population Policies Vary in the Middle East." *Population Today* (April): 3.

Rowland, Mary. 1993. "Making Executives Take a Stake." *New York Times* (May 9): D3.

Rubin, Lillian. 1992. *Worlds of Pain: Life in the Working Class Family,* rev. ed. New York: Basic Books.

Ruggles, Stephen. 1994. "The Origins of African-American Family Structure." *American Sociological Review* 59: 136–51.

Russell, D. E. H. 1974. *Rebellion, Revolution, and Armed Force.* New York: Academic Press.

Safran, Claire. 1988. "Hidden Lessons: Do Little Boys Get a Better Education than Little Girls?" Pp. 35–7 in *Racism and Sexism: An Integrated Study,* edited by Paula S. Rothenberg. New York: St. Martin's Press.

Sagarin, Edward. 1975. *Deviants and Deviance: An Introduction to the Study of Disvalued People.* New York: Praeger.

Sahlins, Marshall. 1972. *Stone Age Economics.* Chicago: Aldine.

Salgado, Sebastiano. 1993. *Workers: An Archaeology of the Modern Age.* New York: Aperture.

Samuelson, Robert J. 1993. "Health Care." *Newsweek* (October 4): 30–5.

Sanchez, Laura. 1993. "Women's Power and the Gendered Division of Domestic Labor in the Third World." *Gender and Society* 7: 434–59.

Sassen, Saskia. 1993. *The Global City: New York, London, Tokyo.* Princeton: Princeton University Press.

Sassen, Saskia and Alejandro Portes. 1993. "Miami: A New Global City?" *Contemporary Sociology* 22: 471–77.

Schaie, K. Warner. 1990. "Intellectual Development in Adulthood." Pp. 291–309 in *Handbook of the Psychology of Aging,* 3rd ed., edited by James A. Birren and K. Warner Schaie. San Diego: Academic Press.

Schmidt, Alvin John. 1989. *Veiled and Silenced: How Culture Shaped Sexist Theology.* Macon, GA: Macon University Press.

Schneider, Jeffrey M. 1989. "Tracking: A National Perspective." *Equity and Choice* 6(1): 11–17.

Schoen, Robert and Robin M. Weinick. 1993. "Partner Choice in Marriages and Cohabitations." *Journal of Marriage and the Family* 55: 408–14.

Schor, Juliet B. 1992. *The Overworked American: The Unexpected Decline of Leisure.* New York: Basic Books.

Schultze, Quenton. 1991. *The Business of Popular Religion: Televangelism and American Culture.* Grand Rapids, MI: Baker Book House.

Schuman, Howard and Shirley Hatchett. 1974. *Black Radical Attitudes: Trends and Complexities.* Ann Arbor, MI: Institute for Social Research.

Schuman, Howard and Cheryl Reiger. 1992. "Historical Analogies, Generational Effects, and Attitudes toward War." *American Sociological Review* 57: 315–326.

Schuman, Howard and Jacqueline Scott. 1989. "Generations and Collective Memories." *American Sociological Review* 54:359–81.

Schur, Edwin M. 1965. *Crimes without Victims: Deviant Behavior and Public Policy.* Englewood Cliffs, NJ: Prentice Hall.

Schwebel, Andrew I., Mark A. Fine, and Maureen A. Renner. 1991. "A Study of Perceptions of the Stepparent Role." *Journal of Family Issues* 12: 43–57.

Sciolino, Elaine. 1993. "An Operator for the Pentagon." *New York Times* (December 17): A1, B12.

Seltzer, Judith A. and Yvonne Brandreth. 1994. "What Fathers Say about Involvement with Children after Separation." *Journal of Family Issues* 15: 49–77.

Semyonov, Moshe and Yinon Cohen. 1990. "Ethnic Discrimination and the Income of Major-ity-Group Workers." *American Sociological Review* 55: 107–14.

Service, Elman. 1975. *Origins of the State and Civilization: The Process of Cultural Evolution.* New York: W. W. Norton.

Shaver, Philip, Cindy Hazan, and Donna Bradshaw. 1988. "Love as Attachment." Pp. 68–99 in *The Psychology of Love,* edited by Robert J. Sternberg and Michael L. Barnes. New Haven: Yale University Press.

Shaw, Clifford R. and Henry D. McKay. 1929. *Delinquency Areas.* Chicago: University of Chicago Press.

Sheldon, William H., Emil M. Harte, and Eugene McDermott. *Varieties of Delinquent Experience.* New York: Harper & Row.

Shenon, Philip. 1994a. "Burmese Using Forced Labor on Tourist Projects." *New York Times* (July 17): A3.

_____. 1994b. "A Chinese Bias against Girls Creates a Surplus of Bachelors." *New York Times* (August 16): A1.

Silberman, Charles E. 1969. *Crisis in the Classroom.* New York: Random House.

Silver, Catherine. 1992. "Personality Structure and Aging Style." *Journal of Aging Studies* 6: 333–50.

Simmel, Georg. 1955 [1908]. *Conflict and the Web of Group Affiliations.* New York: Free Press.

Simmons, Leo. 1945. *The Role of the Aged in Primitive Society.* New Haven: Yale University Press.

Simon, Rita J., Angela J. Scanlan, and Pamela S. Nadell. 1993. "Rabbis and Ministers: Women of the Book and the Cloth." *Sociology of Religion* 54: 114–122.

Simonton, Dean Keith. 1990. "Creativity in the Later Years: Optimistic Prospects for Achievement." *Gerontologist* 30: 626–31.

Simpson, Ida Harper, David Stark, and Robert A. Jackson. 1988. "Class Identification Processes." *American Sociological Review* 53: 284–93.

Sjoberg, Gideon. 1960. *The Preindustrial City.* New York: Free Press.

Skerry, Peter. 1993. *Mexican Americans: The Ambivalent Minority.* New York: Basic Books.

Skocpol, Theda. 1979. *States and Social Revolution.* Cambridge, MA: Cambridge University Press.

_____. 1980. "Political Response to Capitalist Crisis: Neo-Marxist Theories of the State and the

Case of the New Deal." *Politics and Society* 10: 155–201.

Skolnick, Arlene. 1991. *Embattled Paradise.* New York: Basic Books.

Smolowe, Jill. 1993. "Danger in the Safety Zone." *Time* (August 23): 29–33.

Solomon, Andrew. 1993. "Young Russia's Defiant Decadence." *New York Times Magazine* (July 18): 16.

Sontag, Deborah. 1993. "Immigrants Forgoing Citizenship While Pursuing the American Dream." *New York Times* (July 25): A1, A33.

South, Scott J. 1993. "Racial and Ethnic Differences in the Decision to Marry." *Journal of Marriage and the Family* 55: 357–70.

Spencer, Herbert. 1898. *The Principles of Sociology.* 3 vols. New York: Appleton Century Crofts.

Spindler, George D. 1963. *Education and Culture.* New York: Holt, Rinehart & Winston.

Spindler, Konrad. 1994. *The Man in the Ice.* London: Weindenfeld & Nicholson.

Spitze, Glenna. 1988. "Women's Employment and Family Relations." *Journal of Marriage and the Family* 50: 595–618.

Spock, Benjamin. 1989. *Dr. Spock on Parenting.* New York: Simon & Schuster.

Spretnak, Charlene, ed. 1982. *The Politics of Women's Spirituality: Essays on the Rise of Spiritual Power within the Feminist Movement.* New York: Doubieday.

Squier, D. Ann and Jill S. Quadagno. 1988. "The Italian American Family." Pp. 109–140 in *Ethnic Families in America,* edited by Charles H. Mindel, Robert W. Habenstein, and Roosevelt Wright Jr. 3rd ed. New York: Elsevier.

Stacey, Judith. 1990. *Brave New Families.* New York: Basic Books.

———. 1993. "Good Riddance to 'The Family': A Response to David Popenoe." *Journal of Marriage and the Family* 55: 445–47.

Starhawk. 1979. *The Spiral Dance: A Rebirth of the Ancient Religion of the Great Goddess.* San Francisco: Harper & Row.

———. 1982. *Dreaming the Dark: Magic, Sex, and Politics.* Boston: Beacon Press.

Statistical Abstract of the United States 1992, 112th ed. Bureau of the Census. Washington, DC: U.S. Government Printing Office.

Steinfels, Peter. 1993. "2 Authors' Contention That America Has Become More God-Fearing, Not Less So, Has Set Off a Debate." *New York Times* (February 20): A8.

Stellway, Richard J. 1990. *Christiantown, USA.* New York: Haworth Press.

Stent, Angela. 1993. "Treacherous Transition." *New York Times* (December 20): A19.

Stevens, William K. 1993. "Ozone-Depleting Chemicals Building Up at Slower Pace." *New York Times* (August 26): A1, A18.

Stevens-Arroyo, Antonio M. 1980. *Prophets Denied Honor.* Maryknoll, NY: Orbis Books.

———. 1987. "Cahensly Revisited? The National Pastoral Encounter of American Hispanic Catholics." *Migration World* XV (Fall) 3: 16–19.

———. 1994. "The Emergence of a Social Identity among Latino Catholics: An Appraisal." In *Hispanic Catholics in the United States,* vol. 3, edited by Jay Dolan and Alan Figueroa Deck, S. J. South Bend, IN: University of Notre Dame Press.

Stevens-Arroyo, Antonio M. and Anna Maria Diaz-Ramirez. 1980. "The Hispanic Model of Church: A People on the March." *New Catholic World* (July/Aug): 153–57.

Stinchcombe, Arthur L. 1990. *Information and Organizations.* Berkeley: University of California Press.

Storr, Anthony. 1988. *Solitude.* New York: Free Press.

Straus, Murray A. and Richard J. Gelles, eds. 1990. *Physical Violence in American Families.* New Brunswick, NJ: Transaction Publishers.

Strout, Cushing. 1974. *The New Heaven and New Earth: Political Religion in America.* New York: Harper & Row.

Stryker, Sheldon. 1980. *Symbolic Interactionism: A Social Structural Version.* Menlo Park, CA: Benjamin/Cummings.

———. 1987. "The Vitalization of Symbolic Interactionism." *Social Psychology Quarterly* 50: 83–94.

Sudnow, David. 1967. *Passing On: The Social Organization of Dying.* Englewood Cliffs, NJ: Prentice Hall.

Sullivan, Mercer L. 1989. *"Getting Paid": Youth Crime and Work in the Inner City.* Ithaca, NY: Cornell University Press.

Sumner, William Graham. 1906. *Folkways.* Boston: Ginn.

Sutherland, Edwin H. 1939. *Principles of Criminology.* Philadelphia: J. B. Lippincott.

———. 1951. "Critique of Sheldon's Varieties of Delinquent Youth." *American Sociological Review* 16: 10–13.

_____. 1983. *White Collar Crime.* New Haven: Yale University Press.

Swanson, Guy E. 1960. *The Birth of the Gods: The Origins of Primitive Religion.* Ann Arbor: University of Michigan Press.

Szasz, Thomas. 1974. *The Myth of Mental Illness: Foundations of a Theory of Personal Conduct,* rev. ed. New York: Harper & Row.

Tamir, Lois M. 1989. "Modern Myths about Men at Midlife: An Assessment." Pp. 157-179 in *Midlife Myths,* edited by Ski Hunter and Martin Sundel. Newbury Park, CA: Sage Publications.

Tannen, Deborah. 1990. *You Just Don't Understand.* New York: William Morrow.

_____. 1993. "Wears Jump Suit. Sensible Shoes. Uses Husband's Last Name." *New York Times Magazine* (June 30): 18.

Tawney, R. H. 1926. *Religion and the Rise of Capitalism.* New York: Harcourt Brace.

Taylor, Michael, ed. 1988. *Rationality and Revolution.* Cambridge, England: Cambridge University Press.

Thayer, Stephen. 1988. "Close Encounters." *Psychology Today* (March): 30-36.

Thornton, Arland. 1989. "Changing Attitudes toward Family Issues in the United States." *Journal of Marriage and the Family* 51: 841-1116.

Tienda, Marta and Franklin D. Wilson. 1992. "Migration and the Earnings of Hispanic Men." *American Sociological Review* 57: 661-78.

Tilly, Charles. 1993. *European Revolutions, 1492-1992.* Cambridge, MA: Basil Blackwell.

Toffler, Alvin and Heidi Toffler. 1993. "Societies at Hyper Speed." *New York Times* (October 31): E17.

Trebbi, Diana. 1990. "Women-Church: Catholic Women Produce an Alternative Spirituality." Chap. 17 in *In Gods We Trust: New Patterns of Religious Pluralism in America,* 2nd ed. New Brunswick, NJ: Transaction Publishers.

Trent, James W. and Leland L. Medzger. 1968. *Beyond High School.* San Francisco: Jossey-Bass.

Tucker, M. Belinda and Claudia Mitchell-Kernan. 1990. "New Trends in Black American Interracial Marriage: The Social Structural Context." *Journal of Marriage and the Family.*

Tumin, Melvin M. 1953. "Some Principles of Stratification: A Critical Analysis." *American Sociological Review* 18: 378-94.

Turner, Ralph H. and Lewis Killian. 1987. *Collective Behavior,* 3rd ed. Englewood Cliffs, NJ: Prentice Hall.

Tylor, Edward B. 1871. *Primitive Culture.* London: Murry.

Uchitelle, Louis. 1993. "Temporary Workers Are on the Increase in Nation's Factories." *New York Times* (July 6): A1, D2.

_____. 1994. "Moonlighting Plus: 3-Job Families on the Rise." *New York Times* (August 16): A1, D18.

Ulrich, Patricia. 1988. "The Determinents of Depression in Two-Income Families." *Journal of Marriage and the Family* 50: 121-31.

U.S. Bureau of the Census. 1993. "Hispanic Americans Today." *Current Population Reports* P23-183. Washington, DC: U.S. Government Printing Office.

U.S. Department of Commerce. 1993. "School Enrollment—Social and Economic Characteristics of Students: October 1991." Current Population Reports P20-469. Washington, DC: U.S. Government Printing Office.

U.S. Department of Education. 1987. *Schools That Work: Educating Disadvantaged Children.* Washington, DC: U.S. Government Printing Office.

U.S. Department of Education. 1993a. "Public and Private Elementary and Secondary Education Statistics: School Year 1992-93." Washington, DC: U.S. Government Printing Office.

U.S. Department of Education. 1993b. "National Excellence: A Case for Developing America's Talent." Washington, DC: U.S. Government Printing Office.

Useem, Michael. 1984. *The Inner Circle: Large Corporations and the Rise of Political Activity in the U.S. and U.K.* New York: Oxford University Press.

Vaillant, George. 1977. *Adaptation to Life.* Boston: Little, Brown.

van Gennep, Arnold. 1960. *The Rites of Passage,* translated by Monika B. Vizedoni and Gabrielle L. Caffee. Chicago: University of Chicago Press.

Vanfossen, Beth E., James D. Jones, and Loan Z. Spade. 1987. "Curriculum Tracking and Status Maintenance." *Sociology of Education* 60: 104-22.

Vannoy-Hiller, Dana and William Philliber. 1989. *Equal Partners.* Newbury Park, CA: Sage Publications.

Veblen, Thorstein. 1953 [1899]. *The Theory of the Leisure Class.* New York: Mentor.

Veves, Michael. 1989. "Beyond Tracking: A Teacher's View." *Equity and Choice* 6, 1: 18-22.

Vogel, Ezra P. 1980. *Japan as Number One.* New York: Harper & Row.

Voll, John O. 1991. "Fundamentalism in the Sunni Arab World: Egypt and the Sudan." Pp. 345–401 in *Fundamentalisms Observed,* edited by Martin E. Marty and R. Scott Appleby. Chicago: University of Chicago Press.

Wagner, Melinda Bollar. 1990. *God's Schools: Choice and Compromise in American Society.* New Brunswick, NJ: Rutgers University Press.

Walder, Andrew G. 1992. "Property Rights and Stratification in Socialist Redistributive Economies." *American Sociological Review* 57: 524–39.

Wallace, Ruth. 1992. *They Call Her Pastor: A New Role for Catholic Women.* Albany: State University of New York.

_____. 1993. "The Social Construction of a New Leadership Role: Catholic Women Pastors." *Sociology of Religion* 54: 114–122.

Waller, Willard. 1951. *The Family: A Dynamic Interpretation,* revised by Reuben Hill. New York: Dryden.

Wallis, Roy. 1977. "Scientology: Therapeutic Cult to Religious Sect." *Sociology* 9: 89–99.

Warner, Lloyd W. and Paul Lunt. 1941. *The Social Life of a Modern Community.* New Haven: Yale University Press.

Warner, R. Stephen. 1988. *New Wine in Old Wineskins: Evangelicals and Liberals in a Small-Town Church.* Berkeley: University of California Press.

_____. 1990. "Mirror for American Protestantism: Mendocino Presbyterian Church in the Sixties and Seventies." In *The Mainstream Protestant Decline: The Presbyterian Predicament,* edited by Milton J. Coalter, John M. Mulder, and Louis B. Weeks. Louisville, KY: Westminster/John Knox Press.

_____. 1991. "Oenology: The Making of New Wine." Pp. 174–99 in *The Case for the Case Study,* edited by Joe R. Feagin, Anthony M. Orum, and Gideon Sjoberg. Chapel Hill: University of North Carolina Press.

_____. 1993. "Work in Progress toward a New Paradigm for the Sociological Study of Religion in the United States." *American Journal of Sociology* 98: 1044–93.

Watson, Graham and Robert M. Seiler. 1992. *Text in Context: Contributions to Ethnomethodology.* Newbury Park, CA: Sage Publications.

Watt, David Harrington. 1991. *A Transforming Faith: Explorations of Twentieth-Century American Evangelicalism.* New Brunswick, NJ: Rutgers University Press.

Weaver, Ross Lee. 1990. "Separate Is Not Equal." *Principal* 69 (5): 40, 42.

Weber, Marianne. 1975 [1926]. *Max Weber: A Biography.* New York: John Wiley.

Weber, Max. 1946 [1914]. "Class, Status, Party." Pp. 180–95 in *From Max Weber: Essays in Sociology,* edited by Hans H. Gerth and C. Wright Mills. New York: Oxford University Press.

_____. 1946 [1919]. "Politics as a Vocation." Pp.78–128 in *From Max Weber: Essays in Sociology,* edited by Hans H. Gerth and C. Wright Mills. New York: Oxford University Press.

_____. 1947 [1925]. *The Theory of Social and Economic Organization,* translated by A. M. Henderson and Talcott Parsons. New York: Free Press.

_____. 1949 [1903–1917]. *The Methodology of the Social Sciences,* translated and edited by Edward A. Shils and Henry A. Finch. New York: Free Press.

_____. 1958 [1904]. *The Protestant Ethic and the Spirit of Capitalism,* translated and edited by Talcott Parsons. New York: Scribner's.

_____. 1963 [1922]. *The Sociology of Religion,* translated by Ephraim Fischoff. Boston: Beacon Press.

Weber, Timothy P. 1992. "Finding Someone to Blame: Fundamentalism and Anti-Semitic Conspiracy Theories in the 1930s." *Fides et Historia* XXIV (Summer).

Weg, Ruth B. 1990. "Sensuality/Sexuality in the Middle Years." Pp. 31–50 in *Midlife Myths,* edited by Ski Hunter and Martin Sundel. Newbury Park, CA: Sage Publications.

Weinberg, Richard A. 1989. "Intelligence and I.Q.: Landmark Issues and Great Debates." *American Psychologist* 44: 98–104.

Weiner, Tim. 1993. "In 1990, U.S. Was Still Training Salvador Civilians Tied to Killings." *New York Times* (December 14): A1, A11.

Weisburd, David, Stanton Wheeler, Elin Waring, and Nancy Bode. 1991. *Crimes of the Middle Classes.* New Haven: Yale University Press.

Weiss, Robert S. 1990. *Staying the Course.* New York: Free Press.

Welsh, Sharon B. 1985. *Communities of Resistance and Solidarity: A Feminist Liberation Theology.* Maryknoll, NY: Orbis Books.

Wheeler, Stanton, Kenneth Mann, and Austin Sarat. 1988. *Sitting in Judgment.* New Haven: Yale University Press.

Whitaker, Mark. 1993. "White and Black Lies." *Newsweek* (November 15): 52–54.

White, Ronald C., Jr. and C. Howard Hopkins. 1976. *The Social Gospel: Religion and Reform in Changing America.* Philadelphia: Temple University Press.

Whyte, Martin King. 1990. *Dating, Mating, and Marriage.* Hawthorne, NY: Aldine de Gruyter.

Wilkie, Jane Riblett. 1993. "Changes in U.S. Men's Attitudes toward the Family Provider Role, 1972–1989." *Gender and Society* 7: 261–79.

Williams, David R. 1992. "Socioeconomic Differences in Health." *Social Psychology Quarterly* 53: 81–99.

Williams, Terry. 1989. *Cocaine Kids.* Reading, MA: Addison-Wesley.

Willie, Charles V. 1978. *The Sociology of Urban Education.* Lexington, MA: Lexington Books.

Willis, Paul. 1990. *Common Ground.* Boulder, CO: Westview Press.

Willis, Sherry L., Gina M. Jay, Manfred Diehl, and Michael Marsiske. 1992. "Longitudinal Change and Prediction of Everyday Task Competence in the Elderly." *Research on Aging* 14: 68–91.

Wills, Gary. 1990. *Under God: Religion and American Politics.* New York: Simon & Schuster.

Wilson, Edward O. 1975. *Sociobiology: A New Synthesis.* Cambridge, MA: Harvard University Press.

———. 1978. *On Human Nature.* Cambridge, MA: Harvard University Press.

———. 1993. "Is Humanity Suicidal?" *New York Times Magazine* (May 30): 24.

Wilson, Franklin D. 1985. "The Impact of School Segregation Programs on White Public Enrollment, 1968–1976." *Sociology of Education* 58: 137–53.

Wilson, James Q. 1990. *What Government Agencies Do and How They Do It.* New York: Basic Books.

———. 1993. *The Moral Sense.* New York: Basic Books.

Wilson, John. 1978. *Religion in America.* Englewood, NJ: Prentice Hall.

Wilson, Kenneth L. 1979. "The Effects of Race and Class on Black Educational Achievement." *Sociology of Education* 52: 84–98.

Wilson, William Julius. 1979. *The Declining Significance of Race.* Chicago: University of Chicago Press.

Wirth, Louis. 1928. *The Ghetto.* Chicago: University of Chicago Press.

———. 1945. "The Problem of Minority Groups." Pp. 347–72 in *The Science of Man in the World Crisis,* edited by Ralph Linton. New York: Columbia University Press.

Witt, Linda, Karen M. Paget, and Glenna Matthews. 1993. *Running as a Woman: Gender and Power in American Politics.* New York: Free Press.

Wogaman, J. Phillip. 1989. "Christianity and Sociopolitical Thought." In *Religious Issues and Interreligious Dialogue: An Analysis and Sourcebook of Developments since 1945,* edited by Charles Wei-hsun Fu and Gerhard E. Speigler. New York: Greenwood Press.

Wolf, Rosalie and Edward R. McCarthy. 1991. "Elder Abuse." Pp. 481–501 in *Growing Old in America,* edited by Beth B. Hess and Elizabeth Markson. New Brunswick, NJ: Transaction Publishers.

Wolff, Kurt H., ed. 1960. *Émile Durkheim, 1858–1917: A Collection of Essays.* Columbus: Ohio State University Press.

Woll, Stanley B. and Peter Young. 1989. "Looking for Mr. or Mrs. Right: Self-Presentation in Videodating." *Journal of Marriage and the Family* 51: 483–88.

Woodward, Kenneth L. 1993a. "Dead End for the Mainline?" *Newsweek* (August 9): 46–48.

———. 1993b. "Mixed Blessings." *Newsweek* (August 16): 39–44.

Wright, Erik Olin. 1993. "Typologies, Scales, and Class Analysis: A Comment on Halaby and Weakliem's 'Ownership and Authority in the Earnings Function.'" *American Sociological Review* 58: 31–4.

Wright, Erik Olin and Donmoon Cho. 1992. "The Relative Permeability of Class Boundaries to Cross-Class Friendships." *American Sociological Review* 57: 85–102.

Wright, Lawrence. 1994. "One Drop of Blood," *New Yorker* (July 25): 46–55.

Wu, Lawrence L. and Brian C. Martinson. 1993. "Family Structure and the Risk of Premarital Birth." *American Sociological Review* 58: 210–32.

Wuthnow, Robert. 1978. *Experimentation in American Religion.* Berkeley: University of California Press.

———. 1988. *The Restructuring of American Religion: Society and Faith since World War II.* Princeton: Princeton University Press.

———. 1989. *The Struggle for America's Soul: Evangelicals, Liberals, and Secularism.* Grand Rapids, MI: William B. Eerdmans.

_____. 1991. *Acts of Compassion: Caring for Others and Helping Ourselves.* Princeton: Princeton University Press.

_____. 1992. *Rediscovering the Sacred: Perspectives on Religion in Contemporary Society.* Grand Rapids, MI: William B. Eerdmans.

_____. 1993. *Christianity in the 21st Century: Reflections on the Challenges Ahead.* New York: Oxford University Press.

Yablonsky, Lewis. 1969. *The Tunnel Back.* Garden City, NY: Doubleday.

Yee, Barbara W. K. 1992. "Markers of Successful Aging among Southeast Asian Refugees." *Women and Therapy* 12: 6–9.

Yinger, J. Milton. 1960. "Contraculture and Subculture." *American Sociological Review* 25: 625–35.

_____. 1977. "Countercultures and Social Change." *American Sociological Review* 42: 833–53.

Yorburg, Betty. 1969. *Utopia and Reality: A Collective Portrait of American Socialists.* New York: Columbia University Press.

_____. 1973. *The Changing Family.* New York: Columbia University Press.

_____. 1974. *Sexual Identity: Sex Roles and Social Change.* New York: John Wiley.

_____. 1975. "The Nuclear and the Extended Family: An Area of Conceptual Confusion." *Journal of Comparative Family Studies* 6: 1–14.

_____. 1983. *Families and Societies.* New York: Columbia University Press.

_____. 1993. *Family Relationships.* New York: St. Martin's Press.

Zald, Mayer N. and John D. McCarthy. 1979. *The Dynamics of Social Movements.* Cambridge, MA: Winthrop.

Zigler, Edward. 1993. "Head Start, the Whole Story." *New York Times* (July 24): A19.

Zigler, Edward and Sally J. Styfco. 1993. *Head Start and Beyond.* New Haven: Yale University Press.

Zimmerman, Shirley L. 1992. *Family Policies and Family Well-Being: The Role of Political Culture.* Newbury Park, CA: Sage Publications.

Zimring, Franklin E. and Gordon Hawkins. 1992. *Prison Population and Criminal Justice Policy in California: Issues and Options.* Berkeley: University of California Press.

Zola, Irving. 1966. "Medicine as an Institution of Social Control." *American Sociological Review* 31: 115–30.

Index

Boldface page numbers indicate glossary terms.

ability grouping, 400, **405**-406, 414, 417
abolitionism, 436-437
absent role definitions, role conflict and, 118-119, 121
acculturation, of minorities, 260-**261,** 262, 263, 264, 398
achieved status, **85,** 230, 332, 394
achievement, 40, 122, 261, 348
achievement motivation, **166**-167
activism, 165, **166**-167
adapting, individual ways of, 125
adolescent sexual activity, risk factors for, 32
Adorno, Theodore, 256, 257
adult education, 419-422
age cohort, **191**
agricultural societies, 146, **154**-157, 158, 162, 163, 164, 167, 172, 196, 275; deviance in, 215, 228-229; education in, 395, 403-404, 405; families in, 291-292, 297, 300, 301, 304, 305, 306, 307, 312; inequality in, 328, 334, 339, 340, 353; power in, 365, 366, 369-371, 372; premarital sexual behavior in, 295-296; religion in, 432-433; women in, 265, 269
AIDS, 294-295, 309, 413
Albigensian Heresy, 433
alienation, **349**-350, 353
alternative family forms, 305-311
altruistic suicide, **12**
ambiguous role definitions, role conflict and, 118-119, 121
American Sociological Association, 16, 19, 20
Amy, Douglas J., 374-375
animism, **431**
anomic suicide, **11**
anomie, **11,** 118, 172, 395; deviance and, 223-224, 227, 231; urban values and, 124-126

anthropology: sociology and, 17, 19, 227, 275, 403; types of human societies and, 144-178
applied sociology, **21**
artifacts, **77,** 147
ascribed status, **85,** 230, 332, 394; minorities and, 247, 251
assets, family, 339
assimilation, of minorities, 260-261, 265
attitudes, toward minorities, 262-263
authoritarian childrearing, 301, **302,** 304, 305, 306
authoritarian government, **364,** 371, 372, 375
authoritarian personality, **256,** 258, 270, 271, 275
authoritarianism, 121, 165, **168;** deviance and, 214, 228; education and, 395, 400, 401; religion and, 444, 445; social class and, 343, 344, 348, 351, 353
authoritative childrearing, 302, **304,** 306
authority, **329;** family forms and, 291; types of, 365-368, 369, 372
autocracy, **369,** 370

B

baby boom generation, 185, 187, 192, 193; religion and, 441, 444, 446
Baumrind, Diana, 301-302
Becker, Howard S., 224
Bellah, Robert N., 439
biological bases, of families, 287-288
biological theories, of deviance, 218-221, 227
blacks, in Congress, 268; as presidential candidates, 248
Buddhism, 432, 446, 449
burdens, older people as, 272-273
bureaucracy, **6,** **100**-102, 103

T

Credits & Acknowledgments (continued from copyright page)

xxviii Busch Gardens; 14 "A Pioneer Woman Sociologist" from *Sociological Lives,* ed. by Matilda White Riley, © 1988 by Sage Publications, reprinted by permission of Sage Publications, Inc.; 32 Figure 2.1 adapted from "Adolescent Sexual Activity: An Ecological, Risk-Factor Approach" by Stephen A. Small and Tom Luster, *Journal of Marriage and the Family 56* (1994), pp. 181-192, copyright 1994 by the National Council on Family Relations, 3989 Central Ave. NE, Suite 550, Minneapolis, MN 55421, reprinted by permission; 58 Figure 2.2 reproduced with the permission of The Alan Guttmacher Institute from *Sex and America's Teenagers,* New York, 1994; 98 Figure 3.3 "Generations and Gender Equality" from November 1993 issue, *American Demographics* magazine, © 1993, reprinted with permission; 125 Table 4.2 "Individual Ways of Adapting" adapted with the permission of The Free Press, a Division of Simon & Schuster, from *Social Theory and Social Structure* by Robert K. Merton, copyright © 1968, 1967 by Robert K. Merton; 128 "The Goldfish-Swallowing Fad" from Jack Levin, *Sociological Snapshots,* pp. 30-31, copyright © 1993 by Pine Forge Press, reprinted by permission of Pine Forge Press; 142 SuperStock; 197 Figure 6.1 "Projected World Population by Region, Central Scenario, 1990, 2030, and 2100" from "The Future of World Population" by Wolfgang Lutz, *Population Bulletin 49*(1) (June 1994), reprinted by permission of the Population Reference Bureau, Inc.; 200 Figure 6.2 "The Total Fertility Rate of Women on Welfare," from the *New York Times,* June 19, 1994, copyright © 1994 by the New York Times Company, reprinted by permission; 201 Figure 6.3 "Life Expectancy for World Regions, 1994" from "The Future of World Population" by Wolfgang Lutz, *Population Bulletin 49*(1) (June 1994), reprinted by permission of the Population Reference Bureau, Inc.; 202 Figure 6.4 "Total Fertility Rates for World Regions, 1994" from "The Future of World Population" by Wolfgang Lutz, *Population Bulletin 49*(1) (June 1994), reprinted by permission of the Population Reference Bureau, Inc.; 205 "The Latent Functions of Technological Development" from "Heartbreaking Fight Unfolds in Hospital for Valdez Otters" by Charles McCoy, *Wall Street Journal,* January 20, 1989, reprinted by permission of the *Wall Street Journal,* © 1989 Dow Jones & Company, Inc., all rights reserved worldwide; 217 Table 7.1 "Fear and Violence at School," from the *New York Times,* April 21, 1993, copyright © 1993 by the New York Times Company, reprinted by permission; 225 "Mobility and Nonconformity" from "End of the Run" by Nancy Gibbs, *Time,* June 27, 1994, copyright 1994 Time Inc., reprinted by permission; 236 Figure 7.1 "Crime and Punishment" from *Time,* February 7, 1994, copyright 1994 Time Inc., reprinted by permission; 258 "Ethnic Conflict in Africa" from "Africa Tries Democracy, Finding Hope and Peril" by John Darnton, *New York Times,* June 21, 1994, copyright © 1994 by the New York Times Company, reprinted by permission; 284 Liliana Nieto Del Rio/J. B. Pictures; 294 Figure 9.1 "Sexual Activity of Teenagers" reproduced with the permission of The Alan Guttmacher Institute from *Sex and America's Teenagers,* New York, 1994; 300 Figure 9.2 "Percentage of Household Chores Done by Mothers with Husband Present" from "Family Diversity and the Division of Domestic Labor: How Much Have Things Really Changed?" by David H. Demo and Alan C. Acock, *Family Relations 42*(3), pp. 323-331, copyright 1993 by the National Council on Family Relations, 3989 Central Ave. NE, Suite 550, Minneapolis, MN 55421, reprinted by permission; 302 Figure 9.3 "Primary Care Providers for Preschool Children While Mothers Work, 1991" from "Where's Papa?" by Martin O'Connell, *Population Trends and Public Policy* (Washington, DC: Population Reference Bureau, 1993), reprinted by permission; 303 "Psychologically Correct Parenting" from "Kids Acting Up? Don't Yell, Validate Their Tiny Feelings" by Cynthia Crossen, *Wall Street Journal,* December 10, 1991, reprinted by permission of the *Wall Street Journal,* © 1991 Dow Jones & Company, Inc., all rights reserved worldwide; 315 Figure 9.4 "Changing Shares